Autism Spectrum Disorder: An Evidence-Based Approach

Autism Spectrum Disorder: An Evidence-Based Approach

Editor: Collin Flowers

AMERICAN
MEDICAL PUBLISHERS
www.americanmedicalpublishers.com

AMERICAN
MEDICAL PUBLISHERS
www.americanmedicalpublishers.com

Cataloging-in-Publication Data

Autism spectrum disorder : an evidence-based approach / edited by Collin Flowers.
p. cm.
Includes bibliographical references and index.
ISBN 978-1-63927-900-5
1. Autism spectrum disorders. 2. Autism spectrum disorders--Diagnosis. 3. Autism spectrum disorders--Treatment.
4. Evidence-based medicine. 5. Evidence-based psychiatry. 6. Psychiatry. I. Flowers, Collin.
RC553.A88 A98 2023
616.858 82--dc23

American Medical Publishers,
41 Flatbush Avenue,
1st Floor, New York,
NY 11217, USA

ISBN 978-1-63927-900-5 (Hardback)

Contents

Preface

The purpose of the book is to provide a glimpse into the dynamics and to present opinions and studies of some of the scientists engaged in the development of new ideas in the field from very different standpoints. This book will prove useful to students and researchers owing to its high content quality.

Autism spectrum disorder (ASD) refers to a type of condition, associated with brain development that affects how a person perceives and interacts with others. This condition can create difficulties in social interaction and communication. It also involves recurring and limited behavioral patterns. The risk factors of ASD include family history, preterm births, the child's gender, the age of the parents, etc. ASD is diagnosed by a thorough examination of a person's behavior and growth, and it is typically diagnosed by the age of two. The most successful therapies of ASD include occupational therapy, physical therapy, applied behavioral analysis, pharmacological therapy and speech therapy. The goal of the treatment is to reduce the negative effects and related deficits of ASD. The treatment also emphasizes on increasing functional independence and quality of life. This book contains some path-breaking studies on autism spectrum disorder. It provides significant information to help develop a good understanding of this medical condition. The extensive content of this book provides the readers with a thorough understanding of the condition.

At the end, I would like to appreciate all the efforts made by the authors in completing their chapters professionally. I express my deepest gratitude to all of them for contributing to this book by sharing their valuable works. A special thanks to my family and friends for their constant support in this journey.

Editor

A Complementary Sensory Tool for Children with Autism Spectrum Disorders

Sabina Barrios-Fernández [1,*], Margarita Gozalo [2], Beatriz Díaz-González [3] and Andrés García-Gómez [4]

1 Medical-Surgical Therapeutics Department, University of Extremadura, 10003 Cáceres, Spain
2 Psychology and Anthropology Department, University of Extremadura, 10003 Cáceres, Spain; mgozalo@unex.es
3 Nursing and Occupational Therapy College, University of Extremadura, 10003 Cáceres, Spain; bdiazgon@alumnos.unex.es
4 Education Sciences Department, University of Extremadura, 10003 Cáceres, Spain; agarcil9@unex.es
* Correspondence: sabinabarrios@unex.es

Abstract: Background: Sensory integration (SI) issues are widely described in people with autism spectrum disorder (ASD), impacting in their daily life and occupations. To improve their quality of life and occupational performance, we need to improve clinical and educational evaluation and intervention processes. We aim to develop a tool for measuring SI issues for Spanish children and adolescents with ASD diagnosis, to be used as a complementary tool to complete the Rivière's Autism Spectrum Inventory, a widely used instrument in Spanish speaking places to describe the severity of ASD symptoms, recently updated with a new sensory scale with three dimensions. Methods: 458 Spanish participants complemented the new questionnaire, initially formed by 73 items with a 1–5 Likert scale. Results: The instrument finally was composed of 41 items grouped in three factors: modulation disorders (13 items), discrimination disorders (13 items), and sensory-based motor disorders (15 items). The goodness-of-fit indices from factor analyses, reliability, and the analysis of the questionnaire's classification capability offered good values. Conclusions: The new questionnaire shows good psychometric properties and seems to be a good complementary tool to complete new the sensory scale in the Rivière's Autism Spectrum Inventory.

Keywords: sensory processing; emotional regulation; assessment; autism spectrum disorders

1. Introduction

1.1. Sensory Integration Process

Sensory integration (SI) is "the neurological process that organizes sensations from one's own body (internal) and the environment (external) and makes it possible to use the body effectively within the environment" [1] (p. 11). An adequate organization of sensory information is necessary for producing adaptive responses in daily life, which includes different end products: motor, cognitive, behavioral, emotional, or learning outcomes [2]. SI is considered a prerequisite so that more complex functions, as perceptual-motor and cognitive ones, can be appropriately developed [3].

The SI process runs through a series of stages. Firstly, the sensory organs capture fragments of sensory information, which can have either an internal or an external origin. Later, that information is integrated in the central nervous system (CNS) to become a meaningful whole [4]. The SI process takes place in different brain structures in a coordinated way, classifying, and organizing the sensory flow through a series of stages. Firstly, in registration, the CNS detects the sensory sensations from our sensory receptors and we become aware of those sensations [5]. Next, in modulation, the CNS regulates and processes the sensory stimuli [6]. Then, during discrimination the CNS distinguishes between different sensory stimuli, perceiving their specific qualities and becoming meaningful [6–8]. Finally, we elicit a response, intended to adaptive, which can include attention, organization, self-esteem, self-confidence, movement, reasoning, and learning outcomes [1,7,9]. Within that end products, and in the group of adaptive motor-based responses, we must refer to praxis. Praxis is the ability to conceptualize, plan, and execute unusual motor actions. Thus, it allows us to organize and manage a purposeful interaction with the physical world, thus involving both motor and cognitive skills [8,10].

Although traditionally we have focused in five senses (vision, hearing, smell, taste, and touch), there are three more sensory systems essential to be successful in daily life: proprioception, vestibular system, and interoception. Proprioceptive sense reports on sensations from muscles, ligaments, and joints, providing information about the compression and stretching of muscles and joints. Proprioception and touch together form the somatosensory pathway, considered essential for praxis and movement [11,12]. The vestibular system provides information on movement, gravity and balance, so it is crucial for the building of spatial and temporal relationships [13]. It also provides information about the speed and the direction of the head movement and our position with relation to gravity [9]. Interoception sense processes sensory stimuli within the body, including body sensations (hunger, thirst, body temperature, heart, breathing rate, etc.) and emotional states (happiness, sadness, shame, anger), being intimately related to self-regulation and well-being [14,15].

1.2. Sensory Processing Disorders

When sensations flow in an organized and integrated way, our brain can use those sensations to form perceptions, behaviors, and learning; when the flow of sensations is disorganized, perception, behavior, and learning are like a traffic jam at a rush hour [16]. Therefore, when SI is not working properly, motor, cognitive, emotional, behavioral, and adaptive issues produce a decrease in daily living functioning and learning [17–20]. This dysfunction can be mild, medium, or severe [21]. Sensory processing disorder (SPD) is a neurological disorder in which the ability to process and interpret sensory stimuli results in abnormal responses, causing a decrease in the quality of life and occupational performance [22,23]. Several models have been developed to understand the SPD [1,6,24], being Miller's model one of the most accepted. According to it, SPD can be classified into three categories with their corresponding subtypes: sensory modulation disorders, sensory discrimination disorders, and sensory-based motor disorders. Sensory modulation disorders happen when the CNS has problems in regulating the sensory information (degree, nature, or intensity) resulting in the following subtypes: sensory over-responsivity (exaggerated response), sensory under-responsivity (lack or insufficient response), or sensory craving (desperate seeking for sensory information). Sensory discrimination disorders happen when there is difficulty interpreting the qualities of the sensory stimuli. As a result, the responses are often slow, and sometimes, wrong. Finally, sensory-based motor disorders cause difficulty with motor planning and movement, resulting in postural disorder or dyspraxia subtypes [6,25].

1.3. Autism Spectrum Disorders and SPD Relationships

Taking the latest version of the Diagnostic and Statistical Manual of Mental Disorders (DSM-5) as a reference [26], ASD are included in the neurodevelopmental disorders group, and they are defined by the presence of (a) persistent deficits in social communication and interaction, and (b) restricted, repetitive patterns of behavior, interests, or activities. Within the (b) criterion and, for the first time in the DSM, sensory abnormalities were included as "Hyper- or hyporeactivity to sensory input or unusual interest in sensory aspects of the environment (e.g., apparent indifference to pain/temperature, adverse response to specific sounds or textures, excessive smelling or touching of objects, visual fascination with lights or movement)" (p. 50).

With regards to etiology, and although it is widely recognized that genetic and environmental factors and their interactions contribute to the phenotypes of ASD, the precise causal mechanisms keep still unclear [27]. On a neuroanatomical basis, it is hypothesized that ASD symptoms should be a consequence of brain disconnection since hypomyelination of the brain nerves occurs simultaneously with the main behavioral symptoms [28]. Other studies complement this hypoconnectivity hypothesis by suggesting that in addition to hypoconnectivity in some regions of the cerebral cortex and at an interhemispheric level, a compensatory hyperconnectivity between the thalamus and the cerebral cortex, explaining sensory, and social symptoms [29]. Under this assumption, sensory issues in ASD have as origin atypical connectivity of neuronal structures. Nevertheless, it seems that topography of hypoconnectivity in ASD is unique and different from other conditions, such as SPD. In ASD, areas related to socio-emotional processing are highly affected; whereas, in SPD, there is lower connectivity in the brain's perception and integration pathways, which serve as connections for the auditory, visual, and somatosensory systems involved in SI [30].

SI issues are commonly reported in ASD, compared to their peers [31]. Various studies have tried to explain the most frequent sensory profiles or those issues that cause the biggest issues in children with ASD, as well as the proposals of intervention to improve their occupational performance [19,31–37]. With regards to ASD specific sensory profiles, hyporeactivity/under-responsivity is one of the most consistent issues found [24], although hyperreactivity/over-responsivity and sensory seeking have been also reported [38]. Several studies have found relationships between the core symptoms of ASD and sensory impairments, such as repetitive behaviors [34,39], with social communication and interaction [31,40,41], but also, with movement issues, including coordination, planning, and timing [42,43], impacting in their daily life [44]. With regards to the interventions, some of the studies focused on Ayres's Sensory Integration Therapy [36,45], and others in using specific sensory techniques and environmental modifications, thus the promotion of ecological approaches to improve occupational performance [4,37].

1.4. Autism Spectrum Disorders and SPD Assessment

There are different tools to measure SI functioning, including questionnaires, observational tools, and comprehensive tests administered to the children or adolescents. Some reviews have been performed to resume information about SI tools, noticing that there are a large number of proposals [46,47]. Other reviews have checked for the most used SI tools in ASD, providing information about their characteristics and limitations [48–50]. Some of the most representative instruments are the Sensory Profile (SP) [51] and its second version (SP2) [52], a group of standardized questionnaires for assessing sensory processing including the infant, toddler, child, short, and school companion forms, from birth to 14.11 years. The Sensory Processing Measure (SPM), formed by a set of questionnaires to assess SI in home and the school, in children between 5–12 years. It also includes self-evaluation forms to be completed by the children and adolescents. There is a preschool version from 2–5 years [53]. The Sensory Integration and Praxis Test (SIPT) is a comprehensive test formed by 17 subtests to assess visual, tactile, kinesthetic, and motor tasks in children from 4–8.11 years [16]. There are several emerging SI assessment tools. The Sensory Processing 3-Dimensions (SP3D) is a tool composed of a series of task to elicit typical and atypical behavioral responses in children, covering sensory modulation, discrimination, and sensory-based motor disorders; and by a questionnaire with five subscales: sensory over-responsiveness, sensory under-responsiveness, sensory craving, postural disorder, dyspraxia, and sensory discrimination disorder [25,54]. The Evaluation in Ayres Sensory Integration (EASI) is a comprehensive assessment test for SI which includes measures related to sensory perception, sensory responsiveness, postural, ocular and bilateral integration, and praxis [24,55].

Tools for ASD assessment, including detection [56,57], diagnosis and measuring changes after interventions [58,59] are also available. In any case, the assessment of the severity of ASD should be complete and comprehensive and must include the measure of the SI and its impact in daily life. Within these tools, the Autism Spectrum Disorders Inventory developed by Rivière [60,61], is a widely used tool both in Spain and Latin America. It examines the severity of ASD by establishing four disease groups: relationship disorders, communication disorders, anticipation and flexibility, and symbolization, resulting in 12 dimensions, all of which can be scored from 0 to 8 points. The Rivière's Autism Spectrum Inventory was set up before the importance of the SI was spread so, recently, a new sensory scale has been incorporated [62] updating the tool to the current knowledge of ASD. Now it is formed by five disease groups and 15 dimensions (Figure 1). An advantage of the Rivière's Autism Spectrum Inventory is the fact that, as being designed by severity levels, it can help the clinicians' in their judgment to determine the levels of severity required in DSM-5 [26]. However, and although this instrument explains the four levels of affectation in each dimension, it does not define specific behaviors to observe, so using complementary tools to collect information is strongly recommended.

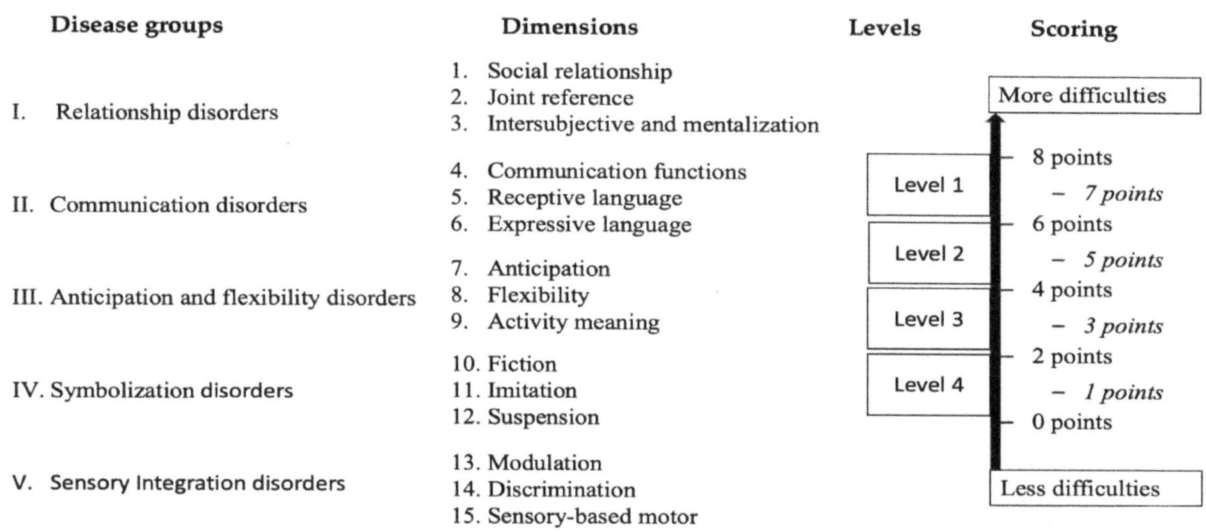

Figure 1. Summary of Rivière's Autism Spectrum Inventory [60,61]. Disease groups from I–IV with their 12 dimensions correspond to Rivière's original version. The V scale with the dimensions 13–15 was added by García-Gómez [62]. Preferred scores for rating the Inventory are the even ones, while odd scores are used to describe intermediate stages.

1.5. Aim

We aim to create a questionnaire to be used as a support for scoring the new sensory scale in the Rivière's Autism Spectrum Inventory, a widely used tool to assess ASD severity in Spanish speaking places.

2. Methods

2.1. Participants

The sample was formed by 458 children and adolescents (308 males, 68.7%, and 144 females, 31.3%) from 4 to 19 years ($x = 9.6$, $dt = 4.42$). Of these, 259 were individuals with typical development (57.2%), 145 presented ASD clinical diagnosis (32%) and 54 had other diagnoses different than ASD resulting in intellectual, sensory, and/or motor disabilities (11.95%).

2.2. Procedure

After conducting a literature review, a group of experts in the fields of Occupational Therapy and Psychology, with clinical experience, created a preliminary version of the tool composed of 73 items. Then a pilot study was carried out with 31 ASD families with diagnosed children. The 50 items with the best indicators were selected. Participants were recruited using the snowball technique in the case of typical development children, and through different associations, in the case of diagnosed children. The data collection was carried out between May and August 2020. This protocol adheres to the updates of the Declaration of Helsinki, and the study was approved by the Committee on Biomedical Ethics of the University of Extremadura (97/2020).

Our instrument, the Behavioral Observation on Sensory Stimuli Questionnaire for Parents (BOSS-P) was administered to the families. They were also asked for socio-demographic data, including age, sex, clinical diagnosis, intellectual capacity, language level, comorbidities, and the need for aids in their daily life. Once the questionnaire was administered to the sample, the items were analyzed by the group of experts, discarding those which did not fit on the theoretical model, being the final version composed of 41 items (Supplementary Table S1). The BOSS-P was administered together with the Sensory Profile 2 (SP2) Short Form [63,64] to 31 participants, to obtain validity indicators.

2.3. Instrument

The BOSS-P, a new instrument to better characterize ASD children and adolescents to fulfil the three new sensory dimensions from Rivière's Autism Spectrum Inventory based on Miller's model, must be completed interviewing with main caregivers, which may answer the 41 items through a Likert scale with five response options, from 1 to 5 (higher scores mean greater SI dysfunction). It takes about 25–30 min to complete the interview.

2.4. Statistics

To perform the validation process of the BOSS-P we have carried out: (1) an exploratory factor analysis (EFA), (2) confirmatory factor analysis (CFA), (3) reliability analysis, (4) the assessment of concurrent validity through the correlations with the SP2, and (5) provide descriptive statistics from the typical development and the ASD subsamples.

Because we are handling ordinal variables from a Likert-type scale with five response categories, the EFA was carried out with the FACTOR software [65–67] using polychoric correlations and robust methods [68]. Items with factorial weights below 0.30 were excluded. The CFA was carried out with the IBM SPSS AMOS™ 24 [69] using the Maximum Likelihood estimation procedure, suitable for Likert-type scales of five response categories. The CFA supports the factorial solution provided by the EFA and also offers the model of relations between the variables that best fits with the data [70–72].

The evaluation of the model fit was made taking into account the Chi-Square divided by degrees of freedom (CMIN/DF) and the p of Chi-square following Byrne's criteria [73]. The statistical p of Chi-square is dependent on the sample size, so it was convenient to use other goodness-of-fit indicators choosing the Tucker–Lewis index (TLI), the comparative fit index (CFI) following Hu and Bentler's criteria [74], the root-mean-square error of approximation (RMSEA), and the root-mean-square residuals (RMSR) [75,76].

Ordinal alpha coefficients were calculated [77,78] to assess reliability, considering values >0.70 acceptable and >0.90, excellent [79]. The analysis of the correlations between our tool and the SP2, the descriptive statistics of the subsamples and the relative operating characteristic (ROC) analysis were carried out to check the instrument's ability to classify between the two subsamples, using the IBM SPSS™ 24 [80] statistical package. Cohen's d statistic [81] was also calculated to check the magnitude of the effect size of the differences between the subsamples scores.

3. Results

3.1. Exploratory Factor Analysis

After administering the experimental version of the questionnaire to the sample, a solution of 41 items grouped into three correlated factors was obtained. Bartlett's (5025.4; $df = 820$; $p = 0.000$) and Kaiser–Meyer–Olkin test (0.912) statistics showed a very good sample suitability [82]. In Table 1, can be found both the rotated factorial matrix and factorial weights of each item. The three factors obtained represent (F1) modulation disorders with 13 items, (F2) discrimination disorders with 13 items, and (F3) sensory-based motor disorders with 15 items.

Table 1. Rotated factorial matrix and factorial weights of each item.

Items	F1	F2	F3
1. Shows disproportionate reactions if touched.	0.491		
2. Shows panic reactions to loud noises.	0.624		
3. Shows rejection of water when showering or washing.	0.340		
4. He is bothered by noisy and crowded places.	0.829		
5. When something goes wrong, it takes a long time to calm down.	0.566		
6. Shows discomfort with activities that involve spinning.	0.507		
7. Cannot concentrate or perform tasks when background noise.	0.627		
8. He gets agitated in the presence of very powerful light sources.	0.760		
9. Frequently touches or puts body parts or objects in his mouth.	0.394		
10. He is bothered with strong smells.	0.702		
11. Some clothes bother him; he feels itchy about some fabrics.	0.730		
12. He dislikes personal hygiene or grooming activities.	0.452		
13. Quick movements are unpleasant for him.	0.643		
14. Attends to his name or when he is called.		0.492	
15. Communicates feelings aimed at satisfying basic needs.		0.620	
16. Realizes when he is tired or exhausted.		0.639	
17. Shows comfort when hugged by parents or close relatives.		0.837	
18. Shows satisfaction when basic needs are met		0.959	
19. When he is disconsolate, he gets calmed by his parents.		0.720	
20. Expresses enjoyment or feels comfortable in certain situations.		0.897	
21. Can perceive danger in situations that could harm.		0.475	
22. Can identify basic emotions in himself and others.		0.442	
23. Can orientate himself in the environment.		0.418	
24. Notices that his heart is racing when he is tired or excited.		0.522	
25. Recognizes the elements that make him nervous.		0.578	
26. Has difficulty in recognizing people's faces.		0.374	
27. Has difficulty identifying parts of his own body.			0.655
28. Presents inability to reproduce speech movements.			0.737
29. Can ride a bicycle, rollerblades or a skateboard.			0.623
30. Can perform simple motor imitations.			0.724
31. Can fasten buttons or make loops to get dressed.			0.927
32. Can stack small blocks or string beads on a string.			0.569
33. Can use cutlery with both hands.			0.634
34. Can make copies from simple drawings.			0.930
35. Shows clumsiness in typing or using the computer keyboard.			0.814
36. Shows insecurity going downstairs/hills, holds on to railings.			0.485
37. Can adjust his strength when grasping objects.			0.452
38. Can cut with scissors properly for his age.			0.929
39. Can draw or colour within the proposed margins.			0.924
40. Can follow motor imitations containing multiple steps.			0.892
41. Can complete drawings with one half of it missing.			0.930

(F1) Modulation disorders; (F2) discrimination disorders; and (F3) sensory-based motor disorders. Items translated for readability; no cross-cultural adaptation performed.

With regards to the correlation between factors, moderate relationships were found between F1–F2 (0.38); F1–F3 (0.61), and F2–F3 (0.53) [81], which was to be expected since they are different stages within the same neurobiological process.

3.2. *Confirmatory Factor Analysis*

The CFA confirms the exploratory factorial solution revealing three latent variables which group the 41 observable variables (items). Figure 2 shows the graphical representation of the analyzed model, being (F1) modulation disorders, (F2) discrimination disorders, and (F3) sensory-based motor disorders. The factorial weights of every item and the covariation relations between the latent variables are shown.

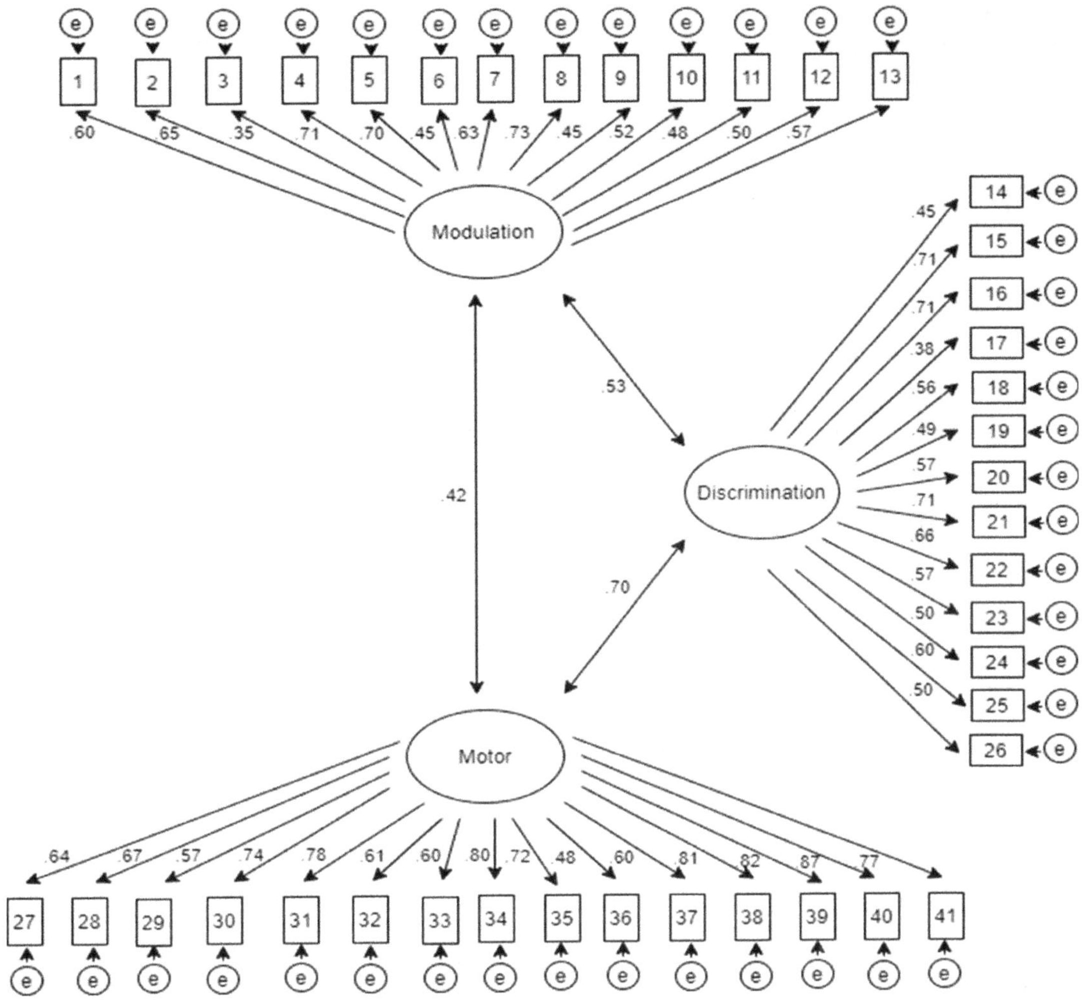

Figure 2. The Behavioral Observation on Sensory Stimuli Questionnaire for Parents' (BOSS-P) graphical representation after confirmatory factor analysis (CFA).

In Table 2, are represented the goodness-of-fit indices from the CFA, showing good values.

Table 2. BOSS-P goodness-of-fit indices from the confirmatory factor analysis (CFA).

Indices	Cut-Off	Value
CMIN/DF	<2	1.995
p (χ^2)	>0.05	0.000
TLI	>0.90	0.912
CFI	>0.90	0.925
RMSEA	<0.06	0.047 (0.043–0.051)
RMSR	<0.08	0.071

p (χ^2): chi-squared probability; CFI: comparative fit index; NNFI: non-normed fit index, RMSEA: root mean square error of approximation; RMSR: root mean square of residuals.

3.3. *Reliability*

To analyze the concurrent validity, we compared the BOSS-P with the SP2, a tool for SI assessment validated for Spanish children and adolescents. Both questionnaires were administered to 31 participants with ASD to study their correlations. As shown in Table 3, the modulation disorders factor (F1) from the BOSS-P was the only with significant and moderate correlations with the factors analyzed in the SP2.

Table 3. Correlation matrix between the Behavioral Observation on Sensory Stimuli Questionnaire for Parents (BOSS-P) and the Short Sensory Profile 2 (SP2).

	BOSS-P				SP2		
	F1	**F2**	**F3**	**Total**	**Sensory**	**Behavioral**	**Total**
F1	1						
F2	−0.076	1					
F3	−0.134	0.297	1				
Total	0.438 *	0.636 **	0.701 **	1			
Sensory	0.448 *	0.084	0.027	0.309	1		
Behaviour	0.600 **	0.034	0.147	0.446 *	0.613 **	1	
total	0.590 **	0.063	0.103	0.426 *	0.879 **	0.915 **	1

*. Correlation is significant at the 0.05 level (2-tailed). **. Correlation is significant at the 0.01 level (2-tailed) F1 = Modulation Disorders factor; F2 = Discrimination Disorders factor; F3 = Sensory-Based Motor Disorders factor; Sensory = Sensory Processing; Behavioral = Behavioral Responses associated with Sensory Processing.

3.4. *Questionnaire's Capability to Classify between ASD and Typical Development*

Descriptive statistics of participants with ASD (n = 145) and with typical development (n = 259) subsamples are shown in Table 4. It can be checked that both, mean and standard deviation of every subsample offer different scores.

Table 4. Descriptive statistics of ASD and typical development samples.

	Autism Spectrum Disorder				Typical Development			
	F1	**F2**	**F3**	**Total**	**F1**	**F2**	**F3**	**Total**
x	33.8	31.9	40.3	106	24.8	20.5	23.1	68.4
SD	8.9	8.0	11.9	19	7.7	5.5	7.8	16.0

x: mean; SD: standard deviation.

In Figure 3, graphical representation and statistics from ROC curves are provided. The area under the curve (AUC) shows differences with large effect magnitudes between the three factors, being the BOSS-P total score the most capable dimension to establish a correct classification of subjects according to their reference group.

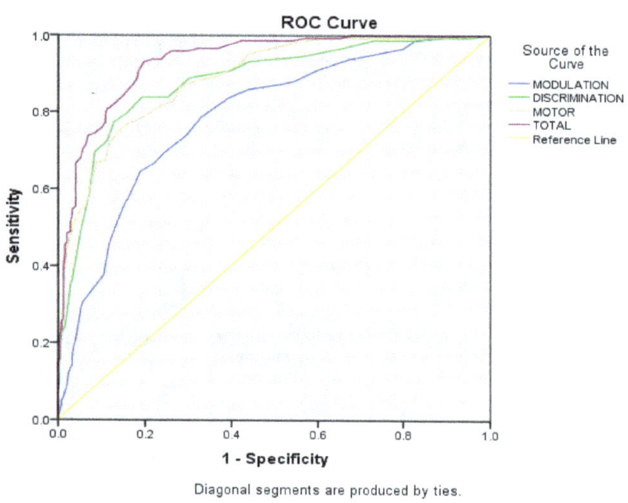

(a)

Dimensions	AUC (CI 95%)	p	d
Modulation	0.80 (0.75–0.84)	0.000	1.190
Discrimination	0.88 (0.84–0.91)	0.000	1.669
Motor	0.89 (0.85–0.92)	0.000	1.735
Total	0.93 (0.91–0.96)	0.000	2.176

AUC = Area under the curve; CI = confidence interval; p = significance level; d = size effect following Cohen criteria [81].

(b)

Figure 3. Graphical representation (**a**) and statistics (**b**) from the receiver operating characteristic (ROC) curves.

Considering the Rivière's Autism Spectrum Inventory scoring system, an approximation to the level of SI severity using the level of affectation in the Rivière's inventory and the BOSS-P interquartile scores was obtained in the ASD sample (see Table 5).

Table 5. Combination of the level of affectation in the Rivière's Inventory and the Behavioral Observation on Sensory Stimuli Questionnaire for Parents' (BOSS-P) interquartile scores.

		BOSS-P		
		F1	**F2**	**F3**
Rivière's inventory levels of severity	1 (8 points)	>40	>36	>50
	2 (6 points)	34–40	30–36	40–50
	3 (4 points)	27–34	27–30	31.5–40
	4 (2 points)	<27	<27	<31.5

F1 = modulation disorders factor; F2 = discrimination disorders factor; F3 = sensory-based motor disorders factor.

4. Discussion

4.1. About the BOSS-P Questionnaire

We aimed to create a questionnaire to support the new SI scale [62] added to the Rivière's Autism Spectrum Inventory [60,61]. The Rivière's Inventory is a widely used instrument in Spain and Latin America, which allows us to establish the level of the ASD severity, in line with the levels proposed in the DSM-5 [26]. The Rivière's Inventory is useful both during the diagnosis and intervention processes.

The BOSS-P is a screening instrument, administered through an interview with parents or carers, which is not intended to replace other comprehensive assessments, existing or emerging, with good psychometric properties on SI. However, our instrument has several advantages: (1) it is a quick test which is administered in 25–30 min; (2) that does not require specific training; (3) is open access; (4) is a complete tool, as it assesses items within the three areas described by Miller [6]: sensory modulation, sensory discrimination, and sensory-based motor disorders; (5) with good psychometric properties in terms of validity, reliability, and discrimination capacity; (6) created in Spain and therefore, adapted to the cultural characteristics of this country; (7) which fills a gap in terms of SI tools in Spanish-speaking population; and (8) which complements a psychological test widely used in the Spanish-speaking world, the Rivière's Inventory for people with ASD.

We have also provided an attempt to the combined use of the BOSS-P and the Rivière's Inventory, by linking the Rivière's level of severity and the BOSS-P quartile scores. Our instrument showed good psychometric values, offering a factorial structure formed by the three groups proposed by Miller [6]. These data are interesting because let us verify that Miller's model is consistent in different cultures and because. The BOSS-P's ability to classify between participants with ASD and typical development children seems adequate (AUC = 0.938), corresponding to a large effect size between the scores of both subsamples (d = 2.176) [83].

4.2. The BOSS-P and Other Instruments

Some reviews have found that psychometric properties of some of the SI tools are from poor to moderate, so the professionals must use the obtained data with caution [48,50], selecting appropriate SI assessments depending on the detected SI needs [47]. However, as aforementioned, there are few available instruments for Spanish children and adolescents. According to our best knowledge, neither the SIPT—considered as a Gold Standard for SI assessment [84]—nor the SPM are available for Spanish population, while the SP3D and the EASI are not yet published, being the SP2 the only tool of choice in Spain. The SP2 Spanish version covers a little shorter age range than the original, from 3 to 14.11 years. The BOSS-P covers from 4 to 19 years, a wider range including the full adolescent stage. The correlations between the BOSS-P and the SP2 only find relationships in modulation disorders, which could lead us to consider the necessity of using different tools to obtain information about SI if using the SP2.

Concerning its psychometric properties, the BOSS-P items present excellent internal consistency (alpha > 0.87), similar or superior other questionnaires used in the international context [46]. The ability of the questionnaire to discriminate between sub-samples offers a large effect size (d = 2.176), which is slightly higher than the size effect of the difference reported in other instruments [85].

4.3. Limitations and Future Lines

This research has some limitations. The information was completed through parents, and although instruments completed by families are considered to be valid [86], we must be careful because some parents should overestimate or underestimate the development of their children [87]. The sample was one of convenience. Another limitation was that we could not perform a test–retest. As future lines, we will try to improve the psychometric properties of the questionnaire, as well as to perform studies for its use in other Spanish-speaking countries different than Spain.

5. Conclusions

The preliminary study of the psychometric properties of Behavioral Observation on Sensory Stimuli Questionnaire for Parents (BOSS-P) shows good values for its use in Spanish children and adolescents diagnosed with ASD between 4 and 19 years. This tool was designed to help clinicians and educational professionals to establish the level of severity in children and adolescents with ASD diagnosis through the new SI scale in the Rivière's Autism Spectrum Inventory.

Author Contributions: Conceptualization, S.B.-F., M.G., and B.D.-G.; Methodology, A.G.-G.; Software, A.G.-G.; Formal analysis, A.G.-G.; Writing—original draft preparation, S.B.-F., M.G.; Writing—review and editing, S.B.-F. and M.G.; Supervision, A.G.-G. All authors have read and agreed to the published version of the manuscript.

Acknowledgments: We want to thank all the participants who kindly dedicated their time to help us in this research.

References

1. Ayres, A.J. *Sensory Integration and Learning Disorders*; Western Psychological Services: Los Angeles, CA, USA, 1972; ISBN 978-0-87424-303-1.
2. Humphries, T.; Wright, M.; McDougall, B.; Vertes, J. The Efficacy of Sensory Integration Therapy for Children with Learning Disability. *Phys. Occup. Ther. Pediatr.* **1990**, *10*, 1–17. [CrossRef]
3. Williams, M.S.; Shellenberger, S. *The Alert Program for Self-Regulation*; TherapyWorks Inc.: Albuquerque, NM, USA, 1995; ISBN 978-0-9643041-1-6.
4. Dunn, W. Supporting Children to Participate Successfully in Everyday Life by Using Sensory Processing Knowledge. *Infants Young Child.* **2007**, *20*, 84–101. [CrossRef]
5. Kilroy, E.; Aziz-Zadeh, L.; Cermak, S.A. Ayres Theories of Autism and Sensory Integration Revisited: What Contemporary Neuroscience Has to Say. *Brain Sci.* **2019**, *9*, 68. [CrossRef]
6. Miller, L.J.; Anzalone, M.E.; Lane, S.J.; Cermak, S.A.; Osten, E.T. Concept Evolution in Sensory Integration: A Proposed Nosology for Diagnosis. *Am. J. Occup. Ther.* **2007**, *61*, 135–140. [CrossRef]
7. Sher, B. *Everyday Games for Sensory Processing Disorder: 100 Playful Activities to Empower Children with Sensory Differences*; Althea Press: Berkeley, CA, USA, 2016; ISBN 978-1-62315-700-5.
8. Lane, S.J.; Bundy, A.C. *Kids Can Be Kids: A Childhood Occupations Approach*; Lane, S., Bundy, A.C., Eds.; F.A. Davis Co.: Philadelphia, PA, USA, 2012; ISBN 978-0-8036-1228-0.
9. Lane, S.J.; Mailloux, Z.; Schoen, S.; Bundy, A.; May-Benson, T.A.; Parham, L.D.; Roley, S.S.; Schaaf, R.C. Neural Foundations of Ayres Sensory Integration®. *Brain Sci.* **2019**, *9*, 153. [CrossRef]
10. Cermak, S.A. Reflections on 25 Years of Dyspraxia Research. In *Ayres Dyspraxia Monograph*; Pediatric Therapy Network: Torrance, CA, USA, 2011.
11. Ackerley, R.; Kavounoudias, A. The role of tactile afference in shaping motor behaviour and implications for prosthetic innovation. *Neuropsychologia* **2015**, *79*, 192–205. [CrossRef]

12. Beaudry Bellefeuille, I.; Sánchez Padrón, O. *Tengo Duendes en Las Piernas*; Nobel: Oviedo, Spain, 2011; ISBN 978-84-8459-654-7.
13. Pfeiffer, C.; Serino, A.; Blanke, O. The vestibular system: A spatial reference for bodily self-consciousness. *Front. Integr. Neurosci.* **2014**, *8*, 31. [CrossRef]
14. Mahler, K.J.; Craig, A.D. *Interoception: The Eighth Sensory System: Practical Solutions for Improving Self-Regulation, Self-Awareness and Social Understanding of Individuals with Autism Spectrum and Related Disorders*; AAPC Publishing: Shawnee Mission, KS, USA, 2016; ISBN 978-1-942197-14-0.
15. Farb, N.A.S.; Daubenmier, J.; Price, C.J.; Gard, T.; E Kerr, C.; Dunn, B.D.; Klein, A.C.; Paulus, M.P.; Mehling, W.E. Interoception, contemplative practice, and health. *Front. Psychol.* **2015**, *6*, 763. [CrossRef]
16. Ayres, A.J. *Sensory Integration and Praxis Tests*; Western Psychological Services: Los Angeles, CA, USA, 1989.
17. Gourley, L.; Wind, C.; Henninger, E.M.; Chinitz, S. Sensory Processing Difficulties, Behavioral Problems, and Parental Stress in a Clinical Population of Young Children. *J. Child Fam. Stud.* **2013**, *22*, 912–921. [CrossRef]
18. Miller, L.J.; Nielsen, D.M.; Schoen, S.; Brett-Green, B.A. Perspectives on sensory processing disorder: A call for translational research. *Front. Integr. Neurosci.* **2009**, *3*, 3. [CrossRef]
19. Galiana-Simal, A.; Vela-Romero, M.; Romero-Vela, V.M.; Oliver-Tercero, N.; García-Olmo, V.; Benito-Castellanos, P.J.; Muñoz-Martinez, V.; Beato-Fernandez, L. Sensory processing disorder: Key points of a frequent alteration in neurodevelopmental disorders. *Cogent Med.* **2020**, *7*. [CrossRef]
20. Butera, C.; Ring, P.; Sideris, J.; Jayashankar, A.; Kilroy, E.; Harrison, L.; Cermak, S.; Aziz-Zadeh, L. Impact of Sensory Processing on School Performance Outcomes in High Functioning Individuals with Autism Spectrum Disorder. *Mind Brain Educ.* **2020**, *14*, 243–254. [CrossRef]
21. Baranek, G.T.; David, F.J.; Poe, M.D.; Stone, W.L.; Watson, L.R. Sensory Experiences Questionnaire: Discriminating sensory features in young children with autism, developmental delays, and typical development. *J. Child Psychol. Psychiatry* **2006**, *47*, 591–601. [CrossRef] [PubMed]
22. Dunn, W. The Sensations of Everyday Life: Empirical, Theoretical, and Pragmatic Considerations. *Am. J. Occup. Ther.* **2001**, *55*, 608–620. [CrossRef] [PubMed]
23. Ismael, N.; Lawson, L.M.; Hartwell, J. Relationship Between Sensory Processing and Participation in Daily Occupations for Children with Autism Spectrum Disorder: A Systematic Review of Studies That Used Dunn's Sensory Processing Framework. *Am. J. Occup. Ther.* **2018**, *72*. [CrossRef]
24. Schaaf, R.C.; Mailloux, Z. *Clinician's Guide for Implementing Ayres Sensory Integration: Promoting Participation for Children with Autism*; AOTA Press: Bethesda, MD, USA, 2015; ISBN 978-1-56900-365-7.
25. Mulligan, S.; A Schoen, S.; Miller, L.J.; Valdez, A.; Magalhaes, D. The Sensory Processing 3-Dimensions Scale: Initial Studies of Reliability and Item Analyses. *Open J. Occup. Ther.* **2019**, *7*, 4. [CrossRef]
26. APA. *Diagnostic and Statistical Manual of Mental Disorders*, 5th ed.; American Psychiatric Association: Washington, DC, USA, 2013; p. 5.
27. Bölte, S.; Girdler, S.; Marschik, P.B. The contribution of environmental exposure to the etiology of autism spectrum disorder. *Cell. Mol. Life Sci.* **2019**, *76*, 1275–1297. [CrossRef]
28. Steinman, G.; Mankuta, D. Molecular biology of autism's etiology—An alternative mechanism. *Med. Hypotheses* **2019**, *130*, 109–272. [CrossRef]
29. Linke, A.C.; Keehn, R.J.J.; Pueschel, E.B.; Fishman, I.; Müller, R.-A. Children with ASD show links between aberrant sound processing, social symptoms, and atypical auditory interhemispheric and thalamocortical functional connectivity. *Dev. Cogn. Neurosci.* **2018**, *29*, 117–126. [CrossRef]
30. Chang, Y.-S.; Owen, J.P.; Desai, S.S.; Hill, S.S.; Arnett, A.B.; Harris, J.; Marco, E.J.; Mukherjee, P. Autism and Sensory Processing Disorders: Shared White Matter Disruption in Sensory Pathways but Divergent Connectivity in Social-Emotional Pathways. *PLoS ONE* **2014**, *9*, e103038. [CrossRef]
31. Schaaf, R.C.; Lane, A.E. Toward a Best-Practice Protocol for Assessment of Sensory Features in ASD. *J. Autism Dev. Disord.* **2015**, *45*, 1380–1395. [CrossRef] [PubMed]
32. Posar, A.; Visconti, P. Sensory abnormalities in children with autism spectrum disorder. *J. Pediatr.* **2018**, *94*, 342–350. [CrossRef]
33. Marco, E.J.; Hinkley, L.B.N.; Hill, S.S.; Nagarajan, S.S. Sensory Processing in Autism: A Review of Neurophysiologic Findings. *Pediatr. Res.* **2011**, *69*, 48R–54R. [CrossRef] [PubMed]
34. Suarez, M.A. Sensory Processing in Children with Autism Spectrum Disorders and Impact on Functioning. *Pediatr. Clin. North Am.* **2012**, *59*, 203–214. [CrossRef] [PubMed]

35. Glod, M.; Riby, D.M.; Rodgers, J. Sensory processing profiles and autistic symptoms as predictive factors in autism spectrum disorder and Williams syndrome. *J. Intellect. Disabil. Res.* **2020**, *64*, 657–665. [CrossRef] [PubMed]
36. Schoen, S.; Lane, S.J.; Mailloux, Z.; May-Benson, T.; Parham, L.D.; Roley, S.S.; Schaaf, R.C. A systematic review of ayres sensory integration intervention for children with autism. *Autism Res.* **2019**, *12*, 6–19. [CrossRef] [PubMed]
37. Bodison, S.C.; Parham, L.D. Specific Sensory Techniques and Sensory Environmental Modifications for Children and Youth with Sensory Integration Difficulties: A Systematic Review. *Am. J. Occup. Ther.* **2017**, *72*, 72011–90040. [CrossRef]
38. Ben-Sasson, A.; Hen, L.; Fluss, R.; Cermak, S.A.; Engel-Yeger, B.; Gal, E. A Meta-Analysis of Sensory Modulation Symptoms in Individuals with Autism Spectrum Disorders. *J. Autism Dev. Disord.* **2009**, *39*, 1–11. [CrossRef]
39. Di Renzo, M.; Di Castelbianco, F.B.; Vanadia, E.; Petrillo, M.; Racinaro, L.; Rea, M. Sensory Processing and Repetitive Behaviors in Clinical Assessment of Preschool Children with Autism Spectrum Disorder. *J. Child Adolesc. Behav.* **2017**, *5*, 5. [CrossRef]
40. Dakopolos, A.J.; Jahromi, L.B. Differences in sensory responses among children with autism spectrum disorder and typical development: Links to joint attention and social competence. *Infant Child Dev.* **2018**, *28*, e2117. [CrossRef]
41. Thye, M.D.; Bednarz, H.M.; Herringshaw, A.J.; Sartin, E.B.; Kana, R.K. The impact of atypical sensory processing on social impairments in autism spectrum disorder. *Dev. Cogn. Neurosci.* **2018**, *29*, 151–167. [CrossRef] [PubMed]
42. Miller, M.; Chukoskie, L.; Zinni, M.; Townsend, J.; Trauner, D. Dyspraxia, motor function and visual–motor integration in autism. *Behav. Brain Res.* **2014**, *269*, 95–102. [CrossRef] [PubMed]
43. Kaur, M.; Srinivasan, S.M.; Bhat, A.N. Comparing motor performance, praxis, coordination, and interpersonal synchrony between children with and without Autism Spectrum Disorder (ASD). *Res. Dev. Disabil.* **2018**, *72*, 79–95. [CrossRef] [PubMed]
44. Günal, A.; Bumin, G.; Huri, M. The Effects of Motor and Cognitive Impairments on Daily Living Activities and Quality of Life in Children with Autism. *J. Occup. Ther. Sch. Early Interv.* **2019**, *12*, 444–454. [CrossRef]
45. Wong, C.; Odom, S.L.; Hume, K.A.; Cox, A.W.; Fettig, A.; Kucharczyk, S.; Brock, M.E.; Plavnick, J.B.; Fleury, V.P.; Schultz, T.R. Evidence-Based Practices for Children, Youth, and Young Adults with Autism Spectrum Disorder: A Comprehensive Review. *J. Autism Dev. Disord.* **2015**, *45*, 1951–1966. [CrossRef]
46. Jorquera-Cabrera, S.; Romero-Ayuso, D.; Rodriguez-Gil, G.; Triviño-Juárez, J.-M. Assessment of Sensory Processing Characteristics in Children between 3 and 11 Years Old: A Systematic Review. *Front. Pediatr.* **2017**, *5*, 57. [CrossRef]
47. Eeles, A.L.; Spittle, A.J.; Anderson, P.J.; Brown, N.; Lee, K.J.; Boyd, R.; Doyle, L.W. Assessments of sensory processing in infants: A systematic review. *Dev. Med. Child Neurol.* **2012**, *55*, 314–326. [CrossRef]
48. Burns, C.O.; Dixon, D.R.; Novack, M.; Granpeesheh, D. A Systematic Review of Assessments for Sensory Processing Abnormalities in Autism Spectrum Disorder. *Rev. J. Autism Dev. Disord.* **2017**, *4*, 209–224. [CrossRef]
49. Dubois, D.; Lymer, E.; Gibson, B.E.; Desarkar, P.; Nalder, E.J. Assessing Sensory Processing Dysfunction in Adults and Adolescents with Autism Spectrum Disorder: A Scoping Review. *Brain Sci.* **2017**, *7*, 108. [CrossRef]
50. Yeung, L.H.J.; Thomacos, N. Assessments of sensory processing in infants and children with autism spectrum disorder between 0–12 years old: A scoping review. *Res. Autism Spectr. Disord.* **2020**, *72*, 101517. [CrossRef]
51. Dunn, W. *Sensory Profile User's Manual*; Pearson Psychcop: San Antonio, TX, USA, 1999.
52. Dunn, W. *Sensory Profile 2 Manual*; Pearson Psychcop: San Antonio, TX, USA, 2014.
53. Parham, L.D.; Ecker, C.; Miller Kuhaneck, H.; Henry, D.A.; Glennon, T.J. *Sensory Processing Measure (SPM): Manual*; Western Psychological Services: Los Angeles, CA, USA, 2007.
54. Mulligan, S.; Schoen, S.; Miller, L. Scientific Research Panel 304C Reliability and Item Analyses of the Sensory Processing 3-Dimensions Scale. *Am. J. Occup. Ther.* **2018**, *72*, 7211500055. [CrossRef]
55. Mailloux, Z.; Parham, L.D.; Roley, S.S.; Ruzzano, L.; Schaaf, R.C. Introduction to the Evaluation in Ayres Sensory Integration® (EASI). *Am. J. Occup. Ther.* **2017**, *72*, 72011–95030. [CrossRef]
56. Petrocchi, S.; Levante, A.; Lecciso, F. Systematic Review of Level 1 and Level 2 Screening Tools for Autism Spectrum Disorders in Toddlers. *Brain Sci.* **2020**, *10*, 180. [CrossRef]

57. Towle, P.O.; Patrick, P.A. Autism Spectrum Disorder Screening Instruments for Very Young Children: A Systematic Review. *Autism Res. Treat.* **2016**, *2016*, 1–29. [CrossRef]
58. Payakachat, N.; Tilford, J.M.; Kovacs, E.; Kuhlthau, K. Autism spectrum disorders: A review of measures for clinical, health services and cost–effectiveness applications. *Expert Rev. Pharm. Outcomes Res.* **2012**, *12*, 485–503. [CrossRef]
59. Randall, M.; Egberts, K.J.; Samtani, A.; Scholten, R.J.; Hooft, L.; Livingstone, N.; Sterling-Levis, K.; Woolfenden, S.; Williams, K. Diagnostic tests for autism spectrum disorder (ASD) in preschool children. *Cochrane Database Syst. Rev.* **2018**, *7*, CD009044. [CrossRef]
60. Rivière, Á. Tratamiento y Definición del Espectro Autista. In *Tratamiento del Autismo. Nuevas Perspectivas*; Instituto de Migraciones y Servicios Sociales: Madrid, Spain, 1998; ISBN 84-88986-70-X.
61. Rivière, A. *IDEA: Inventario de Espectro Autista*; Fundec: Buenos Aires, Argentina, 2002.
62. García-Gómez, A. A proposal of three additional dimensions to the Rivière's Autism Spectrum Inventory. *Psicol. Educ.* in press. [CrossRef]
63. Williams, Z.J.; Failla, M.D.; Gotham, K.O.; Woynaroski, T.G.; Cascio, C. Psychometric Evaluation of the Short Sensory Profile in Youth with Autism Spectrum Disorder. *J. Autism Dev. Disord.* **2018**, *48*, 4231–4249. [CrossRef]
64. Dunn, W. *Perfil Sensorial 2 Breve*; Adaptación Española; Pearson Psychcop: Madrid, Spain, 2016; ISBN 978-84-9035-547-3.
65. Ferrando, P.J.; Lorenzo-Seva, U. Program FACTOR at 10: Origins, development and future directions. *Psicothema* **2017**, *29*, 236–240.
66. Lorenzo-Seva, U.; Ferrando, P.J. Factor: A computer program to fit the exploratory factor analysis model. *Behav. Res. Methods* **2006**, *38*, 88–91. [CrossRef]
67. Manual of the Program. Available online: http://psico.fcep.urv.es/utilitats/factor/documentation/Manual-of-the-Factor-Program-v92.pdf (accessed on 20 August 2020).
68. Timmerman, M.E.; Lorenzo-Seva, U. Dimensionality assessment of ordered polytomous items with parallel analysis. *Psychol. Methods* **2011**, *16*, 209–220. [CrossRef] [PubMed]
69. Arbuckle, J. *Amos 24.0 User's Guide*; IBM SPSS: Chicago, IL, USA, 2015.
70. Flora, D.B.; LaBrish, C.; Chalmers, R.P. Old and New Ideas for Data Screening and Assumption Testing for Exploratory and Confirmatory Factor Analysis. *Front. Psychol.* **2012**, *3*, 3. [CrossRef]
71. Lloret-Segura, S.; Ferreres-Traver, A.; Hernández-Baeza, A.; Tomás-Marco, I. Exploratory Item Factor Analysis: A practical guide revised and updated. *An. Psicol.* **2014**, *30*, 1151–1169. [CrossRef]
72. Ferrando, P.J.; Anguiano-Carrasco, C. Factor analysis as a research technique in psychology. *Pap. Psicólogo* **2010**, *31*, 18–33.
73. Byrne, B.M. A Primer of LISREL. In *Texto original: Basic Applications and Programming for Confirmatory Factor Analytic Models*; Springer: New York, NY, USA, 1989; ISBN 978-1-4613-8887-6.
74. Hu, L.-T.; Bentler, P.M. Cutoff criteria for fit indexes in covariance structure analysis: Conventional criteria versus new alternatives. *Struct. Equ. Model. Multidiscip. J.* **1999**, *6*, 1–55.
75. Hair, J.F. *Multivariate Data Analysis: A Global Perspective*; Pearson Education: London, UK, 2010; ISBN 978-0-13-515309-3.
76. Browne, M.W.; Cudeck, R. Alternative Ways of Assessing Model Fit. *Sociol. Methods Res.* **1992**, *21*, 230–258. [CrossRef]
77. Gadermann, A.M.; Guhn, M.; Zumbo, B.D. Ordinal Alpha. *Encycl. Qual. Life Well Being Res.* **2014**, 4513–4515. [CrossRef]
78. Oliden, P.E.; Zumbo, B.D. Reliability coefficients for ordinal response scales. *Psicothema* **2008**, *20*, 896–901.
79. Pallant, J. *SPSS Survival Manual: A Step by Step Guide to Data Analysis Using IBM SPSS*, 5th ed.; McGraw Hill: Berkshire, UK, 2013; ISBN 978-0-335-26258-8.
80. IBM Corp IBM SPSS Statistics for Windows, Version 24.0. Available online: https://he02.tci-thaijo.org/index.php/ramajournal/statistical_software_references_format (accessed on 22 August 2020).
81. Cohen, J. Statistical Power Analysis for the Behavioral Sciences. Lawrence Earlbaum Associates Hillsdale, NJ, USA. Available online: http://www.utstat.toronto.edu/~{}brunner/oldclass/378f16/readings/CohenPower.pdf (accessed on 15 October 2020).
82. Jöreskog, K.G.; Sörbom, D. *LISREL 8: Structural Equation Modeling with the SIMPLIS Command Language*; Scientific Software International: Lincolnwood, IL, USA, 1993; ISBN 978-0-89498-033-6.

83. Salgado, J.F. Transforming the Area under the Normal Curve (AUC) into Cohen's d, Pearson's r pb, Odds-Ratio, and Natural Log Odds-Ratio: Two Conversion Tables. *Eur. J. Psychol. Appl. Leg. Context* **2018**, *10*, 35–47. [CrossRef]
84. Roley, S.S.; Blanche, E.I.; Schaaf, R.C. *Understanding the Nature of Sensory Integration with Diverse Populations*; PRO-ED: Indianapolis, IN, USA, 2007; ISBN 978-1-4164-0332-6.
85. Schoen, S.; Miller, L.J.; Sullivan, J.C. Measurement in Sensory Modulation: The Sensory Processing Scale Assessment. *Am. J. Occup. Ther.* **2014**, *68*, 522–530. [CrossRef]
86. Ministerio de Sanidad, Servicios Sociales e Igualdad. *Salud Mental y Calidad de Vida en la Población Infantil*; Serie Informes Monográficos no2; Ministerio de Sanidad, Servicios Sociales e Igualdad: Madrid, Spain, 2014.
87. Van Gameren-Oosterom, H.B.; Van Dommelen, P.; Schönbeck, Y.; Oudesluys-Murphy, A.M.; Van Wouwe, J.P.; Buitendijk, S.E. Prevalence of Overweight in Dutch Children with Down Syndrome. *Pediatrics* **2012**, *130*, e1520–e1526. [CrossRef] [PubMed]

2

Role of Oligodendrocytes and Myelin in the Pathophysiology of Autism Spectrum Disorder

Alma Y. Galvez-Contreras [1,*], David Zarate-Lopez [2,3], Ana L. Torres-Chavez [2,3] and Oscar Gonzalez-Perez [2,*]

1 Department of Neuroscience, Centro Universitario de Ciencias de la Salud, University of Guadalajara, Guadalajara 44340, Mexico
2 Laboratory of Neuroscience, School of Psychology, University of Colima, Colima 28040, Mexico; dzarate@ucol.mx (D.Z.-L.); torres_chavez@ucol.mx (A.L.T.-C.)
3 Physiological Sciences PhD Program, School of Medicine, University of Colima, Colima 28040, Mexico
* Correspondence: alma.galvez@academicos.udg.mx (A.Y.G.-C.); osglez@ucol.mx (O.G.-P.)

Abstract: Autism Spectrum Disorder (ASD) is an early neurodevelopmental disorder that involves deficits in interpersonal communication, social interaction, and repetitive behaviors. Although ASD pathophysiology is still uncertain, alterations in the abnormal development of the frontal lobe, limbic areas, and putamen generate an imbalance between inhibition and excitation of neuronal activity. Interestingly, recent findings suggest that a disruption in neuronal connectivity is associated with neural alterations in white matter production and myelination in diverse brain regions of patients with ASD. This review is aimed to summarize the most recent evidence that supports the notion that abnormalities in the oligodendrocyte generation and axonal myelination in specific brain regions are involved in the pathophysiology of ASD. Fundamental molecular mediators of these pathological processes are also examined. Determining the role of alterations in oligodendrogenesis and myelination is a fundamental step to understand the pathophysiology of ASD and identify possible therapeutic targets.

Keywords: oligodendrogenesis; myelination; epidermal growth factor; insulin-like growth factor

1. Introduction

In 1943, Kanner described the first symptoms of Autism Spectrum Disorder (ASD) as an innate disturbance of affective contact. In 1944, Hans Asperger included a psychopathic disturbance of social interaction in the symptomatology of ASD [1]. To date, ASD is considered an early neurodevelopmental disorder [1], which is characterized by substantial deficits in social interaction and communication associated with repetitive and restricted behaviors [2]. The incidence of ASD around the world is 1 per 160 children [3] but some epidemiological variations have been reported among world regions [3,4]. Possible explanations for this variability include dissimilarity in methods, variations in diagnostic or community identification, and potential risk factors [5]. To date, the Diagnostic and Statistical Manual of Mental Disorders (DSM-5), ASD comprises only two symptomatic domains: deficits in communication and social interaction, and repetitive and restricted behavior [6]. Thus, the current ASD definition includes autistic disorder, Asperger's disorder, pervasive developmental disorder not otherwise specified (PDD-NOS), Rett's disorder, and childhood disintegrative disorder, which represent a moderate variation in ASD diagnosis with respect to the previous DSM version [7]. Throughout life, the clinical course of ASD is variable and includes a wide range of clinical manifestations [8], including poor social skills, language, intellectual disabilities, sensory abnormalities (hyper- or hypo-sensory responsiveness), motor tics, and gross motor discoordination [8–11]. Nevertheless,

ASD is a heterogeneous disorder with many inter-subject dissimilarities in social behaviors that some authors have associated with a combination of genetic variants that contribute to different phenotypic outcomes [12,13].

During the first years of life, the clinical symptoms correlate with two pathophysiological abnormalities in the brain. The overgrowth of certain brain regions precedes some symptoms of ASD and also coincides with periods of high neural plasticity [14,15]. From prenatal stages to birth, a slight delay in neural development is observed, which seems to be compensated by an accelerated brain growth during the first years of life [16,17]. This rapid overgrowth tends to reduce during the second and third years of life [14]. From the 5th to 16th year of life, this abnormal brain growth ceases and tends to normalize when compared to typically developing subjects [14,18]. In adults, some structures, such as the frontal lobe, cerebellum, and amygdala, show a normal or reduced volume as compared to typically developing subjects [19–22]. Recently, it has been reported that children with ASD show significant alterations in the connectivity between the right insula with the supramarginal gyrus and left superior frontal gyrus [23]. Adolescents with ASD also show age-dependent alterations in the connectivity between the frontal lobe and parietal region [24], which supports the notion that ASD is a dynamic developmental syndrome. Some of these anatomical abnormalities have been associated with extensive changes in myelination, excessive oxidative stress [25], glial activation [26], minicolumn pathology [27], abnormal neurogenesis, and neuronal migration [28,29]. Because the cerebral size in patients with ASD often correlates with functional deficits [30,31], these changes in the brain-growth pattern seem to be crucial to understand the symptomatology and etiology of ASD.

In the postnatal brain, white matter enlargement is one of the biological events that produces considerable changes in the volume of brain regions [32]. In the human brain, myelination is mostly a postnatal process that reaches its highest during childhood and continues until early adulthood [33]. Hence, myelination and oligodendrogenesis appear to be crucial events that notably modify several neuroanatomical structures. Increasing evidence suggests that this dynamic process may be disrupted in the ASD brain [34]. Patients with ASD show enlarged cerebellar and cerebral white matter structures and this increase occurs during the first years of life. This brain overgrowth of white matter observed in ASD is not sustained throughout life and tends to be smaller with age [14]. A pilot study in children diagnosed with autism between 4 and 6 years suggested that alterations in axons and myelin of the *corona radiata* appear to be associated with the clinical severity of ASD [35]. Additional evidence in adolescents indicates that ASD brains show fewer axons, less axonal volume, and a low density of white matter tracts in the corpus callosum, frontal-occipital fasciculus, right uncinate fasciculus, and right arcuate fasciculus [36]. Interestingly, pathological changes in the cytoarchitecture of white matter in all brain lobes [30] and altered myelination rate in corpus callosum [1,37] may explain the dysfunctional connectivity found in medial parietal and temporoparietal regions [16]. These structural disruptions have also been correlated to parental age [38] and may explain the severity of stereotypes and deficits in social interaction [31]. In contrast, clinical data indicate that the improvement in ASD symptoms is associated with white matter recovery [39]. In this review, we described the general pathogenesis and neuroanatomical changes found in several regions of the ASD brain and many of these areas correspond to white matter regions. Thus, we explained proteins, genes, and signaling pathways that regulate the oligodendroglial process, which in some cases are coincidentally affected in ASD. Finally, we compiled the most recent evidence that suggests a role for myelination and oligodendrocytes in the pathogenesis of ASD. Taken together, these reports suggest that some pathological changes observed in the white matter may explain the abnormal brain development related to ASD.

2. Pathophysiological Basis of ASD

ASD is considered by some authors as a brain connectivity disorder that, in turn, modifies the inhibition/excitation balance. Some reports sustain that the neuronal hypoconnectivity in frontal areas and fusiform face area observed in ASD patients [40] may explain the morphological alteration in brain size and interhemispheric connections [41–43]. This balance between neuronal inhibition and excitation is coordinated by several biological and molecular processes that modify synapse structure and brain plasticity [44], which may affect the frontotemporal, frontolimbic, frontoparietal, and interhemispheric connections [21]. Intriguingly, some local neuronal circuits in the frontal lobe are overconnected, whereas long-range connections (cortico-parietal, sub-cortical systems, and inter-hemispheric tracts) seem to be reduced in ASD patients [16,21,45,46].

However, abnormalities in neuronal connections per se cannot explain all the functional changes observed in ASD, and emerging evidence suggests that glial cells may play a pivotal role in neuroanatomical and behavioral changes found in ASD. Astrocytes and oligodendrocytes may contribute to neurochemical imbalances described in the autistic brain by disrupting neurotransmission or modifying axonal conduction. In mice models for ASD, the genetic depletion of glutamate transporter-1 (GLT-1) in astrocytes increases excitatory neurotransmission that is related to a high frequency of repetitive behaviors [44], whereas phosphatase and tensin homolog (PTEN) mislocation produces precocious maturation of oligodendrocytes that is associated with aberrant myelination [47]. A recent report suggests that a mutation in the eukaryotic translation initiation factor 4E (eIF4E) in microglia produces sex-dependent ASD-like behaviors by modifying synaptic development and function in male mice [48]. Therefore, neuroinflammation and pro-inflammatory cytokines released by microglia can alter gliotransmission, ion-channel expression, brain plasticity, and oxidative stress that may also lead to behavioral dysfunctions [49]. Interestingly, oxidative stress has also been implicated in the pathophysiological process of ASD by affecting the myelination process [50,51].

In this regard, oxidant radicals can damage the oligodendrocyte population that fails to differentiate into myelin-forming mature oligodendrocytes and increase a significant proliferation of oligodendrocyte precursor cells (OPCs) that, in turn, impair the whole myelination process [52]. Thus, oligodendrocytes are a very susceptible cell lineage to oxidant radicals because they have low levels of glutathione (a highly efficient antioxidant molecule) and elevated amounts of sphingolipids [53,54]. Therefore, oligodendrocytes represent a plausible cellular target for the oxidative stress identified in the ASD brain.

Abnormal development in the white matter and myelination has been found in animal models of ASD [55–59] and humans [60,61]. Neuroimaging studies support the notion that ASD patients have a complex and dynamic disorder [62] in which the level of white matter involvement is associated with clinical severity [60,63–69]. ASD patients show extensive alterations in the white matter of several cortical and subcortical regions, such as the orbitofrontal cortex [70], anterior cingulate cortex and lateral prefrontal cortex [61], external capsule [71,72], arcuate fasciculus [73–75], ventral temporal gyrus [60,76], temporo-parietal junctions [60,72,77], amygdala [60], occipitofrontal fasciculus [60], occipitotemporal gyrus [77], thalamus [78], superior and middle cerebellar peduncle [79,80], medial lemniscus [81], and the corticospinal tract [82–84] (Figure 1). However, some clinical reports have shown contradictory findings in the myelination process of ASD brains. From childhood to adolescence, the inferior longitudinal fasciculus shows pathological changes in the white matter density [83–90] (Table 1). The uncinate fasciculus of ASD patients younger than 15 years may show increased or decreased white matter density [64,65,74,75,91], but, after age 15, only an increase in the white matter has been found [87]. ASD patients older than 15 years may also have high white matter density in the lingual gyrus [78], amygdala-fusiform pathway, and left hippocampi-fusiform pathway [92].

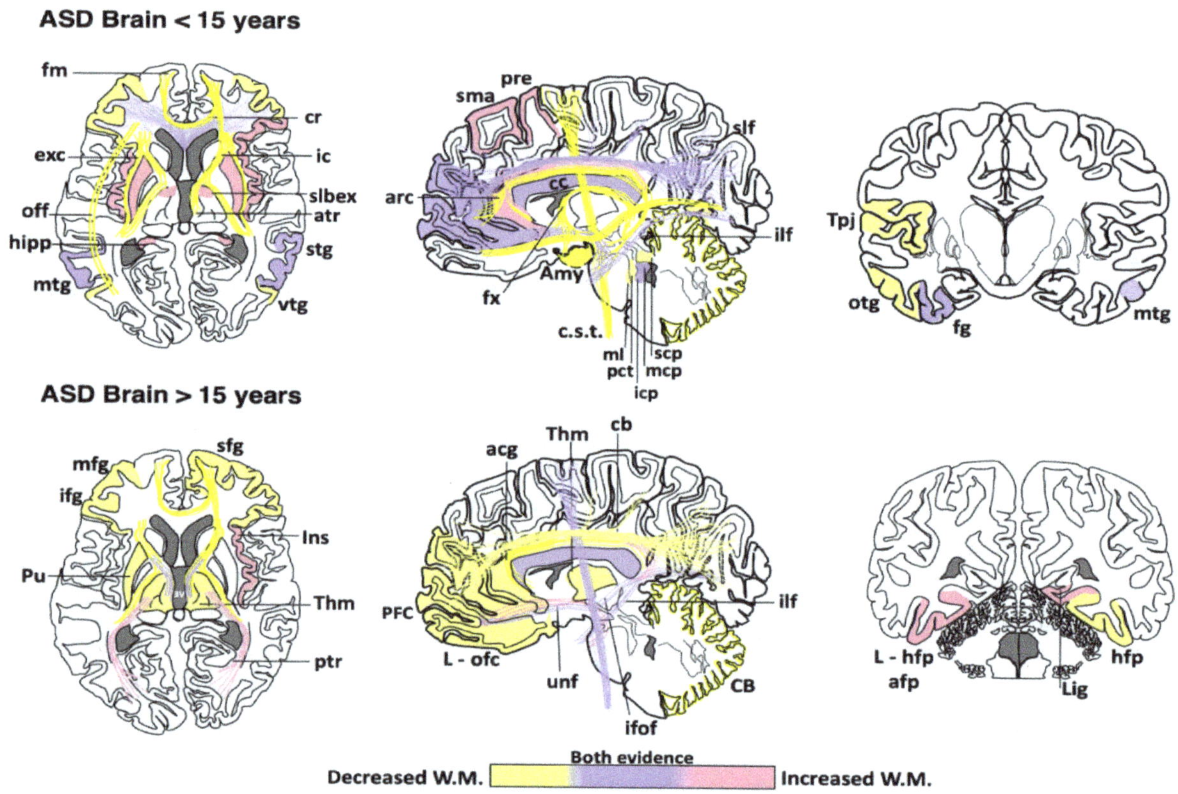

Figure 1. Cortical areas, subcortical areas and white matter tracts affected in patients with Autism Spectrum Disorder (ASD). White matter areas with the most noticeable changes are represented in the three anatomical planes of the human brain: axial, sagittal, and coronal, respectively. Brain schemes also indicate the most common myelination changes that occur in ASD patients during two different stages of development [21,30,36,60,64,65,67,70–109]. acg: anterior cingulate gyrus; afp: amygdala-fusiform pathway; Amy: amygdala; atr: anterior thalamic radiation; arc: arcuate fasciculus; CB: cerebellum; cb: cingulum bundle; cc: corpus callosum; c.s.t.: corticospinal tract; cr: corona radiata; exc: external capsule; fm: forceps minor; fx: fornix; fg: fusiform gyrus; hipp: hippocampus; icp: inferior cerebellar peduncle; ifof: inferior fronto-occipital fasciculus; ifg: inferior frontal gyrus; Ins: insula; ic: internal capsule; L-hfp: left hippocampus-fusiform pathway; L-ilf: Left inferior longitudinal fasciculus; L-ofc: left orbitofrontal cortex; lig: lingual gyrus; ml: medial lemniscus; mcp: middle cerebellar peduncle; mtg: middle frontal gyrus; mtg: middle temporal gyrus; off: occipitofrontal fasciculus; otg: occipitotemporal gyrus; pct: pontine crossing tracts; ptr: posterior thalamic radiation; pre: precentral area; PFC: prefrontal cortex; Pu: putamen; slbex: sub-lobar extranuclear area; scp: superior cerebellar peduncle; sfg: superior frontal gyrus; slf: superior longitudinal fasciculus; stg: superior temporal gyrus; sma: supplementary motor area; Tpj: temporoparietal junction; Thm: thalamus; unf: uncinate fasciculus; vtg: ventral temporal gyrus.

Table 1. Main changes observed in white matter regions of the ASD human brain. Age categorization was used to highlight the findings described in children and early adolescence (<15 years) vs. those observed in late adolescence and adults (>15 years). Asterisks indicate the brain regions where contradictory findings have been reported [21,30,36,60,64,65,67,70–109].

Age	Affected Brain Regions in ASD
<15 years	Increased white matter density: Supplementary motor area, left precentral, superior longitudinal fasciculus *, left cingulum *, right cingulate gyrus, prefrontal cortex *, radiate volume, corpus callosum *, right inferior frontal gyrus, putamen, insula, sublobar extranuclear area, right superior temporal gyrus, hippocampus, middle temporal gyrus *, fusiform gyrus, uncinate fasciculus *, inferior longitudinal fasciculus *, bilateral middle *, and left inferior cerebellar peduncle. Reduced white matter density: Superior longitudinal fasciculus *, cingulum *, cingulate gyrus, prefrontal cortex *, corona radiata, middle frontal gyrus, corpus callosum *, arcuate fasciculus, inferior frontal gyrus, forceps minor, fornix, anterior thalamic radiation, internal and external capsule, superior temporal gyrus, superior temporal sulcus, temporoparietal junctions, middle temporal gyrus *, right inferior frontal gyrus-middle temporal gyrus tracts, bilateral inferior frontal gyrus-fusiform gyrus tracts, inferior fronto-occipital fasciculus, occipitotemporal gyrus, uncinate fasciculus *, inferior longitudinal fasciculus *, amygdala, inferior temporal gyrus, bilateral superior, middle * and right inferior cerebellar peduncle, pontine crossing tracts and medial lemniscus, cerebellum, and corticospinal tract.
>15 years	Increased white matter density: Corpus callosum *, anterior and posterior thalamic radiation, right insula, bilateral amygdala-fusiform pathways temporal, left hippocampus-fusiform pathways, temporal segment of Superior longitudinal fasciculus *, right lingual gyrus, uncinate fasciculus, inferior fronto-occipital fasciculus *, inferior longitudinal fasciculus, and corticospinal tract *. Reduced white matter density: Superior longitudinal fasciculus, intraparietal sulcus, cingulum, anterior cingulate gyrus, right superior frontal gyrus, prefrontal cortex, middle frontal gyrus, corpus callosum *, left orbitofrontal cortex, inferior frontal gyrus, left putamen tracts, thalamus, forceps minor, anterior thalamic radiation, internal capsule, right hippocampus-fusiform pathway, inferior fronto-occipital fasciculus *, cerebellum, and corticospinal tract *.

Although a reduction in the white matter density and impaired structural integrity of corpus callosum appears to be a consistent finding throughout the clinical evolution of ASD [64,71,72,74,77,79,82–84,99–102], some clinical studies have found an increase in the genu and midbody subregion of the corpus callosum [94] or the entire corpus callosum [78]. This evidence indicates that white matter alterations might not be present in the whole white matter or restricted to certain portions of the corpus callosum [89,110,111]. The disparity in these clinical findings may be due to multiple factors, including age range, specific diagnosis, comorbidities, medication, gender, type of imaging, or sample size. Other factors such as inter-individual differences, nurture, and epigenetic factors can also explain the discrepancy among clinical studies. Nevertheless, these differences also suggest that ASD might be associated with abnormalities in the myelination process, which is a very dynamic event. Therefore, multicenter longitudinal studies are required to fully establish which brain regions are more susceptible to determine whether alterations in certain brain regions may be linked to some specific ASD phenotypes.

3. Role of Oligodendrocytes in ASD: Cellular and Molecular Evidence

In animal models of ASD, reduction in the proliferation of oligodendroglial cells and low levels of myelin basic protein (MBP) has also been implicated in ASD pathogenesis [55]. Oligodendrocytes are glial cells that myelinate the brain and spinal cord to insulate axons electrically and provide neurons with trophic and metabolic factors. Mature oligodendrocytes originate from OPCs that, throughout life, preserve the population of myelinating oligodendrocytes [112]. OPCs are a persistent cell population that consists of around 5% to 10% of the total number of cells in the adult brain [113,114]. White-matter regions contain a high number of oligodendrocytes and OPCs that are in contact with axons, which facilitate neuronal communication [115]. Migrating and resident OPCs express the plated-derived growth factor receptor alpha (PDGFRα) and the oligodendrocyte transcription factor 2 (Olig2), and NG2 proteoglycan (Figure 2), which are cell markers of these progenitor cells [29,116]. Remarkably, a subpopulation of NG2-expressing cells (NG2 glia) establish synaptic junctions with local neurons and modulates axonal conduction by releasing glutamate and stimulating α-Amino-3-hydroxy-5-methyl-4-isoxazole propionic acid (AMPA) receptors [117–119]. Experimental evidence has suggested that disruption in neuron–glia interactions promotes autistic-like features [120]. However, it is unknown whether NG2 glia or glial transmission is implicated directly in the pathophysiology or clinical manifestations of ASD patients.

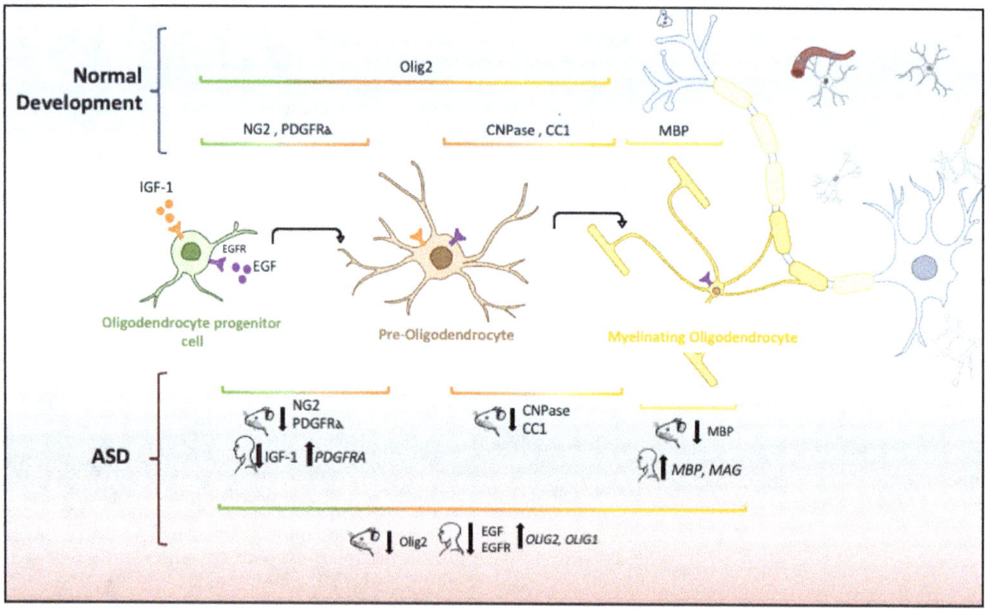

Figure 2. Oligodendrocyte lineage and molecular markers (genes or proteins) expressed under physiological and ASD conditions. Each human and mouse illustration indicates whether the molecular abnormality was found in clinical or experimental conditions [29,55,56,121–124].

The aberrant development of white matter found in patients with ASD (Figure 1) and disrupted protein levels in oligodendrocytes in ASD mice models (Figure 2) are suggestive of disruptions in the maturation of oligodendrocytes [40], which may convey changes in the white matter of corpus callosum and other white matter regions [21,36,40]. Deletions and duplications in the chromosome 15q11.2 region have been described in autistic patients and associated with alterations in myelination and abnormal development of the corpus callosum [125]. In humans, deletion carriers of 15q11.2 present a reduced volume of white matter [126]. This chromosomal region encodes CYFIP1 (Cytoplasmatic FMRP interacting protein 1), a protein that regulates cytoskeletal dynamics and protein translation. In mice, *Cyfip1* mutation reduces the myelin thickness and impairs neuronal connectivity in the corpus callosum that, in turn, produces aberrant behaviors and poor motor coordination in these mice [127]. Interestingly, deletions in chromosome 7 (7q11.23) have been associated with Williams Syndrome, a neurodevelopmental genetic disorder characterized by hypersociability and higher empathy [128,129], which has been also related to a decrease in the volume of white matter [130]. Therefore, disruptions in the myelination process could be associated with impairments in different chromosomes that, in turn, produce deficient electrical transmission resulting in impaired neurotransmitter release and behavioral manifestations [115].

Chromodomain helicase DNA binding proteins 7 (CHD-7) and 8 (CHD-8) are nucleosome remodeling factors that spatially and temporally control gene expression. CHD-7 is highly expressed in myelinating oligodendrocytes and its deficit or malfunction strongly compromises the myelination and remyelination process [131]. Transgenic *Chd7* mice demonstrate that this nucleosome remodeling factor is necessary throughout life for the transcription of *Sox10*, *Nkx2-2*, and *Gpr17* genes that regulate oligodendrocyte differentiation, and its inactivation decreases OPC survival and differentiation in cortex and corpus callosum via cellular tumor antigen p53 (Trp53) [131]. In contrast, CHD-8 is highly expressed in the early prenatal period and progressively decreases at later stages of development [132], but it remains highly expressed in the OPCs of adult white matter in the corpus callosum, optic nerve, and spinal cord [133]. CHD-8 regulates several genes associated with neurodevelopmental and synaptic functions that are affected in autism [134]. Interestingly, a clinical report found that *CHD8* mutations seem to be responsible for some phenotypic characteristics: macrocephaly and wide occipitofrontal circumference (head with a relatively large occipitofrontal diameter) and clinical behaviors (anxiety and social deficit) that have been associated with ASD [132,134]. A study in human neural stem cells and mid fetal human brain shows that the *CHD8* remodeling factor together with *ANK2*, *CUL3*, *DYRK1A*, *GRIN2B*, *KATNAL2*, *POGZ*, *SCN2A*, and *TBR1* are considered genetic risk factors to develop ASD [135]. Hence, this evidence suggests that *CHD7*/*CHD8* genes not only regulate the oligodendroglia differentiation and myelination but also provide some phenotypical features observed in people with ASD (macrocephaly, sleep dysfunction, growth retardation, and intellectual disability) [133,136].

Several growth factors regulate the proliferation and maturation of OPCs in the developing and adult brain. At the same time, systemic and local alterations in growth factors appear to be involved in the progression and severity of some psychiatric disorders [137]. Low levels of insulin-like growth factor 1 (IGF-1) reduce oligodendroglia survival [138] and cause OPCs to fail to differentiate into mature oligodendrocytes via bone morphogenetic protein (BMP) activation by up-regulating Noggin, Smad6, and Smad7 [139]. *Igf1* knockout mice show a reduction in the volume of the corpus callosum and anterior commissure that is associated with defectively myelinated axons and a decrease in the oligodendrocyte population [140]. Postnatally, these subjects also show fewer OPCs and mature oligodendrocytes that correlate with reduced expression of myelin proteins (MBP and the myelin proteolipid protein-PLP) [141]. Interestingly, children with ASD show low levels of IGF-1 in cerebrospinal fluid as compared with typically developing subjects [121,122]. In addition, low levels of IGF-1 are associated with deficient myelination and disorganization of neuronal circuits [142]. These pathological changes at the early stages of neurodevelopment may explain the impairment in synaptic development, inappropriate nerve conduction, and deficient axonal myelination frequently observed in ASD [142]. Therefore, IGF-1 and its signaling pathway are crucial for adequate axonal myelination and oligodendrocyte differentiation, but, when disrupted, white matter alterations, learning deficits, and ASD-like behaviors arise. To date, there are some experimental approaches to target the IGF-1 deficiency associated with ASD. The administration of IGF-1 for two weeks in Shank3-deficient mice, an ASD mouse model, notably improves the neuronal function by enhancing the long-term potentiation (LTP) and decreasing stereotypical behaviors [143]. Therefore, IGF-1 can be considered a promising therapeutic target, but further research is needed before using it in patients with ASD.

The Epidermal Growth Factor (EGF) and its receptors (ErbB 1–4) help preserve the oligodendrocyte population and repair demyelinating lesions by promoting proliferation, migration, and differentiation of OPCs in the adult brain [144–147]. Low levels of EGF and HER1 (ErbB1 in rodents) have been found in adults with high-functioning ASD [123]. In children, EGF levels correlate negatively with hyperactivity, tiptoe walking, and other motor signs [124]. Furthermore, the high expression of HER1 in children is correlated with high symptom severity (hyperactivity, conversational language, attention, eye contact, sound sensitivity, and expressive language) [148]. The interaction between neuregulin and ErbB4 protein, another member of the EGFR family, modifies the excitability of GABAergic neurons by increasing the inhibitory transmission [44,149]. GABAergic interneurons regulate cortical plasticity and cognitive flexibility in the frontal or parietal cortex [44]. Although the role of EGF in ASD has not been directly determined, this evidence suggests that changes in the ErbB family members or their ligands can modify the cortical plasticity and myelination as observed in ASD.

Both EGF and IGF-1 activate the PI3K/Akt/mTOR signaling pathway that regulates several intracellular functions, including cell growth, proliferation, differentiation, motility, survival, metabolism, and protein synthesis [150]. Akt/mTOR hyperactivity is commonly found in T cells [151] and peripheral blood [152] of patients with ASD. This hyperphosphorylation can, in turn, generate a deficiency of PTEN protein, a key negative regulator of the PI3K/Akt pathway [151], which results in Akt overactivation and increases the activity of mTOR [151,153]. The long-term activation of the Akt pathway prevents glutamate-mediated apoptosis in immature oligodendrocytes, which may induce aberrant myelination patterns [154]. Remarkably, patients with ASD and macrocephaly commonly show *PTEN* mutations [155]. In mice, disruption of PTEN activity by increasing Akt phosphorylation at Ser437 produces severe changes in the population of OPCs and in the genes and proteins involved in myelination (MBP, PLP, and myelin-associated glycoprotein-MAG), which induces social deficits that mimic some symptoms of ASD [156], such as increased anxiety and reduced social interest [153]. Interestingly, these animals also show aberrant myelin deposits adjacent to axons, increased volume of the corpus callosum, and brain enlargement [47,156,157]. Suppression of Akt/mTOR signaling improves ASD-associated symptoms in *Pten* knockout mice [153]. Therefore, *PTEN* alterations may be implicated in the pathogenesis of white matter abnormalities and behavioral symptoms observed in ASD [47,156,157]. A possible explanation for the low levels of IGF-1 and EGF reported in patients with ASD, despite the hyperactivity of the AKT/mTOR pathway, could be the interaction of receptors with other ligands as a compensatory mechanism, for instance, the IGF receptor (IGF1R) also interacts with insulin and insulin-like growth factor 2 (IGF-II) [158], whereas the EGFR has an affinity for other ligands such as TGF-α and HB-EGF [159].

MAPK/ERK is another signaling pathway activated by IGF-1 and EGF [160] that regulates the differentiation, migration, proliferation, and survival of oligodendrocytes in the adult brain [161]. The MAPK/ERK signaling pathway also determines the morphology of oligodendrocytes [161] and regulates myelin synthesis [162] by promoting the activation of transcriptional factors (ELK1, AP2-complex, and CREB) that are necessary for the expression of MBP [162]. Interestingly, the crosstalk between PI3K/Akt/mTOR and MAPK pathways [163] controls the synthesis of oligodendroglia proteins [164] and OPCs proliferation [165]. However, while the role of MAPK/ERK in myelination and oligodendrocytes is well known, there is not enough evidence to clearly define the link between this signaling pathway and ASD. Hence, further research is required to elucidate this question.

4. Conclusions

ASD is a clinically heterogeneous disorder that seems to have a multifactorial origin. Typically, ASD has been considered as a brain connectivity disorder that produces a disparity in the inhibition/excitation balance. However, emerging evidence suggests that oligodendroglial cells play a role in the etiology of ASD. Oligodendrocytes insulate axons electrically and provide neurons with trophic factors that guarantee proper neurotransmission and axonal conduction in the white matter. Patients with ASD show an aberrant growth pattern in several white-matter regions that varies throughout life. During the first 15 years of life, axon tracts in the arcuate fasciculus, occipitofrontal fasciculus, and external capsule show a significant hypomyelination, whereas the fusiform gyrus and hippocampal area show a substantial increase in their myelin volume (Figure 1). In both cases, these alterations tend to normalize throughout development. Intriguingly, other brain regions such as cerebellum, cingulum, and internal capsule remain hypomyelinated. This atypical myelination pattern has been linked to several factors, including gene disruption and epigenetic factors. Some genes and growth factors implicated in this abnormal myelination process include Olig1, Olig2, *Sox10*, *PGFRA*, *Nkx2-2*, *Gpr17*, IGF-1, and EGF. Hence, this emerging evidence supports the notion that oligodendrogenesis and neural myelination may play a pivotal role in the pathophysiology of ASD and its clinical presentation. Understanding the molecular mediators involved in abnormal myelination patterns in the ASD brain may represent an initial step to design therapeutic targets that help improve social skills and disruptive behaviors observed in these patients.

Author Contributions: Writing—original draft, Writing—review & editing, A.Y.G.-C.; Writing—original draft, D.Z.-L.; Writing—original draft, A.L.T.-C.; Writing—original draft, Writing—review and editing, O.G.-P. All authors have read and agreed to the published version of the manuscript.

References

1. Parellada, M.; Penzol, M.J.; Pina, L.; Moreno, C.; González-Vioque, E.; Zalsman, G.; Arango, C. The neurobiology of autism spectrum disorders. *Eur. Psychiatry* **2014**, *29*, 11–19. [CrossRef]
2. Carlisi, C.O.; Norman, L.J.; Lukito, S.S.; Radua, J.; Mataix-Cols, D.; Rubia, K. Comparative multimodal meta-analysis of structural and functional brain abnormalities in autism spectrum disorder and obsessive-compulsive disorder. *Biol. Psychiatry* **2017**, *82*, 83–102. [CrossRef] [PubMed]
3. Elsabbagh, M.; Divan, G.; Koh, Y.J.; Kim, Y.S.; Kauchali, S.; Marcín, C.; Montiel-Nava, C.; Patel, V.; Paula, C.S.; Wang, C.; et al. Global prevalence of autism and other pervasive developmental disorders. *Autism Res.* **2012**, *5*, 160–179. [CrossRef] [PubMed]
4. Baxter, A.J.; Brugha, T.S.; Erskine, H.E.; Scheurer, R.W.; Vos, T.; Scott, J.G. The epidemiology and global burden of autism spectrum disorders. *Psychol. Med.* **2015**, *45*, 601–613. [CrossRef] [PubMed]
5. Rice, C.E.; Rosanoff, M.; Dawson, G.; Durkin, M.S.; Croen, L.A.; Singer, A.; Yeargin-Allsopp, M. Evaluating changes in the prevalence of the autism spectrum disorders (ASDs). *Public Health Rev.* **2012**, *34*, 1–22. [CrossRef]
6. American Psychiatric Association. *Diagnostic and Statistical Manual of Mental Disorders (DSM-5)*; American Psychiatric Publishing: Washington, DC, USA, 2013; ISBN 9780890425541.
7. Harstad, E.B.; Fogler, J.; Sideridis, G.; Weas, S.; Mauras, C.; Barbaresi, W.J. Comparing diagnostic outcomes of autism spectrum disorder using DSM-IV-TR and DSM-5 criteria. *J. Autism Dev. Disord.* **2015**, *45*, 1437–1450. [CrossRef]
8. Masi, A.; DeMayo, M.M.; Glozier, N.; Guastella, A.J. An overview of autism spectrum disorder, heterogeneity and treatment options. *Neurosci. Bull.* **2017**, *33*, 183–193. [CrossRef]
9. Balasco, L.; Provenzano, G.; Bozzi, Y. Sensory abnormalities in autism spectrum disorders: A focus on the tactile domain, from genetic mouse models to the clinic. *Front. Psychiatry* **2020**, *10*, 1–17. [CrossRef]
10. Mosconi, M.W.; Sweeney, J.A. Sensorimotor dysfunctions as primary features of autism spectrum disorders. *Sci. China Life Sci.* **2015**, *58*, 1016–1023. [CrossRef]
11. Baum, S.H.; Stevenson, R.A.; Wallace, M.T. Behavioral, perceptual, and neural alterations in sensory and multisensory function in autism spectrum disorder. *Prog. Neurobiol.* **2015**, *134*, 140–160. [CrossRef]
12. Girirajan, S.; Rosenfeld, J.A.; Coe, B.P.; Parikh, S.; Friedman, N.; Goldstein, A.; Filipink, R.A.; McConnell, J.S.; Angle, B.; Meschino, W.S.; et al. Phenotypic heterogeneity of genomic disorders and rare copy-number variants. *N. Engl. J. Med.* **2012**, *367*, 1321–1331. [CrossRef] [PubMed]
13. Rylaarsdam, L.; Guemez-Gamboa, A. Genetic causes and modifiers of autism spectrum disorder. *Front. Cell. Neurosci.* **2019**, *13*. [CrossRef] [PubMed]
14. Courchesne, E.; Karns, C.M.; Davis, H.R.; Ziccardi, R.; Carper, R.A.; Tigue, Z.D.; Chisum, H.J.; Moses, P.; Pierce, K.; Lord, C.; et al. Unusual brain growth patterns in early life in patients with autistic disorder: An MRI study. *Neurology* **2001**, *57*, 245–254. [CrossRef] [PubMed]
15. Courchesne, E.; Carper, R.; Akshoomoff, N. Evidence of brain overgrowth in the first year of life in autism. *J. Am. Med. Assoc.* **2003**, *290*, 337–344. [CrossRef] [PubMed]
16. Courchesne, E.; Pierce, K. Why the frontal cortex in autism might be talking only to itself: Local over-connectivity but long-distance disconnection. *Curr. Opin. Neurobiol.* **2005**, *15*, 225–230. [CrossRef] [PubMed]
17. Courchesne, E.; Pierce, K.; Schumann, C.M.; Redcay, E.; Buckwalter, J.A.; Kennedy, D.P.; Morgan, J. Mapping early brain development in autism. *Neuron* **2007**, *56*, 399–413. [CrossRef]
18. Courchesne, E.; Campbell, K.; Solso, S. Brain growth across the life span in autism: Age-specific changes in anatomical pathology. *Brain Res.* **2011**, *1380*, 138–145. [CrossRef]
19. Morgan, J.T.; Barger, N.; Amaral, D.G.; Schumann, C.M. Stereological study of amygdala glial populations in adolescents and adults with autism spectrum disorder. *PLoS ONE* **2014**, *9*, e110356. [CrossRef]
20. McAlonan, G.M.; Daly, E.; Kumari, V.; Critchley, H.D.; Van Amelsvoort, T.; Suckling, J.; Simmons, A.; Sigmundsson, T.; Greenwood, K.; Russell, A.; et al. Brain anatomy and sensorimotor gating in Asperger's syndrome. *Brain* **2002**, *127*, 1594–1606. [CrossRef]

21. Bloemen, O.J.N.; Deeley, Q.; Sundram, F.; Daly, E.M.; Barker, G.J.; Jones, D.K.; Van Amelsvoort, T.A.M.J.; Schmitz, N.; Robertson, D.; Murphy, K.C.; et al. White matter integrity in Asperger syndrome: A preliminary diffusion tensor magnetic resonance imaging study in adults. *Autism Res.* **2010**, *3*, 203–213. [CrossRef]
22. Schmitz, N.; Daly, E.; Murphy, D. Frontal anatomy and reaction time in Autism. *Neurosci. Lett.* **2007**, *412*, 12–17. [CrossRef] [PubMed]
23. Rashid, B.; Blanken, L.M.E.; Muetzel, R.L.; Miller, R.; Damaraju, E.; Arbabshirani, M.R.; Erhardt, E.B.; Verhulst, F.C.; van der Lugt, A.; Jaddoe, V.W.V.; et al. Connectivity dynamics in typical development and its relationship to autistic traits and autism spectrum disorder. *Hum. Brain Mapp.* **2018**, *39*, 3127–3142. [CrossRef] [PubMed]
24. Lawrence, K.E.; Hernandez, L.M.; Bookheimer, S.Y.; Dapretto, M. Atypical longitudinal development of functional connectivity in adolescents with autism spectrum disorder. *Autism Res.* **2019**, *12*, 53–65. [CrossRef] [PubMed]
25. Chauhan, A.; Chauhan, V. Oxidative stress in autism. *Pathophysiology* **2006**, *13*, 171–181. [CrossRef] [PubMed]
26. Zeidán-Chuliá, F.; Salmina, A.B.; Malinovskaya, N.A.; Noda, M.; Verkhratsky, A.; Moreira, J.C.F. The glial perspective of autism spectrum disorders. *Neurosci. Biobehav. Rev.* **2014**, *38*, 160–172. [CrossRef] [PubMed]
27. Casanova, M.F.; Buxhoeveden, D.P.; Switala, A.E.; Roy, E. Minicolumnar pathology in autism. *Neurology* **2002**, *58*, 428–432. [CrossRef] [PubMed]
28. Wegiel, J.; Kuchna, I.; Nowicki, K.; Imaki, H.; Wegiel, J.; Marchi, E.; Ma, S.Y.; Chauhan, A.; Chauhan, V.; Bobrowicz, T.W.; et al. The neuropathology of autism: Defects of neurogenesis and neuronal migration, and dysplastic changes. *Acta Neuropathol.* **2010**, *119*, 755–770. [CrossRef]
29. Zeidán-Chuliá, F.; de Oliveira, B.H.N.; Casanova, M.F.; Casanova, E.L.; Noda, M.; Salmina, A.B.; Verkhratsky, A. Up-regulation of oligodendrocyte lineage markers in the cerebellum of autistic patients: Evidence from network analysis of gene expression. *Mol. Neurobiol.* **2016**, *53*, 4019–4025. [CrossRef]
30. Herbert, M.R.; Ziegler, D.A.; Makris, N.; Filipek, P.A.; Kemper, T.L.; Normandin, J.J.; Sanders, H.A.; Kennedy, D.N.; Caviness, V.S. Localization of white matter volume increase in autism and developmental language disorder. *Ann. Neurol.* **2004**, *55*, 530–540. [CrossRef]
31. Hong, S.J.; Hyung, B.; Paquola, C.; Bernhardt, B.C. The superficial white matter in autism and its role in connectivity anomalies and symptom severity. *Cereb. Cortex* **2019**, *29*, 4415–4425. [CrossRef]
32. Mengler, L.; Khmelinskii, A.; Diedenhofen, M.; Po, C.; Staring, M.; Lelieveldt, B.P.F.; Hoehn, M. Brain maturation of the adolescent rat cortex and striatum: Changes in volume and myelination. *Neuroimage* **2014**, *84*, 35–44. [CrossRef] [PubMed]
33. Tomassy, G.S.; Dershowitz, L.B.; Arlotta, P. Diversity matters: A revised guide to myelination. *Trends Cell Biol.* **2016**, *26*, 135–147. [CrossRef] [PubMed]
34. Herbert, M.R.; Ziegler, D.A.; Deutsch, C.K.; O'Brien, L.M.; Lange, N.; Bakardjiev, A.; Hodgson, J.; Adrien, K.T.; Steele, S.; Makris, N.; et al. Dissociations of cerebral cortex, subcortical and cerebral white matter volumes in autistic boys. *Brain* **2003**, *126*, 1182–1192. [CrossRef] [PubMed]
35. Carmody, D.P.; Lewis, M. Regional white matter development in children with autism spectrum disorders. *Dev. Psychobiol.* **2010**, *52*, 755–763. [CrossRef] [PubMed]
36. Dimond, D.; Schuetze, M.; Smith, R.E.; Dhollander, T.; Cho, I.; Vinette, S.; Ten Eycke, K.; Lebel, C.; McCrimmon, A.; Dewey, D.; et al. Reduced white matter fiber density in autism spectrum disorder. *Cereb. Cortex* **2019**, *29*, 1–11. [CrossRef]
37. DiCicco-Bloom, E.; Lord, C.; Zwaigenbaum, L.; Courchesne, E.; Dager, S.R.; Schmitz, C.; Schultz, R.T.; Crawley, J.; Young, L.J. The developmental neurobiology of autism spectrum disorder. *J. Neurosci.* **2006**, *26*, 6897–6906. [CrossRef]
38. Yassin, W.; Kojima, M.; Owada, K.; Kuwabara, H.; Gonoi, W.; Aoki, Y.; Takao, H.; Natsubori, T.; Iwashiro, N.; Kasai, K.; et al. Paternal age contribution to brain white matter aberrations in autism spectrum disorder. *Psychiatry Clin. Neurosci.* **2019**, *73*, 649–659. [CrossRef]
39. Swanson, M.R.; Hazlett, H.C. White matter as a monitoring biomarker for neurodevelopmental disorder intervention studies. *J. Neurodev. Disord.* **2019**, *11*, 1–11. [CrossRef]
40. Hughes, J.R. Autism: The first firm finding = underconnectivity? *Epilepsy Behav.* **2007**, *11*, 20–24. [CrossRef]
41. Boger-Megiddo, I.; Shaw, D.W.W.; Friedman, S.D.; Sparks, B.F.; Artru, A.A.; Giedd, J.N.; Dawson, G.; Dager, S.R. Corpus callosum morphometrics in young children with autism spectrum disorder. *J. Autism Dev. Disord.* **2006**, *36*, 733–739. [CrossRef]

42. Dawson, G.; Munson, J.; Webb, S.J.; Nalty, T.; Abbott, R.; Toth, K. Rate of head growth decelerates and symptoms worsen in the second year of life in autism. *Biol Psychiatry* **2007**, *61*, 458–464. [CrossRef] [PubMed]
43. Wolff, J.J.; Gu, H.; Gerig, G.; Elison, J.T.; Styner, M.; Gouttard, S.; Botteron, K.N.; Dager, S.R.; Dawson, G.; Estes, A.M.; et al. Differences in white matter fiber tract development present from 6 to 24 months in infants with autism. *Am. J. Psychiatry* **2012**, *169*, 589–600. [CrossRef] [PubMed]
44. Lee, E.; Lee, J.; Kim, E. Excitation/inhibition imbalance in animal models of autism spectrum disorders. *Biol. Psychiatry* **2017**, *81*, 838–847. [CrossRef]
45. Ecker, C.; Ronan, L.; Feng, Y.; Daly, E.; Murphy, C.; Ginestet, C.E.; Brammer, M.; Fletcher, P.C.; Bullmore, E.T.; Suckling, J.; et al. Intrinsic gray-matter connectivity of the brain in adults with autism spectrum disorder. *Proc. Natl. Acad. Sci. USA* **2013**, *110*, 13222–13227. [CrossRef] [PubMed]
46. O'Reilly, C.; Lewis, J.D.; Elsabbagh, M. Is functional brain connectivity atypical in autism? A systematic review of EEG and MEG studies. *PLoS ONE* **2017**, *12*, e0175870. [CrossRef]
47. Lee, H.; Thacker, S.; Sarn, N.; Dutta, R.; Eng, C. Constitutional mislocalization of Pten drives precocious maturation in oligodendrocytes and aberrant myelination in model of autism spectrum disorder. *Transl. Psychiatry* **2019**, *9*, 13. [CrossRef]
48. Xu, Z.X.; Kim, G.H.; Tan, J.W.; Riso, A.E.; Sun, Y.; Xu, E.Y.; Liao, G.Y.; Xu, H.; Lee, S.H.; Do, N.Y.; et al. Elevated protein synthesis in microglia causes autism-like synaptic and behavioral aberrations. *Nat. Commun.* **2020**, *11*. [CrossRef]
49. Kim, Y.S.; Choi, J.; Yoon, B.E. Neuron-glia interactions in neurodevelopmental disorders. *Cells* **2020**, *9*, 2176. [CrossRef]
50. Chauhan, A.; Chauhan, W.; Brown, W.T. Autism oxidative stress, inflamation and Immune abnormalities. In *CRC Press*; Evans, T.A., Perry, G., Smith, M.A., Salomon, R.G., McGinnis, W.R., Sajdel-Sulkowska, M., Zhu, X., Eds.; CRC Press: Boca Raton, FL, USA, 2010; pp. 1–34. ISBN 9781420068818.
51. Yui, K.; Kawasaki, Y.; Yamada, H.; Ogawa, S. Oxidative stress and nitric oxide in autism spectrum disorder and other neuropsychiatric disorders. *CNS Neurol. Disord. Drug Targets* **2016**, *15*, 587–596. [CrossRef]
52. Back, S.A. White matter injury in the preterm infant: Pathology and mechanisms. *Acta Neuropathol.* **2017**, *134*, 331–349. [CrossRef]
53. Thorburne, S.K.; Juurlink, B.H.J. Low glutathione and high iron govern the susceptibility of oligodendroglial precursors to oxidative stress. *J. Neurochem.* **1996**, *67*, 1014–1022. [CrossRef] [PubMed]
54. McTigue, D.M.; Tripathi, R.B. The life, death, and replacement of oligodendrocytes in the adult CNS. *J. Neurochem.* **2008**, *107*, 1–19. [CrossRef] [PubMed]
55. Graciarena, M.; Seiffe, A.; Nait-Oumesmar, B.; Depino, A.M. Hypomyelination and oligodendroglial alterations in a mouse model of autism spectrum disorder. *Front. Cell. Neurosci.* **2019**, *12*, 1–11. [CrossRef]
56. Khanbabaei, M.; Hughes, E.; Ellegood, J.; Qiu, L.R.; Yip, R.; Dobry, J.; Murari, K.; Lerch, J.P.; Rho, J.M.; Cheng, N. Precocious myelination in a mouse model of autism. *Transl. Psychiatry* **2019**, *9*, 251. [CrossRef]
57. Cartocci, V.; Catallo, M.; Tempestilli, M.; Segatto, M.; Pfrieger, F.W.; Bronzuoli, M.R.; Scuderi, C.; Servadio, M.; Trezza, V.; Pallottini, V. Altered brain cholesterol/isoprenoid metabolism in a rat model of autism spectrum disorders. *Neuroscience* **2018**, *372*, 27–37. [CrossRef]
58. Pacey, L.K.K.; Xuan, I.C.Y.; Guan, S.; Sussman, D.; Henkelman, R.M.; Chen, Y.; Thomsen, C.; Hampson, D.R. Delayed myelination in a mouse model of fragile X syndrome. *Hum. Mol. Genet.* **2013**, *22*, 3920–3930. [CrossRef] [PubMed]
59. Meikle, L.; Talos, D.M.; Onda, H.; Pollizzi, K.; Rotenberg, A.; Sahin, M.; Jensen, F.E.; Kwiatkowski, D.J. A mouse model of tuberous sclerosis: Neuronal loss of Tsc1 causes dysplastic and ectopic neurons, reduced myelination, seizure activity, and limited survival. *J. Neurosci.* **2007**, *27*, 5546–5558. [CrossRef] [PubMed]
60. Noriuchi, M.; Kikuchi, Y.; Yoshiura, T.; Kira, R.; Shigeto, H.; Hara, T.; Tobimatsu, S.; Kamio, Y. Altered white matter fractional anisotropy and social impairment in children with autism spectrum disorder. *Brain Res.* **2010**, *1362*, 141–149. [CrossRef] [PubMed]
61. Zikopoulos, B.; García-Cabezas, M.Á.; Barbas, H. Parallel trends in cortical gray and white matter architecture and connections in primates allow fine study of pathways in humans and reveal network disruptions in autism. *PLoS Biol.* **2018**, *16*, 1–43. [CrossRef]
62. Ha, S.; Sohn, I.; Kim, N.; Sim, H.J.; Cheon, K. Characteristics of brains in autism spectrum disorder: Structure, function and connectivity across the lifespan. *Exp. Neurobiol.* **2015**, *24*, 273–284. [CrossRef]

63. Wolff, J.J.; Gerig, G.; Lewis, J.D.; Soda, T.; Styner, M.A.; Vachet, C.; Botteron, K.N.; Elison, J.T.; Dager, S.R.; Estes, A.M.; et al. Altered corpus callosum morphology associated with autism over the first 2 years of life. *Brain* **2015**, *138*, 2046–2058. [CrossRef] [PubMed]
64. Cheon, K.A.; Kim, Y.S.; Oh, S.H.; Park, S.Y.; Yoon, H.W.; Herrington, J.; Nair, A.; Koh, Y.J.; Jang, D.P.; Kim, Y.B.; et al. Involvement of the anterior thalamic radiation in boys with high functioning autism spectrum disorders: A diffusion tensor imaging study. *Brain Res.* **2011**, *1417*, 77–86. [CrossRef] [PubMed]
65. Kumar, A.; Sundaram, S.K.; Sivaswamy, L.; Behen, M.E.; Makki, M.I.; Ager, J.; Janisse, J.; Chugani, H.T.; Chugani, D.C. Alterations in frontal lobe tracts and corpus callosum in young children with autism spectrum disorder. *Cereb. Cortex* **2010**, *20*, 2103–2113. [CrossRef] [PubMed]
66. Schaer, M.; Ottet, M.-C.; Scariati, E.; Dukes, D.; Franchini, M.; Eliez, S.; Glaser, B. Decreased frontal gyrification correlates with altered connectivity in children with autism. *Front. Hum. Neurosci.* **2013**, *7*, 1–13. [CrossRef] [PubMed]
67. Ikuta, T.; Shafritz, K.M.; Bregman, J.; Peters, B.D.; Gruner, P.; Malhotra, A.K.; Szeszko, P.R. Abnormal cingulum bundle development in autism: A probabilistic tractography study. *Psychiatry Res. Neuroimaging* **2014**, *221*, 63–68. [CrossRef]
68. Nair, A.; Treiber, J.M.; Shukla, D.K.; Shih, P.; Müller, R.A. Impaired thalamocortical connectivity in autism spectrum disorder: A study of functional and anatomical connectivity. *Brain* **2013**, *136*, 1942–1955. [CrossRef]
69. Pardini, M.; Elia, M.; Garaci, F.G.; Guida, S.; Coniglione, F.; Krueger, F.; Benassi, F.; Emberti Gialloreti, L. Long-term cognitive and behavioral therapies, combined with augmentative communication, are related to uncinate fasciculus integrity in autism. *J. Autism Dev. Disord.* **2012**, *42*, 585–592. [CrossRef]
70. Pardini, M.; Garaci, F.G.; Bonzano, L.; Roccatagliata, L.; Palmieri, M.G.; Pompili, E.; Coniglione, F.; Krueger, F.; Ludovici, A.; Floris, R.; et al. White matter reduced streamline coherence in young men with autism and mental retardation. *Eur. J. Neurol.* **2009**, *16*, 1185–1190. [CrossRef]
71. McAlonan, G.M.; Cheung, C.; Cheung, V.; Wong, N.; Suckling, J.; Chua, S.E. Differential effects on white-matter systems in high-functioning autism and Asperger's syndrome. *Psychol. Med.* **2009**, *39*, 1885–1893. [CrossRef]
72. Barnea-Goraly, N.; Lotspeich, L.J.; Reiss, A.L. Similar white matter aberrations in children with autism and their unaffected siblings. *Arch. Gen. Psychiatry* **2010**, *67*, 1052. [CrossRef]
73. Fletcher, P.T.; Whitaker, R.T.; Tao, R.; DuBray, M.B.; Froehlich, A.; Ravichandran, C.; Alexander, A.L.; Bigler, E.D.; Lange, N.; Lainhart, J.E. Microstructural connectivity of the arcuate fasciculus in adolescents with high-functioning autism. *Neuroimage* **2010**, *51*, 1117–1125. [CrossRef] [PubMed]
74. Jeong, J.W.; Kumar, A.K.; Sundaram, S.K.; Chugani, H.T.; Chugani, D.C. Sharp curvature of frontal lobe white matter pathways in children with autism spectrum disorders: Tract-based morphometry analysis. *Am. J. Neuroradiol.* **2011**, *32*, 1600–1606. [CrossRef] [PubMed]
75. Lo, Y.C.; Soong, W.T.; Gau, S.S.F.; Wu, Y.Y.; Lai, M.C.; Yeh, F.C.; Chiang, W.Y.; Kuo, L.W.; Jaw, F.S.; Tseng, W.Y.I. The loss of asymmetry and reduced interhemispheric connectivity in adolescents with autism: A study using diffusion spectrum imaging tractography. *Psychiatry Res. Neuroimaging* **2011**, *192*, 60–66. [CrossRef] [PubMed]
76. Cheung, C.; Chua, S.E.; Cheung, V.; Khong, P.L.; Tai, K.S.; Wong, T.K.W.; Ho, T.P.; McAlonan, G.M. White matter fractional anisotrophy differences and correlates of diagnostic symptoms in autism. *J. Child Psychol. Psychiatry Allied Discip.* **2009**, *50*, 1102–1112. [CrossRef]
77. Barnea-Goraly, N.; Kwon, H.; Menon, V.; Eliez, S.; Lotspeich, L.; Reiss, A.L. White matter structure in autism: Preliminary evidence from diffusion tensor imaging. *Biol. Psychiatry* **2004**, *55*, 323–326. [CrossRef]
78. Ecker, C.; Rocha-Rego, V.; Johnston, P.; Mourao-Miranda, J.; Marquand, A.; Daly, E.M.; Brammer, M.J.; Murphy, C.; Murphy, D.G. Investigating the predictive value of whole-brain structural MR scans in autism: A pattern classification approach. *Neuroimage* **2010**, *49*, 44–56. [CrossRef]
79. Shukla, D.K.; Keehn, B.; Lincoln, A.J.; Müller, R.A. White matter compromise of callosal and subcortical fiber tracts in children with autism spectrum disorder: A diffusion tensor imaging study. *J. Am. Acad. Child Adolesc. Psychiatry* **2010**, *49*, 1269–1278. [CrossRef]
80. Sivaswamy, L.; Kumar, A.; Rajan, D.; Behen, M.; Muzik, O.; Chugani, D.; Chugani, H. A diffusion tensor imaging study of the cerebellar pathways in children with autism spectrum disorder. *J. Child Neurol.* **2010**, *25*, 1223–1231. [CrossRef]
81. Yu, Q.; Peng, Y.; Kang, H.; Peng, Q.; Ouyang, M.; Slinger, M.; Hu, D.; Shou, H.; Fang, F.; Huang, H. Differential white matter maturation from birth to 8 years of age. *Cereb. Cortex* **2020**, *30*, 2674–2690. [CrossRef]

82. Brito, A.R.; Vasconcelos, M.M.; Domingues, R.C.; Hygino Da Cruz, L.C.; Rodrigues, L.D.S.; Gasparetto, E.L.; Calçada, C.A.B.P. Diffusion tensor imaging findings in school-aged autistic children. *J. Neuroimaging* **2009**, *19*, 337–343. [CrossRef]
83. Jou, R.J.; Mateljevic, N.; Kaiser, M.D.; Sugrue, D.R.; Volkmar, F.R.; Pelphrey, K.A. Structural neural phenotype of autism: Preliminary evidence from a diffusion tensor imaging study using tract-based spatial statistics. *Am. J. Neuroradiol.* **2011**, *32*, 1607–1613. [CrossRef] [PubMed]
84. Shukla, D.K.; Keehn, B.; Müller, R.A. Tract-specific analyses of diffusion tensor imaging show widespread white matter compromise in autism spectrum disorder. *J. Child Psychol. Psychiatry Allied Discip.* **2011**, *52*, 286–295. [CrossRef] [PubMed]
85. Sahyoun, C.P.; Belliveau, J.W.; Mody, M. White matter integrity and pictorial reasoning in high-functioning children with autism. *Brain Cogn.* **2010**, *73*, 180–188. [CrossRef] [PubMed]
86. Ameis, S.H.; Fan, J.; Rockel, C.; Voineskos, A.N.; Lobaugh, N.J.; Soorya, L.; Wang, A.T.; Hollander, E.; Anagnostou, E. Impaired structural connectivity of socio-emotional circuits in autism spectrum disorders: A diffusion tensor imaging study. *PLoS ONE* **2011**, *6*, e28044. [CrossRef] [PubMed]
87. Thomas, C.; Humphreys, K.; Jung, K.J.; Minshew, N.; Behrmann, M. The anatomy of the callosal and visual-association pathways in high-functioning autism: A DTI tractography study. *Cortex* **2011**, *47*, 863–873. [CrossRef]
88. Itahashi, T.; Yamada, T.; Nakamura, M.; Watanabe, H.; Yamagata, B.; Jimbo, D.; Shioda, S.; Kuroda, M.; Toriizuka, K.; Kato, N.; et al. Linked alterations in gray and white matter morphology in adults with high-functioning autism spectrum disorder: A multimodal brain imaging study. *Neuroimage Clin.* **2015**, *7*, 155–169. [CrossRef]
89. Roine, U.; Salmi, J.; Roine, T.; Wendt, T.N.-v.; Leppämäki, S.; Rintahaka, P.; Tani, P.; Leemans, A.; Sams, M. Constrained spherical deconvolution-based tractography and tract-based spatial statistics show abnormal microstructural organization in Asperger syndrome. *Mol. Autism* **2015**, *6*. [CrossRef]
90. Karahanoğlu, F.I.; Baran, B.; Nguyen, Q.T.H.; Meskaldji, D.E.; Yendiki, A.; Vangel, M.; Santangelo, S.L.; Manoach, D.S. Diffusion-weighted imaging evidence of altered white matter development from late childhood to early adulthood in autism spectrum disorder. *Neuroimage Clin.* **2018**, *19*, 840–847. [CrossRef]
91. Poustka, L.; Jennen-Steinmetz, C.; Henze, R.; Vomstein, K.; Haffner, J.; Sieltjes, B. Fronto-temporal disconnectivity and symptom severity in children with autism spectrum disorder. *World J. Biol. Psychiatry* **2012**, *13*, 269–280. [CrossRef]
92. Conturo, T.E.; Williams, D.L.; Smith, C.D.; Gultepe, E.; Akbudak, E.; Minshew, N.J. Neuronal fiber pathway abnormalities in autism: An initial MRI diffusion tensor tracking study of hippocampo-fusiform and amygdalo-fusiform pathways. *J. Int. Neuropsychol. Soc.* **2008**, *14*, 933–946. [CrossRef]
93. Cheng, Y.; Chou, K.H.; Chen, I.Y.; Fan, Y.T.; Decety, J.; Lin, C.P. Atypical development of white matter microstructure in adolescents with autism spectrum disorders. *Neuroimage* **2010**, *50*, 873–882. [CrossRef] [PubMed]
94. Weinstein, M.; Ben-Sira, L.; Levy, Y.; Zachor, D.A.; Itzhak, E.B.e.n.; Artzi, M.; Tarrasch, R.; Eksteine, P.M.; Hendler, T.; Bashat, D. Ben Abnormal white matter integrity in young children with autism. *Hum. Brain Mapp.* **2011**, *32*, 534–543. [CrossRef] [PubMed]
95. Mengotti, P.; D'Agostini, S.; Terlevic, R.; De Colle, C.; Biasizzo, E.; Londero, D.; Ferro, A.; Rambaldelli, G.; Balestrieri, M.; Zanini, S.; et al. Altered white matter integrity and development in children with autism: A combined voxel-based morphometry and diffusion imaging study. *Brain Res. Bull.* **2011**, *84*, 189–195. [CrossRef] [PubMed]
96. Ke, X.; Tang, T.; Hong, S.; Hang, Y.; Zou, B.; Li, H.; Zhou, Z.; Ruan, Z.; Lu, Z.; Tao, G.; et al. White matter impairments in autism, evidence from voxel-based morphometry and diffusion tensor imaging. *Brain Res.* **2009**, *1265*, 171–177. [CrossRef] [PubMed]
97. Li, Y.; Zhou, Z.; Chang, C.; Qian, L.; Li, C.; Xiao, T.; Xiao, X.; Chu, K.; Fang, H.; Ke, X. Anomalies in uncinate fasciculus development and social defects in preschoolers with autism spectrum disorder. *BMC Psychiatry* **2019**, *19*, 1–9. [CrossRef] [PubMed]
98. Sahyoun, C.P.; Belliveau, J.W.; Soulières, I.; Schwartz, S.; Mody, M. Neuroimaging of the functional and structural networks underlying visuospatial vs. linguistic reasoning in high-functioning autism. *Neuropsychologia* **2010**, *48*, 86–95. [CrossRef]

99. Vidal, C.N.; Nicolson, R.; DeVito, T.J.; Hayashi, K.M.; Geaga, J.A.; Drost, D.J.; Williamson, P.C.; Rajakumar, N.; Sui, Y.; Dutton, R.A.; et al. Mapping corpus callosum deficits in autism: An index of aberrant cortical connectivity. *Biol. Psychiatry* **2006**, *60*, 218–225. [CrossRef]
100. Frazier, T.W.; Keshavan, M.S.; Minshew, N.J.; Hardan, A.Y. A two-year longitudinal MRI study of the corpus callosum in autism. *J. Autism Dev. Disord.* **2012**, *42*, 2312–2322. [CrossRef]
101. Hardan, A.Y.; Pabalan, M.; Gupta, N.; Bansal, R.; Melhem, N.M.; Fedorov, S.; Keshavan, M.S.; Minshew, N.J. Corpus callosum volume in children with autism. *Psychiatry Res. Neuroimaging* **2009**, *174*, 57–61. [CrossRef]
102. Hong, S.; Ke, X.; Tang, T.; Hang, Y.; Chu, K.; Huang, H.; Ruan, Z.; Lu, Z.; Tao, G.; Liu, Y. Detecting abnormalities of corpus callosum connectivity in autism using magnetic resonance imaging and diffusion tensor tractography. *Psychiatry Res. Neuroimaging* **2011**, *194*, 333–339. [CrossRef]
103. Jou, R.J.; Jackowski, A.P.; Papademetris, X.; Rajeevan, N.; Staib, L.H.; Volkmar, F.R. Diffusion tensor imaging in autism spectrum disorders: Preliminary evidence of abnormal neural connectivity. *Aust. N. Z. J. Psychiatry* **2011**, *45*, 153–162. [CrossRef]
104. Thakkar, K.N.; Polli, F.E.; Joseph, R.M.; Tuch, D.S.; Hadjikhani, N.; Barton, J.J.S.; Manoach, D.S. Response monitoring, repetitive behaviour and anterior cingulate abnormalities in autism spectrum disorders (ASD). *Brain* **2008**, *131*, 2464–2478. [CrossRef]
105. Haigh, S.M.; Keller, T.A.; Minshew, N.J.; Eack, S.M. Reduced white matter integrity and deficits in neuropsychological functioning in adults with autism spectrum disorder. *Autism Res.* **2020**, *13*, 702–714. [CrossRef]
106. Catani, M.; Jones, D.K.; Daly, E.; Embiricos, N.; Deeley, Q.; Pugliese, L.; Curran, S.; Robertson, D.; Murphy, D.G.M. Altered cerebellar feedback projections in Asperger syndrome. *Neuroimage* **2008**, *41*, 1184–1191. [CrossRef]
107. Hardan, A.Y.; Minshew, N.J.; Keshavan, M.S. Corpus callosum size in autism. *Neurology* **2000**, *55*, 1033–1036. [CrossRef]
108. Piven, J.; Bailey, J.; Ranson, B.J.; Arndt, S. An MRI study of the corpus callosum in autism. *Am. J. Psychiatry* **1997**, *154*, 1051–1056. [CrossRef]
109. Langen, M.; Leemans, A.; Johnston, P.; Ecker, C.; Daly, E.; Murphy, C.M.; Dell'Acqua, F.; Durston, S.; Murphy, D.G.M. Fronto-striatal circuitry and inhibitory control in autism: Findings from diffusion tensor imaging tractography. *Cortex* **2012**, *48*, 183–193. [CrossRef]
110. Libero, L.E.; DeRamus, T.P.; Lahti, A.C.; Deshpande, G.; Kana, R.K. Multimodal neuroimaging based classification of autism spectrum disorder using anatomical, neurochemical, and white matter correlates. *Cortex* **2015**, *66*, 46–59. [CrossRef]
111. Haigh, S.M.; Eack, S.M.; Keller, T.; Minshew, N.J.; Behrmann, M. White matter structure in schizophrenia and autism: Abnormal diffusion across the brain in schizophrenia. *Neuropsychologia* **2019**, *135*, 107233. [CrossRef]
112. Bradl, M.; Lassmann, H. Oligodendrocytes: Biology and pathology. *Acta Neuropathol.* **2010**, *119*, 37–53. [CrossRef]
113. Dulamea, A. The contribution of oligodendrocytes and oligodendrocyte progenitor cells to central nervous system repair in multiple sclerosis: Perspectives for remyelination therapeutic strategies. *Neural Regen. Res.* **2017**, *12*, 1939. [CrossRef]
114. Tiane, A.; Schepers, M.; Rombaut, B.; Hupperts, R.; Prickaerts, J.; Hellings, N.; van den Hove, D.; Vanmierlo, T. From OPC to oligodendrocyte: An Epigenetic journey. *Cells* **2019**, *8*, 1236. [CrossRef]
115. Alexander, A.L.; Hurley, S.A.; Samsonov, A.A.; Adluru, N.; Hosseinbor, A.P.; Mossahebi, P.; Tromp, D.P.M.; Zakszewski, E.; Field, A.S. Characterization of cerebral white matter properties using quantitative magnetic resonance imaging stains. *Brain Connect.* **2011**, *1*, 423–446. [CrossRef]
116. Menn, B.; Garcia-Verdugo, J.M.; Yaschine, C.; Gonzalez-Perez, O.; Rowitch, D.; Alvarez-Buylla, A. Origin of oligodendrocytes in the subventricular zone of the adult brain. *J. Neurosci.* **2006**, *26*, 7907–7918. [CrossRef]
117. Bergles, D.E.; Roberts, J.D.B.; Somogyl, P.; Jahr, C.E. Glutamatergic synapses on oligodendrocyte precursor cells in the hippocampus. *Nature* **2000**, *405*, 187–191. [CrossRef]
118. Kukley, M.; Capetillo-Zarate, E.; Dietrich, D. Vesicular glutamate release from axons in white matter. *Nat. Neurosci.* **2007**, *10*, 311–320. [CrossRef]
119. Ziskin, J.L.; Nishiyama, A.; Rubio, M.; Fukaya, M.; Bergles, D.E. Vesicular release of glutamate from unmyelinated axons in white matter. *Nat. Neurosci.* **2007**, *10*, 321–330. [CrossRef]

120. Bronzuoli, M.R.; Facchinetti, R.; Ingrassia, D.; Sarvadio, M.; Schiavi, S.; Steardo, L.; Verkhratsky, A.; Trezza, V.; Scuderi, C. Neuroglia in the autistic brain: Evidence from a preclinical model 11 medical and health sciences 1109 neurosciences 17 psychology and cognitive sciences 1701 psychology. *Mol. Autism* **2018**, *9*, 1–17. [CrossRef]
121. Riikonen, R.; Makkonen, I.; Vanhala, R.; Turpeinen, U.; Kuikka, J.; Kokki, H. Cerebrospinal fluid insulin-like growth factors IGF-1 and IGF-2 in infantile autism. *Dev. Med. Child Neurol.* **2006**, *48*, 751–755. [CrossRef]
122. Vanhala, R.; Turpeinen, U.; Riikonen, R. Low levels of insulin-like growth factor-I in cerebrospinal fluid in children with autism. *Dev. Med. Child Neurol.* **2007**, *43*, 614–616. [CrossRef]
123. Suzuki, K.; Hashimoto, K.; Iwata, Y.; Nakamura, K.; Tsujii, M.; Tsuchiya, K.J.; Sekine, Y.; Suda, S.; Sugihara, G.; Matsuzaki, H.; et al. Decreased serum levels of epidermal growth factor in adult subjects with high-functioning autism. *Biol. Psychiatry* **2007**, *62*, 267–269. [CrossRef] [PubMed]
124. Russo, A.J. Decreased epidermal growth factor (EGF) associated with HMGB1 and increased hyperactivity in children with autism. *Biomark. Insights* **2013**, *8*, 35–41. [CrossRef] [PubMed]
125. Silva, A.I.; Ulfarsson, M.O.; Stefansson, H.; Gustafsson, O.; Walters, G.B.; Linden, D.E.J.; Wilkinson, L.S.; Drakesmith, M.; Owen, M.J.; Hall, J.; et al. Reciprocal white matter changes associated with copy number variation at 15q11.2 BP1-BP2: A diffusion tensor imaging study. *Biol. Psychiatry* **2019**, *85*, 563–572. [CrossRef] [PubMed]
126. Stefansson, H.; Meyer-Lindenberg, A.; Steinberg, S.; Magnusdottir, B.; Morgen, K.; Arnarsdottir, S.; Bjornsdottir, G.; Walters, G.B.; Jonsdottir, G.A.; Doyle, O.M.; et al. CNVs conferring risk of autism or schizophrenia affect cognition in controls. *Nature* **2014**, *505*, 361–366. [CrossRef] [PubMed]
127. Domínguez-Iturza, N.; Lo, A.C.; Shah, D.; Armendáriz, M.; Vannelli, A.; Mercaldo, V.; Trusel, M.; Li, K.W.; Gastaldo, D.; Santos, A.R.; et al. The autism- and schizophrenia-associated protein CYFIP1 regulates bilateral brain connectivity and behaviour. *Nat. Commun.* **2019**, *10*, 1–13. [CrossRef]
128. Nir, A.; Barak, B. White matter alterations in Williams syndrome related to behavioral and motor impairments. *Glia* **2021**, *69*, 5–19. [CrossRef]
129. Morris, C.A. Introduction: Williams syndrome. *Am. J. Med. Genet. Part C Semin. Med. Genet.* **2010**, *154*, 203–208. [CrossRef]
130. Osório, A.; Soares, J.M.; Prieto, M.F.; Vasconcelos, C.; Fernandes, C.; Sousa, S.; Carracedo, Á.; Gonçalves, Ó.F.; Sampaio, A. Cerebral and cerebellar MRI volumes in Williams syndrome. *Res. Dev. Disabil.* **2014**, *35*, 922–928. [CrossRef]
131. Marie, C.; Clavairoly, A.; Frah, M.; Hmidan, H.; Yan, J.; Zhao, C.; Van Steenwinckel, J.; Daveau, R.; Zalc, B.; Hassan, B.; et al. Oligodendrocyte precursor survival and differentiation requires chromatin remodeling by Chd7 and Chd8. *Proc. Natl. Acad. Sci. USA* **2018**, *115*, E8246–E8255. [CrossRef]
132. Bernier, R.; Golzio, C.; Xiong, B.; Stessman, H.A.; Coe, B.P.; Penn, O.; Witherspoon, K.; Gerdts, J.; Baker, C.; Vulto-Van Silfhout, A.T.; et al. Disruptive CHD8 mutations define a subtype of autism early in development. *Cell* **2014**, *158*, 263–276. [CrossRef]
133. Zhao, C.; Dong, C.; Frah, M.; Deng, Y.; Marie, C.; Zhang, F.; Xu, L.; Ma, Z.; Dong, X.; Lin, Y.; et al. Dual requirement of CHD8 for chromatin landscape establishment and histone methyltransferase recruitment to promote CNS myelination and repair. *Dev. Cell* **2018**, *45*, 753–768. [CrossRef]
134. Platt, R.J.; Zhou, Y.; Slaymaker, I.M.; Shetty, A.S.; Weisbach, N.R.; Kim, J.A.; Sharma, J.; Desai, M.; Sood, S.; Kempton, H.R.; et al. Chd8 mutation leads to autistic-like behaviors and impaired striatal circuits. *Cell Rep.* **2017**, *19*, 335–350. [CrossRef]
135. Cotney, J.; Muhle, R.A.; Sanders, S.J.; Liu, L.; Willsey, A.J.; Niu, W.; Liu, W.; Klei, L.; Lei, J.; Yin, J.; et al. The autism-associated chromatin modifier CHD8 regulates other autism risk genes during human neurodevelopment. *Nat. Commun.* **2015**, *6*, 6404. [CrossRef]
136. Xu, Q.; Liu, Y.Y.; Wang, X.; Tan, G.H.; Li, H.P.; Hulbert, S.W.; Li, C.Y.; Hu, C.C.; Xiong, Z.Q.; Xu, X.; et al. Autism-associated CHD8 deficiency impairs axon development and migration of cortical neurons. *Mol. Autism* **2018**, *9*, 1–17. [CrossRef]
137. Galvez-Contreras, A.Y.; Campos-Ordonez, T.; Gonzalez-Castaneda, R.E.; Gonzalez-Perez, O. Alterations of growth factors in autism and attention-deficit/hyperactivity disorder. *Front. Psychiatry* **2017**, *8*, 1–8. [CrossRef]
138. Baumann, N.; Pham-Dinh, D. Biology of oligodendrocyte and myelin in the mammalian central nervous system. *Physiol. Rev.* **2001**, *81*, 871–927. [CrossRef]

139. Hsieh, J.; Aimone, J.B.; Kaspar, B.K.; Kuwabara, T.; Nakashima, K.; Gage, F.H. IGF-I instructs multipotent adult neural progenitor cells to become oligodendrocytes. *J. Cell Biol.* **2004**, *164*, 111–122. [CrossRef]
140. Beck, K.D.; Powell-Braxtont, L.; Widmer, H.R.; Valverde, J.; Hefti, F. Igf1 gene disruption results in reduced brain size, CNS hypomyelination, and loss of hippocampal granule and striatal parvalbumin-containing neurons. *Neuron* **1995**, *14*, 717–730. [CrossRef]
141. Ye, P.; Li, L.; Richards, R.G.; DiAugustine, R.P.; D'Ercole, A.J. Myelination is altered in insulin-like growth factor-I null mutant mice. *J. Neurosci.* **2002**, *22*, 6041–6051. [CrossRef]
142. Steinman, G. Plausible etiology of brain dysconnectivity in autism—Review and prospectus. *Med. Hypotheses* **2015**, *85*, 405–407. [CrossRef]
143. Bozdagi, O.; Tavassoli, T.; Buxbaum, J.D. Insulin-like growth factor-1 rescues synaptic and motor deficits in a mouse model of autism and developmental delay. *Mol. Autism* **2013**, *4*, 3–6. [CrossRef] [PubMed]
144. Gonzalez-Perez, O.; Romero-Rodriguez, R.; Soriano-Navarro, M.; Garcia-Verdugo, J.M.; Alvarez-Buylla, A. Epidermal growth factor induces the progeny of subventricular zone type B cells to migrate and differentiate into oligodendrocytes. *Stem Cells* **2009**, *27*, 2032–2043. [CrossRef]
145. Gonzalez-Perez, O.; Quiñones-Hinojosa, A. Dose-dependent effect of EGF on migration and differentiation of adult subventricular zone astrocytes. *Glia* **2010**, *58*, 975–983. [CrossRef] [PubMed]
146. Gonzalez-Perez, O.; Alvarez-Buylla, A. Oligodendrogenesis in the subventricular zone and the role of epidermal growth factor. *Brain Res. Rev.* **2011**, *67*, 147–156. [CrossRef] [PubMed]
147. Galvez-Contreras, A.Y.; Quiñones-Hinojosa, A.; Gonzalez-Perez, O. The role of EGFR and ErbB family related proteins in the oligodendrocyte specification in germinal niches of the adult mammalian brain. *Front. Cell. Neurosci.* **2013**, *7*, 258. [CrossRef] [PubMed]
148. Russo, A.J. Increased epidermal growth factor receptor (EGFR) associated with hepatocyte growth factor (HGF) and symptom severity in children with autism spectrum disorders (ASDs). *J. Cent. Nerv. Syst. Dis.* **2014**, *6*, 79–83. [CrossRef]
149. Kaphzan, H.; Hernandez, P.; Jung, J.I.; Cowansage, K.K.; Deinhardt, K.; Chao, M.V.; Abel, T.; Klann, E. Reversal of impaired hippocampal long-term potentiation and contextual fear memory deficits in angelman syndrome model mice by ErbB inhibitors. *Biol. Psychiatry* **2012**, *72*, 182–190. [CrossRef]
150. Chen, J.; Alberts, I.; Li, X. Dysregulation of the IGF-I/PI3K/AKT/mTOR signaling pathway in autism spectrum disorders. *Int. J. Dev. Neurosci.* **2014**, *35*, 35–41. [CrossRef]
151. Onore, C.; Yang, H.; Van de Water, J.; Ashwood, P. Dynamic Akt/mTOR signaling in children with autism spectrum disorder. *Front. Pediatr.* **2017**, *5*, 1–9. [CrossRef]
152. Cuscó, I.; Medrano, A.; Gener, B.; Vilardell, M.; Gallastegui, F.; Villa, O.; González, E.; Rodríguez-Santiago, B.; Vilella, E.; Del Campo, M.; et al. Autism-specific copy number variants further implicate the phosphatidylinositol signaling pathway and the glutamatergic synapse in the etiology of the disorder. *Hum. Mol. Genet.* **2009**, *18*, 1795–1804. [CrossRef]
153. Zhou, J.; Blundell, J.; Ogawa, S.; Kwon, C.H.; Zhang, W.; Sinton, C.; Powell, C.M.; Parada, L.F. Pharmacological inhibition of mTORCl suppresses anatomical, cellular, and behavioral abnormalities in neural-specific PTEN knock-out mice. *J. Neurosci.* **2009**, *29*, 1773–1783. [CrossRef]
154. Ness, J.K.; Mitchell, N.E.; Wood, T.L. IGF-I and NT-3 signaling pathways in developing oligodendrocytes: Differential regulation and activation of receptors and the downstream effector akt. *Dev. Neurosci.* **2002**, *24*, 437–445. [CrossRef]
155. Butler, M.G.; Dazouki, M.J.; Zhou, X.P.; Talebizadeh, Z.; Brown, M.; Takahashi, T.N.; Miles, J.H.; Wang, C.H.; Stratton, R.; Pilarski, R.; et al. Subset of individuals with autism spectrum disorders and extreme macrocephaly associated with germline PTEN tumour suppressor gene mutations. *J. Med. Genet.* **2005**, *42*, 318–321. [CrossRef]
156. Tilot, A.K.; Gaugler, M.K.; Yu, Q.; Romigh, T.; Yu, W.; Miller, R.H.; Frazier, T.W.; Eng, C. Germline disruption of Pten localization causes enhanced sex-dependent social motivation and increased glial production. *Hum. Mol. Genet.* **2014**, *23*, 3212–3227. [CrossRef]
157. Frazier, T.W.; Embacher, R.; Tilot, A.K.; Koenig, K.; Mester, J.; Eng, C. Molecular and phenotypic abnormalities in individuals with germline heterozygous PTEN mutations and autism. *Mol. Psychiatry* **2015**, *20*, 1132–1138. [CrossRef]
158. Jones, J.I.; Clemmons, D.R. Insulin-like growth factors and their binding proteins: Biological actions. *Endocr. Rev.* **1995**, *16*, 3–34. [CrossRef]

159. Linggi, B.; Carpenter, G. ErbB receptors: New insights on mechanisms and biology. *Trends Cell Biol.* **2006**, *16*, 649–656. [CrossRef]
160. Galvez-Contreras, A.Y.; Campos-Ordonez, T.; Lopez-Virgen, V.; Gomez-Plascencia, J.; Ramos-Zuniga, R.; Gonzalez-Perez, O. Growth factors as clinical biomarkers of prognosis and diagnosis in psychiatric disorders. *Cytokine Growth Factor Rev.* **2016**, *32*, 85–96. [CrossRef]
161. Furusho, M.; Dupree, J.L.; Nave, K.A.; Bansal, R. Fibroblast growth factor receptor signaling in oligodendrocytes regulates myelin sheath thickness. *J. Neurosci.* **2012**, *32*, 6631–6641. [CrossRef]
162. Ishii, A.; Furusho, M.; Bansal, R. Sustained activation of ERK1/2 MAPK in oligodendrocytes and schwann cells enhances myelin growth and stimulates oligodendrocyte progenitor expansion. *J. Neurosci.* **2013**, *33*, 175–186. [CrossRef]
163. Ishii, A.; Fyffe-Maricich, S.L.; Furusho, M.; Miller, R.H.; Bansal, R. ERK1/ERK2 MAPK signaling is required to increase myelin thickness independent of oligodendrocyte differentiation and initiation of myelination. *J. Neurosci.* **2012**, *32*, 8855–8864. [CrossRef] [PubMed]
164. Bibollet-Bahena, O.; Almazan, G. IGF-1-stimulated protein synthesis in oligodendrocyte progenitors requires PI3K/mTOR/Akt and MEK/ERK pathways. *J. Neurochem.* **2009**, *109*, 1440–1451. [CrossRef] [PubMed]
165. Cui, Q.L.; Almazan, G. IGF-I-induced oligodendrocyte progenitor proliferation requires PI3K/Akt, MEK/ERK, and Src-like tyrosine kinases. *J. Neurochem.* **2007**, *100*, 1480–1493. [CrossRef] [PubMed]

3

Investigating Autism-Related Symptoms in Children with Prader-Willi Syndrome

Jeffrey A. Bennett [1,2], Sandra Hodgetts [3], Michelle L. Mackenzie [1], Andrea M. Haqq [1,*,†] and Lonnie Zwaigenbaum [1,2,†]

1 Department of Pediatrics, Faculty of Medicine and Dentistry, University of Alberta, 11405 87 Avenue, Edmonton, AB T6G1C9, Canada; jabennet@ualberta.ca (J.A.B.); michelle.mackenzie@ualberta.ca (M.L.M.); lonnie.zwaigenbaum@albertahealthservices.ca (L.Z.)

2 Autism Research Centre-E209, Glenrose Rehabilitation Hospital, 10230 111 Avenue, Edmonton, AB T5G 0B7, Canada

3 Faculty of Rehabilitation Medicine, University of Alberta, 8205 114 Street, Edmonton, AB T6G 2G4, Canada; sandra.hodgetts@ualberta.ca

* Correspondence: haqq@ualberta.ca

† These authors contributed equally to this work.

Academic Editor: Merlin G. Butler

Abstract: Prader-Willi syndrome (PWS), a rare genetic disorder caused by the lack of expression of paternal genes from chromosome 15q11-13, has been investigated for autism spectrum disorder (ASD) symptomatology in various studies. However, previous findings have been variable, and no studies investigating ASD symptomatology in PWS have exclusively studied children. We aimed to characterize social communication functioning and other ASD-related symptoms in children with PWS, and assessed agreement across measures and rates of ASD diagnosis. Measures included the Autism Diagnostic Observation Schedule-2 (ADOS-2), the Social Communication Questionnaire (SCQ), Social Responsiveness Scale-2 (SRS-2), Social Skills Improvement System-Rating Scales (SSIS-RS), and the Vineland Adaptive Behavioral Scales-II (VABS-II). General adaptive and intellectual skills were also assessed. Clinical best estimate (CBE) diagnosis was determined by an experienced developmental pediatrician, based on history and review of all available study measures, and taking into account overall developmental level. Participants included 10 children with PWS, aged 3 to 12 years. Three of the 10 children were male and genetic subtypes were two deletion (DEL) and eight uniparental disomy (UPD) (with a total of 6 female UPD cases). Although 8 of the 10 children exceeded cut-offs on at least one of the ASD assessments, agreement between parent questionnaires (SCQ, SRS-2, SSIS-RS) and observational assessment (ADOS-2) was very poor. None of the children were assigned a CBE diagnosis of ASD, with the caveat that the risk may have been lower because of the predominance of girls in the sample. The lack of agreement between the assessments emphasizes the complexity of interpreting ASD symptom measures in children with PWS.

Keywords: Prader-Willi syndrome; PWS; social communication; Autism Diagnostic Observation Schedule; ADOS; autism spectrum disorder; ASD

1. Introduction

Prader-Willi syndrome (PWS) is a genetic disorder caused by the absence of expression of the paternal contribution of chromosome 15q11-13. The majority of cases are due to deletion (DEL; 65%–75%) or uniparental disomy (UPD; 20%–30%), with a small minority (1%–3%) due to rare imprinting center defects [1]. The PWS phenotype includes hypotonia and failure to thrive during infancy, followed in early childhood by hyperphagia and an insatiable appetite which can lead to morbid obesity if left unchecked [1]. Cognitive disability and problem behaviors are also common and, for some families, represent greater challenges than the food-seeking behaviors [2].

Although variable, the PWS phenotype overlaps to some degree with autism spectrum disorder (ASD), a neurodevelopmental disorder characterized by the presence of symptoms in two core domains: social communication impairment and restricted and repetitive behaviors and interests. Indeed, the prevalence of ASD in PWS has been estimated at 26.7% based on exceeding clinical cut-points on relevant ASD assessments [3]. Also, ASD in the UPD genetic subtype (35.3%; two maternal copies of chromosome 15 present) is almost twice as common as in the DEL subtype (18.3%) [3]. This may be partially due to a genetic finding that overexpression of chromosome 15 is associated with higher rates of ASD [4]. The estimated prevalence of ASD in PWS is significantly higher than the current prevalence estimate of about 1.5% for ASD in the general population [5]. To receive an ASD diagnosis, symptoms in both domains must be present during the early developmental period; however, they may not be fully recognized until a child is older and social demands exceed their capacity [1]. Nevertheless, early social communication impairments (including reduced gazing towards faces and directed vocalizations [6], and reduced response to name being called [7]) in children who later receive a diagnosis of ASD have been reported as early as 12 months. Indeed, ASD diagnosis can be reliably made by 18 to 24 months in a clinical setting. Earlier recognition of ASD is important as studies have demonstrated that early intervention for ASD yields more favorable outcomes [8].

Despite a recent increase of research investigating symptoms of ASD in PWS, no studies have focused on young children with PWS. Eight years of age is the youngest mean age in a study investigating ASD in individuals with PWS [9]. The expression of ASD in PWS may change over development, with two studies reporting more prominent symptoms in adolescents and adults with PWS compared to younger children. Lo et al. [10] reported that none of the 22 children with PWS, ages 7–9, exceeded the cut-off for ASD on the Diagnostic Interview for Social and Communication Disorders (DISCO); however, 24 of 44 of the individuals aged 10–17 years old exceeded the cut-off for ASD. Additionally, Akefeldt and Gillberg [11] reported lower average scores (3.4; SD = 4.4) in toddlers with PWS (mean age = 2.1 years; range = 0.8–3.7 years) compared to the older individuals (19.1; SD = 10.7) with PWS (mean age 18.4 years; range = 4.2–36.3 years) on the Autism Spectrum Screening Questionnaire (ASSQ) [12]. However, this tool was designed to assess children ages 6 to 17 years old with normal intelligence to mild cognitive disability, raising concerns about the validity of the ASSQ in this sample.

Assessments commonly used to investigate ASD symptomatology and adaptive functioning in individuals with PWS include the Social Responsiveness Scale [13,14], Social Communication Questionnaire [15,16], and Vineland Adaptive Behavior Scales [13,17]. A recent systematic review [3] found that few studies investigating ASD in PWS have included the Autism Diagnostic Observation Schedule (ADOS) [18] or the Autism Diagnostic Interview-Revised (ADI-R) [19], considered to be gold standard measures of ASD symptoms based on excellent sensitivity and specificity in differentiating ASD from other developmental disorders [20]. Moreover, rates of ASD reported in PWS are generally not based on ICD or DSM-based clinical diagnoses, but are rather based on clinical cut-offs on proxy measures such as the Social Communication Questionnaire (SCQ) [3]. This is problematic, as no single measure can be used as a proxy for diagnosis.

The primary goal of this study was to characterize ASD symptoms in children ages 3 to 12 with PWS using the ADOS, 2nd edition (ADOS-2) [21], and other standardized ASD assessment tools. As a secondary objective, we investigated other aspects of social-communication development in children with PWS, and compared the agreement between various ASD assessment tools and categorical ASD diagnosis by clinical best estimate (CBE). Based on previous studies, we hypothesized elevated rates of ASD symptomatology in children with PWS, as has been found in adolescents and adults with PWS. We also expected ASD symptoms to be present in some children with PWS who do not have a diagnosis of ASD. Furthermore, we expected a moderate agreement between the various ASD tools used to assess ASD symptomatology in children with PWS.

2. Results

2.1. Demographics

There were a total of 10 participants, all of whom resided in western Canada (Alberta (n = 8); British Columbia (n = 1); Saskatchewan (n = 1)). Nine of the ten patients with PWS in the age range who were contacted directly through a regional specialty clinic agreed to participate in the study. One additional child was recruited through a provincial PWS group. The cohort included seven females and three males, with a mean age of 6.77 years old (SD = 2.85). Participant genetic subtype was confirmed by genetic testing completed previously, or through confirmation of genetic testing by the participants' health-care provider. Only two participants were the DEL subtype; the other eight were the UPD subtype. Each participant completed all of the assessments. Table 1 provides a summary of the study results, including the mean, standard error of the mean, and standard deviation, as well as the minimum and maximum scores attained for all measures. The average full scale IQ (FSIQ) was 63.38 (SD = 17.42), which falls within the range for individuals with PWS reported in a review by Cassidy and colleagues [1]. A negative correlation between age and FSIQ was found (Spearman's $\rho = -0.815$, $p = 0.004$).

Table 1. Results from assessments, given as mean (SE; SD) and range.

	Mean (SE; SD)	Min–Max
Age	6.77 (2.85)	3.42–11.75
# (%) male	3 (30)	–
# (%) UPD	8 (80)	–
FSIQ	64.70 (5.05; 15.96)	40–92
ADOS-2 Severity score	3.00 (0.42; 1.33)	1–5
ADOS-2 SA Severity score	3.50 (0.56; 1.78)	2–7
ADOS-2 RRB Severity score	4.70 (0.80; 2.54)	0–7
SCQ raw score	11.90 (2.20; 6.95)	5–21
SRS-2 Overall T-score	62.70 (3.98; 12.56)	43–85
SRS-2: Social Awareness T-score	61.60 (4.16; 13.16)	43–81
SRS-2: Social Cognition T-score	61.00 (4.83; 15.27)	40–94
SRS-2: Social Communication T-score	61.70 (4.04; 12.78)	43–86
SRS-2: Social Motivation T-score	56.10 (2.47; 7.81)	43–67
SRS-2: RRB T-score	65.80 (4.20; 13.28)	48–88
SSIS-RS: Social skills percentile	23.10 (7.02; 22.18)	2–64
SSIS-RS: Problem behaviors percentile	80.00 (7.06; 22.32)	42–99
SSIS-RS: ASD raw score	19.00 (2.53; 8.01)	8–31
Vineland-II Composite standard score	80.40 (3.57; 11.29)	60–96
Vineland-II: Communication standard score	85.20 (4.60; 14.56)	59–100
Vineland-II: Daily Living Skills standard score	86.50 (3.60; 11.38)	68–101
Vineland-II: Socialization standard score	83.20 (4.79; 15.14)	57–108
Vineland-II: Motor standard score	77.20 (2.59; 8.19)	67–91

n = 10 for all assessments; SE = Standard Error (of the mean); SD = Standard Deviation (of the sample); FSIQ = Full-scale IQ (based on WPPSI/WISC scores); ADOS-2 = Autism Diagnostic Observation Schedule-2; SA = Social Affect; RRB = Restricted and Repetitive Behaviors; SRS-2 = Social Responsiveness Scale-2; SCQ = Social Communication Questionnaire; SSIS-RS = Social Skills Improvement System-Rating Scales.

2.2. Assessments

Table 2 gives detailed results for every participant on each of the ASD assessments, including an indication of which scores exceeded clinical cut-offs. In total, three of 10 children (all 3 female UPD) scored above the cut-off for ASD on the ADOS-2 symptom severity score. However, two of those three children (P8 and P9) scored 0 in the restricted and repetitive behaviors (RRB) domain, which would suggest that ASD is not present, as under DSM-5 observable symptoms are expected in both the social affect (SA) and RRB domains.

Table 2. Individual participant score profiles.

ID	Sub-Type	Sex	FSIQ	ADOS Module	ADOS SA	ADOS RRB	ADOS Overall	SCQ	SRS AWR	SRS COG	SRS COM	SRS MOT	SRS RRB	SRS Overall	SSIS SS	SSIS PB	SSIS ASD	CBE
1	DEL	F	92	2	2	6	2	6	54	56	55	51	62	56	25	53	11	N
2	UPD	M	63	2	2	5	1	6	43	54	48	57	56	52	50	56	16	N
3	UPD	F	77	2	4	6	*4*	5	49	40	43	43	48	43	64	42	8	N
4	UPD	M	82	2	2	6	2	*14*	66	63	57	47	64	59	18	90	*21*	N
5	UPD	F	69	2	2	6	2	9	57	53	64	54	58	*62*	14	98	*20*	N
6	UPD	F	56	2	3	6	3	*13*	68	77	71	64	82	*75*	8	97	*26*	N
7	DEL	M	65	3	4	5	3	*20*	67	55	65	67	66	*65*	2	99	*31*	N
8	UPD	F	47	1	6	0	*5*	*14*	81	67	73	64	80	*75*	4	96	*21*	N
9	UPD	F	56	3	7	0	*5*	6	50	51	55	60	54	55	44	71	8	N
10	UPD	F	40	3	3	7	3	*26*	81	94	86	54	88	*85*	2	98	*23*	N

Subtype: DEL = deletion ; UPD = uniparental disomy; Sex: M=Male, F = Female; ADOS-SA = ADOS-2 Social Affect Severity Score; ADOS-RRB = ADOS-2 Restricted or Repetitive Behavior Severity Score; SCQ = SCQ Raw Score; SRS-AWR = SRS-2 Social Awareness T-score; SRS-COG = SRS-2 Social Cognition T-score; SRS-COM = SRS-2 Social Communication T-score; SRS-MOT = SRS-2 Social Motivation T-score; SRS-RRB = SRS-2 Restricted or Repetitive Behaviors T-score; SSIS-SS = SSIS-RS Social Skills Percentile; SSIS-PB = SSIS-RS Problem Behaviors Percentile; SSIS-ASD = SSIS-RS ASD Subscale Raw; CBE = Clinical Best Estimate; ADOS-2: scores of >3 are associated with ASD; SCQ: scores of ≥12 are associated with ASD; SRS-2: scores <60 are not associated with ASD, 60–65 are associated with mild to moderate impairment in social responsiveness, 66–75 are associated with substantial impairment in social responsiveness and ASD, >75 are associated with severe impairment in social responsiveness and ASD; SSIS-RS: overall score for the following age ranges represents the average amount of ASD behaviors; any score above or below these ranges indicate above or below average ASD symptoms, respectively: age 3–5 years: 4–16; age 5–12 years: 3–14; CBE: N = does not qualify for ASD diagnosis, Y = does qualify for ASD diagnosis; * Scores that exceed cut-off for ASD are ***bolded and italicized*** *. Note: The individuals were ordered from youngest (ID = 1) to oldest (ID = 10) in order to give a sense of participant age (range = 3–12 years); to maintain anonymity (due to the rarity of PWS), participant ages not listed; rather, ordered by age.

2.2.1. ASD Cut-Off Scores

Five children exceeded the cut-off SRS-2 score associated with ASD in the general population, four of whom also exceeded cut-off on the SCQ. With respect to the separate domains, social motivation showed the least impairment (T-score = 56.10), while the RRB domain showed the most impairment (T-score = 65.80). No differences were detected among SRS-2 domain means, based on a non-parametric Kruskal-Wallis Test. It should be noted that, although a modified cut-off score of 12 was used for the SCQ, using the original cut-off score of 15 did not add meaningful clarification to the overall scores or patterns of agreement between assessments. Six of 10 children (1 male DEL, 1 male DEL, 4 female UPD) had above average ASD symptoms on the SSIS-RS ASD subscale. These six children also exceeded cut-off on the SCQ and/or the SRS-2.

2.2.2. Clinical Best Estimate

None of the participants met clinical best estimate (CBE) criteria for ASD based on DSM-5, largely because of inconsistency across measures. Detailed case descriptions of each participant (P) are provided below. To maintain confidentiality, age and gender cannot be reported, although the participants are ordered from youngest (P1) to oldest (P10) to provide a sense of relative age. Each profile describes the unique or extreme findings from each child.

2.2.3. Case Study Descriptions

P1 (female DEL) was the youngest individual in our study. The assessment results from this participant were not indicative of ASD. The Restricted or Repetitive Behaviors and Interests (RRB) sections on both the ADOS-2 and SRS-2 confirmed mild impairment in this symptom domain, but the ADOS-SA domain was low at a severity score of 2. The SSIS-RS percentiles and Vineland-II scores were average, with the exception of the Vineland-II motor skills domain, which was more than one standard deviation below the normative standard.

P2 (male UPD) did not exceed cut-off for ASD on any of the assessments. Again, the SSIS-RS and Vineland-II results were all close to the normative standard, with the exception of motor skills on the Vineland-II.

P3 (female UPD) had parent-reported symptoms from the three ASD questionnaires (SCQ, SRS-2, and SSIS-RS) that were the lowest in the entire sample. Indeed, she had among the most favourable scores on the SSIS-RS and Vineland-II of all participants, scoring above the normative standard on all domains except Vineland-II socialization and Vineland-II motor skills domains, both of which were less than one standard deviation below age-related norms. In contrast, P3 is the only child who exceeded the ASD threshold on both the SA and RRB domains of the ADOS-2, albeit with an overall severity score right at the cut-off associated with ASD.

P4 (male UPD) had SCQ and SSIS-RS ASD subdomain scores that exceeded the cut-off for ASD, while his SRS-2 score was one point below cut-off. The SRS-2 domains that elevated the overall scores included social awareness, social cognition, and RRBs. He also scored below the sample mean on the social skills subdomain of the SSIS-RS (18th percentile), and higher on the problem behaviors subdomain (90th percentile). However, he was assessed as having social-communicative symptoms well below the level associated with ASD (ADOS-SA severity score = 2, and overall severity score = 2), although RRB symptoms were observed. As well, Vineland-II social and communicative domains were rated as close to average.

P5 (female UPD) had similar results as P4: low ADOS-2 scores, despite exceeding cut-off for ASD on two of the three parent-report questionnaires. Critically, the SCQ score was three points below the cut-off associated with ASD and the SRS-2 overall score was only two points above cut-off. She also scored low on the social skills domain of the SSIS-RS (14th percentile), and very high on the problem behaviors domain (98th percentile). Additionally, the Vineland-II scores were all below the sample mean, with motor skills being the most affected.

P6 (female UPD) was assessed as having social-communication symptoms below the level associated with ASD (severity score = 3) on the ADOS, despite RRB symptoms (severity score = 6). However, she was rated as having high levels of symptoms on all three questionnaires. The SRS-2 scores were especially high, with the overall score one point below the severe range. These scores were largely driven by the RRB and the social cognition subdomains, both of which fell in the severe range; comparatively, the social motivation subdomain only showed mild impairment. Additionally, the SSIS-RS social skills (8th percentile) and problem behavior (97th percentile) were both indicative of significant social impairments. Despite the high scores on the questionnaires, P6 scored within one SD of age norms on the communication and daily living skills domains on the Vineland-II, although more than one standard deviation lower on the socialization and motor skills domains. Full scale IQ was 56, so clinically, social impairments were felt to relate, at least in part, to intellectual impairments.

P7 (male DEL) also scored below the clinical threshold on the ADOS-2, with an overall severity score of 3, despite symptoms observed in both domains. He exceeded the cut-off for ASD on all three questionnaires. On the SSIS-RS, this child was rated at the 2nd percentile on the social skills domain, >99th percentile for the problem behaviors domain, and the highest raw score on the ASD subdomain. The participant's SCQ score was also elevated. Interestingly, all of the subdomains on the SRS-2 were extremely similar (scores ranged from 65–67), with the exception of social cognition, which was below cut-off.

P8 (female UPD) had an overall symptom severity rating of 5, above the level associated with ASD, although with no symptoms observed in the RRB domain (severity score = 0). The parent report on the SRS-2 did suggest severe impairments in the RRB subdomain, with overall SRS-2 score at the upper end of the moderate range. SSIS-RS social skills (4th percentile) and problem behaviors (96th percentile) were also indicative of social impairment, and the ASD subscale score was very high as well. She scored over two standard deviations below the normative standard on the communication domain of the Vineland-II, and had slightly higher scores in the other three domains. Other factors taken in consideration in the CBE process included cognitive delay (FSIQ = 47).

P9 (female UPD) had high levels of symptoms rated on the SA domain of the ADOS (severity score = 7), but no observed RRB symptoms (severity score = 0). As well, she had among the lowest scores on the SSIS-RS ASD domain, the SCQ, and the SRS-2, including on the RRB domain. The only SRS-2 subdomain that exceeded cut-off for ASD was social motivation, albeit by one point.

P10 (female UPD) had symptoms rated in both SA (severity score = 3) and RRB. (severity score = 7) of the ADOS, although the overall severity was subthreshold for ASD (severity score = 3). Scores were also elevated on the SCQ and SRS-2. This child's SSIS-RS ASD score was also well above cut-off, and the SSIS-RS social skills (2nd percentile) and problem behaviors (98th percentile) also showed significant impairment. She also had the lowest adaptive behavior composite score on the Vineland-II, with the socialization and communication scores almost three standard deviations below standard. However, the clinician responsible for CBE diagnosis concluded that impairments in socialization and communication were largely attributable to intellectual disability (FSIQ = 40), and that this child did not meet DSM-5 criteria for ASD.

2.3. *Agreement among Measures*

The three questionnaires (SRS-2, SCQ, and SSIS-RS) all had acceptable agreement with one another (see Table 3). Cohen's κ for the SCQ and SSIS-RS, as well as for the SRS-2 and SSIS-RS, was calculated to be 0.80 (SE = 0.19), and κ for the SCQ and SRS-2 was calculated to be 0.60 (SE = 0.25). Notably, a total of six children exceeded the cut-off on the SSIS-RS; 4 of 6 children exceeded the cut-off on both the SRS-2 and SCQ, a fifth on the SRS-2 but not the SCQ, and the sixth on the SCQ but not the SRS-2. However, agreement between the three questionnaires and the ADOS-2 was poor. Cohen's κ for the ADOS-2 vs. the SCQ, SRS-2, and SSRI-RS were calculated to be −0.20 (SE = 0.28), −0.20 (SE = 0.28), and −0.30 (SE = 0.28), respectively.

Table 3. Agreement among Measures.

Measures	Kohen's κ	Standard Error
SCQ/SRS-2	0.60	0.25
SCQ/SSIS-RS	0.80	0.19
SRS-2/SSIS-RS	0.80	0.19
SCQ/ADOS-2	−0.20	0.28
SRS-2/ADOS-2	−0.20	0.28
SSIS-RS/ADOS-2	−0.30	0.28

3. Discussion

Our main findings were that (1) ASD symptomatology and social competence in children with PWS were highly variable; (2) While there was moderate to high agreement among parent-report measures of ASD symptoms and social behaviors ($\kappa = 0.6$–0.8), agreement between these measures and ASD symptom severity as observed on the ADOS-2 was poor ($\kappa < 0.0$) (see Table 3). Six of the 10 children (1 male DEL, 1 male DEL, 4 female UPD) exceeded the cut-off for ASD on at least one of the parent-report measures (and 4 of 10 on all three). In contrast, 3 of 10 (all female UPD) had observable symptom severity at the level associated with ASD diagnosis on the ADOS-2, only one of whom had elevated symptoms in both domains. Moreover, only 1 of the 3 children with elevated ASD symptom severity on the ADOS-2 met the scoring cut-off suggestive of ASD on *any* of the parent report measures (not the same child with elevated symptoms on both ADOS-2 domains). Thus, while most (8 of 10) participants had evidence of ASD symptoms on at least one study measure, there was poor agreement between measures and thus, inconsistent findings that complicated clinical diagnostic judgement. Indeed, none of the participants were assigned a clinical diagnosis of ASD. One child (P8) with elevated symptoms on both the ADOS-2 (albeit not both domains) and the parent report measures had an FSIQ of 47, and thus, the clinical presentation was complicated by intellectual disability. This child's inability to perform numerous tasks made the interpretation of social skills deficits more challenging. Although the clinical diagnostic status of this child may be equivocal, the pattern of scoring overall on study measures indicated considerable variability in profile, poor agreement between parent-report measures, and direct behavioral observation (i.e., using the ADOS-2), and raises important questions about the clinical interpretation and even the validity of available ASD symptom measures in this population. Finally, there was a negative correlation between age and FSIQ (Spearman's $\rho = -0.815$, $p = 0.004$ in this small sample).

In our study, sample means on ASD assessments in children with PWS were less indicative of ASD than have been previously reported in adolescents and adults with PWS. For example, Zyga et al. [14] and Dimitropoulos et al. [13] used the SRS to assess samples with a mean age over 10 years of age, and found average scores of 82.18 and 76.31, respectively. Both of these scores fall in the severe range on the SRS-2, whereas the average score from our population was 62.70, which falls in the mild range. Dimitropoulos et al. [13] and Milner et al. [17] also used the Vineland-II in their samples of adolescents and adults with PWS, and reported average composite scores of 65.15 and 62.60, respectively. Meanwhile, our sample had an average score of 80.40, over one standard deviation above results from these previously published studies. Lastly, Zyga et al. [14] reported that 8 of 14 adolescents (57.14%) met criteria for ASD on the ADOS, whereas only 3 of 10 (30%) from our cohort met criteria (actually only 1 of 10 (10%), considering that P8 and P9 did not pass cut-off on the RRB domain). These findings indicate interesting differences in ASD symptoms and adaptive functioning between age groups (children vs. adolescents and adults). However, other potential confounders, such as growth hormone treatment or exposure to other interventions, cannot be ruled out.

There were marked discrepancies between direct observational assessment and parent report in the assessment of ASD in PWS in our study. Notably, previous research in non-PWS samples indicates that both parent reports and observational data are essential to valid diagnostic assessment for ASD [22]. In a recent systematic review of ASD in PWS, Bennett et al. [3] reported that most studies investigating ASD in PWS are based on single measures, with parent reports more common than observational assessment (i.e., ADOS-2). Given that parent reports may be less resource-intensive and require less specialized training, they may be more feasible to administer in a clinical program serving a rare population such as PWS. However, given the limited agreement across parent reports and direct observational measures in our sample, further research may be needed to verify which assessments are most accurate and informative in the clinical diagnostic assessment of ASD in PWS.

Another possible explanation for the discrepancy between the results from the ADOS-2 and the parent-report assessments could be the distinction between what a child 'can do' and 'typically does'. The AODS-2 is a 30 to 45-minute observational assessment designed to elicit certain responses from children. Since some children with PWS are more comfortable associating with adults than same-age peers, the ADOS-2 interaction potentially provides a more comfortable situation than their usual social experiences. Parent-report measures, on the other hand, focus on the frequency of the child's social behaviors in their real-life settings, which may be influenced by both ability and opportunities/contexts. Another possible explanation for poor agreement between the SCQ questionnaire and ADOS-2 is that the restrictive repetitive behaviors on the SCQ (which are more prevalent in PWS) are not as heavily weighted on the ADOS-2. However, it would be difficult to know whether any of these possibilities are valid without further research to probe discrepancies between the various ASD assessments employed in this study.

Lack of agreement between ASD assessment measures has been reported in studies investigating ASD in other genetic syndromes, specifically Fragile-X syndrome [23]. These studies indicate poor agreement between the ADOS-2 and SCQ (Cohen's $\kappa = 0.33$ for girls, 0.13 for boys). Additionally, using a combination of the ADI-R, ADOS, and DSM-IV criteria, Harris et al. [24] reported that in a group of 63 males with Fragile X syndrome, 15 participants (24%) met criteria for ASD on all three assessments, while an additional 28 individuals (44%) met criteria on only one or two of the assessments. One potential explanation for these findings is that each genetic syndrome manifests its own set of complex behaviors which are not typical in the general population, some of which may overlap with ASD, even when the full ASD phenotype is not present [25,26]. The overlap in phenotype places individuals with a genetic syndrome closer to ASD cut-off scores on particular measures than typically developing individuals, even in the absence of an ASD diagnosis. Another contributor to higher scores on ASD assessments may be the degree of intellectual disability. Indeed, the SCQ manual [27] mentions that non-ASD individuals with lower IQ (50–69) obtained higher scores on the SCQ (11.40; SD = 5.87), which is quite similar to the results in our study (mean IQ = 63.38; mean SCQ score = 11.90). The SRS-2 manual [28] gives similar caution to its use in individuals with an IQ less than 70. Both overlapping phenotype and intellectual disability may affect the ability for these assessments to reliably detect ASD in PWS.

Limitations to this study include the sample demographics, limited sample size, and cross-sectional design. The limited number of children available for the study resulted in uneven distribution in both gender and genetic subtype. Our study included three boys and seven girls, whereas the gender distribution in the PWS population is roughly equal. Given that ASD is recognized four times more in males than females [5], the high number of females in the study may have reduced the likelihood of ASD diagnosis. The ratio of 7:3 in favor of girls (in our study) is not an extreme variation, which would be expected about 17% of the time based on the binomial distribution. As well, the presence of ASD symptoms on the questionnaire measures and the ADOS did not seem to predominantly characterize males, albeit with only 3 in the sample. ASD in general is less common in females, although sex differences in ASD symptoms are generally not reported in PWS studies [3]. As well, although recruitment involved every known child with PWS in our study age-range, there was an unexpected distribution of eight UPD and two DEL cases in our sample. It has been reported that the UPD genetic subtype is associated with a higher level of ASD symptoms than the DEL subtype [3,29,30]. This sample characteristic might have been expected to lead to a higher level of ASD symptomatology. Notably, 1 of 2 (50%) DEL cases exceeded the cut-off on multiple ASD assessments, whereas 7 of 8 (88%) UPD exceeded the cut-off on at least one of the ASD assessments. It is important to note that it is unlikely that recruitment was biased to include more UPD children, given that 9 of 10 parents initially contacted agreed to participate in the study, without prior knowledge of genetic subtype from those contacting the participants. Notably, within the DEL subtype, there are two types of deletions: the longer type 1, and relatively shorter type 2. Some studies have found differences between type 1 and type 2, with type 1 typically showing greater overall impairment as well as ASD-related impairments [17,31–34]. However, we were unable to distinguish between the 2 types in our study, as the sample population had not received the necessary genotyping. Individuals with truncating mutations on the paternal allele of MAGEL2, a gene within the PWS domain, were recently found to exhibit both features of PWS and autism [35]. The overall implication is that our current limited sample was predominantly female UPD which may have influenced ASD symptom levels, although the two factors (sex and genetic subtype) would have been expected to shift the distribution in opposite directions. Our subsample of 6 girls with UPD is a relatively large grouping of this rarer subtype, and may provide a useful detailed clinical reference for other such patients. Critically, this study was originally intended to make group comparisons between UPD, DEL, and an ASD comparison group, but lacked an available adequate sample size due to lack of children with PWS in the region. Although descriptive studies are able to provide a wealth of information regarding smaller samples in order to generate hypotheses and ideas, they lack the statistical power to compare results to other groups, such as an ASD comparison group. A matched control group could have helped shed further insight into both the ASD symptoms and the relative strengths and weaknesses identified in this study. As well, our clinical best estimate (CBE) was done by an experienced developmental paediatrician, who reviewed all results, watched videotapes of the ADOS-2 assessments and met with individual patients for further discussion. However, there was no second rater that would have been necessary to determine reliability of the CBE in this study. Finally, the negative correlation between age and IQ in children with PWS is of interest, but is difficult to interpret in this small sample, which does not allow us to parse potential confounding effects of sex, genetic subtype, and obesity. A longitudinal design would also be helpful to discriminate possible factors involved in the negative correlation between age and IQ, and to determine if ASD symptoms in PWS are exacerbated with age.

4. Materials and Methods

4.1. Study Design

This cross-sectional study was conducted in Edmonton, AB, Canada. Individuals aged 3 to 12 with PWS were recruited for this study from local and regional care providers, as well as provincial PWS groups. The ratio of UPD to deletion cases of PWS (and girls versus boys) was the result of random chance; those who met study inclusion criteria from the local area were recruited. Parents agreed to receive a report of their child's performance and to be referred for further assessment and treatment if indicated clinically by the findings. Ethical approval was received from the local Health Research Ethics Board Health Panel (Study ID: Pro00051250; Approved 7 January 2015) at the University of Alberta. Parents gave informed consent for their children prior to participation in this study.

4.2. Assessments

All assessments were administered by experienced research psychometrists, who had been trained to reliability on each of the measures (including research reliability on the ADOS-2). Data collection was blinded to genetic subtype to avoid bias. A developmental paediatrician with 20 years experience in ASD diagnosis (LZ) reviewed case files and ADOS videos to determine whether criteria were met for ASD for each participant (hereafter, 'clinical best estimate' diagnosis).

4.2.1. Autism Diagnostic Observation Schedule-2

The Autism Diagnostic Observation Schedule, 2nd edition (ADOS-2) [21] is a semi-structured interactive assessment that provides an opportunity to observe behaviors relevant to ASD diagnosis. Items are scored from 0–3 or 0–2, with '0' representing a continuum of behavior not generally associated with ASD; a code of '1' generally indicates mild impairment of a nature that may be observed in persons with ASD; a code of '2' indicates definite impairment in that area; a code of '3' represents more profound impairment, although for the purpose of the scoring algorithm, scores of '3' are converted to '2'. The ADOS-2 provides a total score for social affect (SA) and restricted and repetitive behaviors (RRB) symptoms, each of which can be translated into a standardized severity score on a scale of 1 to 10. There is also an overall severity score, with $\geq$4 indicative of ASD. Because the severity of SA symptoms is rated based on ten algorithm items and RRB severity is based on four items, the overall severity score is more heavily weighted towards the SA domain. Additionally, since the RRB domain only consists of 4 algorithm items, if all items are scored '0', the severity is 0, whereas any item scored '1' leads to a severity rating of 5. Thus, the RRB severity scores are highly sensitive to scoring on individual items, and must be interpreted with caution. The ADOS-2 has been validated for ages 12 months to adulthood. One of 5 modules is administered, based on age and verbal fluency; Only modules 1 to 3 were administered in our study. Module 1 is designed for individuals with no speech or single words; Module 2 is for individuals with phrase speech; and Module 3 is for individuals with fluent speech and typically less than 14 years of age.

4.2.2. Social Communication Questionnaire

The Social Communication Questionnaire (SCQ) [27] is a 40-item parent questionnaire used to screen for autistic symptomatology; it is derived from the Autism Diagnostic Interview-Revised (ADI-R), a semi-structured interview used in ASD diagnosis [19]. The SCQ, which uses a yes/no parent response form, was chosen over the ADI-R to be more time-feasible for parents (10 minutes for the SCQ vs. 2 h for the ADI-R). Raw scores of 15 or greater are indicative of ASD. A study released after the publication of the SCQ indicates that a cut-off of 12 greatly improves the sensitivity of the assessment when used in combination with the ADOS, particularly for younger children [36].

4.2.3. Social Responsiveness Scale-2

The Social Responsiveness Scale, 2nd edition (SRS-2) [28] is a questionnaire completed by a primary caregiver and/or a teacher that provides an overall rating of social impairment as well as scores on 5 ASD-specific subdomains: (1) Social Awareness; (2) Social Cognition; (3) Social Communication; (4) Social Motivation; and (5) Restricted or Repetitive Behaviors (RRBs). It is designed to assess individuals from age 2.5 years to adulthood. Total scores on the SRS-2 are standardized as T-scores, based on age and gender, and are further separated into four levels: <60 (Within normal limits; generally not associated with ASD); 60 to 65 (Mild range; indicates deficiencies in reciprocal social behavior that may lead to mild to moderate interference with everyday social interactions); 66 to 75 (Moderate range; indicates deficiencies in reciprocal social interaction that lead to substantial interference with everyday social interaction, and are typical for children with ASD of moderate severity); and >75 (Severe range; indicates deficiencies in reciprocal social interaction that lead to severe interference with everyday social interaction, and are strongly associated with a clinical diagnosis of ASD).

4.2.4. Social Skills Improvement System-Rating Scales

The Social Skills Improvement System-Rating Scales (SSIS-RS) [37] was selected to provide information on a broad range of social behaviours; i.e., not only those specifically impaired in ASD. It is a parent questionnaire that can be administered for children between the ages of 3 and 18. The SSIS-RS provides percentiles for social skills (higher scores indicate more advanced social skills) as well as problem behaviors (higher scores indicate increased problem behaviors), normed by gender and age. There is also a subscale to indicate ASD symptoms (rated as below average, average, or above average). Although the SSIS-RS has not previously been reported in a PWS population, it has been widely used in the ASD population and determined to be a valid research tool for measuring social skills [38]. Furthermore, this questionnaire also assesses non-ASD related social impairments that might be present in PWS.

4.2.5. Vineland Adaptive Behavior Scales-II

The Vineland Adaptive Behavior Scales, 2nd edition (Vineland-II) [39] is a parent interview that quantifies their child's current adaptive behaviors. It provides a composite score, plus sub-scores in the following domains: (1) Daily Living Skills; (2) Socialization; (3) Communication; and (4) Motor Skills. Scores are based on a standardized scale with a mean of 100, and standard deviation of 15. It has been validated for all ages and specifically for individuals with ASD [40].

4.2.6. Wechsler Preschool and Primary Scale of Intelligence-III/ Wechsler Intelligence Scale for Children-IV

The Wechsler Preschool and Primary Scale of Intelligence, 3rd edition (WPPSI-III) [41] and Wechsler Intelligence Scale for Children, 4th edition (WISC-IV) [42] are individually administered measures of cognitive abilities that yield full-scale IQ. The WPPSI-III has been validated in children from age 2 to 7 years, and the WICS-IV has been validated in children from age 6 to 16 years. Both the WPSSI-III and WISC-IV have been used previously to assess patients with PWS and ASD [13,14,43].

4.3. Analytic Approach

Descriptive data from the ADOS-2, the 3 questionnaires (SCQ, SRS-2, and SSIS-RS), and the Vineland-II were provided for each child. Clinical best estimate (CBE) ASD diagnosis included a video review of each participant's ADOS-2, review of the questionnaires, and in person meeting with the parent and child. Any test result exceeding previously recommended ASD clinical cut-offs were considered in relation to CBE. Summary statistics were calculated for each assessment, including mean, standard deviation, standard error of the mean, and range. Additional analyses were performed using SPSS version 22 to compare performance among domains within measures. Experiment-wise alpha was set at $p < 0.05$ for all statistical analyses, which were completed using non-parametric tests due to the small sample size and associated non-normal distribution of study measures across our sample.

5. Conclusions

Our data suggest variable ASD symptomatology in children with PWS, with caveats related to the sex and genetic subtype composition of our small sample. Further research is necessary to identify the most appropriate tools to assess ASD in PWS. In particular, the disparity in agreement between direct observational assessment and parent reports warrants investigation into appropriate assessment of ASD in children with PWS.

Acknowledgments: Most importantly, we are grateful for the children with Prader-Willi syndrome and their families for coming, some from great distances, to participate. The research was funded by the Women and Children's Health Research Institute (WCHRI) from the University of Alberta, Department of Pediatrics. Andrea M. Haqq is also supported by the Canadian Institutes of Health Research (CIHR). Lonnie Zwaigenbaum is supported by the Stollery Children's Hospital Foundation Chair in Autism Research, which contributed funding toward Open Access publication.

Author Contributions: Jeffrey A. Bennett, Sandra Hodgetts, Michelle L. Mackenzie, Andrea M. Haqq, and Lonnie Zwaigenbaum designed the research study. Jeffrey A. Bennett performed the research. Jeffrey A. Bennett, Andrea M. Haqq, and Lonnie Zwaigenbaum analyzed the data. Jeffrey A. Bennett wrote the paper. Sandra Hodgetts, Michelle L. Mackenzie, Andrea M. Haqq, and Lonnie Zwaigenbaum all contributed to revisions of the paper. All authors read and approved the final manuscript.

Abbreviations

ADI-R	autism diagnostic interview-revised
ADOS-2	autism diagnostic observation schedule, 2nd edition
ASD	autism spectrum disorder
CBE	clinical best estimate
DEL	deletion (genetic subtype)
PWS:	Prader-Willi syndrome
RRB	restricted or repetitive behaviors
SCQ	Social Communication Questionnaire
SRS-2	Social Responsiveness Scale-2
SSIS-RS	Social Skills Improvement System-Rating Scales
UPD	uniparental disomy (genetic subtype)

References

1. Cassidy, S.B.; Schwartz, S.; Miller, J.L.; Driscoll, D.J. Prader-Willi syndrome. *Genet. Med.* **2012**, *14*, 10–26. [CrossRef] [PubMed]
2. Dykens, E.M.; Maxwell, M.A.; Pantino, E.; Kossler, R.; Roof, E. Assessment of hyperphagia in Prader-Willi syndrome. *Obesity* **2007**, *15*, 1816–1826. [CrossRef] [PubMed]
3. Bennett, J.A.; Germani, T.; Zwaigenbaum, L.; Haqq, A.M. Autism spectrum disorder in Prader-Willi syndrome: A systematic review. *Am. J. Med. Genet. A* **2015**, *167*, 2936–2944. [CrossRef] [PubMed]
4. Vorstman, J.A.; Staal, W.G.; van Daalen, E.; van Engeland, H.; Hochstenbach, P.F.; Franke, L. Identification of novel autism candidate regions through analysis of reported cytogenetic abnormalities associated with autism. *Mol. Psychiatry* **2006**, *11*, 18–28. [CrossRef] [PubMed]
5. Developmental Disabilities Monitoring Network Surveillance Year Principal Investigators; Centers for Disease Control and Prevention. Prevalence of autism spectrum disorder among children aged 8 years—Autism and developmental disabilities monitoring network, 11 sites, United States, 2010. *MMWR Surveill. Summ.* **2014**, *63*, 1–21.
6. Ozonoff, S.; Iosif, A.M.; Baguio, F.; Cook, I.C.; Hill, M.M.; Hutman, T.; Rogers, S.J.; Rozga, A.; Sangha, S.; Sigman, M.; et al. A prospective study of the emergence of early behavioral signs of autism. *J. Am. Acad. Child Adolesc. Psychiatry* **2010**, *49*, 256–266. [CrossRef] [PubMed]
7. Zwaigenbaum, L.; Bryson, S.; Rogers, T.; Roberts, W.; Brian, J.; Szatmari, P. Behavioral manifestations of autism in the first year of life. *Int. J. Dev. Neurosci.* **2005**, *23*, 143–152. [CrossRef] [PubMed]
8. Anagnostou, E.; Zwaigenbaum, L.; Szatmari, P.; Fombonne, E.; Fernandez, B.A.; Woodbury-Smith, M.; Brian, J.; Bryson, S.; Smith, I.M.; Drmic, I. Autism spectrum disorder: Advances in evidence-based practice. *Can. Med. Assoc. J.* **2014**, *186*, 509–519. [CrossRef] [PubMed]
9. Ali, D.H.; Effat, S.; Afifi, H. Prader-Willi syndrome psychobehavioral profile in a clinic based sample. *Eur. Psychiatry* **2013**, *28*, 1. [CrossRef]
10. Lo, S.T.; Siemensma, E.; Collin, P.; Hokken-Koelega, A. Impaired theory of mind and symptoms of autism spectrum disorder in children with Prader-Willi syndrome. *Res. Dev. Disabil.* **2013**, *34*, 2764–2773. [CrossRef] [PubMed]
11. Akefeldt, A.; Gillberg, C. Behavior and personality characteristics of children and young adults with Prader-Willi syndrome: A controlled study. *J. Am. Acad. Child Adolesc. Psychiatry* **1999**, *38*, 761–769. [CrossRef] [PubMed]
12. Ehlers, S.; Gillberg, C.; Wing, L. A screening questionnaire for asperger syndrome and other high-functioning autism spectrum disorders in school age children. *J. Autism Dev. Disord.* **1999**, *29*, 129–141. [CrossRef] [PubMed]
13. Dimitropoulos, A.; Ho, A.; Feldman, B. Social responsiveness and competence in Prader-Willi syndrome: Direct comparison to autism spectrum disorder. *J. Autism Dev. Disord.* **2013**, *43*, 103–113. [CrossRef] [PubMed]
14. Zyga, O.; Russ, S.; Ievers-Landis, C.E.; Dimitropoulos, A. Assessment of pretend play in Prader–Willi syndrome: A direct comparison to autism spectrum disorder. *J. Autism Dev. Disord.* **2014**, *45*, 975–987. [CrossRef] [PubMed]

15. Veltman, M.W.; Thompson, R.J.; Roberts, S.E.; Thomas, N.S.; Whittington, J.; Bolton, P.F. Prader-Willi syndrome—A study comparing deletion and uniparental disomy cases with reference to autism spectrum disorders. *Eur. Child Adolesc. Psychiatry* **2004**, *13*, 42–50. [CrossRef] [PubMed]
16. Moss, J.; Oliver, C.; Arron, K.; Burbidge, C.; Berg, K. The prevalence and phenomenology of repetitive behavior in genetic syndromes. *J. Autism Dev. Disord.* **2009**, *39*, 572–588. [CrossRef] [PubMed]
17. Milner, K.M.; Craig, E.E.; Thompson, R.J.; Veltman, M.W.; Thomas, N.S.; Roberts, S.; Bellamy, M.; Curran, S.R.; Sporikou, C.M.; Bolton, P.F. Prader-Willi syndrome: Intellectual abilities and behavioural features by genetic subtype. *J. Child Psychol. Psychiatry* **2005**, *46*, 1089–1096. [CrossRef] [PubMed]
18. Lord, C.; Rutter, M.; DiLavore, P.C.; Risi, S. *Autism Diagnostic Observation Schedule (ADOS) Manual*, 4th ed.; Western Psychological Services: Los Angeles, CA, USA, 2006.
19. Rutter, M.; le Couteur, A.; Lord, C. *Autism Diagnostic Interview-Revised (ADI-R)*; Western Psychological Services: Los Angeles, CA, USA, 2003.
20. Falkmer, T.; Anderson, K.; Falkmer, M.; Horlin, C. Diagnostic procedures in autism spectrum disorders: A systematic literature review. *Eur. Child Adolesc. Psychiatry* **2013**, *22*, 329–340. [CrossRef] [PubMed]
21. Lord, C.; Rutter, M.; DiLavore, P.C.; Risi, S.; Gotham, K.; Bishop, S. *Autism Diagnostic Observation Schedule, Second Edition (ADOS-2) Manual (Part 1): Modules 1–4*; Western Psychological Services: Torrence, CA, USA, 2012.
22. Risi, S.; Lord, C.; Gotham, K.; Corsello, C.; Chrysler, C.; Szatmari, P.; Cook, E.H., Jr.; Leventhal, B.L.; Pickles, A. Combining information from multiple sources in the diagnosis of autism spectrum disorders. *J. Am. Acad. Child Adolesc. Psychiatry* **2006**, *45*, 1094–1103. [CrossRef] [PubMed]
23. Hall, S.S.; Lightbody, A.A.; Hirt, M.; Rezvani, A.; Reiss, A.L. Autism in fragile X syndrome: A category mistake? *J. Am. Acad. Child Adolesc. Psychiatry* **2010**, *49*, 921–933. [CrossRef] [PubMed]
24. Harris, S.W.; Hessl, D.; Goodlin-Jones, B.; Ferranti, J.; Bacalman, S.; Barbato, I.; Tassone, F.; Hagerman, P.J.; Herman, H.; Hagerman, R.J. Autism profiles of males with fragile X syndrome. *Am. J. Ment. Retard* **2008**, *113*, 427–438. [CrossRef] [PubMed]
25. Cornish, K.; Turk, J.; Hagerman, R. The fragile X continuum: New advances and perspectives. *J. Intell. Disabil. Res.* **2008**, *52*, 469–482. [CrossRef] [PubMed]
26. Cornish, K.; Turk, J.; Levitas, A. Fragile X syndrome and autism: Common developmental pathways? *Curr. Pediatr. Rev.* **2007**, *3*, 61–68. [CrossRef]
27. Rutter, M.; Bailey, A.; Lord, C. *The Social Communication Questionnaire (SCQ)*; Western Psychological Services: Los Angeles, CA, USA, 2003.
28. Constantino, J.N.; Gruber, C.P. *Social Responsiveness Scale-2 (SRS-2) Manual*; Western Psychological Services: Los Angeles, CA, USA, 2012.
29. Dykens, E.M.; Lee, E.; Roof, E. Prader-Willi syndrome and autism spectrum disorders: An evolving story. *J. Neurodev. Disord.* **2011**, *3*, 225–237. [CrossRef] [PubMed]
30. Dimitropoulos, A.; Schultz, R.T. Autistic-like symptomatology in Prader-Willi syndrome: A review of recent findings. *Curr. Psychiatry Rep.* **2007**, *9*, 159–164. [CrossRef] [PubMed]
31. Dykens, E.M.; Roof, E. Behavior in Prader-Willi syndrome: Relationship to genetic subtypes and age. *J. Child Psychol. Psychiatry* **2008**, *49*, 1001–1008. [CrossRef] [PubMed]
32. Butler, M.G.; Bittel, D.C.; Kibiryeva, N.; Talebizadeh, Z.; Thompson, T. Behavioral differences among subjects with Prader-Willi syndrome and type I or type II deletion and maternal disomy. *Pediatrics* **2004**, *113*, 565–573. [CrossRef] [PubMed]
33. Bittel, D.C.; Kibiryeva, N.; Butler, M.G. Expression of 4 genes between chromosome 15 breakpoints 1 and 2 and behavioral outcomes in Prader-Willi syndrome. *Pediatrics* **2006**, *118*, 1276–1283. [CrossRef] [PubMed]
34. Zarcone, J.; Napolitano, D.; Peterson, C.; Breidbord, J.; Ferraioli, S.; Caruso-Anderson, M.; Holsen, L.; Butler, M.G.; Thompson, T. The relationship between compulsive behaviour and academic achievement across the three genetic subtypes of Prader-Willi syndrome. *J. Intellect. Disabil. Res.* **2007**, *51*, 478–487. [CrossRef] [PubMed]
35. Schaaf, C.P.; Gonzalez-Garay, M.L.; Xia, F.; Potocki, L.; Gripp, K.W.; Zhang, B.; Peters, B.A.; McElwain, M.A.; Drmanac, R.; Beaudet, A.L.; et al. Truncating mutations of Magel2 cause Prader-Willi phenotypes and autism. *Nat. Genet.* **2013**, *45*, 1405–1408. [CrossRef] [PubMed]

36. Corsello, C.; Hus, V.; Pickles, A.; Risi, S.; Cook, E.H.; Leventhal, B.L.; Lord, C. Between a roc and a hard place: Decision making and making decisions about using the SCQ. *J. Child Psychol. Psychiatry* **2007**, *48*, 932–940. [CrossRef] [PubMed]
37. Gresham, F.M.; Elliot, S.N. *Social Skills Improvement System: Rating scales manual*; NCS Pearson, Inc.: Minneapolis, MN, USA, 2008.
38. Anagnostou, E.; Jones, N.; Huerta, M.; Halladay, A.K.; Wang, P.; Scahill, L.; Horrigan, J.P.; Kasari, C.; Lord, C.; Choi, D.; et al. Measuring social communication behaviors as a treatment endpoint in individuals with autism spectrum disorder. *Autism* **2014**, *19*, 622–636. [CrossRef] [PubMed]
39. Sparrow, S.; Cicchetti, D.; Balla, D.A. *Vineland Adaptive Behavior Scales: Second Edition (Vineland II), Survey Interview Form*; Pearson Assessments: Livonia, MN, USA, 2005.
40. Carter, A.S.; Volkmar, F.R.; Sparrow, S.S.; Wang, J.-J.; Lord, C.; Dawson, G.; Fombonne, E.; Loveland, K.; Mesibov, G.; Schopler, E. The Vineland Adaptive Behavior Scales: Supplementary norms for individuals with autism. *J. Autism Dev. Disord.* **1998**, *28*, 287–302. [CrossRef] [PubMed]
41. Wechsler, D. *Wechsler Preschool and Primary Scale of Intelligence (WPPSI-III)*, 3rd ed.; Pearson Psychological Corporation: San Antonio, TX, USA, 2002.
42. Wechsler, D. *Wechsler Intelligence Scale for Children (WISC-IV)*, 4th ed.; Pearson Psychological Corporation: San Antonio, TX, USA, 2003.
43. Song, D.K.; Sawada, M.; Yokota, S.; Kuroda, K.; Uenishi, H.; Kanazawa, T.; Ogata, H.; Ihara, H.; Nagai, T.; Shimoda, K. Comparative analysis of autistic traits and behavioral disorders in Prader-Willi syndrome and Asperger disorder. *Am. J. Med. Genet. A* **2015**, *167*, 64–68. [CrossRef] [PubMed]

4

Alexithymia Profile in Relation to Negative Affect in Parents of Autistic and Typically Developing Young Children

Elisa Leonardi [1], Antonio Cerasa [1,2], Francesca Isabella Famà [1], Cristina Carrozza [1], Letteria Spadaro [1], Renato Scifo [3], Sabrina Baieli [3], Flavia Marino [1], Gennaro Tartarisco [1], David Vagni [1], Giovanni Pioggia [1,†] and Liliana Ruta [1,*,†]

1 Institute for Biomedical Research and Innovation (IRIB), National Research Council of Italy, 98164 Messina, Italy; elisa.leonardi@istitutomarino.it (E.L.); antonio.cerasa@irib.cnr.it (A.C.); francescaisabella.fama@istitutomarino.it (F.I.F.); cristina.carrozza@istitutomarino.it (C.C.); spadarolia@gmail.com (L.S.); flavia.marino@irib.cnr.it (F.M.); gennaro.tartarisco@irib.cnr.it) (G.T.); david.vagni@irib.cnr.it (D.V.); giovanni.pioggia@irib.cnr.it (G.P.)

2 S. Anna Institute and Research in Advanced Neurorehabilitation (RAN), 88900 Crotone, Italy

3 Centre for Autism Spectrum Disorders, Child Psychiatry Unit, Provincial Health Service of Catania (ASP CT), 95100 Catania, Italy; renato.scifo@aspct.it (R.S.); sabrina.baieli@aspct.it (S.B.)

* Correspondence: liliana.ruta@irib.cnr.it

† These Authors contributed equally to the study.

Abstract: In our study, we explored the construct of alexithymia in parents of children with and without ASD using a multi-method approach based on self-rated and external rater assessment. We also assessed the level of self-report measures of negative affect states such as trait anxiety and depression, and investigated the correlation between the alexithymia construct, trait anxiety, and depression within the broader autism phenotype (BAP). A total sample of 100 parents (25 mothers and 25 fathers in each group) were administered the TAS-20 and the TSIA to measure self-reported and observer-rated alexithymia traits, as well as self-report measures of anxiety and depression. Study results showed that the TSIA but not the TAS-20 was able to detect significant group differences in alexithymia traits among parents of children with and without ASD, with parents of ASD children displaying significantly higher levels of alexithymia. Furthermore, differently from the TAS-20, no significant correlations between the TSIA and measures of anxiety and depression were detected. Taken together, our results suggest the importance of using multi-method approaches to control for potential measurement bias and to detect psychological constructs such as alexithymia in subclinical samples such as parents of children with ASD.

Keywords: autism; alexithymia; anxiety; depression; TAS-20; TSIA; parents; broader autism phenotype

1. Introduction

Alexithymia literally means "absence of words for emotions". It is a personality construct, normally distributed in the general population [1,2], characterized by deficits identifying and describing one's own emotions and feelings, problems distinguishing between feelings and bodily sensations of emotional arousal, lack of fantasy, externally oriented cognitive style, and impairment in cognitively mapping their feeling states onto internal bodily responses [3–6]. Difficulties in emotional awareness may have a negative impact on subjective emotion regulation [7] and, in turn, may compromise the understanding of others' emotions, giving rise to problems in social interaction. It has been reported, indeed, that individuals with alexithymia show difficulties distinguishing and appreciating emotions expressed by others, and consequently, they are likely to show nonempathic and idiosyncratic socio-emotional responses [8]. Deficits in empathy, specifically in the cognitive component of recognizing and understanding others emotions, have also been reported as one of the distinctive features of autism spectrum disorders (ASD) [9–13], a neurodevelopmental condition characterized by socio-communicative impairments and restricted and repetitive patterns of behaviors and interests [14]. A significant association between ASD and alexithymia has been reported, with at least half of individuals with ASD experiencing co-occurring alexithymia [15–19]. The interrelationship between the two conditions is complex, and it is still debated whether alexithymia and ASD share common etiological roots or if, instead, alexithymia is a symptomatological manifestation within the ASD neuropsychological functioning [20]. Some broad genetic and neurobiological overlapping between the two conditions have been reported, including the involvement of the serotonin and oxytocin systems, and brain areas related to emotion processing, specifically the amygdala, cingulate, and prefrontal cortex [21]. It has been suggested that a common genetic vulnerability between autism and alexithymia could lead to atypical brain networks, associated in turn with different behavioral patterns that manifest themselves mainly with symptoms of alexithymia, autism, or both [22,23]. At the behavioral level, the intersection between alexithymia and ASD is equally controversial and questions the role of alexithymia in relation to emotion recognition and interoception (the ability to interpret the internal state of the body). Indeed, the abilities to perceive one's own emotions and bodily signals are closely interrelated in social-emotional development [24]. Some studies, comparing individuals with and without ASD on alexithymia, have found that alexithymia, rather than autism per se, predicts difficulties in facial emotion recognition [17], while other evidence in nonclinical samples reported that autism traits more than alexithymia were a stronger predictor of atypical empathy [25]. In relation to interoception, across clinical and nonclinical samples, alexithymia, but not autism, has been associated with impaired interoception [23,24]. Furthermore, alexithymia associated traits have also been reported in relatives of individuals with ASD [26] who show subclinical autism traits, reported as the broader autism phenotype (BAP) [27–31]. The BAP is characterized by below the diagnostic threshold social and cognitive deficits, restricted behavior patterns, ASD-like personality characteristics, and psychiatric difficulties in relatives of autistic individuals [28–37]. Furthermore, higher levels of alexithymia in fathers of children with ASD were related to higher severity on the repetitive behavior domain in their children [38]. The most widely used questionnaire to evaluate alexithymia is the Toronto Alexithymia Scale (TAS-20) [39]. The TAS-20 is a self-report measure consisting of 20 items rated on a five-point Likert scale. The higher the score on the TAS-20, the greater the alexithymia traits. Although consistent empirical evidence over the past 25 year period has confirmed the reliability and validity of the TAS-20 to tap into the alexithymia construct [40], some concerns about applying a self-report measure to individuals who have difficulties identifying their own emotional states and lack the appropriate insight on this impairment, have been raised. Self-assessment of the interoceptive deficit in alexithymia would, in fact, imply a self-reliance bias being that the main characteristic of alexithymia is exactly the absence of recognition of one's feelings and bodily sensations [19,41–43]. Another shortcoming of the TAS-20 is that the measure does not include the dimension of the imaginative processes, which represents one of the facets of the complex alexithymia construct. Furthermore, scores at the TAS-20 have been correlated with negative affect states, particularly depression and anxiety. This association may be partially explained by a neuropsychological overlap between these dimensions, being that impairment in interoception is frequently associated with negative affect [44], but might also be related to a negativity response bias due to the self- report nature of the TAS-20 [45–47]. To overcome this limitation, in 2006, Bagby, Taylor, and Parker developed the Toronto structured interview for Alexithymia (TSIA) [48], a structured interview consisting of 24 questions and carried out by an external examiner who scores the items based on the individual responses across four core domains such as difficulty identifying feelings (DIF), difficulty describing feelings (DDF), externally oriented thinking (EOT), and imaginal processes (IMP). Several studies have confirmed the internal and convergent validity as well as cultural stability of the TAS-20 and the TSIA in nonclinical populations, as well as clinical patients, and have suggested that the TSIA is able to more reliably assess the "fantasy" facet of the alexithymia construct and to better disentangle negative affect states such as depression and anxiety that may partially overlap with the alexithymia construct [48–53].

To the best of our knowledge, the only study assessing alexithymia in family members using the TSIA was conducted in parents of anorexic daughters [54], reported significantly higher levels of alexithymia using the observer-rated measure as compared to the self-report measure in parents of the clinical group. Also, as far as we are aware, no studies assessing the alexithymia profile through both self-report and interviewer-administered measures in relatives of ASD individuals have been conducted. Hence, in our study, we used both the TAS-20 and the TSIA to investigate alexithymia in parents of children with and without ASD. Furthermore, since it has been demonstrated an association between alexithymia as measured by the TAS-20 and negative affect states, a secondary goal of the study is to explore the association between both self-report and rater-assessed alexithymia scores and measures of depression and trait anxiety. Previous findings have reported, in fact, significantly higher self-reported levels of trait anxiety and depression symptoms in parents of children with ASD [55–60] and it may be relevant to investigate the overlapping alexithymia construct in relation to these dimensions within the BAP trying to disentangle potential biases related to the administration method.

We expect that parents of ASD children, compared to parents of typically developing children, present higher levels of alexithymia at both the TAS-20 and the TSIA, and that the TSIA, in particular, will be able to keep aside co-occurrent traits of depression and anxiety.

2. Methods

2.1. Participants

Parents were enrolled and tested in the context of an ongoing study on young children with and without ASD, aged between 3 and 6 years of age, both males and females (30% females in the ASD group and 48% females in the TD group). Parents of children with ASD were recruited and tested at the clinical facilities of the Institute for Research and Innovation in Biomedicine of the National Research Council of Italy (IRIB-CNR) in Messina and at the Centre for Autism Spectrum Disorders, Child Psychiatry Unit, Provincial Health Service (ASP-CT) in Catania, Italy. Parents of typically developing children (TD) were recruited and tested in three different mainstream nursery schools and primary schools in Messina. Inclusion criteria in both the ASD and TD parent groups were: (1) biological parents; (2) native Italian speakers; (3) between the age of 25 and 55 years. Specific inclusion criterion in the ASD parent group was having a child with a confirmed clinical diagnosis of ASD according to the Diagnostic and Statistical Manual of Mental Disorders, Fifth Edition [14], while exclusion criteria in the TD parents group were having a child with a clinical diagnosis of neurodevelopmental conditions (such as language and/or motor delay, ADHD, etc.) and a family history of intellectual disabilities, language delay and ASD. A total sample of 112 parents were recruited. According to the inclusion and exclusion criteria, 12 parents (8 parents in the TD group and 5 parents in the ASD group) were excluded for the following reasons: four couples of parents (2 couples in each group) were adoptive parents; two couples of parents of TD children had a first degree relative with ASD; one parent (mother) in the TD group presented a mild intellectual disability; one parent (mother) in the ASD group was a foreigner and had significant difficulties with understanding written and spoken Italian language and finally 4 couples of parents (3 couples in the TD group and 1 couple in the ASD group) who initially agreed to participate, subsequently refused to contribute to the study. A final sample of 50 parents (25 mothers and 25 fathers) of ASD children and 50 parents of TD children (25 mothers and 25 fathers) were fully tested and analyzed in the study.

The study received ethical clearance by the Ethics Committees of CNR (ethical clearance, 01.08.2018) and ASP-CT (Prot. N. 498), respectively, and all the caregivers signed an informed consent to participate in the study.

2.2. Measures and Procedures

All enrolled subjects completed the following neuropsychological assessment battery: (1) the State Trait Anxiety Inventory-Form Y (STAI-Y), a self-report questionnaire which consists of 20 questions scored on a 4-point Likert-type scale, ranging from 1 to 4 (from "almost never" to "almost always"). The total score at the STAI-Y ranges from 20 to 80, with scores >40 indicating above-average levels of anxiety. (2) The Beck Depression Inventory (BDI-II) is a self-report questionnaire with 21 items, rated on a 4-point scale from 0 to 3, based on the diagnostic criteria for depressive disorders. Inventory cutoffs are: 0–13: minimal depression, 14–19: mild depression, 20–28: moderate depression, and 29–63: severe depression [61,62]; (3) The Toronto Alexithymia Scale (TAS-20) [39] is a self-report scale comprised of 20 items. Each item is rated on a five-point Likert scale ranging from 1 ("strongly disagree") to 5 ("strongly agree"). The TAS-20 is a reliable and valid measure of emotion processing in adults and includes a total score and three subscales: Difficulty Identifying Feelings (DIF), Difficulty Describing Feelings (DDF), and Externally-Oriented Thinking (EOT). The empirically derived cutoff score of 61 is used for identifying individuals with "high" versus "low" alexithymia. (4) The Toronto Structured Interview for Alexithymia (TSIA) is a structured interview with prompts and probes which incorporates the same three subscales included in the TAS-20 (DIF, DDF, and EOT, respectively), and an extra subscale investigating Imaginal Processes (IMP). The TSIA consists of 24 items, six items for each of the four salient facets of the alexithymia construct; (5) the "Reading the Mind in the Eyes" Test Revised (Eyes Test) [63]. In the Eyes Test, the participant is presented with a series of 36 black and white photographs of the eye-region of different actors and actresses and is asked to choose which of four words best describes what the person in the photograph is thinking or feeling. We implemented the test on an iPad tablet 9.7 in and collected both accuracy (number of correct answers) and reaction time (RT = length of time taken to answer in seconds); (6) the Wechsler Abbreviated Scale of Intelligence Second Edition (WASI-II) [64] to assess the intelligent quotient (IQ) in all the participants. All questionnaires were administered in a standardized way and in the same sequence to all participants. Assessment administration took about 2 h and was split into two sessions over two consecutive days. In the first session, participants filled in the TAS-20, the STAI-Y and the BDI-II, while during the second visit, the TSIA and the WASI-II were administered by an experienced clinical neuropsychologist (E.L.), specially trained on the administration procedures and scoring of the measures.

2.3. Statistical Analysis

Statistical analyses were performed using SPSS Version 23.0. Kolmogorov–Smirnov test was carried out and confirmed the assumptions of normality for all variables. A chi-square test was used for categorical variables, while the Mann–Whitney U-test was run for ordinal variables. An independent two-sample t-test was used to analyze between-group differences for continuous, normally distributed variables. The t-test's effect size was calculated using Cohen d, where an effect size value of 0.2 is considered a small effect, of 0.5 is considered a medium effect, and values of 0.8 and above are considered large effects. Pearson's correlations between TAS-20 and TSIA total scores and their dimensions, correlations between TAS-20 and TSIA and correlations of TSIA and TAS-20 with BDI-II and STAI-Y2 respectively, were performed.

All statistical analyses were 2-tailed; α levels were corrected for multiple comparisons using hierarchical Sidak correction. We used two primary measures (TAS-20 and TSIA) for fathers' and mothers' questionnaires respectively, therefore, we had 4 primary variables, and we set $\alpha_c < 0.013$. Only if the total score is significant, we analyzed the sub-scales for each measure. TAS-20 has 3 sub-scales and TSIA has 6 sub-scales, therefore $\alpha_c < 0.017$ for the first sub-scales analysis and $\alpha_c < 0.009$

for the second one. The Eyes Test accuracy and reaction Time were added as secondary measures of the BAP and $\alpha_c < 0.01$ was set. In the ancillary correlation analyses, we used a similar procedure setting $\alpha_c < 0.003$ for the correlation among Eyes Test, STAI-Y and BDI-II with TAS-20 and TSIA total scores, $\alpha_c < 0.009$ and $\alpha_c < 0.004$ for the correlation among Eyes Test, STAI-Y and BDI-II with TAS-20 and TSIA sub-scales.

3. Results

Table 1 shows the demographic and clinical characteristics of the sample. Parents of children with and without ASD did not differ as regards to descriptive variables and IQ. Parents on the ASD group were characterized by significantly higher levels of trait anxiety (both for mothers and fathers) and depression (more evident in the mothers) with respect to TD parents. Furthermore, mothers of ASD children were significantly slower than mothers of TD children in recognizing emotions from the eyes. Inter-correlations among TAS-20 and TSIA with their respective subscales were all statistically significant (all p-values < 0.001) and correlations ranged from moderate to high (from $r = 0.59$ to $r = 0.80$ for the TAS-20 and from $r = 0.65$ to $r = 0.82$ for the TSIA in the ASD parent group and from $r = 0.66$ to $r = 0.77$ for the TAS-20 and from $r = 0.61$ to $r = 0.73$ for the TSIA in the TD parent group). The TAS-20 demonstrated also a modest association with the TSIA ($r = 0.40$; $p = 0.001$ and $r = 0.44$; $p = 0.001$ in the ASD and TD parent group respectively), confirming convergent validity of the two measures. On the TAS-20 total score and subscales, no significant between-group difference has been detected, neither in the mothers nor in the fathers (Table 2). Conversely, using the TSIA, we found a significant group difference on the total score, with parents in the ASD group scoring significantly higher (i.e., demonstrating more alexithymia traits) than parents in the TD group ($p = 0.003$ and $p = 0.0001$ for mothers and fathers respectively). Furthermore, investigating the TSIA subdomains, mothers on the ASD group scored significantly higher in the "operative thinking (OT)" subscale ($p = 0.004$), while fathers on the ASD group, showed significantly higher scores in all the subscales apart from the "difficulty identifying feelings (DIF)" subscale (all p's < 0.009). When we analyzed the correlations between the TAS-20 and the TSIA (and their subscales) with the negative effect self-report measures (STAI-Y and the BDI-II) separately in the ASD and TD parent samples, additional significant findings were detected. In the ASD parent group, measures of anxiety and depression were significantly associated to the TAS-20 total scores in both mothers ($r = 0.58$, $p < 0.0001$ and $r = 0.61$, $p < 0.0001$ respectively) and fathers ($r = 0.37$, $p = 0.02$ and $r = 0.36$, $p = 0.03$ respectively). However, in the ASD father group, statistical significance did not survive correction for multiple comparisons. Comparable results were obtained in the TD parent group, with a significant positive association between the TAS-20 total scores and the STAI-Y and BDI-II scores in both mothers ($r = 0.45$, $p = 0.002$ and $r = 0.36$, $p = 0.01$ respectively) and fathers ($r = 0.51$, $p < 0.0001$ and $r = 0.31$, $p = 0.03$ respectively). However, in both mothers and fathers, correlations between the TAS-20 and the BDI-II did not survive the threshold for multiple comparisons. Conversely, we did not observe any significant relationship between the TSIA total scores and measures of anxiety and depression in neither group. Correlations between the alexithymia scales (and subscales) and the anxiety and depression measures, corrected for multiple comparisons, are reported in Tables 3 and 4. As an ancillary analysis, to explore if the group difference on the Eyes Test RT in mothers was driving the group differences found on alexithymia, anxiety, and depression, we analyzed the relationship between these measures in the ASD group. We found no significant correlations between the Eyes Test RT and the other measures (Eyes Test RT vs. TAS-20 total score: $r = -0.13$, $p = 0.3$; vs. TSIA total score: $r = -0.12$, $p = 0.4$; vs. STAI-Y: $r = -0.06$, $p = 0.6$; vs. BDI-II: $r = -0.16$, $p = 0.2$).

Table 1. Descriptive and neuropsychological characteristics in parents of ASD and TD children.

	ASD (n = 50)	TD (n = 50)	p-Level	d's Cohen
Age Mother	38.3 ± 4.8	39.9 ± 5.3	0.31 *	-
Age Father	41.7 ± 8.4	43.2 ± 5.2	0.95 *	-
Education Mother	3 [2–5]	5 [2–6]	0.05 °	-
Education Father	3 [2–6]	3 [2–6]	0.66 °	-
Verbal IQ Mother	97.8 ± 8.9	98.8 ± 9.9	0.67 *	0.11
Performance IQ Mother	102.1 ± 12.5	101.7 ± 13.9	0.91 *	0.02
Total IQ Mother	100.1 ± 10.3	104.7 ± 22.7	0.3 *	0.26
Verbal IQ Father	97.9 ± 8.1	95.6 ± 8.3	0.31 *	0.28
Performance IQ Father	101.7 ± 12.2	105.7 ± 12.2	0.23 *	0.32
Total IQ Father	103.5 ± 23.8	104.4 ± 8.4	0.53 *	0.05
STAI-Y Mother	50.3 ± 10.9	43.9 ± 7.8	0.002 *	0.68
STAI-Y Father	49.5 ± 9.6	44.8 ± 7.9	0.01 *	0.54
BDI-II Mother	11.4 ± 8.8	7.2 ± 5.9	0.01 *	0.56
BDI-II Father	7.6 ± 6.3	4.8 ± 4.6	0.03	0.51
Eyes Test Accuracy Mother	22.6 ± 4.2	22.4 ± 4.4	0.93	0.02
Eyes Test RT Mother	328.3 ± 185.2	230.2 ± 82.7	0.005	0.68
Eyes Test Accuracy Father	20.8 ± 4.1	22.1 ± 3.5	0.23	0.31
Eyes Test RT Father	257.8 ± 88.6	247.3 ± 49.9	0.59	0.14

Data are given as mean values (SD), percentage or median [range] as appropriate. § chi-square test; ° = Mann–Whitney U-test; * = Two sample t-test. ASD, autism spectrum disorders; TD, typical development; education labels, 1 = primary school; 2 = secondary school; 3 = high school; 4 = bachelor degree; 5 = master degree; IQ, intelligent quotient; STAI-Y, State Trait Anxiety Inventory-Form Y; BDI-II, Beck depression inventory; eyes test accuracy, number of correct answers; eyes test RT, length of time taken to answer in seconds.

Table 2. Alexithymia profile in parents of ASD and TD children.

	ASD (Mean ± SD)	TD (Mean ± SD)	p-Level *	d's Cohen
	Toronto Alexithymia Scale (TAS-20)			
Total score Mother	39.6 ± 12.3	39.1 ± 9.5	0.79	0.05
DIF Mother	12.1 ± 5.5	11.4 ± 4.8	0.53	0.13
DDF Mother	10.3 ± 4.6	10.3 ± 4.5	0.97	0.01
EOT Mother	17.5 ± 4.2	17.1 ± 4.3	0.65	0.09
Total score Father	42.3 ± 10.8	40.9 ± 9.9	0.53	0.13
DIF Father	11.4 ± 5.2	11.4 ± 4.7	0.99	0.01
DDF Father	11.4 ± 4.4	10.6 ± 9.1	0.38	0.11
EOT Father	19.4 ± 4.7	19.1 ± 3.9	0.68	0.07
	Toronto Structured Interview for Alexithymia (TSIA)			
DIF Mother	1.6 ± 1.5	0.9 ± 0.7	0.02	0.6
DDF Mother	2.2 ± 2.3	1.6 ± 1.9	0.22	0.29
EOT Mother	2.9 ± 1.9	2.1 ± 1.7	0.04	0.44
IMP Mother	3.8 ± 1.9	2.7 ± 2.0	0.02	0.56
AA Mother	3.8 ± 3.0	2.5 ± 2.4	0.04	0.48
OT Mother	6.7 ± 2.9	4.8 ± 2.5	**0.004**	**0.71**
Total score Mother	10.5 ± 4.6	7.3 ± 4.4	**0.003**	**0.71**
DIF Father	2.3 ± 2.6	1.0 ± 1.6	0.04	0.6
DDF Father	3.8 ± 3.3	1.3 ± 1.5	**0.001**	**0.97**
EOT Father	4.2 ± 2.8	2.3 ± 1.5	**0.006**	**0.85**
IMP Father	4.2 ± 2.3	2.1 ± 1.2	**0.001**	**1.15**
AA Father	5.9 ± 5.3	2.3 ± 2.4	**0.004**	**0.87**
OT Father	8.5 ± 4.5	4.4 ± 2.1	**0.0001**	**1.16**
Total score Father	14.9 ± 9.1	6.7 ± 3.7	**0.0001**	**1.19**

DIF, difficulty identifying feelings; DDF, difficulty describing feelings (DDF); OT, externally-oriented thinking; IMP, imaginal processing; AA, affect awareness; OT, operative thinking. * α levels are corrected for multiple comparisons using hierarchical Sidak correction. An $\alpha_c < 0.01$ was set for the TAS-20 total score and subscales and for the TSIA total score and an $\alpha_c < 0.009$ was set for the TSIA subscales.

Table 3. Correlations between alexithymia scales, trait anxiety, and depression in parents of ASD children.

ASD Parent Group	STAI-Y Mother	STAI-Y Father	BDI-II Mother	BDI-II Father
Toronto Alexithymia Scale (TAS-20)				
Total score Mother	$r = 0.58$		$r = 0.61$	
	$p < 0.0001$		$p < 0.0001$	
DIF Mother	$r = 0.67$		$r = 0.73$	
	$p < 0.0001$		$p < 0.0001$	
DDF Mother	$r = 0.46$		$r = 0.54$	
	$p = 0.002$		$p < 0.0001$	
EOT Mother	$r = 0.09$		$r = 0.21$	
	$p = 0.54$		$p = 0.19$	
Total score Father		$r = 0.37$		$r = 0.36$
		$p = 0.02$		$p = 0.03$
DIF Father		$r = 0.32$		$r = 0.45$
		$p = 0.04$		$p = 0.005$
DDF Father		$r = 0.33$		$r = 0.21$
		$p = 0.04$		$p = 0.21$
EOT Father		$r = 0.18$		$r = 0.13$
		$p = 0.27$		$p = 0.43$
Toronto Structured Interview for Alexithymia (TSIA)				
Total score Mother	$r = 0.11$		$r = 0.15$	
	$p = 0.51$		$p = 0.35$	
DIF Mother	$r = 0.31$		$r = 0.25$	
	$p = 0.07$		$p = 0.13$	
DDF Mother	$r = 0.11$		$r = 0.11$	
	$p = 0.52$		$p = 0.49$	
EOT Mother	$r = 0.15$		$r = 0.21$	
	$p = 0.39$		$p = 0.22$	
IMP Mother	$r = 0.24$		$r = 0.17$	
	$p = 0.15$		$p = 0.32$	
AA Mother	$r = 0.23$		$r = 0.22$	
	$p = 0.16$		$p = 0.19$	
OT Mother	$r = 0.07$		$r = 0.35$	
	$p = 0.07$		$p = 0.04$	
Total score Father		$r = 0.13$		$r = 0.17$
		$p = 0.51$		$p = 0.36$
DIF Father		$r = 0.07$		$r = 0.25$
		$p = 0.7$		$p = 0.19$
DDF Father		$r = 0.38$		$r = 0.08$
		$p = 0.04$		$p = 0.68$
EOT Father		$r = 0.21$		$r = 0.03$
		$p = 0.28$		$p = 0.88$
IMP Father		$r = 0.05$		$R = -0.26$
		$p = 0.81$		$p = 0.18$
AA Father		$r = 0.28$		$r = 0.05$
		$p = 0.13$		$p = 0.81$
OT Father		$r = 0.11$		$R = -0.17$
		$p = 0.59$		$p = 0.41$

DIF, difficulty identifying feelings; DDF, difficulty describing feelings (DDF); OT, externally-oriented thinking; IMP, imaginal processing; AA, affect awareness; OT: operative thinking. * α levels were corrected for multiple comparisons using hierarchical Sidak correction. We set an $\alpha_c < 0.006$ for the correlation among STAI-Y and BDI-II with TAS-20 and TSIA total scores and an $\alpha_c < 0.009$ for the correlation among STAI-Y and BDI-II with TAS-20 and TSIA subscales.

Table 4. Correlations between alexithymia scales, trait anxiety, and depression in parents of TD children.

TD Parent Group	STAI-Y Mother	STAI-Y Father	BDI-II Mother	BDI-II Father
		Toronto Alexithymia Scale (TAS-20)		
Total score Mother	**$r = 0.45$** **$p = 0.002$**		$r = 0.36$ $p = 0.01$	
DIF Mother	**$r = 0.37$** **$p = 0.008$**		$r = 0.28$ $p = 0.06$	
DDF Mother	$r = 0.35$ $p = 0.01$		$r = 0.26$ $p = 0.07$	
EOT Mother	$r = 0.11$ $p = 0.43$		$r = 0.21$ $p = 0.15$	
Total score Father		$r = 0.51$ $p < 0.0001$		$r = 0.31$ $p = 0.03$
DIF Father		$r = 0.42$ $p = 0.003$		$r = 0.4$ $p = 0.007$
DDF Father		$r = 0.45$ $p = 0.002$		$r = 0.39$ $p = 0.007$
EOT Father		$r = 0.41$ $p = 0.004$		$r = 0.11$ $p = 0.47$
		Toronto Structured Interview for Alexithymia (TSIA)		
Total score Mother	$r = 0.43$ $p = 0.01$		$r = 0.45$ $p = 0.007$	
DIF Mother	$r = 0.29$ $p = 0.1$		$r = 0.43$ $p = 0.01$	
DDF Mother	$r = 0.28$ $p = 0.11$		$r = 0.39$ $p = 0.02$	
EOT Mother	$r = 0.42$ $p = 0.01$		$r = 0.41$ $p = 0.02$	
IMP Mother	$r = 0.19$ $p = 0.28$		$r = 0.005$ $p = 0.98$	
AA Mother	$r = 0.32$ $p = 0.06$		$r = 0.45$ **$p = 0.008$**	
OT Mother	$r = 0.43$ $p = 0.01$		$r = 0.35$ $p = 0.04$	
Total score Father		$r = 0.42$ $p = 0.04$		$r = 0.36$ $p = 0.09$
DIF Father		$r = 0.39$ $p = 0.06$		$r = 0.43$ $p = 0.04$
DDF Father		$r = 0.4$ $p = 0.05$		$r = 0.25$ $p = 0.25$
EOT Father		$r = 0.03$ $p = 0.87$		$r = 0.02$ $p = 0.92$
IMP Father		$r = 0.21$ $p = 0.34$		$r = 0.19$ $p = 0.37$
AA Father		$r = 0.51$ $p = 0.01$		$r = 0.44$ $p = 0.03$
OT Father		$r = 0.15$ $p = 0.49$		$r = 0.13$ $p = 0.54$

DIF, difficulty identifying feelings; DDF, difficulty describing feelings (DDF); OT, externally-oriented thinking; IMP, imaginal processing; AA, affect awareness; OT, operative thinking. * α levels were corrected for multiple comparisons using hierarchical Sidak correction. We set an α_c <0.006 for the correlation among STAI-Y and BDI-II with TAS-20 and TSIA total scores and an α_c <0.009 for the correlation among STAI-Y and BDI-II with TAS-20 and TSIA subscales.

4. Discussion

In our study, we explored the construct of alexithymia in parents of children with and without ASD using a multi-method approach based on self-rated and external rater assessment. Both the TAS-20 and the TSIA were administered to all the participants showing that the TSIA but not the TAS-20 was able to detect significant group differences in alexithymia traits among parents of children with and without ASD, with parents of ASD children displaying significantly higher levels of alexithymia as reflected by the total score and the subscale scores, especially for fathers. This result suggests that the assessment method has an impact on the capacity to detect alexithymic traits in subclinical populations such as parents of ASD children. The TAS-20, in fact, implies that people are aware and able to identify and describe their own feelings and strongly relies on the self-perception of the subject. Individuals with higher alexithymia traits may lack awareness of their own difficulties because of their meta-emotional impairment [65], and a structured interview such as the TSIA may possibly avoid this bias, as the examiner can use probes and examples to more in-depth assess the presence and degree of alexithymia. This result is in line with previous evidence, in a different clinical sample, reporting that parents of anorexic daughters display significantly higher alexithymia traits at the TSIA as compared to the TAS-20 [54]. Furthermore, we explored the dimensions of negative affect and trait anxiety in our sample of parents, and in agreement with previous studies, we found significantly higher levels of self-reported trait anxiety and depression in parents of children with ASD (both in mothers and fathers), compared with parents of TD children. Last but not least, we analyzed the correlation between measures of alexithymia and self-report measures of depression and trait anxiety to investigate if negative affect may influence rater's answers to the TAS-20. We found that the TAS-20 total score and the subscales "difficulty identifying feelings (DIF)" and "difficulty describing feelings (DDF)", but not the TSIA total and subscale scores, were strongly associated with measures of both anxiety and depression in mothers of ASD children. Similar results were observed in the TD parent group, with the TAS-20 being strongly associated with anxiety traits and depression, especially in fathers, and the TSIA showing no significant correlations (apart from the subscale "affect awareness" which was associated with depression in mothers). These findings may suggest that symptoms related to negative emotional states such as reduced cognitive flexibility, emotional awareness, and affective range may influence self-rated responses on the TAS-20. Co-occurring anxiety and depression, in fact, may affect the way one's emotions are self-judged and instead, having a structured interview such as the TSIA, may ensure a more objective and reliable assessment of the facets related to alexithymia reducing the potential misinterpretation of one's emotional state due to self-judgment in relation to negative affect. In line with our results, previous evidence reported that negative affectivity influences the rater's self-report on the TAS-20 items, especially on the DIF and DDF factor subscales, while no association between the TSIA scores and scores at the STAI-Y and the DBI-II was found [46,49,53].

Finally, to explore if aspects of the broader autism phenotype (BAP) in the ASD parent group would account for the results obtained on the alexithymia and negative affect dimensions, we used the Eyes Test to measure emotion recognition and Theory of Mind (ToM) abilities in both groups. Previous evidence, reported impairment in emotion recognition at the Eyes Test in parents of ASD children [66]. We found that mothers of ASD children were significantly slower than mothers of TD children in detecting emotional, mental states from eyes, but no relationship between this measure and measures of alexithymia, anxiety, and depression was found, suggesting that in our ASD parent sample, atypical empathy is not associated to alexithymia traits nor to negative affectivity. Our results, in the light of the mixed findings reported in the literature about the influence of alexithymia on atypical empathy [17,25,67], clearly indicate that measuring these two constructs in relation to autism traits is not simple and generalization from clinical samples to sub-clinical samples such as parents of ASD children to the general population poses complex conceptual and methodological issues that should be taken into account.

Some limitations should be considered with regard to the study and the use of the TSIA. Firstly, the study sample size was relatively small, although rigorously selected according to precise inclusion and exclusion criteria to avoid sampling bias; furthermore, there was no opportunity to conduct a specific psychometric and clinical evaluation on the TD children, to exclude not diagnosed neuropsychiatric conditions, which may have influenced the responses in the TD parent group. Finally, in relation to the use of the TSIA, it should be considered that the time needed to complete the interview, as well as the need for appropriate training in administration procedures and scoring, make the use of the TSIA still limited and more difficult in clinical practice. Further studies are warranted to replicate these results and to generalize these findings from clinical samples to the general population.

5. Conclusions

Our study explored the construct of alexithymia in parents of children with and without ASD using a multi-method approach, and also investigated the correlation between the alexithymia construct, trait anxiety, and depression within the broader autism phenotype (BAP). Based on our findings, in subclinical populations such as parents of children with ASD, the use of an external-rater assessment should be considered to allow a more accurate detection of the presence and degree of alexithymia and to disentangle potential influences of negative affect states and trait anxiety on the alexithymia dimension.

Author Contributions: E.L. participated in the study design, enrolled and tested the participants and contributed to the manuscript draft. L.R. designed and supervised the study and drafted the manuscript. A.C. conducted the statistical analysis and participated in the manuscript draft. F.M., F.I.F., C.C., L.S., S.B., and R.S. helped with participants' enrollment and contributed with data interpretation. D.V. and G.T. contributed with statistical analysis and statistical data interpretations. G.P. contributed in the coordination of the study. All authors read and approved the final manuscript.

Acknowledgments: We acknowledge all the parents who volunteered to participate in the study.

References

1. Eccleston, D. *Disorders of Affect Regulation: Alexithymia in Medical and Psychiatric Illness*; Taylor, G.J., Bagby, R.M., Parker, J.D.A., Eds.; Cambridge University Press: Cambridge, UK, 1998; ISBN 0-521-45610-X.
2. Franz, M.; Popp, K.; Schaefer, R.; Sitte, W.; Schneider, C.; Hardt, J.; Decker, O.; Braehler, E. Alexithymia in the German general population. *Soc. Psychiatry Psychiatr. Epidemiol.* **2008**, *43*, 54–62. [CrossRef] [PubMed]
3. Taylor, G.J.; Michael Bagby, R.; Parker, J.D.A. The Alexithymia Construct: A Potential Paradigm for Psychosomatic Medicine. *Psychosomatics* **1991**, *32*, 153–164. [CrossRef]
4. Parker, J.D.A.; Taylor, G.J.; Bagby, R.M. The 20-Item Toronto Alexithymia Scale. *J. Psychosom. Res.* **2003**, *55*, 269–275. [CrossRef]
5. Picardi, A.; Toni, A.; Caroppo, E. Stability of Alexithymia and Its Relationships with the 'Big Five' Factors, Temperament, Character, and Attachment Style. *Psychother. Psychosom.* **2005**, *74*, 371–378. [CrossRef] [PubMed]
6. Vermeulen, N.; Luminet, O.; Corneille, O. Alexithymia and the automatic processing of affective information: Evidence from the affective priming paradigm. *Cogn. Emot.* **2006**, *20*, 64–91. [CrossRef]
7. Connelly, M.; Denney, D.R. Regulation of emotions during experimental stress in alexithymia. *J. Psychosom. Res.* **2007**, *62*, 649–656. [CrossRef] [PubMed]
8. FeldmanHall, O.; Dalgleish, T.; Mobbs, D. Alexithymia decreases altruism in real social decisions. *Cortex* **2013**, *49*, 899–904. [CrossRef] [PubMed]
9. Baron-Cohen, S.; Wheelwright, S. The Empathy Quotient: An Investigation of Adults with Asperger Syndrome or High Functioning Autism, and Normal Sex Differences. *J. Autism Dev. Disord.* **2004**, *34*, 163–175. [CrossRef]
10. Auyeung, B.; Baron-Cohen, S.; Ashwin, E.; Knickmeyer, R.; Taylor, K.; Hackett, G. Fetal testosterone and autistic traits. *Br. J. Psychol.* **2009**, *100*, 1–22. [CrossRef]
11. Lombardo, M.V.; Barnes, J.L.; Wheelwright, S.J.; Baron-Cohen, S. Self-Referential Cognition and Empathy in Autism. *PLoS ONE* **2007**, *2*, e883. [CrossRef] [PubMed]
12. Sucksmith, E.; Allison, C.; Baron-Cohen, S.; Chakrabarti, B.; Hoekstra, R.A. Empathy and emotion recognition in people with autism, first-degree relatives, and controls. *Neuropsychologia* **2013**, *51*, 98–105. [CrossRef] [PubMed]

13. Aaron, R.V.; Benson, T.L.; Park, S. Investigating the role of alexithymia on the empathic deficits found in schizotypy and autism spectrum traits. *Pers. Individ. Dif.* **2015**, *77*, 215–220. [CrossRef]
14. American Psychiatric Association. DSM-5 Diagnostic Classification. In *Diagnostic and Statistical Manual of Mental Disorders*; American Psychiatric Association: Washington, DC, USA, 2013.
15. Hill, E.; Berthoz, S.; Frith, U. Brief Report: Cognitive Processing of Own Emotions in Individuals with Autistic Spectrum Disorder and in Their Relatives. *J. Autism Dev. Disord.* **2004**, *34*, 229–235. [CrossRef] [PubMed]
16. Berthoz, S.; Hill, E.L. The validity of using self-reports to assess emotion regulation abilities in adults with autism spectrum disorder. *Eur. Psychiatry* **2005**, *20*, 291–298. [CrossRef] [PubMed]
17. Cook, R.; Brewer, R.; Shah, P.; Bird, G. Alexithymia, Not Autism, Predicts Poor Recognition of Emotional Facial Expressions. *Psychol. Sci.* **2013**, *24*, 723–732. [CrossRef]
18. Griffin, C.; Lombardo, M.V.; Auyeung, B. Alexithymia in children with and without autism spectrum disorders. *Autism Res.* **2016**, *9*, 773–780. [CrossRef]
19. Gaigg, S.B.; Cornell, A.S.F.; Bird, G. The psychophysiological mechanisms of alexithymia in autism spectrum disorder. *Autism* **2018**, *22*, 227–231. [CrossRef]
20. Kinnaird, E.; Stewart, C.; Tchanturia, K. Investigating alexithymia in autism: A systematic review and meta-analysis. *Eur. Psychiatry* **2019**, *55*, 80–89. [CrossRef]
21. Poquérusse, J.; Pastore, L.; Dellantonio, S.; Esposito, G. Alexithymia and Autism Spectrum Disorder: A Complex Relationship. *Front. Psychol.* **2018**, *9*, 1–10. [CrossRef]
22. Bird, G.; Cook, R. Mixed emotions: The contribution of alexithymia to the emotional symptoms of autism. *Transl. Psychiatry* **2013**, *3*, e285. [CrossRef]
23. Shah, P.; Hall, R.; Catmur, C.; Bird, G. Alexithymia, not autism, is associated with impaired interoception. *Cortex* **2016**, *81*, 215–220. [CrossRef] [PubMed]
24. Livingston, L.A.; Livingston, L.M. Commentary: Alexithymia, not autism, is associated with impaired interoception. *Front. Psychol.* **2016**, *7*, 7–9. [CrossRef] [PubMed]
25. Shah, P.; Livingston, L.A.; Callan, M.J.; Player, L. Trait Autism is a Better Predictor of Empathy than Alexithymia. *J. Autism Dev. Disord.* **2019**, *49*, 3956–3964. [CrossRef] [PubMed]
26. Berthoz, S.; Lalanne, C.; Crane, L.; Hill, E.L. Investigating emotional impairments in adults with autism spectrum disorders and the broader autism phenotype. *Psychiatry Res.* **2013**, *208*, 257–264. [CrossRef]
27. Bailey, A.; Le Couteur, A.; Gottesman, I.; Bolton, P.; Simonoff, E.; Yuzda, E.; Rutter, M. Autism as a strongly genetic disorder: Evidence from a British twin study. *Psychol. Med.* **1995**, *25*, 63–77. [CrossRef]
28. Bolton, P.; Macdonald, H.; Pickles, A.; Rios, P.; Goode, S.; Crowson, M.; Bailey, A.; Rutter, M. A Case-Control Family History Study of Autism. *J. Child Psychol. Psychiatry* **1994**, *35*, 877–900. [CrossRef]
29. Piven, J.; Palmer, P.; Jacobi, D.; Childress, D.; Arndt, S. Broader autism phenotype: Evidence from a family history study of multiple-incidence autism families. *Am. J. Psychiatry* **1997**, *154*, 185–190. [CrossRef] [PubMed]
30. Piven, J. The broad autism phenotype: A complementary strategy for molecular genetic studies of autism. *Am. J. Med. Genet.* **2001**, *105*, 34–35. [CrossRef]
31. Szatmari, P.; MacLean, J.E.; Jones, M.B.; Bryson, S.E.; Zwaigenbaum, L.; Bartolucci, G.; Mahoney, W.J.; Tuff, L. The Familial Aggregation of the Lesser Variant in Biological and Nonbiological Relatives of PDD Probands: A Family History Study. *J. Child Psychol. Psychiatry* **2000**, *41*, 579–586. [CrossRef]
32. Landa, R.; Piven, J.; Wzorek, M.M.; Gayle, J.O.; Chase, G.A.; Folstein, S.E. Social language use in parents of autistic individuals. *Psychol. Med.* **1992**, *22*, 245–254. [CrossRef]
33. Piven, J.; Wzorek, M.; Landa, R.; Lainhart, J.; Bolton, P.; Chase, G.A.; Folstein, S. Personality characteristics of the parents of autistic individuals. *Psychol. Med.* **1994**, *24*, 783–795. [CrossRef] [PubMed]
34. Hurley, R.S.E.; Losh, M.; Parlier, M.; Reznick, J.S.; Piven, J. The Broad Autism Phenotype Questionnaire. *J. Autism Dev. Disord.* **2007**, *37*, 1679–1690. [CrossRef] [PubMed]
35. Wolff, S.; Narayan, S.; Moyes, B. Personality Characteristics of Parents of Autistic Children: A Controlled Study. *J. Child Psychol. Psychiatry* **1988**, *29*, 143–153. [CrossRef]
36. Murphy, M.; Bolton, P.F.; Pickles, A.; Fombonne, E.; Piven, J.; Rutter, M. Personality traits of the relatives of autistic probands. *Psychol. Med.* **2000**, *30*, 1411–1424. [CrossRef]

37. Yirmiya, N.; Shaked, M. Psychiatric disorders in parents of children with autism: A meta-analysis. *J. Child Psychol. Psychiatry* **2005**, *46*, 69–83. [CrossRef]
38. Papageorgiou, V.; Georgiades, S.; Mavreas, V. Brief report: Cross-cultural evidence for the heterogeneity of the restricted, repetitive behaviours and interests domain of autism: A Greek study. *J. Autism Dev. Disord.* **2008**, *38*, 558–561. [CrossRef]
39. Bagby, R.M.; Parker, J.D.A.; Taylor, G.J. The twenty-item Toronto Alexithymia scale—I. Item selection and cross-validation of the factor structure. *J. Psychosom. Res.* **1994**, *38*, 23–32. [CrossRef]
40. Bagby, R.M.; Parker, J.D.A.; Taylor, G.J. Twenty-five years with the 20-item Toronto Alexithymia Scale. *J. Psychosom. Res.* **2020**, *131*, 109940. [CrossRef] [PubMed]
41. Lane, R.D.; Weihs, K.L.; Herring, A.; Hishaw, A.; Smith, R. Affective agnosia: Expansion of the alexithymia construct and a new opportunity to integrate and extend Freud's legacy. *Neurosci. Biobehav. Rev.* **2015**, *55*, 594–611. [CrossRef]
42. Luminet, O.; Taylor, G.; Bagby, R. Assessment of alexithymia: Self-report and observer-rated measures. In *The Handbook of Emotional Intelligence: Theory, Development, Assessment, and Application at Home, School, and in the Workplace*; Bar-On, R., Parker, J.D.A., Eds.; Jossey-Bass: San Francisco, CA, USA, 2000; pp. 301–319.
43. Meganck, R.; Vanheule, S.; Desmet, M. Factorial Validity and Measurement Invariance of the 20-Item Toronto Alexithymia Scale in Clinical and Nonclinical Samples. *Assessment* **2008**, *15*, 36–47. [CrossRef]
44. Mikhailova, E.S.; Vladimirova, T.V.; Iznak, A.F.; Tsusulkovskaya, E.J.; Sushko, N.V. Abnormal recognition of facial expression of emotions in depressed patients with major depression disorder and schizotypal personality disorder. *Biol. Psychiatry* **1996**, *40*, 697–705. [CrossRef]
45. Leising, D.; Grande, T.; Faber, R. The Toronto Alexithymia Scale (TAS-20): A measure of general psychological distress. *J. Res. Pers.* **2009**, *43*, 707–710. [CrossRef]
46. Lumley, M.A. Alexithymia and negative emotional conditions. *J. Psychosom. Res.* **2000**, *49*, 51–54. [CrossRef]
47. Marchesi, C.; Giaracuni, G.; Paraggio, C.; Ossola, P.; Tonna, M.; De Panfilis, C. Pre-morbid alexithymia in panic disorder: A cohort study. *Psychiatry Res.* **2014**, *215*, 141–145. [CrossRef] [PubMed]
48. Bagby, R.M.; Taylor, G.J.; Parker, J.D.A.; Dickens, S.E. The development of the Toronto structured interview for Alexithymia: Item selection, factor structure, reliability and concurrent validity. *Psychother. Psychosom.* **2006**. [CrossRef]
49. Caretti, V.; Porcelli, P.; Solano, L.; Schimmenti, A.; Bagby, R.M.; Taylor, G.J. Reliability and validity of the Toronto Structured Interview for Alexithymia in a mixed clinical and nonclinical sample from Italy. *Psychiatry Res.* **2011**, *187*, 432–436. [CrossRef]
50. Grabe, H.J.; Löbel, S.; Dittrich, D.; Bagby, R.M.; Taylor, G.J.; Quilty, L.C.; Spitzer, C.; Barnow, S.; Mathier, F.; Jenewein, J.; et al. The German version of the Toronto Structured Interview for Alexithymia: Factor structure, reliability, and concurrent validity in a psychiatric patient sample. *Compr. Psychiatry* **2009**, *50*, 424–430. [CrossRef] [PubMed]
51. Inslegers, R.; Meganck, R.; Ooms, E.; Vanheule, S.; Taylor, G.J.; Bagby, R.M.; De Fruyt, F.; Desmet, M. The Dutch Language Version of the Toronto Structured Interview for Alexithymia: Reliability, Factor Structure and Concurrent Validity. *Psychol. Belg.* **2013**, *53*, 93. [CrossRef]
52. Rosenberg, N.; Rufer, M.; Lichev, V.; Ihme, K.; Grabe, H.J.; Kugel, H.; Kersting, A.; Suslow, T. Observer-Rated Alexithymia and its Relationship with the Five-Factor-Model of Personality. *Psychol. Belg.* **2016**, *56*, 118–134. [CrossRef] [PubMed]
53. Montebarocci, O.; Surcinelli, P. Correlations between TSIA and TAS-20 and their relation to self-reported negative affect: A study using a multi-method approach in the assessment of alexithymia in a nonclinical sample from Italy. *Psychiatry Res.* **2018**, *270*, 187–193. [CrossRef]
54. Mannarini, S.; Nacinovich, R.; Bomba, M.; Balottin, L. Alexithymia in parents and adolescent anorexic daughters: Comparing the responses to TSIA and TAS-20 scales. *Neuropsychiatr. Dis. Treat.* **2014**, *10*, 1941–1951. [CrossRef] [PubMed]
55. Piven, J.; Chase, G.A.; Landa, R.; Wzorek, M.; Gayle, J.; Cloud, D.; Folstein, S. Psychiatric Disorders in the Parents of Autistic Individuals. *J. Am. Acad. Child Adolesc. Psychiatry* **1991**, *30*, 471–478. [CrossRef] [PubMed]
56. Bitsika, V.; Sharpley, C.F. Stress, Anxiety and Depression Among Parents of Children With Autism Spectrum Disorder. *Aust. J. Guid. Couns.* **2004**, *14*, 151–161. [CrossRef]

57. Hamlyn-Wright, S.; Draghi-Lorenz, R.; Ellis, J. Locus of control fails to mediate between stress and anxiety and depression in parents of children with a developmental disorder. *Autism* **2007**, *11*, 489–501. [CrossRef] [PubMed]
58. Kuusikko-Gauffin, S.; Pollock-Wurman, R.; Mattila, M.-L.; Jussila, K.; Ebeling, H.; Pauls, D.; Moilanen, I. Social Anxiety in Parents of High-Functioning Children with Autism and Asperger Syndrome. *J. Autism Dev. Disord.* **2013**, *43*, 521–529. [CrossRef]
59. Al-Farsi, O.; Al-Farsi, Y.; Al-Sharbati, M.; Al-Adawi, S. Stress, anxiety, and depression among parents of children with autism spectrum disorder in Oman: A case-control study. *Neuropsychiatr. Dis. Treat.* **2016**, *12*, 1943–1951. [CrossRef]
60. Schnabel, A.; Youssef, G.J.; Hallford, D.J.; Hartley, E.J.; McGillivray, J.A.; Stewart, M.; Forbes, D.; Austin, D.W. Psychopathology in parents of children with autism spectrum disorder: A systematic review and meta-analysis of prevalence. *Autism* **2020**, *24*, 26–40. [CrossRef]
61. Beck, A.T.; Steer, R.A.; Brown, G.K. *Manual for the Beck Depression Inventory-II*; Psychological Corporation: San Antonio, TX, USA, 1996; ISBN 0158018389.
62. Sica, C.; Ghisi, M. *The Italian versions of the Beck Anxiety Inventory and the Beck Depression Inventory-II: Psychometric Properties and Discriminant Power*; Lange, M.A., Ed.; Nova Science: Hauppauge, NY, USA, 2007; ISBN 1-60021-571-8 (Hardcover), 978-1-60021-571-1 (Hardcover).
63. Baron-Cohen, S.; Wheelwright, S.; Hill, J.; Raste, Y.; Plumb, I. The "Reading the Mind in the Eyes" Test revised version: A study with normal adults, and adults with Asperger syndrome or high-functioning autism. *J. Child Psychol. Psychiatry.* **2001**, *42*, 241–251. [CrossRef]
64. Wechsler, D. *Wechsler Abbreviated Scale of Intelligence–Second Edition (WASI-II)*; NCS Pearson: San Antonio, TX, USA, 2011.
65. Lundh, L.-G.; Johnsson, A.; Sundqvist, K.; Olsson, H. Alexithymia, memory of emotion, emotional awareness, and perfectionism. *Emotion* **2002**, *2*, 361–379. [CrossRef]
66. Baron-Cohen, S.; Hammer, J. Parents of Children with Asperger Syndrome: What is the Cognitive Phenotype? *J. Cogn. Neurosci.* **1997**, *9*, 548–554. [CrossRef]
67. Oakley, B.F.M.; Brewer, R.; Bird, G.; Catmur, C. Theory of mind is not theory of emotion: A cautionary note on the reading the mind in the eyes test. *J. Abnorm. Psychol.* **2016**, *125*, 818–823. [CrossRef] [PubMed]

5

Developing Employment Environments where Individuals with ASD Thrive: Using Machine Learning to Explore Employer Policies and Practices

Amy Jane Griffiths [1,*], Amy Hurley Hanson [2], Cristina M. Giannantonio [2], Sneha Kohli Mathur [1], Kayleigh Hyde [3] and Erik Linstead [4]

1 Attallah College of Educational Studies, Chapman University, One University Drive, Orange, CA 92866, USA; mathu109@mail.chapman.edu
2 Argyros School of Business and Economics, Chapman University, One University Drive, Orange, CA 92866, USA; ahurley@chapman.edu (A.H.H.); giannant@chapman.edu (C.M.G.)
3 Schmid College of Science and Technology, Chapman University, One University Drive, Orange, CA 92866, USA; khyde@chapman.edu
4 Fowler School of Engineering, Chapman University, One University Drive, Orange, CA 92866, USA; linstead@chapman.edu
* Correspondence: agriffit@chapman.edu

Abstract: An online survey instrument was developed to assess employers' perspectives on hiring job candidates with Autism Spectrum Disorder (ASD). The investigators used K-means clustering to categorize companies in clusters based on their hiring practices related to individuals with ASD. This methodology allowed the investigators to assess and compare the various factors of businesses that successfully hire employees with ASD versus those that do not. The cluster analysis indicated that company structures, policies and practices, and perceptions, as well as the needs of employers and employees, were important in determining who would successfully hire individuals with ASD. Key areas that require focused policies and practices include recruitment and hiring, training, accessibility and accommodations, and retention and advancement.

Keywords: autism spectrum disorder; machine learning; employment

1. Introduction

Research suggests that competitive employment may be difficult to attain for individuals with Autism Spectrum Disorder (ASD). Although companies are beginning to recognize the value of hiring employees with ASD, the academic literature on the benefits and current practices of recruiting people with ASD is limited [1,2]. Providing supportive employment services for adults with ASD is seen as a positive investment. Individuals with ASD can typically gain employment with the right support [3]. Research indicates that employees with ASD have many skills that can contribute a great deal to the workforce. Despite the skill sets of individuals with ASD, the unemployment and underemployment rates for these individuals, as compared to the general population, remains staggeringly low [4–10]. This discrepancy suggests that it is critical to understand employers' perspectives and experiences, so that hiring practices and outcomes may be improved for both organizations and employees with ASD.

2. Background

Organizations' interest in hiring neurodiverse individuals, including those with ASD, has increased [2]. This interest is due in part to companies recognizing the value of hiring employees with ASD. Research indicates that employees with ASD typically pay close attention to detail, enjoy certain job tasks that other employees may find repetitive or socially isolating, and bring a different perspective to issues, allowing for innovative solutions to common problems [3,11]. Research also suggests that employees with ASD have high levels of trustworthiness, integrity, and honesty. They are reliable, precise, efficient, and consistent [4,7,12,13].

Additionally, employees with ASD may demonstrate "above standard" workplace performance compared to their counterparts related to increased attention to detail, work ethic, and quality of work [9]. Employees with ASD have been found to have fewer absences and are more likely to arrive at work on time than other employees [12,14,15]). Research has also found that employees with autism have dramatically lower turnover rates than neurotypical employees. Turnover is a large expense for organizations. In some industries, such as software, the turnover rate is close to fifteen percent nationally. Employees with autism have a seven percent turnover rate. The costs of replacing a worker earning less than $50,000 are estimated to be twenty percent of their annual salary [16]. As salaries rise, so do the costs of replacing those employees.

Moreover, an increase in the employment of people with ASD can lead to significant economic benefits to society [3,17–19]. A study in Australia found that reducing the unemployment of people with ASD by one-third would lead to a $43 billion increase in the Australian Gross Domestic Product [20]. The Dandelion Employment Program in Australia calculates that every 100 individuals with ASD who were previously unemployed, and who participate in the program for three years, save the Australian government over six million dollars in the form of tax gains, savings in welfare benefits, and savings in unemployment services costs.

Despite these individual positive qualities, and benefits to organizations and society, many individuals with ASD remain unemployed, underemployed, and underpaid. Recent unemployment statistics for adults with ASD reveal that 85% are unemployed (National Autistic Society, 2016). Research has shown that many individuals with ASD have never been members of the labor force [21]. The authors of [10] found that thirty-five percent of young adults with autism have never held a job, been members of the labor force, or attended educational programs after high school [10,21]. A study of 200 transition-age young adults with ASD found that 81% were unemployed [22].

Understanding the factors that contribute to unemployment is critical. The number of people affected by Autism Spectrum Disorder (ASD) is estimated in the tens of millions worldwide and 3.5 million in the United States [2]. Moreover, it is predicted that over the next decade, close to half a million children with ASD will reach adulthood (https://www.cdc.gov/ncbddd/autism/index.html). If they cannot be employed and live independently, the services they will require will place a financial toll on families and society [3]. Supporting an individual with ASD may exceed two million dollars throughout their lifetime [17]. The total cost of ASD support services in the U.S. exceeds 236 billion dollars annually [17]. This number is expected to rise to one trillion dollars by 2025 [4]. There are additional financial and non-financial costs that are difficult to measure, such as income losses for individuals with ASD and their families, as well as the emotional and psychological costs associated with long term unemployment [1].

Research must examine why organizations hire individuals with ASD and the barriers to their employment [2]. The literature on the employment of people with disabilities has found that, although many employers say they are willing to hire those with disabilities, their actual hiring practices do not show efforts in this area [23–25]. Employer's attitudes and perceptions towards people with disabilities, and organizational practices and policies, are two significant barriers to employment success [23]. This paper examines the role of employers' attitudes, perceptions, organizational practices, and policies on the hiring and retention of employees with ASD.

2.1. *Research on Employer Attitudes and Perceptions*

The literature on employer attitudes and perceptions towards employees with ASD is limited. However, there are studies in the disabilities literature that may lend insight into employers' attitudes and perceptions of individuals with ASD. Investigators at Cornell University surveyed over 800 private sector employers and over 400 federal sector employers in regard to actual hiring and retention processes for employees with disabilities [26,27].

When considering hiring individuals with disabilities, employers have several concerns. These concerns include potential legal risks, the time and effort to supervise and train, safety issues, the financial burden of accommodations, and the belief that they would never be able to terminate the disabled employee once hired [24,28–31]. Specifically looking at ASD, the authors of [32] found that employers who do not hire employees with ASD tend to have the following concerns; focusing on the employee's ability to adapt to work situations, a concern for adverse outcomes, and a lower interest in receiving new information and training. A study focusing on employees with Asperger's Syndrome (now categorized as ASD), found that employers' resistance and negative attitudes about the (perceived) need to provide accommodations, concerns about high costs, low productivity, and high turnover, as well as the need to provide outside supports, were associated with lower rates of hiring and higher rates of termination of individuals with ASD [7].

However, research has contradicted employer attitudes and perceptions that hiring adults with ASD may result in a loss of productivity and increased costs associated with workplace modifications and additional training and supervision. A few studies have compared the job performance ratings of employees with and without ASD [3]. Managers tended to rate the job performance of the employee with ASD as average or above average [11,14,33]. The authors of [34] compared employees with and without ASD on the extent to which they met standard requirements for good workplace performance. They found that employees with ASD performed at an "above standard level" regarding attention to detail, work ethic, and quality of work. This study found that employers do not incur additional costs when employing an adult with ASD over and above that of any new employee. They also found that while they may require some workplace modifications, supervision, and training, there is no significant difference between them and their colleagues concerning weekly employment, supervision, and training costs. Twaronite found that those with ASD were able to identify process improvements that cut training time in half (https://wwTw.ey.com/en_us/diversity-inclusiveness/six-ways-to-advance-disability-inclusion-in-your-organization). They also found that quality of work, efficiency, and productivity was equal to their other employees. JP Morgan & Chase Company has employed over 70 individuals with ASD over the past three years (https://www.forbes.com/sites/jpmorganchase/2017/06/05/how-jpmorgan-chases-autism-at-work-program-is-helping-to-win-top-tech-talent/#660a965830bb). Representatives of JP Morgan & Chase Company report that their employees with ASD are producing forty-eight to one-hundred-and-forty percent more work than their neurotypical colleagues (https://fortune.com/2018/06/24/where-autistic-workers-thrive/). They anticipate hiring hundreds more individuals with ASD globally in the coming years. A survey of employers who had hired individuals with ASD found that fifty-seven percent of employers reported no additional costs from hiring an individual with ASD and did not require assistance from tax incentives to hire them (https://askjan.org/topics/costs.cfm). Consequently, at the organizational level, these results contradict employers' attitudes and perceptions that hiring adults with ASD may result in a loss of productivity and increased costs associated with workplace modifications and additional training and supervision.

2.2. *Research on Employer Practices and Policies*

Research on employers' practices and policies to support employees with ASD is in its infancy. Although many organizations have created hiring initiatives to hire individuals with disabilities, some are beginning to focus on explicitly hiring individuals with ASD [27]. Organizational practices and policies may influence all stages of employment. A holistic approach to hiring for employees with ASD should be encouraged [35]. To better assist organizations in improving their employment practices, the barriers and facilitators to hiring individuals with ASD must be understood [2].

Much attention has focused on how the traditional selection interview may operate as a barrier to employment for individuals with ASD. The authors of [36] note that one of the obstacles to hiring neurodiverse employees is the traditional interview process. Current recruitment interview processes have not been found to provide adequate accommodations for neurodiverse individuals [37,38]. The authors of [36,39] found that the employment interview poses a unique barrier for individuals with ASD. Their research found that it is difficult for individuals with autism to navigate the social cues present during an interview. Research has found that individuals with ASD experience high anxiety during employment interviews [4,40]. A study of adults with ASD participating in an interview process found that 100% of the participants found that their high levels of anxiety negatively influenced their experience with the interview process. The participants also reported that their anxiety negatively affected their communication and performance in the interview (https://search.proquest.com/openview/b2bf39c3621955296526edd36f51dde6/1?pq-origsite=gscholar&cbl=18750&diss=y). The study also found that all participants viewed the interview as a negative experience due to issues of verbal and nonverbal communication, the process of the interview, and anxiety. For example, when companies use online applications, candidates may not be able to complete the application without adaptive technology, such as talk-to-text software. This can prevent a potential employee from even being eligible for an interview. Some organizations replace traditional interviews with opportunities for applicants with ASD to engage in a job trial or to demonstrate their skills with alternative methods [27].

The work in [35] found that, in Australia and Sweden, employers reported that knowledge and understanding of ASD, work environment, and job match led to successful employment of individuals with ASD. The authors of [35] noted that, when employees had a working knowledge of the needs of individuals with ASD, they fostered successful workplace relationships, minimized misunderstandings, and increased communication. The authors of [41], who interviewed employment support service providers, found that accommodations need to begin during the hiring process, not after the person has been hired. Some organizations may benefit from using support specialists in the hiring process. Support specialists help employers to see how the organization can successfully hire individuals with disabilities, including ASD. They will also assist them with training other employees and needed accommodations [42–48]. When education comes directly from employment support specialists during the hiring process, employers feel more confident about hiring employees with ASD. Employers reported that having an employment support specialist allows them to have someone to rely on. Employers can then ask disability-related questions, understand accommodation needs, and ease legal concerns [31,42,48–50]. Research is needed that examines organizational policies and practices that lead to successful employment outcomes for individuals with ASD [2].

2.3. Current Study

The literature explores employer perspectives and practices in regard to hiring employees with disabilities. There is limited research on employer factors that contribute to successful hiring and retention practices of employees with ASD, specifically. In this study, we used K-means clustering, a form of unsupervised machine learning, to categorize companies in different clusters based on their response to an online survey. This analysis allowed us to assess and compare aspects of businesses that successfully hire employees with ASD versus those that do not. Clustering algorithms aim to partition the dataset into groups (clusters) in which members of each group are similar to those in their cluster and dissimilar to those in other clusters. This type of analysis allows for a better understanding of the characteristics of those companies that are more successful in hiring employees with ASD.

3. Data

An online survey instrument was developed to assess employers' perspectives on hiring candidates with "High Functioning" Autism Spectrum Disorder (HFASD). This term was used to provide a brief descriptor of a particular group of individuals with ASD (i.e., those with average to above-average cognitive skills). However, the term HFASD can be problematic, as the term suggests those with average or above cognitive skills perform well in other functional areas, while the evidence indicates this is a poor predictor of functional skills [51]. To ameliorate some of these concerns, while still maintaining a "short descriptor", investigators clearly defined what was meant by HFASD as it related to the survey. Example behaviors based on the Diagnostic and Statistical Manual of mental disorders, 5th edition [52] were described in the survey and included areas of difficulty in functional domains. Specifically, for the purposes of this study, a person with HFASD is defined as someone who has identified themselves as having Autism, Aspergers, or HFASD has approximately average intellectual ability (when compared to peers) but may have marked difficulties in social interactions, including communication. The employee may have difficulty initiating or responding to social interactions, or may not seem interested in interacting with colleagues or customers. The person may be able to have a conversation when necessary, but may have difficulty keeping the conversation going or knowing how and when to end the conversation. The person may require a structured environment and/or schedule and may not deal well with change. The person may have difficulty with organization and planning.

A review of the literature was conducted to identify related studies across various stakeholders [53,54] to develop a basic framework and a list of questions. Questions used to assess these perspectives were organized into several categories including employer background and characteristics of employees; policies and practices related to recruitment and hiring; training, accessibility, and accommodations; and retention and advancement; barriers and facilitators to hiring individuals with ASD; and finally, the employer needs to improve hiring outcomes for individuals with ASD.

Employers from five local businesses agreed to participate as early reviewers and provided feedback about content as well as readability. A staff member from one local business volunteered to take the survey, along with the authors, and read aloud and answered each question on the computer and verbally. The volunteer asked questions for clarification and provided feedback during the process. In addition, the research team completed the survey multiple times, taking on varying respondent perspectives (e.g., employers with experience in hiring individuals with ASD, employers who had no experience) to assess whether the survey branching logic was appropriate; also discussed were potential answers, the survey flow, and whether the questions were sequenced in a logical order based on earlier responses. All pretest feedback was considered and resulted in multiple revisions. After obtaining Institutional Review Board approval, the survey instrument was finalized and placed in an electronic survey platform (Qualtrics), and a unique resource locator (URL) was created.

To access a broad range of employers across a larger geographical region, the team utilized the Qualtrics research services to recruit survey respondents. An invitation was sent out through their platform. The request to complete the survey included a statement regarding the researchers' interest in the employer's opinions on organizational practices, policies, and needs, related to employing people with ASD. However, it was made clear that the employer did not have to have experience hiring an individual with ASD to participate. Respondents were selected if they had a significant role in hiring decisions for their company. The survey link was active and open for three weeks. Participants were able to direct any questions or concerns to the authors; however, no questions or concerns were received.

The survey research methodology involved a traditional analytical process. The researchers had knowledge only about the demographic categories that the respondents provided, and no other identifying information was provided. Quantitative and qualitative data were collected via the survey. Quantitative data were obtained primarily through forced-choice or ranking questions. For most items, standard survey nomenclature (e.g., Likert scales) was used. Specifically, for the policy- and practices-related questions, respondents were asked if a particular policy or practice was not in place, being considered, in place but not effective, in place and somewhat effective, or in place and very effective. When asked about barriers and facilitators, employers were given a range of options to choose from, and an "other" or short text box was available for many questions so that respondents could provide a more detailed response [55]. For example, when asked, "Do any of the following pose a barrier to employment or advancement for people with ASD in your organization?" Respondents could select all that apply from a range of options including (but not limited to) cost of accommodations, cost of training/additional supervision, attitudes/stereotypes, lack of requisite skills among individuals with ASD, productive and performance of an individual, etc. All of the response options are based on previous research described above. When explicitly asked about employer needs related to hiring individuals with ASD, employers were asked a variety of questions about training, tax incentives and support, and experience with incentive and support programs. For example, employers were asked, "If an agency were to provide training and support for employing people with ASD, what would make it worthwhile for your organization to utilize the training?" Employers were able to select all applicable response options including the training would be free of cost, the training would be in partnership with a well-respected community organization concerning HFASD, and the training would be tailored to my company's needs. They were also asked if they would be willing to pay for training to assist their company in hiring individuals with ASD. The results of the quantitative data analysis are reported in this paper.

The instrument consisted of 50 to 80 questions, depending on the participant's hiring experience. Specifically, the number of items offered to each respondent varied based on his or her experience with hiring individuals with High Functioning ASD (HFASD). It took approximately 20 min to complete the survey online, and a total of 285 respondents completed the online survey. Of the 285 respondents, 166 (58%) indicated they had hired at least one individual with HFASD in the past five years. Of the 285 respondents, 120 possessed a high school diploma, 36 held an associates degree, 107 held a bachelors degree or higher, and the remainder indicated "other" as their highest level of education. Of the respondents, 14 worked for organizations with 15 or less employees, 7 at organizations with 16–49 employees, 26 at organizations with 50–99 employees, 26 at organizations with 100–499 employees, 13 at organizations with 500–999 employees, and the remainder at organizations with 1000 or more employees.

To create the data matrix, 41 questions and sub-questions from the survey were used to create a binary variable for each item. For each variable, a 1 indicated a favorable response in relation to HFASD. The variables were then broken into five categories: (1) Hiring (n = 15), (2) Training (n = 8), (3) Accommodations (n = 8), (4) Retention (n = 10), and (5) Perceptions (n = 18). To reduce the dimensions of the dataset, the average score for each respondent in each of the four categories was calculated. Creating an average score for each category also helped to normalize the data. Because the number of variables differed among the categories, using a count (as opposed to an average score) would put more weight on the categories with more variables. For example, if a respondent had a favorable response for seven of the Hiring variables, he or she would have a Hiring score of 7/15 = 0.47. After assessing the cluster model, all clusters had virtually the same Perception score, which led to overlapping clusters. Thus, the Perception scores from the final data matrix were excluded. Having a dataset with large dimensions often leads to a sparse dataspace (all objects may seem dissimilar in this space) and analysis results that may be true with higher dimensionality but that will not necessarily hold in a lower dimensional space. Thus, the final data matrix was a 285 $\times$ 4 dimensional matrix that represents the average scores of 285 employers' responses to the 41 questions mapped to 4 categories. The variable descriptions and survey averages for each category can be found in Tables 1–4.

Table 1. Accommodation.

Description	Survey Average
Regularly reviews the accessibility of its online application system to people with visual, hearing, finger dexterity, and cognitive impairments	61.0%
Analyzes our job descriptions to determine whether the responsibilities could be broken down into discrete tasks that could be performed by an individual with ASD	61.0%
Provides advance notice to job applicants that reasonable accommodations are provided during the job application process	68.0%
Evaluates pre-employment occupational screenings to ensure they are unbiased	71.0%
Has company-wide fund to provide accommodations for people with disabilities	61.0%
Has a designated office or person to address accommodation questions	69.0%
Has an established grievance procedure to address reasonable accommodation issues	70.0%

Table 2. Hiring.

Description	Survey Average
Hired someone with ASD in the last 5 years	58.0%
Actively recruits people with ASD	53.0%
Works with community organizations that promote hiring of people with ASD	57.0%
Includes people with ASD explicitly in its diversity and inclusion plan	58.0%
Has explicit organizational goals related to the recruitment or hiring of people with ASD	54.0%
Includes progress toward hiring goals for people with ASD in the performance appraisals of senior management	52.0%
Participates in internships that target people with ASD	53.0%
Has senior management that demonstrates a strong commitment to ASD hiring	56.0%
Utilizes tax incentives for hiring people with disabilities	54.0%
Requires subcontractors/suppliers to adhere to disability nondiscrimination requirements	56.0%
Does not automatically exclude job applicants with a history of unemployment	79.0%
Does not automatically exclude job applicants with a large gap in employment	76.0%
Has company initiative to hire people with HFASD	53.0%
Works with universities to hire people with HFASD	49.0%
Uses social media ads to recruit people with HFASD	45.0%

Table 3. Retention.

Description	Survey Average
Has a formal mentoring program to support employees with ASD	53.0%
Encourages flexible work arrangements for all employees with ASD (e.g., flextime, part-time, telecommuting)	62.0%
Offers special career planning and development tools for employees with ASD	55.0%
Has an ASD-focused employee network (e.g., employee resource group or affinity group)	52.0%
Invites employees to confidentially disclose whether they have a disability (e.g., staff surveys)	73.0%
Has explicit organizational goals related to retention or advancement of employees with ASD	54.0%
Includes progress toward retention of advancement goals for employees with ASD in the performance appraisals of senior management	54.0%
Allows an employee to exceed the maximum duration of medical leave as an accommodation	54.0%
Has defined career paths at our company for all employees	75.0%
Opportunities for advancement of employees with HFASD	61.0%

Table 4. Training.

Description	Survey Average
Offers ASD awareness and sensitivity training (internal)	60.0%
Offers ASD awareness and sensitivity training (external)	51.0%
Trains HR staff and supervisors on effective interviewing of people with ASD	62.0%
Trains HR staff and supervisors on inclusion practices of people with ASD in the workplace	62.0%
Requires training for supervisors on legal requirements of disability and non-discrimination and accommodation	68.0%
Includes ASD awareness and sensitivity as a topic in training for managers/ supervisors	58.0%
In contract with an agency that can help our business provide the support needed for working with employees with ASD now and in the future	52.0%

4. Methods

K-means is an unsupervised learning algorithm that is capable of discerning latent clusters in data [56]. We chose this algorithm for our analysis based on data visualizations which showed no irregular shapes or non-homogeneous behavior which would require a more sophisticated technique. Unlike supervised learning (classification), which requires labeled data to measure the accuracy of prediction, unsupervised learning methods are instead assessed on the "goodness" of the clusters identified using one or more common quantitative metrics, such as silhouette score. K-means requires a single parameter, k, as input, which represents the number of clusters to be fit to the data. The algorithm then proceeds as follows.

1. A centroid (mean) for each of the k clusters is assigned by randomly selecting a data point from the data.
2. Every other data point is assigned to the cluster whose centroid is closest. Distance can be calculated using any valid distance metric, with Euclidean and Cosine distance being popular choices.
3. The centroids are reevaluated by averaging each data point assigned to a specific cluster.
4. Steps 2 and 3 are repeated, alternating between assigning data points to their nearest centroids, and then reevaluating the value of the centroids based on the new assignments. When the centroids no longer change, or the cluster assignments for the data points become static, the algorithm terminates.

For the work presented here, we found the most likely number of clusters to be five. This was calculated by using the gap statistic [57], a common technique for assessing the number of latent clusters in unsupervised machine learning. This was further validated using the Hopkins statistic, which denotes the overall likelihood that the data can be partitioned into clusters. For the data presented here, the Hopkins score was 0.72, indicating that the dataset exhibits strong clustering tendency.

With clustering, the lack of labeled data means there is not an independent data set to validate accuracy. Instead, silhouette scores [58] were used to measure how well the clusters explained the latent structure of the data. Silhouette scores quantify how similar a data point is to the other points in its cluster compared to those represented in other nearby clusters. The silhouette scores vary from -1 to $+1$, with values close to 1 suggesting that the point is well clustered and a negative silhouette as suggesting that the data point likely should not belong to its assigned cluster. The mean silhouette score for our model was 0.54.

5. Model Results

The data from the complete set of respondents were partitioned into five clusters and visualized in Figure 1, with average category scores listed in Table 5. The remaining figures (presented according to cluster) provide a visualization of the individual cluster average category scores, with the last (presented at the end of this section) that shows all graphs on the same axis for comparison.

Table 5. Cluster average scores.

Cluster	Size	Accommodation	Hiring	Retention	Training
1	41	0.67	0.21	0.28	0.11
2	32	0.84	0.56	0.78	0.70
3	62	0.10	0.12	0.06	0.04
4	24	0.30	0.34	0.25	0.61
5	126	0.97	0.95	0.97	0.98

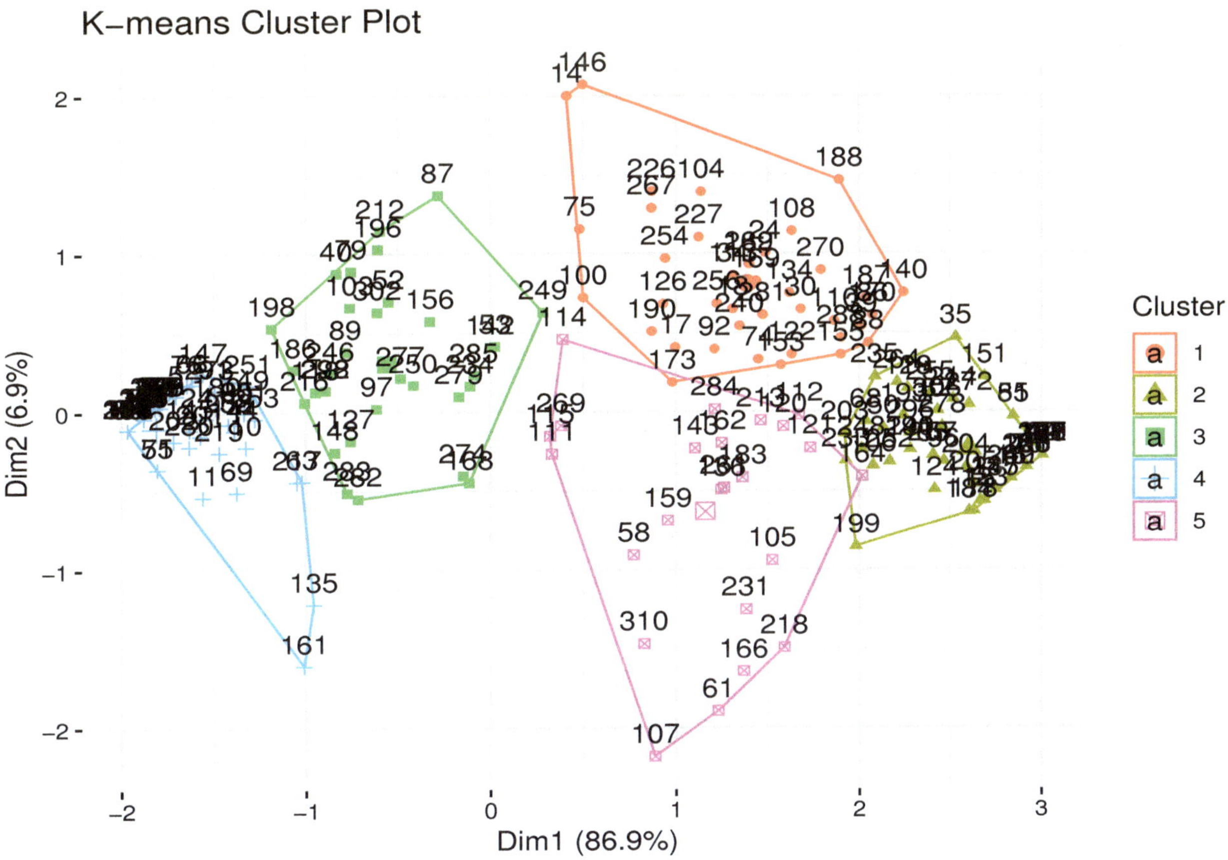

Figure 1. Employer K-means cluster plot.

5.1. Cluster 1

The 41 employer respondents in Cluster 1 (14.0% of sample) had only 29.0% in a management/owner role, while 54.0% were in a human resource/recruiting position. Although employers in Cluster 1 had the lowest five-year hiring rates (24.0% vs. survey average 58.0%) for individuals with high functioning ASD, they are able to offer full-time employment to those they do hire. Almost all, 98.0%, of the employers in Cluster 1 have high functioning ASD employees employed full time. In the past two years, 63.0% of employers in Cluster 1 have hired more than 11 employees.

This cluster had employers in 19 out of the 24 different industries listed and a company size of 218 employees on average (survey average 285 employees). Most respondents in all clusters and the survey were representing health care/social assistance employers. Only the health care/social assistance and construction industries represented at least 10.0% of Cluster 1. A college degree is required by 32.0% of employers in Cluster 1, and 63.0% require a high school diploma for employment. Employers in this cluster had 5.0% in the Southwest, 12.0% in the Northeast, 22.0% in the Southeast, 24.0% in the Midwest, and 34.0% located in the West.

Employers in this cluster do not have policies and practices to foster hiring, retaining, or training employees with high functioning ASD (significantly lower than survey averages for all variables). No employers in Cluster 1 had a hiring initiative for high functioning ASD or a job-related training program for employees with high functioning ASD (compared to 53.0% and 56% of survey respondents, respectively).

Employers in this cluster have most accommodations in place for high functioning ASD comparable to the survey averages. Only the following four accommodation variables were significantly higher than the average for the survey. More than 80.0% of employers in Cluster 1 allow an employee to exceed the maximum duration of medical leave as an accommodation, have an established grievance procedure to address reasonable accommodation issues, have a designated office to address accommodation questions, and provide advance notice to job applicants that reasonable accommodations are provided during the job application process (Figure 2).

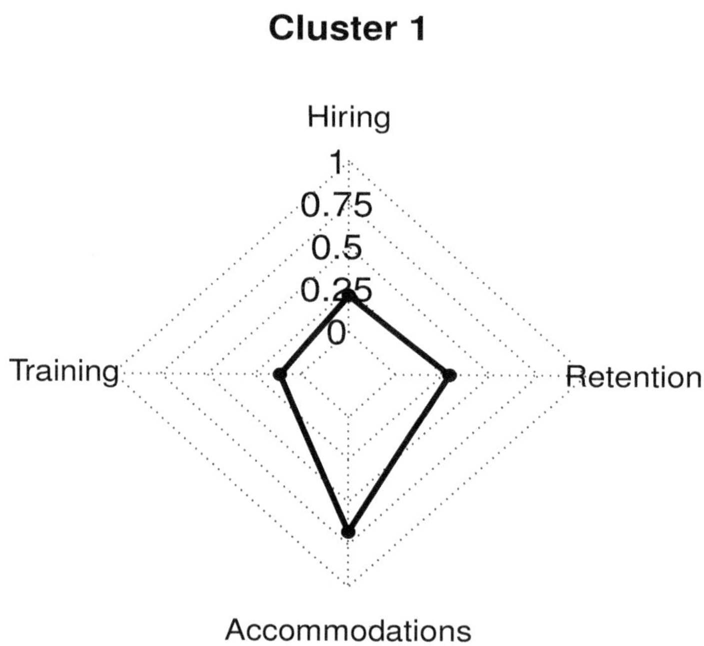

Figure 2. Cluster 1 radar graph.

5.2. Cluster 2

The 32 employer respondents in Cluster 2 (11.0% of sample) had 44.0% in a management/owner role, while 53.0% were in a human resource/recruiting position. Respondents in Cluster 2 had a five-year high functioning ASD hiring rate above the survey average (66.0% vs. survey average 58.0%). Cluster 2 had 72.0% of respondents who were involved in the hiring process for less than 10 years (survey average 64.0%). In this cluster, 72.0% of employers have hired over 11 employees in the last 2 years.

This cluster had employers in 18 out of the 24 different industries listed and had a company size of 400 employees on average (40.0% higher than the survey average of 285 employees). Cluster 2 had the highest number, 24.0%, of employers having over 1000 employees compared to the other clusters. Only the insurance/finance (12.0%) and health care/social assistance (16.0%) industries represented at least 10.0% of Cluster 2. A high school diploma is required by 47.0% of employers in Cluster 2, and a college degree is needed for 50.0% of employers in this cluster. Employers in Cluster 2 had

3.0% in the Southwest, 16.0% in the Midwest, 25.0% in the West, 28.0% in the Northeast, and 28.0% in the Southeast.

Cluster 2 employers had most hiring practices similar to the survey averages. Of these employers, 75.0% had senior management that exhibited a strong commitment to high functioning ASD hiring and recruitment (survey average of 56.0%); however, only 25.0% of employers in this cluster require suppliers/subcontractors to follow disability non-discrimination requirements (survey average of 56.0%). Cluster 2 have employers who have human resource staff and supervisors training on high functioning ASD sensitivity and awareness approximately 20.0% more than the survey average. However, only 19.0% do the training internally (survey average of 60.0%). Employers in Cluster 2 also impart training on effective inclusion and interviewing practices for employees with high functioning ASD approximately 20.0% more than the average for survey. In addition, this cluster had about 20.0% higher instances of favorable policies and procedures regarding accommodations and accessibility than the averages for the survey. More than 90.0% of Cluster 2 employers have a defined career path for every employee, have opportunities for advancement for employees with high functioning ASD, and invite employees to confidentially disclose whether they have a disability (Figure 3).

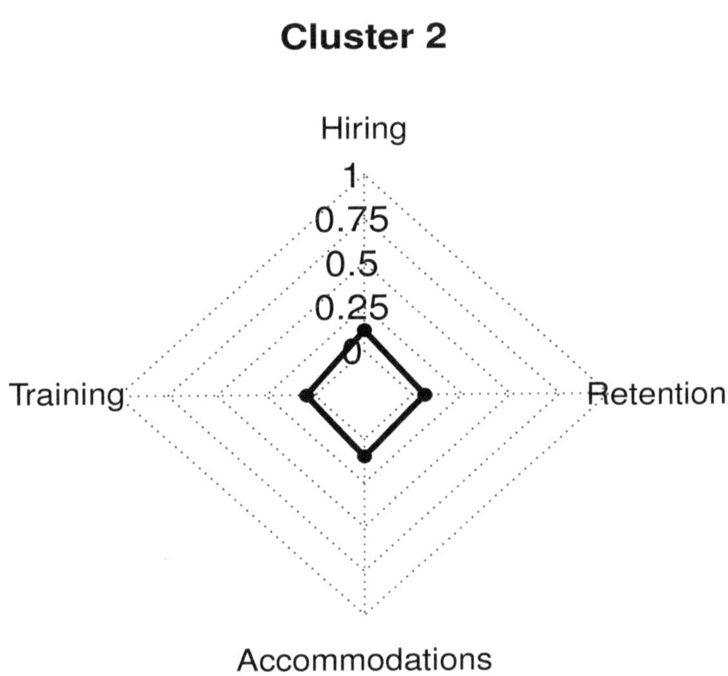

Figure 3. Cluster 2 radar graph.

5.3. Cluster 3

The 62 employer respondents in Cluster 3 (22.0% of sample) had 45.0% in a management/owner role, while 42.0% were in a human resource/recruiting position. Employers in Cluster 3 had a five-year high functioning ASD hiring rate below the survey average (42.0% vs. survey average 58.0%). Cluster 3 had 52.0% of respondents who were involved in the hiring process for less than 10 years (survey average 64.0%). In this cluster, only 42.0% of employers have hired over 11 employees in the last 2 years.

Cluster 3 had employers in 15 out of the 24 different industries listed and had a company size of 108 employees on average (62.0% lower than the survey average of 285 employees). Only the construction (11.0%), Other (13.0%), and health care/social assistance (19.0%) industries represented at least 10.0% of Cluster 3. A high school diploma is required by 55.0% of employers in Cluster 3, and a college degree is needed for only 29.0% of employers in this cluster. Over half of the employers in Cluster 3 were located in the eastern United States. This cluster had 6.0% in the Southwest, 15.0% in the Midwest, 18.0% in the West, 29.0% in the Northeast, and 35.0% in the Southeast.

Cluster 3 only had two policies and procedures, in any category, that were within 40% of the average for the survey: 47.0% do not automatically exclude applicants with a large gap in employment (76.0% survey average), and 45.0% do not automatically exclude applicants with a history of unemployment (79.0% survey average).

Employers in this cluster had very few favorable hiring policies and procedures in place for individuals with high functioning ASD. Only the following three hiring variables were in place for more than 10.0% of employers in Cluster 3: 11.0% actively recruit individuals with high functioning ASD, 13.0% require suppliers/subcontractors to follow disability non-discrimination requirements, and 46.0% do not automatically exclude applicants with a gap in employment or a history of unemployment. The single training variable present in more than 10.0% of Cluster 3 employers was the 23.0% that train supervisors on the legal requirements related to disability, non-discrimination, and accommodation.

Cluster 3 employers also had few favorable accommodations and accessibility policies and procedures in place for individuals with high functioning ASD. Only the following two accommodations variables were in place for more than 10.0% of employers in Cluster 3: 23.0% allow employees to exceed the maximum medical leave duration, and 19.0% evaluate pre-employment occupational screenings to verify they are unbiased.

This cluster only had two favorable policies related to retention of employees with high functioning ASD present in more than 10.0% of employers: 25.0% invite employees to confidentially disclose whether they have a disability, and have a defined career path for all employees (Figure 4).

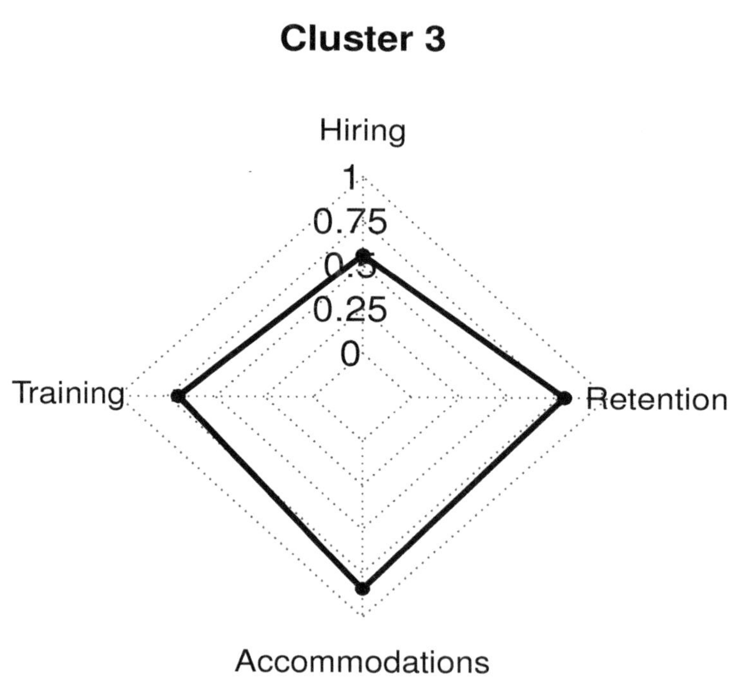

Figure 4. Cluster 3 radar graph.

5.4. Cluster 4

The 28 employer respondents in Cluster 4 (8.0% of sample) had 33.0% in a management/owner role, while 67.0% were in a human resource/recruiting position. Employers in Cluster 4 had a five-year high functioning ASD hiring rate below the survey average (46.0% vs. survey average 58.0%). Cluster 4 had 67.0% of respondents who were involved in the hiring process for less than 10 years (survey average 64.0%). In this cluster, 54.0% of employers have hired less than 11 employees in the last 2 years.

Cluster 4 had employers in 13 out of the 24 different industries listed and had a company size of 250 employees on average (survey average of 285 employees). Only the retail trade (12.0%) and health care/social assistance (29.0%) industries represented at least 10.0% of Cluster 4. A high school diploma is required by only 38.0% of employers in Cluster 4, and a college degree is needed for 63.0% of employers in this cluster. Over half of the employers in Cluster 4 were located in the eastern United States. This cluster had 8.0% in the Midwest, 13.0% in the Southwest, 21.0% in the West, 29.0% in the Northeast, and 29.0% in the Southeast.

Most employers in in Cluster 4 had training policies and procedures in place within 10.0% of the survey averages. There were four training policies in place in ~20.0% more employers than the survey averages: work with an agency to provide the support needed for working with individuals with high functioning ASD, train human resource supervisors and staff on effective inclusion and inclusion practices, and offer sensitivity and awareness training internally.

The majority of employers in Cluster 4 did not have policies in place to stimulate accommodating, hiring, or retaining individuals with high functioning ASD. Nearly all hiring procedures related to employees with high functioning ASD were approximately 20.0–40.0% below the average for the survey. Only one hiring variable had an average comparable to to the survey average: 50.0% actively recruit employees with high functioning ASD (53.0% survey average)

All accommodations and accessibility variables were approximately 30.0–44.0% below the survey average for employers in Cluster 4. All but one retention policies were 30.0–45.0% below the survey average: 54.0% of employers provide a defined career path for all employees (Figure 5).

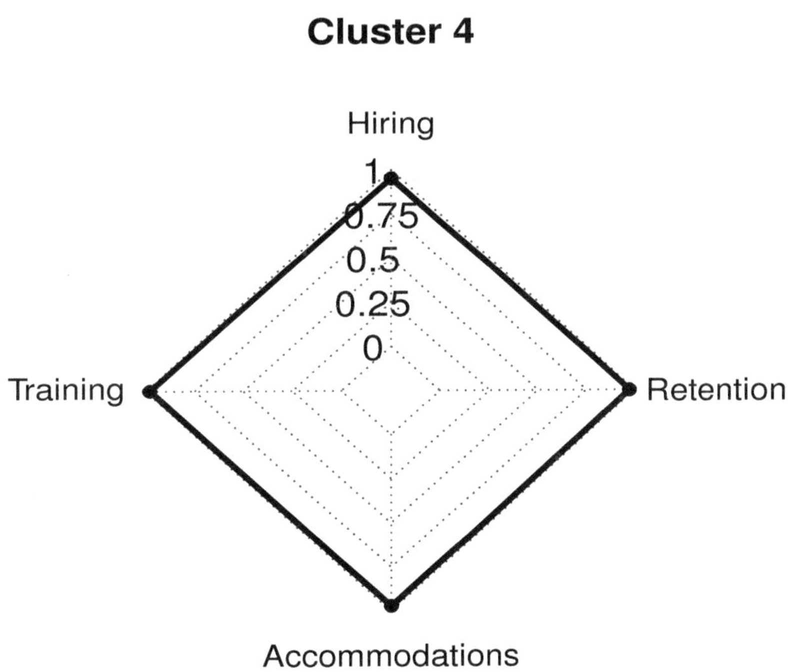

Figure 5. Cluster 4 radar graph.

5.5. Cluster 5

Cluster 5 is the largest cluster of the model. The 126 employer respondents in Cluster 5 (44.0% of sample) had 40.0% in a management/owner role, while 56.0% were in a human resource/recruiting position. Employers in Cluster 5 had a five-year high functioning ASD hiring rate far above the survey average (86.0% vs. survey average 58.0%). Cluster 5 had 75.0% of respondents who were involved in the hiring process for less than 10 years. This is consistent with the work in [59], which found employers newer to the hiring process were more likely to hire an individual with high functioning ASD. In this cluster, 71.0% of employers have hired over 11 employees in the last 2 years.

This cluster had employers in all 24 different industries listed and had a company size of 375 employees on average. The average company size is higher than the survey average of 285 employees, but comparable to the that of Cluster 2 (400 employees). Cluster 5 had 19.0% of employers with over 1000 employees compared to the other clusters. Only the educational services (12.0%) and health care/social assistance (20.0%) industries represented at least 10.0% of Cluster 5. A high school diploma is required by 29.0% of employers in Cluster 5, and a college degree is needed for 64.0% of employers in this cluster. Most employers in this cluster were located in the eastern United States. Employers in Cluster 5 had 7.0% in the Southwest, 15.0% in the West, 18.0% in the Midwest, 22.0% in the Northeast, and 40.0% in the Southeast.

Cluster 5 employers had very high rates of favorable policies and practices in place for individuals with high functioning ASD. The following three polices were in place for *all* employers in this cluster; have a company-wide initiative to higher employees with high functioning ASD, offer a job-related training program for individuals with high functioning ASD, and include individuals with high functioning ASD explicitly in their diversity and inclusion plan.

All but two hiring policies and procedures in place for more than 90% of the Cluster 5 employers: 82.0% have relationships with community organizations that promote the employment of individuals with high functioning ASD, and 88.0% actively recruit individuals with high functioning ASD. Every accommodation, retention, and training policies included in the survey were in place for almost all, 94.0%, of Cluster 5 employers (Figure 6).

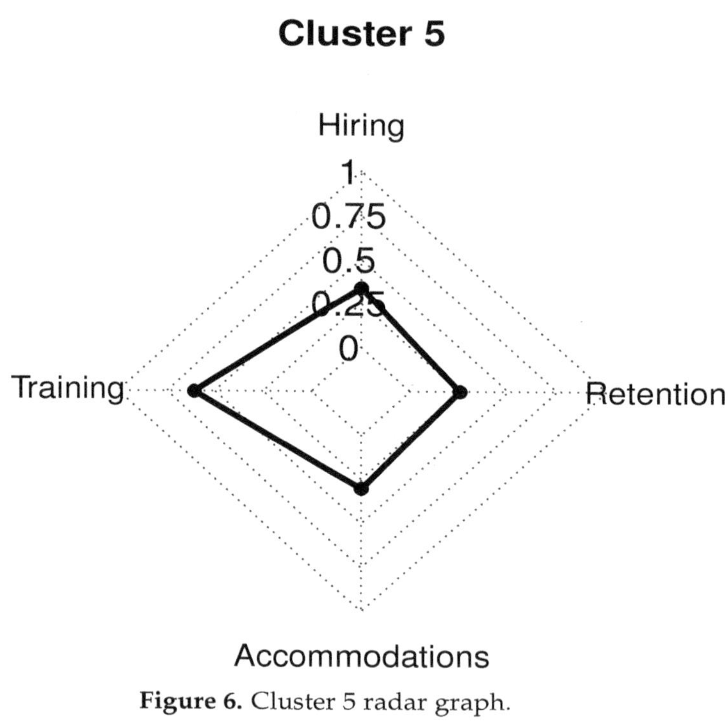

Figure 6. Cluster 5 radar graph.

5.6. Summary of Cluster Comparisons

Most of the respondents were employed in Human Resources and/or Recruiting, which was consistent across all clusters. Cluster 5 had the highest high functioning ASD hiring rate for the past five years, at 86.0%, and, surprisingly also had the most cluster members. The two largest clusters (3 and 5) also had the most extreme average scores for each category. This could indicate that employers tend to have either extremely favorable policies and practices in place or none at all. The most prevalent industry in the survey and all clusters was health care/social assistance, but the cluster with the highest rate of high functioning ASD employment (Cluster 5) did not have the highest rate of health care/social assistance.

Only two clusters (2 and 5) have employment rates above the survey average of 58.0%. These also are the only two clusters with an average company size above the survey average. Although large companies hire more employees, over 50.0% of employers in both of these clusters require a college degree for entry-level jobs. Clusters 1 and 3 had the lowest rates of hiring high function ASD (24.0% and 26.0%, respectively) and are the only two clusters with rates for requiring a college degree below 50.0% (32.0% and 29.0%, respectively). Figure 7 shows all graphs on the same axis.

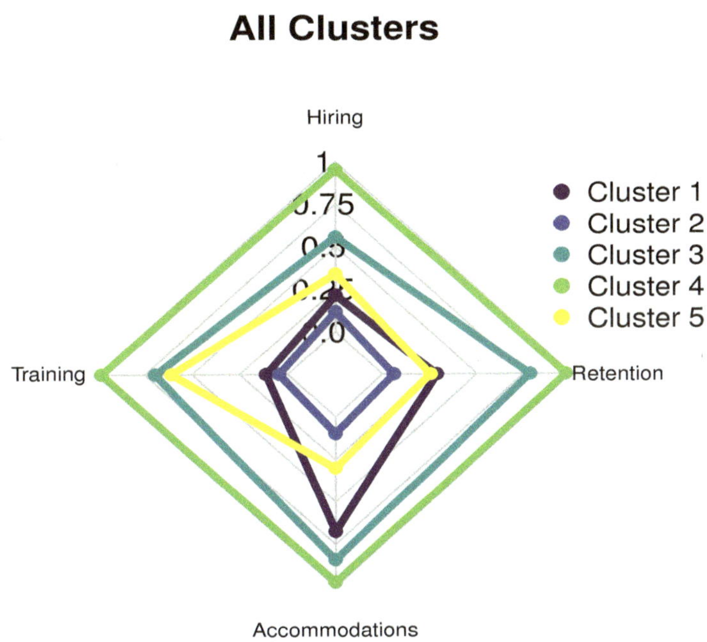

Figure 7. Radar graph for all clusters.

6. Discussion

Although Cluster 3 had the lowest overall score across four categories (hiring, training, accommodation, and retention), Cluster 1 had the lowest hiring rate for individuals with ASD. For this reason, Cluster 1 was compared to Cluster 5, which had the highest hiring rate for individuals with ASD. Cluster 5 also offered a sharp contrast to Cluster 1 in the number of policies in place in support of employees with ASD. Comparing the company structures, policies and practices, perceptions, and needs of employers and employees within these two clusters allows a determination of best practices for companies that are looking to improve their employment rates of individuals with ASD.

6.1. Company Structure, Policies, and Practices

Given that company size and job structures affect hiring practices, company data across the two clusters are included. For size, 58.5% of companies in Cluster 1 had more than 50 employees, compared to 75.3% of Cluster 5 companies. This is important to note, as larger companies may have more opportunities to hire employees with ASD. There also was a difference between job availability and skill sets needed for the different clusters. In Cluster 5, over half of the entry-level jobs require a bachelor's degree (53.2%), whereas, for Cluster 1, only 24.4% require a bachelor's degree, and most require a high school diploma (63.4%). This may be affected by the fact that 70.7% of employers in Cluster 5 work directly with universities to hire employees with HFASD.

In comparison to Cluster 1, companies in Cluster 5 provide their employees with ASD more opportunities for professional growth. For example, 73.0% of Cluster 5 employees with HFASD are paid more now than when they started, and 65.0% of Cluster 5 employees with HFASD have been promoted or had an increase in job responsibilities, versus just 7% in Cluster 1. Further, 50.0% of respondents in Cluster 5 reported that their employees disclosed their HFASD during the application or interview process, rather than after being hired (37.5%) or not at all (12.5%) This could reflect a tendency of the companies in Cluster 5 to be responsive and supportive to a disability disclosure during the interview process.

In Cluster 5, 65.1% of companies created incentives to work at their companies by offering credit-based internships for employees with high functioning ASD, compared to 7.3% in Cluster 1. In addition, about half of the organizations in Cluster 5 show purposeful initiatives to hire employees with high functioning ASD. In contrast, every company in Cluster 1 responded that they did *not* have any purposeful initiatives to hire individuals with high functioning ASD. This indicates that there are no current or future plans for initiatives related to hiring people with high functioning ASD, in contrast to Cluster 5, which included positive responses to many of the initiatives to specifically hire, support, and retain employees with high functioning ASD. One of the few initiatives that 58.6% of Cluster 1 organizations did have was advance notice to job applicants that reasonable accommodations are provided during the job application process. Cluster 1 responses, however, indicated that employers did not offer much beyond this, whereas 81.0% of organizations in Cluster 5 had the accommodations in place. Although none of the companies in Cluster 1 reported having hiring initiatives for employees with high functioning ASD, Cluster 5 reported having specific initiatives to hire employees with high functioning ASD to create a more inclusive workplace (21.0%), because they recognize the skills of employees with high functioning ASD (21.0%), to increase the company's reputation benefits (7.0%), and to decrease employee turnover (2.0%).

Employers in Cluster 1 provide far fewer accommodations than do those in Cluster 5. For example, 81.7% of Cluster 5 employees state that they have a centralized accommodations fund to specifically provide accommodations for employees with disabilities, compared to 39.1% in Cluster 1. Further, just 2.4% of employers in Cluster 5 reported *not* having a designated office or person to address accommodation questions compared to 17.1% in Cluster 1 who do not have a designated accommodation office or person. These data indicate that it may be necessary for employers to provide a menu of accommodation options for their employees, rather than using a one-size-fits-all approach.

Because all respondents in Cluster 1 indicated that they did not have initiatives to specifically hire employees with high functioning ASD, their survey was auto-formatted to skip questions regarding these specific hiring practices. Although this does not allow for comparisons of specific high functioning ASD hiring practices between Clusters 1 and 5, the difference in responses indicates that Cluster 1 companies did not have any initiatives to specifically hire employees with high functioning ASD, while Cluster 5 companies did.

Many employers in Cluster 5 said that they have relationships with community organizations that promote the employment of people with high functioning ASD, with 81.8% that reported that such a program was already in place, and 17.5%, that such a program was being considered. Approximately, 70.7% of Cluster 5 also reported having relationships with universities, with 23.0% that noted that such a program was being considered, and 4.0%, that such a program was not currently in place.

6.2. Perceptions and Attitudes

Questions related to employer attitudes demonstrated, in Cluster 5, a company belief in the high competency of their employees with high functioning ASD. For example, 74.6% of employers in Cluster 5 reported being likely to hire employees with high functioning ASD versus 17.1% of Cluster 1.

In Cluster 5, 65.1% of employees with high functioning ASD have been promoted or taken on additional job responsibilities, whereas only 7.3% of Cluster 1 had. Generally, employers in Cluster 5 reported having supportive coworkers, reflecting a positive work environment as well as an overall positive experience in working with employees with high functioning ASD, with 20.6% rating their experience as positive and 53.2% as very positive. The majority (78.0%) of respondents in Cluster 1 did not have experience with working with high functioning ASD; thus, comparison data were not available.

The data from Cluster 5 demonstrate an inclusive culture in which high functioning ASD training is offered to employees. Employers offer HR and staff training on inclusive practices (80.2%) and legal requirements (77.8%), high functioning ASD sensitivity and awareness training (72.9%), and training related to effective interviewing of potential employees with high functioning ASD (83.4%). In Cluster 1, 87.8% do not offer high functioning ASD sensitivity and awareness training, 87.8% do not have training in effective interviewing of potential employees with high functioning ASD, 63.4% do not require training related to legal requirements and nondiscrimination accommodation, and 90.2% do not train staff on inclusive workplace practices of people with high functioning ASD.

The biggest fears of hiring someone with high functioning ASD were the same for both clusters: high functioning ASD employees would have behaviors that put themselves or others at risk (Cluster 1: 24.0%; Cluster 5: 29.0%) and employees with high functioning ASD would not perform well (Cluster 1: 24.0%; Cluster 5: 23.0%). Despite having the same fears, Cluster 5 businesses responded positively to hiring employees with high functioning ASD.

6.3. *Needs of Employers and Employees*

When asked about obtaining additional training in hiring practices, respondents in Clusters 1 and 5 stated that they would prefer that training in hiring employees with high functioning ASD be free, but only 43.9% of Cluster 1 were willing to pay, whereas 80.0% of Cluster 5 were willing to pay.

Having a supportive environment helps to alleviate stress and boost productivity [35]. In Cluster 5, the majority of high functioning ASD employees seem to need some form of support, but these companies appear to be prepared to provide that support. Cluster 1 has a far lower perceived need of support for high functioning ASD employees, but perhaps employers are simply unaware of the support needed or less open to offering extra support. For the level of support that their employees with high functioning ASD need, 75.6% of Cluster 1 companies did not respond, indicating a lack of experience with high functioning ASD employees. Of those who did respond, their answers were that their employees with high functioning ASD required: no support (7.3%), some support (12.2%), substantial support (2.4%), or very substantial support (2.4%). In Cluster 5, 12.1% did not respond, but the remaining responded: no support (6.3%), some support (30.2%), substantial support (28.6%), or very substantial support (19.8%). In Cluster 5, 47.6% reported that high functioning ASD employees are in a job-related training program, whereas, in Cluster 1, employers responded that none of their employees with high functioning ASD is in a job-related training program. After considering the notable factors in the in-depth cluster comparisons and reviewing the literature in the field, the researchers identified best practices in employment that would likely lead to the successful hiring of individuals with ASD. These components were organized under a summary of best practices for improving employment, to assist with applying the study outcomes to the field and presented in Table 6.

Table 6. Practices for improving employment of individuals with high functioning ASD.

Category	Practice	Supporting Citations
Recruitment and Hiring	Foster relationships with community organizations for recruitment of employees with ASD. Encourage relationships with universities and employment agencies to help bridge the gap between college and employment and allow for a smoother transition. Have a supportive interview process. It is not enough to simply note that accommodations will be provided during interview (e.g., Cluster 1); more is needed Have specific hiring and retention practices and policies related to ASD employees, along with training for managers, hiring personnel (specify who)	Culler et al. (2011); Fraser et al. (2010); Fraser et al. (2011); Gewurtz et al. (2018); Graffam et al. (2002); Peck & Kirkbride (2001); Wiggett-Barnard and Swarts (2012)
Training	Make hiring personnel, managers, and employees aware of the many positive professional traits that employees with ASD have; foster an inclusive workplace that reflects a belief in the high competency of employees. Provide training about the myths of ASD employment "challenges".	Fraser et al. (2011); Lengnick-Hall et al. (2008); Lopez & Keenan (2014); Luecking (2011); Nesbitt (2000); Peck & Kirkbride (2001); Richards (2012)
Accessibility & Accommodations	Provide a menu of options, rather than just a few, that the employer believes are effective, for individuals to hire and retain employees with ASD. Offer for-credit internships; this creates more of an incentive to work there and can provide a transition opportunity for employees with ASD to adjust to the work environment. Provide the same professional growth opportunities for ASD as for neurotypical colleagues.	Project SEARCH [60]; Taube (2014) [61]
Retention & Advancement	Create and monitor a professional growth plan. Support employers (encourage ride-sharing, peer mentor/support, relationships of open communication and trust). Partner with or provide an on-site job training program.	Lindsay et al. (2019); Wiggett-Barnard and Swarts (2012)

7. Conclusions

This study supports some of the findings of the research on employer perspectives on hiring employees with ASD [7,25,32], but also expands upon Lindsay et al.'s study by using machine learning to analyze trends in businesses that have successfully hired and retained employees with ASD [27]. To foster such diversity and inclusion, it is critical to understand the needs of both the employees and employers. The results of this analysis may be utilized to make suggestions for stakeholders who are working to make improvements to the employment of individuals with high functioning ASD.

The comparison of clusters of employers with the highest and lowest rates of employing individuals with ASD revealed company policies and practices that can be effective for hiring, training, and retaining employees with ASD. The results show that purposeful diversity initiatives and relationships with community organizations that promote ASD are likely effective in increasing employment for those with ASD. Offering disability and diversity training is also helpful for understanding the needs of employees with ASD. These steps may affect perceptions and attitudes as well, as shown through the belief in high competency of employees with ASD; promotions; and supportive, positive coworker experiences. These results are promising for developing recommendations that can be implemented to increase employment opportunities for individuals with ASD on a large scale. More research, however, needs to be conducted to continue to identify best practices for supporting employees with ASD. As these recommendations are further researched and refined, employers will need training and support to translate these concepts into practice.

Author Contributions: Conceptualization, A.J.G., A.H.H., and C.M.G.; data curation, A.J.G., A.H.H., and C.M.G.; methodology, K.H. and E.L.; software, K.H. and E.L.; writing—original draft preparation, A.J.G., A.H.H., C.M.G., S.K.M., and K.H.; writing—review and editing, A.J.G., A.H.H., C.M.G., S.M., K.H., and E.L. All authors have read and agreed to the published version of the manuscript.

Abbreviations

The following abbreviations are used in this manuscript.

ASD	Autism Spectrum Disorder
HFASD	High Functioning Autism Spectrum Disorder
HR	Human Resources

References

1. Hurley-Hanson, A.E.; Giannantonio, C.M.; Griffiths, A.J. *Autism in the Workplace: Creating Positive Employment and Career Outcomes for Generation A*; Palgrave Macmillan: Basingstoke, UK, 2020.
2. Hedley, D.; Uljarević, M.; Cameron, L.; Halder, S.; Richdale, A.; Dissanayake, C. Employment programmes and interventions targeting adults with autism spectrum disorder: A systematic review of the literature. *Autism* **2017**, *21*, 929–941. [CrossRef]
3. Jacob, A.; Scott, M.; Falkmer, M.; Falkmer, T. The costs and benefits of employing an adult with autism spectrum disorder: A systematic review. *PLoS ONE* **2015**, *10*, e0139896. [CrossRef] [PubMed]
4. Baldwin, S.; Costley, D.; Warren, A. Employment activities and experiences of adults with high-functioning Autism and Asperger's disorder. *J. Autism Dev. Disord.* **2014**, *44*, 2440–2449. [CrossRef] [PubMed]
5. Kreiger, B.; Kinebanian, A.; Prodinger, B.; Heigl, F. Becoming a member of the workforce: Perceptions of adults with Asperger syndrome. *Work* **2012**, *43*, 141–157. [CrossRef] [PubMed]
6. Nord, D.K.; Stancliffe, R.J.; Nye-Legerman, K.; Hewitt, A.S. Employment in the community for people with and without autism: A comparative analysis. *Res. Autism Spectr. Disord.* **2016**, *24*, 11–16. [CrossRef]
7. Richards, J. Examining the exclusion of employees with Asperger syndrome from the workplace. *Pers. Rev.* **2012**, *41*, 630–646. [CrossRef]

8. Roux, A.M.; Shattuck, P.T.; Cooper, B.P.; Anderson, K.A.; Wagner, M.; Narendorf, S.C. Postsecondary employment experiences among young adults with an Autism Spectrum Disorder RH: Employment in young adults with autism. *J. Am. Acad. Child Adolesc. Psychiatry* **2013**, *52*, 931–939. [CrossRef]
9. Scott, M.; Falkmer, M.; Girdler, S.; Falkmer, T. Viewpoints on factors for successful employment for adults with autism spectrum disorder. *PLoS ONE* **2015**, *10*, e0139281.
10. Shattuck, P.T.; Narendorf, S.C.; Cooper, B.; Sterzing, P.R.; Wagner, M.; Taylor, J.L. Postsecondary education and employment among youth with an autism spectrum disorder. *Pediatrics* **2012**, *129*, 1042–1049. [CrossRef]
11. Hagner, D.; Cooney, B.F. "I do that for everybody": Supervising employees with autism. *Focus Autism Other Dev. Disabil.* **2005**, *20*, 91–97. [CrossRef]
12. Hendricks, D. Employment and adults with autism spectrum disorders: Challenges and strategies for success. *J. Vocat. Rehabil.* **2010**, *32*, 125–134. [CrossRef]
13. de Schipper, E.; Mahdi, S.; de Vries, P.; Granlund, M.; Holmann, M.; Karande, S.; Almodayfer, O.; Shulman, C.; Tonge, B.; Wong, V.; et al. Functioning and disability in Autism Spectrum Disorder: A worldwide survey of experts. *Autism Res.* **2016**, *9*, 959–969. [CrossRef] [PubMed]
14. Hillier, A.; Campbell, H.; Mastriani, K.; Izzo, M.V.; Kool-Tucker, A.K.; Cherry, L.; Beversdorf, D.Q. Two-Year Evaluation of a Vocational Support Program for Adults on the Autism Spectrum. *Career Dev. Except. Individ.* **2007**, *30*, 35–47. [CrossRef]
15. Howlin, P.; Alcock, J.; Burkin, C. An 8 year follow-up of a specialist supported employment service for high-ability adults with autism or Asperger syndrome. *Autism* **2005**, *9*, 533–549. [CrossRef] [PubMed]
16. Boushey, H.; Glynn, S.J. There are significant business costs to replacing employees. *Cent. Am. Prog.* **2012**, *16*, 1–9.
17. Buescher, A.V.; Cidav, Z.; Knapp, M.; Mandell, D.S. Costs of autism spectrum disorders in the United Kingdom and the United States. *JAMA Pediatr.* **2014**, *168*, 721–728. [CrossRef]
18. Kemper, A.; Stolarick, K.; Milway, J.B.; Treviranus, J. *Releasing Constraints: Projecting the Economic Impacts of Increased Accessibility in Ontario*; Martin Prosperity Institute: Toronto, ON, Canada, 2009.
19. Knapp, M.; Romeo, R.; Beecham, J. Economic cost of autism in the UK. *Autism* **2009**, *13*, 317–336. [CrossRef]
20. Lee, E.A.; Black, M.H.; Tan, T.; Falkmer, T.; Girdler, S. "I'm destined to ace this": Work experience placement during high school for individuals with autism spectrum disorder. *J. Autism Dev. Disord.* **2019**, *49*, 3089–3101. [CrossRef]
21. Cidav, Z.; Marcus, S.C.; Mandell, D.S. Implications of childhood autism for parental employment and earnings. *Pediatrics* **2012**, *129*, 617–623. [CrossRef]
22. Gewurtz, R.E.; Langan, S.; Shand, D. Hiring people with disabilities: A scoping review. *Work* **2016**, *54*, 135–148. [CrossRef]
23. Chen, J.L.; Leader, G.; Sung, C.; Leahy, M. Trends in Employment for Individuals with Autism Spectrum Disorder: A Review of the Research Literature. *Rev. J. Autism Dev. Disord.* **2015**, *2*, 115–127. [CrossRef]
24. Hernandez, B.; Keys, C.; Balcazar, F. Employer attitudes toward workers with disabilities and their ADA employment rights: A literature review. *J. Rehabil.* **2000**, *66*, 4–16.
25. López, B.; Keenan, L. Barriers to employment in autism: Future challenges to implementing the Adult Autism Strategy. In *Autism Research Network*; University of Portsmouth: Portsmouth, UK, 2014.
26. Bruyere, S.M. *Disability Employment Policies and Practices in Private and Federal Sector Organizations*; Cornell University: Ithaca, NY, USA, 2000.
27. Lindsay, S.; Cagliostro, E.; Leck, J.; Shen, W.; Stinson, J. Employers' perspectives of including young people with disabilities in the workforce, disability disclosure and providing accommodations. *J. Vocat. Rehabil.* **2019**, *50*, 141–156. [CrossRef]
28. Kaye, H.S.; Jans, L.H.; Jones, E.C. Why don't employers hire and retain workers with disabilities? *J. Occup. Rehabil.* **2011**, *21*, 526–536. [CrossRef] [PubMed]
29. Loprest, P.; Maag, E. Issues in Job Search and Work, Accommodation. *Res. Soc. Sci. Disabil.* **2003**, *3*, 87–108.
30. Morgan, R.L.; Alexander, M. The employer's perception: Employment of individuals with developmental disabilities. *J. Vocat. Rehabil.* **2005**, *23*, 39–49.
31. Peck, B.; Kirkbride, L.T. Why businesses don't employ people with disabilities. *J. Vocat. Rehabil.* **2001**, *16*, 71–75.
32. Nesbitt, S. Why and why not? Factors influencing employment for individuals with Asperger syndrome. *Autism* **2000**, *4*, 357–369. [CrossRef]

33. Unger, D.D. Employers' attitudes toward persons with disabilities in the workforce: Myths or realities? *Focus Autism Other Dev. Disabil.* **2002**, *17*, 2–10. [CrossRef]
34. Scott, M.; Jacob, A.; Hendrie, D.; Parsons, R.; Girdler, S.; Falkmer, T. Employers' perception of the costs and the benefits of hiring individuals with autism spectrum disorder in open employment in Australia. *PLoS ONE* **2017**, *12*, e0177607. [CrossRef]
35. Dreaver, J.; Thompson, C.; Girdler, S.; Adolfsson, M.; Black, M.H.; Falkmer, M. Success Factors Enabling Employment for Adults on the Autism Spectrum from Employers' Perspective. *J. Autism Dev. Disord.* **2019**, *50*, 1657–1667. [CrossRef] [PubMed]
36. Austin, R.D.; Pisano, G.P. Neurodiversity as a competitive advantage. *Harv. Bus. Rev.* **2017**, *95*, 96–103.
37. Demer, L. The Autism Spectrum: Human Rights Perspectives. *Pediatrics* **2018**, *141*, 369–374. [CrossRef]
38. Hensel, W.F. People with Autism spectrum disorder in the workplace: An expanding legal frontier. *Harv. Civ.-Rights-Civ. Lib. Law Rev.* **2017**, *52*, 74–103.
39. Vogus, T.J.; Lounds-Taylor, J. Flipping the script: Bringing an organizational perspective to the study of autism at work. *Autism* **2018**, *22*, 514–516. [CrossRef] [PubMed]
40. Hara, K.; Bigham, J.P. Introducing people with ASD to crowd work. In Proceedings of the 19th International ACM SIGACCESS Conference on Computers and Accessibility, Baltimore, MD, USA, 29 October–1 November 2017; pp. 42–51.
41. Gerhardt, P.F.; Lainer, I. Addressing the needs of adolescents and adults with autism: A crisis on the horizon. *J. Contemp. Psychother.* **2011**, *41*, 37–45. [CrossRef]
42. Fraser, R.; Ajzen, I.; Johnson, K.; Hebert, J.; Chan, F. Understanding employers' hiring intention in relation to qualified workers with disabilities. *J. Vocat. Rehabil.* **2011**, *35*, 1–11. [CrossRef]
43. Bricout, J.C.; Bentley, K.J. Disability status and perceptions of employability by employers. *Soc. Work. Res.* **2000**, *24*, 87–95. [CrossRef]
44. Chan, F.; Strauser, D.; Maher, P.; Lee, E.J.; Jones, R.; Johnson, E.T. Demand-side factors related to employment of people with disabilities: A survey of employers in the Midwest region of the United States. *J. Occup. Rehabil.* **2010**, *20*, 412–419. [CrossRef]
45. Hand, C.; Tryssenaar, J. Small business employers' views on hiring individuals with mental illness. *Psychiatr. Rehabil. J.* **2006**, *29*, 166. [CrossRef]
46. Hazer, J.T.; Bedell, K.V. Effects of seeking accommodation and disability on preemployment evaluations. *J. Appl. Soc. Psychol.* **2000**, *30*, 1201–1223. [CrossRef]
47. Jasper, C.R.; Waldhart, P. Employer attitudes on hiring employees with disabilities in the leisure and hospitality industry. *Int. J. Contemp. Hosp. Manag.* **2013**, *25*, 577–594. [CrossRef]
48. Wiggett-Barnard, C.; Swartz, L. What facilitates the entry of persons with disabilities into South African companies? *Disabil. Rehabil.* **2012**, *34*, 1016–1023. [CrossRef]
49. Culler, K.H.; Wang, Y.C.; Byers, K.; Trierweiler, R. Barriers and facilitators of return to work for individuals with strokes: perspectives of the stroke survivor, vocational specialist, and employer. *Top. Stroke Rehabil.* **2011**, *18*, 325–340. [CrossRef]
50. Graffam, J.; Shinkfield, A.; Smith, K.; Polzin, U. Factors that influence employer decisions in hiring and retaining an employee with a disability. *J. Vocat. Rehabil.* **2002**, *17*, 175–181.
51. Alvares, G.A.; Bebbington, K.; Cleary, D.; Evans, K.; Glasson, E.J.; Maybery, M.T.; Pillar, S.; Uljarevic, M.; Varcin, K.; Wray, J.; Whitehouse, A.J. The misnomer of 'high functioning autism': Intelligence is an imprecise predictor of functional abilities at diagnosis. *Autism* **2020**, *24*, 221–232. [CrossRef]
52. American Psychiatric Association. *Diagnostic and Statistical Manual of Mental Disorders*, 5th ed.; American Psychiatric Publishing: Washington, DC, USA, 2013.
53. Erickson, W.A.; von Schrader, S.; Bruyère, S.M.; VanLooy, S.A. The employment environment: Employer perspectives, policies, and practices regarding the employment of persons with disabilities. *Rehabil. Couns. Bull.* **2014**, *57*, 195–208. [CrossRef]
54. Newman, L.; Wagner, M.; Knokey, A.M.; Marder, C.; Nagle, K.; Shaver, D.; Wei, X. *The Post-High School Outcomes of Young Adults with Disabilities up to 8 Years after High School: A Report from the National Longitudinal Transition Study-2 (NLTS2). NCSER 2011–3005*; National Center for Special Education Research: Washington, DC, USA, 2011.
55. Dillman, D.A.; Smyth, J.D.; Christian, L.M. *Internet, Phone, Mail, and Mixed-Mode Surveys: The Tailored Design Method*; John Wiley & Sons: Hoboken, NJ, USA, 2014.

56. MacQueen, J. Some methods for classification and analysis of multivariate observations. In Proceedings of the Fifth Berkeley Symposium on Mathematical Statistics and Probability, Berkeley, CA, USA, 21 June–18 July 1965; University of California: Oakland, CA, USA, 1967; Volume 1, pp. 281–297.
57. Tibshirani, R.; Walther, G.; Hastie, T. Estimating the number of clusters in a data set via the gap statistic. *J. R. Stat. Soc. Ser. (Stat. Methodol.)* **2001**, *63*, 411–423. [CrossRef]
58. Rousseeuw, P.J. Silhouettes: A graphical aid to the interpretation and validation of cluster analysis. *J. Comput. Appl. Math.* **1987**, *20*, 53–65. [CrossRef]
59. Hyde, K.; Griffiths, A.J.; Giannantonio, C.; Hurley-Hanson, A.; Linstead, E. Predicting employer recruitment of individuals with autism spectrum disorders with decision trees. In Proceedings of the 2018 17th IEEE International Conference on Machine Learning and Applications (ICMLA), Orlando, FL, USA, 17–20 December 2018; pp. 1366–1370.
60. Wehman, P.; Schall, C.; McDonough, J.; Molinelli, A.; Riehle, E.; Ham, W.; Thiss, W.R. Project SEARCH for youth with autism spectrum disorders: Increasing competitive employment on transition from high school. *J. Posit. Behav. Interv.* **2013**, *15*, 144–155. [CrossRef]
61. Taube, A. *Two MIT Grads Founded A Startup That Almost Exclusively Employs People On The Autism Spectrum*; Organization for Autism Research: Arlington County, VA, USA, 2014.

6

Grammatical Comprehension in Italian Children with Autism Spectrum Disorder

Jessica Barsotti [1], Gloria Mangani [1], Roberta Nencioli [1], Lucia Pfanner [1], Raffaella Tancredi [1], Angela Cosenza [1], Gianluca Sesso [1], Antonio Narzisi [1], Filippo Muratori [1,2,*], Paola Cipriani [1] and Anna Maria Chilosi [1]

1 IRCCS Stella Maris Foundation, Calambrone, 56018 Pisa, Italy; jessica.barsotti@fsm.unipi.it (J.B.); gloria.man96@hotmail.it (G.M.); roberta.nencioli@fsm.unipi.it (R.N.); lucia.pfanner@fsm.unipi.it (L.P.); raffaella.tancredi@fsm.unipi.it (R.T.); angela.cosenza@fsm.unipi.it (A.C.); gianluca.sesso@fsm.unipi.it (G.S.); antonio.narzisi@fsm.unipi.it (A.N.); paola.cipriani@fsm.unipi.it (P.C.); anna.chilosi@fsm.unipi.it (A.M.C.)

2 Department of Clinical and Experimental Medicine, University of Pisa, Via Savi, 10, 56126 Pisa, Italy

* Correspondence: filippo.muratori@fsm.unipi.it

Abstract: Language deficits represent one of the most relevant factors that determine the clinical phenotype of children with autism spectrum disorder (ASD). The main aim of the research was to study the grammatical comprehension of children with ASD. A sample of 70 well-diagnosed children (60 boys and 10 girls; aged 4.9–8 years) were prospectively recruited. The results showed that language comprehension is the most impaired language domain in ASD. These findings have important clinical implications, since the persistence of grammatical receptive deficits may have a negative impact on social, adaptive and learning achievements. As for the grammatical profiles, persistent difficulties were found during the school-age years in morphological and syntactic decoding in children with relatively preserved cognitive and expressive language skills. These data and the lack of a statistically significant correlation between the severity of ASD symptoms and language skills are in line with the DSM-5 (Diagnostic and Statistical Manual of Mental Disorders, Fifth Edition) perspective that considers the socio-communication disorder as a nuclear feature of ASD and the language disorder as a specifier of the diagnosis and not as a secondary symptom anymore. The presence of receptive difficulties in school-age ASD children with relatively preserved non-verbal cognitive abilities provides important hints to establish rehabilitative treatments.

Keywords: autism spectrum disorder; language profiles; grammatical comprehension

1. Introduction

Children with autism spectrum disorder (ASD) show heterogeneous functional profiles and outcomes [1,2]. Language deficits represent one of the most relevant factors that determine the clinical phenotype of children with ASD. Language deficits in ASD children can be described as a continuum, as on one hand there are non-verbal or minimally verbal children or those who do not acquire verbal language (in variable percentages up to 50% according to different studies) [3–8], and on the other hand there are children with formally appropriate but pragmatically inadequate language [9,10]. Within this continuum, highly variable language profiles can be found, with children exhibiting language delay, children with language disorders, and those who, despite reaching their first language milestones (i.e., speaking their first words between 12 and 18 months), later experience an arrest or a regression in language development.

Though communication and language in children with ASD have been extensively investigated [4,9–13], the nature of the language deficit still remains an open issue. According to the DSM-5 [14], social communication disorder is considered a nuclear feature of ASD, while language disorder is only defined as a "specifier" of the condition. Some authors consider language disorders and ASD as potentially comorbid conditions [10,15] and use the term ASD-LI to refer to individuals with ASD who have impairments in structural language, regardless of their overall cognitive functioning.

The majority of published studies report that, in ASD, receptive language is more impaired than expressive language [5,11,16–21], but this finding has not been completely confirmed [22,23]. Moreover, the issue of the discrepancy between receptive and expressive competences is still unclear in terms of whether it should be considered as a possible marker of ASD, or whether both receptive and expressive language difficulties are comorbid to ASD.

Receptive language disorders in children with ASD are part of a wide and more complex phenotype characterized by pragmatic and neuropsychological deficits that may impair the acquisition of verbal comprehension. According to Tager-Flusberg and colleagues [24], the ASD's problems of language comprehension are especially present in everyday situations, rather than during single-word comprehension testing. Children with ASD exhibit impairments in the ability to decode relevant contextual cues and deficits in social attention [25–28], whereas typically developing (TD) children are able from an early age to identify and select salient sensory stimuli and crucial social cues that are relevant both for comprehension and communication [29,30].

Grammatical comprehension, as a specific language skill that is required for decoding verbal messages in interactions, would represent a crucial matter of research in the field of ASD. However, it is worth noticing that relatively few studies are available which assess the comprehension of someone with ASD by means of specific tasks that differentially evaluate their lexical and grammatical skills. The evaluation of receptive abilities in children with ASD is of crucial importance in the clinical context in order to more clearly define the language profile, which has always been considered a paramount prognostic marker of development. Indeed, minimally verbal children with ASD exhibit a greater severity of autistic symptoms and globally worse clinical outcomes [31] than those with normal or mildly delayed language development, for whom an outcome could be more satisfactory [32]. Considering the above mentioned prognostic significance of language skills on the developmental perspective of children with ASD, the aims of the present study were:

1. To assess grammatical receptive skills in relation to other language abilities;
2. To investigate the relative contributions of non-verbal cognitive abilities and the severity of autistic symptoms on the language profile of children with ASD;
3. To examine the qualitative and quantitative differences in grammatical comprehension between ASD and TD children.

2. Materials and Methods

2.1. Sample

The present study was conducted on a sample of 70 children (60 boys) aged 4.9–8 years (mean age: 6.3 years; SD: 11 months; age range: 4.9–8 years) prospectively recruited at IRCCS Stella Maris Foundation (Calambrone, Pisa, Italy) from February 2009 to May 2018.

Inclusion criteria were as follows:

- A diagnosis of either autistic disorder according to DSM-IV-TR criteria or autism spectrum disorder according to DSM-5 criteria;
- Average or borderline non-verbal intellectual or developmental functioning level assessed through standardized psychometric tests;
- Expressive language at the level of multiword productions.

In order to qualitatively analyze grammatical comprehension, a subsample of 54 children with ASD and performance IQ ≥ 85 was selected and compared to 54 age- and sex-matched typically developing (TD) children. TD children were recruited from kindergarten and elementary schools in the area of Pisa, excluding subjects exposed to bilingualism.

Both groups were subdivided into four age groups at 12 months intervals, from 4.10 to 8 years. Informed written consent was obtained from the parents of all participants. This study was approved by the Pediatric Ethical Committee of the Tuscany Region (approval number: 178/2016) and was conducted according to the Helsinki Declaration.

2.2. Tests and Procedures

Grammatical comprehension was assessed using the Grammatical Comprehension Test for Children (Test Comprensione Grammaticale per Bambini; TCGB) [33] standardized on Italian children aged 3.6–8 years. The TCGB is a picture multiple-choice language test composed of 76 sentences pertaining to eight main blocks of grammatical structures: locatives, inflectionals, both affirmative and negative actives and passives, relatives and datives. Within each block of structures, the clauses differ not only in grammatical complexity, but also in semantic complexity (i.e., irreversible vs. reversible and probable vs. improbable clauses).

Children with ASD also underwent a comprehensive assessment of language skills by means of a receptive vocabulary test (PPVT-R: Peabody Picture Vocabulary Test—Revised) [34], an expressive picture naming test (One-Word Picture Vocabulary Test) [35] and the analysis of spontaneous language performed according to a six level rating system (Grid of Analysis of Spontaneous speech—GASS) [36,37]. For a detailed description of the TCGB and GASS, see Tables S1 and S2 in the Supplementary Materials. For all language tests, *z*-scores below—1.5 SD of the mean were considered as deficient.

Wechsler Preschool and Primary Scale of Intelligence, 3rd Ed (WPPSI-III, [38]) performance IQ, the Perceptual Reasoning Index at WISC-IV [39] or Griffiths [40] developmental quotient of the performance scale were used as measures of the non-verbal intellectual functioning level.

Finally, the Autism Diagnostic Observation Schedule-Generic (ADOS-G) [41] and Autism Diagnostic Observation Schedule-Second Edition (ADOS-2) [42] semi-structured observations were performed in ASD children for the evaluation of the autistic symptomatology severity.

2.3. Statistical Analysis

Skewness and Kurtosis statistics did not demonstrate a normal distribution for language-related variables, thus non-parametric tests were utilized. On the whole sample of 70 children with ASD, Spearman's rank correlation coefficients between the grammatical comprehension non-verbal cognitive scores and ADOS severity scores were calculated. The Mann–Whitney U test was used to compare: (1) the non-verbal cognitive scores between children who performed averagely in the TCGB and children whose performances were classed as deficient; (2) the TCGB scores between the 54 ASD and the 54 TD children. The Kruskal–Wallis test for independent samples was also used to assess significant differences between the four age groups (5, 6, 7 and 8-year-old groups) of 54 children with ASD and 54 TD controls. Statistical analyses were performed using SPSS 21 software (IBM SPSS Statistics, Chicago, IL, USA).

3. Results

3.1. Language Profiles

Considering the mean z scores of the whole sample (see Table 1), grammatical comprehension appeared the most impaired domain compared to the other language measures. The TGCB mean total z score and the mean z score of the different structures (with the exception of active negative sentences) fell below −1.5 SD of the mean. Sixty-three percent of children with ASD had impaired grammatical comprehension. As for the vocabulary measures, the mean receptive lexical quotient at the PPVT was in the borderline range, with 56% of children showing an impaired performance. The expressive vocabulary scores were in the average range both for high and low frequency words (only 18% of children exhibited an impaired performance). According to the GASS, expressive language was at level 4, which corresponds to a deficient control of complex grammar, and only 14% of children had a more severe deficit.

Table 1. Sample characteristics ($n = 70$).

Children's Language, Cognitive and ADS Profiles	Mean	SD	Mean z Score
Age	76.43	11.80	-
Grammatical Comprehension (TCGB)	20.33	11.27	−3.25
Locative	2.55	2.14	−1.66
Inflectional	3.29	2.47	−2.55
Affirmative Active	1.99	1.98	−2.59
Negative Active	1.90	1.68	−0.86
Affirmative Passive	3.31	2.29	−2.58
Negative Passive	2.74	1.79	−2.61
Relative	2.59	1.85	−2.97
Dative	1.96	1.33	−4.73
Receptive Vocabulary (QL PPVT-R)	80.72	11.12	−1.22
Grammatical production level (GASS)	4.18	0.62	-
Expressive Vocabulary for high-frequency words (Brizzolara)	13.58	5.27	−0.38
Expressive Vocabulary for low-frequency words (Brizzolara)	32.32	6.09	−0.77
NVIQ	100.62	14.66	-
ADOS Comparison Score	5.30	1.42	-

Abbreviations: SD: standard deviation; NVIQ: non-verbal intelligence quotient.

3.2. *Correlations between Language Measures, Non-Verbal Cognitive Skills and Autistic Symptoms Severity*

Statistically significant correlations were found between the non-verbal IQ and total TCGB scores ($p = 0.020$). Non-verbal IQ was also correlated with active negative and passive negative clauses ($p = 0.000$ and $p = 0.023$, respectively). However, it is worth noting that non-verbal cognitive abilities did not differ significantly between ASD children with average and impaired comprehensions ($p = 0.073$).

The severity of the autistic symptoms assessed through the ADOS was low/moderate and did not correlate significantly with any expressive and receptive language measure.

3.3. *Grammatical Comprehension Profiles of ASD and TD Children*

The subsample of 54 children with ASD with a non-verbal IQ ≥ 85, was subdivided into four age groups (i.e., 5, 6, 7 and 8-year-old groups). These subgroups did not differ significantly in terms of non-verbal cognitive abilities ($p = 0.296$) or the severity of autistic symptoms ($p = 0.212$).

As displayed in Table 2 and Figure 1, the comparison between ASD and TD children showed that ASD children had significantly lower scores than TD children for most types of grammatical clauses at different ages. As expected, performances of both ASD and TD children changed with age; however, the ASD children's performances changed at a significantly slower rate compared to the TD children. In the 5-year-old subgroup, statistically significant differences emerged for affirmative active, negative passive and dative clauses, whereas, in the 6- and 7-year-old subgroup, ASD children scored significantly lower than TD children in all types of clauses (with the exception of negative active clauses). The 8-year-old subgroup showed a significant reduction in their error scores, compared to 5- and 6-year-old children ($p = 0.030$ and $p = 0.010$, respectively). Nonetheless, significant differences between ASD and TD children were still evident for locative, affirmative passive, relative and dative clauses. Considering the semantic and grammatical complexity of the different clause types (for details see Table 3), markedly significant differences between ASD and TD children were observed for the more complex but not for the simpler sentences (i.e., verbal vs. nominal inflexions, projective vs. topological locatives, semantically improbable vs. probable and neutral active affirmative clauses, reversible vs. irreversible clauses) [33]. The comparison between the reversible and irreversible clauses total scores showed a highly significant difference between TD and ASD children in the comprehension of reversible clauses ($p = 0.000$), but not in irreversible clauses ($p = 0.834$).

Table 2. Comparison between typically developing (TD) and autism spectrum disorder (ASD) children in the different age ranges.

Grammatical Comprehension	5 Years			6 Years			7 Years			8 Years		
	TD ($n = 21$)	ASD ($n = 21$)	p	TD ($n = 14$)	ASD ($n = 14$)	p	TD ($n = 12$)	ASD ($n = 12$)	p	TD ($n = 7$)	ASD ($n = 7$)	p
TCGB Total score	14.00 (6.51)	21.38 (8.95)	0.004	6.86 (2.64)	20.68 (3.27)	0.000	2.79 (1.12)	14.00 (7.48)	0.000	2.21 (2.02)	9.14 (4.92)	0.005
Locative	1.79 (1.52)	2.38 (1.84)	ns	1.00 (0.70)	2.11 (1.36)	0.012	0.38 (0.57)	2.17 (1.70)	0.002	0.14 (0.24)	1.14 (0.85)	0.011
Inflectional	3.21 (2.22)	3.60 (2.40)	ns	1.04 (1.15)	2.33 (0.62)	0.002	0.29 (0.33)	2.42 (1.04)	0.000	0.29 (0.39)	0.57 (0.45)	ns
Affirmative Active	0.88 (0.74)	2.29 (1.55)	0.001	0.61 (0.56)	1.61 (1.66)	0.043	0.25 (0.50)	1.08 (1.28)	0.047	0.21 (0.57)	0.64 (0.80)	ns
Negative Active	1.71 (1.27)	2.07 (1.54)	ns	1.25 (1.03)	1.64 (1.26)	ns	0.46 (0.58)	1.00 (1.19)	ns	0.50 (0.58)	0.79 (0.99)	ns
Affirmative Pass.	2.45 (2.64)	3.19 (2.11)	ns	1.07 (1.47)	3.71 (2.55)	0.003	0.38 (0.38)	3.00 (2.13)	0.000	0.29 (0.57)	2.00 (1.68)	0.025
Negative Passive	1.64 (1.43)	2.71 (1.51)	0.023	0.71 (0.80)	3.07 (1.20)	0.000	0.42 (0.51)	1.79 (1.47)	0.006	0.43 (0.53)	1.21 (1.55)	ns
Relative	1.74 (1.34)	2.74 (1.86)	ns	0.93 (0.92)	3.11 (1.91)	0.001	0.50 (0.56)	1.50 (1.46)	0.038	0.29 (0.39)	1.71 (0.81)	0.001
Dative	0.57 (0.81)	2.38 (1.22)	0.000	0.25 (0.38)	2.04 (1.42)	0.000	0.13 (0.31)	0.92 (0.63)	0.001	0.07 (0.19)	1.07 (0.67)	0.003

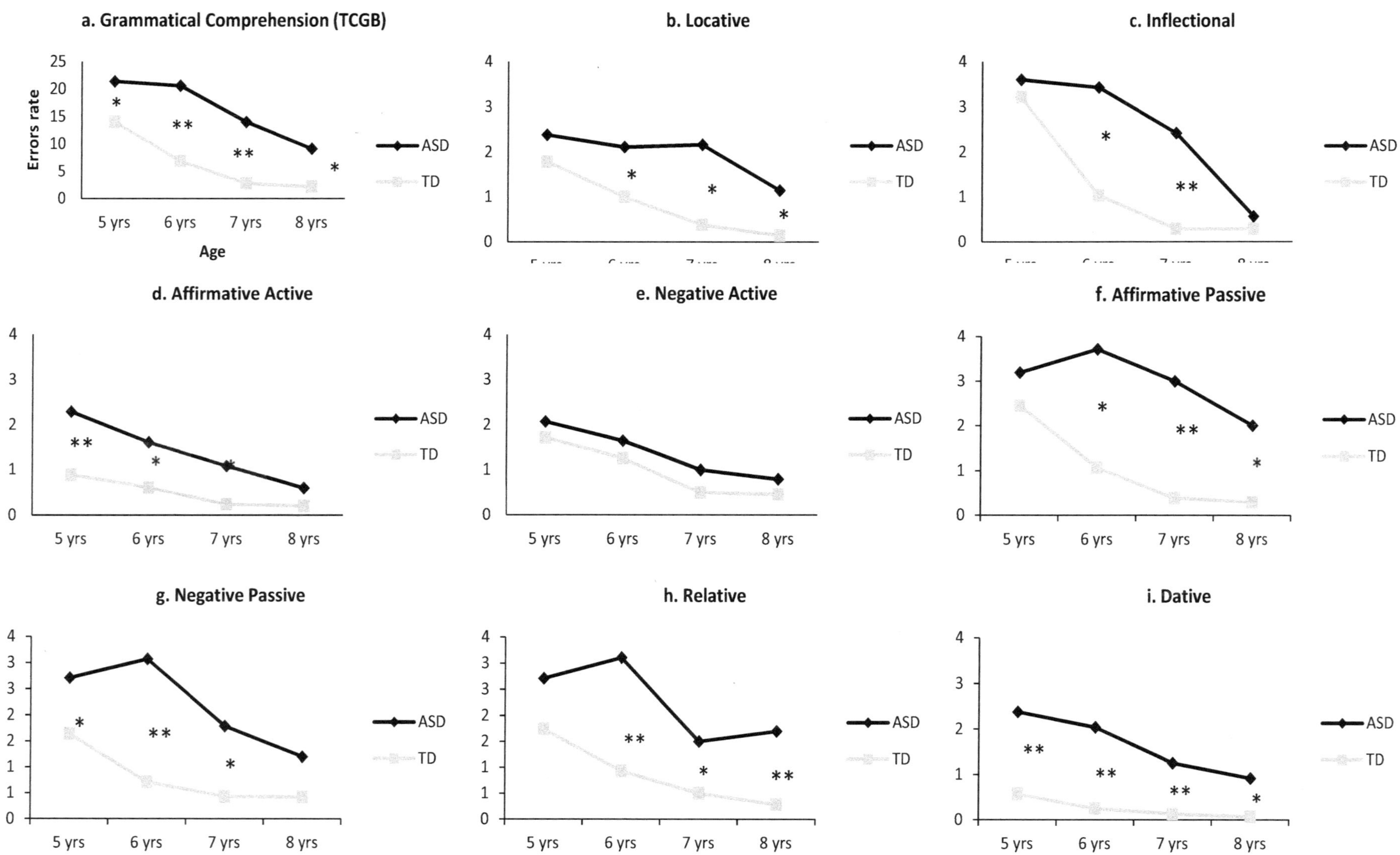

Figure 1. ASD and TD children's total (**a**) and single clause type (**b–i**) error scores (* $p \leq 0.05$; ** $p \leq 0.001$). Abbreviation: yrs: years.

Table 3. Comparison between ASD and TD children: qualitative assessment of the clause type related subcategories.

Structure	Sub-Categories	TD (n = 54)	ASD (n = 54)	Mann–Whitney Test
Locative	topological	0.12 (0.34)	0.42 (0.88)	0.021
	projective	0.94 (1.07)	1.57 (1.31)	0.009
Inflectional	nominal	0.07 (0.20)	0.16 (0.50)	ns
	verbal	0.84 (1.14)	1.80 (1.46)	0.000
	possessive	0.70 (1.16)	0.89 (0.92)	0.027
Affirmative Active	SV (reflexive)	0.08 (0.30)	0.41 (0.46)	0.000
	reversible probable	0.11 (0.21)	0.05 (0.18)	0.048
	reversible neutral	0.13 (0.28)	0.28 (0.50)	ns
	reversible improbable	0.07 (0.26)	0.54 (0.66)	0.000
	reversible with subject object inanimate-animate	0.19 (0.37)	0.30 (0.65)	ns
Negative Active	SV	0.01 (0.07)	0.13 (0.48)	0.041
	SVO irreversible	0.50 (0.67)	0.43 (0.65)	ns
	SVO reversible	0.65 (0.84)	1.00 (0.92)	0.023
Affirmative Passive	irreversible	0.53 (1.08)	0.40 (0.53)	ns
	reversible probable	0.22 (0.49)	0.94 (1.06)	0.000
	reversible improbable	0.35 (0.55)	0.95 (0.84)	0.000
	reversible neutral	0.25 (0.59)	0.78 (1.02)	0.000
Negative Passive	SV	0.10 (0.36)	0.77 (0.72)	0.000
	SVA irreversible	0.34 (0.53)	0.55 (0.68)	ns
	SVA reversible	0.53 (0.88)	1.05 (0.96)	0.002
Relative	embedded	0.61 (0.70)	1.44 (1.09)	0.000
	right branching	0.45 (0.75)	0.92 (1.12)	0.022
Dative	AAA	0.26 (0.56)	0.92 (0.85)	0.000
	AIA	0.07 (0.24)	0.86 (0.88)	0.000

Abbreviations: SV: subject verb; SVO: subject verb object; SVA: subject verb agent; AAA: animate animate animate; AIA: animate inanimate animate.

4. Discussion

The present research is the first Italian study aimed at assessing grammatical comprehension in children with ASD. Our results support the hypothesis proposed by some authors [9,11,17,20,43] that language comprehension would be the most impaired language domain in autism, in spite of its highly heterogeneous linguistic phenotype [1]. Around two thirds of our patients exhibited an impaired grammatical comprehension, whereas grammatical production was impaired in only 14% of children. Additionally, in the lexical domain, receptive skills were more impaired than expressive ones. However, the deficit of language comprehension was not homogeneous, since receptive grammar was more impaired than receptive vocabulary. The above language profile differs from the one usually observed in children with a primary developmental language disorder, which is generally characterized by better receptive abilities as opposed to expressive language abilities [16,44–46]. The discrepancy between receptive and expressive skills in children with ASD is, however, still a debated issue, because it is not clear whether it could be considered a specific marker of ASD.

As for the relationship between language and non-verbal cognitive abilities, a positive correlation between non-verbal intellectual functioning and grammatical comprehension was found, but non-verbal cognitive abilities did not differ statistically between children with a normal comprehension and those with an impaired comprehension. These apparently conflicting findings suggest that the grammar comprehension deficit is quite specific in children with ASD, and, thus, is relatively independent from non-verbal cognitive skills. This evidence is in line with the results of a study conducted on a sample of ASD children with average or borderline intellectual functioning [43] in which non-verbal IQ explained a limited amount of the variance of language scores.

The lack of statistically significant correlations between the severity of ASD symptoms and language skills seems to confirm the DSM-5's choice to let language deficits outside the nuclear symptoms of autism. In this way, the DSM-5 avoids the risk of automatically establishing an overlap between communication and structural language skills.

4.1. Grammatical Comprehension Profiles in Children with ASD and TD

To date, the qualitative assessment of grammatical decoding strategies in children with ASD has generally been carried out on English-speaking subjects [47–49], with few reports in the recent literature [50]. In the present Italian study, the qualitative assessment of language comprehension showed significant differences between TD and ASD children. The latter showed both delayed and atypical receptive grammatical skills.

Data on the development of grammatical comprehension in TD children show a significant change between 5 and 6 years of age, a period characterized by an increasing integration of the different decoding strategies, and by a sharp reduction in the inter-individual variability. By 7 or 8 years old, TD children show a further increase in their capacity to generalize the use of linguistic principles and rules for decoding more complex grammatical structures [33]. In children with ASD, improvements in grammatical comprehension occurred around 7 or 8 years of age, but their receptive skills remained significantly impaired in comparison to TD children. This result has important clinical implications, since the persistence of grammatical receptive deficits may have a negative impact on social, adaptive and learning achievements during the school-age years [43,51,52].

As for the grammatical profiles, persistent difficulties were found in morphological (i.e., inflectional clauses) and syntactic decoding (i.e., locative, passive, relative and dative clauses). Similar to what was observed in TD children, the comprehension of active negative sentences was more difficult than the comprehension of active affirmative sentences. This might be due to the poor representability of negative actions and to the fact that decoding of such structures requires inferential reasoning (e.g., the correct answer for the sentence "the child does not eat the soup" is represented by a picture in which the child is eating an ice-cream).

Relative, passive and dative clauses were more difficult for children with ASD than for TD children. In the case of relative clauses, the persistence of difficulties up to 8 years of age probably depends on their length and structural complexity. For passive and dative clauses, the crucial factor may be the reversibility of actions. The significant difficulty in decoding reversible, but not irreversible sentences, which characterizes the profiles of children with ASD, is an important result because it suggests the presence of a specific linguistic deficit. In fact, in reversible sentences the roles of the agent or patient of the action are interchangeable, as they are both animate referents (e.g., "the girl pushes the boy" or vice versa). Therefore, decoding these sentences is crucially based on the word order, that is, on syntactic strategies. Conversely, in irreversible sentences, the agent and patient roles are not interchangeable, because of semantic restrictions linked to the animate/inanimate nature of referents (e.g., "the car is washed by the boy"). In this case, lexical factors can drive the sentence decoding. Difficulties in processing reversible sentences have also been described [47] in a study reporting that impairments in reversible sentence comprehension was greater than expected from the global level of receptive skills. We would suggest that ASD children with average or borderline intellectual functioning may be able to process lexical information, while showing difficulties to acquire an integrate system for decoding morpho-syntactic information.

4.2. Limitations

This study presents several limitations. A first limitation is that the non-verbal IQ tests we chose to administer require verbal comprehension skills to follow the instructions, which might have contributed to the positive correlation between the non-verbal IQ scores and the grammatical comprehension scores. Another limit is the typology of our structured picture-based comprehension test, which does not tap into ecologically natural and contextual-based comprehension abilities, thus not providing a comprehensive profile of ASD children's receptive skills.

Finally, although there was no a priori restriction on patient selection according to the severity of autistic symptomatology applied in the present study, the children with ASD showed a low to moderate severity of autistic symptomatology. This may be due to the fact that only patients who were able to complete the structured language evaluation were included, creating a bias in the selection of the sample. Patients on the autism spectrum exhibit quite heterogeneous clinical pictures, while the present study focuses on the language comprehension of intellectually unimpaired verbal children with a low/moderate severity of autistic symptoms. Hence, our results may not be generalizable to the whole population of patients with ASD.

5. Conclusions

Our results are in line with the DSM-5 perspective according which emphasizes that the socio-communication disorder is a nuclear feature of ASD, whereas the language disorder should be considered as a specifier of the diagnosis, not a nuclear deficit or a secondary symptom. Among the language abilities we have described, a specific receptive grammatical deficit was found, whilst cognitive and expressive language are relatively preserved. It would be important in the future to evaluate the relationship between language comprehension and some neuropsychological abilities, such as working memory and executive functions to shed some light on the nature of the comprehension deficits in children with ASD.

The presence of receptive difficulties in school-age ASD children with relatively preserved non-verbal cognitive abilities provides important hints about treatment. Receptive language difficulties, when not associated with expressive deficits, may go unnoticed [43] and may be neglected despite their relevance in everyday life functioning, communication and social interaction. Early support to aid in the acquisition of adequate receptive language skills is crucial for further development. Moreover, as grammatical comprehension difficulties tend to persist in ASD children up to school-age (when generally speech therapy gradually diminishes), a specific intervention on both oral and written receptive skills is mandatory.

Author Contributions: Conceptualization, J.B., R.N., L.P., R.T., A.N., F.M. and A.M.C.; Data curation, J.B., G.M., R.N., L.P., R.T., A.C. and A.N.; Methodology, J.B., G.M. and A.M.C.; Supervision, A.N., F.M., P.C. and A.M.C.; Writing—original draft, J.B., G.M., R.N., L.P., G.S. and A.M.C.; Writing—review and editing, J.B., R.N., L.P., G.S., A.N., F.M., P.C. and A.M.C. All authors have read and agreed to the published version of the manuscript.

Acknowledgments: We would like to acknowledge the children and families who participated in this study, we also thank Linda Tieu for English editing.

References

1. Lombardo, M.V.; Pierce, K.; Eyler, L.; Carter Barnes, C.; Ahrebs-Barbeau, C.; Solso, S.; Campbell, K.; Courchesne, E. Different functional neural substrates for good and poor language outcome in autism. *Neuron* **2015**, *86*, 567–577. [CrossRef]
2. Lombardo, M.V.; Lai, M.; Baron-Cohen, S. Big data approaches to decomposing heterogeneity across the autism spectrum. *Mol. Psychiatry* **2019**, *24*, 1435–1450. [CrossRef]
3. Rapin, I. *Preschool Children with Inadequate Communication: Developmental Language Disorder, Autism, Low IQ*; Mac Keith: London, UK, 1996.
4. Wetherby, A.M.; Prizant, B.M.; Schuler, A.L. Understanding the nature of communication and language impairments. In *Autism Spectrum Disorders: A Transactional Developmental Perspective*; Wetherby, A., Prizant, B.M., Eds.; Paul H. Brookes Publishing: Baltimore, MD, USA, 2000; pp. 109–142.
5. Boucher, J. Research Review: Structural language in autistic spectrum disorder—characteristics and causes. *J. Child Psychol. Psychiatry* **2012**, *53*, 219–233. [CrossRef]
6. Anderson, D.K.; Lord, C.; Risi, S.; Di Lavore, P.S.; Shulman, C.; Thurm, A.; Welch, K.; Pickles, A. Patterns of growth in verbal abilities among children with autism spectrum disorder. *J. Consult. Clin. Psychol.* **2007**, *75*, 594–604. [CrossRef] [PubMed]
7. Gotham, K.; Pickles, A.; Lord, C. Trajectories of autism severity in children using standardized ADOS scores. *Pediatrics* **2012**, *130*, 1278–1284. [CrossRef] [PubMed]
8. Pickles, A.; Anderson, D.K.; Lord, C. Heterogeneity and plasticity in the development of language: A 17-year follow-up of children referred early for possible autism. *J. Child Psychol. Psychiatry* **2014**, *5*, 1354–1362. [CrossRef] [PubMed]
9. Tager-Flusberg, H.; Caronna, E. Language disorders: Autism and other pervasive developmental disorders. *Pediatr. Clin. N. Am.* **2007**, *54*, 469–481. [CrossRef] [PubMed]
10. Tager-Flusberg, H. Defining language impairments in a subgroup of children with autism spectrum disorder. *Sci. China Life Sci.* **2015**, *58*, 1044–1052. [CrossRef]
11. Mitchell, S.; Brian, J.; Zwaigenbaum, L.; Roberts, W.; Szatmari, P.; Smith, I.; Bryson, S. Early language and communication development of infants later diagnosed with autism spectrum disorder. *J. Dev. Behav. Pediatr.* **2006**, *27*, 69–78. [CrossRef]
12. Kjellmer, L.; Hedvall, A.; Fernell, E.; Gillberg, C.; Norrelgen, F. Language and communication skills in preschool children with autism spectrum disorders: Contribution of cognition, severity of autism symptoms, and adaptive functioning to the variability. *Res. Dev. Disabil.* **2012**, *33*, 172–180. [CrossRef]
13. Tager-Flusberg, H. On the nature of linguistic functioning in early infantile autism. *J. Autism Dev. Disord.* **1981**, *54*, 469–481. [CrossRef] [PubMed]
14. American Psychiatric Association (APA). *Diagnostic and Statistical Manual of Mental Disorders*, 5th ed.; American Psychiatry Association: Washington, DC, USA, 2013.
15. Williams, D.; Botting, N.; Boucher, J. Language in autism and specific language impairment: Where are the links? *Psychol. Bull.* **2008**, *134*, 944–963. [CrossRef] [PubMed]
16. Davidson, M.M.; Ellis Weismer, S. A discrepancy in comprehension and production in early language development in ASD: Is it clinically relevant? *J. Autism Dev. Disord.* **2017**, *47*, 2163–2175. [CrossRef] [PubMed]
17. Hudry, K.; Leadbitter, K.; Temple, K.; Slonims, V.; McConachie, H.; Aldre, C.; Howlin, P.; Charman, T. Preschoolers with autism show greater impairment in receptive compared with expressive language abilities. *Int. J. Lang. Commun. Disord.* **2010**, *45*, 681–690. [CrossRef]

18. Seol, K.I.; Song, S.H.; Kim, K.L.; Oh, S.T.; Kim, Y.T.; Im, W.Y.; Song, D.H.; Cheon, K.A. A comparison of receptive-expressive language profiles between toddlers with autism spectrum disorder and developmental language delay. *Yonsei Med. J.* **2014**, *55*, 1721–1728. [CrossRef]
19. Woynarosky, T.; Yoder, P.; Watson, L.R. Atypical cross-modal profiles and longitudinal associations between vocabulary scores in initially minimally verbal children with ASD. *Autism Res.* **2016**, *9*, 301–310. [CrossRef]
20. Charman, T.; Drew, A.; Baird, C.; Baird, G. Measuring early language development in preschool children with autism spectrum disorder using the MacArthur Communicative Development Inventory (Infant Form). *J. Child Lang.* **2003**, *30*, 213–236. [CrossRef]
21. Ellis Weismer, S.; Lord, C.; Esler, A. Early language patterns of toddlers on the autism spectrum compared to toddlers with developmental delay. *J. Autism Dev. Disord.* **2010**, *40*, 1259–1273. [CrossRef]
22. Kwok, E.Y.L.; Brown, H.M.; Smyth, R.E.; Cardy, J.O. Meta-analysis of receptive and expressive language skills in autism spectrum disorder. *Res. Autism Spectr. Disord.* **2015**, *9*, 202–222. [CrossRef]
23. Reinhartsen, D.B.; Tapia, A.L.; Watson, L.; Crais, E.; Bradley, C.; Fairchild, J.; Herring, A.H.; Daniels, J. Expressive Dominant Versus Receptive Dominant Language Patterns in Young Children: Findings from the Study to Explore Early Development. *J. Autism Dev. Disord.* **2019**, *49*, 2447–2460. [CrossRef]
24. Tager-Flusberg, H.; Paul, R.; Lord, C. Language and Communication in Autism. In *Handbook of Autism and Pervasive Developmental Disorders: Diagnosis, Development, Neurobiology, and Behavior*; Volkmar, F.R., Paul, R., Klin, A., Cohen, D., Eds.; John Wiley & Sons Inc.: Hoboken, NJ, USA, 2005; pp. 335–364.
25. Young, N.; Hudry, K.; Trembath, D.; Vivanti, G. Children With Autism Show Reduced Information Seeking When Learning New Tasks. *Am. J. Intellect. Dev. Disabil.* **2016**, *121*, 65–73. [CrossRef] [PubMed]
26. Cornew, L.; Dobkins, K.R.; Akshoomoff, N.; McCleery, J.P.; Carver, I.J. Atypical social referencing in infant siblings of children with Autism Spectrum Disorders. *J. Autism Dev. Disord.* **2012**, *42*, 2611–2621. [CrossRef] [PubMed]
27. Scambler, D.; Hepburn, S.; Rutherford, M.; Wehner, E.; Rogers, S. Emotional responsivity in children with autism, children with other developmental disabilities, and children with typical development. *J. Autism Dev. Disord.* **2007**, *37*, 553–563. [CrossRef] [PubMed]
28. Volkmar, F.R. Understanding the social brain in autism. *Dev. Psychobiol.* **2011**, *53*, 428–434. [CrossRef]
29. Menyuk, P. *Language Development: Knowledgeand Use*; Addison-Wesley Longman: Chicago, IL, USA, 1988.
30. Menyuk, P.; Liebergott, J.W.; Schultz, M.C. *Early Language Development in Full-Term and Premature Infants*; Psychology Press: New York, NY, USA, 2014.
31. Tager-Flusberg, H.; Kasari, C. Minimally verbal school-aged children with autism spectrum disorder: The Neglected End of the Spectrum. *Autism Res.* **2013**, *6*, 468–478. [CrossRef]
32. Fein, D.; Barton, M.; Eigsti, I.M.; Kelley, E.; Naigles, L.; Schultz, R.T. Optimal outcome in individuals with a history of autism. *J. Child Psychol. Psychiatry* **2013**, *54*, 195–205. [CrossRef]
33. Chilosi, A.M.; Cipriani, P. *TCGB Test di Comprensione Grammaticale Per Bambini*; Edizioni Del Cerro: Tirrenia, Pisa, Italy, 2006.
34. Dunn, L.M.; Dunn, L.M. *Peabody Picture Vocabulary Test*; Guidance Associates: Wilmingston, DE, USA, 1981.
35. Brizzolara, D. *Test di Vocabolario Figurato*; Technical Report of the Research Project 500.4/62.1/1134; Italian Department of Health to IRCCS Stella Maris: Calambrone, Pisa, Italy, 1989.
36. Cipriani, P.; Chilosi, A.M.; Bottari, P.; Pfanner, L. *L'acquisizione Della Morfosintassi Dell'italiano: Fasi e Processi*; Uipress: Padova, Italy, 1993.
37. Cipriani, P.; Chilosi, A.M.; Pfanner, L.; Villani, S.; Bottari, P. Il ritardo di linguaggio in età precoce: Profili evolutivi e indici di rischio. In *Indici di Rischio Nel Primo Sviluppo Del Linguaggio*; Caselli, C., Capirci, O., Eds.; Franco Angeli: Milano, Italy, 2002; pp. 95–108.
38. Wechsler, D. *Wechsler Preschool and Primary Scale of Intelligence*, 3rd ed.; Harcourt Assessment: San Antonio, TX, USA, 2002.
39. Wechsler, D. *Wechsler Intelligence Scale for Children*, 4th ed.; Psychological Corporation: San Antonio, TX, USA, 2003.
40. Griffiths, R. *The Abilities of Young Children: A Comprehensive System of Mental Measurement for the First Eight Years of Life (Revised Edition)*; Bucks: A.R.I.C.D. Test Agency Limited: London, UK, 1984.

41. Lord, C.; Risi, S.; Lambrecht, L.; Cook, E.H.; Leventhal, B.L.; DiLavore, P.C.; Pickles, A.; Rutter, M. The Autism Diagnostic Observation Schedule-Generic: A Standard Measure of Social and Communication Deficits Associated with the Spectrum of Autism. *J. Autism Dev. Disord.* **2000**, *30*, 205–223. [CrossRef]
42. Lord, C.; Rutter, M.; DiLavore, P.C.; Risi, S.; Luyster, R.J.; Gotham, K.; Bishop, S.L.; Guthrie, W. *ADOS-2—Autism Diagnostic Observation Schedule-Second Edition*; Colombi, C., Tancredi, R., Persico, A., Faggioli, R., Eds.; Hogrefe: Göttingen, Germany, 2013.
43. Kjellmer, L.; Fernell, E.; Gillberg, C.; Norrelgen, F. Speech and language profiles in 4- to 6-year-old children with early diagnosis of autism spectrum disorder without intellectual disability. *Neuropsychiatr. Dis. Treat.* **2018**, *14*, 2415–2427. [CrossRef]
44. Rapin, I. Language and its development in the autism spectrum disorders. In *Language: Normal and Pathological Development*; Riva, D., Rapin, I., Zardini, G., Eds.; John Libbey Eurotext: Montrange, France, 2006; pp. 121–137.
45. Rapin, I.; Allen, D.A.; Aram, D.M.; Dunn, M.A.; Fein, D.; Morris, R.; Waterhouse, L. Classification issues, in Rapin, I. In *Preschool Children with Inadequate Communication*; MacKeith: London, UK, 1996; pp. 190–201.
46. Chilosi, A.M.; Pfanner, L.; Pecini, C.; Salvadorini, R.; Casalini, C.; Brizzolara, D.; Cipriani, P. Which linguistic measures distinguish transient from persistent language problems in Late Talkers from 2 to 4 years? A study on Italian speaking children. *Res. Dev. Disabil.* **2019**, *89*, 59–68. [CrossRef]
47. Paul, R.; Fischer, M.L.; Cohen, D.J. Brief Report: Sentence comprehension strategies in children with autism and specific language disorders. *J. Autism Dev. Disord.* **1988**, *18*, 669–679. [CrossRef]
48. Prior, M.R.; Hall, L.C. Comprehension of transitive and intransitive phrases by autistic, retarded, and normal children. *J. Commun. Disord.* **1979**, *12*, 103–111. [CrossRef]
49. Tager-Flusberg, H. Sentence comprehension in autistic children. *Appl. Psycholinguist.* **1981**, *2*, 5–24. [CrossRef]
50. Kover, S.T.; Haebig, E.; Oakes, A.; McDuffie, A.; Hagerman, R.J.; Abbeduto, L. Sentence comprehension in boys with autism spectrum disorder. *Am. J. Speech Lang. Pathol.* **2014**, *23*, 385–394. [CrossRef] [PubMed]
51. Catts, H.W.; Fey, M.E.; Tomblin, J.B.; Zhang, X. A longitudinal investigation of reading outcomes in children with language impairments. *J. Speech Lang. Hear. Res.* **2002**, *45*, 1142–1157. [CrossRef]
52. Stothard, S.E.; Snowling, M.J.; Bishop, D.V.; Chipchase, B.B.; Kaplan, C.A. Language-impaired preschoolers: A follow-up into adolescence. *J. Speech Lang. Hear. Res.* **1998**, *41*, 407–418. [CrossRef]

7

Explaining Age at Autism Spectrum Diagnosis in Children with Migrant and Non-Migrant Background in Austria

Patricia Garcia Primo [1], Christoph Weber [1,2], Manuel Posada de la Paz [3,*], Johannes Fellinger [1,4,5], Anna Dirmhirn [4] and Daniel Holzinger [1,4,6]

1 Research Institute of Developmental Medicine, Johannes Kepler University, 4020 Linz, Austria; patricia.garcia_primo@jku.at (P.G.P.); christoph.weber@ph-ooe.at (C.W.); Johannes.Fellinger@bblinz.at (J.F.); Daniel.Holzinger@bblinz.at (D.H.)

2 Department for Inclusive Education, University of Education Upper Austria, 4020 Linz, Austria

3 Institute of Rare Diseases Research (IIER) & CIBERER, Instituto de Salud Carlos III, 28029 Madrid, Spain

4 Institut für Sinnes- und Sprachneurologie, Konventhospital Barmherzige Brüder, 4020 Linz, Austria; Anna.Dirmhirn@bblinz.at

5 Division of Social Psychiatry, Medical University of Vienna, 1010 Vienna, Austria

6 Institute of Linguistics, Karl-Franzens University of Graz, 8010 Graz, Austria

* Correspondence: mposada@isciii.es

Abstract: This study explored (i) differences in age at Autism Spectrum Disorder (ASD) diagnosis between children with and without a migrant background in the main diagnostic centre for ASD in Upper Austria (ii) factors related to the age at diagnosis and (iii) whether specific factors differed between the two groups. A retrospective chart analysis included all children who received their first diagnosis before the age of 10 years (n = 211) between 2013 and 2018. Children with a migrant background were diagnosed 13 months earlier than those without (r = 0.278, $p < 0.001$), and had more severe delays in language, more severe autism, no Asperger's syndrome, lower parental educational level and more frequent referrals by paediatricians. For the total sample, expressive language delay, severity of restricted and repetitive behaviours, higher nonverbal development, and paediatric referrals explained earlier diagnoses. There was a stronger effect of parental education and weaker effect of language impairment on age at ASD diagnosis in children with a migrant background. In conclusion, no delay in diagnosing ASD in children with a migrant background in a country with universal health care and an established system of paediatric developmental surveillance was found. Awareness of ASD, including Asperger's syndrome, should be raised among families and healthcare professionals.

Keywords: migration; autism; diagnosis; Europe; health system

1. Introduction

(1) Prevalence of Autism Spectrum Disorder (ASD): The prevalence of ASD has risen in the last decade, with current rates of 1/59 in North America [1] and similar rates reported in Europe [2–5]. In the absence of ASD prevalence studies in Austria, epidemiological studies must be consulted [6], which would indicate a number of approximately 80,000 individuals with ASD diagnosis in this country—clearly a number that has a considerable impact on the national health and social systems. *ASD and migration.* A growing number of European studies, particularly from Nordic countries, suggests an increased frequency of autism in children of immigrant parents [7–10]. However, a recent systematic review of ASD prevalence and migration status in Europe has shown no simple, linear relationship between prevalence or risk of ASD and immigrant status [11,12]. Earlier data from North

American studies tend not to support this finding [13,14], whereas a recent ADDM (Autism and Developmental Disabilities Monitoring Network) study has shown a higher ASD prevalence in black children as compared to their white peers [15]. In Europe, the number of immigrants is substantial and also on the rise. In 2018, 22.3 million people with citizenship of a non-member country (4.4% of the EU-28 population) resided in an EU member state. Additionally, 17.6 million people in the EU were citizens of another EU member state [16]. Within the EU, Austria has one of the highest proportions of migrants (23.3%) [17]. The proportion of children who do not use German as their primary family language is 26% across all school types and 31% in primary schools [18].

(2) Age at ASD diagnosis and predictors: The increase in ASD prevalence has been accompanied by a decrease in the age at diagnosis in many countries [11,19], although there are exceptions [9]. Early ASD diagnosis is the gateway to support services [20] and interventions. Growing evidence points to the beneficial effects of enrolment at younger age in autism intervention on (a) the child's long-term outcomes [4,21,22], (b) the family's coping skills [23,24] and (c) costs to society [25,26]. Timely access to ASD diagnosis and support requires equitable access to health services, which is also one of the principles of the World Health Organisation (WHO) for universal health coverage [27]. Specific factors that affect the age at ASD diagnosis have been identified in several studies and are mainly related to clinical ASD presentation [28]. Severe language delay and more severe repetitive behaviours have been shown to be very common symptoms that prompt early medical consultation and diagnosis at a younger age. Hearing impairment and intellectual disability [28,29] have been found to delay identification of ASD in many cases. However, a low level of intellectual functioning can also stimulate earlier developmental investigation and earlier autism diagnosis [30–32]. Particular characteristics that are related to the child's family such as living in under-resourced or rural areas [28], low parental occupational level [33] and/or lower socioeconomic status [34,35] have more recently been identified as factors related to later ASD diagnosis. Furthermore, characteristics of the health system (mainly presence or absence of universal coverage), and whether it has a tradition of surveillance or screening programmes, must be considered.

(3) Migration and age at diagnosis: Lastly, migration status may also be a cause of delayed diagnosis [28,36–41]. Several studies in the USA have shown that children from immigrant families are more likely to be diagnosed later (mostly after the age of 4) than their non-migrant peers [28,33,37,39,41]. Although these data show an association between parental immigration and delay of autism diagnosis in North America, a limited number of studies has investigated this outside the United States [42]. To our knowledge, in Europe only one study in the Netherlands has explored this research question; the authors concluded that the immigrant sample did not differ in age at ASD diagnosis from the non-immigrant sample [43]. The following specific factors related to the age at ASD diagnosis in children from immigrant families have been reported [44]: firstly, a lack of knowledge of the host country language can restrict access to ASD awareness campaigns and education about ASD [44–47]. In addition, culture-related differences, such as parental feelings of shame and guilt related to child disability, have been described between families of children with developmental disabilities and the values and expectations of service providers [48–50]. A lack of understanding of the host country's health care system and community stigma can also prevent parents from seeking care [49,51]. Negative perceptions of services and a poor understanding of rehabilitation concepts can also delay access to specialised health services, and parents with a migration background have reported perceived discrimination by service providers [52]. Furthermore, culturally shaped interpretations of child behaviours (e.g., social communication) can influence the parents' seeking of medical advice [53]. As a consequence, professional organisations such as the American Psychological Association increasingly emphasise the importance of accounting for cultural differences in both professional practices and research [54].

(4) Health Care Services for Children with ASD in Upper Austria: The Austrian federal state of Upper Austria (1.48 million inhabitants) has a high proportion of immigration. In Upper Austria, 31% of all primary school children have a family language other than German [18]. The Austrian federal state

of Upper Austria provides an extensive network of healthcare institutions and a universal-coverage health insurance system. The social system in Austria offers free public early intervention for all children with developmental delays. In Upper Austria, a paediatric well-baby check-up program is provided free of charge from birth to school entry (at the age of 6 years) and is well accepted by families. An important element of this programme is a specific language screening programme (SPES) that was developed in 2007 by the Institute of Neurology of Language and Senses (ISSN) to identify children with increased risk for persisting language difficulties at the 2- and 3-year paediatric check-ups. The SPES language screening is used on a voluntary basis by the majority of paediatricians. Children who fail the short assessment of receptive vocabulary are referred for further neurodevelopmental assessment. By use of this screening the age of autism diagnosis could be significantly decreased within the last decade. About 50% of all children live in rural areas (i.e., thinly populated areas; 12% of these children do not use German as their primary family language), 13% live in the city of Linz, where the proportion of children with a family language other than German is 56% [55].

The out-patient clinic of the ISSN, situated within a public general hospital in the city of Linz, has been the major clinical focus for developmental disorders for the local community in Upper Austria in the last decade. It is the main centre where the complex multidisciplinary diagnostic evaluation needed for ASD diagnosis is regularly conducted [56]. In the associated Autism Centre, ASD-specific early intervention—following primarily the Early Start Denver Model—is provided [57]. In the last decade, the percentage of patients with a migrant background using the diagnostic clinic has risen from about 40% to 50%. Thus, data from this clinic's medical charts lend themselves to investigating factors that may determine a possible relationship between immigrant status and access to diagnosis.

Aim and Hypotheses

This study aimed to explore (i) whether there are differences in terms of age at ASD diagnosis between children with or without a migrant background at the principal diagnostic centre for ASD in Upper Austria, (ii) what factors might be correlated with the age at diagnosis of these children and (iii) whether predictors of age at diagnosis differ between children with and without a migrant background.

2. Methods

2.1. Study Design

A cross sectional study was used. All children of parents with and without a migrant background (see definition below) who attended the diagnostic centre of the ISSN in the study period (01-01-2013 to 31-12-2018) and received an ICD-10- diagnosis (International Classification of Diseases, 10th Revision [58]) of ASD (F84) for the first time before the age of 10 years were considered in the study.

Migration background cannot be sufficiently defined by citizenship, since there are many families with parents born outside Austria (and even more second-generation families) who have Austrian citizenship. The ISSN medical records did not contain systematic information on the parents' and children's places of birth, but detailed information about the language(s) spoken in the family. Therefore, a family was considered to have a migrant background if both parents (or one parent in a single-parent family) used a language other than German as their primary language in the family. There were no members of Austria's autochthonous ethnic minorities in the study sample.

Age of diagnosis was limited to a maximum of 10 years for both samples, since there were only few individual children in our clinical population who received an ASD diagnosis after that age. All ASD cases were evaluated at the ISSN by a developmental paediatrician, a clinical psychologist and a clinical linguist using various standardised tests depending on each child's developmental level and a clinical (non-standardised) interview. The ICD-10 [58] was used as a basis for clinical diagnosis of ASD and for the classification codes in the reports. All clinicians had been trained in the implementation and scoring of the ADOS-2 [59], which was applied in the majority of cases. Main outcomes were summarised in a comprehensive medical report.

2.2. Study Variables

Dependent variable: chronological age of the child at first ASD diagnosis. Independent variables: grouped by (a) sociodemographic, (b) clinical characteristic and (c) referral to diagnosis.

(a) Sociodemographic characteristics: Migration background status was based on language(s) predominantly spoken by the parents in the family as reported by the parents themselves. A family was considered to have a migrant background if both mother and father (or a single parent) used a language other than German as their primary language at home. The languages reported as being used at home by the study population were then categorised into five geographical regions: South-Eastern and Eastern Europe, Western and Northern Europe, Middle and East Asia, West Asia, and others (see Supplement S3). No parent was excluded due to insufficient language skills since translators were always available within the health system. Parental educational level was derived from the information provided by the parents in the registration form prior to clinical evaluation. Parents reported their current occupational level and/or educational background, and this information was then categorised into two levels of education: with or without high school diploma. For the analysis the highest parental educational level (i.e., of either father or mother) was used. Location of family residence was also elicited from the information provided by the parents in the registration form. This data was used to determine the degree of urbanisation of the place of residence (densely populated urban areas vs. thinly populated areas) and to estimate the distance between family residence and diagnostic clinic (in kilometres).

(b) Clinical characteristics: Gender was extracted from the medical record of the child. The non-verbal IQ score is the standardised non-verbal quotient of the child at the time of ASD diagnosis, either extracted directly from the evaluation report or calculated using the well-known quotient formula with the non-verbal developmental age of the child divided by the chronological age indicated in the report. The most common standardised cognitive tests reported were Mullen Scales of Early Learning (MSEL) [60], the Bayley Scales of Infant Development III [61] and the Hamburg-Wechsler Intelligenz test IV [62], depending on the child's age and level of functioning. Language Scores (Receptive and Expressive): receptive (RL) and expressive (EL) language developmental quotient scores, usually assessed by use of the MSEL, were either obtained directly from the diagnostic report or calculated from age-equivalent scores (age-equivalent scores/chronological age × 100) when the clinician indicated the language level of the child in months (usually based on a standardised language test, but also according to clinical picture when administration of a test was not possible due to the characteristics of the child) (PGP and DH). Language skills where assessed by linguists experienced in multilingualism in the child's primary language. If necessary, interpreters were used and parental observations were taken into consideration. Children with a developmental quotient below 50 were considered to have a moderate or severe delay. Variables of ASD Subtype: ICD-10 Code diagnosis of ASD (F84) ADOS Calibrated Severity Scores (CSS) for Social Affect (SA) and Restricted and Repetitive Behaviours (RRB) were transformed as appropriate from the original SA and RRB raw scores of the clinical report, following the indications of Gotham et al. [63], based on the child age, module and/or version of ADOS administered and reported in the clinical record (PGP and DH). A change in the clinical diagnostic procedure within the study period (from ADOS-G to ADOS-2) [64] was taken into account by the calibrated severity scores.

(c) Referral to diagnosis was either directly stated by the parents in the registration form or reported to the clinician at the evaluation (and therefore included in the diagnostic report).

2.3. Procedures

The clinical charts of all cases were revised and abstracted by researchers with considerable knowledge and experience in the field of neurodevelopmental disorders. To ensure accuracy, reliability and consistency in data abstraction, we developed, tested and revised a Record Review Protocol (RCR) following best practice [65,66]. An initial list of variables to be captured was tested in a small pilot study, discussed by the research team, and adjusted where necessary. In the case of conflicting or uncertain information in the medical charts, consensus decisions (PGM, DH) were made. The information that was reviewed referred to demographic and clinical characteristics of the children and their families and to the system of referral for ASD diagnosis.

Ethics: This study was approved by the ethics committee (Ethikkommission der Medizinischen Fakultät der Johannes Kepler Universität), Nr. 1140/2020 Version 3, following the rules of the Declaration of Helsinki of 1975 revised in 2013 [67].

2.4. Statistical Analysis

First, we separately calculated descriptive statistics (means, standard deviations for continuous variables and percentages for categorical variables) of all study variables for children with and without a migration background. Second, bivariate correlations were calculated between the age at diagnosis and the sociodemographic and clinical variables. This was done for the total sample and also separately according to migration status. In order to test for differences in correlations between the migrant and non-migrant groups, a Wald χ^2-test was carried out. Correlations were also calculated for different age groups in order to identify possible age-dependent predictors of the age at diagnosis. For all bivariate analyses we calculated effect size measures in a correlation metric, more specifically, Pearson's r for the association between continuous variables, point biserial correlation for the association between binary variable and continuous variables and phi or Cramer's V for the association between categorical variables. Finally, we used linear regression models to evaluate the effects of all predictors simultaneously. We also tested whether the association between predictors and age at diagnosis differed by migrant status. This was achieved by including interaction terms (e.g., migrant × sex) in the regression models [68]. We report unstandardised regression coefficients (b) and their standard errors (SE) and standardised coefficients (β) that have the same metric as correlation coefficients and could likewise be interpreted as effect size measures [69,70]. Several study variables had a high number of missing values (e.g., 42% missing values for parental education; see also Table 1). Preliminary analysis indicated that missingness depended on other variables (i.e., missing at random [71]). For example, children with missing values for parental education were diagnosed later (M = 52 months vs. M = 44 months). Thus, in order to avoid bias and a loss of statistical power, we used multiple imputation (MI)—a state-of-the-art technique for dealing with missing data—to replace missing values [71]. Firstly, the missing data was imputed by available data, and several imputed data sets were generated. Secondly, analyses were carried out for all data sets, and lastly the results of all data sets were pooled and final coefficients and standard errors were computed according to Rubin's combination rules [72]. Specifically, we used the blimp software [71,73], which implements a multiple imputation by chained equations (MICE) algorithm. All study variables were used for the imputation models, and imputations were carried out separately for the migrant and non-migrant groups. In order to obtain accurate standard errors, 200 imputed data sets were generated [74]. M*plus* 8.2. [75] was used for all analyses based on imputed data. Due to the non-normal distribution of the dependent variable of age at diagnosis (skewness = 1.411, kurtosis = 1.424), a maximum-likelihood estimation with robust standard errors (MLR) was used. Only descriptive results are reported for non-imputed data. These analyses were carried out using SPSS 26 and Jamovi [76].

Table 1. Sample characteristics by migration status.

	Values	%M	Total (n = 211) M (SD) or n (%)	Non-Migrants (n = 91) M (SD) or n (%)	Migrants (n = 120) M (SD) or n (%)	Difference *ES r* [a]	Difference *p*
Age at Diagnosis	12–119 m.o.	0%	46.7 (22.80)	53.96 (26.86)	41.19 (17.33)	0.278	<0.001
Sociodemographic Characteristics							
Family Residence in Urban Area	No/Yes	0%	148 (70.1%)	51 (56.0%)	97 (80.8%)	0.268	<0.001
Distance to Hospital	0–187 km	0%	38.27 (37.50)	49.27 (41.67)	29.93 (31.73)	0.256	<0.001
Parental Level of Education above High School	No/Yes	41%	37 (30.1%)	23 (42.6%)	14 (20.3%)	0.241	0.007
Clinical Characteristics							
Male Gender	No/Yes	0%	174 (82.5%)	77 (84.6%)	97 (80.8%)	0.049	0.474
Non-Verbal Developmental Quotient, (D/IQ)	16–122	13%	62.26 (18.89)	65.5 (21.15)	59.67 (16.56)	0.155	0.036
D/IQ 50 or Below	No/Yes	13%	37 (20.1%)	16 (19.8%)	21 (20.4%)	0.008	0.915
Expressive Language Quotient (ELQ)	13–128	15%	46.38 (24.44)	57.42 (28.93)	39.34 (18.46)	0.340	<0.001
ELQ 50 or Below	No/Yes	15%	118 (65.9%)	37 (49.3%)	81 (77.90%)	0.297	<0.001
Receptive Language Quotient (RLQ)	15–133	15%	48.25 (24.65)	59.6 (29.04)	40.75 (18.23)	0.355	<0.001
RLQ Score 50 or Below	No/Yes	15%	116 (64.8%)	36 (47.4%)	80 (77.70%)	0.314	<0.001
ADOS-Calibrated Severity Scores—Total CSS							
Social Affect—CSS	1–10	18%	6.35 (2.19)	5.83 (2.16)	6.71 (2.15)	0.591.	0.041
Repetitive Behaviour—CSS	1–10	18%	5.85 (1.8)	5.76 (1.86)	5.91 (1.86)	0.009.	0.198
ICD-10 ASD Code							
Autism Disorder		0%	122 (57.80%)	38 (41.8%)	84 (70.00%)	0.385	<0.001
Asperger's Disorder			21 (10%)	20 (22%)	1 (0.80%)		
PDD-nos			68 (32.20%)	33 (36.2%)	35 (29.20%)		
Referral to Diagnosis							
Referred by Paediatrician	No/Yes	27%	76 (36%)	23 (25.3%)	53 (44.2%)	0.289	<0.001

Note. %M = percentage missing values, M = mean, SD = standard deviation. [a] Effect size estimates for differences between migrants and non-migrants in a correlation metric.

3. Results

3.1. Descriptive Results

In Table 1 the descriptive results (based on non-imputed data) both for the total sample and for the non-migrant and migrant subsamples separately are shown. Results based on imputed data are provided in the Supplement (S1).

Of the 211 children in the sample, 58% received a diagnosis of autistic disorder, 10% of Asperger's disorder, and 32% of Pervasive Developmental Disorder–Not Otherwise Specified (PDD-NOS). Children with autistic disorder were diagnosed at an average age of 39.4 months, followed by children with PDD-NOS (50.8 months) and children with Asperger's disorder (75.9 months). Notably, children with Asperger's disorder were almost exclusively from the non-migrant group; only one case in the children with migrant background subsample had received an Asperger's disorder diagnosis. The difference in the ICD-10 ASD type between the non-migrant and migrant groups is highly significant (Cramer's V = 0.385, $p < 0.001$).

The mean age at diagnosis was 46.7 months (SD = 22.8) for the total sample. Values ranged from 12 to 119 months. The non-migrant group was diagnosed at a mean age of 54 months as compared to 41.2 months for the migrant group. Thus, children with a migration background received their autism diagnosis significantly earlier (difference of about 13 months) than those without (r = 0.278, $p < 0.001$). The distributions of the age at diagnosis for the total sample and the migration-status subsamples are shown in Figure 1. The sample with a migrant background is characterised by a reduced distribution with a stronger concentration around ages 2–4 and a smaller proportion of children diagnosed with ASD at a later age.

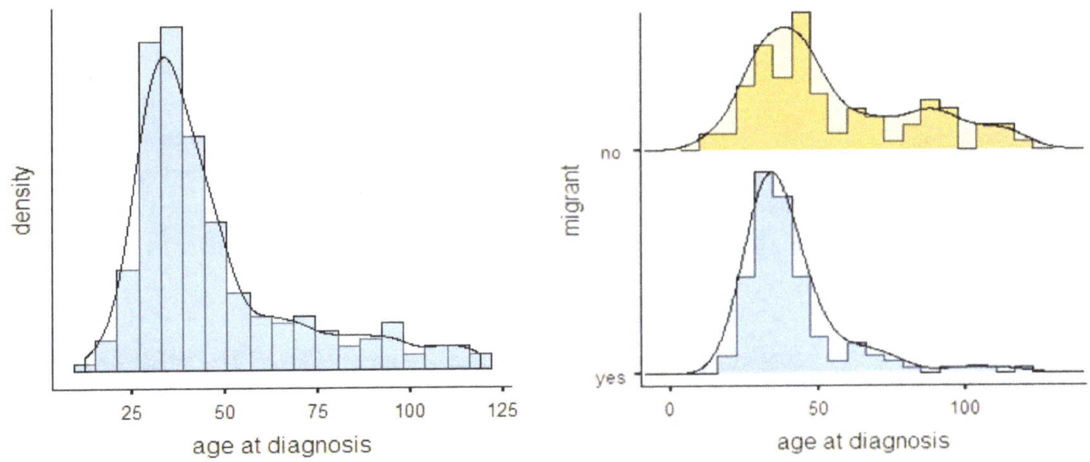

Figure 1. Age at diagnosis distribution histogram and density plot for total sample and split by migrant status.

3.2. Bivariate Analysis

In the total sample, there are moderate correlations between age at diagnosis and language scores. Children with lower expressive (r = 0.423, $p < 0.001$) and receptive (r = 0.355, $p < 0.001$) language scores were diagnosed significantly earlier. There is also a moderate correlation between RB-CSS and age at diagnosis (r = −0.370, $p < 0.001$). Children with higher RB-CSS received their diagnosis significantly earlier than those with lower RB-CSS. Similarly, analysis revealed a weak correlation between SA-CSS and age at diagnosis (r = −0.158, $p < 0.05$); more specifically, diagnosis occurred earlier in the case of higher severity scores for social affect. Finally, children who were referred by a paediatrician received their diagnoses earlier (r = −0.255, $p < 0.001$, M 40.78 months) than the rest of the sample (M 51.16 months). Table 2 shows the correlations between age at diagnosis and predictor variables for the total sample and the migration-status subsamples.

Table 2. Correlations between sample characteristics and age at diagnosis separated by migration status.

	Total	Non-Migrants	Migrants	Correlation Difference between Groups [a]
Sociodemographic Characteristics	r	r	r	*p*
Family Residence in Urban Area	−0.132	−0.073	−0.047	0.684
Distance Between Home And Hospital in Km	0.031	−0.050	−0.034	0.740
Parental Level of Education above High School	0.100	0.198	−0.169 *	0.035
Clinical Characteristics				
Male Gender	0.011	0.095	−0.048	0.252
Non-Verbal Developmental Quotient (IQ)	0.065	0.123	−0.131	0.136
Expressive Language Quotient (ELQ)	0.423 ***	0.443 ***	0.216	0.014
Receptive Language Quotient (RLQ)	0.355 ***	0.341 ***	0.177	0.059
ADOS-Calibrated Severity Scores—Total CSS				
Social Affect—CSS	−0.158 *	0.011	−0.263 **	0.206
Repetitive Behaviour—CSS	−0.370 ***	−0.446 ***	−0.326 ***	0.186
Referred by Paediatrician	−0.255 ***	−0.195	−0.220 *	0.707

Note. Correlations are based on multiple imputed data. [a] *p*-values for correlation differences between migrants and non-migrants are based on a Wald χ^2-Test. *** $p < 0.001$, ** $p < 0.01$, * $p < 0.05$.

There are some notable differences between the strengths of the correlations with age of diagnosis between children with and without a migrant background. First, for migrant-background children there is a negative association between age at diagnosis and parental education (r = −0.169, $p < 0.05$). Thus, children of parents with migrant status who had at least graduated high school were diagnosed at an earlier age than children of parents with migration background who had no high school diploma. In contrast, this association is of comparable strength but of opposite direction and not statistically significant in the non-migrant subsample (r = 0.198, $p > 0.05$). Second, the correlations between both ELQ and RLQ and age at diagnosis are of moderate strength and statistically significant for the non-migrant group (ELQ, r = 0.443, $p < 0.001$; RLQ, r = 0.341, $p < 0.001$), but weaker and non-significant for the migrant group (ELQ, r = 0.216, $p < 0.10$; RLQ, r = 0.177, $p > 0.05$). Finally, it is interesting to note that the correlation between SA-CSS and age at diagnosis is significant for the migrant subsample (r = −0.263, $p < 0.01$), but not for non-migrant subsample (r = 0.011, $p > 0.05$). However, these two correlations do not differ significantly.

Table 3 presents the results of exploring age effects on the correlations between the predictors and age at diagnosis for two subsamples defined by age at diagnosis (<48 months vs. ≥48 months) and migration status. Note that these analyses suffer somewhat from small sample sizes (e.g., n = 23 for the migrant group in the "age at diagnosis ≥ 48 months" subsample). Nonetheless, there are several interesting results. First, there is no significant correlation between age at diagnosis and ELQ and RLQ, respectively, in the younger subsample, neither for children with nor for those without a migrant background. These correlations are only significant for non-migrant-background children in the older group (ELQ, r = 0.462, $p < 0.001$; RLQ, r = 0.346, $p < 0.05$). Thus, non-migrant-background children aged ≥ 48 months at diagnosis received their diagnoses earlier, the lower their language scores were. A somewhat similar pattern—although individual correlations are not significant—was found for the correlations between RLQ and age at diagnosis in the migrant group. RLQ and age at diagnosis correlate moderately (r = 0.332; $p < 0.10$) for migrant-background children aged ≥ 48 months at diagnosis, but not for those who received their diagnosis before 48 months (r = −0.122; $p > 0.05$). Second, the RB-CSS is only correlated with age at diagnosis for children who received their diagnosis at the age of 48 months or later. In detail, there are moderate to strong correlations between RB-CSS and age at diagnosis for children both with (r = −0.530, $p < 0.01$) and without (r = −0.477, $p < 0.001$) a migrant background. In the subsample of children who were younger at diagnosis, these correlations are much smaller and not significant (correlation differences between age subsamples are significant). Finally, there is a negative and significant small correlation between age at diagnosis and distance between home and hospital in the older non-migrant subsample (r = −0.282, $p < 0.05$). Thus, children from this subsample received their diagnoses later, the closer they lived to the hospital. For children with a migrant background in this age group, the correlation is not significant and positive (r = 0.179, $p > 0.05$). The correlations differ marginally ($p < 0.10$).

Table 3. Correlations between sample characteristics and age at diagnosis according to migration status and age-at-diagnosis subsample.

	Age at Diagnosis < 48 Months		Age at Diagnosis ≥ 48 Months		Correlation Differences between Groups (p-Values) [a]			
	(1) Non-Migrants (n = 50)	(2) Migrants (n = 97)	(3) Non-Migrants (n = 41)	(4) Migrants (n = 23)				
Sociodemographic Characteristics	r	r	r	r	1, 2	3, 4	1, 3	2, 4
Family Residence in Urban Area	−0.079	0.167	0.033	−0.114	0.244	0.597	0.700	0.461
Home Distance to Hospital in km	−0.009	−0.122	−0.282*	0.179	0.711	0.059	0.118	0.265
Parental Level of Education above High School	0.037	−0.094	0.167	−0.197	0.574	0.204	0.418	0.559
Clinical Characteristics								
Male Gender	0.090	0.034	−0.124	−0.200	0.680	0.848	0.355	0.204
Non-Verbal Developmental Quotient (IQ)	0.066	−0.150	0.168	0.235	0.305	0.989	0.371	0.213
Expressive Language Quotient (ELQ)	0.097	−0.172	0.462 ***	0.186	0.249	0.158	0.006	0.284
Receptive Language Quotient (RLQ)	0.007	−0.122	0.346 *	0.332	0.662	0.659	0.037	0.097
ADOS-Calibrated Severity Scores—Total CSS								
Social Affect—CSS	−0.111	−0.128	0.144	0.023	0.916	0.623	0.294	0.779
Repetitive Behaviour—CSS	0.125	0.002	−0.477 ***	−0.530 **	0.531	0.989	0.003	0.045
Referred by Paediatrician	−0.085	−0.026	−0.087	−0.148	0.702	0.836	0.785	0.550

Note. Correlations are based on multiple imputed data. [a] p-values for correlation differences between groups are based on a Wald χ^2-Test. *** $p < 0.001$, ** $p < 0.01$, * $p < 0.05$.

3.3. Regression Analysis

The results of the regression models are shown in Table 4. Due to the high correlation between ELQ and RLQ (r = 0.84), a unique composite language score (Language Quotient, LQ = (RLQ + ELQ)/2) was used in the regression models. All 10 predictors explain 34.6% of the variance in age at diagnosis. In accordance with the bivariate results, the LQ turned out to be the best predictor (β = 0.389, $p < 0.001$), followed by RB-CSS (β = −0.301, $p < 0.001$) and referral by paediatrician (β = −0.206, $p < 0.01$). Interestingly, the association between IQ and age at diagnosis, which was not significant in the bivariate analysis, is negative and statistically significant (β = −0.175, $p < 0.05$), when we control for other predictors. In fact, the association becomes significant as soon as we control for LQ; thus, given a constant LQ, the higher the IQ, the younger the child at diagnosis.

Table 4. Regression model for age at diagnosis.

	b (SE)	β	95%-CI
Sociodemographic Characteristics			
Family Residence in Urban Area	1.139 (3.457)	0.023	(−0.113, 0.159)
Distance between Home and Hospital in km	−0.020 (0.038)	−0.033	(−0.156, 0.089)
Parental Level of Education above High School	−3.719 (4.103)	−0.073	(−0.231, 0.085)
Migration Status	−6.228 (3.305)	−0.136	(−0.275, 0.004)
Clinical Characteristics			
Male Gender	1.539 (3.433)	0.026	(−0.087, 0.138)
Non-Verbal Developmental Quotient	−0.219 * (0.098)	−0.175	(−0.336, −0.014)
Language Composite (Expressive and Receptive)	0.363 *** (0.090)	0.389	(0.204, 0.574)
ADOS-Calibrated Severity Scores—Total CSS			
Social Affect—CSS	−0.133 (0.739)	−0.013	(−0.157, 0.131)
Repetitive Behaviour—CSS	−3.575 *** (0.941)	−0.301	(−0.452, −0.150)
Referred by Paediatrician	−9.370 ** (3.375)	−0.206	(−0.349, −0.063)
R^2		0.346	

Note. Results are based on multiple imputed data. 95%-CI = 95% confidence interval for β. *** $p < 0.001$, ** $p < 0.01$, * $p < 0.05$.

The regression model shows that migrant status is only marginally significantly associated with age at diagnosis (β = −0.136, $p < 0.10$) once other predictors have been controlled for. In detail, the difference in age at diagnosis, which amounted to about 13 months in the bivariate case (see Table 1), decreases to 6 months (b = −6.228) when other predictors are being controlled for. Again, the LQ is primarily responsible for differences between the bivariate and the multivariate analyses. Once we control for LQ, the difference between migration status and age at diagnosis decreases to roughly 7 months (b = −6.686, $p < 0.05$). Thus, about half of the difference in the age at diagnosis between the migrant and non-migrant groups is due to lower language scores of the migrant subsample.

In order to analyse possible differences in the associations between age at diagnosis and the independent variables between the migrant and non-migrant groups, we applied a series of regression models including interaction terms (for detailed results see Supplement S2). None of the interaction effects were significant. Thus, in contrast to the bivariate results (Table 2), no differences between the migrant and non-migrant subsamples in the associations between age at diagnosis and independent variables were found in the multivariate models.

Finally, some further analyses were performed to better understand the negative IQ effect in the multivariate regression model. In detail, we included an interaction term between IQ and LQ, which turned out to be statistically significant (b = 0.007, $p < 0.01$). In order to interpret this interaction, we plotted the simple slopes, that is, the associations of IQ and age at diagnosis for both high (=M + SD) and low (=M − SD) levels of LQ. Figure 2 shows that there is no association between IQ and age at diagnosis for children with high LQ. This association is negative and significant at low LQ levels. Thus, children with high IQ and low LQ were diagnosed the earliest.

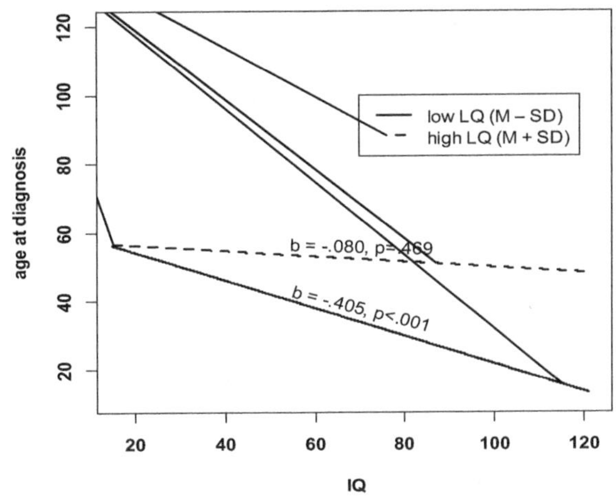

Figure 2. Interaction between LQ and IQ. Note. M = mean, SD = standard deviation. IQ = Non-Verbal Developmental Quotient. LQ = composite language score. b = unstandardised regression coefficient for IQ at high levels of LQ (M + SD) and low levels of LQ (M – SD).

4. Discussion

The aim of this study was to investigate and compare age at diagnosis of autism spectrum disorders in children with or without a migrant background from an intake population of an outpatient clinic for developmental disorders in Austria and to examine the impact of sociodemographic variables, child characteristics and referral factors on age at diagnosis. We carried out a retrospective chart analysis including all children who received an ASD diagnosis before the age of 10 years for the first time.

Notably, our results demonstrate a higher percentage of children with (57%) than without (43%) a migrant background being diagnosed with ASD in our clinic. This contrasts with a reverse ratio of about 30:70 of primary non-German to German family language in Austria. On the one hand, this might be explained by the high percentage of immigrant families (56%) in the city of Linz and a closer distance to the diagnostic centre facilitating service use. On the other hand, the high percentage of children with migrant background might also be due to a higher prevalence of ASD in migrant populations, as described by some of the European studies [8,10]. Additionally, clinical experience shows a high uptake of medical referrals among families with a migrant background. In our sample, a significantly higher number of migrant- than non-migrant-background families reported that their child had been referred to the clinic by a paediatrician. There also seems to be a general tendency for families with a migrant background to use primary paediatric care more often and longer [77] than non-migrant-background families; the latter are more likely to consult general practitioners, who are often less well trained in identifying developmental disorders. Finally, the large proportion of ASD diagnoses in children with a migrant background is probably also related to free access to health care in Austria. Studies in countries without universal health care have shown that children with ethnic and racial differences are less often diagnosed with ASD [78].

Our main finding is that for the total study sample, children with a migrant background received the ASD diagnosis significantly earlier than the rest of the sample. However, in the younger subsample, diagnosed before 48 months of age, the mean age at diagnosis was almost identical for the migrant and non-migrant groups (34.4 and 34.6 months, respectively). For the total sample, the significantly younger mean age at diagnosis in the subsample with a migrant background is due to a lack of children with less severe autism symptomatology (Asperger disorder), who are usually presented to the clinic at an age older than 4 years. In any case, contrary to findings in other health systems [78], there are no disparities in early access to diagnosis of ASD in Austria, where free health care and a medical surveillance system (preventive medical check-ups) are provided for all.

In accordance with the literature [8,79,80], we found significant differences in clinical symptomatology between migrant- and non-migrant-background children diagnosed with ASD. The sample with a migrant background demonstrated significantly longer delays in language as well as more severe autism and tended to be more delayed in their nonverbal cognitive development. The differences in language development persisted after reducing the sample to those diagnosed before the age of 4 years. A comparison of the distribution of autism subtypes (according to ICD_10) showed an almost complete absence of diagnoses of Asperger's disorder in children with a migrant background (n = 1) in contrast to the non-migrant subsample (n = 21). This accords with the results of Lehti et al. in 2015 [10], who found in a national birth cohort study of children diagnosed with Asperger's disorder in Finland a significantly decreased likelihood of diagnosis in children whose parents were immigrants (adjusted odds ratio 0.2, 95% CI 0.1–0.4). The higher likelihood of childhood autism versus Asperger's disorder syndrome in children with a migrant background might be related to specific risk factors associated with childhood autism (but not with Asperger's disorder) that occur more frequently in the migrant population, such as perinatal complications, low birth weight and lower gestational age [9,81]. However, we strongly suspect that our results also reflect service utilisation. Underdiagnoses might be due to less awareness of milder forms of ASD in the migrant-background subsample with a significantly lower level of parental education. In addition, the culturally shaped appearance of Asperger's disorder and communication problems between health professionals and parents and children might be other reasons for a lower number of this type of diagnosis.

Bivariate and multivariate analyses that identified factors correlated with delayed age at diagnosis for the total sample demonstrated a strong impact of the severity of language problems (expressive and/or receptive) on earlier ASD diagnosis. Severe delays in expressive language are easily noticed both by parents and by professionals in health and education systems and have been described as the most frequently observed symptoms of ASD that prompt medical consultation [82]. They have also been shown to be an important marker of non-apparent (invisible) developmental disorders [83]. In concordance with the findings of other studies, the severity of restricted and repetitive behaviours is another factor significantly related to earlier diagnosis of ASD, which is most likely a consequence of their obvious character compared to the often more subtle peculiarities in social communication. In addition, RBBs are often perceived as a cause of stress by the families and might therefore lead to external help being sought. The third-strongest factor related to earlier diagnosis was referral by a primary care paediatrician. Despite possible challenges in providing language- and culturally appropriate screening [78], well-trained paediatricians play an important role in reducing barriers to (early) ASD diagnosis. Finally, higher levels of intellectual functioning were found to be correlated with younger age at diagnosis, especially in children with seriously delayed language development, but it is also seen with average language scores. A severe language delay combined with significantly higher cognitive development may be even more obvious to parents and referring primary care professionals than a generalised developmental delay associated with a stronger need for explanation. With an expected majority of male gender in the sample, gender was not found to correlate significantly with age at diagnosis. Interestingly, parental education and the distance between the family's place of residence and the diagnostic centre did not add significantly to explaining the variance in age at ASD diagnosis.

A comparison of factors related to age at identification of ASD in the migrant and non-migrant samples mostly showed significantly stronger effects of parental education in the group with a migration background. However, the correlation was small. In migrant-background families, educational disparities are often linked to pronounced deficits in (spoken and written) language that might have a particularly strong effect on access to health information.

The severity of (primarily expressive) language delay had significantly stronger effects on delayed ASD diagnosis in the non-migrant sample. This effect is almost exclusively observed in the older subsample (>4 years), where—due to the much higher number of children with Asperger's disorder—variance in language development was significantly higher in the non-migrant sample. In school children with a migrant background, parents and professionals in health and education might ascribe language difficulties to bilingual language acquisition rather than to a developmental disorder. However, given the small size of the sample of older children with a migrant background ($n = 23$), results must be interpreted with caution. The minimal differences in factors explaining age at autism diagnosis between children with and without a migrant background are most likely a consequence of equitable access to medical care and a model of early identification with strong involvement of primary paediatric care that is well accepted.

The almost complete lack of significant effects of variables associated with age at diagnosis in the younger subsample is surprising at first glance. However, the variance in age at diagnosis was very small in the group aged younger than 4 years and probably related to the fact that paediatric screenings (mainly for expressive and receptive language) are usually offered at the ages of 2 and 3 years. Earlier referrals are highly unlikely. Furthermore, kindergarten, where autistic symptoms might be noticed, typically starts at the age of three. Long waiting periods for diagnostic services due to insufficient resources can cause inequalities and might be another reason that complicates the finding of significant predictors. The retrospective medical chart analysis presented has some limitations. Firstly, due to sample recruitment from a single clinic, effects of specific clinic-related factors on the age at diagnosis cannot be excluded. Secondly, another limitation of this study is its reliance on self-reported data about the parental level of occupation, since other information about Socioeconomic Status (SES), such as income or highest parental education, was not included in the medical charts. Even for information on parental occupation, data extracted from medical reports were very incomplete. Missing data, including those for other variables, were reported, and multiple imputations was used for missing values to avoid bias. Analyses of correlates of age at diagnosis by splitting the sample into two age subsamples and by migration status were interpreted with caution due to the small sizes of some of the subsamples.

5. Conclusions

This is one of the rare studies investigating age at diagnosis in children with a migrant background in Europe. Our findings highlight that for them the diagnosis of ASD is not delayed in Upper Austria, where universal health care includes a system of preventive medical check-ups provided mainly by paediatricians during the first years of life. Specific effects of lower parental education on age at diagnosis in families with a migrant background point to the importance of utilising existing preventive systems for systematic ASD screening and to the need to improve parent education on child development and health care services. The almost complete absence of diagnoses of milder forms of ASD (Asperger's disorder) in children with a migrant background demonstrates the need for improving awareness of the whole autism spectrum by training professionals in health care and education and extending education to parents. Restricted and repetitive behaviours, language delay, and the combination of severe language delay with a relatively higher nonverbal development are possible symptoms of autism that can be used to identify ASD by observation by parents or professionals and by their inclusion in systematic screening tools.

For children both with and without a migrant background, referrals by primary care paediatricians significantly decreased age at diagnosis. A universal implementation of a streamlined model from systematic screening to timely diagnosis is expected to further reduce age at ASD diagnosis and to facilitate earlier access to specialised intervention.

Author Contributions: P.G.P. and D.H. designed the study; P.G.P. and D.H. did the retrospective data analysis; C.W. did the statistical analysis; P.G.P., D.H. and C.W. wrote the paper; M.P.d.l.P. and J.F. were advising, all authors contributed with the revisions. All authors have read and agreed to the published version of the manuscript.

Acknowledgments: We thank the Federal Institute for Education Research, Innovation and Development of the Austrian School System for providing some statidistical information included in the introduction.

References

1. Christensen, D.L.; Maenner, M.J.; Bilder, D.; Constantino, J.N.; Daniels, J.; Durkin, M.S.; Fitzgerald, R.T.; Kurzius-Spencer, M.; Pettygrove, S.D.; Robinson, C.; et al. Prevalence and Characteristics of Autism Spectrum Disorder Among Children Aged 4 Years-Early Autism and Developmental Disabilities Monitoring Network, Seven Sites, United States, 2010, 2012, and 2014. MMWR. *Surveill. Summ.* **2019**, *68*, 1–19. [CrossRef] [PubMed]
2. Atladottir, H.O.; Schendel, D.E.; Henriksen, T.B.; Hjort, L.; Parner, E.T. Gestational Age and Autism Spectrum Disorder: Trends in Risk Over Time. *Autism Res.* **2016**, *9*, 224–231. [CrossRef] [PubMed]
3. Boilson, A.M.; Staines, A.; Ramirez, A.; Posada, M.; Sweeney, M.R. Operationalisation of the European Protocol for Autism Prevalence (EPAP) for Autism Spectrum Disorder Prevalence Measurement in Ireland. *J. Autism Dev. Disord.* **2016**, *46*, 3054–3067. [CrossRef]
4. Reichow, B. Overview of meta-analyses on early intensive behavioral intervention for young children with autism spectrum disorders. *J. Autism Dev. Disord.* **2012**, *42*, 512–520. [CrossRef] [PubMed]
5. Rydzewska, E.; Hughes-McCormack, L.A.; Gillberg, C.; Henderson, A.; MacIntyre, C.; Rintoul, J.; Cooper, S.-A. Age at identification, prevalence and general health of children with autism: Observational study of a whole country population. *BMJ Open* **2019**, *9*, e025904. [CrossRef]
6. Bejarano-Martin, A.; Canal-Bedia, R.; Magan-Maganto, M.; Fernandez-Alvarez, C.; Cilleros-Martin, M.V.; Sanchez-Gomez, M.C.; Garcia-Primo, P.; Rose-Sweeney, M.; Boilson, A.; Linertova, R.; et al. Early Detection, Diagnosis and Intervention Services for Young Children with Autism Spectrum Disorder in the European Union (ASDEU): Family and Professional Perspectives. *J. Autism Dev. Disord.* **2019**. [CrossRef]
7. Allison, C.; Williams, J.; Scott, F.; Stott, C.; Bolton, P.; Baron-Cohen, S.; Brayne, C. The Childhood Asperger Syndrome Test (CAST): Test-Retest Reliability in a High Scoring Sample. *Autism Int. J. Res. Pract.* **2007**, *11*, 173–185. [CrossRef]
8. Bolton, S.; McDonald, D.; Curtis, E.; Kelly, S.; Gallagher, L. Autism in a recently arrived immigrant population. *Eur. J. Pediatr.* **2014**, *173*, 337–343. [CrossRef]
9. Haglund, N.G.S.; Kallen, K.B.M. Risk factors for autism and Asperger syndrome. Perinatal factors and migration. *Autism Int. J. Res. Pract.* **2011**, *15*, 163–183. [CrossRef]
10. Lehti, V.; Hinkka-Yli-Salomaki, S.; Cheslack-Postava, K.; Gissler, M.; Brown, A.S.; Sourander, A. The risk of childhood autism among second-generation migrants in Finland: A case-control study. *BMC Pediatr.* **2013**, *13*, 171. [CrossRef]
11. Fuentes, J.; Basurko, A.; Isasa, I.; Galende, I.; Muguerza, M.D.; García-Primo, P.; García, J.; Fernández-Álvarez, C.J.; Canal-Bedia, R.; La Posada de Paz, M. The ASDEU autism prevalence study in northern Spain. *Eur. Child Adolesc. Psychiatry* **2020**. [CrossRef]
12. Kawa, R.; Saemundsen, E.; Loa Jonsdottir, S.; Hellendoorn, A.; Lemcke, S.; Canal-Bedia, R.; Garcia-Primo, P.; Moilanen, I. European studies on prevalence and risk of autism spectrum disorders according to immigrant status-a review. *Eur. J. Public Health* **2017**, *27*, 101–110. [CrossRef]
13. Croen, L.A.; Grether, J.K.; Hoogstrate, J.; Selvin, S. The changing prevalence of autism in California. *J. Autism Dev. Disord.* **2002**, *32*, 207–215. [CrossRef] [PubMed]
14. Yeargin-Allsopp, M.; Rice, C.; Karapurkar, T.; Doernberg, N.; Boyle, C.; Murphy, C. Prevalence of autism in a US metropolitan area. *JAMA* **2003**, *289*, 49–55. [CrossRef] [PubMed]
15. Nevison, C.; Zahorodny, W. Race/Ethnicity-Resolved Time Trends in United States ASD Prevalence Estimates from IDEA and ADDM. *J. Autism Dev. Disord.* **2019**, *49*, 4721–4730. [CrossRef]
16. EUROSTAT. Migration and Migrant Population Statistics. Available online: https://ec.europa.eu/eurostat/statistics-explained/index.php/Migration_and_migrant_population_statistics#Migrant_population:_22.3_million_non-EU_citizens_living_in_the_EU_on_1_January_2018 (accessed on 4 April 2020).
17. Bundesministerium Europäische und Internationale Angelegenheiten. Statistisches Jahrbuch "migration & Integration 2019": Integrationsbericht 2019. Available online: https://www.bmeia.gv.at/integration/integrationsbericht/ (accessed on 4 April 2020).
18. Bundesministerium Europäische und Internationale Angelegenheiten. Österreich Integrationsbericht 2019: Integrationsbericht 2019: Integration in Österreich-Zahlen, Entwicklungen, Schwerpunkte.

Available online: https://www.bmeia.gv.at/fileadmin/user_upload/Zentrale/Integration/Integrationsbericht_2019/Migration-Integration-2019.pdf (accessed on 4 April 2020).

19. Hertz-Picciotto, I.; Delwiche, L. The rise in autism and the role of age at diagnosis. *Epidemiology* **2009**, *20*, 84–90. [CrossRef]
20. Russell, G.; Norwich, B. Dilemmas, diagnosis and de-stigmatization: Parental perspectives on the diagnosis of autism spectrum disorders. *Clin. Child Psychol. Psychiatry* **2012**, *17*, 229–245. [CrossRef]
21. Dawson, G. Recent advances in research on early detection, causes, biology, and treatment of autism spectrum disorders. *Curr. Opin. Neurol.* **2010**, *23*, 95–96. [CrossRef]
22. Warren, Z.; McPheeters, M.L.; Sathe, N.; Foss-Feig, J.H.; Glasser, A.; Veenstra-Vanderweele, J. A systematic review of early intensive intervention for autism spectrum disorders. *Pediatrics* **2011**, *127*, e1303–e1311. [CrossRef]
23. Hayes, S.A.; Watson, S.L. The impact of parenting stress: A meta-analysis of studies comparing the experience of parenting stress in parents of children with and without autism spectrum disorder. *J. Autism Dev. Disord.* **2013**, *43*, 629–642. [CrossRef]
24. Koegel, L.K.; Koegel, R.L.; Ashbaugh, K.; Bradshaw, J. The importance of early identification and intervention for children with or at risk for autism spectrum disorders. *Int. J. Speech-Lang. Pathol.* **2014**, *16*, 50–56. [CrossRef] [PubMed]
25. Horlin, C.; Falkmer, M.; Parsons, R.; Albrecht, M.A.; Falkmer, T. The cost of autism spectrum disorders. *PLoS ONE* **2014**, *9*, e106552. [CrossRef] [PubMed]
26. Jacobson, J.W.; Mulick, J.A. System and cost research issues in treatments for people with autistic disorders. *J. Autism Dev. Disord.* **2000**, *30*, 585–593. [CrossRef] [PubMed]
27. Evans, D.B.; Hsu, J.; Boerma, T. Universal health coverage and universal access. *Bull. World Health Organ.* **2013**, *91*, 546–546A. [CrossRef]
28. Mandell, D.S.; Novak, M.M.; Zubritsky, C.D. Factors associated with age of diagnosis among children with autism spectrum disorders. *Pediatrics* **2005**, *116*, 1480–1486. [CrossRef]
29. Szymanski, C.A.; Brice, P.J.; Lam, K.H.; Hotto, S.A. Deaf children with autism spectrum disorders. *J. Autism Dev. Disord.* **2012**, *42*, 2027–2037. [CrossRef]
30. Bickel, J.; Bridgemohan, C.; Sideridis, G.; Huntington, N. Child and family characteristics associated with age of diagnosis of an autism spectrum disorder in a tertiary care setting. *J. Dev. Behav. Pediatr.* **2015**, *36*, 1–7. [CrossRef]
31. Eriksson, M.A.; Westerlund, J.; Hedvall, Å.; Åmark, P.; Gillberg, C.; Fernell, E. Medical conditions affect the outcome of early intervention in preschool children with autism spectrum disorders. *Eur. Child Adolesc. Psychiatry* **2013**, *22*, 23–33. [CrossRef]
32. Simonoff, E.; Pickles, A.; Charman, T.; Chandler, S.; Loucas, T.; Baird, G. Psychiatric disorders in children with autism spectrum disorders: Prevalence, comorbidity, and associated factors in a population-derived sample. *J. Am. Acad. Child Adolesc. Psychiatry* **2008**, *47*, 921–929. [CrossRef]
33. Harstad, E.; Huntington, N.; Bacic, J.; Barbaresi, W. Disparity of care for children with parent-reported autism spectrum disorders. *Acad. Pediatr.* **2013**, *13*, 334–339. [CrossRef]
34. Delobel-Ayoub, M.; Ehlinger, V.; Klapouszczak, D.; Maffre, T.; Raynaud, J.-P.; Delpierre, C.; Arnaud, C. Socioeconomic Disparities and Prevalence of Autism Spectrum Disorders and Intellectual Disability. *PLoS ONE* **2015**, *10*, e0141964. [CrossRef] [PubMed]
35. Durkin, M.S.; Maenner, M.J.; Meaney, F.J.; Levy, S.E.; DiGuiseppi, C.; Nicholas, J.S.; Kirby, R.S.; Pinto-Martin, J.A.; Schieve, L.A. Socioeconomic inequality in the prevalence of autism spectrum disorder: Evidence from a U.S. cross-sectional study. *PLoS ONE* **2010**, *5*, e11551. [CrossRef] [PubMed]
36. Chaidez, V.; Hansen, R.L.; Hertz-Picciotto, I. Autism spectrum disorders in Hispanics and non-Hispanics. *Autism Int. J. Res. Pract.* **2012**, *16*, 381–397. [CrossRef] [PubMed]
37. Daniels, A.M.; Mandell, D.S. Explaining differences in age at autism spectrum disorder diagnosis: A critical review. *Autism Int. J. Res. Pract.* **2014**, *18*, 583–597. [CrossRef]
38. Mandell, D.S.; Listerud, J.; Levy, S.E.; Pinto-Martin, J.A. Race differences in the age at diagnosis among medicaid-eligible children with autism. *J. Am. Acad. Child Adolesc. Psychiatry* **2002**, *41*, 1447–1453. [CrossRef]

39. Mandell, D.S.; Morales, K.H.; Xie, M.; Lawer, L.J.; Stahmer, A.C.; Marcus, S.C. Age of diagnosis among Medicaid-enrolled children with autism, 2001–2004. *Psychiatr. Serv.* **2010**, *61*, 822–829. [CrossRef]
40. Rivard, M.; Millau, M.; Magnan, C.; Mello, C.; Boulé, M. Snakes and Ladders: Barriers and Facilitators Experienced by Immigrant Families when Accessing an Autism Spectrum Disorder Diagnosis. *J. Dev. Phys. Disabil.* **2019**, *31*, 519–539. [CrossRef]
41. Valicenti-McDermott, M.; Hottinger, K.; Seijo, R.; Shulman, L. Age at diagnosis of autism spectrum disorders. *J. Pediatr.* **2012**, *161*, 554–556. [CrossRef]
42. Samadi, S.A.; McConkey, R. Autism in developing countries: Lessons from iran. *Autism Res. Treat.* **2011**, *2011*, 145359. [CrossRef]
43. VanDenHeuvel, A.; Fitzgerald, M.; Greiner, B.; Perry, I.J. Screening for autistic spectrum disorder at the 18-month developmental assessment: A population-based study. *Ir. Med. J* **2007**, *100*, 565–567.
44. Liptak, G.S.; Benzoni, L.B.; Mruzek, D.W.; Nolan, K.W.; Thingvoll, M.A.; Wade, C.M.; Fryer, G.E. Disparities in diagnosis and access to health services for children with autism: Data from the National Survey of Children's Health. *J. Dev. Behav. Pediatr.* **2008**, *29*, 152–160. [CrossRef] [PubMed]
45. Hussein, A.M.; Pellicano, E.; Crane, L. Understanding and awareness of autism among Somali parents living in the United Kingdom. *Autism Int. J. Res. Pract.* **2019**, *23*, 1408–1418. [CrossRef] [PubMed]
46. Sritharan, B.; Koola, M.M. Barriers faced by immigrant families of children with autism: A program to address the challenges. *Asian J. Psychiatry* **2019**, *39*, 53–57. [CrossRef]
47. Zuckerman, K.E.; Sinche, B.; Mejia, A.; Cobian, M.; Becker, T.; Nicolaidis, C. Latino parents' perspectives on barriers to autism diagnosis. *Acad. Pediatr.* **2014**, *14*, 301–308. [CrossRef] [PubMed]
48. Bailey, D.B.; Skinner, D.; Correa, V.; Arcia, E.; Reyes-Blanes, M.E.; Rodriguez, P.; Vázquez-Montilla, E.; Skinner, M. Needs and supports reported by Latino families of young children with developmental disabilities. *Am. J. Ment. Retard.* **1999**, *104*, 437–451. [CrossRef]
49. Dyches, T.T.; Wilder, L.K.; Sudweeks, R.R.; Obiakor, F.E.; Algozzine, B. Multicultural issues in autism. *J. Autism Dev. Disord.* **2004**, *34*, 211–222. [CrossRef]
50. Rogers-Dulan, J.; Blacher, J. African American families, religion, and disability: A conceptual framework. *Ment. Retard.* **1995**, *33*, 226–238.
51. Matson, J.L.; Matheis, M.; Burns, C.O.; Esposito, G.; Venuti, P.; Pisula, E.; Misiak, A.; Kalyva, E.; Tsakiris, V.; Kamio, Y.; et al. Examining cross-cultural differences in autism spectrum disorder: A multinational comparison from Greece, Italy, Japan, Poland, and the United States. *Eur. Psychiatry J. Assoc. Eur. Psychiatr.* **2017**, *42*, 70–76. [CrossRef]
52. Pondé, M.P.; Rousseau, C.; Carlos, M.A.C. Pervasive developmental disorder in the children of immigrant parents: Comparison of different assessment instruments. *Arq. Neuropsiquiatr.* **2013**, *71*, 877–882. [CrossRef]
53. Carruthers, S.; Kinnaird, E.; Rudra, A.; Smith, P.; Allison, C.; Auyeung, B.; Chakrabarti, B.; Wakabayashi, A.; Baron-Cohen, S.; Bakolis, I.; et al. A cross-cultural study of autistic traits across India, Japan and the UK. *Mol. Autism* **2018**, *9*, 52. [CrossRef]
54. American Psychological Association. Ethical Principles of Psychologists and Code of Conduct (2002, Amended Effective 1 June 2010, and 1 January 2017). 2017. Available online: https://www.apa.org/ethics/code/ethics-code-2017.pdf (accessed on 14 July 2020).
55. STATcube- Statistical Database of STATISCS AUSTRIA. Available online: http://www.statistik.at/web_en/publications_services/statcube/index.html (accessed on 14 July 2020).
56. Fellinger, J.; Holzinger, D. Creating innovative clinical and service models for communication: Institut fuer Sinnes- und Sprachneurologie. *J. Dev. Behav. Pediatr.* **2014**, *35*, 148–153. [CrossRef] [PubMed]
57. Holzinger, D.; Laister, D.; Vivanti, G.; Barbaresi, W.J.; Fellinger, J. Feasibility and Outcomes of the Early Start Denver Model Implemented with Low Intensity in a Community Setting in Austria. *J. Dev. Behav. Pediatr.* **2019**, *40*, 354–363. [CrossRef] [PubMed]
58. World Health Organization; Ebrary, Inc. *The ICD-10 Classification of Mental and Behavioural Disorders: Diagnostic Criteria for Research*; World Health Organization: Geneva, Switzerland, 1993; ISBN 9789241544559.
59. Poustka, L. *ADOS-2: Diagnostische Beobachtungsskala für Autistische Störungen 2*; Hogrefe: Göttingen, Germany, 2015.
60. Mullen, E.M. *Mullen Scales of Early Learning (AGS ed.)*; American Guidance Service Inc.: Circle Pines, MN, USA, 1995.

61. Bayley scales of infant and toddler development. In *Harcourt Assessment*; Springer: Boston, MA, USA, 2006.
62. Petermann, F.; Petermann, U.J. *Hamburg Wechsler Intelligenztest für Kinder IV (HAWIK-IV)*; Huber: Bern, Switzerland, 2008.
63. Gotham, K.; Pickles, A.; Lord, C. Standardizing ADOS scores for a measure of severity in autism spectrum disorders. *J. Autism Dev. Disord.* **2009**, *39*, 693–705. [CrossRef] [PubMed]
64. Lord, C.; Rutter, M.; Le, C.A. Autism Diagnostic Interview-Revised: A revised version of a diagnostic interview for caregivers of individuals with possible pervasive developmental disorders. *J. Autism Dev. Disord.* **1994**, *24*, 659–685. [CrossRef] [PubMed]
65. Gearing, R.E.; Mian, I.A.; Barber, J.; Ickowicz, A. A methodology for conducting retrospective chart review research in child and adolescent psychiatry. *J. Can. Acad. Child Adolesc. Psychiatry = J. de l'Academie canadienne de psychiatrie de l'enfant et de l'adolescent* **2006**, *15*, 126–134.
66. Vassar, M.; Holzmann, M. The retrospective chart review: Important methodological considerations. *J. Educ. Eval. Health Prof.* **2013**, *10*, 12. [CrossRef]
67. The World Medical Association, Inc. (WMA). WMA DoH Übersetzung DE_Rev 190905: Declaration of Helsinki of 1975, 2013 Reviewed 2013. Available online: https://www.wma.net/policy/hb-e-version-2019/ (accessed on 14 July 2020).
68. Cohen, J.; Cohen, P.; West, S.G.; Aiken, L.S. *Applied Multiple Regression/Correlation Analysis for the Behavioral Sciences*, 3rd ed.; Routledge, Taylor & Francis Group: New York, NY, USA; London, UK, 2003; ISBN 9780805822236.
69. Kelley, K.; Preacher, K.J. On effect size. *Psychol. Methods* **2012**, *17*, 137–152. [CrossRef]
70. Peterson, R.A.; Brown, S.P. On the use of beta coefficients in meta-analysis. *J. Appl. Psychol.* **2005**, *90*, 175–181. [CrossRef]
71. Enders, C.K. Multiple imputation as a flexible tool for missing data handling in clinical research. *Behav. Res. Ther.* **2017**, *98*, 4–18. [CrossRef]
72. Rubin, D.B. *Multiple Imputation for Nonresponse in Surveys, [Book on Demand]*; John Wiley: Hoboken, NJ, USA, 2011; ISBN 978-0-471-65574-9.
73. Keller, B.T.; Enders, C.K. Blimp User's Manual (Version 1.0), Los Angeles, CA, USA. 2017. Available online: http://www.appliedmissingdata.com/blimpuserguide-4.pdf (accessed on 14 July 2020).
74. von Hippel, P.T. How Many Imputations Do You Need? A Two-stage Calculation Using a Quadratic Rule. *Sociol. Methods Res.* **2018**. [CrossRef]
75. Muthén, L.K.; Muthén, B.O. *Mplus User's Guide*, 8th ed.; Muthén & Muthén: Los Angeles, CA, USA, 1998–2017.
76. The Jamovi Project. Jamovi. (Version 1.1), 2019, Sydney, Australia. Available online: https://www.jamovi.org/about.html (accessed on 14 July 2020).
77. Schenk, L.; Kamtsiuris, P.; Ellert, U. Ambulante Versorgung von Kindern mit Migrationshintergrund–Inanspruchnahme und Zufriedenheit. *Gesundheitswesen* **2009**, *71*. [CrossRef]
78. Zuckerman, K.E.; Mattox, K.; Donelan, K.; Batbayar, O.; Baghaee, A.; Bethell, C. Pediatrician identification of Latino children at risk for autism spectrum disorder. *Pediatrics* **2013**, *132*, 445–453. [CrossRef] [PubMed]
79. Magnusson, C.; Rai, D.; Goodman, A.; Lundberg, M.; Idring, S.; Svensson, A.; Koupil, I.; Serlachius, E.; Dalman, C. Migration and autism spectrum disorder: Population-based study. *Br. J. Psychiatry* **2012**, *201*, 109–115. [CrossRef] [PubMed]
80. Magnusson, M.; Rasmussen, F.; Sundelin, C. Early identification of children with communication disabilities–evaluation of a screening programme in a Swedish county. *Acta Paediatr.* **1996**, *85*, 1319–1326. [CrossRef] [PubMed]
81. Lampi, K.M.; Lehtonen, L.; Tran, P.L.; Suominen, A.; Lehti, V.; Banerjee, P.N.; Gissler, M.; Brown, A.S.; Sourander, A. Risk of autism spectrum disorders in low birth weight and small for gestational age infants. *J. Pediatr.* **2012**, *161*, 830–836. [CrossRef]

82. Kiing, J.S.H.; Neihart, M.; Chan, Y.-H. Teachers' role in identifying young children at risk for developmental delay and disabilities: Usefulness of the Parents Evaluation of Developmental Status tool. *Child Care Health Dev.* **2019**, *45*, 637–643. [CrossRef]
83. Henrichs, J.; Rescorla, L.; Donkersloot, C.; Schenk, J.J.; Raat, H.; Jaddoe, V.W.V.; Hofman, A.; Verhulst, F.C.; Tiemeier, H. Early Vocabulary Delay and Behavioral/Emotional Problems in Early Childhood: The Generation R Study. *J. Speech Lang. Hear. Res.* **2013**, *56*, 553–566. [CrossRef]

8

Examining the Overlap between Autism Spectrum Disorder and 22q11.2 Deletion Syndrome

Opal Ousley [1,*], A. Nichole Evans [2], Samuel Fernandez-Carriba [2,3], Erica L. Smearman [4], Kimberly Rockers [1,5], Michael J. Morrier [1], David W. Evans [6], Karlene Coleman [2] and Joseph Cubells [1,5]

1 Emory Autism Center, Department of Psychiatry and Behavioral Sciences, Emory University School of Medicine, 1551 Shoup Court, Atlanta, GA 30322, USA; kimberly.rockers@gmail.com (K.R.); mmorrier@emory.edu (M.J.M.); jcubell@emory.edu (J.C.)
2 Marcus Autism Center, Children's Healthcare of Atlanta, 1920 Briarcliff Road, Atlanta, GA 30329, USA; andrea.evans@choa.org (A.N.E.); samuel.fernandez-carriba@emory.edu (S.F.-C.); karlene.coleman@choa.org (K.C.)
3 Marcus Autism Center, Department of Pediatrics, Emory University School of Medicine, 1920 Briarcliff Road, Atlanta, GA 30329, USA
4 Department of Psychology, Emory University, Psychology and Interdisciplinary Studies (PAIS) Building, 36 Eagle Row, Atlanta, GA 30322, USA; esmearm@emory.edu
5 Department of Human Genetics, Emory University School of Medicine, 615 Michael Street, Whitehead Biomedical Research Building, Suite 301, Atlanta, GA 30322, USA
6 Department of Psychology, Bucknell University, 1 Dent Drive, Lewisburg, PA 17837, USA; dwevans@bucknell.edu
* Correspondence: oousley@emory.edu

Academic Editor: Merlin G. Butler

Abstract: 22q11.2 deletion syndrome (22q11.2DS) is a genomic disorder reported to associate with autism spectrum disorders (ASDs) in 15–50% of cases; however, others suggest that individuals with 22q11.2DS present psychiatric or behavioral features associated with ASDs, but do not meet full criteria for ASD diagnoses. Such wide variability in findings may arise in part due to methodological differences across studies. Our study sought to determine whether individuals with 22q11.2DS meet strict ASD diagnostic criteria using research-based guidelines from the Collaborative Programs of Excellence in Autism (CPEA), which required a gathering of information from three sources: the Autism Diagnostic Interview-Revised (ADI-R), the Autism Diagnostic Observational Schedule (ADOS), and a clinician's best-estimate diagnosis. Our study examined a cohort of children, adolescents, and young adults (n = 56) with 22q11.2DS, who were ascertained irrespective of parents' behavioral or developmental concerns, and found that 17.9% (n = 10) of the participants met CPEA criteria for an ASD diagnosis, and that a majority showed some level of social-communication impairment or the presence of repetitive behaviors. We conclude that strictly defined ASDs occur in a substantial proportion of individuals with 22q11.2DS, and recommend that all individuals with 22q11.2DS be screened for ASDs during early childhood.

Keywords: 22q11.2 deletion; autism; autism spectrum; diagnosis; copy number variation; CNV; Research Domain Criteria; RDoC

1. Introduction

22q11.2 deletion syndrome (22q11.2DS) is among a growing number of genomic disorders that associate with autism spectrum disorders (ASDs) [1]. 22q11.2DS, also referred to as DiGeorge syndrome, or velo-cardio-facial syndrome (VCFS), occurs in approximately 1/4000 live births [2–5], making it the most common recurrent copy-number variant (CNV) associated with developmental disorders described to date. 22q11.2DS arises from an interstitial deletion of up to 3 Mb of DNA on chromosome 22q11.2 and produces a diverse range of physical, behavioral, social, and neurocognitive impairments [2,5–7], which overlap with the social-communication impairments found among patients with ASD [7–9].

While previous studies have described both the presence of ASDs among individuals with 22q11.2DS and the presence of 22q11.2DS among individuals diagnosed with ASD, there is no consensus on the rate of co-occurrence [10]. Previous studies have reported that 15–50% of those with 22q11.2DS also have an ASD [8,9,11], and that between 0.3% and 1% of individuals with an ASD also have 22q11.2DS [12,13]—an approximately 10–40-fold increase relative to the general population. The substantial discrepancies in reported rates of ASDs in 22q11.2DS could reflect methodological differences across studies, including the use of varied subject ascertainment methods and diagnostic assessment approaches [8]. However, some researchers argue that, although ASD-like symptoms are present in individuals with 22q11.2DS, these individuals do not truly meet criteria for an ASD, and may represent misclassified persons with, for example, prodromal symptoms of schizophrenia [14,15].

This issue resembles the ongoing debate faced by Fragile X syndrome (FXS) researchers, on the association between ASD and FXS [16–18]. Although debate over the overlap between FXS and autism continues, the clinical evaluation of individuals with ASD now regularly includes molecular testing for FXS. Furthermore, basic research on FXS has led to the testing of novel psychopharmacological interventions for FXS that appear to impact ASD-related symptoms [19,20]. Thus, the value of understanding relationships among molecularly defined genetic and genomic disorders and ASD is abundantly clear.

Our study aims to clarify the association between 22q11.2DS and ASD by applying rigorous, research-based diagnostic methods applied to a cohort of individuals ascertained solely on the basis of a molecular diagnosis of 22q11.2DS. We sought to determine the proportion of individuals with 22q11.2DS who meet research criteria for an ASD diagnosis according to the guidelines set forth by the Collaborative Programs of Excellence in Autism (CPEA) Simons Simplex Collection study (Simons Foundation Autism Research Initiative) [21]. The CPEA guidelines require individuals to meet cutoff scores on gold standard observational and parent report measures (i.e., the Autism Diagnostic Interview-Revised (ADI-R) [22] and Autism Diagnostic Observation Schedule (ADOS) [23]) in conjunction with clinicians' best-estimate consensus diagnosis in order to receive a research-based diagnosis of ASD. We assessed 56 children, adolescents, and young adults with fluorescent in situ hybridization (FISH) confirmed 22q11.2DS, ascertained from a registry of all cases of 22q11.2DS diagnosed at Children's Healthcare of Atlanta since the mid-1990s. We hypothesized that we would identify strictly defined ASDs in a substantial proportion of patients with 22q11.2DS.

2. Results

We found that a substantial number of individuals with 22q11.2DS within our sample met strictly defined ASD (17.9%, n = 10; 2.3:1 male to female ratio), using rigorous research diagnostic criteria, and that a significant level of ASD-related symptoms occurred for a portion of our sample, even in the absence of an ASD diagnosis. An additional subset of individuals did not meet overall autism or ASD cutoffs on the standardized assessments. Details of these findings are outlined below and depicted in Figures 1–4.

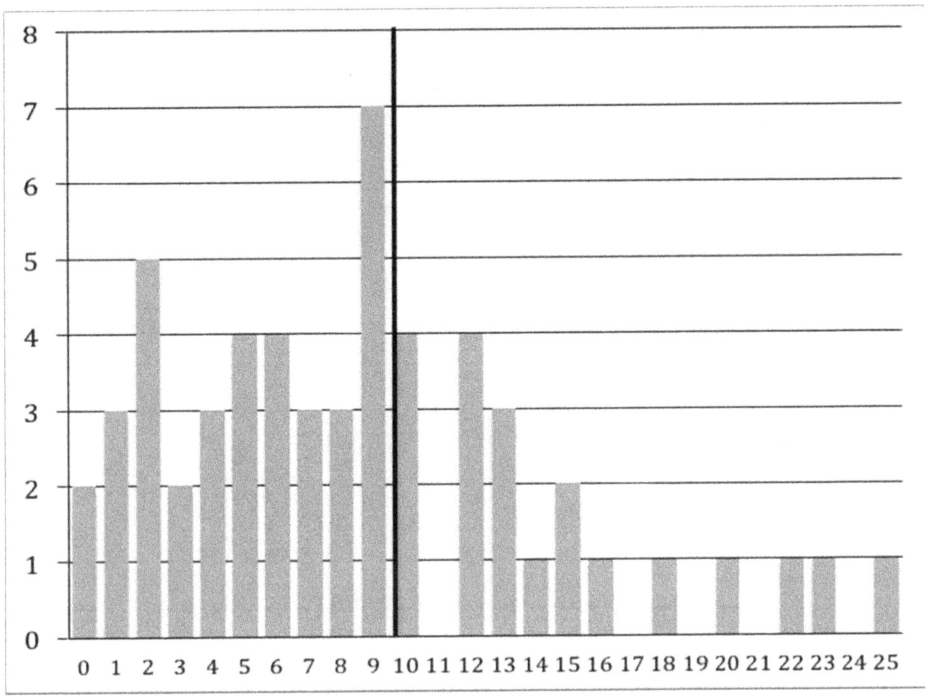

Figure 1. Figure 1 shows the broad range of Autism Diagnostic Interview-Revised (ADI-R) Reciprocal Social Interaction algorithm total scores (0–25; the autism spectrum disorder (ASD) cutoff score $\geq$ 10 is indicated by the black vertical line). The x-axis shows the algorithm score, and the y-axis indicates the number of individuals with each score.

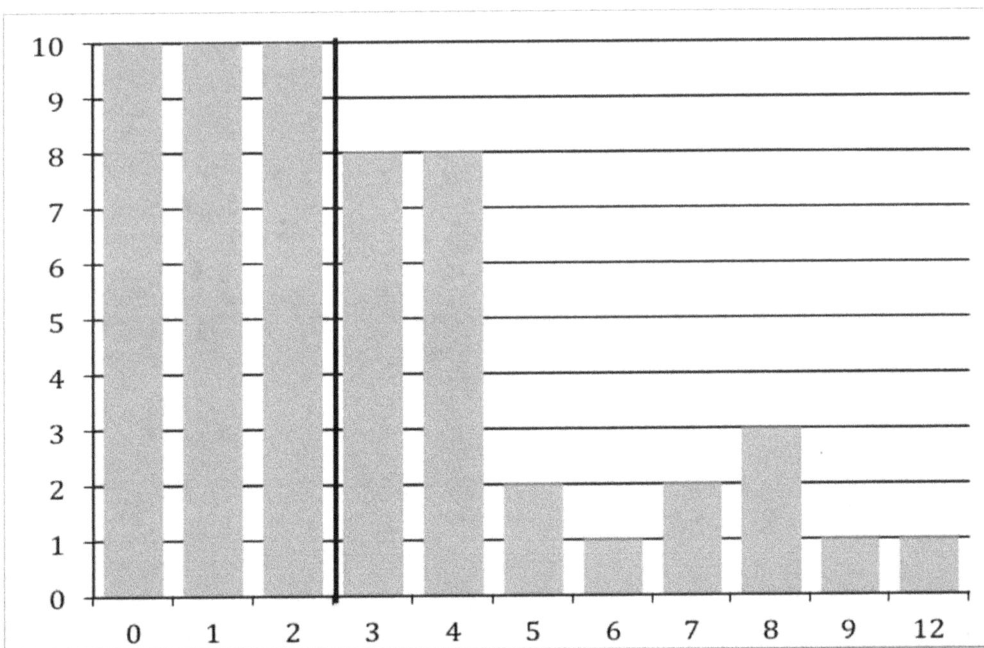

Figure 2. Figure 2 shows the broad range of ADI-R Restricted, Repetitive, and Stereotyped Behavior algorithm total scores (0–12; the ASD cutoff score $\geq$3 is indicated by the black vertical line). The x-axis shows the algorithm score, and the y-axis indicates the number of individuals with each score.

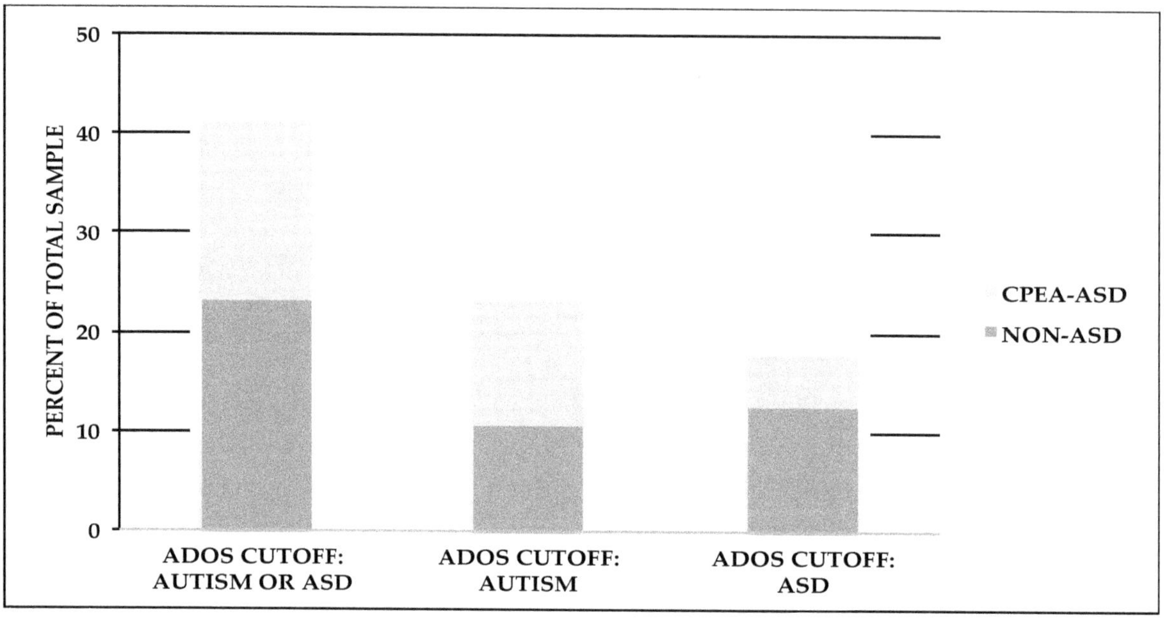

Figure 3. Figure 3 shows the percentages of individuals meeting the Autism Diagnostic Observational Schedule (ADOS) cutoff criteria. Within each cutoff category, diagnostic groups are designated as those who either met the Collaborative Programs of Excellence in Autism (CPEA) criteria for an ASD diagnosis (CPEA-ASD), or those who did not meet these criteria (non-ASD).

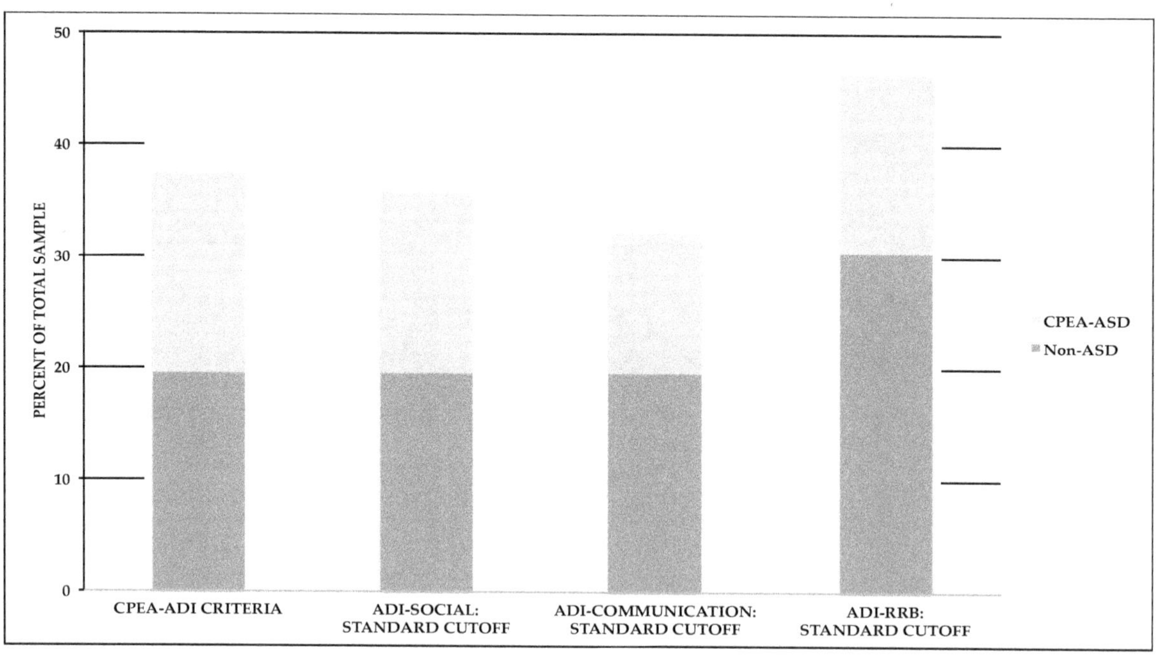

Figure 4. Figure 4 shows the percentages of individuals meeting ADI-R criteria set forth by the CPEA (CPEA-ADI) or standard ADI-R domain cutoff scores. Within each cutoff category, diagnostic groups are designated as those who met CPEA-ASD criteria or those who did not meet these criteria (non-ASD).

As described in the Materials and Methods section, we examined various cutoff scores for the Autism Diagnostic Observation Schedule (ADOS) and the Autism Diagnostic Interview-Revised (ADI-R), and determined who met CPEA criteria for an ASD diagnosis. A majority of individuals (n = 53) completed either ADOS Modules 3 or 4, which is given to children or adults, respectively, with language fluency. Three individuals completed either Module 1 (n = 2) or Module 2 (n = 1), which is given to individuals with no speech/single words or phrase speech, respectively. Examination of the

ADOS scores revealed that 23.2% (n = 13) of the participants met the autism cutoff score and 17.9% (n = 10) met the ASD cutoff score, for a total of 41.1% (n = 23). We also found that more than a third of the study participants (37.5%, n = 21) met ADI-R criteria as specified by the CPEA criteria, which follows either the standard ADI-R cutoff scoring parameters for autism (17.9%, n = 10) or a more flexible set of parameters (19.6%, n = 11; following Risi et al.; see Methods section below) [24]. An examination of each ADI-R domain score revealed that 35.7% (n = 20) met the ADI-R Reciprocal Social Interaction domain cutoff score, 32.1% (n = 18) met the ADI-R Communication domain cutoff score, and 46.4% (n = 26) met the Restricted, Repetitive, and Stereotyped Behavior domain cutoff score. Moreover, 66.1% (n = 37) of our total sample met cutoff scores for at least one of the social, communication, or repetitive behavior domains on the ADI-R. A wide range of algorithm scores was obtained for the ADI-R: Reciprocal Social Interaction range = 0–25, Communication range (verbal algorithm) = 0–18 (n = 53) and Communication range (nonverbal algorithm) = 0–12 (n = 3), and Restricted, Repetitive, and Stereotyped Behavior range = 0–12. The range of scores for the Reciprocal Social Interaction algorithm is shown below in Figure 1, whereas the range for the Restricted, Repetitive, and Stereotyped Behavior algorithm score is shown in Figure 2.

We also examined the presence of a strictly defined ASD using the CPEA guidelines, which required us to examine cutoff scores on the both the ADI-R and ADOS, in conjunction with best-estimate Diagnostic and Statistical Manual of Mental Disorders, Fourth Edition (DSM-IV) diagnosis [21,25]. We found that, of 56 participants, 17.9% (n = 10) met CPEA research-based criteria for a strictly defined ASD. That is, each participant met cutoff criteria for both the ADI-R and ADOS, and received a best-estimate diagnosis of a DSM-IV ASD. Our participants meeting CPEA criteria included individuals with a best-estimate diagnosis of DSM-IV Autistic Disorder or PDD-NOS. Although DSM-IV Asperger's Disorder would have qualified as a CPEA diagnosis, no participants in this sample met Asperger's diagnostic criteria. For those individuals who did not meet CPEA diagnostic criteria, two subsets emerged. In one subset (39.3%, n = 22), neither the ADI-R nor the ADOS overall cutoff scores were met; in the second subset (42.9%, n = 24), overall cutoff scores were met for at least one of the standardized instruments. Thus, even in the absence of a CPEA-ASD diagnosis, a significant minority of individuals met ADOS cutoff scores, or ADI-R cutoff scores, depicted in Figures 3 and 4.

3. Discussion

Debate continues regarding the association between 22q11.2DS and ASDs. While multiple studies show that individuals with 22q11.2DS present with ASD-like symptomatology, not all studies find that such individuals qualify for a formal diagnosis of an ASD [26]. Our study attempts to resolve these discrepant findings by considering ascertainment bias and drawing from a strict and thorough research-based definition of ASD, as outlined by CPEA guidelines, which require individuals to attain cutoff scores for an ASD from both the ADI-R and ADOS as well as a clinician's best estimate diagnosis of DSM-IV Autism, Asperger's Disorder, or PDD-NOS. Our findings showed that a substantial proportion of study participants with 22q11.2DS met research-based CPEA criteria for an ASD, supporting an association between 22q11.2DS and ASD. We also found in our sample that significant social and communication impairments, as well as restricted and repetitive behaviors, occurred in the absence of an ASD diagnosis.

Our finding that 17.9% of study participants with 22q11.2DS met research CPEA criteria for an ASD diagnosis falls within the range of prior studies reporting that 15–50% of individuals meet diagnostic criteria for an ASD [8,9,11]. To obtain a conservative estimate of ASD in individuals with 22q11.2DS, we chose (1) to use the CPEA research criteria; and (2) to recruit from a hospital and medical clinic database of individuals with 22q11.2DS, with a molecular diagnosis of the disorder as the only criterion for participation. We thus avoided the potential ascertainment bias inherent in studying subjects independently seeking behavioral, mental health, or neurodevelopmental evaluations. Importantly, while this is not an epidemiologic study and individuals in this sample may not be representative of all individuals with 22q11.2DS, a substantial portion of participants met

ASD criteria, suggesting the presence of an association. We also found that almost 40% of 22q11.2DS participants met neither the ADI-R nor the ADOS overall cutoffs for autism or ASD, but that more than 60% met at least one domain cutoff on the ADI-R.

These findings should be considered in light of the RDoC (Research Domain Criteria) initiative of the National Institutes of Mental Health [27]. Here, we applied a conservative threshold for ASD diagnosis. We recognize, however, that neurodevelopmental disorders are characterized by deviations and delays on dimensional traits that extend well into the general population [28,29]. Thus, understanding the morbidity of CNV syndromes requires an appreciation for the more subtle deviations and delays that may arise throughout development, reflecting, for example, a psychiatric prodrome. In some instances, even probands with de novo mutations that appear clinically unaffected nonetheless exhibit a "shift" in symptom expression relative to non-carrier first-degree relatives [30,31]. It is important therefore to bear in mind the impact of a CNV as it increases risk—both in terms of traditional clinical thresholds and categories, as well as dimensions of cognitive, social, motor, and behavioral phenotypes.

Our study's limitations include its cross-sectional design, which precludes examination of behavioral trajectories or emergence of ASD-related symptoms. Additionally, although the presence of co-morbid diagnoses was not the focus of this paper, individuals with 22q11.2DS are at risk for symptoms that extend beyond an ASD diagnosis, including schizophrenia spectrum disorder, depressive disorders, and anxiety disorders [21,32]. We do not yet know precisely how the presence of an ASD diagnosis or ASD symptoms in the absence of an ASD diagnosis affects the emergence of these additional disorders, and only longitudinal studies will allow us to understand these associations. Further, our study relied on the DSM-IV diagnostic system, which closely mirrors the International Classification of Diseases (ICD-10) published by the World Health Organization; however, we did not re-code our autism diagnoses based on the revised specifications for "autism spectrum disorder" outlined in the Diagnostic and Statistical Manual, Fifth Edition (DSM-5). We would predict that our findings would be similar using the DSM-5 criteria, which were developed in part based on prior research from the ADOS, ADI-R, and CPEA [21,23,24]. Future studies examining the various diagnostic classification systems are needed, however, to verify the stability of our findings.

Findings from this study have both clinical and scientific relevance. Because this study supports an association between 22q11.2DS and ASD, we recommend that individuals with 22q11.2DS (1) receive earlier evaluations for ASDs and (2) receive targeted interventions and therapies, such as pharmacological and behavioral approaches, which, when started earlier, may lead to more positive long-term outcomes [9,19]. Furthermore, clinicians evaluating or treating patients with ASDs should consider diagnostic testing for 22q11.2DS (and other CNV disorders), particularly when other associated features such as congenital heart defects, velo-palatal pathology, and immune-related difficulties are present. Awareness of the association between 22q11.2DS and ASDs may also lead to specific hypotheses regarding the etiology and final common pathways that increase risk for childhood social disability and ASDs [33,34].

4. Materials and Methods

4.1. Participants

4.1.1. Overview

This study evaluated 56 participants between the ages of 6–29 who were diagnosed with 22q11.2DS and who had participated in a larger study investigating neuropsychological and behavioral outcomes in 22q11.2DS [21,35]. All individuals in the study underwent neurocognitive screening and diagnostic assessments for ASD, which included the Autism Diagnostic Interview- Revised (ADI-R) [22] and the Autism Diagnostic Observation Schedule (ADOS) [23]. Data collection procedures were approved by the Emory University Institutional Review Board (#IRB00024756).

4.1.2. Recruitment and Eligibility

We recruited study participants from a children's 22q11.2DS medical clinic and hospital case registry maintained at the Children's Healthcare of Atlanta, which also includes adult subjects who were first diagnosed with 22q11.2DS in a congenital heart defects follow-up clinic. These clinics serve all of metro Atlanta and pull from a large regional catchment area in the Southeastern United States. For all study participants, the diagnosis of 22q11.2DS was identified by FISH using the standard *TUPLE* probe (LSI TUPLE1(22q11.2)/ARSA(22q13.3); Abbott Molecular #05J21-028; Abbott Park, IL, USA). This probe detects the common 3 Mb and 1.5 Mb deletions, which account for approximately 90% of the deletions observed in the clinically ascertained in the DiGeorge and velo-cardio-facial syndrome populations, but does not distinguish between these deletions.

Having a diagnosis of 22q11.2DS was the primary eligibility requirement for each study, and recruitment occurred without regard to the level of behavioral, developmental, or medical difficulties. The adolescent/adult participants were recruited for a longitudinal study of psychiatric symptoms in 22q11.2DS, and the child participants were recruited for a longitudinal study investigating language development. A majority of subjects (n = 51) were ascertained directly from this case registry, based on age eligibility. Five other participants were referred directly to the study from the Children's Healthcare of Atlanta 22q11.2DS multidisciplinary medical clinic or an adult congenital heart clinic, which follows children formerly served at Children's Healthcare of Atlanta. Additionally, no subjects in the study were from the same family.

4.1.3. Demographic Characteristics

Our 56 participants include an adolescent/adult group (n = 32; mean age = 19.21, SD = 4.12; range = 14–29) and a child group (n = 24; mean age = 9.58, SD = 1.91; range = 6–11). For the adult group, females comprise 53.13% (n = 17) of the group, while among children, females comprise 45.83% (n = 11). The majority of our adult participants are Caucasian (78.12%, n = 25) with three additional ethnicities represented: African-American (12.50%, n = 4), Hispanic (6.25%, n = 2), and Asian (3.12%, n = 1). Similarly among our child participants, Caucasian (70.83%, n = 17) is the majority, with four additional ethnicities represented: Hispanic (12.50%, n = 3), African-American (8.33%, n = 2), Asian (4.16%, n = 1), and bi-racial: African-American and Caucasian (4.16%, n = 1). Parent-reported medical, developmental and family history is provided in Table 1, which indicates a high rate of cardiac, immune, and palatal problems in the study participants. Parents also commonly reported a history of speech delay and ADHD in the study participants, although a history of known autism spectrum disorder was reported for only one participant. Parents reported ADHD as the most common disorder among family members (i.e., parents or siblings); only one family member was known to have 22q11.2DS.

For the adolescent/adult group, the estimated Verbal IQ (VIQ) was based on the Vocabulary and Similarities subtests from either the Wechsler Adult Intelligence Scale–Third Edition (WAIS-III) or the Wechsler Intelligence Scale for Children-Third Edition (WISC-III), depending on chronological age. To calculate the estimated VIQ, we converted the T-scores from these subtests to standard scores, and calculated their average (i.e., mean VIQ = 84.61, SD = 16.81; range = 57–120; n = 32). We also converted the WAIS-III or WISC-III Block Design T-score to a standard score to determine an estimated nonverbal IQ (NVIQ) (i.e., mean NVIQ = 73.29, SD = 14.96; range = 55–100; n = 32). For the child group, we used the Differential Ability Scales–Second Edition (DAS-II) Verbal score as the indicator of VIQ (i.e., mean VIQ = 72.87; SD = 17.60; range = 3–98; n = 23) and used the DAS-II Pattern Construction score to estimate NVIQ (i.e., mean NVIQ = 79.48, SD = 15.69; range = 43–102; n = 22). The sample sizes used to calculate the children's VIQ and NVIQ mean scores vary by one and two data points, respectively, due to missing data.

Table 1. Parent report of known medical, developmental, and family history.

	Child	Adult	Total	Family
	n = 24	*n* = 32	*n* = 56	
Mean age (Standard deviation)	9.58 (1.91)	19.21 (4.12)	15.1 (5.85)	-
Gender				
Female, n (percent, %)	11 (45.8)	17 (53.1)	28 (50.0)	-
Male, n (%)	13 (54.2)	15 (46.9)	28 (50.0)	-
Congenital heart defect n (%)	16 (66.7)	17 (53.1)	33 (58.9)	1 (1.8)
Immune deficiency n (%)	15 (62.5)	14 (43.8)	29 (51.8)	0 (0)
Palatal anomalies n (%)	11 (45.8)	19 (59.4)	30 (53.6)	0 (0)
Speech-language delay n (%)	17 (70.8)	15 (46.9)	32 (57.1)	8 (14.3)
Attention Deficit/Hyperactivity Disorder (ADHD) n (%)	11 (45.8)	7 (21.9)	18 (32.1)	12 (21.4)
Autism spectrum diagnosis (known prior to study entry) n (%)	0 (0)	1 (3.1)	1 (1.8)	2 (3.6)
22q11.2 deletion n (%)	24 (100)	32(100)	56 (100)	1 (1.8)

4.2. Diagnostic Procedures

We applied a strict, research-based definition of ASD, as designated by CPEA guidelines and outlined by the Simons Simplex Collection study (Simons Foundation Autism Research Initiative), previously described [21]. Essentially, these criteria require participants to attain cutoff scores for an autism spectrum disorder from all of the following sources: (1) the Autism Diagnostic Interview-Revised (ADI-R); (2) the Autism Diagnostic Observation Schedule (ADOS); and (3) the clinician's best estimate DSM-IV diagnosis, which considers a hierarchical classification strategy for identifying autism, Asperger's Disorder, or PDD-NOS [25]. To achieve the clinician's best estimate diagnosis, two clinicians conducted a case conference during which they reviewed all diagnostic and neurocognitive assessments available.

4.3. Diagnostic Assessments

The diagnostic assessments included the Autism Diagnostic Interview-Revised (ADI-R) and the Autism Diagnostic Observation Schedule (ADOS) [22,23]. The ADI-R is a semi-structured interview used to evaluate autistic symptomatology and, in particular, to differentiate between autism and other developmental disorders [22]. It is used for a wide range of ages, with a minimum mental age of 18 months. As such, both adults and children were assessed with the ADI-R. This interview evaluates three functional domains: Reciprocal Social Interaction, Communication skills, and Restricted, Repetitive, and Stereotyped behaviors. We classified participants as meeting CPEA-ADI-R cutoff criteria if they met either the standard ADI-R cutoff scores, or an additional set of cutoff scores suggested by Risi et al. [24]. The standard cutoff scores included (1) the total Social algorithm score $\geq$10; (2) the total (verbal) Communication algorithm score $\geq$8 or the total (nonverbal) Communication algorithm score $\geq$7; and (3) the total Restricted, Repetitive and Stereotyped behaviors algorithm score $\geq$3 [22]. ADI-R cutoff rule, as designated by the Collaborative Programs of Excellence in Autism (CPEA), required that one of the following conditions be met: (1) meeting standard cutoffs for both Social and Communication domains; (2) meeting the standard cutoff for the Social domain and within 2 points of the standard Communication domain cutoff; (3) meeting the standard cutoff for Communication domain and within

2 points of standard Social domain cutoff; or (4) meeting the standard cutoff within 1 point for both the Social and Communication domains [24].

The Autism Diagnostic Observation Schedule (ADOS) is a semi-structured assessment that uses tasks and play activities to elicit social communication and interaction [23,36]. Observations are made concerning social and communication behaviors associated with ASD. Its structure allows for diagnoses across all ages, developmental stages, and language abilities and includes four different modules (1–4) dependent on age, development, and language ability [36]. We used ADOS for both adults and children. For this study, we used the revised algorithms for Modules 1, 2, and 3 were used based on Gotham et al. [23], whereas the standard algorithm for Module 4 was used. Please note, although we used the first edition of the ADOS in combination with the revised algorithms, these revised algorithms are parallel to the cutoffs used for the second revision of the ADOS (i.e., ADOS-2).

Modules 1–3 consist of two subdomains, Social Affect and Restricted, Repetitive, and Stereotyped Behavior, which yield one collapsed score, with two cutoffs provided: an autism cutoff score and an ASD cutoff. For Module 4, scores are obtained for two subdomains, Communication and Social, in addition to a combined subdomain score, Communication plus Social. Two cutoff scores are provided for each domain: autism and ASD. Individuals must meet all three cutoff scores in order to receive an ADOS classification of either autism or ASD.

These cutoffs differ according to which module is used. Modules 1, 2, and 3 derive a Total raw score from the Social Affect algorithm score and the Restricted, Repetitive, and Stereotyped Behaviors algorithm score. Module 1 (n = 2) is for those without no speech or single words, who do not use phrase speech consistently (total raw score $\geq$16 = autism, $\geq$11 = ASD). Module 2 (n = 1) is for those who use phrase speech but are not verbally fluent (Total raw score $\geq$9 = autism, $\geq$8 = ASD). Module 3 (n = 23) is for verbally fluent children (Total raw score $\geq$9 = autism, $\geq$7 = ASD). Module 4 (n = 30) is for verbally fluent adults and adolescents. Scoring parameters for Module 4 include the following: Communication total raw score $\geq$3 = autism, $\geq$2 = ASD; Social total raw score $\geq$6 = autism, $\geq$4 = ASD; Communication and Social total raw score $\geq$10 = autism, $\geq$7 = ASD [23].

Acknowledgments: This work was supported in part by the Robert W. Woodruff Foundation, Predictive Medicine Grant, awarded to Cubells and Ousley; a Simons Foundation Junior Investigator Award and a NARSAD award to Ousley. The NARSAD award provided some funds for open access publishing. We would like to thank Karen Wallace (Emory Autism Center, Department of Psychiatry and Behavioral Sciences, Emory School of Medicine, Atlanta, GA, USA) for her assistance in recruiting families and organizing the study. In addition, we would like to express our gratitude to all children, adults, and families who participated in the study.

Author Contributions: Opal Ousley and Joseph Cubells conceived and designed the experiments; Kimberly Rockers, Samuel Fernandez-Carriba, and Michael J. Morrier performed the experiments; Opal Ousley, A. Nichole Evans, Samuel Fernandez-Carriba, Erica L. Smearman, Kimberly Rockers and Karlene Coleman contributed to the data analysis; Opal Ousley, A. Nichole Evans, David W. Evans and Joseph Cubells contributed to the interpretation of the data analysis; all authors contributed to writing and editing the paper.

Abbreviations

22q11.2DS	22q11.2 Deletion Syndrome
FISH	Fluorescent In Situ Hybridization
ASD	Autism Spectrum Disorder
ADOS	Autism Diagnostic Observation Schedule
ADI-R	Autism Diagnostic Interview-Revised
CNV	Copy Number Variation
PDD-NOS	Pervasive Developmental Disorder-Not Otherwise Specified
RDoC	Research Domain Criteria
DSM-IV	Diagnostic and Statistical Manual of Mental Disorders, Fourth edition

References

1. Artigas-Pallares, J.; Gabau-Vila, E.; Guitart-Feliubadalo, M. Syndromic autism: II. Genetic syndromes associated with autism. *Rev. Neurol.* **2005**, *40*, S151–S162. [PubMed]
2. Bassett, A.S.; McDonald-McGinn, D.M.; Devriendt, K.; Digilio, M.C.; Goldenberg, P.; Habel, A.; Vorstman, J. Practical guidelines for managing patients with 22q11.2 deletion syndrome. *J. Pediatr.* **2011**, *159*, 332–339. [CrossRef] [PubMed]
3. Botto, L.D.; May, K.; Fernhoff, P.M.; Correa, A.; Coleman, K.; Rasmussen, S.A.; Merritt, R.K.; O'Leary, L.A.; Wong, L.Y.; Elixson, E.M.; et al. A population-based study of the 22q11.2 deletion: Phenotype, incidence, and contribution to major birth defects in the population. *Pediatrics* **2003**, *112*, 101–107. [CrossRef] [PubMed]
4. Oskarsdottir, S.; Vujic, M.; Fasth, A. Incidence and prevalence of the 22q11 deletion syndrome: A population-based study in Western Sweden. *Arch. Dis. Child.* **2004**, *89*, 148–151. [CrossRef] [PubMed]
5. Tezenas Du Montcel, S.; Mendizabai, H.; Ayme, S.; Levy, A.; Philip, N. Prevalence of 22q11 microdeletion. *J. Med. Genet.* **1996**, *33*, 719. [CrossRef] [PubMed]
6. Gothelf, D.; Frisch, A.; Michaelovsky, E.; Weizman, A.; Shprintzen, R.J. Velo-Cardio-Facial Syndrome. *J. Ment. Health Res. Intellect. Disabil.* **2009**, *2*, 149–167. [CrossRef] [PubMed]
7. Ousley, O.; Rockers, K.; Dell, M.L.; Coleman, K.; Cubells, J.F. A review of neurocognitive and behavioral profiles associated with 22q11 deletion syndrome: Implications for clinical evaluation and treatment. *Curr. Psychiatry Rep.* **2007**, *9*, 148–158. [CrossRef] [PubMed]
8. Fine, S.E.; Weissman, A.; Gerdes, M.; Pinto-Martin, J.; Zackai, E.H.; McDonald-McGinn, D.M.; Emanuel, B.S. Autism spectrum disorders and symptoms in children with molecularly confirmed 22q11.2 deletion syndrome. *J. Autism Dev. Disord.* **2005**, *35*, 461–470. [CrossRef] [PubMed]
9. Vorstman, J.A.; Morcus, M.E.; Duijff, S.N.; Klaassen, P.W.; Heineman-de Boer, J.A.; Beemer, F.A.; van Engeland, H. The 22q11.2 deletion in children: High rate of autistic disorders and early onset of psychotic symptoms. *J. Am. Acad. Child Adolesc. Psychiatry* **2006**, *45*, 1104–1113. [CrossRef] [PubMed]
10. Bruining, H.; de Sonneville, L.; Swaab, H.; de Jonge, M.; Kas, M.; van Engeland, H.; Vorstman, J. Dissecting the clinical heterogeneity of autism spectrum disorders through defined genotypes. *PLoS ONE* **2010**, *5*, e10887. [CrossRef] [PubMed]
11. Antshel, K.M.; Aneja, A.; Strunge, L.; Peebles, J.; Fremont, W.P.; Stallone, K.; Kates, W.R. Autistic spectrum disorders in velo-cardio facial syndrome (22q11.2 deletion). *J. Autism Dev. Disord.* **2007**, *37*, 1776–1786. [CrossRef] [PubMed]
12. Bassett, A.S.; Costain, G.; Fung, W.L.; Russell, K.J.; Pierce, L.; Kapadia, R.; Carter, R.F.; Chow, E.W.; Forsythe, P.J. Clinically detectable copy number variations in a Canadian catchment population of schizophrenia. *J. Psychiatr. Res.* **2010**, *44*, 1005–1009. [CrossRef] [PubMed]
13. Levinson, D.F.; Duan, J.; Oh, S.; Wang, K.; Sanders, A.R.; Shi, J.; Zhang, N.; Mowry, B.J.; Olincy, A.; Amin, F.; et al. Copy number variants in schizophrenia: Confirmation of five previous findings and new evidence for 3q29 microdeletions and VIPR2 duplications. *Am. J. Psychiatry* **2011**, *168*, 302–316. [CrossRef] [PubMed]
14. Karayiorgou, M.; Simon, T.J.; Gogos, J.A. 22q11.2 microdeletions: Linking DNA structural variation to brain dysfunction and schizophrenia. *Nat. Rev. Neurosci.* **2010**, *11*, 402–416. [CrossRef] [PubMed]
15. Ogilvie, C.M.; Moore, J.; Daker, M.; Palferman, S.; Docherty, Z. Chromosome 22q11 deletions are not found in autistic patients identified using strict diagnostic criteria. *Am. J. Med. Genet.* **2000**, *96*, 15–17. [CrossRef]
16. Einfeld, S.; Molony, H.; Hall, W. Autism is not associated with the fragile X syndrome. *Am. J. Med. Genet.* **1989**, *34*, 187–193. [CrossRef] [PubMed]
17. Fisch, G.S. Is autism associated with the fragile X syndrome? *Am. J. Med. Genet.* **1992**, *43*, 47–55. [CrossRef] [PubMed]
18. Hall, S.S.; Lightbody, A.A.; Hirt, M.; Rezvani, A.; Reiss, A.L. Autism in fragile X syndrome: A category mistake? *J. Am. Acad. Child Adolesc. Psychiatry* **2010**, *49*, 921–933. [CrossRef] [PubMed]
19. McCary, L.M.; Roberts, J.E. Early identification of autism in fragile X syndrome: A review. *J. Intellect. Disabil. Res.* **2012**, *57*, 803–814. [CrossRef] [PubMed]
20. Schaefer, G.B.; Mendelsohn, N.J. Genetics evaluation for the etiologic diagnosis of autism spectrum disorders. *Genet. Med.* **2008**, *10*, 4–12. [CrossRef] [PubMed]

21. Ousley, O.Y.; Smearman, E.; Fernandez-Carriba, S.; Rockers, K.A.; Coleman, K.; Walker, E.F.; Cubells, J.F. Axis I psychiatric diagnoses in adolescents and young adults with 22q11 deletion syndrome. *Eur. Psychiatry* **2013**, *28*, 417–422. [CrossRef] [PubMed]
22. Lord, C.; Rutter, M.; Le Couteur, A. Autism diagnostic interview-revised: A revised version of a diagnostic interview for caregivers of individuals with possible pervasive developmental disorders. *J. Autism Dev. Disord.* **1994**, *24*, 659–685. [CrossRef] [PubMed]
23. Gotham, K.; Risi, S.; Pickles, A.; Lord, C. The autism diagnostic observation schedule: Revised algorithms for improved diagnostic validity. *J. Autism Dev. Disord.* **2007**, *7*, 613–627. [CrossRef] [PubMed]
24. Risi, S.; Lord, C.; Gotham, K.; Corsello, C.; Chrysler, C.; Szatmari, P.; Cook, E.H.; Leventhal, B.L.; Pickles, A. Combining information from multiple sources in the diagnosis of autism spectrum disorders. *J. Am. Acad. Child Adolesc. Psychiatry* **2006**, *45*, 1094–1103. [CrossRef] [PubMed]
25. American Psychiatric Association. *DSM-IV: Diagnostic and Statistical Manual*; American Psychiatric Association: Washington, DC, USA, 1994.
26. Wang, P.P.; Woodin, M.F.; Kreps-Falk, R.; Moss, E.M. Research on behavioral phenotypes: Velocardiofacial syndrome (deletion 22q11.2). *Dev. Med. Child Neurol.* **2000**, *42*, 422–427. [CrossRef] [PubMed]
27. Cuthbert, B.N.; Insel, T.R. Toward the future of psychiatric diagnosis: The seven pillars of RDoC. *BMC Med.* **2013**, *11*, 126. [CrossRef] [PubMed]
28. Constantino, J.N.; Todd, R.D. Autistic traits in the general population: A twin study. *Arch. Gen. Psychiatry* **2003**, *60*, 524–530. [CrossRef] [PubMed]
29. Evans, D.W.; Uljarevic, M.; Lusk, L.G.; Loth, E.; Frazier, T. Development of two dimensional measures of restricted and repetitive behaviors in parents and children. *J. Am. Acad. Child Adolesc. Psychiatry* **2017**, *56*, 51–58. [CrossRef] [PubMed]
30. Moreno-De-Luca, A.; Myers, S.M.; Challman, T.D.; Moreno-De-Luca, D.; Evans, D.W.; Ledbetter, D.H. Developmental brain dysfunction (DBD): Revival and expansion of an old concept based on new genetic evidence. *Lancet Neurol.* **2013**, *12*, 406–414. [CrossRef]
31. Moreno-De-Luca, A.; Evans, D.W.; Boomer, K.; Hanson, E.; Bernier, R.; Goin-Kochel, R.; Myers, S.M.; Challman, T.D.; Moreno-de-Luca, D.; Spiro, J.; et al. Parental cognitive, behavioral and motor profiles impact the neurodevelopmental profile of individuals with de novo mutations. *JAMA Psychiatry* **2015**, *72*, 119–126. [CrossRef] [PubMed]
32. Jonas, R.K.; Montojo, C.A.; Bearden, C.E. The 22q11.2 deletion syndrome as a window into complex neuropsychiatric disorders over the lifespan. *Biol. Psychiatry* **2014**, *75*, 351–360. [CrossRef] [PubMed]
33. Grayton, H.M.; Fernandes, C.; Rujescu, D.; Collier, D.A. Copy number variations in neurodevelopmental disorders. *Prog. Neurobiol.* **2012**, *99*, 81–91. [CrossRef] [PubMed]
34. Karam, C.S.; Ballon, J.S.; Bivens, N.M.; Freyberg, Z.; Girgis, R.R.; Lizardi-Ortiz, J.E.; Javitch, J.A. Signaling pathways in schizophrenia: Emerging targets and therapeutic strategies. *Trends Pharmacol. Sci.* **2010**, *31*, 381–390. [CrossRef] [PubMed]
35. Rockers, K.; Ousley, O.; Sutton, T.; Schoenberg, E.; Coleman, K.; Walker, E.; Cubells, J.F. Performance on the modified card sorting test and its relation to psychopathology in adolescents and young adults with 22q11.2 deletion syndrome. *J. Intellect. Disabil. Res.* **2009**, *53*, 665–676. [CrossRef] [PubMed]
36. Lord, C; Rutter, M.; DiLavore, P.; Risi, S. *Autism Diagnostic Observation Schedule Manual*; Western Psychological Services: Los Angeles, CA, USA, 1999.

9

The Role of Executive Functions in the Development of Empathy and its Association with Externalizing Behaviors in Children with Neurodevelopmental Disorders and Other Psychiatric Comorbidities

Chiara Cristofani [1,†], Gianluca Sesso [1,2,†], Paola Cristofani [1], Pamela Fantozzi [1], Emanuela Inguaggiato [1], Pietro Muratori [1], Antonio Narzisi [1], Chiara Pfanner [1], Simone Pisano [3,4], Lisa Polidori [1], Laura Ruglioni [1], Elena Valente [1], Gabriele Masi [1] and Annarita Milone [1,*]

1 IRCCS Stella Maris Foundation, 56128 Pisa (Calambrone), Italy; ccristofani@fsm.unipi.it (C.C.); gsesso@fsm.unipi.it (G.S.); pcristofani@fsm.unipi.it (P.C.); pfantozzi@fsm.unipi.it (P.F.); einguaggiato@fsm.unipi.it (E.I.); pmuratori@fsm.unipi.it (P.M.); anarzisi@fsm.unipi.it (A.N.); cpfanner@fsm.unipi.it (C.P.); lpolidori@fsm.unipi.it (L.P.); lruglioni@fsm.unipi.it (L.R.); evalente@fsm.unipi.it (E.V.); gmasi@fsm.unipi.it (G.M.)

2 Department of Clinical and Experimental Medicine, University of Pisa, 56126 Pisa, Italy

3 Department of Neuroscience, AORN Santobono-Pausilipon, 80122 Naples, Italy; pisano.simone@gmail.com

4 Department of Translational Medical Sciences, Federico II University, 80138 Naples, Italy

* Correspondence: annarita.milone@fsm.unipi.it

† These authors contributed equally to this work.

Abstract: Executive functions have been previously shown to correlate with empathic attitudes and prosocial behaviors. People with higher levels of executive functions, as a whole, may better regulate their emotions and reduce perceived distress during the empathetic processes. Our goal was to explore the relationship between empathy and executive functioning in a sample of children and adolescents diagnosed with Attention Deficit and Hyperactivity Disorder alone or associated with comorbid Disruptive Behavior Disorders and/or Autism Spectrum Disorder. We also aimed to examine the role of empathic dimensions and executive skills in regulating externalizing behaviors. The 151 participants with ADHD were assigned to four groups according to their psychiatric comorbidity (either "pure" or with ASD and/or ODD/CD) and assessed by means of either parent- or self-reported questionnaires, namely the BRIEF−2, the BES, and the IRI. No questionnaire was found to discriminate between the four groups. Affective Empathy was found to positively correlate with Emotional and Behavioral Regulation competences. Furthermore, Aggressiveness and Oppositional Defiant Problems were positively associated with Executive Emotional and Behavioral Regulation competences. On the other hand, Rule-Breaking Behaviors and Conduct Problems were negatively associated with Affective Empathy and with Behavioral skills. Our study provides an additional contribution for a better understanding of the complex relationship between empathic competence and executive functions, showing that executive functioning and empathic attitudes interact with each other to regulate aggressive behaviors. This study further corroborates developmental models of empathy and their clinical implications, for which externalizing behaviors could be attenuated by enhancing executive functioning skills.

Keywords: empathy; executive functions; attention deficit and hyperactivity disorder; autism spectrum disorder; disruptive behavior disorders

1. Introduction

Feeling empathy for someone means understanding his/her emotions and/or personally experiencing the same; it means creating a customized space in one's own inner world to host the world of the other. In other words, it refers to the ability to share and comprehend another person's thoughts and moods [1]. Feeling and understanding the emotions of others are important assumptions to guide one's actions in a prosocial sense and, particularly, to avoid those behaviors that can cause harm and suffering to the other. The cognitive facet of empathy implies the ability to understand the inner situation of the other and to take his/her own perspective [2]. On the other hand, the affective component of empathy is defined as the ability to share the emotional state of others [3]. The latter implies the involvement of limbic and paralimbic structures and develops earlier than the cognitive one, which assumes a fine-tuned maturation of prefrontal and temporal networks [4].

In light of the close association of empathy with contextual factors, early childhood experiences and social behaviors, it is direct to assume that psychopathological conditions are often convoyed by empathy deficits [5,6]. Empathy deficits have been implicated in several neurodevelopmental disorders, among which autism spectrum disorder (ASD) is the most studied [7–9]. ASD have been primarily associated with cognitive empathy deficits [9,10] but the potential role of affective empathy in this framework has been questioned [11].

The reduction or absence of empathy represents the cornerstone of Conduct Disorders (CD) characterized by disruptive and antisocial behaviors [12]. Adults with psychopathic traits show a selective deficit of the affective component of empathy related to impaired emotional responses to facial expressions of feelings of sadness and fear [13–15], which is likely due to dysfunctional neuronal circuits underlying the amygdala [16]. A recent study by our group [17] confirmed these findings in a cohort of young boys with CD, corroborating the association between callous-unemotional (CU) traits and affective empathic attitudes. Interestingly, studies aimed at outlining the differences between children with CD and CU traits and ASD [18] show that, while psychopathy seems to be best characterized by a preserved understanding of what the other thinks, with a deficient capacity to share compassionate feelings towards the others, ASD specifically lacks the ability to take others' perspective. Conversely, a study conducted by Mazza et al., 2014 [11] on a group of adolescents with ASD reported a difficulty in cognitive empathy and a deficit in affective empathy specific for the negative emotional valence, assuming, also for these subjects, the existence of an atypical function and structure of the amygdala [19].

Some evidence has also shown that empathy is compromised in a proportion of children with Attention Deficit and Hyperactivity Disorder (ADHD); in particular, lower levels of social perspective taking are observed [20–22]. Indeed, young people with ADHD may have low cognitive empathic attitudes, as demonstrated for instance by the frequently observed unawareness of other children playing the same game [23]. Further corroborating evidence appeared in a recent study by Maoz et al., 2019 [24], who confirmed the existence of a global deficit in both components of empathy by using the Interpersonal Reactivity Index [25] in its self-report form. In another study conducted by the same research group [26], differences in the empathic profile are identified between the Combined and the Inattentive subtypes of ADHD, identifying a greater impairment in the former for all scales of the IRI questionnaire. According to Uekermann et al., 2010 [27], these deficits might be explained at least in part by the impulsive response modalities typically found in ADHD patients, and thus may be linked to dysfunctions of the fronto-striatal brain networks, functionally related to empathic processing and executive functioning. Interestingly, Barkley, 2006 [28], argues that behavioral inhibition deficits, the core symptoms of ADHD children, might impair social cognition skills, but how much they could affect empathic abilities still remains an unsolved question.

Despite the identification of selective or global impairments of empathy in clinical settings, functional studies, aimed at assessing brain correlates of the experience of feeling the emotions of others, found that empathic attitudes are activated through an emotional processing which is regulated both by bottom-up and top-down circuitry within the prefrontal and limbic cortex [29].

An early influential theory, the Perception-Action Model by Preston and de Waal, 2002 [30], based on an evolutionary perspective, proposed that empathy is considered an uncontrolled response that operates automatically and develops early in life. More recently, the Russian Doll Model by the same authors [31] questioned this simplistic view and posited that bottom-up routes of empathic processing and top-down executive modulators are two interrelated systems that develop sequentially. This model has included executive functions as a regulating factor and considered it as a fundamental ground for the development of cognitive empathy [31–33].

According to the Russian Doll Model, several components of the empathic response, which have been added layer by layer during evolution, remain functionally integrated [34]. At its core is the perception-action mechanism, which induces a similar emotional state in the observer as in the target. Indeed, its basic expressions are motor mimicry and emotional contagion, representing the functional reactions of newborns and infants according to Hoffman's developmental theory of empathy [35]. On the other hand, the external layers of the doll, such as empathic concern and perspective taking, are grounded on the previously described socio-affective basis but require a fine-tuned regulation of emotional responses and a distinct perception between self and cognition. Although the outer layers of the doll depend on prefrontal circuitry, they remain functionally connected to the basic perception-action mechanism [31]. Therefore, cognitive empathic attitudes are supported by the neural regions that underlie working memory, executive functioning, emotional regulation and visuo-spatial processing, overpowering the affective representations of the other in a top-to-bottom fashion [31,36]. In other words, the effective control of empathic responses is thus obtained through the executive functioning regulation system, which allows a fine adaptation and modulation of the sharing experience.

A stepwise transition from immature forms of emotional contagion to more sophisticated expressions of prosocial attitudes, as brilliantly theorized by Hoffman's developmental theory of empathy [37], may be indeed paralleled by the progressive maturation of prefrontal circuitry and executive functions (EF) required to perform a fine-tuned control of such responses. Interestingly, a discrete amount of studies, conducted in community and clinical samples, has repeatedly shown that EF as a whole can modulate empathic attitudes, or in other words people with higher EF competences may better regulate their emotions and reduce perceived distress during the empathic processes [38–46]. Moreover, Gökçen et al. [43,44] found positive correlations between EF and empathic attitudes in individuals with ASD traits, suggesting the role of EF in regulating empathic competences in neurodevelopmental disorders. Similarly, a recent study in ADHD patients versus healthy controls by Abdel-Hamid et al., 2019 [47], found significant positive correlations between theory of mind (ToM) and empathy competences and EF performances in the ADHD group but not in the control group. In a recent review, which analyzed fifteen studies conducted on ADHD samples, with or without comorbidities and included mostly male children, Pineda-Alhucema et al., 2018 [48], found the EF most correlated with ToM were inhibitory control, working memory, cognitive flexibility and attention (for further updated details on the relationship between EF and ToM please refer to Andreou et al. 2020 [49]).

It should be noted, however, that in these studies, EF were variably measured through different neuropsychological tasks, such as the Go/No-Go test and the Wisconsin Card Sorting Test, which assess specific EF such as Cognitive Flexibility and Working Memory in laboratory settings. No study, however, used caregiver-reported measures of behavioral patterns for children and adolescents to evaluate EF in everyday life environments. Given the centrality of EFs in controlling behaviors in everyday life, relying only on laboratory measures of EF performances, detected with clinical tests, may limit the confidence and completeness of the clinical evaluation. The measures based on performances, in fact, depict only limited aspects of the EF system in a narrow time frame and do not fully capture the integrated multidimensional decision-making process based on an analysis of the priority which is often that of real life situations [50].

A recent meta-analysis [29] summarized these results, corroborating the evidence that empathy is strongly related to EF, and interestingly its cognitive facet is more closely related to executive skills than the affective one. Particularly, strong relationships were found between cognitive empathy and specific subcomponents of EF, including Inhibitory Control, Working Memory and Cognitive Flexibility, while affective empathy would only correlate to Inhibitory Control. Despite this, it should be observed that this meta-analysis did not consider further subdivisions of EF in their subgroup analyses, such as emotional regulation abilities and several other metacognitive skills. Moreover, no significant effect of age was demonstrated, though a considerable heterogeneity in the age range of samples of included studies is noticeable. Another potential source of bias was the inclusion of the results of three unpublished dissertations. Finally, many of these studies are made up of heterogeneous samples, while the meta-analysis does not take into account psychiatric comorbidities. The authors emphasized indeed that this field of research is still under open investigation, since the results of single studies are somewhat inconsistent and inadequate to draw definite conclusions.

The present study aims to explore possible relationships between the different facets of empathy and the specific subcomponents of EF in a clinical sample of children and adolescents primarily diagnosed with ADHD, compared to children with comorbid ASD or ODD/CD or both. EF profiles have been evaluated through the Behavior Rating Inventory of Executive Function (BRIEF) [51] questionnaire, which provides a structured assessment of EF behaviors in everyday life environments. Since the EF deficits can strongly affect the cognitive and behavioral manifestations of ADHD and ASD [52,53], our aim was indeed to investigate if and how EF are associated with the dimensions of empathy within these neurodevelopmental disorders.

Moreover, the current study examined the role of empathic dimensions and executive skills in regulating the externalizing behaviors typical of some clinical manifestations of ADHD and ODD/CD, such as for instance aggression, oppositional behaviors and rule transgression. It is believed, in fact, that emotional regulation plays an important role in inhibiting aggressive behaviors by implementing perspective-taking abilities and empathic concern towards the others [54].

2. Methods

2.1. Participants and Diagnostic Procedures

Our study included 151 drug-naïve participants (137 boys, age range 6–18 years old, mean age 9.51 ± 2.64 years) recruited in our third-level Department of Child and Adolescent Psychiatry from March 2019 to December 2019. Subjects underwent a multi-dimensional assessment, through individual clinical evaluations and observations of social interactions within a group of peers, in order to thoroughly investigate ASD symptomatology. The diagnoses were made according to the Diagnostic and Statistical Manual of Mental Disorders–Fifth edition (DSM−5) [55], based on medical history, clinical observations, a structured interview, the Kiddie Schedule for Affective Disorders and Schizophrenia–Present and Lifetime version (K-SADS-PL) [56], and clinical questionnaires, namely the Child Behavior Checklist and the Social Communication Questionnaire, commonly used to assist the diagnostic process.

The Child Behavior Checklist for ages 6 to 18 years (CBCL–6/18) [57,58] is a 118-item scale, completed by parents, with 8 different syndromes scales, a Total Problem Score and two broad-band scores designated as Internalizing Problems and Externalizing Problems. The reliability coefficients (Cronbach's alpha) of the original validation study were 0.82, 0.81 and 0.82, respectively. The Social Communication Questionnaire (SCQ) [59] is a widely used screening measure for ASD. It was designed as a questionnaire version of the Autism Diagnostic Interview–Revised (ADI-R) [60], the gold standard developmental history measure that is widely used in research and often in clinical practice. Caregivers can rate the individual's lifetime and/or current characteristics. Compared to other rating scales, the development research was significantly more robust, including good diagnostic validation on participants, and it has been widely adopted by both the research and clinical community worldwide.

Patients were included if they received a diagnosis of ADHD, with or without comorbid psychiatric conditions, including ODD/CD and ASD. The latter was suspected based on either medical history and clinical observations or a total SCQ score above the cut-off value and later confirmed through the administration of the Autism Diagnostic Observation Schedule–Second Edition (ADOS-2) [61]. The exclusion criteria were as follows: presence of comorbid intellectual disability, as detected through formal psychometric assessment by means of the WISC-IV, i.e., when either the Full-Scale Intelligence Quotient or the General Ability Index were below than 70 points; younger than 6 years old or older than 18 years old; current or previous use of psychoactive medications; neurologic impairments or neurodegenerative conditions.

We identified four clinical groups in our samples: "pure" ADHD group (namely, without comorbid ASD and/or ODD/CD, here-in-after referred as the ADHD alone group), including 64 subjects (12.5% girls, mean age 10.02 ± 2.49 years); comorbid ADHD + ODD/CD group (here-in-after referred as the ADHD+ODD/CD group), including 43 subjects (9.3% girls, mean age 9.37 ± 2.95 years); comorbid ADHD + ASD group (here-in-after referred as the ADHD+ASD group), including 19 subjects (5.26% girls, mean age 9.58 ± 2.69 years); comorbid ADHD + ASD + ODD/CD group (here-in-after referred as the ADHD+ODD/CD+ASD group), including 25 subjects (4% girls, mean age 8.40 ± 2.24 years). All participants and parents were informed about assessment instruments and participated voluntarily in the study after written informed consent was obtained for assessment procedures from parents of all children. The study conformed to the Declaration of Helsinki and the Regional Ethics Committee for Clinical Trials of Tuscany, Pediatric Ethics Committee section, approved the study (ethical approval code: GENCU/03/2019).

2.2. *Clinical Assessment*

Patients' clinical profiles were also assessed by means of several questionnaires, either through self or parental reports. Particularly, the Italian versions of the following measures were used: the Behavior Rating Inventory of Executive Functions–Second version (BRIEF-2) [51] administered to parents of all included children for the assessment of EF profiles; the Antisocial Process Screening Device (APSD) [62] administered to parents of all included children for the evaluation of CU traits; the Basic Empathy Scale (BES) [12], administered to parents of all children aged 11 years old or less, and the Interpersonal Reactivity Index (IRI) [25], administered in its self-report version to adolescents aged 12 years old or more, for the assessment of empathic competences.

The Behavior Rating Inventory of Executive Function–Second version (BRIEF-2) [51] is the updated version of the BRIEF questionnaire which provides a structured assessment of executive function behaviors in everyday life environments, allowing the identification of helpful clinical manifestations in different contexts, i.e., home and school. In its parent-report version that was used in the present study, this tool has been validated for 5- to 18-year-old children and adolescents. BRIEF-2 is a multi-dimensional measure and items are nearly equally distributed across nine factors, each referring to specific executive functions: Inhibit, Self-Monitor, Shift, Emotional Control, Initiate, Working Memory, Plan/Organize, Task Monitor, Organization of Materials. Three composite scales are also identifiable, each including at least two factors: Behavioral Regulation Index (BRI) (including Inhibit and Self-Monitor), Emotional Regulation Index (ERI) (Shift and Emotional Control) and Cognitive Regulation Index (CRI) (Initiate, Working Memory, Plan/Organize, Task Monitor, Organization of Materials). A Global Executive Composite (GEC) score is also computed as sum of the three aforementioned composite indexes.

The Antisocial Process Screening Device (APSD) [62] is a 20-item clinician-administered rating scale normed on a community sample of pre-adolescent children. The available version of the APSD was designed to be completed by parents and teachers; the former was used in the present study. Items are rated on a three-point Likert scale and the scale consists of three main dimensions, based on factor analysis: Narcissism, Impulsivity and Callous-Unemotional. There is substantial support for the validity of the APSD for distinguishing sub-groups of antisocial youths with more severe and aggressive behavior, with characteristics similar to adults with psychopathy [63] (Cronbach's $\alpha = 0.86$).

The Basic Empathy Scale (BES) [12] is a self- or parent-reported questionnaire, the latter being used in this study, for children and/or adolescents composed of 20 items distributed across two subscales, respectively, referring to the affective and cognitive components of empathy. Both exploratory and confirmatory analyses of the original validation established good internal consistency for each subscale with Cronbach's α ranging from 0.79 to 0.85. The Interpersonal Reactivity Index (IRI) was originally developed by Davis, 1980 [25], as a self-reported questionnaire for adults and subsequently adapted for adolescents by Litvack-Miller and colleagues [64]; it is composed of 28 items distributed across four subscales, respectively referring to Fantasy and Perspective-Taking (combined into the Cognitive Empathy subscale), Empathic Concern and Personal Distress (combined into the Affective Empathy subscale).

2.3. *Data Analysis*

Statistical analyses were performed by means of MatLab® (MathWorks, Natick, MA, USA) and RStudio® (RStudio Inc., Boston, MA, USA) software. For each clinical variable with continuous distribution, outliers were defined as observations lying outside the range between [first quartile − 1.5 * interquartile range] and [third quartile + 1.5 * interquartile range] and removed. For each BRIEF-2 subscale-related variable, observations were removed whether the corresponding values at either the Infrequency or the Inconsistency scale was higher than 99° percentile of normalized data. As for the BES and the IRI questionnaires, z-scores were computed for each subscales, i.e., the Cognitive and the Affective Empathy scales; thus, z-scores of the two questionnaires were merged together so that a single pair of variables assessing cognitive and affective empathy was available for all subjects irrespectively of the age.

Analyses of Variance (ANOVA) were used to assess significant differences (p-value < 0.05) between clinical variables with continuous distribution. A Tukey post-hoc test was used whenever the ANOVA led to a statistically significant result in order to identify significant comparisons between variables. Spearman's ranks correlation coefficients were estimated to detect significant relationships between rank values of questionnaire variables. Benjamini and Hochberg's False Discovery Rate (FDR) correction method [65] for multiple comparisons was applied after assessing significant differences at a traditional significance level of 5%.

Finally, four linear regression models were applied to identify statistically significant relationships between selected subscales of the administered questionnaires. Namely, four subscales of the CBCL (Aggressive Behavior [AB], Rule-Breaking Behavior [RBB], Oppositional Defiant Problems [ODP], Conduct Problems [CP]) were included as dependent variables of the models, whilst the three main indexes of the BRIEF (Behavioral, Emotional and Cognitive Regulation Indexes), the z-scores of the two subscales of the merged Empathy Questionnaire (Affective and Cognitive Empathy) and the SCQ total scores were used as independent variables of the models.

3. Results

3.1. *Questionnaires*

Scores obtained by the four clinical groups in the aforementioned questionnaires are reported in Figure 1A–C. No significant differences could be detected in the APSD (Figure 1A) and in the SCQ questionnaires (Figure 1B). Finally, no significant difference emerged neither in the Affective nor in the Cognitive Empathy subscales, neither of the two Empathy questionnaires considered individually (BES and IRI–data not shown) nor in the merged one (Figure 1C).

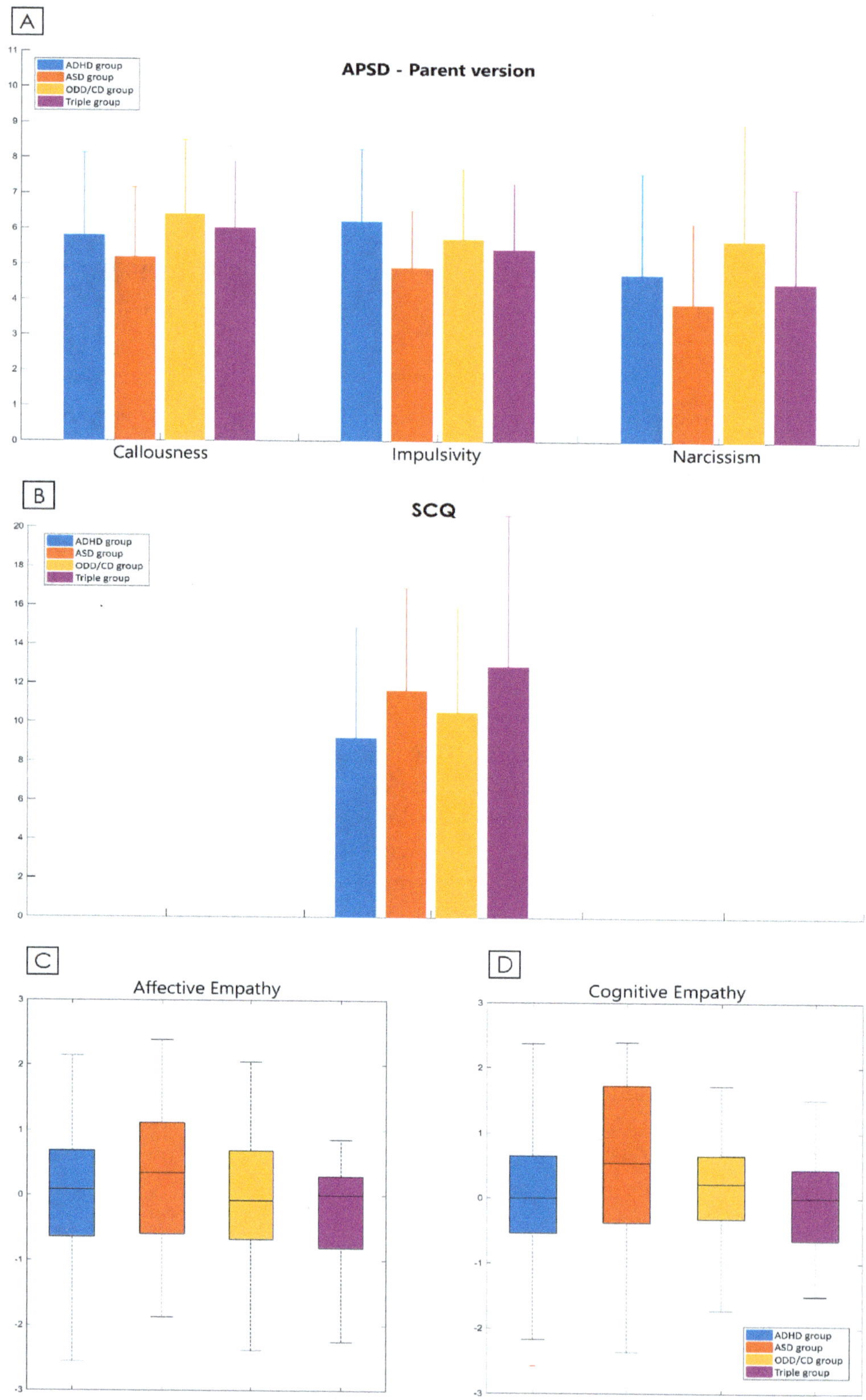

Figure 1. Questionnaires. Scores obtained by the four clinical groups in the Antisocial Process Screening Device (APSD, (**A**)), the Social Communication Questionnaire (SCQ, (**B**)) and the merged Empathy Questionnaire (**C**) are here illustrated. Scores are compared between ADHD group (blue bars), ASD group (red bars), ODD/CD group (yellow bars) and Triple group (purple bars). Graphs represent means with standard deviation bars, except for (**D**) where boxplots represent medians and first and third quartiles with minimum/maximum bars.

3.2. Correlations

Significant correlations between BRIEF-2-related subscales and APSD, SCQ and Empathy questionnaires are illustrated in Figure 2. Briefly, the Callousness subscale of the APSD was positively associated with the Inhibit and Self-Monitor scales of the BRIEF-2, while the Impulsivity subscale was positively correlated with all scales of the questionnaire. Similar findings were reported for the Narcissism subscale of the APSD, which was positively associated to most subscales of the BRIEF-2 across its three dimensions. The SCQ total score was positively associated to the Emotional and Behavioral Regulation related subscales of the BRIEF-2 and with the Initiate and Plan/Organize subscales. Finally, no significant correlations emerged for the Cognitive Empathy scale, while the Affective Empathy scale was negatively correlated with the Inhibit, the Self-Monitor and the Emotional Control subscales of the BRIEF-2.

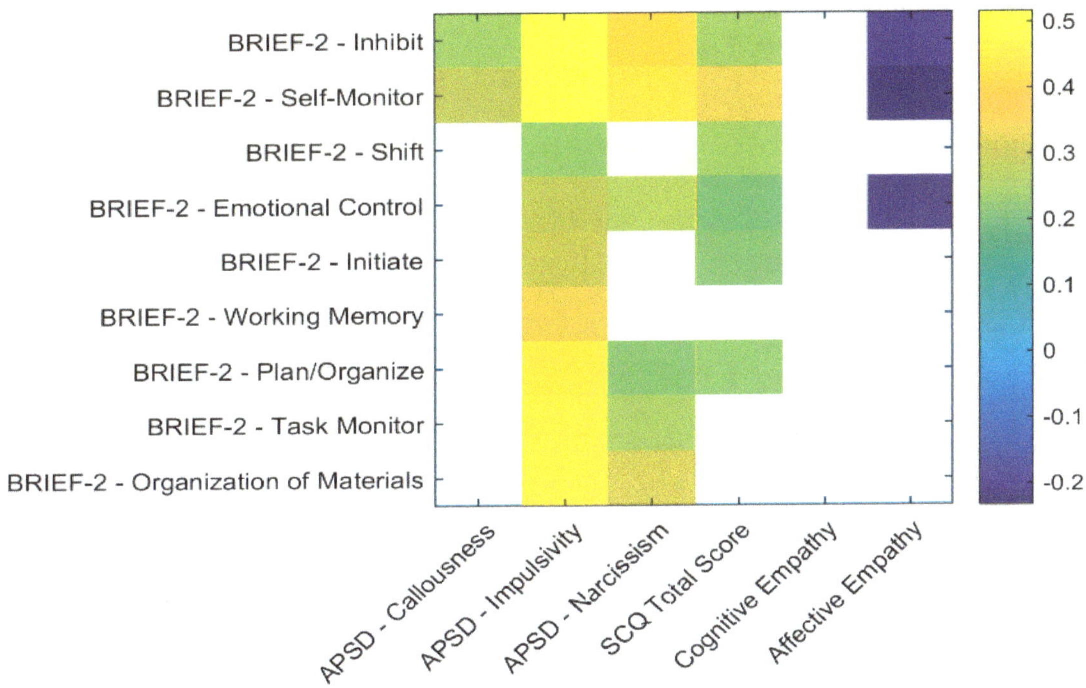

Figure 2. Correlations.

Pearson's linear correlation coefficients were here represented as colored boxes to show only significant relationships between continuous variables of selected questionnaires. The traditional significance level of 5% was corrected by means of Bonferroni's correction method for multiple comparisons. A color legend bar is displayed on the right.

3.3. Regression Models

Finally, a linear regression model was applied to identify statistical relationships between four aggressive/disruptive behavior-related CBCL subscales (AB, RBB, ODP, CP), as dependent variables, and several subscales from the other questionnaires, as independent variables, namely: the three main indexes of the BRIEF-2 (Behavioral, Emotional and Cognitive Regulation Indexes), the two Empathy subscales (Affective and Cognitive Empathy scales) and the SCQ total score.

As displayed in Table 1A–D, a significant positive association was found between both AB (Table 1A) and ODP (Table 1B) subscales of the CBCL, and the Behavioral and Emotional Regulation Indexes of the BRIEF-2. A significant positive relationship emerged, instead, between the RBB (Table 1C) and the CP (Table 1D) subscales of the CBCL, and the Behavioral—but not the Emotional—Regulation Index of the BRIEF-2, while a significant negative relationship was found for the Affective—but not the Cognitive—Empathy subscale.

Table 1. Linear Regression Models.

A. CBCL-AB	**Estimates**	**β-Coefficients**	**Standard Errors**	***p*-Values**
Intercept	26.3134	0.0000	4.9028	4.21×10^{-7} ***
BRIEF-2-BRI	0.7645	0.3891	0.1843	6.49×10^{-5} ***
BRIEF-2-CRI	0.0667	0.2932	0.0715	0.3525
BRIEF-2-ERI	0.4610	0.0753	0.1481	0.0023 **
Affective Empathy	−1.2782	−0.1137	0.9909	0.1996
Cognitive Empathy	0.6295	0.0580	0.9616	0.5139
SCQ Score	−0.0541	−0.0306	0.1317	0.6816
B. CBCL-ODP	**Estimates**	**β-Coefficients**	**Standard Errors**	***p*-Values**
Intercept	35.6661	0.0000	3.8429	1.23×10^{-15} ***
BRIEF-2-BRI	0.5471	0.3891	0.1445	0.0002 ***
BRIEF-2-CRI	0.0535	0.2932	0.0560	0.3420
BRIEF-2-ERI	0.3042	0.0753	0.1161	0.0099 **
Affective Empathy	−0.9299	−0.1137	0.7767	0.2336
Cognitive Empathy	0.1635	0.0580	0.7537	0.8285
SCQ Score	0.0105	−0.0306	0.1032	0.9186
C. CBCL-RBB	**Estimates**	**β-Coefficients**	**Standard Errors**	***p*-Values**
Intercept	38.4738	0.0000	3.6169	$<2 \times 10^{-16}$ ***
BRIEF-2-BRI	0.6978	0.3891	0.1355	1.11×10^{-6} ***
BRIEF-2-CRI	0.0355	0.2932	0.0526	0.5008
BRIEF-2-ERI	0.0637	0.0753	0.1091	0.5606
Affective Empathy	−1.5698	−0.1137	0.7326	0.0343 *
Cognitive Empathy	−0.0574	0.0580	0.7121	0.9359
SCQ Score	−0.0296	−0.0306	0.0968	0.7599
D. CBCL-CP	**Estimates**	**β-Coefficients**	**Standard Errors**	***p*-Values**
Intercept	37.5833	0.0000	3.7916	$<2 \times 10^{-16}$ ***
BRIEF-2-BRI	0.7870	0.3891	0.1424	2.12×10^{-7} ***
BRIEF-2-CRI	−0.0062	0.2932	0.0547	0.9096
BRIEF-2-ERI	0.1749	0.0753	0.1165	0.1359
Affective Empathy	−1.7449	−0.1137	0.7665	0.0247 *
Cognitive Empathy	−0.3663	0.0580	0.7409	0.6220
SCQ Score	−0.1235	−0.0306	0.1008	0.2229

Estimates, standard errors and *p*-values are here presented for four linear regression models between selected subscales of the administered questionnaires. Four subscales of the Child Behavior Checklist questionnaire, namely Aggressive Behaviors (**A**), Oppositional-Defiant Problems (**B**), Rule-Breaking Behaviors (**C**), and Conduct Problems (**D**), were included as dependent variables of the models. The three main indexes of the Behavior Rating Inventory of Executive Functions-Second version (Behavioral, Emotional and Cognitive Regulation Indexes), the two subscales of the Empathy questionnaire (Affective and Cognitive Empathy), and the Social Communication Questionnaire total scores were used as independent variables of the model. * *p*-values < 0.05, ** *p*-values < 0.01, *** *p*-values < 0.001.

4. Discussion

The first aim of the present study was to explore possible relationships between the different aspects of empathy and specific subcomponents of EF in children and adolescents with ADHD alone, ADHD and ODD/CD and/or ASD. To this aim, our effort was to achieve at least three major objectives: (1) to assess empathic attitudes, CU traits, antisocial behaviors and socio-relational skills in our four groups of patients; (2) to identify potential relationships between these variables and the EF profiles; (3) to explore the interrelated role of the cognitive and affective dimensions of empathy and the EF in regulating antisocial behaviors and aggressiveness. To the best of our knowledge, this is the first study of the kind performed in such a multi-structured sample of children and adolescents.

First, none of the questionnaires used in our study was individually able to discriminate between the four clinical groups. The SCQ is a clinical checklist, based on parents or caregivers report, aimed at identifying the presence of abnormal social and communicative behaviors. Although the SCQ is used as a screening tool for ASD symptoms, the lack of significant differences in our sample between ADHD patients with or without ASD suggests that the social functioning deficits reported in ADHD patients [21], at least in their parents' judgement, were severe enough to mitigate the difference among groups. It is also likely, however, that, since parents of ADHD children, with or without ASD, are usually more aware of, and worried about, the behavioral consequences of the disorder, socio-communication difficulties could go unnoticed even in patients with a confirmed diagnosis of ASD. A complementary but not alternative explanation may be that our high-functioning ASD patients did not exhibit such a great severity of social and communicative symptoms [66,67], so that caregivers could not be fully aware of their functional consequences.

Similarly, no significant differences emerged between groups in the two questionnaires assessing CU traits. Our finding may suggest that these traits may be trans-nosographic and thus be present not exclusively in ODD/CD, but also in ADHD [68] and in ASD patients [69]. As for the Empathy questionnaires, neither the BES and IRI nor the merged version of the two, did show any significant differences between the four clinical groups. Unfortunately, few data are available in the literature on the empathic attitudes of ADHD children with comorbid psychiatric conditions [70]. One would expect, based on previous findings on non-comorbid conditions, a greater impairment of the affective component for subjects with ADHD in comorbidity with behavioral disorders [17], while a greater impairment of the cognitive component in subjects with ADHD+ASD [10,18]. Our results could be interpreted in light of the subtle complexity of empathy deficits in these neurodevelopmental disorders, which limited the likelihood to find significant differences among comorbid conditions. It should be also taken into account that all our subjects were diagnosed with ADHD and this shared clinical condition may have obscured possible differences among groups. However, this finding further supports the notion that comorbid conditions are not the simple summation of two different disorders. In light of this, ADHD + ASD patients are not simply ASD patients with an additional ADHD, but a specific phenotype, possibly with a lesser cognitive empathic deficit or greater affective empathic impairment. Similarly, ADHD + ODD/CD patients may present a lesser affective empathic deficit or greater cognitive empathic impairment. This hypothesis should be tested by comparing "pure" ASD and ODD/CD with patients with ADHD and comorbidity conditions. Interestingly, recent studies shed some light on future research about specific empathy impairments in ASD and ODD/CD individuals, suggesting that different mechanisms and factors may be involved in empathic problems in such conditions [71,72].

The principal goal of the present study was to assess the reciprocal relationship between empathic attitudes and EF in ADHD patients. A recent meta-analysis [29], mainly including studies performed on healthy subjects, found positive correlations between empathic competences and EF. Gökçen et al. [43,44] reported similar findings in individuals with ASD traits, suggesting the role of EF in regulating empathic competences in neurodevelopmental disorders. Similarly, a more recent study by Abdel-Hamid et al., 2019 [47], identified in ADHD patients, but not in healthy controls, overlapping significant correlations between theory of mind and empathy measures and EF performances at the Trail Making Test, which specifically assesses Cognitive Flexibility and Working Memory skills. As for the so-called "hot" EF, that is the process underlying the affective modulation of behavioral responses [73,74], Miranda et al., 2017 [75], observed significant correlations between social cognition deficits, assessed by means of a specific subscale of the NEPSY–II test [76], and the BRIEF inhibition and emotional control scales in an ADHD sample, while the former are linked to metacognitive deficits in high functioning ASD patients.

In our sample, affective empathic competences, assessed through the BES and the IRI questionnaires, are negatively correlated with Emotional and Behavioral Regulation impairments, identified through the BRIEF-2 questionnaire. The greater the difficulties in "hot" EF, the lower the empathic attitudes, or, in other words, individuals with severe deficits in the EF profile exhibited lower scores on Empathy questionnaires. Nonetheless, no significant correlations were found neither for EF metacognitive domains nor with the cognitive empathy subscale.

Our results suggest that inhibitory and emotional control play an important role in regulating externalizing behavior, even controlling for empathic competences. As stated above, empathic attitudes are activated through an emotional processing which is regulated both by bottom-up and top-down circuitry within the prefrontal and limbic cortex [29,77]. This effective control is achieved through EF modulation, allowing for a fine adjustment of the sharing experience [33]. It should be noted that bottom-up and top-down processes are hardly separable when examined on a behavioral level. Nonetheless, the Russian Doll Model by Preston and de Waal [31] recently posited that top-down executive regulation of empathic processing develops later than bottom-up routes, which are responsible for uncontrolled empathic responses that operates automatically. This model is in line with the Hoffman's developmental theory of empathy [37], according to which Emotional Contagion would develop earlier than more regulated forms of empathic attitude towards the others.

Our results indicate that EF are more strongly related to the affective empathy than to the cognitive one, which is in disagreement with the results of the aforementioned meta-analysis [29]. Nonetheless, it should be emphasized that the studies of this meta-analysis did not include ADHD patients, who could exhibit such a severe impairment in their EF and a deficit in their cognitive empathic competences, that reciprocal associations would not result in statistical significance. In other words, we posit that ADHD patients are somewhat constrained by their executive dysfunction in an underdevelopment of their empathic attitude, which would be limited to the expression of an emotional contagion from the other.

Furthermore, significant positive relationships were found between several variables of the APSD questionnaire and the BRIEF-2 subscales related to the Emotional and Behavioral Regulation domains. Namely, the higher the scores in CU traits-related questionnaires, the higher the impairment in the Emotional-Behavioral Regulation competences. This finding is in line with a recent study assessing the relationship between CU traits and parent ratings of EF [78]. In particular, this study [78] highlights how CU traits are related to emotional self-regulation, but not to the EF performance scales. Since parental ratings are believed to capture EF behavioral representations, these clinical ratings may be more closely associated with behavioral representations of CU traits, which are also identified by the parents' report [78].

Finally, in our research, we tried to investigate, in a clinical sample of ADHD patients with psychiatric comorbidities, the relationships between two of the fundamental psychological grounds in the neuropsychologic developmental milestones of children and adolescents, namely EF and empathic attitudes, and how they reciprocally interact to regulate behavioral self-regulation and aggressiveness. Our results confirm a strong and finely structured relationship between these variables, being aggressive behaviors and related disturbances significantly influenced by these underlying processes. Our work highlights two different interactions between EF and empathy to regulate social behaviors in ADHD, where a dysfunction of these elements is essential for aggressive and antisocial behaviors to be carried out towards the others.

A first model identifies aggressiveness and oppositional problems, as indexed through the CBCL questionnaire, mainly associated with difficulties in executive emotional-behavioral regulation processes (such as impulse control and the ability to appropriately regulate one's behavior according to the context), but not with dimensions of empathy. Interestingly, reactive aggressiveness usually emerges as an impulsive response to hostile-perceived environmental events, often precipitated by irritability and tantrums [79]. This type of aggressiveness has been related to an orbito-frontal cortical dysfunction, for its primary role in adapting system reactivity to stress events [9,17,80].

On the other hand, rule-breaking behaviors and conduct disorders, as indexed through the CBCL questionnaire, likely relate to a proactive type of aggressiveness, which is associated to the activation of self-oriented behaviors to take advantage for personal purposes to the achievement of benefits at the emotional expense of the others' perspective [79]. Our study confirms that these aspects possibly relate to low levels of affective, but not cognitive, empathy and to impaired behavioral, but not emotional, regulation functioning. It has been hypothesized that proactive aggressiveness might be caused by dysfunctional mechanisms of violence inhibition, which are usually activated by others' discomfort signs, such as fear and sadness [15]. A deficient activation of this self-control mechanism is usually attributed to abnormal responses of the limbic system, particularly of the amygdala, which have been linked to antisocial behaviors in psychopathy [14,15].

Our results are thus in line with previous studies and further elucidate the complex and intriguing relationships between empathic attitudes and EF. In other words, it seems that both impaired behavioral self-regulation and difficulties in the emotional sharing of others' internal state may lead to a down-regulation of proactive aggressiveness inhibition systems, while emotional and behavioral regulation functioning systems are essential in preventing more reactive forms of aggressiveness towards the others. Thus, the multifaceted interactions of both "hot" EF and empathic attitudes have a central role in regulating prosocial behaviors.

Our study displays, however, a number of limitations that might undermine the robustness of our conclusions; notably, a marked discrepancy in group size, particularly between the "pure" ADHD and ADHD+ODD/CD+ASD groups, and the absence of a control group of healthy children. The purpose of this preliminary study was, indeed, to explore the issues addressed above; therefore, further studies on larger samples, possibly including heathy controls, a greater number of girls and ASD patients, and children with limited prosocial emotions, will be performed to confirm the results.

5. Conclusions

In conclusion, our study provides a further contribution for a better understanding of the complex and intriguing relationship between empathic competence and executive skills. These evidences could be beneficial for the definition of treatment strategies aimed at attenuating externalizing behaviors. Aggressive behaviors would, indeed, be modified by an empathic attitude-oriented approach, which should focus on the underlying executive dysfunction. To sum up, we showed that executive functioning and empathic attitudes interact with each other to regulate aggressive behaviors, being the former more related to reactive aggressiveness and the latter to proactive aggressiveness.

Author Contributions: Conceptualization: C.C., G.S., P.C., P.F., E.I., P.M., A.N., S.P., G.M. and A.M.; methodology: C.C., G.S., P.F., E.I., A.N., C.P., L.P., L.R., E.V., G.M. and A.M.; writing draft: C.C., G.S., P.C., P.F., P.M., A.N., S.P., G.M. and A.M. All authors have read and agreed to the published version of the manuscript.

Acknowledgments: We wish to acknowledge all the patients, family members and research staff from all the units that participated in the study.

References

1. Decety, J.; Moriguchi, Y. The empathic brain and its dysfunction in psychiatric populations: Implications for intervention across different clinical conditions. *Biopsychosoc. Med.* **2007**, *1*, 22. [CrossRef] [PubMed]
2. Zahn-Waxler, C.; Robinson, J.L.; Emde, R.N. The development of empathy in twins. *Dev. Psychol.* **1992**, *28*, 1038–1047. [CrossRef]
3. Knafo, A.; Zahn-Waxler, C.; Van Hulle, C.; Robinson, J.A.L.; Rhee, S.H. The developmental origins of a disposition toward empathy: Genetic and environmental contributions. *Emotion* **2008**, *8*, 737–752. [CrossRef] [PubMed]
4. Singer, T.; Seymour, B.; O'Doherty, J.P.; Stephan, K.E.; Dolan, R.J.; Frith, C.D. Empathic neural responses are modulated by the perceived fairness of others. *Nature* **2006**, *439*, 466–469. [CrossRef]
5. Muratori, P.; Lochman, J.E.; Lai, E.; Milone, A.; Nocentini, A.; Pisano, S.; Righini, E.; Masi, G. Which dimension of parenting predicts the change of callous unemotional traits in children with disruptive behavior disorder? *Compr. Psychiatry* **2016**, *69*, 202–210. [CrossRef]
6. Gonzalez-Liencres, C.; Shamay-Tsoory, S.G.; Brüne, M. Towards a neuroscience of empathy: Ontogeny, phylogeny, brain mechanisms, context and psychopathology. *Neurosci. Biobehav. Rev.* **2013**, *37*, 1537–1548. [CrossRef]
7. Vellante, M.; Baron-Cohen, S.; Melis, M.; Marrone, M.; Petretto, D.R.; Masala, C.; Preti, A. The "Reading the Mind in the Eyes" test: Systematic review of psychometric properties and a validation study in Italy. *Cogn. Neuropsychiatry* **2013**, *18*, 326–354. [CrossRef]

8. Preti, A.; Vellante, M.; Baron-Cohen, S.; Zucca, G.; Petretto, D.R.; Masala, C. The Empathy Quotient: A cross-cultural comparison of the Italian version. *Cogn. Neuropsychiatry* **2011**, *16*, 50–70. [CrossRef]
9. Blair, R.J.R. Responding to the emotions of others: Dissociating forms of empathy through the study of typical and psychiatric populations. *Conscious. Cogn.* **2005**, *14*, 698–718. [CrossRef]
10. Bons, D.; van den Broek, E.; Scheepers, F.; Herpers, P.; Rommelse, N.; Buitelaaar, J.K. Motor, emotional, and cognitive empathy in children and adolescents with autism spectrum disorder and conduct disorder. *J. Abnorm. Child Psychol.* **2013**, *41*, 425–443. [CrossRef]
11. Mazza, M.; Pino, M.C.; Mariano, M.; Tempesta, D.; Ferrara, M.; De Berardis, D.; Masedu, F.; Valenti, M. Affective and cognitive empathy in adolescents with autism spectrum disorder. *Front. Hum. Neurosci.* **2014**, *8*, 791. [CrossRef] [PubMed]
12. Jolliffe, D.; Farrington, D.P. Development and validation of the Basic Empathy Scale. *J. Adolesc.* **2006**, *29*, 589–611. [CrossRef] [PubMed]
13. Loney, B.R.; Frick, P.J.; Clements, C.B.; Ellis, M.L.; Kerlin, K. Callous-Unemotional Traits, Impulsivity, and Emotional Processing in Adolescents With Antisocial Behavior Problems. *J. Clin. Child Adolesc. Psychol.* **2003**, *32*, 66–80. [CrossRef] [PubMed]
14. Dadds, M.R.; Perry, Y.; Hawes, D.J.; Merz, S.; Riddell, A.C.; Haines, D.J.; Solak, E. Attention to the eyes and fear-recognition deficits in child psychopathy. *Br. J. Psychiatry* **2006**, *189*, 280–281. [CrossRef]
15. Blair, R.J.R. Neurocognitive models of aggression, the antisocial personality disorders, and psychopathy. *J. Neurol. Neurosurg. Psychiatry* **2001**, *71*, 727–731. [CrossRef] [PubMed]
16. Blair, R.J.R. The amygdala and ventromedial prefrontal cortex in morality and psychopathy n.d. *Trends Cogn. Sci.* **2007**, *11*, 387–392. [CrossRef]
17. Milone, A.; Cerniglia, L.; Cristofani, C.; Inguaggiato, E.; Levantini, V.; Masi, G. Empathy in youths with conduct disorder and callous-unemotional traits. *Neural Plast.* **2019**, *2019*. [CrossRef]
18. Jones, A.P.; Happé, F.G.E.; Gilbert, F.; Burnett, S.; Viding, E. Feeling, caring, knowing: Different types of empathy deficit in boys with psychopathic tendencies and autism spectrum disorder. *J. Child Psychol. Psychiatry* **2010**, *51*, 1188–1197. [CrossRef]
19. Ashwin, C.; Chapman, E.; Colle, L.; Baron-Cohen, S. Impaired recognition of negative basic emotions in autism: A test of the amygdala theory. *Soc. Neurosci.* **2006**, *1*, 349–363. [CrossRef]
20. Braaten, E.; Rosen, L.A. Self-regulation of affect in attention deficit-hyperactivity disorder (ADHD) and non-ADHD boys: Differences in empathic responding. *J. Consult. Clin. Psychol.* **2000**, *68*, 313–321. [CrossRef]
21. Nijmeijer, J.S.; Minderaa, R.B.; Buitelaar, J.K.; Mulligan, A.; Hartman, C.A.; Hoekstra, P.J. Attention-deficit/hyperactivity disorder and social dysfunctioning. *Clin. Psychol. Rev.* **2008**, *28*, 692–708. [CrossRef] [PubMed]
22. Abikoff, H.; Hechtman, L.; Klein, R.G.; Gallagher, R.; Fleiss, K.; Etcovitch, J.; Cousins, L.; Greenfield, B.; Martin, D.; Pollack, S. Social functioning in children with ADHD treated with long-term methylphenidate and multimodal psychosocial treatment. *J. Am. Acad. Child Adolesc. Psychiatry* **2004**, *43*, 820–829. [CrossRef] [PubMed]
23. Cordier, R.; Bundy, A.; Hocking, C.; Einfeld, S. Empathy in the play of children with attention deficit hyperactivity disorder. *OTJR Occup. Particip. Health* **2010**, *30*, 122–132. [CrossRef]
24. Maoz, H.; Gvirts, H.Z.; Sheffer, M.; Bloch, Y. Theory of Mind and Empathy in Children With ADHD. *J. Atten. Disord.* **2019**, *23*, 1331–1338. [CrossRef] [PubMed]
25. Davis, A. multidimensional approach to individual difference in empathy. *JSAS Cat. Sel. Doc. Psychol.* **1980**, *10*, 85.
26. Maoz, H.; Tsviban, L.; Gvirts, H.Z.; Shamay-Tsoory, S.G.; Levkovitz, Y.; Watemberg, N.; Bloch, Y. Stimulants improve theory of mind in children with attention deficit/hyperactivity disorder. *J. Psychopharmacol.* **2014**, *28*, 212–219. [CrossRef]
27. Uekermann, J.; Kraemer, M.; Krankenhaus, A.K.; Abdel-Hamid, M.; Hebebrand, J.; Daum, I.; Wiltfang, J.; Kis, B. Social cognition in attention-deficit hyperactivity disorder (ADHD). *Neurosci. Biobehav. Rev.* **2009**, *34*, 734–743. [CrossRef]

28. Barkley, R.A. The relevance of the Still lectures to attention-deficit/hyperactivity disorder: A commentary. *J. Atten. Disord.* **2006**, *10*, 137–140. [CrossRef]
29. Yan, Z.; Hong, S.; Liu, F.; Su, Y. A meta-analysis of the relationship between empathy and executive function. *PsyCh J.* **2020**, *9*, 34–43. [CrossRef]
30. Preston, S.D.; de Waal, F.B.M. Empathy: Its ultimate and proximate bases. *Behav. Brain Sci.* **2002**, *25*, 1–20. [CrossRef]
31. de Waal, F.B.M.; Preston, S.D. Mammalian empathy: Behavioural manifestations and neural basis. *Nat. Rev. Neurosci.* **2017**, *18*, 498–509. [CrossRef] [PubMed]
32. Decety, J.; Meyer, M. From emotion resonance to empathic understanding: A social developmental neuroscience account. *Dev. Psychopathol.* **2008**, *20*, 1053–1080. [CrossRef] [PubMed]
33. Heyes, C. Empathy is not in our genes. *Neurosci. Biobehav. Rev.* **2018**, *95*, 499–507. [CrossRef] [PubMed]
34. de Waal, F.B.M. Putting the altruism back into altruism: The evolution of empathy. *Annu. Rev. Psychol.* **2008**, *59*, 279–300. [CrossRef]
35. Hoffman, M.L. Prosocial behavior and empathy: Developmental processes. *Int. Encycl. Soc. Behav. Sci.* **2001**, 12230–12233. [CrossRef]
36. Shamay-Tsoory, S.G. The neural bases for empathy. *Neuroscientist* **2011**, *17*, 18–24. [CrossRef]
37. Hoffman, M.L. The contribution of empathy to justice and moral judgment. In *Empathy and Its Development*; Eisenberg, N., Strayer, J., Eds.; University of Cambridge Press: Cambridge, UK, 1987; pp. 47–80.
38. Ze, O.; Thoma, P.; Suchan, B. Cognitive and affective empathy in younger and older individuals. *Aging Ment. Health* **2014**, *18*, 929–935. [CrossRef]
39. Valiente, C.; Eisenberg, N.; Fabes, R.A.; Shepard, S.A.; Cumberland, A.; Losoya, S.H. Prediction of children's empathy-related responding from their effortful control and parents' expressivity. *Dev. Psychol.* **2004**, *40*, 911–926. [CrossRef]
40. Spinella, M. Self-rated executive function: Development of the executive function index. *Int. J. Neurosci.* **2005**, *115*, 649–667. [CrossRef]
41. Eisenberg, N.; Okun, M.A. The relations of dispositional regulation and emotionality to elders' empathy-related responding and affect while volunteering. *J. Pers.* **1996**, *64*, 157–183. [CrossRef]
42. Gao, Z.; Ye, T.; Shen, M.; Perry, A. Working memory capacity of biological movements predicts empathy traits. *Psychon. Bull. Rev.* **2016**, *23*, 468–475. [CrossRef] [PubMed]
43. Gökçen, E.; Petrides, K.V.; Hudry, K.; Frederickson, N.; Smillie, L.D. Sub-threshold autism traits: The role of trait emotional intelligence and cognitive flexibility. *Br. J. Psychol.* **2014**, *105*, 187–199. [CrossRef] [PubMed]
44. Gökçen, E.; Frederickson, N.; Petrides, K.V. Theory of mind and executive control deficits in typically developing adults and adolescents with high levels of autism traits. *J. Autism Dev. Disord.* **2016**, *46*, 2072–2087. [CrossRef] [PubMed]
45. Huang, H.; Su, Y.; Jin, J. Empathy-related responding in chinese toddlers: Factorial structure and cognitive contributors. *Infant Child Dev.* **2017**, *26*, e1983. [CrossRef] [PubMed]
46. Jenkins, L.N.; Demaray, M.K.; Tennant, J. Social, emotional, and cognitive factors associated with bullying. *School Psych. Rev.* **2017**, *46*, 42–64. [CrossRef]
47. Abdel-Hamid, M.; Niklewski, F.; Heßmann, P.; Guberina, N.; Kownatka, M.; Kraemer, M.; Scherbaum, N.; Dziobek, I.; Bartels, C.; Wiltfang, J.; et al. Impaired empathy but no theory of mind deficits in adult attention deficit hyperactivity disorder. *Brain Behav.* **2019**, *9*, e01401. [CrossRef]
48. Pineda-Alhucema, W.; Aristizabal, E.; Escudero-Cabarcas, J.; Acosta-López, J.E.; Vélez, J.I. Executive function and theory of mind in children with ADHD: A systematic review. *Neuropsychol. Rev.* **2018**, *28*, 341–358. [CrossRef]
49. Andreou, M.; Skrimpa, V. Theory of mind deficits and neurophysiological operations in autism spectrum disorders: A review. *Brain Sci.* **2020**, *10*, 393. [CrossRef]
50. Goldberg, E.; Podell, K. Adaptive decision making, ecological validity, and the frontal lobes. *J. Clin. Exp. Neuropsychol.* **2000**, *22*, 56–68. [CrossRef]
51. Gioia, G.; Isquith, P.; Guy, S.; Kenworthy, L. *BRIEF-2: Behavior Rating Inventory of Executive Function: Professional Manual*; Psychological Assessment Resources: Lutz, FL, USA, 2015.

52. Van der Meere, J.; Marzocchi, G.M.; De Meo, T. Response inhibition and attention deficit hyperactivity disorder with and without oppositional defiant disorder screened from a community sample. *Dev. Neuropsychol.* **2005**, *28*, 459–472. [CrossRef] [PubMed]
53. Willcutt, E.G.; Doyle, A.E.; Nigg, J.T.; Faraone, S.V.; Pennington, B.F. Validity of the executive function theory of attention-deficit/hyperactivity disorder: A meta-analytic review. *Biol. Psychiatry* **2005**, *57*, 1336–1346. [CrossRef] [PubMed]
54. Marton, I.; Wiener, J.; Rogers, M.; Moore, C.; Tannock, R. Empathy and social perspective taking in children with attention-deficit/ hyperactivity disorder. *J. Abnorm. Child Psychol.* **2009**, *37*, 107–118. [CrossRef] [PubMed]
55. American Psychological Association. *Diagnostic and Statistical Manual of Mental Disorders*, 5th ed.; American Psychological Association: Washington, DC, USA, 2013.
56. Kaufman, J.; Birmaher, B.; Brent, D.; Rao, U.; Flynn, C.; Moreci, P.; Williamson, D.; Ryan, N. Schedule for affective disorders and schizophrenia for school-age children-present and lifetime version (K-SADS-PL): Initial reliability and validity data. *J. Am. Acad. Child Adolesc. Psychiatry* **1997**, *36*, 980–988. [CrossRef]
57. Pandolfi, V.; Magyar, C.I. Child behavior checklist for ages 6–18. In *Encyclopedia of Autism Spectrum Disorders*; Volkmar, F.R., Ed.; Springer: New York, NY, USA, 2013; pp. 581–587. [CrossRef]
58. Achenbach, T.; Rescorla, L. *Manual for the ASEBA School-Age Forms and Profiles: An Integrated System of Multi-Informant Assessment*; Research Center for Children, Youth, & Families, University of Vermont: Burlington, VT, USA, 2001.
59. Rutter, M.; Bailey, A.; Lord, C. *The Social Communication Questionnaire Manual*; Western Psychological Services: Los Angeles, CA, USA, 2003.
60. Rutter, M.; LeCouteur, A.; Lord, C. *Autism Diagnostic Interview-Revised*; Western Psychological Services: Los Angeles, CA, USA, 2003.
61. Lord, C.; Rutter, M.; DiLavore, P.; Risi, S.; Gotham, K.; Bishop, S. *Autism Diagnostic Observation Schedule (ADOS-2)*, 2nd ed.; Western Psychological Services: Los Angeles, CA, USA, 2012; Available online: https://www.wpspublish.com/ados-2-autism-diagnostic-observation-schedule-second-edition (accessed on 22 February 2020).
62. Frick, P.; Hare, R. *Antisocial Process. Screening Device: APSD*; Multi-Health Systems: Toronto, ON, Canada, 2001.
63. Masi, G.; Milone, A.; Brovedani, P.; Pisano, S.; Muratori, P. Psychiatric evaluation of youths with disruptive behavior disorders and psychopathic traits: A critical review of assessment measures. *Neurosci. Biobehav. Rev.* **2018**, *91*, 21–33. [CrossRef] [PubMed]
64. Litvack-Miller, W.; McDougall, D.; Romney, D.M. The structure of empathy during middle childhood and its relationship to prosocial behavior. *Genet. Soc. Gen. Psychol. Monogr.* **1997**, *123*, 303–324.
65. Benjamini, Y.; Hochberg, Y. Controlling the false discovery rate: A practical and powerful approach to multiple testing. *J. R. Stat. Soc.* **1995**, *57*, 289–300. [CrossRef]
66. Mouti, A.; Dryer, R.; Kohn, M. Differentiating autism spectrum disorder from ADHD using the social communication questionnaire. *J. Atten. Disord.* **2019**, *23*, 828–837. [CrossRef]
67. Narzisi, A.; Posada, M.; Barbieri, F.; Chericoni, N.; Ciuffolini, D.; Pinzino, M.; Romano, R.; Scattoni, M.L.; Tancredi, R.; Calderoni, S.; et al. Prevalence of autism spectrum disorder in a large Italian catchment area: A school-based population study within the ASDEU project. *Epidemiol. Psychiatr. Sci.* **2018**, *29*, e5. [CrossRef]
68. Tye, C.; Bedford, R.; Asherson, P.; Ashwood, K.L.; Azadi, B.; Bolton, P.; McLoughlin, G. Callous-unemotional traits moderate executive function in children with ASD and ADHD: A pilot event-related potential study. *Dev. Cogn. Neurosci.* **2017**, *26*, 84–90. [CrossRef]
69. Herpers, P.C.M.; Rommelse, N.N.J.; Bons, D.M.A.; Buitelaar, J.K.; Scheepers, F.E. Callous-unemotional traits as a cross-disorders construct. *Soc. Psychiatry Psychiatr. Epidemiol.* **2012**, *47*, 2045–2064. [CrossRef]
70. Ay, M.G.; Kiliç, B.G. Factors associated with empathy among adolescents with attention deficit hyperactivity disorder. *Turk Psikiyatr. Derg.* **2019**, *30*, 260–267. [CrossRef]
71. Song, Y.; Nie, T.; Shi, W.; Zhao, X.; Yang, Y. Empathy impairment in individuals with autism spectrum conditions from a multidimensional perspective: A meta-analysis. *Front. Psychol.* **2019**, *10*, 1902. [CrossRef] [PubMed]
72. Pijper, J.; de Wied, M.; van Rijn, S.; van Goozen, S.; Swaab, H.; Meeus, W. Executive attention and empathy-related responses in boys with oppositional defiant disorder or conduct disorder, with and without comorbid anxiety disorder. *Child Psychiatry Hum. Dev.* **2018**, *49*, 956–965. [CrossRef] [PubMed]

73. Zelazo, P.D.; Carlson, S.M. Hot and cool executive function in childhood and adolescence: Development and plasticity. *Child Dev. Perspect.* **2012**, *6*, 354–360. [CrossRef]
74. Zelazo, P.D. Executive function and psychopathology: A neurodevelopmental perspective. *Annu. Rev. Clin. Psychol.* **2020**, *16*, 431–454. [CrossRef]
75. Miranda, A.; Berenguer, C.; Roselló, B.; Baixauli, I.; Colomer, C. Social cognition in children with high-functioning autism spectrum disorder and attention-deficit/hyperactivity disorder. associations with executive functions. *Front. Psychol.* **2017**, *8*, 1035. [CrossRef]
76. Brooks, B.L.; Sherman, E.M.S.; Strauss, E. NEPSY-II: A Developmental neuropsychological assessment, second edition. *Child Neuropsychol.* **2010**, *16*, 80–101. [CrossRef]
77. Fassino, S. Empatia e strategie dell'incoraggiamento nel processo di cambiamento. *Riv. Psicol. Indiv.* **2009**, *63*, 49–63.
78. Rizeq, J.; Toplak, M.E.; Ledochowski, J.; Basile, A.; Andrade, B.F. Developmental neuropsychology callous-unemotional traits and executive functions are unique correlates of disruptive behavior in children. *Dev. Neuropsychol.* **2020**, *45*, 154–166. [CrossRef]
79. Lambruschi, F.; Muratori, P. *Psicopatologia e Psicoterapia dei Disturbi della Condotta*; Carocci: Rome, Italy, 2013.
80. Blair, R.J.R.; Peschardt, K.S.; Budhani, S.; Mitchell, D.G.V.; Pine, D.S. The development of psychopathy. *J. Child Psychol. Psychiatry* **2006**, *47*, 262–276. [CrossRef]

10

Association of Autism Onset, Epilepsy and Behavior in a Community of Adults with Autism and Severe Intellectual Disability

Stefano Damiani [1,*], Pietro Leali [2], Guido Nosari [3], Monica Caviglia [4], Mariangela V. Puci [5], Maria Cristina Monti [5], Natascia Brondino [1] and Pierluigi Politi [1]

1 Department of Brain and Behavioral Sciences, University of Pavia, 27100 Pavia, Italy; natascia.brondino@unipv.it (N.B.); pierluigi.politi@unipv.it (P.P.)
2 Faculty of Medicine, University of Pavia, 27100 Pavia, Italy; leali.pietro@gmail.com
3 Department of Neurosciences and Mental Health, IRCCS Ca' Granda Ospedale Maggiore Policlinico, 20122 Milan, Italy; guido.nosari@gmail.com
4 RSD Cascina Rossago, 27050 Ponte Nizza, Italy; mo.caviglia@gmail.com
5 Department of Public Health, Experimental and Forensic Medicine, University of Pavia, 27100 Pavia, Italy; mariangela.puci@unipv.it (M.V.P.); cristina.monti@unipv.it (M.C.M.)
* Correspondence: stefano.damiani01@ateneopv.it

Abstract: Autism spectrum disorders (ASDs) are hard to characterize due to their clinical heterogeneity. Whether epilepsy and other highly prevalent comorbidities may be related to specific subphenotypes such as regressive ASD (i.e., the onset of symptoms after a period of apparently typical development) is controversial and yet to be determined. Such discrepancies may be related to the fact that age, level of cognitive functioning, and environmental variables are often not taken into account. We considered a sample of 20 subjects (i) between 20 and 55 years of age, (ii) with severe/profound intellectual disability, (iii) living in the same rural context of a farm community. As a primary aim, we tested for the association between epilepsy and regressive ASD. Secondly, we explored differences in behavioral and pharmacological profiles related to the presence of each of these conditions, as worse behavioral profiles have been separately associated with both epilepsy and regressive ASD in previous studies. An initial trend was observed for associations between the presence of epilepsy and regressive ASD (odds ratio: 5.33; 95% CI: 0.62–45.41, p-value: 0.086). Secondly, subjects with either regressive ASD or epilepsy showed worse behavioral profiles (despite the higher pharmacotherapy they received). These preliminary results, which need to be further confirmed, suggest the presence of specific associations of different clinical conditions in subjects with rarely investigated phenotypes.

Keywords: autism in adulthood; intellectual disability; regressive autism; epilepsy; challenging behaviors

1. Introduction

Autism spectrum disorder (ASD) is a neurodevelopmental condition whose phenotype encompasses various degrees of disability. Its growing prevalence has recently reached an estimate of 1 over 40 children [1]. ASD is associated with a wide range of comorbidities, among which intellectual disability (ID) or "low-functioning" ASD, epilepsy, and psychiatric disorders are the most frequent [2,3]. Compared to their "high-functioning" counterparts, low-functioning ASD individuals tend to exhibit more severe symptomatology and represent approximately 50% of the ASD population [4]. Few studies have been conducted on this 50% of the ASD population with comorbid ID, with its poor clinical outcomes and, thus, higher need for effective therapeutical strategies [5]. Similar to ID, epilepsy is also associated with challenging behaviors in individuals with ASD and ID [6]. Moreover, congenital autism spectrum disorders (CASD, when the core symptoms are evident from the very early life stages) may show different clinical presentations from regressive autism disorders (RASD, when the child loses abilities and milestones that were already achieved) [7]. In spite of the well-established presence of shared mechanisms between epilepsy and the autism spectrum being taken as a whole [8], the degree of association between epilepsy and RASD is not fully understood, with the few studies on this topic mostly focused on children [9,10].

A categorization of ASD subphenotypes is highly needed. This explorative study describes the clinical profile of 20 adults with ASD and severe/profound ID by assessing the presence of epilepsy and their history of RASD. The primary aim is to assess (i) the chance of these two conditions occurring together and (ii) the impact of each condition over the clinical picture in order to test whether epilepsy or RASD may be associated with the individuals' behavior. Both these features are hence compared to individual behaviors and pharmacotherapy, expecting worse profiles in subjects with epilepsy or RASD.

2. Materials and Methods

2.1. *Study Design*

This work is an observational retrospective study. We conducted a thorough data collection for each subject in two ways: (i) The number of seizures and sleep-disturbed nights were collected from the clinical records of each subject from January 2012 to December 2017 and sorted in 72 monthly timepoints for a total of 6 years; (ii) at the end of this time-window, behavioral profiles were assessed with the aberrant behavior checklist (ABC) [11] and data concerning antipsychotic, antidepressant, benzodiazepine, and anticonvulsant therapy were recorded.

2.2. *Participants*

Participants were recruited from Cascina Rossago, a farm community located in a rural area in the province of Pavia, Italy. For each subject, the legal representative gave his informed consent for inclusion before participation in the study. The study was conducted in accordance with the Declaration of Helsinki, and the protocol was approved by the Ethics Committee of IRCSS San Matteo, Pavia, Italy. This facility setting is meant to promote the active involvement of the user in farming activities such as fruit harvesting, breeding, and gardening. Moreover, sports and artistic workshops such as painting and drawing, music courses, pottery, basketball, and pool swimming are provided. The location is surrounded by nature: a rural environment was chosen both to avoid external disturbing factors such as city-life distress and to favor natural circadian and seasonal rhythms. This community was considered ideal for the purpose of our research for multiple reasons. Firstly, it is committed to offering lifelong care and working plans to adult ASD patients with severe to profound ID. The same living environment, activities, and diet are hence available for all the subjects. Secondly, each patient was constantly monitored by healthcare professionals, with accurate and detailed medical records. The main sample characteristics are shown in Table 1. RASD and epilepsy were considered as primary factors to present more specific information regarding the subsamples.

Table 1. Sample characteristics.

	All Subjects	Groups Stratified by Absence/Presence of Epilepsy			Groups Stratified by Autism Onset		
	(n = 20)	Absence (n = 9)	Presence (n = 11)	Absence vs. Presence *p*-Value	CASD (n = 9)	RASD (n = 11)	CASD vs. RASD *p*-Value
Age—mean ± SD	37.5 ± 9.5	36.33 ± 3.9	38.5 ± 2.4	0.632 †	36. 6 ± 8.1	38.3 ± 10.8	0.698 †
Sex—n (%)							
Male	15 (75.0)	6 (66.7)	9 (81.8)	0.617 #	5 (55.6)	10 (90.9)	0.127 #
BMI (kg/m^2)—mean ± SD	25.3 ± 4.2	24.8 ± 3.8	25.7 ± 4.7	0.649 †	26.1 ± 3.3	25.4 ± 4.6	0.553 †
Drug therapy—n (%)							
anticonvulsant	12 (60.0)	4 (44.4)	8 (72.7)	0.362 #	4 (44.4)	8 (72.7)	0.362 #
benzodiazepine	11 (55.0)	3 (33.3)	8 (72.7)	0.175 #	3 (33.3)	8 (72.7)	0.175 #
Antidepressant	6 (30.0)	2 (22.2)	4 (36.4)	0.642 #	2 (22.2)	4 (36.4)	0.642 #
antipsychotic	10 (50.0)	4 (44.4)	6 (54.6)	0.999 #	4 (44.4)	6 (54.6)	0.999 #

† Student's *t*-test # Fisher's exact test; CASD = congenital autism spectrum disorder; RASD = regressive autism spectrum disorder.

2.3. Materials

Epilepsy—A subject was considered epileptic if the diagnosis from a specialized neurological center was present. The patient's legal representatives were contacted to further confirm the anamnestic data and to provide the official documentation confirming the clinical history. The retrospective analysis of the data allowed us to reconstruct the number of seizures suffered by each subject monthly. Taking into account the numerical limits of the sample in contrast with the detailed temporal data, a graphic illustration of the epilepsy trends was produced as a useful tool to promptly understand and visualize the differences between the two cohorts.

CASD/RASD—In relation to the diagnosis of RASD, early life medical records were available for all the subjects. According to the commonly agreed definition [12], we classified patients who initially reached cognitive and behavioral milestones but experienced a setback before the age of 3 as RASD.

2.4. Pharmacological Treatments

In our sample, 18 of the 20 participants were on psychopharmacological therapy. Antipsychotics were necessary for 10 subjects to support educational interventions for challenging behaviors. Anticonvulsants and benzodiazepines were used to control seizures in the majority of cases. In subjects without epilepsy (4 cases), these drugs were administered with the aim of controlling impulsive and self-harming behaviors [13].

2.5. Data Analyses

To describe the sample, we calculated summary statistics that are expressed as means, standard deviations (SD), median and 25th–75th percentiles or percentages, as appropriate. A Shapiro–Wilk test was used to test the normality of the data. We used Fisher's exact test for categorical variables and Student's *t*-test or the Mann–Whitney test, as appropriate, for the quantitative ones. Odds ratio (OR) with 95% confidence interval (CI) was calculated to evaluate the associations between epilepsy and RASD/CASD. Statistical analysis was conducted using STATA/SE for Windows, version 15 (StataCorp, College Station, TX, USA). A p-value <0.05 was considered significant.

3. Results

The mean age of the whole sample was 37.5 ± 9.48 years (range 23–55 years), 15 (75%) were males. For all patients, the mean BMI was 25.30 ± 4.21 kg/m^2. Information about drug therapy revealed that 60% of patients consumed antiepileptic drugs, 55% benzodiazepines, 30% antidepressants, and 50%

psychiatric drugs (Table 1). Table 1 shows patient characteristics for all subjects, stratified by the presence of epilepsy and CASD/RASD conditions. The history of registered epileptic seizures is graphically reported in Figure 1.

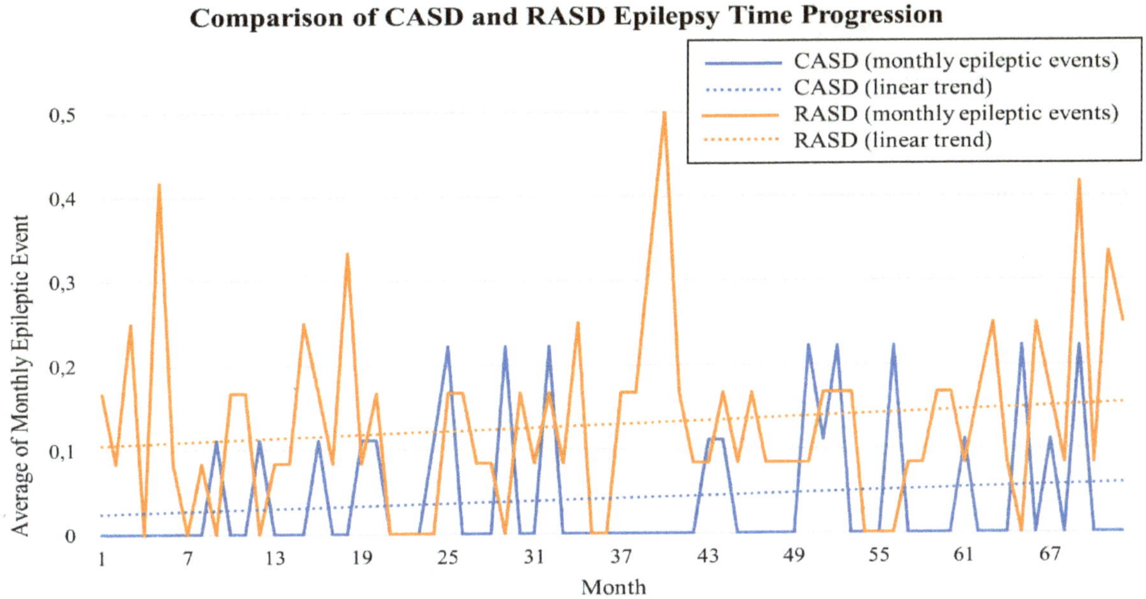

Figure 1. The graph represents oscillations in the presentation of epileptic events in CASD and RASD groups during the 6-year interval. The more frequent and higher spikes suggest a greater occurrence of seizures in the RASD group. Conversely, the seizure-free period reaches the zero level more often and for longer timespans in the CASD group. This trend tends to remain stable across the period of observation.

Six subjects had no history of epilepsy or RASD, three had only epilepsy, three had only RASD, and eight had both epilepsy and RASD (Figure 2A). The odds ratio was computed to check for associations between the presence of epilepsy and RASD (OR: 5.33; 95% CI: 0.62–45.41, *p*-value: 0.086).

The ABC median subscores were higher in epileptic patients versus nonepileptic patients and in the RASD group versus the CASD group (Table 2). No statistically significant difference was appreciated, but a trend was observed, for which each condition tends to increase the severity of challenging behaviors (all the ABC median subscores are higher in both epilepsy and RASD groups; see Figure 2).

Table 2. Aberrant behavior checklist (ABC) subscales scores.

	All Subjects	Groups Stratified by Absence/Presence of Epilepsy			Groups Stratified by Autism Onset		
	(n = 20)	Absence (n = 9)	Presence (n = 11)	Absence vs. Presence *p*-Value	CASD (n = 9)	RASD (n = 11)	CASD vs. RASD *p*-Value
Hyperactivity Mean ± SD	21.05 ± 7.56	19.0 ± 9.0	22.73 ± 6.08	0.270	17.56 ± 8.29	23.9 ± 5.80	0.056
Median (IQR)	21.0 (16.0–25.5)	17.0 (15.0–25.0)	22.0 (18.0–26.0)		17.0 (14.0–23.0)	24.0 (19.0–30.0)	
Irritability Mean ± SD	22.25 ± 8.65	19.67 ± 10.37	24.36 ± 6.73	0.209	19.56 ± 10.19	24.45 ± 6.87	0.261
Median (IQR)	21.5 (18.0–29.0)	18.0 (15.0–29.0)	23.0 (19.0–29.0)		18.0 (13.0–26.5)	23.0 (19.0–32.0)	
Lethargy Mean ± SD	20.65 ± 9.45	19.22 ± 11.34	21.82 ± 7.96	0.469	18.56 ± 11.86	22.36 ± 7.06	0.370
Median (IQR)	19.5 (16.5–26.0)	17.0 (11.0–25.0)	20.0 (18.0–26.0)		17.0 (9.0–29.5)	22.0 (18.0–26.0)	

Table 2. *Cont.*

	All Subjects	Groups Stratified by Absence/Presence of Epilepsy			Groups Stratified by Autism Onset		
	(n = 20)	Absence (n = 9)	Presence (n = 11)	Absence vs. Presence *p*-Value	CASD (n = 9)	RASD (n = 11)	CASD vs. RASD *p*-Value
Stereotypy							
Mean ± SD	11.15 ± 3.99	10.22 ± 4.71	11.91 ± 3.33	0.377	9.89 ± 4.51	12.18 ± 3.37	0.230
Median (IQR)	11.0 (7.0–14.0)	10.0 (7.0–14.0)	12.0 (9.0–14.0)		10.0 (7.0–13.0)	13.0 (9.0–14.0)	
Inappropriate speech							
Mean ± SD	5.85 ± 3.10	5.0 ± 2.92	6.55 ± 3.21	0.267	4.67 ± 2.50	6.82 ± 3.31	0.175
Median (IQR)	5.0 (4.0–7.5)	5.0 (4.0–6.0)	6.0 (4.0–9.0)		5 (2.5–6.5)	6.0 (4.0–11.0)	

p-values obtained from Mann–Whitney U-tests. CASD = congenital autism spectrum disorder; RASD = regressive autism spectrum disorder.

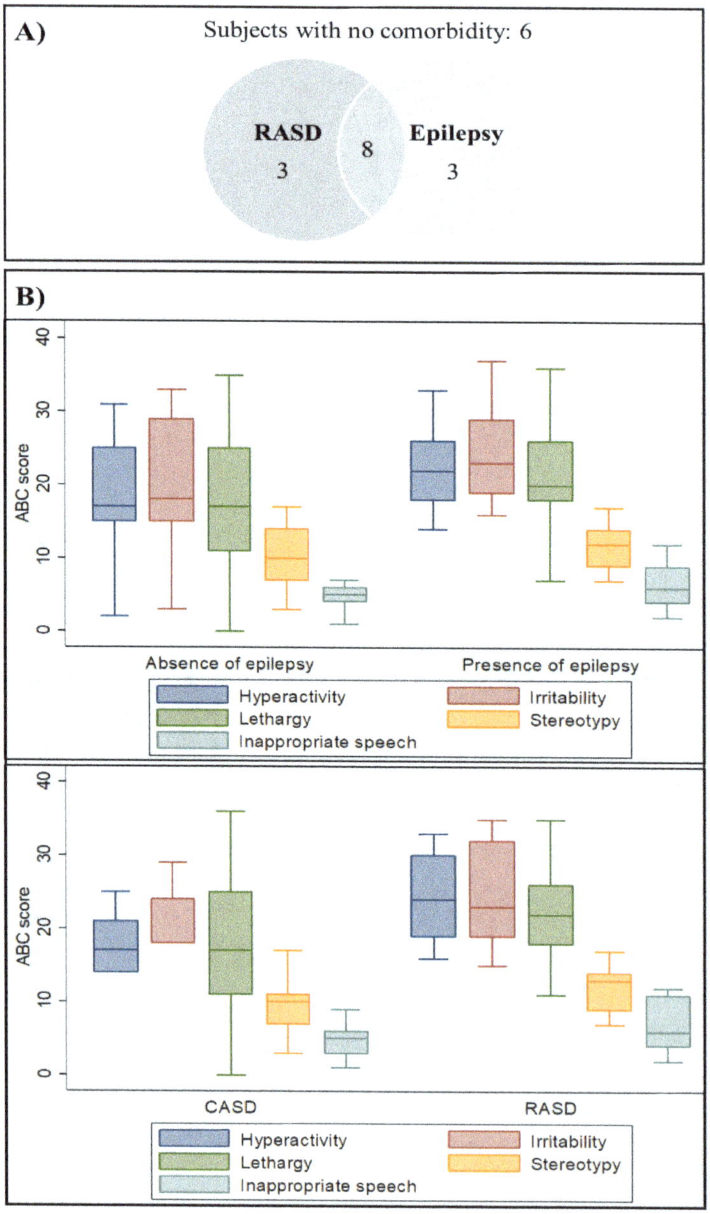

Figure 2. (**A**) Number of subjects with RASD, epilepsy, and both conditions are displayed. (**B**) Boxplots representing the difference of ABC median scores and the 25th–75th percentile of ABC scores in subjects stratified by epilepsy absent/present and CADS/RASD.

4. Discussion

We analyzed a sample of adult patients with ASD and ID who are stably living within the setting of a farm community. The main purpose of our study is to assess the association between autism onset and epilepsy and the impact of these conditions on behavioral profiles. Even though limitations such as the sample size did not allow the emergence of statistically significant results, the RASD subjects were 5 times more likely to also have a diagnosis of epilepsy.

We retrospectively measured the average of monthly epileptic events, i.e., any type of seizure, to better describe the presence of epileptic events and their frequency. RASD patients experienced a greater number of events, with fewer and shorter epilepsy-free periods. The three CASD subjects with epilepsy seemed to respond better to pharmacotherapy, with better control of the seizures.

Concerning behavioral profiles, even if differences in the ABC domains did not reach statistical significance, both RASD and epilepsy groups scored higher in each of these subscores. This trend is important, especially considering that the behavioral impairments are observed despite the higher pharmacotherapy that the RASD and epilepsy groups are undergoing. In fact, these subjects are more likely to consume not only anticonvulsants/mood stabilizers and benzodiazepines (which would be intuitive due to the epileptic risk), but also antipsychotics and antidepressants, which were initiated to better control problem behaviors and dysregulated moods, respectively. Autism and epilepsy share several neurobiological pathways [14]. An increased association between RASD and epilepsy may be determined by severe brain damage (for instance, after encephalitis, which is a risk factor for both autism [15] and epilepsy [16]) occurring in the first years of life. For instance, in our sample, two subjects suffered acute infection-related, early age neuroinflammation, after which seizures and regression arose.

The main limitation of this study is the low sample size, which does not allow us to hypothesize more complex assumptions based on the statistical significance of the findings due to excessively wide confidence intervals. The restrictive inclusion criteria and the same living and care conditions allowed to exclude several confounding factors, such as the variability given by differences in cognitive profiles, environments, diets, and therapeutical/educational approaches. However, high intersubject variability in behavioral and pharmacological profiles was measured despite these highly specific criteria.

5. Conclusions

Our findings show that (i) RASD and epilepsy tend to present together in a subsample of subjects with ASD and ID, (ii) RASD is associated with poorer control of epileptic symptoms, and (iii) RASD and epilepsy tend to worsen the behavioral prognosis, requiring more psychopharmacological therapies to compensate the clinical problems. Even though previous studies concerning the association between RASD and epilepsy yielded controversial results, the apparently contrasting findings may be attributed to the often-neglected differences between different life-phases (children versus adults) and levels of cognitive functioning. Carefully considering age and the presence of ID as influencing factors may hence help to shed light on this relatively uncharted but promising field of investigation in order to refine clinical classifications and tailor individualized treatments. These results invite us to further explore the subject, with the aim of determining whether the occurrence of different symptoms in autistic subpopulations may eventually lead to the individuation of ASD phenotypes.

Author Contributions: Conceptualization, S.D.; methodology, M.V.P. and M.C.M.; formal analysis, M.V.P. and M.C.M.; investigation, P.L. and N.B.; resources, M.C.; data curation, G.N.; writing—original draft preparation, P.L.; writing—review and editing, S.D. and G.N.; visualization, S.D. and P.L.; supervision, M.C. and P.P.; project administration, P.P. All authors have read and agreed to the published version of the manuscript.

References

1. Xu, G.; Strathearn, L.; Liu, B.; O'brien, M.; Kopelman, T.G.; Zhu, J.; Snetselaar, L.G.; Bao, W. Prevalence and treatment patterns of autism spectrum disorder in the United States, 2016. *JAMA Pediatrics* **2019**, *173*, 153–159. [CrossRef] [PubMed]

2. Cervantes, P.E.; Matson, J.L. Comorbid symptomology in adults with autism spectrum disorder and intellectual disability. *J. Autism Dev. Disord.* **2015**, *45*, 3961–3970. [CrossRef] [PubMed]
3. Mannion, A.; Leader, G. Comorbidity in autism spectrum disorder: A literature review. *Res. Autism Spectr. Disord.* **2013**, *7*, 1595–1616. [CrossRef]
4. Matson, J.L.; Shoemaker, M. Intellectual disability and its relationship to autism spectrum disorders. *Res. Dev. Disabil.* **2009**, *30*, 1107–1114. [CrossRef] [PubMed]
5. Feldman, M.; Bosett, J.; Collet, C.; Burnham-Riosa, P. Where are persons with intellectual disabilities in medical research? A survey of published clinical trials. *J. Intellect. Disabil. Res.* **2014**, *58*, 800–809. [CrossRef] [PubMed]
6. Smith, K.R.; Matson, J.L. Behavior problems: Differences among intellectually disabled adults with co-morbid autism spectrum disorders and epilepsy. *Res. Dev. Disabil.* **2010**, *31*, 1062–1069. [CrossRef] [PubMed]
7. Rogers, S.J. Developmental regression in autism spectrum disorders. *Ment. Retard. Dev. Disabil. Res. Rev.* **2004**, *10*, 139–143. [CrossRef] [PubMed]
8. Richard, A.E.; Scheffer, I.E.; Wilson, S.J. Features of the broader autism phenotype in people with epilepsy support shared mechanisms between epilepsy and autism spectrum disorder. *Neurosci. Biobehav. Rev.* **2017**, *75*, 203–233. [CrossRef] [PubMed]
9. Hrdlicka, M. EEG abnormalities, epilepsy and regression in autism: A review. *Neuroendocrinol. Lett.* **2008**, *29*, 405. [PubMed]
10. Trauner, D.A. Behavioral correlates of epileptiform abnormalities in autism. *Epilepsy Behav.* **2015**, *47*, 163–166. [CrossRef] [PubMed]
11. Kaat, A.J.; Lecavalier, L.; Aman, M.G. Validity of the aberrant behavior checklist in children with autism spectrum disorder. *J. Autism Dev. Disord.* **2014**, *44*, 1103–1116. [CrossRef] [PubMed]
12. Stefanatos, G.A. Regression in autistic spectrum disorders. *Neuropsychol. Rev.* **2008**, *18*, 305–319. [CrossRef] [PubMed]
13. Ji, N.Y.; Findling, R.L. Pharmacotherapy for mental health problems in people with intellectual disability. *Curr. Opin. Psychiatry* **2016**, *29*, 103–125. [CrossRef] [PubMed]
14. Lee, B.H.; Smith, T.; Paciorkowski, A.R. Autism spectrum disorder and epilepsy: Disorders with a shared biology. *Epilepsy Behav.* **2015**, *47*, 191–201. [CrossRef] [PubMed]
15. Kern, J.K.; Geier, D.A.; Sykes, L.K.; Geier, M.R. Relevance of neuroinflammation and encephalitis in autism. *Front. Cell. Neurosci.* **2015**, *9*, 519. [CrossRef]
16. Klein, P.; Dingledine, R.; Aronica, E.; Bernard, C.; Blumcke, I.; Boison, D.; Brodie, M.J.; Brooks-Kayal, A.R.; Engel, J., Jr.; Forcelli, P.A.; et al. Commonalities in epileptogenic processes from different acute brain insults: Do they translate? *Epilepsia* **2018**, *59*, 37–66. [CrossRef]

11

Autism and Intellectual Disability Associated with Mitochondrial Disease and Hyperlactacidemia

José Guevara-Campos [1], Lucía González-Guevara [2] and Omar Cauli [3,*]

1 "Felipe Guevara Rojas" Hospital, Pediatrics Service, University of Oriente, El Tigre-Anzoátegui, 6034 Venezuela, Spain; joguevara90@hotmail.com
2 "Felipe Guevara Rojas" Hospital, Epilepsy and Encephalography Unit, El Tigre-Anzoátegui, 6034 Venezuela, Spain; proyectoasociacion@hotmail.com
3 Department of Nursing, University of Valencia, 46010 Valencia, Spain
* Author to whom correspondence should be addressed; omar.cauli@uv.es

Academic Editor: Merlin G. Butler

Abstract: Autism spectrum disorder (ASD) with intellectual disability (ID) is a life-long debilitating condition, which is characterized by cognitive function impairment and other neurological signs. Children with ASD-ID typically attain motor skills with a significant delay. A sub-group of ASD-IDs has been linked to hyperlactacidemia and alterations in mitochondrial respiratory chain activity. The objective of this report is to describe the clinical features of patients with these comorbidities in order to shed light on difficult diagnostic and therapeutic approaches in such patients. We reported the different clinical features of children with ID associated with hyperlactacidemia and deficiencies in mitochondrial respiratory chain complex II–IV activity whose clinical presentations are commonly associated with the classic spectrum of mitochondrial diseases. We concluded that patients with ASD and ID presenting with persistent hyperlactacidemia should be evaluated for mitochondrial disorders. Administration of carnitine, coenzyme Q10, and folic acid is partially beneficial, although more studies are needed to assess the efficacy of this vitamin/cofactor treatment combination.

Keywords: autism; possible mitochondrial disease; vitamins; intellectual disability; muscular tone

---

1. Introduction

Intellectual disability (ID) represents a significant social and economic burden; About 3% of the Western population is diagnosed with ID, and these patients require lifelong care [1–3]. An individual is considered to have an ID based on the following three criteria: (1) An intellectual functioning level (IQ) below 70; (2) Significant limitations exist in two or more adaptive skill areas (communication, self-care, home living, social skills, leisure, health and safety, self-direction, functional academics, community use, and work); and (3) the condition manifests itself before the age of 18 [4,5]. ID is sometimes associated with autism spectrum disorders (ASDs), behavioral disorders (hyperactivity, irritability, and self-injurious behavior), epilepsy, and/or other neurological disabilities (ataxia, hypotonia, sensorial alterations), all resulting in psychological, social, and economic burdens [1,6,7]. There are also some genetic causes of ID, which constitute 30%–50% of cases [3,7–9], however in the majority of instances the etiology is unknown. Assessment of molecular defects that result in synaptic deficits as well as defining suitable therapeutic treatments for these deficits remains a challenge [10].

Mitochondrial diseases can develop because of mitochondrial (mtDNA) or nuclear DNA (nDNA) mutations, however in many cases no mutations are found. These mutations are uncommon in the general population and have an estimated prevalence of around 1:8500 [11]. The extremely heterogeneous clinical presentation of mtDNA and nDNA mutations often causes diagnostic difficulties and thus many patients are diagnosed with mitochondrial disease without identifying the mtDNA or nDNA mutation responsible for the ASD-ID [2]. Additionally, the same genetic mutation can give rise to multiple varied phenotypes [12]. Mitochondrial respiratory chain (electron transport chain; ETC) disorders can be difficult to recognize clinically because of their diverse symptoms and clinical presentations and, as we report here, the diagnosis is often reached late in childhood.

Histopathological, biochemical, and genetic findings [13,14] are normally used to aid final diagnosis of possible, probable, or definite mitochondrial disease. The clinical presentation almost always widely varies, making definitive diagnosis of these mitochondrial disorders challenging [15] and although various criteria and checklists have been established these are more reflective of adult disease [13,14,16]. Patients with mitochondrial disease often show signs and symptoms such as heart, pancreas, or liver dysfunction, growth retardation, and fatigability, but sometimes the semiology is different from classical mitochondrial diseases and patients show symptoms associated with neurological deficits such as ID, ASD, abnormal muscle tone, seizures, extrapyramidal movements, and autonomic and ocular dysfunction [17,18].

Here, we report the interesting cases of three patients diagnosed with developmental delay, ID and ASD, and also with a possible mitochondrial disease accompanied by an ETC deficiency accompanied by hyperlactacidemia [14]. These cases have an unusual clinical presentation, which would not normally lead to suspicion of mitochondrial disease. For instance, fewer than three organ systems were involved, and red-flags for neurological involvement *i.e.*, cerebral stroke-like lesions in a nonvascular pattern, basal ganglia disease, recurrent encephalopathy, neurodegeneration, epilepsia partialis continua, myoclonus, ataxia, magnetic resonance imaging (MRI) findings consistent with Leigh disease, *etc.*, were not present [2]. We provide useful clinical evidence that patients presenting only ID and an alteration in muscular tone but in the absence of any other systemic signs may, according to the current classification of these disorders, also have a mitochondrial ETC disorder [14]. Children with ID and ASD who show no systemic signs should therefore be evaluated for comorbid mitochondrial disorders. In addition we describe some beneficial effects of combined pharmacological treatment with antipsychotic drugs and vitamins.

2. Results

2.1. Medical History and Clinical Examination

Patient 1: A 17-month-old boy was referred to the neuropediatrician because of generalized hypotonia and reduced cranial growth perimeter. He was the full-term product of a third pregnancy (preceded by a spontaneous miscarriage) resulting from a non-consanguineous relationship. His birth weight was 4.2 kg (60th percentile) and height was 51 cm (50th percentile), he had normal immunization and had an Apgar score of 9. However, he showed global developmental delay according to the Peabody Developmental Motor Scale 2 (PDMS-2) and the Battelle developmental inventory 2 (BDI-2; see Section 4.1).

Head support was achieved at seven months, with stable seating and autonomous position attained at 12 months; he started to walk autonomously at 30 months, and his first raw words appeared at 12 months. There was no family history of metabolic or neurological disease. Upon physical examination, his weight was 10 kg (50–75th percentile), height was 72 cm (90th percentile), head circumference was 41.5 cm (10th percentile, microcephaly), and his general condition was regular except for generalized hypotonia and loss of strength in the upper part of his lower-limbs but with normal deep tendon I/IV reflexes. No dysmorphic features, skin blemishes, or cardiopulmonary alterations were observed.

Patient 2: A two-year-old girl was referred to the neuropediatrician for psychomotor delay and generalized hypotonia. She was the term product of a first pregnancy resulting from a non-consanguineous relationship. Her birth weight was 2.7 kg (10th percentile), her height was 50 cm (50th percentile), and she had normal immunization. At birth, her Apgar score was 7 because of a delayed birth cry. Head support was achieved at 12 months, with a stable seating position achieved for the first time at 24 months, and autonomous walking at 30 months. Her first raw words appeared at 12 months but she did not produce complete sentences. She exhibited global developmental delay according to the PDMS-2 scale and BDI-2 inventory (see Section 4.1).

There was a family history of diabetes (four aunts and her maternal grandfather). Upon physical examination she had a weight of 13.5 kg (50–75th percentile), a height of 93 cm (90th percentile), head circumference of 43 cm (10th percentile, microcephaly), hypertonia in the left hemibody, and deep tendon hyperreflexia in her left-hand side limbs. There were no dysmorphic features, skin blemishes, or pulmonary alterations, and although her mitral valve was hyperelastic it was competent. Her thorax radiography, karyotype, and the EEG were normal, but an MRI showed ventriculomegaly with a prominent cisterna magna but without signs of displacement or compression (Figure 1A). Her associated clinical features are summarized in Table 1.

Table 1. Summary of the clinical features of the three patients described in this case study.

ID	Patient 1	Patient 2	Patient 3
	Severe	Moderate	Severe
Hypotonia	YES	YES (hypertonia at 1.5 months in the left hemibody)	YES
EEG Alteration	NO	NO	YES
Seizure	NO	NO	NO
Developmental Delay (Before age 5)	YES	YES	YES
Behavioral Problem (Irritability)	YES	NO	YES
PDD-NOS (According to DMS-IV)	YES (fulfilled 2 criteria of ASD diagnosis: Qualitative abnormalities in communication and reciprocal social interaction)	YES (fulfilled 1 criterion of ASD diagnosis: Qualitative abnormalities in communication)	YES (fulfilled 2 criteria of ASD diagnosis: Qualitative abnormalities in communication and reciprocal social interaction)
Microcephaly	YES	YES	NO
MRI Alteration (Ventricle enlargement)	YES	YES	YES

ID: Intellectual disability; EEG: Electroencephalography; PDD-NOS: Pervasive developmental disorder-not otherwise specified; DMS-IV: Diagnostic and statistical manual of mental disorders, fourth edition; and MRI: Magnetic resonance imaging.

Patient 3: A 19-month-old boy was referred to the neuropediatrician for psychomotor delay because he was unable to maintain an autonomous seating position or to autonomously walk, and he made poor visual contact and could not pronounce any words. He was the term product of a first pregnancy resulting from a non-consanguineous relationship, and there was no family history of metabolic or neurological diseases. His birth weight was 2.9 kg (50th percentile), his height was 74 cm (50th percentile), he received normal immunization, and his Apgar score was 9. He started to autonomously stand up from the age of three and there was autonomous ambulation at 40 months. His first raw words appeared at 12 months but he did not communicate intentionally or make any sentences. He exhibited global developmental delay according to the PDMS-2 scale and BDI-2 inventory (see Section 4.1), which was later defined as severe ID.

Upon physical examination his weight was 15 kg (50–75th percentile), height was 83 cm (90th percentile), and he had a normal head circumference of 47 cm. He presented moderate generalized hypotonia accompanied by a reduction of strength in his upper limbs and hyperreflexia (deep tendon II/IV reflexes). There were no dysmorphic features, skin blemishes, visceromegaly, or cardiopulmonary alterations. His thorax radiography and karyotype were normal, but a brain MRI showed cerebral atrophy, prominent cisterna magna, and a moderately increased ventricular volume (Figure 1B). An EEG during natural sleep showed generalized spikes of slow waves (1–2 Hz high voltage), although he never presented seizures. He was diagnosed with severe psychomotor delay, ID, and a possible mitochondrial disease due to decreased mitochondrial respiratory chain complex I activity. His clinical features are summarized in Table 1.

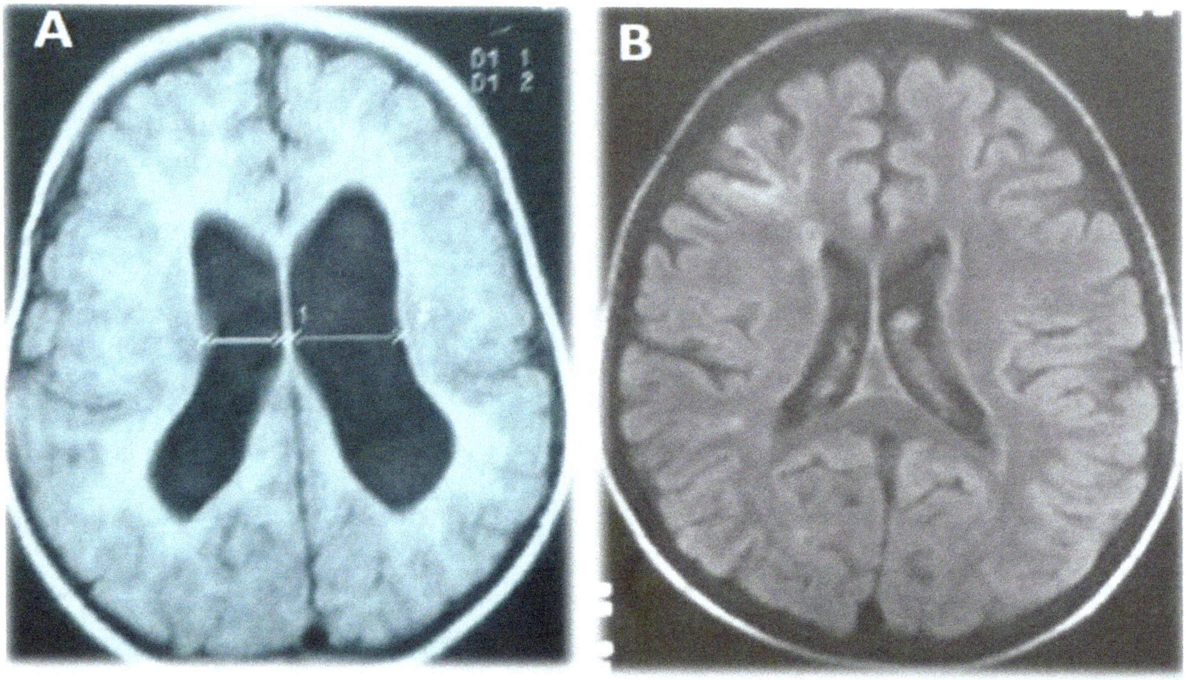

Figure 1. Magnetic resonance image of patient 2 (**A**) and 3 (**B**) showing an increase in lateral cerebral ventricle volume, diffuse enlargement of the cortical spaces, and cortical atrophy.

2.2. Blood and Muscle Laboratory Tests

Blood laboratory test results were normal for hemoglobin, hematocrit, leukocytes, platelets, glucose, urea, creatinine, alkaline phosphatase, alanine and aspartate transaminases (AST and ALT, respectively), total bilirubin concentration, cholesterol (above 145 mg/dL), ammonia, thyroid hormones, and thyrotropin for all three patients. The concentration of organic acids in urine, biotinidase, and cystine/homocysteine, acylcarnitine panel as well as all amino acids (including alanine) were also within the normal range. Due to persistent hyperlactacidemia (analysis was repeated three times on different days) and the clinical phenotypes of all three patients, femoral muscle biopsies were taken to evaluate any metabolic or histological alterations suggestive of a mitochondrial disorders; we measured mitochondrial ETC complex activity at three years for patient 1, 3.5 years for patient 2, and at 2.4 years for patient 3.

Patient 1: Blood gas analysis showed metabolic acidosis with pH 7.20, partial pressure of carbon dioxide (PCO_2) was 50 mmHg, partial pressure of oxygen (PO_2) was 134 mmHg, bicarbonate (HCO_3^-) was 17.6 mEq/L, and the base excess (BE) was −6.8 mEq/L. Serum electrolytes were normal average (sodium, potassium, and chlorine were 139, 4.80 and 105 mEq/L, respectively). Further tests revealed elevated levels of fasting lactate (2.96 mM; normal range 0.95–2.30), postprandial lactate (3.84 mM; normal range 1.95–3.0), fasting pyruvate (0.1 mM; normal range 0.05–0.09), postprandial pyruvate (0.15 mM; normal range 0.08–0.13), fasting lactate pyruvate ratio (29.6), and postprandial lactate pyruvate ratio (25.6). These details are summarized in Table 2.

Analysis of the muscle homogenate revealed a 30%–50% reduction in the enzymatic complexes II, III, and IV, and a slight reduction (12%) in coenzyme Q10 concentration (CoQ10). Mild and non-specific histological alterations in muscle fiber size were observed by optical microscopy. No known mtDNA mutations were found. The final diagnosis was severe ID (35th IQ percentile at age five), a possible mitochondrial disease (based on current diagnostic criteria [13,14]), a pervasive developmental disorder not otherwise specified (according to the DMS-IV criteria and the Autism Diagnostic Interview—Revised), and microcephaly.

Table 2. Metabolic energy study performed on muscle biopsy samples. The enzymatic activity of mitochondrial respiratory chain complexes (I–IV) was corrected for the presence of citrate synthase (CS). Succinate dehydrogenase activity was assessed in the presence of phenazine methosulfate, which acts as part of the electron transfer system. The measurement unit for each enzyme/complex activity was mU/U, and this was normalized to CS activity. Lactate values and the lactate/pyruvate ratio found in the plasma are shown. Values that are underlined represent those that are outside the normal range for children without mitochondrial disease.

Enzyme Activity or Metabolite Concentration	Patient 1	Patient 2	Patient 3	Control Values
NADH: Cit C oxidoreductase (Complex I + III) (mU/U CS)	156	310	253	107–560
Succinate: Cit C oxidoreductase (Complex II + III) (mU/U CS)	49	111	35	75–149
Succinate: DCPIP oxidoreductase (Complex II) (mU/U CS)	29	48	27	33–69
Succinate Dehydrogenase (mU/U CS)	74	119	79	57–239
Decylubiquinone: Cytochrome C oxidoreductase (Complex III) (mU/U CS)	498	597	615	610–1760
Cytochrome C oxidase (Complex IV) (mU/U CS)	287	501	291	590–1300
Coenzyme Q10 (nmol/U CS)	2.3	2.6	2.9	2.6–8.4
Citrate Synthase (nmol/min/mg)	243.7	125.7	350	71–200
Fasting Lactate (mM)	2.96	2.64	4.56	<2.30
Postprandial Lactate (mM)	3.84	2.82	5.15	<3
Fasting lactate/pyruvate ratio	29.6	47.7	14.2	10–15
Postprandial lactate/pyruvate ratio	25.6	42.2	24.5	10–15

Patient 2: Blood gas analysis showed the following: pH 7.35, PCO_2: 26.8 mmHg, PO_2: 98.9 mmHg, HCO_3: 24.3 mEq/L, and BE: −0.3 mEq/L (as shown in Table 2). Sodium, potassium, and chlorine serum electrolytes were 136, 4.93, and 102 mEq/L, respectively. Fasting lactate was elevated at 2.64 mM, while fasting pyruvate and the fasting lactate pyruvate ratio (0.06 mM and 47.67, respectively, were within the normal range). No histological alterations were observed by optical microscopy. Analysis of the muscle homogenate revealed a significant reduction in the activity of the mitochondrial respiratory chain enzymatic complexes III (decylubiquinol cytochrome c oxidoreductase) and IV (cytochrome c oxidase) to within 5% and 15% of the lower limit of their normal ranges, respectively (Table 2). No known mtDNA mutations were found and the final diagnosis was moderate ID (50th IQ percentile at age five), microcephaly, a pervasive developmental disorder not otherwise specified (using DMS-IV and the criteria of Autism Diagnostic Interview—Revised), and based on current diagnostic criteria [13,14], a possible mitochondrial disease.

Patient 3: Blood gas analysis showed metabolic acidosis with pH 7.33, PCO_2 of 25 mmHg, PO_2 of 90 mmHg, HCO_3 at 17.5 mEq/L, and a BE of −5.5 mEq/L. Serum electrolytes were: sodium 144 mEq/L, potassium: 4.7 mEq/L, and chlorine: 101 mEq/L. Other tests revealed significantly elevated fasting lactate (4.56 mM; normal range 0.95–2.30), postprandial lactate (5.15 mM; normal range 1.95–3.0), and fasting pyruvate (0.21 mM; normal range 0.08–0.10). Postprandial pyruvate was slightly above normal (0.15 mM; normal range 0.08–0.13), and fasting lactate pyruvate and postprandial lactate/pyruvate ratios were normal (14.2 and 24.5, respectively). Analysis of the muscle homogenate revealed a significant reduction (by 20%–45%) in the activity of mitochondrial respiratory chain complexes II and IV/I as well as increased CS. These data are summarized in Table 2. Optical microscopy revealed mild and non-specific histological variations in muscular fiber size. No known mtDNA mutations were found. The final diagnosis was moderate ID (55th IQ percentile at age five), a pervasive developmental disorder not otherwise specified (defined by the DMS IV and the criteria of Autism Diagnostic Interview—Revised), and a possible mitochondrial disease based on current diagnostic criteria [13,14].

2.3. Pharmacological Treatment

All three patients were started on the same initial treatment regime of 50 mg/Kg/day L-carnitine, a vitamin B complex (50 mg each of vitamin B1and B2, 15 mg B3, 2 mg B6, and 10 mg B12), and 30 mg CoQ10 divided twice daily, and 5 mg folic acid given once a day.

Patient 1: After one year of pharmacological treatment his intellectual abilities improved and he reached the 45th IQ percentile. This patient is currently seven years old and does not show any motor delay, motor alterations, or hypotonia. He recently displayed a behavioral disorder characterized by hyperactivity and irritability (as defined by the fifth edition of the diagnostic and statistical manual of mental disorders [DSM-5] by the American psychiatric association [19]), which was accompanied by psychotic reactions. These symptoms, as well as a sleep problem, greatly improved after he was started on risperidone (0.5 mg twice a day). It is unlikely that this antipsychotic drug caused the improvement of his ID because these changes were present before risperidone therapy, rather it is more likely that risperidone allowed him to be more responsive to other therapeutic interventions, and gave him a better ability to demonstrate his cognitive status when assessed. His intellectual abilities still remain stable (an additional year after the implementation of initial pharmacological treatment), however, he still uses very few words and is not able to construct complete sentences; he attends a special school to which he has adapted well.

Patient 2: This patient is currently nine years old and she attends a special school; She now walks autonomously with mild ataxia and instability. Once she started pharmacological treatment both signs (ataxia and tremor) disappeared, if CoQ10 is withdrawn she becomes ataxic and a strong hand tremor ensues. She is able to construct simple sentences and to communicate verbally; she understands verbal instructions and presents moderate ID that improved after treatment, reaching the 60th IQ percentile after 10 months of pharmacological treatment. After an additional year of this treatment her ID remains stable and although her hypertonia improved it still remains present at the lower limb level. This patient has never been referred for behavioral or sleep problems.

Patient 3: This patient is currently six years old and he attends a special school, which he has accepted well. His language is very poor and he displays episodes of irritability that improved following administration of 0.75 mg risperidone twice a day. Similar to patient 1, improvement of cognitive status was not due to risperidone treatment since it was started eight months after starting the mitochondrial drug combination treatment. ID also improved by 10 IQ points with this pharmacological treatment compared to before starting treatment (he reached the 60th IQ percentile, compared to the 50th measured a year before treatment started).

3. Discussion

Mitochondrial respiratory chain complex disorders are the most prevalent group of inherited neurometabolic diseases [2,3]. Classically, their clinical manifestation includes central and peripheral neurological manifestations, usually associated with the involvement of other organs including the eye, heart, liver, and kidneys, and may cause diabetes mellitus and/or sensorineural deafness. Patients with ID and a mitochondrial disease generally present several symptoms which are rarely observed in idiopathic ID, which can include tremor, ataxia, pancreatic or liver dysfunction, cardiac or hematological alterations, growth retardation, and/or ophthalmological or auditory signs [16,20–22]. Mitochondrial diseases are caused by abnormalities in the mitochondrial ETC, and may be accompanied by ID and an ASD in some individuals. Hypotonia with a long delay in motor development milestones such as head support, or stable autonomous seating and walking, can also suggest the presence of a mitochondrial disorder.

All three patients described in this study fulfilled the criteria for global developmental delay (under age five) and ID (over age five) according to the consensual terminology [23]. Their cranial MRIs showed a symmetrical increase in lateral cerebral ventricle volume and there was cortical atrophy in case 3. Interestingly, in addition to general hypotonia on the right side of her body, patient 2 also showed additional spasticity on the left side. This clinical finding probably represents a prior insult to the right hemisphere, as shown by asymmetry of lateral ventricles in her MRI image. Non-specific global MRI abnormalities such as abnormal or delayed myelination, atrophy, ventricle enlargement, or specific brain structural changes are common in patients with mitochondrial disorders and/or ID, especially those with clinical central nervous system involvement [16,24,25]. However, specific MRI findings (lesions in specific brain areas) are more likely to be associated with syndromic phenotypes, as in the case of MELAS (mitochondrial encephalomyopathy, lactic acidosis, and stroke-like episodes), Leigh, or Pearson/Kearns-Sayre syndromes [24,26,27]. Nonetheless, it should be stressed that brain MRI results can also appear normal in some patients with mitochondrial diseases.

Microcephaly, which was present in patients 1 and 2, has been described in both mitochondrial disorders and in ID cases [28], but its significance is poorly understood in terms of clinical presentation. Additionally, many patients with ID and mitochondrial disorders also have epilepsy [29] although, as reported here, EEG activity was abnormal in patient 3 and he had no clinical seizures, meaning that the lack of epilepsy does not exclude a mitochondrial disorder diagnosis. Some patients with mitochondrial diseases have hyperlactacidemia, which can be interpreted as a sign of mitochondrial metabolism impairment [30]. However, an increase in plasma lactate concentration is observable in many acute or chronic diseases and lactic acid in blood can be found within the normal range in some patients with mitochondrial disorders [2]. A persistent increase in plasma lactate concentration was found in all three cases and was accompanied by variable changes in pyruvate concentration (a slight increase in case 1, normal range in case 2, and a strong increase in case 3). Persistent hyperlactacidemia and an increased lactate/pyruvate ratio suggested to us that we should evaluate the presence of mitochondrial alterations by analyzing ETC activity in muscle tissue.

Our experience suggests that measuring the ratio of fasting lactate/pyruvate is recommendable in patients with ID with suspected mitochondrial disorders in order to further direct the diagnosis towards more relevant assays (*i.e.*, muscle biopsy, a detailed MRI/MRS study, or more sophisticated physiological measurements). In many cases a mitochondrial protein mutation is likely responsible for the clinical phenotype but in others, as reported here, no known mutations can be identified [31,32]. Based on these difficulties, and given that classical mitochondrial diseases affect only a small number of individuals with ID and ASD, we cannot exclude *de novo* mutations or secondary mitochondrial dysfunction in these patients. When these types of changes occur, they are accompanied by genetic abnormalities or biochemical defects in respiratory chain enzymes. Patient 1 and 3 had a 25%–50% complex II–IV deficiency, patient 1 also had slightly diminished levels of muscular CoQ10 (by 12%), and patient 2 displayed a 5%–15% decrease in complex III and IV activity. These biochemical findings are rare and add clinical relevance to this report since complex I deficiency is the most commonly observed deficit, and it presents either alone or in association with other respiratory complex deficits [33]. These cases adds new information compared to the previous reported cases of ASD and mitochondrial disease since the typical reported features such as gastro-intestinal symptoms (red-flags for, other organ involvement (eyes, liver, hearth, *etc.*) and regression were missing in these patients [21].

Pharmacological treatment for these patients remains limited, and a Cochrane Collaboration systematic review [34] concluded that there is currently no clear evidence supporting the systemic use of such interventions in patients with mitochondrial disorders. Symptomatic therapy can be effective in some patients with mitochondrial disorders [32,35] however a limited, or no, clinical effect is observed in the majority of cases [34]. It is clear that the efficacy of these treatments needs to be confirmed by randomized clinical trials performed in homogeneous study samples (with clinical features similar to the patients described in this report), which have clinically relevant primary endpoints. The limited size of our series limits our ability to recommend the use of any pharmacological treatments to treat patients with similar mitochondrial diseases. However, the treatments we administered to our patients could be described as almost empirical: there is currently very little evidence in the literature for drug combinations, which have a beneficial effect for such cases, and there are no FDA-approved drugs for this patient profile.

The administration of vitamins B1, B2, B3, folic acid (vitamin B9), carnitine, and Coenzyme Q, and their dosage was selected on the basis of the few reports we did find that show some benefit in patients with mitochondrial disease, as reviewed elsewhere [36,37]. Vitamin B6 and B12 were chosen because they have shown some benefit in patients with ASD and mitochondrial dysfunction [32,38]. Encouragingly, we observed a general (although variable) clinical improvement after pharmacological treatment with this combination, and interestingly, this beneficial effect was observed for ID (a condition which is classically considered to be stable over time and rarely scored after pharmacological treatment in this subgroup of patients), ASD, and in muscular tone signs. In contrast, other CNS manifestations such as sleep problems, irritability, and hyperactivity only improved following the administration of the neuroleptic drug risperidone. These results, although limited to case reports, suggest that administration of this mitochondrial "cocktail" as a symptomatic treatment can have some beneficial effects.

Undoubtedly the efficacy of this treatment should be evaluated in a large sample of patients with concomitant ID, ASD, hyperlactacidemia, and possible mitochondrial disorders. It is important to note that mitochondrial energy metabolism disorders may be missed in children with ID-ASD because its symptoms overlap with idiopathic ID, ASD, and other developmental disorders and secondary mitochondrial dysfunctions cannot be completely ruled out in these patients since their clinical phenotype fulfills that of a possible mitochondrial disorder [14]. In conclusion, our report supports the idea that some children with ID, ASD, and hyperlactacidemia may have a mitochondrial disorder with clinical manifestations different from, or less severe than, those patients with the known phenotypes of other well-characterized mitochondrial diseases.

These data offer clinicians a valuable set of benchmark parameters which can be used as a reference for suspected mitochondrial diseases in patients with ID, ASD, hypotonia, and for those with other non-systemic involvement (besides the muscular and nervous system). However it should be pointed out that these patients manifested additional and diverse clinical signs, *i.e.*, acquired microcephaly, hemi-spasticity, EEG alterations without clinical convulsions, and MRI imaging alterations, and non-specific pervasive developmental disorders (according to DMS-IV). The diagnosis of an associated mitochondrial disorder in patients with ID and ASD is sometimes difficult and requires knowledge of several different clinical presentations (as shown in Table 1). Each of these clinical features is shared by a subgroup of patients with idiopathic ID however these features alone are not sufficient to suggest mitochondrial disease unless other signs and symptoms are present. Despite the biochemical, histological, and genetic limitations that determine the final diagnosis of mitochondrial disease, this etiological possibility must be considered for primary or secondary mitochondrial respiratory chain disorders in children with ID and ASD in order to reach an early diagnosis and start prompt treatment and rehabilitation programs. There is a clear need of more advanced genetic testing of mtDNA and nDNA genes using next generation sequencing to help identify new genetic lesions (mutations) seen in these types of patients.

4. Experimental Section

4.1. Clinical Examinations

Each individual was subjected to a general physical, neurological, and psychological examination performed by a neuropediatrician, neurologist, and psychologist. Developmental delay was assessed under the age of 5 years using the standardized and validated Peabody Developmental Motor Scale 2 (PDMS-2) [39]. The Battelle developmental inventory (BDI-2) [40] was used to perform a comprehensive developmental assessment. The diagnosis of ID was made between 4.5–5 years of age using Raven's Colored Progressive Matrices (CPM) [41]. This is a standardized instrument for assessing non-verbal general intelligence in children aged 5 years and over and for adults with ID for the purposes of clinical investigation. The overall score in each scale/inventory was transferred into a centile using the age-appropriate norms given by this scale. Testing was done in all three patients in order to exclude the common genetic causes of ID, such as fragile X syndrome, Prader–Willi syndrome, MECP2, and karyotype alterations (chromosomal deletions and duplications). Genetic testing for fragile X syndrome, Prader–Willi syndrome, MECP2 were done in University of Alabama (Med. Genomics Lab, Dr. L. Messiaen, Birmingham, USA) after extraction of genomic DNA from peripheral blood samples collected in EDTA (1 mM) in a volume of about 5 mL. Fragile X syndrome was analyzed by Southern blot analysis using primary restriction site EcoRI, (5.2 kb) and EagI (internal methyl-sensitive site) digestion, probed with StB12.3. After this analysis, fragile X syndrome was excluded in all three patients (CGG 29; 30; 48 for patient 1, 2 and 3, respectively). Analysis of MECP2 was performed by amplifying the MECP2-coding exons and flanking intronic sequences. The following primer pair was used to amplify exon 1: forward Rett-EX-1F 5'-GCAGCTCAATGGGGCT-TTCAACTT-3' and reverse Rett-EX-1R 5'-GGCACAGTTA-TGTCTTTAGTCTTTGG-3'. PCR were performed and the products extracted from agarose gel using QIAquick gel extraction kit (Qiagen, Hilden, Germany) according to manufacturer's protocol. Sequencing of the PCR products was performed by ABI prism BigDye Terminator (Applied Biosystem, Foster City, CA, USA) and separated by capillary electrophoresis and detected via laser induced florescence and compared with reference MECP2 sequence. Prader–Willi syndrome (PWS) was performed with the methylation test by Southern blot. For the analysis a double digestion was done with the enzymes Hind III and Hpa II (sensitive to methylation) and subsequent hybridization with the PW71B probe (patients without Prader–Willy or Angelman syndrome displayed a pattern with two bands (6 and 4 kb). Karyotype was performed at Oriente University, Faculty of Medicine in Ciudad Bolivar (Venezuela) by analyzing specimens that were processed using direct methods and unstimulated short-term (24- and 48-h) cultures with G-banding analysis (550–850 band). A minimum of 20 metaphases was required to define a normal karyotype. Analysis of known mitochondrial ASD/ID gene mutations according to patients' phenotype are described in the Section 4.3 Autism spectrum disorder was assessed by Autism Diagnostic Interview—Revised (according to DMS IV criteria).

4.2. Blood Analysis

Blood samples were extracted in both the fasting and postprandial condition for analytical and biochemical assessments. In order to prevent erroneous lactate elevations due to a poor venipuncture technique or because of the use of a tourniquet, an indwelling butterfly needle was placed in order to permit blood sample collection after the patient had settled for 30 min.

4.3. Muscle Tissue Analysis

A quadricep muscle was biopsied and the sample was frozen until analysis with light and electron microscopy, as well as for mtDNA content using real time PCR analysis and for the following mutations: T3271C and A3243G in tRNA-leu (UUR), A8344G and T8356C in tRNA-lys, T8993C and T8993G in subunit 6 of ATPase gene, G3460A and G11778A, mutation at 8993 and common deletion of mitochondrial DNA that causes Kearns-Sayre syndrome (KSS), progressive external ophthalmoplegia (PEO) or Pearson syndrome. MtDNA deletions and depletion were analyzed as previously described [42,43]. The percentage of m.6955G>A transition was analyzed by last-cycle radioactive PCR/RFLP by using primers HmtL6954 (GGATTCATCTTTCTTTTCACCCTAG) and HmtH7114 (TGGCGTAGGTTTGGTCTAGG). HmtL6954 contains a mismatch (G-C) at nucleotide position 6951. The amplicon size is 204 bp and the PCR conditions: 94 °C 2min (94 °C 30 s/55 °C 30 s/72 °C 1 min 30 s) 35 cycles, 72 °C 5 min. 0.5 μL of (α-32P) dCTP at 10 mCi/mL was added to each PCR reaction before the last cycle. The restriction enzyme BlnI (C/CTAGG) cuts the amplicon in two fragments of 183 + 21 bp. The m.6955G>A transition removes the cutting site. The levels of the mutant mtDNA were quantified by using the GelProAnalyzer 4.0 program. The revised human mitochondrial DNA Cambridge reference sequence (GenBank REFSEQ AC_000021.2) was used. All of these mtDNA depletion analyses were negative.

4.4. Determination of Mitochondrial Respiratory Chain Complexes

Small pieces of frozen muscle tissues were homogenized (1/30 weight per volume) in a solution containing 50 mM Tris buffer (pH 7.5), 100 mM potassium chloride, 5 mM $MgCl_2$, and 1 mM ethylenediaminetetraacetic acid using a glass/glass homogenizer. Enzyme activities were assayed at 30 °C using a spectrophotometer and were calibrated against CS activity.

ETC function analysis is presented as enzyme complex activity, namely: Nicotinamide adenine dinucleotide (NADH): Coenzyme Q1-oxidoreductase (complex I), NADH: Cytochrome c-oxidoreductase (complex I + III), succinate: Cytochrome c-oxidoreductase (complex II + III), ubiquinone: Cytochrome c-oxidoreductase (complex III), cytochrome c-oxidase (complex IV), in all cases using CS as a mitochondrial marker enzyme, as previously described [44,45]. The concentration of CoQ10 was determined according to Montero *et al.* [46]. Abnormalities in ETC function were compared to the standard range in age-matched control subjects used in each diagnostic laboratory.

Each patient's parents were requested (and gave) written informed for consent to allow their child's medical information to be anonymously abstracted into a clinical database that contained their medical history, physical examination findings, and the results of neurological, psychological, and metabolic tests. The protocols described in this manuscript follow rules approved by the institute's ethical committee.

5. Conclusions

In conclusion, our experience suggests that children with ID, ASD, and with abnormal neurological or muscular involvement but without other systemic findings should be also evaluated for mitochondrial disorders (blood biochemical screening tests) and these disorders should be included in the differential diagnosis of secondary ID/ASD. Other genetic causes such as single gene disorders with ID or ASD as a feature via candidate gene mutation screening, clinical genetics evaluation and microarray analysis should be performed in patients presenting with these findings. Advanced genetic testing results could impact on clinical care and genetic risk counseling for family members.

Acknowledgments: This work was supported by Grant number UV-INV_PRECOMP13-115500 from The University of Valencia and GV/043 from *Conselleria de Educació-Generalitat Valenciana.*

Author Contributions: José Guevara-Campos, Lucía González-Guevara, and Omar Cauli analyzed the data; Omar Cauli and José Guevara-Campos drafted the manuscript; José Guevara-Campos and Lucía González-Guevara revised the manuscript; Omar Cauli designed and conceived the study and was responsible for obtaining project grant funding for the search for a molecular basis for cognitive impairment in neuropsychiatric disease.

References

1. Jansen, D.E.; Krol, B.; Groothoff, J.W.; Post, D. People with intellectual disability and their health problems: A review of comparative studies. *J. Intellect. Disabil. Res.* **2004**, *48*, 93–102. [CrossRef] [PubMed]
2. Haas, R.H.; Parikh, S.; Falk, M.J.; Saneto, R.P.; Wolf, N.I.; Darin, N.; Cohen, B.H. Mitochondrial disease: A practical approach for primary care physicians. *Pediatrics* **2007**, *120*, 1326–1333. [CrossRef] [PubMed]
3. Sherr, E.H.; Shevell, M.I. Global developmental delay and mental retardation/intellectual disability. In *Pediatric Neurology: Principles and Practice*, 5th ed.; Swaiman, K.F., Ashwal, S., Ferriero, D.M., Schor, N.F., Eds.; Elsevier Saunders: Philadelphia, PA, USA, 2012; pp. 554–574.
4. American Association of Intellectual and Developmental Disabilities (AAIDD). Definition of Intellectual Disability. Available online: http://aaidd.org/intellectual-disability/definition (accessed on 11 July 2013).
5. Luckasson, R.; Reeve, A. Naming, defining, and classifying mental retardation. *Ment. Retard.* **2001**, *39*, 47–52. [CrossRef] [PubMed]
6. Oeseburg, B.; Jansen, D.E.; Groothoff, J.W.; Dijkstra, G.J.; Reijneveld, S.A. Emotional and behavioural problems in adolescents with intellectual disability with and without chronic diseases. *J. Intellect. Disabil. Res.* **2010**, *54*, 81–89. [CrossRef] [PubMed]
7. Van Karnebeek, C.D.; Stockler, S. Treatable inborn errors of metabolism causing intellectual disability: A systematic literature review. *Mol. Genet. Metab.* **2012**, *105*, 368–381.
8. Bokhoven, H. Genetic and epigenetic networks in intellectual disabilities. *Ann. Rev. Genet.* **2011**, *45*, 81–104. [CrossRef] [PubMed]
9. Sherr, E.H.; Michelson, D.J.; Shevell, M.I.; Moeschler, J.B.; Gropman, A.L.; Ashwal, S. Neurodevelopmental disorders and genetic testing: Current approaches and future advances. *Ann. Neurol.* **2013**, *74*, 164–170. [CrossRef] [PubMed]

10. Baker, K.; Raymond, F.L.; Bass, N. Genetic investigation for adults with intellectual disability: Opportunities and challenges. *Curr. Opin. Neurol.* **2012**, *25*, 150–158. [CrossRef] [PubMed]
11. Chinnery, P.F. Mitochondrial disorders overview. In *GeneReviews®*; Pagon, R.A., Adam, M.P., Ardinger, H.H., Bird, T.D., Dolan, C.R., Fong, C.T., Smith, R.J.H., Stephens, K., Eds.; University of Washington: Seattle, WA, USA; pp. 1993–2014.
12. Friedman, S.D.; Shaw, D.W.; Ishak, G.; Gropman, A.L.; Saneto, R.P. The use of neuroimaging in the diagnosis of mitochondrial disease. *Dev. Disabil. Res. Rev.* **2010**, *16*, 129–135. [CrossRef] [PubMed]
13. Bernier, F.P.; Boneh, A.; Dennett, X.; Chow, C.W.; Cleary, M.A.; Thorburn, D.R. Diagnostic criteria for respiratory chain disorders in adults and children. *Neurology* **2002**, *59*, 1406–1411. [CrossRef] [PubMed]
14. Wolf, N.I.; Smeitink, J.A. Mitochondrial disorders: A proposal for consensus diagnostic criteria in infants and children. *Neurology* **2002**, *59*, 1402–1405. [CrossRef] [PubMed]
15. Thorburn, D.R.; Sugiana, C.; Salemi, R.; Kirby, D.M.; Worgan, L.; Ohtake, A.; Ryan, M.T. Biochemical and molecular diagnosis of mitochondrial respiratory chain disorders. *Biochim. Biophys. Acta.* **2004**, *1659*, 121–128. [CrossRef] [PubMed]
16. Verity, C.M.; Winstone, A.M.; Stellitano, L.; Krishnakumar, D.; Will, R.; McFarland, R. The clinical presentation of mitochondrial diseases in children with progressive intellectual and neurological deterioration: A national, prospective, population-based study. *Dev. Med. Child Neurol.* **2010**, *52*, 434–440. [CrossRef] [PubMed]
17. .McFarland, R.; Taylor, R.W.; Turnbull, D.M. A neurological perspective on mitochondrial disease. *Lancet Neurol.* **2010**, *9*, 829–840. [CrossRef] [PubMed]
18. Nissenkorn, A.; Zeharia, A.; Lev, D.; Watemberg, N.; Fattal-Valevski, A.; Barash, V.; Gutman, A.; Harel, S.; Lerman-Sagie, T. Neurologic presentations of mitochondrial disorders. *J. Child Neurol.* **2000**, *15*, 44–48. [CrossRef] [PubMed]
19. American Psychiatric Association. Intellectual disability. In *Diagnostic and Statistical Manual of Mental Disorders*, 5th ed.; American Psychiatric Publication: Arlington, VA, USA, 2013; p. 33.
20. Di Mauro, S.; Schon, E.A. Mitochondrial respiratory-chain diseases. *N. Engl. J. Med.* **2003**, *348*, 2656–2668. [CrossRef] [PubMed]
21. Weissman, J.R.; Kelley, R.I.; Bauman, M.L.; Cohen, B.H.; Murray, K.F.; Mitchell, R.L.; Kern, R.L.; Natowicz, M.R. Mitochondrial disease in autism spectrum disorder patients: A cohort analysis. *PLoS One* **2008**, *3*, e3815. [CrossRef] [PubMed]
22. Zeviani, M.; Carelli, V. Mitochondrial disorders. *Curr. Opin. Neurol.* **2007**, *20*, 564–571. [CrossRef] [PubMed]
23. Shevell, M. Global developmental delay and mental retardation or intellectual disability: Conceptualization, evaluation, and etiology. *Pediatr. Clin. North Am.* **2008**, *55*, 1071–1084. [CrossRef] [PubMed]
24. Valanne, L.; Ketonen, L.; Majander, A.; Suomalainen, A.; Pihko, H. Neuroradiologic findings in children with mitochondrial disorders. *Am. J. Neuroradiol.* **1998**, *19*, 369–377. [PubMed]
25. Barragan-Campos, H.M.; Valee, J.N.; Lo, D.; Barrera-Ramírez, C.F.; Argote-Greene, M.; Sánchez-Guerrero, J.; Estañol, B.; Guillevin, R.; Chiras, J. Brain magnetic resonance imaging findings in patients with mitochondrial cytopathies. *Arch. Neurol.* **2005**, *62*, 737–742. [CrossRef] [PubMed]
26. Gropman, A.L. Neuroimaging in mitochondrial disorders. *Neurotherapeutics* **2013**, *10*, 273–285. [CrossRef] [PubMed]
27. Saneto, R.P.; Friedman, S.D.; Shaw, D.W. Neuroimaging of mitochondrial disease. *Mitochondrion* **2008**, *8*, 396–413. [CrossRef] [PubMed]
28. Watemberg, N.; Silver, S.; Harel, S.; Lerman-Sagie, T. Significance of microcephaly among children with developmental disabilities. *J. Child. Neurol.* **2002**, *17*, 117–122. [CrossRef] [PubMed]
29. Bindoff, L.A.; Engelsen, B.A. Mitochondrial diseases and epilepsy. *Epilepsia* **2012**, *53*, 92–97. [CrossRef] [PubMed]
30. Koenig, M.K. Presentation and diagnosis of mitochondrial disorders in children. *Pediatr. Neurol.* **2008**, *38*, 305–313. [CrossRef] [PubMed]
31. Anitha, A.; Nakamura, K.; Thanseem, I.; Matsuzaki, H.; Miyachi, T.; Tsujii, M.; Iwata, Y.; Suzuki, K.; Sugiyama, T.; Mori, N. Down-regulation of the expression of mitochondrial electron transport complex genes in autism brains. *Brain Pathol.* **2013**, *23*, 294–302. [CrossRef] [PubMed]
32. Rossignol, D.A.; Frye, R.E. Mitochondrial dysfunction in autism spectrum disorders: A systematic review and meta-analysis. *Mol. Psychiatry* **2011**, *17*, 290–314. [CrossRef] [PubMed]

33. Nissenkorn, A.; Zeharia, A.; Lev, D.; Fatal-Valevskic, A.; Barashd, V.; Gutmand, A.; Harelc, S.; Lerman-Sagiea, T. Multiple presentation of mitochondrial disorders. *Arch Dis. Child.* **1999**, *81*, 209–214. [CrossRef] [PubMed]
34. Pfeffer, G.; Majamaa, K.; Turnbull, D.M.; Thorburn, D.; Chinnery, P.F. Treatment for mitochondrial disorders. *Cochrane Database Syst. Rev.* **2012**, *4*, CD004426. [PubMed]
35. Di Mauro, S.; Mancuso, M. Mitochondrial diseases: Therapeutic approaches. *Biosci. Rep.* **2007**, *27*, 125–137. [CrossRef] [PubMed]
36. Chinnery, P.F.; Turnbull, D.M. Epidemiology and treatment of mitochondrial disorders. *Am. J. Med. Genet.* **2001**, *106*, 94–101. [CrossRef] [PubMed]
37. Avula, S.; Parikh, S.; Demarest, S.; Kurz, J.; Gropman, A. Treatment of mitochondrial disorders. *Curr. Treat. Options Neurol.* **2014**, *16*, 292. [CrossRef] [PubMed]
38. Frye, R.E.; Rossignol, D.A. Treatments for biomedical abnormalities associated with autism spectrum disorder. *Front. Pediatr.* **2014**, *2*, 66. [CrossRef] [PubMed]
39. Connolly, B.H.; McClune, N.O.; Gatlin, R. Concurrent validity of the Bayley-III and the peabody developmental motor scale-2. *Pediatr. Phys. Ther.* **2012**, *24*, 345–352. [CrossRef] [PubMed]
40. Goldin, R.L.; Matson, J.L.; Beighley, J.S.; Jang, J. Autism spectrum disorder severityas a predictor of Battelle Developmental Inventory—Second edition (BDI-2) scores in toddlers. *Dev. Neurorehabil.* **2014**, *17*, 39–43. [CrossRef] [PubMed]
41. Raven, J.; Raven, J.C.; Court, J. *Raven Manual: Standard Colored Progressive Matrices*; Oxford Psychologists Press: London, UK, 1998.
42. Herrero-Martín, M.D.; Pineda, M.; Briones, P.; López-Gallardo, E.; Carreras, M.; Benac, M.; Angel Idoate, M.; Vilaseca, M.A.; Artuch, R.; López-Pérez, M.J.; *et al.* A new pathologic mitochondrial DNA mutation in the cytochrome oxidase subunit I (MT-CO1). *Hum. Mutat.* **2008**, *29*, E112–E122. [PubMed]
43. Marcuello, A.; González-Alonso, J.; Calbet, J.A.; Damsgaard, R.; López-Pérez, M.J.; Díez-Sánchez, C. Skeletal muscle mitochondrial DNA content in exercising humans. *J. Appl. Physiol.* **1985**, *99*, 1372–1377. [CrossRef]
44. Genova, M.L.; Castelluccio, C.; Fato, R. Major changes in complex I activity in mitochondria from aged rats may not be detected by direct assay of NADH:coenzyme Q reductase. *Biochem. J.* **1995**, *311*, 105–109. [PubMed]
45. Trumbeckaite, S.; Opalka, J.R.; Neuhof, C.; Zierz, S.; Gellerich, F.N. Different sensitivity of rabbit heart and skeletal muscle to endotoxin-induced impairment of mitochondrial function. *Eur. J. Biochem.* **2001**, *268*, 1422–1429. [CrossRef] [PubMed]
46. Montero, R.; Artuch, R.; Briones, P.; Nascimento, A.; García-Cazorla, A.; Vilaseca, M.A.; Śnchez-Alćzar, J.A.; Navas, P.; Montoya, J.; Pineda, M. Muscle coenzyme Q10 concentrations in patients with probable and definite diagnosis of respiratory chain disorders. *Biofactors.* **2005**, *25*, 109–115. [CrossRef] [PubMed]

12

An Assessment of the Motor Performance Skills of Children with Autism Spectrum Disorder in the Gulf Region

Rehab H. Alsaedi [1,2]

[1] Faculty of Education, Queensland University of Technology (QUT), Brisbane 4059, Australia; r-alsaidi@hotmail.com

[2] Department of Special Education, Taibah University, Madinah 41477, Saudi Arabia

Abstract: This study aims to determine the prevalence, severity, and nature of the motor abnormalities seen in children with autism spectrum disorder (ASD) as well as to elucidate the associated developmental profiles. The short-form of the Bruininks-Oseretsky Test of Motor Proficiency, Second Edition (BOT-2) was used to assess various aspects of the motor performance of 119 children with ASD and 30 typically developing children (age range: 6–12 years) from three Gulf states. The results revealed the high prevalence of motor abnormalities among the ASD group when compared with the normative data derived from the BOT-2 manual as well as with the data concerning the typically developing group. The results also indicated that the motor performance of the children with ASD fell within the below-average range according to the BOT-2 cut-off score. Further, the results suggested that the age variable may influence the overall motor performance of children with ASD, since the children's motor abnormalities may decrease with maturation. The results concerning the specific motor dysfunction profiles seen in individuals with ASD could help practitioners, parents, and educators to better understand the nature of the motor deficits exhibited by children with ASD, which could assist with the design and implementation of treatment and rehabilitation programs for such children. Overall, motor performance represents an important aspect that should be considered during the clinical evaluation of ASD and that should not be ignored during early interventions.

Keywords: motor performance skills; autism spectrum disorder; Gulf; BOT-2

---

1. Introduction

Motor skills are associated with "activities that require a chain of sensory (vision, hearing, touch, and smell), central (brain and nervous systems), and motor mechanisms whereby the performer is able to maintain constant control of the sensory input and in accordance with the goal of the movement" [1]. The child development literature tends to assume that motor ability is an important indicator of overall development, particularly if it is compromised [2]. Indeed, early motor disturbances and delays are likely to have far-reaching consequences for later development, and they may be predictive of developmental disorders in later life [3,4]. Children with autism spectrum disorder (ASD) represent a population likely to experience motor impairments [5].

ASD affects every domain of human existence. An impairment in the motor domain can have profound effects on a child's development in areas such as schooling, socialisation, and communication [6,7]. It has been estimated that "80–90% of children with ASD show some degree of motor abnormality" [8]. However, it should be noted that previous results regarding prevalence rates vary depending on the utilised cut-off scores, diagnoses, and instruments [9].

Motor dysfunction represents an important neurological symptom in those with ASD. A growing body of evidence illustrates the motor difficulties experienced by children with ASD when compared with their typically developing peers [10–13]. However, such difficulties have traditionally been considered secondary aspects of ASD [14].

The only motor abnormalities currently included in the diagnostic criteria for ASD are stereotypical and repetitive behaviours [15]. However, the relevant motor abnormalities are not limited to such behaviours, as individuals with ASD, including children [16], often display motor issues consisting of both delays and deficits. Delays occur in the gross and fine motor skills [12], while deficits manifest in praxis [17], coordination and gait [18], postural control [19], and motor planning [20]).

Little is currently known about the underlying neurobiology of ASD-related motor problems, although the disruptions observed in those with ASD may stem from abnormal brain connectivity [10,21]. Some studies report reduced cerebellar activation in individuals with ASD during motor tasks when compared with neurotypical controls [22,23]. Dysfunctions in the frontostriatal pathways of children with ASD have also been demonstrated [24,25]. Further, the aberrant neural connectivity patterns observed between the cerebellar and frontostriatal pathways indicate the role of the cortical and subcortical structures and the pathways connecting them in controlling the accuracy of motor outputs [21].

Considerable ambiguity persists regarding the nature of such motor abnormalities and whether they are universal and specific to ASD. Some findings indicate that motor impairments constitute a cardinal feature of ASD [10,26–28]. The identified impairments remain consistent across ages and levels of functioning [11,29,30]. Additionally, evidence from prospective studies of at-risk infants indicates motor deficits to have been documented in infants later diagnosed with ASD [31–34]. Therefore, motor symptoms could serve as diagnostic markers and guide the early identification of ASD [26,35,36]. However, other evidence suggests that motor delays can be attributed to developmental disorders in general, meaning that they are not specific to ASD [37].

Some preliminary evidence indicates that motor impairments represent an essential part of a broader autistic phenotype [38], although other studies have not found such impairments to represent an essential aspect [8,37]. It is important to recognise that motor impairments are not limited to one disorder (e.g., ASD), as they are also present in other developmental disorders [9,39–41]. The debate regarding the prevalence and importance of motor deficits is not surprising given that ASD is a spectrum disorder, meaning that every child exhibits a wide variety of symptoms with different degrees of severity. This variability can offer a unique opportunity to identify disorder subtypes [42].

Jeste (2011) offers a number of justifications for investigating motor dysfunction in individuals with ASD [20]. First, motor symptoms are easily quantifiable and so can be objectively measured. Second, motor impairments may elucidate the heterogeneity within the autistic spectrum. Third, the investigation of motor abnormalities may yield insights into the aberrant neural mechanisms underlying ASD and the defining characteristics of the disorder. Fourth, motor performance is critical to the development of a wide variety of skills, which would all benefit from the early identification of deficits and the implementation of appropriate interventions. Lastly, determining when motor deficits manifest in individuals with ASD may assist with the early diagnosis of the disorder [20].

Age might be a critical factor in determining the nature of the motor dysfunction seen in individuals with ASD. However, the available research concerning the developmental acquisition of motor skills by children with ASD is limited. Evidence suggests that the different subsystems supporting motor development mature at different times and rates, which results in nonlinear development [43]; thereby, indicating the dynamic development of motor skills. Thus, Darrah et al. (2003) suggest the adoption of a developmental change perspective rather than one that emphasises the stability of motor development [44].

No firm conclusions regarding the stability or instability of motor performance can yet be drawn in relation to ASD. Some longitudinal studies indicate the persistent and constant nature of impaired motor performance in children with ASD [45]. Further, other longitudinal research confirms that motor problems among preschool children are not always stable, although they do appear to be so in most children with ASD [46]. However, some cross-sectional studies note the changing nature of motor problems in children with ASD, with the prevalence of motor deficits being lower in older children than younger children [16]. In contrast, other studies indicate that motor difficulties become increasingly problematic over time [34]. A number of factors could contribute to this decline in motor performance, including a lack of early intervention programs targeting motor skills and a lack of parental involvement in children's treatment [34].

A growing body of evidence gathered in Western contexts suggests motor abnormalities to be a marker of clinical severity and an important therapeutic target in children with ASD [26,36,47]. However, despite this increasing recognition, the evaluation and intervention processes related to motor abnormalities are still not seen as priorities, meaning that they are unlikely to attract the attention of professionals in our research context (the Gulf region). Indeed, motor dysfunctions arguably represent one of the most commonly overlooked comorbidities associated with ASD in the Gulf context. It is important to conduct research regarding motor performance in individuals with ASD in different cultures so as to achieve a clearer understanding of ASD and its phenotypes in different socio-cultural contexts.

The present study had three main aims. First, to determine the ratio of motor impairments seen in children with ASD, as identified using the short form of the Bruininks-Oseretsky Test of Motor Proficiency, Second Edition (BOT-2) [48]. It was expected that children with ASD would surpass the cut-off point for being "motor impaired". Second, to examine the extent of the differences in the motor performance of children with ASD and typically developing children. It was hypothesised that the motor performance of children with ASD would be significantly worse than that of typically developing children. Third, to investigate the effect of chronological age on the motor performance of children with ASD. Due to the lack of relevant evidence, no predictions were made regarding the relation between motor performance and age.

2. Materials and Methods

2.1. Study Design

This observational study applied a quantitative research approach that entailed the use of a cross-sectional design to characterize the motor proficiency levels of the participants at a given point in time. There were a number of reasons why this particular research approach was chosen. First, the study relied on a quantitative measurement instrument (i.e., the BOT-2) that provided a numerical evaluation of various aspects of the participants' motor performance, which meant that it was possible to objectively assess the performance of the study sample. Second, due to the nature of the research aims, outcomes in the form of numerical values were required to allow for comparisons between the ASD population and the corresponding BOT-2 norms and/or those children without ASD, as well as to reflect the relationship between the participants' age and their test outcomes.

2.2. Participants

Data for the present study were collected in Bahrain, Saudi Arabia, and the United Arab Emirates (UAE). The participants comprised children who were participating in an ongoing large-scale study evaluating neurobehavioral problems in children with ASD. They were recruited through purposive sampling on a voluntary basis.

The initial sample consisted of 235 children, who were divided into the ASD ($n = 180$) and typically developing (TD) ($n = 55$) groups. Among them, 61 children with ASD and 25 TD children were excluded from the final sample. The recruitment process is illustrated in Figure 1.

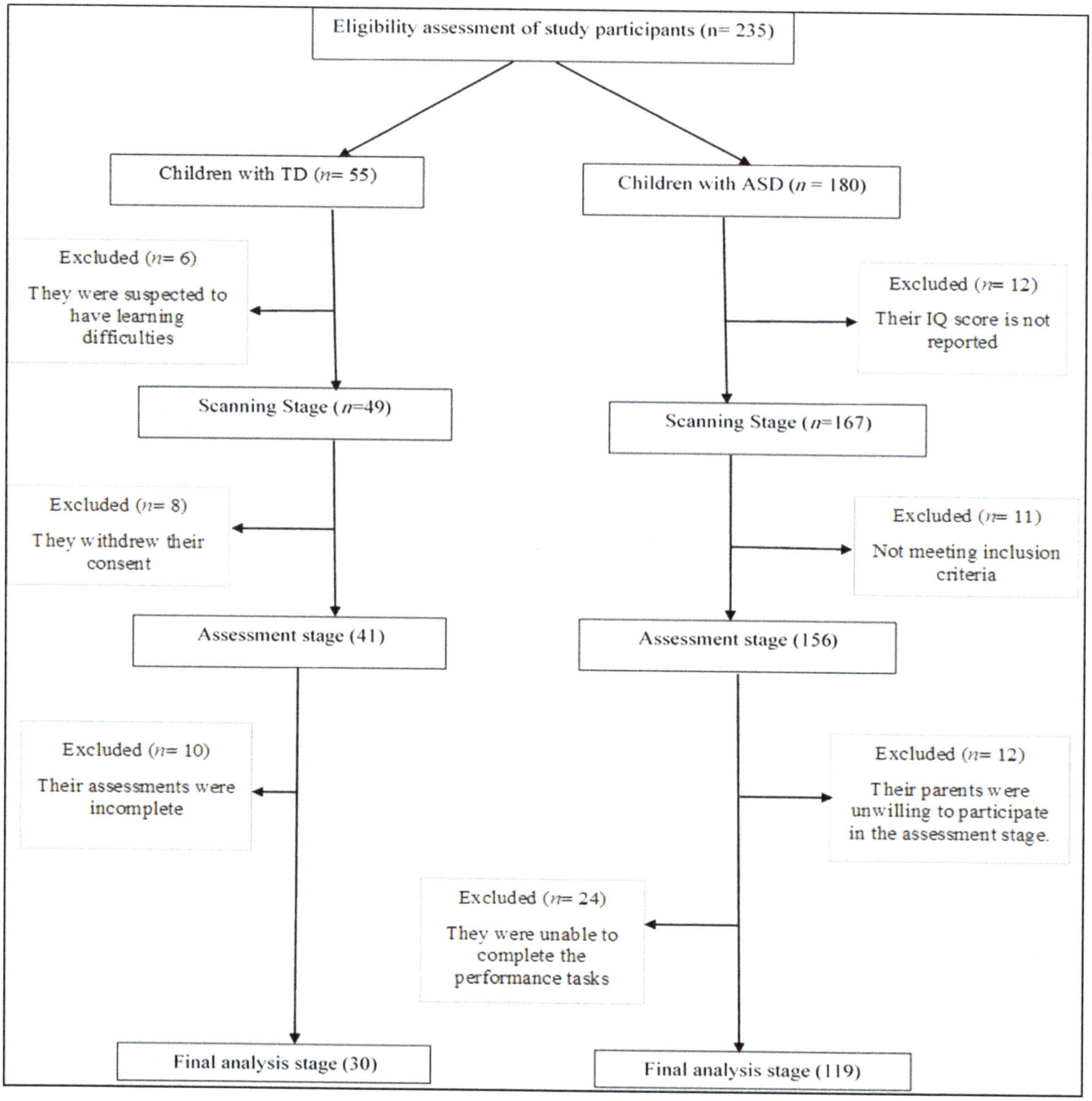

Figure 1. Recruitment of the Participants.

All the children with ASD (age range: 6–12 years; mean age = 8.75 years) had received a formal diagnosis prior to their recruitment for the present study. They attended three different types of educational settings, namely a fully inclusive school (*N* = 26; 21.8%), a partially inclusive school (*N* = 19; 15.9%), or a specialised ASD school or centre (*N* = 74; 62.18%).

The inclusion criteria for the ASD group were as follows. First, all the children with ASD had an IQ score of 70 or above. This IQ-related criterion was required to ensure that they could understand the test items and instructions and so that any identified differences in performance reflected autistic symptomatology rather than general intellectual functioning. The intelligence test scores were obtained from the children's school records. In the three countries of interest, a child's IQ is normally determined by a clinical psychologist or school psychologist using the Arabic version of the Wechsler Intelligence Scale for Children, Third Edition (WISC-III; 1991). Second, they all met the diagnostic criteria for level 1 of the ASD severity scale included within the DSM-5, indicating that they had mild symptoms and required support [49]. Third, all their scores on the Michigan Autism Spectrum Questionnaire

(MASQ) [50] were 22 or above, indicating high-functioning performance. Moreover, they all scored ≥ 71 on the Gilliam Autism Rating Scale—Third Edition (GARS-3) [51], indicating that an ASD diagnosis is very likely.

The exclusion criterion for the ASD group was the presence of comorbid affective and/or behavioural symptoms (e.g., intractable epilepsy, severe self-injury, aggression, uncorrected hearing loss, or visual impairment precluding participation). The absence of such comorbidities was verified by the researcher through interviewing the parents and reviewing the children's medical records.

The comparison (non-ASD or TD) group comprised 30 TD children (age range: 6–12 years; mean age = 9.06 years) recruited from mainstream primary schools. The exclusion criteria were (i) a history of any psychiatric, neurological, or developmental disorder, (ii) a family history of ASD, (iii) a need to regularly use any psychotropic medication, (iv) a physical disability that hinders motor performance, and/or (v) undergoing physical therapy to address motor issues. One obstacle to recruiting a sufficient number of TD participants concerns parents' reluctance to permit their children to participate in research. This reluctance could indicate that parents are concerned about their children's assessment results. Data collection can prove particularly challenging in the Arab context due to recognised delays in certain developmental skills and the potential for stigmatisation.

All the participants (i.e., with and without ASD) were group-wise matched according to their gender, chronological age, handedness (rated using the Edinburgh Handedness Inventory (EHI) [52], non-verbal IQ (assessed using Raven's Coloured Progressive Matrices (RCPM) [53]), and parental education level (see Table 1). The results of the group-wise analyses revealed no significant between-group differences ($p < 0.05$) with regard to any factor relevant to the comparison outcome variables.

Table 1. Demographic and Clinical Characteristics of the Participants.

Comparison Characteristics		Target Group (N = 119) Children with ASD	Control Group (N = 30) TD Children	t/χ^2	p	ES
Continuous variables						
Age (years)		8.72 (1.96) *	9.06 (1.42) *	1.05	0.71	0.21
Non-verbal IQ		29.76 (1.92) *	29.80 (2.64) *	0.69	0.060	0.17
Categorical variables						
Gender	Male	95 (79.8%)	24 (80.0%)	0.00	0.98	-
	Female	24 (20.2%)	6 (20.0%)			
Handedness	Right	104 (87.4%)	23 (76.7%)	2.191	0.14	-
	Lift	15 (12.6%)	7(23.3%)			
Father's education level	Secondary	67 (56.3%)	16 (53.3%)	0.09	0.77	-
	College degree	52 (43.7%)	14 (46.7%)			
Mother's education level	Secondary	78 (65.5%)	20 (66.7%)	0.01	0.91	-
	College degree	41(34.5%)	10 (33.3%)			

Note: * Mean (SD) non-verbal IQ (Raven's raw score range 0–36). The continuous variables are summarised as the mean and standard deviation using t-tests, while the categorical variables are summarised as the count and percentage using the chi-square χ^2. ES = effect size, which is calculated using Cohen's d.

2.3. *Instruments*

This study relied on two types of instruments, namely screening questionnaires, and assessment measures.

2.3.1. Screening Questionnaires

The following three screening questionnaires were used to verify the participant's clinical diagnosis and to determine the severity of their autistic symptoms. The first two measures were completed by at least one parent of each participant with ASD, while the third measure was used by the researcher to independently assess the severity of the ASD symptoms.

1. Gilliam Autism Rating Scale—Third Edition (GARS-3) [51]: After obtaining written permission from the publisher (Pro-Ed), the researcher had previously translated the GARS-3 and made certain cultural adaptations to facilitate its use in the Gulf region. The GARS-3 is a norm-referenced, standardised informant rating scale designed to identify and rate the severity of autism symptomatology in individuals. The GARS-3 items correspond to the diagnostic criteria for ASD set out in the DSM-5 [54]. It consists of 56 Likert-type items that comprise six subtests: restricted/repetitive behaviours (RB; 13 items), social interaction (SI; 14 items), social communication (SC; nine items), emotional responses (ER; eight items), cognitive style (CS; seven items), and maladaptive speech (MS; seven items). The summation of the subscales' scaled scores yields the composite autism index, which is also reported in terms of the standard score, percentile rank, severity level, and probability of ASD. Two autism indices (four or six) can be formed, depending on whether or not the individual is mute. Higher scaled scores indicate increasingly severe autistic symptoms. Caregivers require approximately 5–10 min to complete the measure.
2. Michigan Autism Spectrum Questionnaire (MASQ) [50]: The MASQ is based on the clinical characteristics that may be suggestive of Asperger's syndrome (AS) or high-functioning ASD (HFA). It includes ten items representing two main functional areas: the quality of the social interaction patterns and the style of both the content and form of communication. The items are rated on a four-point (0–3) scale, with their sum yielding the total score (maximum 30). A cut-off score ≥ 22 is recommended to screen for individuals with HFA or AS. Cut-off scores between 14 and 21 are predictive of ASD or pervasive developmental disorder-not otherwise specified (PDD-NOS), while scores < 14 are predictive of other psychiatric disorders.
3. The Clinician-Rated Severity of Autism Spectrum and Social Communication Disorders (CRSASSC) [49]: This two-item scale is used to assess the severity of an individual's autistic symptoms and his/her level of functioning based on the amount of support required due to challenges associated with the social and communication (SC) domain and the restricted interests and repetitive behaviours (RRB) domain, respectively. Each domain is rated on a four-point Likert scale consistent with the DSM-5 diagnostic criteria: 0 (none), 1 (requiring support), 2 (requiring substantial support), or 3 (requiring very substantial support). The clinical criteria may also help to assign a specific functional level to an individual: mild (level 1), moderate (level 2), or severe (level 3). The level of severity for each item should be independently reported, and a combined overall severity score should not be calculated.

2.3.2. Assessment Measures

There are a number of different tools available to assist clinicians and researchers with the evaluation and measurement of different aspects of motor skills development and their contribution to motor performance [55,56]. This study used the following measure.

Bruininks-Oseretsky Test of Motor Proficiency, Second Edition (BOT-2; [48]): The BOT-2 is a standardised, norm-referenced test of motor proficiency used to assess the gross and fine motor skills involved in engaging, goal-directed activities among children aged 4–21 years. It includes eight subtests: fine motor precision, fine motor integration, manual dexterity, bilateral coordination, balance, running speed and agility, and upper-limb coordination and strength. The BOT-2 results in four composite scores and one comprehensive measure of overall motor proficiency. The different administration options include the complete form, the short form, selected composites, and selected subtests. The short form (14 items), which was used in this study, takes 15–20 min to administer, with another five minutes being required to tape off the running course. Liu et al. (2015) noted that it is most efficient for practitioners to evaluate a child using the short form first [56]. The short-form BOT-2 consists of 14 items covering eight subtests and including the widest possible range of abilities to produce sufficiently reliable scores (see Table 2). It is a quick and user-friendly screening tool that provides a single overall motor proficiency score. The total composite score is reported as the standardised score (mean = 50.0, standard deviation = 10.0).

Table 2. Short-Form Items.

The BOT-2 Subtest	Item	Assessment
Subtest 1 *Fine Motor Precision*	Drawing Lines Through Paths Folding Paper	# of Errors # of Errors
Subtest 2 *Fine Motor Integration*	Copying a Square Copying a Star	# of Errors # of Errors
Subtest 3 *Manual Dexterity*	Transferring Pennies	# of Pennies in 15 s
Subtest 4 *Bilateral Coordination*	Jumping in Place-Same Sides Synchronized Tapping Feet and Fingers-Same Sides Synchronized	Repetitions Repetitions
Subtest 5 *Balance*	walking Forward on a Line Standing on One Leg on a Balance Beam-Eyes Open	Steps Time
Subtest 6 *Running Speed Agility*	One-Legged Stationary Hop	# of Hops in 15 s
Subtest 7 *Upper-Limb Coordination*	Dropping and Catching a Ball-Both Hands Dropping a Ball-Alternating Hands	Catches Dribbles
Subtest 8 *Strength*	Full Push-Ups Sit-Ups	# Performed in 30 s # Performed in 30 s

Note: (#) The hash symbol expresses the number of errors made during task completion and the number of tasks completed.

The BOT-2 SF exhibited strong psychometric properties. Its high internal consistency was determined using the stratified alpha method with regard to each composite and the split-half method with regard to each subtest [48]. The alpha value for the total motor composites was found to equal 0.93, while the test-retest correlations were found to be >0.80. Further, the interrater reliability correlations were noted to range between 0.92 and 0.98 [48].

In terms of the validity of the measure, the internal structure of the BOT-2 has been examined using the correlations among the subtest scale scores and the composite scores [57]. The validity of the BOT-2 was also established using a confirmatory factor analysis [58]. The BOT-2 was further determined to be correlated with other measures of motor performance (Bruininks and Bruininks, 2005 [48]. Moreover, the BOT-2 SF was reported to exhibit high sensitivity (84%) but poor specificity (42.9%) with 76.5% accuracy among 153 neurotypical children aged 8–11 years [59]. As per the test manual, the BOT-2 is noted to be able to differentiate between children in different clinical groups, including an ASD group, and children in the normative group.

2.4. Procedures

All the involved procedures were carried out in accordance with the ethical standards of the Queensland University of Technology, the research ethics committee of which approved the study protocol. The children involved in this project participated with the full written informed consent of their parents and legal guardians after the study procedures were explained; however, it was also important that the child participants were asked to give their verbal assent to participate. The parents of children with ASD provided information about the severity of their child's autism by answering the questions on the GARS-3 and MASQ. In addition, the children with ASD underwent an assessment based on the CRSASSC scale that was conducted by the researcher in order to determine the level of severity. Each child was individually evaluated according to the BOT-2 by the researcher in a noise- and distraction-free room at their school. The verbal instructions given were adapted to fit each child's level of language ability. The instructions for the test were also accompanied by photos of a child performing the main components of the test. All scores were recorded and converted into standardised scores according to the procedure described in the test manual. The assessment sessions were scheduled according to the times suggested by the children's parents and teachers. The children were all given adequate praise throughout the test. At the start of the testing session, the children were informed that they could cease to participate at any time and for any reason.

2.5. Analysis

All the data analyses in the present study were performed using the Statistical Package for the Social Sciences (SPSS) version 23.0 (IBM, Chicago, IL, USA). A one-sample z-test was performed to determine whether the mean of the motor scores of the ASD group statistically differed from the corresponding normative mean derived from the standardisation sample, as available in the BOT-2 manual. Further, the BOT-2 cut-off score (40 or less) was used to calculate the proportions of the actual clinical scores (i.e., the proportion of participants who scored below the clinical cut-off point).

Descriptive statistics were calculated concerning the raw scores for all the BOT-2 subtests. The overall differences between the raw scores of the children with ASD on the BOT-2 and those of the typically developing children were analysed by means of an independent samples t-test.

Generally speaking, when performing multiple comparisons using the same data set, the risk of a type I error occurring increases. To overcome this problem, the probabilities were not maintained at the chosen level (0.05), while a Bonferroni adjustment was made to control the overall type I error rate. When performing a Bonferroni adjustment, the alpha is estimated by taking the desired alpha level (0.05) and then dividing it by the number of comparisons being conducted. In the present study, for the multiple comparison analysis of the eight BOT-2 subtests, the significance level was set at $p = 0.006$.

The effect sizes were expressed using Cohen's d [60]. According to Cohen (1988), the magnitude of the effect size can be categorised into one of three graded levels, namely small (0.2–0.5), medium (0.5–0.8) or large (>0.8) [60].

Further, the effect of the age variable on the participants' motor performance was investigated using a regression analysis, with age being considered the predictor variable and the total raw score for each child's motor performance being considered the outcome of interest. The level of statistical significance was set as $p < 0.01$ in order to avoid type I errors.

For linear regression, the effect size was calculated using Cohen's $f2$. According to Cohen's guidelines (1988) concerning the interpretation of the magnitude of the R-squared value, the values of Cohen's $f2 = 0.02$, 0.13 and 0.26 are considered to be small, medium, and large effect size, respectively. The equation to compute Cohen's effect size is ($f2$ = R2/1 – R2) [60].

3. Results

The results of this study are presented in three stages according to the sequence of the research objectives:

3.1. The Proportion of Children with ASD Who Exhibit Motor Impairments

The BOT-2 standardized test was used in this study in order to evaluate motor proficiency in the child participants. Lower scores on the BOT-2 items are considered to be indicative of lower motor performance. On the short form of the BOT-2, the subtests are administered to find the raw scores. Each raw score for the subtests was then converted into a point score using the graded scale provided. The point scores are summed to give the total point score (max = 88), which is in turn converted into the standard score considering age and sex (ranging from 20 to 80), with a mean of 50 (SD = 10). A total composite standard score of 40 or less (one standard deviation below) is classified as indicative of motor impairment. This total motor composite can be reported as a categorical variable with five descriptive categories: well above average "≥70", above average "60–69", average "41–59", below average "31–40", and well below average "≤30". Based on this process, the overall score, which is the sum of the eight subscales, was compared with the BOT-2 norms. Table 3 presents descriptive statistics concerning the total BOT-2 motor composite scores of the children with ASD as well as the results of the z-test comparing their overall motor performance to the performance of the normative test sample.

Table 3. Descriptive Statistics and Z-Test Results Concerning the Total Motor Composite.

BOT-2	ASD Sample (N = 119)					95% Confidence Interval for the Mean		One-Sample Z-Test		
	Min	Max	M	SD	SE	Lower	Upper	Z	p	d
Standard score for the total motor composite *	47.0	85.0	31.90	5.03	0.46	30.98	32.81	−19.74	<0.001	1.81

Note: * A standard score less than 40 is regarded as the cut-off point for an abnormal motor performance.

As shown in Table 3, the mean BOT-2 score of the ASD group for the total motor composite (M = 31.90, SD = 5.03, $p < 0.001$) statistically deviated from the norm with a large effect size; thereby, indicating the presence of motor impairment within the overall level of motor proficiency. In light of the cut-off score set out in the BOT-2 guidelines, 88% of participants with ASD scored below the normal threshold when compared with the normative BOT-2 data. Based on the descriptive standard scoring categories detailed in the BOT-2 guidelines, the children with ASD were classified as displaying a motor performance deficit that fell within the below-average range.

3.2. Comparing the ASD and TD Children Based on the BOT-2 Test Raw Scores

Table 4 shows the participants' mean raw scores and standard deviations on the eight BOT-2 subtests, namely fine motor precision, fine motor integration, manual dexterity, upper-limb coordination, bilateral coordination, balance, running speed and agility, and strength, as well as the total motor composite. It therefore indicates the differences identified between the children in the ASD group and the typically developing children. The highest point score for the test is 88. Higher scores on the BOT-2 items are indicative of higher motor performance, and vice versa.

Table 4. Comparison of the autism spectrum disorder and typically developing groups based on the BOT-2 raw scores and total motor composite.

The BOT-2 Test Scores	ASD Sample (N = 119)		TDC Group (N = 30)		t-Statistic	p	D
	M	SD	M	SD			
Fine Motor Precision	5.38	2.66	10.17	2.10	9.171 ***	<0.001 ***	1.99
Fine Motor Integration	7.43	2.17	9.53	1.36	6.623 ***	<0.001 ***	1.16
Manual Dexterity	3.28	1.62	6.33	1.56	9.322 ***	<0.001 ***	1.92
Bilateral Coordination	4.60	1.68	6.67	0.85	9.489 ***	<0.001 ***	1.55
Balance	5.69	1.10	7.30	0.75	7.563 ***	<0.001 ***	1.71
Running Speed and Agility	3.08	2.03	6.97	1.40	12.267 ***	<0.001 ***	2.23
Upper-Limb Coordination	5.13	2.80	10.20	1.73	12.472 ***	<0.001 ***	2.18
Strength	3.21	2.08	8.97	2.24	13.352 ***	<0.001 ***	2.66
Total Motor Composite	37.79	12.25	66.13	8.24	15.097 ***	<0.001 ***	2.71

Note: *** $p < 0.001$ by independent samples t-test. ADS: Autism spectrum disorder without intellectual disability; TDC: typically developing children; BOT-2: Bruininks-Oseretsky Test of Motor Proficiency, Second Edition; d values are effect sizes (ESs) of ASD versus TDC. Bonferroni correction: $\alpha = 0.05/8 = 0.006$.

The independent samples t-test found significant differences in terms of all the BOT-2 short-form subtests and the total score when comparing the children with ASD and the typically developing children. All the differences are significant at the $p < 0.001$ level, with the size effects on the eight BOT-2 subtests ranging from 1.16 to 2.66 and the total motor composite equalling 2.71 (Cohen's d). This indicates that the children with ASD performed more poorly on the BOT-2 items than the TD controls. The performance on the eight motor subtests was variable. The children with ASD scored their lowest point scores on the strength element of all the subtests (Cohen's $d = 2.66$), while Fine Motor Integration was associated with their highest point scores (Cohen's $d = 1.16$).

3.3. Relationship between Motor Performance and Age

The relationship between the ASD participants' age and their overall motor performance was examined using linear regression analyses. The results indicated the significant main effect of age, which suggested that the children with ASD exhibited age-related gains in terms of their overall motor performance. Indeed, positive correlation was noted between their overall motor performance and their age ($\beta = 0.52$, $p \leq 0.001$, $R^2 = 0.26$, Cohen's $f^2 = 0.36$). This correlation pattern indicated that the children with ASD exhibited fewer deficits during the performance of motor tasks as they aged.

4. Discussion

The results relevant to each aim of the study will be discussed separately in the following subsections

4.1. Prevalence of Children with ASD Who Exhibited Clinically Significant Motor Abnormalities

Our first objective was to identify the prevalence of children with ASD who exhibited clinically significant motor abnormalities. The results indicated that the majority of the ASD sample fell outside the normal range in terms of motor performance. Indeed, the prevalence of children with ASD who exhibited clinically significant motor performance problems was found to be 88%. These children had a score of 40 or less on the total composite, which indicates deficits in their motor skills.

These results regarding the motor impairments seen in children with ASD are consistent with our expectations, since they reflect the motor abnormalities seen in those with autism. Additionally, such findings regarding deficient motor functioning in children with ASD are in line with the findings of several prior studies that relied on a similar measure to the BOT-2 [8,17,29,61–63]. The mean standard score for the overall motor composite in these previous studies ranged from 33.0 to 39.6, indicating the existence of motor impairments among children with ASD. A similar pattern of results was also found in the clinical sample of 45 individuals with autism aged 4 –21 years described in the BOT-2 manual (M = 37.0; SD = 8.4) [48]. The present results are also in line with those of other studies that used different measures [6,11]. However, our results contrast with those found in a study by Hilton et al. (2014) that used the BOT-2 but did not identify a significant deficit in the motor skills of individuals with ASD [64]. However, the small sample size involved in Hilton et al.'s (2014) study should be considered, since they only investigated seven children with ASD.

The motor disruptions seen in children with ASD may be attributed to the increase in the total brain volume seen in such children, as well as to certain affected brain regions that are regularly suspected to be involved in the neural underpinnings of autism, including the cerebellum, basal ganglia, brain stem functions, and alterations in the frontostriatal and frontocerebellar pathways [10,65]. However, the brain mechanisms underlying the motor disruptions observed in those with autism are not conclusive, meaning that they warrant further investigation.

Environmental factors may also contribute to the poor motor skills performance exhibited by those with ASD. An individual's motor skills development stems from the dynamic relationship that exists between organismic and environmental factors; hence, any changes in such properties will influence the acquisition of motor skills [66]. A study by Maksoud (2016) indicated that certain environmental factors might explain the poor performance exhibited by Egyptian children with Down's syndrome in relation to the BOT-2 instrument [67]. These factors included low enhancement and poor support from the parent(s), as well as limited opportunities to practice during the early years of their lives [67].

A proposition drawn from these findings is that these factors may also be applicable to children with ASD.

It is important to note, however, that the prevalence of motor performance abnormalities identified in the context of our research was high when compared to the prevalence reported in other studies [17,61–63]. It is possible that the high frequency of motor performance abnormalities seen in the children with ASD in the present study could be attributed to several factors largely related to the local cultural context.

First, low levels of physical activity can contribute to reducing the motor proficiency of children with ASD. The relationship between an individual's motor proficiency level and his/her level of physical activity was confirmed by Wrotniak, Epstein, Dorn, Jones, and Kondilis (2006) [68]. The majority of families in the Gulf region depend on domestic servants to help care for their children and to do the housework [69]. These domestic servants also typically assist the children with numerous tasks associated with daily living, especially in the case of children who have been diagnosed with a disability. This assistance could involve, for example, buttoning up clothes, zipping up zippers, tying shoes, bathing, feeding, cleaning teeth, and combing hair. Hence, it is possible that the children might come to overly rely on the domestic servants to help them perform everyday activities. This could in turn have a negative impact on the physical activity levels of the children, and therefore adversely affect their motor development.

Second, a lack of opportunities to engage in physical activity/practice responding to physical stimuli could stem from various familial factors. The negative relationship between motor development and insufficient physical activity has been confirmed in the literature [70,71]. The parents of children with ASD in the Arab Gulf region tend toward an overprotective parenting style, and they often exhibit excessive concern about their children's safety when outdoors. This parenting style is likely to have contributed to the children with ASD being less physically active than is ideal and, relatedly, to their insufficient motor skills proficiency [72].

Additionally, children living in the Gulf region tend to only rarely engage in physical activities out in the natural environment. Prior research evidence has suggested that the physical environment that we inhabit can offer both opportunities and barriers in terms of engaging in physical activities [70]. For example, countries in the Gulf region frequently experience very high temperatures during the daytime [73]. Therefore, it is rarely considered safe or appropriate for children to engage in outdoor activities during that time/in such conditions. Children with ASD are particularly prone to being prevented for participating in outdoor activities due to both the perceived inconvenience of them doing so and the associated security concerns. This lack of participation may affect the development of the children's gross motor skills.

Finally, children with ASD typically lack exercise partners of the same age and are frequently isolated from their peers, which means that they generally lack opportunities to engage in social interactions. Unfortunately, children with ASD are particularly susceptible to social exclusion due to both the stigma experienced by their families (i.e., feelings of shame about their child's condition) and the rejection and lack of acceptance shown by their peers (i.e., evasion and discrimination). Some families attempt to keep their children's condition a secret, and hence prevent their children from attending social events and engaging in social interactions with their peers. It has been reported that the lack of a peer exercise partner represents one of the key barriers to physical activity experienced by children with ASD [74]. Such non-participation in peer activities may limit children's opportunities to develop their motor proficiency.

4.2. Distinct Nature of Motor Performance Exhibited by Children with ASD and Typically Developing Children

This study also sought to examine the differences between the motor performance, as assessed using the BOT-2, of children with ASD and typically developing children. The results demonstrated that the children with ASD exhibited weaker motor skills performance than the typically developing children, which indicated deficits in their motor proficiency. The results, therefore, support the findings of prior studies concerning motor behaviours, which indicated a general impairment of motor functioning in individuals with ASD [10,11]. The results contribute to our understanding of definitive areas of motor dysfunction among children with ASD and their long-term developmental consequences. Further, the results add weight to previous insights intended to assist caregivers and therapists in addressing such issues. Overall, the results provide further evidence of the need to reconceptualise ASD to include motor delays and deficits.

When considering all eight subscales used to evaluate the overall motor proficiency of the children with ASD, it appears that the identified motor deficits manifested with different degrees of severity. For instance, fine motor precision tasks require precise control over finger and hand movements. Our results indicated that the children with ASD experienced difficulties drawing lines through paths and folding paper. This finding is in accordance with the notion that individuals with ASD experience difficulties completing tasks that require the planning and sequencing of movement [75]. As some children with ASD also exhibit hypotonia, it is likely that the hypotonia in their hands results in severe fine-motor and graph-motor delays due to an inability to manipulate objects and control a pencil [76]. Such difficulties may lead to problems during many activities associated with daily living, including buttoning clothes and writing.

Fine motor integration skills require the capacity to integrate visual stimuli with motor control. This kind of integration is commonly referred to as "visual motor integration". Our results indicated that the children with ASD were generally unable to perform the hand-eye coordination tasks. This finding is in line with prior evidence that some individuals with ASD exhibit underlying deficits in visual-motor integration [77]. Such deficits may stem from sensory problems since hand-eye coordination requires the assimilation of several types of sensory inputs to direct movement toward the target [78]. Moreover, children with ASD demonstrate delayed manipulation skills, which are also important for activities such as writing and fastening clothing [79]. These fine motor integration skills tend to be affected when an individual with ASD experiences a tactile perception problem, especially when tactile defensiveness is present. Ayres noted that hyper-responsivity to tactile stimuli may render it difficult for younger children to develop in-hand manipulation, fine motor skills, and hand-eye coordination [80]. It has been established that children with ASD often exhibit difficulties with tactile awareness, which may impede their fine motor skills. Thus, it has a bearing on their ability to develop fine motor skills.

Our findings also revealed the impaired performance of the children with ASD on the manual dexterity subtest, which is in line with the results of prior studies [11,14,81,82]. Deficits in manual coordination may occur due to the poor hand-eye coordination typically seen in children with ASD, since good hand-eye coordination allows individuals to pick up small objects and precisely manipulate them. Further, perception-action coupling is crucial to the production of purposeful, coherent movements [14]. However, prior evidence has suggested that such manual coordination deficits may be related to the use of a dual-scored task that involves both spatial accuracy and age-related temporal parameters [14]. Interestingly, a recent study indicated that the worst results for children with ASD were seen in relation to the fine motor skills component, while the gross motor skills component gave rise to the best results [83]. During the indicative qualitative evaluation, the researchers found more children with ASD to be able to manage the manual tasks when provided with unlimited time and support [83]. In contrast, the majority of children with ASD could not manage the gross motor tasks at all [83].

The bilateral coordination subtest concerns the capacity to use both sides of the body in a controlled and organized manner to accomplish a functional task [79]. The results indicated that the children with ASD experienced problems when attempting movements involving both sides of the body. This finding is consistent with the fact that individuals with ASD are typically characterised by poor bilateral coordination [84]. Further, Staples and Reid found that children with ASD experienced difficulty coordinating both sides of their body, or both arms and legs, while performing motor tasks [82]. Bilateral coordination problems may be associated with vestibular dysfunction, as when the vestibular system is unable to adequately integrate information, it can contribute to poor bilateral coordination.

Moreover, the vestibular system allows the two sides of the body to communicate with each other at the level of the brain stem via the vestibular nuclei [85].

The balance subtest evaluates the motor control skills integral to an individual's posture when standing. Balance is necessary for both movement and stillness, which is why it is sometimes referred to as postural control [86,87]. The balance subtest consists of movement activities that measure the stability of the trunk support as well as stasis and movement. Our results suggested that the balance skills of the children with ASD were significantly impaired when compared with the typically developing children, which is in line with the findings of previous studies [10,11,14,81]. However, Ament et al. found that deficits in the balance skills of children with ASD were only demonstrated during static balance tasks and not during dynamic balance tasks [88]. Further, the presence of balance deficits in children with ASD is often interpreted as indicating a deficit in the integration of information obtained from the visual, proprioception and vestibular afferent systems [10,89]. The maintenance of successful postural stability during static balance postures is thought to require the integration of vestibular, somatosensory, and visual inputs. If one of these inputs is impaired or disrupted, then both simple and complex motor tasks prove more difficult [19].

The running speed and agility subtest includes activities that require both speed and agility. Hopping is defined as the elevation of the body off the ground and the subsequent landing on a single foot [90]. It appears to be an extension of the ability to balance while standing on one leg. This type of balance is referred to as "dynamic balance". Our results indicated that the children with ASD experienced difficulty in hopping on one foot when compared with the typically developing children. This is in accordance with prior clinical observations that many autistic children experience great difficulty when hopping [91,92]. For instance, Noterdaeme et al. found that children with ASD experienced difficulties performing motor skills that require standing and hopping on one foot for a predetermined period of time when compared with typically developing children [93]. A similar result was found by Pusponegoro et al., who noted that only five out of 40 (12.5%) children with ASD could hop on one foot without falling over [92]. Comparable to the situation with balance and bilateral coordination, a possible contributing factor to the impairment seen in children with ASD is the vestibular problems they experience. Hopping requires the ability to balance on either foot, which relies heavily on a sensitive vestibular system and motor coordination [94]. The vestibular system also plays an important role in controlling the mutual interaction of sensory inputs and motor outputs [95]. As the ASD population typically exhibits an impairment in vestibular processing that results in poor balance, this impairment may impact the ability of a child with ASD to hop.

The upper-limb coordination (ULC) subtest consists of activities designed to measure visual tracking with coordinated arm and hand movements. Our results revealed that the children with ASD exhibited ULC difficulties, which is consistent with prior evidence that individuals with ASD exhibit poor ULC during visuomotor activities [96]. The results also indicated that the use of both hands to drop and catch a ball proved difficult for the children with ASD [14]. It appears, therefore, that children with ASD experience difficulty completing tasks involving both hands. When attempting to catch a ball with two hands, their arm movements are often poorly coordinated [97,98]. These deficits may be attributed to insufficient information processing [99]. As activities involving ball skills are often social in nature, such motor impairments may result in the exclusion of children with ASD from games, which may disrupt their psychosocial development [98,100].

The strength subtest is intended to assess the trunk flexor muscles and the upper and lower extremity strength. It involves activities such as push-ups and sit-ups. Our results indicated that the children with ASD showed an insufficient level of strength during such activities. They were able to complete fewer push-up and sit-up repetitions than the typically developing children. This is in line with the results obtained by Pan (2014), who found individuals with ASD to be able to complete fewer push-ups and sit-ups than age-matched peers without ASD [29]. The inability to master the push-up skill may indicate weakness in an individual's general upper body condition. Further, difficulty performing sit-ups may result from relatively low middle-body strength [101]. One explanation for the poor performance of the children with ASD in relation to strength skills could be their limited general body strength. Such activities require a great deal of muscle strength, which is also necessary for many aspects of movement and motor control, including postural control, balance, and coordination [102].

4.3. The Relationship between Age and Motor Performance

The final aim of this study was to determine whether the chronological age of the children with ASD affected their overall motor performance. Ultimately, it was determined that age did impact the motor performance of the children with ASD. The total score for motor performance was positively related to the age of the children with ASD. In general, the present results indicate that children with ASD demonstrated fewer deficits during motor tasks with age. This finding is consistent with the general pattern of the developmental acquisition of motor skills with age [43,48]. Relatively few studies have examined age differences in terms of motor performance in those with ASD, although the current results are in line with those of a study by Ming et al. (2007), who found that older children with ASD tend to perform better in relation to the motor skills than younger children with ASD [16]. However, the present results stand in contrast to the results of longitudinal work indicating that these motor deficits remain relatively stable over time in children with ASD [46]. The identified age-related gains could be due to the natural maturity of motor skills or the result of therapeutic interventions [16]. Structural environmental changes may promote motor development in children with ASD. However, the children with ASD in the context in which this study was conducted, whether they exhibited motor deficits or not, were not expected to receive any services to assist with their motor development. Hence, the results of the present study support the hypothesis that the development of fine and gross motor skills is characterized by change rather than stability.

5. Conclusions

The present study outlined the prevalence of motor impairments in children with ASD, as well as the nature of the motor abnormalities seen in school-aged children with ASD when compared to typically developing children, through the use of a standardized test so as to facilitate a better understanding of the motor profiles associated with ASD. An additional focus of the study was the exploration of the relationship between motor performance ability and age. Based on the impairment cut-off detailed in the BOT-2 guidelines, the majority of children with ASD in our sample showed mild to extremely negative deviation from population norms, and therefore were classified as exhibiting a motor performance deficit. This study also found evidence that the children with ASD performed significantly poorer than the typically developing children in relation to all the items of the BOT-2. In addition, the study demonstrated the existence of a positive relationship between age and motor performance ability, which indicated that motor skills may improve as children grow older.

The overall findings of this study served to reinforce and extend the results of prior studies concerning motor abnormalities in those with ASD. In particular, the present findings contributed significantly to our understanding of such motor characteristics in non-Western individuals diagnosed with ASD.

A strength of this study is related to the use of a standardised assessment of motor impairment (i.e., the BOT-2), which is one of the most commonly applied means of evaluating and discriminating motor function in children. However, only the short form of the chosen motor proficiency test (SFBOT-2) was used in this study, which limited our interpretation of the subcategories. However, the use of the SFBOT-2 can be justified based on the findings of our unpublished pilot study, which revealed both the difficulty and the high time requirements associated with applying the full version of the test. Additionally, a number of comorbid psychiatric disorders, including anxiety, could potentially impact children's performance during a motor task [103,104]. However, the results of this study do not contribute to the ongoing discussion regarding the effect of anxiety on test performance. Thus, future studies could examine the possible relationship between anxiety levels and performance levels during motor tasks. Although the severity of the ASD symptoms has been found to be related to the severity of the experienced motor problems [8,105–107], examining this relationship in more detail is beyond the scope of the present study. It does, however, represent an interesting avenue for future studies to explore.

Another limitation of the present study is related to the cross-sectional methodological approach chosen to explore the impact of chronological age on the motor difficulties exhibited by children with ASD, which limited our ability to interpret the findings from a developmental perspective. Future studies should employ a longitudinal design so as to be better able to investigate the developmental trajectories of motor impairments in children with ASD and to provide us with further insights into the mechanisms that underlie such motor disruptions. The final limitation of this study concerned the study sample. Only children with ASD who exhibited an average or above-average IQ were included in the study. Therefore, the findings are limited to that group, and hence are not representative of individuals with ASD who exhibit lower cognitive function. Additionally, the fact that the sample of typically developing children included in the study was relatively small should be considered. Indeed, the typically developing participants in this study may not be representative of the population as a whole.

Despite the above-mentioned limitations, the findings of the present study have a number of important implications for practice. First, the results reported here suggested that motor abnormalities represent a prevalent feature of ASD. However, such problems do not typically form part of the assessments for ASD nor are they typically included in intervention programs. Therefore, the inclusion of a motor assessment in the evaluation protocols associated with ASD should prove highly useful. Second, although motor deficits are present from very early on in the development of children with ASD and may actually reflect an underlying brain deficit, they do not generally represent a key focus for either parents or professionals. It is recommended that motor functioning should be considered during the clinical assessment and management of ASD, and it should not be ignored during early interventions. Further, it is recommended that additional research be undertaken in this regard so as to ensure greater clinical recognition of motor dysfunctions among children with ASD.

Moreover, the wide-ranging implications of poor motor performance on the part of individuals with ASD can extend beyond the motor domain and into the educational, social, cognitive, and behavioural domains. Hence, motor functioning represents another area that we should be mindful of in the clinical context. The identification of motor abnormalities could be a potentially valuable marker of the degree and the nature of the other defining clinical features of ASD. Finally, the results of the present study highlighted the need for increased efforts to improve the clinical surveillance process in order to better identify potential developmental delays or deficits in terms of motor performance, as well as to implement intervention strategies intended to address motor problems, in children with ASD. Early identification and proper intervention with regard to motor problems in children with ASD may lead to such children experiencing improved self-confidence and self-esteem, increased performance quality, and enhanced occupational engagement and social participation.

Acknowledgments: The author would like to thank the parents and staff members from the autism centers and mainstream primary schools in Bahrain, Saudi Arabia, and the UAE. for their assistance with the data collection. This study was conducted as part of the author's PhD thesis.

References

1. Haibach, P.; Reid, G.; Collier, D. *Motor Learning and Development*, 2nd ed.; Human Kineticsl: Champaign, IL, USA, 2017.
2. Piek, J.P.; Hands, B.; Licari, M.K. Assessment of motor functioning in the preschool period. *Neuropsychol. Rev.* **2012**, *22*, 402–413. [CrossRef] [PubMed]
3. Catama Bryan, V.; Calalang Wielm Mae, S.; Cada Renz Karlo, D.; Ballog Angelica, C.; Batton Kaylee, B.; Bigay Ma Lourdes, R.; Borje Denice Jan, J. Motor intervention activities for children with autism spectrum disorders. *Int. J. Res. Stud. Psychol.* **2017**, *6*, 27–42. [CrossRef]
4. Libertus, K.; Hauf, P. Motor skills and their foundational role for perceptual, social, and cognitive development. *Front. Psychol.* **2017**, *8*, 301. [CrossRef] [PubMed]

5. Gowen, E.; Hamilton, A. Motor abilities in autism: A review using a computational context. *J. Autism Dev. Disord.* **2013**, *43*, 323–344. [CrossRef]
6. Abu-Dahab, S.M.N.; Skidmore, E.R.; Holm, M.B.; Rogers, J.C.; Minshew, N.J. Motor and tactile-perceptual skill differences between individuals with high-functioning autism and typically developing individuals ages 5–21. *J. Autism Dev. Disord.* **2013**, *43*, 2241–2248. [CrossRef]
7. Dowd, A.; Rinehart, N.; McGinley, J. Motor function in children with autism: Why is this relevant to psychologists? *Clin. Psychol.* **2010**, *14*, 90–96. [CrossRef]
8. Hilton, C.L.; Zhang, Y.; Whilte, M.R.; Klohr, C.L.; Constantino, J. Motor impairment in sibling pairs concordant and discordant for autism spectrum disorders. *Autism* **2012**, *16*, 430–441. [CrossRef]
9. Van Damme, T.; Simons, J.; Sabbe, B.; Van West, D. Motor abilities of children and adolescents with a psychiatric condition: A systematic literature review. *World J. Psychiatry* **2015**, *5*, 315. [CrossRef]
10. Fournier, K.A.; Hass, C.J.; Naik, S.K.; Lodha, N.; Cauraugh, J.H. Motor coordination in autism spectrum disorders: A synthesis and meta-analysis. *J. Autism Dev. Disord.* **2010**, *40*, 1227–1240. [CrossRef]
11. Green, D.; Charman, T.; Pickles, A.; Chandler, S.; Loucas, T.; Simonoff, E.; Baird, G. Impairment in movement skills of children with autistic spectrum disorders. *Dev. Med. Child Neurol.* **2009**, *51*, 311–316. [CrossRef]
12. Liu, T.; Breslin, C.M. Fine and gross motor performance of the MABC-2 by children with autism spectrum disorder and typically developing children. *Res. Autism Spectr. Disord.* **2013**, *7*, 1244–1249. [CrossRef]
13. Moseley, R.L.; Pulvermueller, F. What can autism teach us about the role of sensorimotor systems in higher cognition? New clues from studies on language, action semantics, and abstract emotional concept processing. *Cortex* **2018**, *100*, 149–190. [CrossRef] [PubMed]
14. Whyatt, C.P.; Craig, C.M. Motor skills in children aged 7–10 years, diagnosed with autism spectrum disorder. *J. Autism Dev. Disord.* **2012**, *42*, 1799–1809. [CrossRef] [PubMed]
15. McCleery, J.P.; Elliott, N.A.; Sampanis, D.S.; Stefanidou, C.A. Motor development and motor resonance difficulties in autism: Relevance to early intervention for language and communication skills. *Front. Integr. Neurosci.* **2013**, *7*, 30. [CrossRef]
16. Ming, X.; Brimacombe, M.; Wagner, G.C. Prevalence of motor impairment in autism spectrum disorders. *Brain Dev.* **2007**, *29*, 565–570. [CrossRef]
17. Dewey, D.; Cantell, M.; Crawford, S.G. Motor and gestural performance in children with autism spectrum disorders, developmental coordination disorder, and/or attention deficit hyperactivity disorder. *J. Int. Neuropsychol. Soc.* **2007**, *13*, 246–256. [CrossRef]
18. Nobile, M.; Perego, P.; Piccinini, L.; Mani, E.; Rossi, A.; Bellina, M.; Molteni, M. Further evidence of complex motor dysfunction in drug naive children with autism using automatic motion analysis of gait. *Autism* **2011**, *15*, 263–283. [CrossRef]
19. Travers, B.G.; Powell, P.S.; Klinger, L.G.; Klinger, M.R. Motor difficulties in autism spectrum disorder: Linking symptom severity and postural stability. *J. Autism Dev. Disord.* **2013**, *43*, 1568–1583. [CrossRef]
20. Jeste, S.S. The neurology of autism spectrum disorders. *Curr. Opin. Neurol.* **2011**, *24*, 132–139. [CrossRef]
21. Stefanatos, G.A. Autism Spectrum Disorders. In *The Neuropsychology of Psychopathology*; Noggle, C., Dean, R., Eds.; Springer Publishing Company: New York, NY, USA, 2013; pp. 97–170.
22. Mostofsky, S.H.; Powell, S.K.; Simmonds, D.J.; Goldberg, M.C.; Caffo, B.; Pekar, J.J. Decreased connectivity and cerebellar activity in autism during motor task performance. *Brain* **2009**, *132*, 2413–2425. [CrossRef]
23. Takarae, Y.; Minshew, N.J.; Luna, B.; Sweeney, J.A. Atypical involvement of frontostriatal systems during sensorimotor control in autism. *Psychiatry Res. Neuroimaging* **2007**, *156*, 117–127. [CrossRef] [PubMed]
24. McAlonan, G.M.; Suckling, J.; Wong, N.; Cheung, V.; Lienenkaemper, N.; Cheung, C.; Chua, S.E. Distinct patterns of grey matter abnormality in high-functioning autism and Asperger's syndrome. *J. Child Psychol. Psychiatry* **2008**, *49*, 1287–1295. [CrossRef] [PubMed]
25. Rinehart, N.J.; Tonge, B.J.; Iansek, R.; McGinley, J.; Brereton, A.V.; Enticott, P.G.; Bradshaw, J.L. Gait function in newly diagnosed children with autism: Cerebellar and basal ganglia related motor disorder. *Dev. Med. Child Neurol.* **2006**, *48*, 819–824. [CrossRef]
26. Cairney, J.; King-Dowling, S. Developmental coordination disorder. In *Comorbid Conditions among Children with Autism Spectrum Disorders*; Matson, J.L., Ed.; Springer: Berlin, Germany, 2016; pp. 303–322.
27. Mosconi, M.W.; Sweeney, J.A. Sensorimotor dysfunctions as primary features of autism spectrum disorders. *Sci. China Life Sci.* **2015**, *58*, 1016–1023. [CrossRef] [PubMed]

28. Pluta, M. Parental perceptions of the effect of child participation in hippotherapy programme on overall improvement of child mental and physical wellbeing. *Ann. UMCS Zootech.* **2011**, *29*, 74–84. [CrossRef]
29. Pan, C.Y. Motor proficiency and physical fitness in adolescent males with and without autism spectrum disorders. *Autism* **2014**, *18*, 156–165. [CrossRef]
30. Travers, B.G.; Kana, R.K.; Klinger, L.G.; Klein, C.L.; Klinger, M.R. Motor learning in individuals with autism spectrum disorder: Activation in superior parietal lobule related to learning and repetitive behaviors. *Autism Res.* **2015**, *8*, 38–51. [CrossRef]
31. Choi, B.; Leech, K.A.; Tager-Flusberg, H.; Nelson, C.A. Development of fine motor skills is associated with expressive language outcomes in infants at high and low risk for autism spectrum disorder. *J. Neurodev. Disord.* **2018**, *10*, 14. [CrossRef]
32. Flanagan, J.E.; Landa, R.; Bhat, A.; Bauman, M. Head lag in infants at risk for autism: A preliminary study. *Am. J. Occup. Ther.* **2012**, *66*, 577–585. [CrossRef]
33. Landa, R.; Garrett-Mayer, E. Development in infants with autism spectrum disorders: A prospective study. *J. Child Psychol. Psychiatry* **2006**, *47*, 629–638. [CrossRef]
34. Lloyd, M.; MacDonald, M.; Lord, C. Motor skills of toddlers with autism spectrum disorders. *Autism* **2013**, *17*, 133–146. [CrossRef] [PubMed]
35. Esposito, G.; Pasca, S. Motor abnormalities as a putative endophenotype for Autism Spectrum Disorders. *Front. Integr. Neurosci.* **2013**, *7*, 43. [CrossRef] [PubMed]
36. Marrus, N.; Eggebrecht, A.T.; Todorov, A.; Elison, J.T.; Wolff, J.J.; Cole, L.; Emerson, R.W. Walking, gross motor development, and brain functional connectivity in infants and toddlers. *Cereb. Cortex* **2017**, *28*, 750–763. [CrossRef] [PubMed]
37. Ozonoff, S.; Young, G.S.; Goldring, S.; Greiss-Hess, L.; Herrera, A.M.; Steele, J.; Rogers, S.J. Gross motor development, movement abnormalities, and early identification of autism. *J. Autism Dev. Disord.* **2008**, *38*, 644–656. [CrossRef] [PubMed]
38. Bhat, A.N.; Galloway, J.C.; Landa, R.J. Relation between early motor delay and later communication delay in infants at risk for autism. *Infant Behav. Dev.* **2012**, *35*, 838–846. [CrossRef]
39. Baranek, G.T.; Parham, L.D.; Bodfish, J.W. Sensory and motor features in autism: Assessment and intervention. In *Handbook of Autism and Pervasive Developmental Disorders*; Volkmar, F., Ed.; John Wiley & Sons: Hoboken, NJ, USA, 2017; pp. 831–857.
40. Setoh, P.; Marschik, P.B.; Einspieler, C.; Esposito, G. Autism spectrum disorder and early motor abnormalities: Connected or coincidental companions? *Res. Dev. Disabil.* **2005**, *60*, 13–15. [CrossRef]
41. Williams JH, G.; Whiten, A.; Singh, T. A systematic review of action imitation in autistic spectrum disorder. *J. Autism Dev. Disord.* **2004**, *34*, 285–299. [CrossRef]
42. Chinello, A.; Di Gangi, V.; Valenza, E. Persistent primary reflexes affect motor acts: Potential implications for autism spectrum disorder. *Res. Dev. Disabil.* **2018**, *83*, 287–295. [CrossRef]
43. Piek, J. *Infant Motor Development*; Human Kinetics: Champaign, IL, USA, 2006.
44. Darrah, J.; Hodge, M.; Magill-Evans, J.; Kembhavi, G. Stability of serial assessments of motor and communication abilities in typically developing infants—Implications for screening. *Early Hum. Dev.* **2003**, *72*, 97–110. [CrossRef]
45. Pless, M.; Carlsson, M.; Sundelin, C.; Persson, K. Preschool children with developmental coordination disorder: A short-term follow-up of motor status at seven to eight years of age. *Acta Paediatr.* **2002**, *91*, 521–528. [CrossRef]
46. Van Waelvelde, H.; Oostra, A.; Dewitte, G.; Van Den Broeck, C.; Jongmans, M.J. Stability of motor problems in young children with or at risk of autism spectrum disorders, ADHD, and/or developmental coordination disorder. *Dev. Med. Child Neurol.* **2010**, *52*, e174–e178. [CrossRef] [PubMed]
47. Baumer, F.; Sahin, M. Neurological comorbidities in autism spectrum disorder. In *Autism Spectrum Disorder*; McDougle, C.J., Ed.; Oxford University Press: Oxford, UK, 2016; pp. 99–116.
48. Bruininks, R.H.; Bruininks, B.D. *Bruininks-Oseretsky Test of Motor Proficiency*, 2nd ed.; Pearson Assessments: Minneapolis, MN, USA, 2005.
49. American Psychiatric Association. DSM-5 Task Force. The Clinician-Rated Severity of Autism Spectrum and Social Communication Disorders. 2013. Available online: http://www.psychiatry.org/dsm5 (accessed on 29 February 2020).

50. Ghaziuddin, M.; Welch, K. The Michigan Autism Spectrum Questionnaire: A Rating Scale for High-Functioning Autism Spectrum Disorders. *Autism Res. Treat.* **2013**, *2013*, 1–5. [CrossRef] [PubMed]
51. Gilliam, J.E. *Gilliam Autism Rating Scale*, 3rd ed.; Pro-Ed: Austin, TX, USA, 2013.
52. Oldfield, R. The assessment and analysis of handedness: The Edinburgh inventory. *Neuropsychologia* **1971**, *9*, 97–113. [CrossRef]
53. Raven, J.; Raven, J.; Court, J. *Manual for Raven's Progressive Matrices and Vocabulary Scales*; Oxford Psychologists Press: Oxford, UK, 1998.
54. American Psychiatric Association. DSM-5 Task Force, & American Psychiatric Association. In *Diagnostic and Statistical Manual of Mental Disorders: DSM-5*, 5th ed.; American Psychiatric Association: Arlington, VA, USA, 2013.
55. Holloway, J.M.; Long, T.M.; Biasini, F. Relationships between gross motor skills and social function in young boys with autism spectrum disorder. *Pediatric Phys. Ther.* **2018**, *30*, 184–190. [CrossRef] [PubMed]
56. Liu, T.; Breslin, C.M.; ElGarhy, S. Methods and Procedures for Measuring Comorbid Disorders: Motor Movement and Activity. In *Comorbid Conditions among Children with Autism Spectrum Disorders*; Matson, J.L., Ed.; Springer: Berlin, Germany, 2015; pp. 91–134.
57. Deitz, J.C.; Kartin, D.; Kopp, K. Review of the Bruininks-Oseretsky test of motor proficiency, (BOT-2). *Phys. Occup. Ther. Pediatr.* **2007**, *27*, 87–102. [CrossRef]
58. Okuda, P.; Pangelinan, M.; Capellini, S.; Cogo-Moreira, H. Motor skills assessments: Support for a general motor factor for the Movement Assessment Battery for Children-2 and the Bruininks-Oseretsky Test of Motor Proficiency-2. *Trends Psychiatry Psychother.* **2019**, *41*, 51–59. [CrossRef]
59. Jírovec, J.; Musálek, M.; Mess, F. Test of motor proficiency second edition (bot-2): Compatibility of the complete and short form and its usefulness for middle-age school children. *Front. Pediatr.* **2019**, *7*, 153. [CrossRef]
60. Cohen, J. *Statistical Power Analysis for the Behavioral Sciences*, 2nd ed.; L. Erlbaum Associates: Hillsdale, NJ, USA, 1988.
61. Hilton, C.L.; Attal, A.; Best, J.R.; Reistetter, T.; Trapani, P.; Collins, D. Exergaming to improve physical and mental fitness in children and adolescents with autism spectrum disorders: Pilot study. *Int. J. Sports Exerc. Med.* **2015**, *1*, 1–6. [CrossRef]
62. Mattard-Labrecque, C.; Amor, L.B.; Couture, M.M. Children with autism and attention difficulties: A pilot study of the association between sensory, motor, and adaptive behaviors. *J. Can. Acad. Child Adolesc. Psychiatry* **2013**, *22*, 139.
63. Olzenak, D.L. Adding Motor Assessment to the Disability Determination Process in School-Aged Children with ASD: Implications for Participation. 2015. Available online: https://ddp.policyresearchinc.org/wp-content/uploads/2015/09/Olzenak_Final-Report.pdf (accessed on 5 December 2019).
64. Hilton, C.L.; Cumpata, K.; Klohr, C.; Gaetke, S.; Artner, A.; Johnson, H.; Dobbs, S. Effects of exergaming on executive function and motor skills in children with autism spectrum disorder: A pilot study. *Am. J. Occup. Ther. Off. Publ. Am. Occup. Ther. Assoc.* **2014**, *68*, 57–65. [CrossRef]
65. Mosconi, M.W.; Takarae, Y.; Sweeney, J.A. Motor functioning and dyspraxia in autism spectrum disorders. In *Autism Spectrum Disorder*; Amaral, D.G., Dawson, G., Geschwind, H.D., Eds.; Oxford University Press: New York, NY, USA, 2011; pp. 355–380.
66. Gaul, D.; Issartel, J. Fine motor skill proficiency in typically developing children: On or off the maturation track? *Hum. Mov. Sci.* **2016**, *46*, 78–85. [CrossRef] [PubMed]
67. Maksoud, G. Fine motor skill proficiency in children with and without down syndrome. *J. Phys. Ther. Health Promot.* **2016**, *4*, 43–50. [CrossRef]
68. Wrotniak, B.H.; Epstein, L.H.; Dorn, J.M.; Jones, K.E.; Kondilis, V.A. The relationship between motor proficiency and physical activity in children. *Pediatrics* **2006**, *118*, e1758–e1765. [CrossRef] [PubMed]
69. Khalifa, B.; Nasser, R. The closeness of the child to the domestic servant and its mediation by negative parenting behaviors in an Arab Gulf country. In Proceedings of the Australasian Conference on Business and Social Sciences, Sydney, Australia, 6 December 2015; pp. 258–269.
70. Duncan, M.J.; Spence, J.C.; Mummery, W.K. Perceived environment and physical activity: A meta-analysis of selected environmental characteristics. *Int. J. Behav. Nutr. Phys. Act.* **2005**, *2*, 11. [CrossRef]
71. Zeng, N.; Ayyub, M.; Sun, H.; Wen, X.; Xiang, P.; Gao, Z. Effects of physical activity on motor skills and cognitive development in early childhood: A systematic review. *Biomed. Res. Int.* **2017**, *2017*, 1–13. [CrossRef]

72. Al-Heizan, M.O.; Al-Abdulwahab, S.S.; Kachanathu, S.J.; Natho, M. Sensory processing dysfunction among Saudi children with and without autism. *J. Phys. Ther. Sci.* **2015**, *27*, 1313–1316. [CrossRef]
73. Alkhalifah, S. Psychometric properties of the Sensory Processing Measure Preschool-Home among Saudi children with autism spectrum disorder: Pilot study. *J. Occup. Ther. Sch. Early Interv.* **2019**, *12*, 401–416. [CrossRef]
74. Must, A.; Phillips, S.; Curtin, C.; Bandini, L.G. Barriers to physical activity in children with autism spectrum disorders: Relationship to physical activity and screen time. *J. Phys. Act. Health* **2015**, *12*, 529–534. [CrossRef]
75. Patz, J.A.; Messina, R.M. Fine motor, oral motor, and self-care development. In *Young Children with Special Needs*, 5th ed.; Hooper, S.R., Umansky, W., Eds.; Pearson: Upper Saddle River, NJ, USA, 2009; pp. 168–235.
76. McCarton, C. Assessment and diagnosis of pervasive developmental disorder. In *Autism Spectrum Disorders*; Hollander, E., Ed.; Dekker: New York, NY, USA, 2003; pp. 101–132.
77. Coffin, A.B.; Myles, B.S.; Rogers, J.; Szakacs, W. Supporting the Writing Skills of Individuals with Autism Spectrum Disorder through Assistive Technologies. In *Technology and the Treatment of Children with Autism Spectrum Disorder*; Cardon, T.A., Ed.; Springer: Berlin, Germany, 2016; pp. 59–73.
78. Abdel Karim, A.E.; Mohammed, A.H. Effectiveness of sensory integration program in motor skills in children with autism. *Egypt. J. Med Hum. Genet.* **2015**, *16*, 375–380. [CrossRef]
79. Betts, D.; Jacobs, D. *Everyday Activities to Help Your Young Child with Autism Live Life to the Full: Simple Exercises to Boost Functional Skills, Sensory Processing, Coordination and Self-Care*; Jessica Kingsley Publishers: London, UK, 2011.
80. Semel, E.; Rosner, S. *Understanding Williams Syndrome: Behavioral Patterns and Interventions*; L. Erlbaum: Mahwah, NJ, USA, 2003.
81. Hilton, C.; Wente, L.; LaVesser, P.; Ito, M.; Reed, C.; Herzberg, G. Relationship between motor skill impairment and severity in children with Asperger syndrome. *Res. Autism Spectr. Disord.* **2007**, *1*, 339–349. [CrossRef]
82. Staples, K.L.; Reid, G. Fundamental movement skills and autism spectrum disorders. *J. Autism Dev. Disord.* **2010**, *40*, 209–217. [CrossRef] [PubMed]
83. Zikl, P.; Petrů, D.; Daňková, A.; Doležalová, H.; Šafaříková, K. Motor skills of children with autistic spectrum disorder. In *SHS Web of Conferences*; EDP Sciences: Les Ulis, France, 2016; Volume 26, p. 1076.
84. Paris, B. Characteristics of autism. In *Exploring the Spectrum of Autism and Pervasive Developmental Disorders*; Murray-Slutsky, C., Paris, B., Eds.; Therapy Skill Builders (Harcourt Health Sciences): San Antonio, TX, USA, 2000; pp. 7–23.
85. Dejean, V.M. *Vestibular Re Integration of the Autistic Child: Developmental Model for Autism*; iUniverse, Inc.: New York, NY, USA, 2008.
86. Coetzee, D. Strength, running speed, agility and balance profiles of 9-to 10-year-old learners: NW-child study. *S. Afr. J. Res. Sport Phys. Educ. Recreat.* **2016**, *38*, 13–30.
87. Deponio, P.; Macintyre, C. *Identifying and Supporting Children with Specific Learning Difficulties: Looking Beyond the Label to Support the Whole Child*; Routledge: London, UK, 2003.
88. Ament, K.; Mejia, A.; Buhlman, R.; Erklin, S.; Caffo, B.; Mostofsky, S.; Wodka, E. Evidence for specificity of motor impairments in catching and balance in children with autism. *J. Autism Dev. Disord.* **2015**, *45*, 742–751. [CrossRef]
89. Molloy, C.A.; Dietrich, K.N.; Bhattacharya, A. Postural stability in children with autism spectrum disorder. *J. Autism Dev. Disord.* **2003**, *33*, 643–652. [CrossRef] [PubMed]
90. Van Sant, A.; Goldberg, C. Normal motor development. In *Pediatric Physical Therapy*; Tecklin, J.S., Ed.; Lippincott Williams & Wilkins: New York, NY, USA, 1999; pp. 22–25.
91. DeLong, G.R. The cerebellum in autism. In *The Neurology of Autism*; Coleman, M., Ed.; Oxford University Press: Oxford, UK, 2005; pp. 75–90.
92. Pusponegoro, H.D.; Efar, P.; Soebadi, A.; Firmansyah, A.; Chen, H.J.; Hung, K.L. Gross motor profile and its association with socialization skills in children with autism spectrum disorders. *Pediatr. Neonatol.* **2016**, *57*, 501–507. [CrossRef] [PubMed]
93. Noterdaeme, M.; Mildenberger, K.; Minow, F.; Amorosa, H. Evaluation of neuromotor deficits in children with autism and children with a specific speech and language disorder. *Eur. Child Adolesc. Psychiatry* **2002**, *11*, 219–225. [CrossRef]
94. Dixon, G.; Addy, L. *Making Inclusion work for Children with Dyspraxia: Practical Strategies for Teachers*; Routledge Falmer: London, UK, 2004.

95. Memari, A.H.; Ghanouni, P.; Shayestehfar, M.; Ghaheri, B. Postural control impairments in individuals with autism spectrum disorder: A critical review of current literature. *Asian J. Sports Med.* **2014**, *5*, e22963. [CrossRef]
96. Bhat, A.N.; Landa, R.J.; Galloway, J.C. Current perspectives on motor functioning in infants, children, and adults with autism spectrum disorders. *Phys. Ther.* **2011**, *91*, 1116–1129. [CrossRef]
97. Attwood, T. *The Complete Guide to Asperger's Syndrome*; Jessica Kingsley Publishers: London, UK, 2006.
98. Baetti, S. Argentinian ambulatory integral model to treat autism spectrum disorders. In *Autism: The Movement Sensing Perspective*; Torres, E.B., Whyatt, C., Eds.; CRC Press; Taylor & Francis Group: Boca Raton, FL, USA, 2017; pp. 253–269.
99. Dirksen, T.; Lussanet, D.; Marc, H.E.; Zentgraf, K.; Slupinski, L.; Wagner, H. Increased Throwing Accuracy Improves Children's Catching Performance in a Ball-Catching Task from the Movement Assessment Battery (MABC-2). *Front. Psychol.* **2016**, *7*, 1122. [CrossRef]
100. Emck, C.; Bosscher, R.; Beek, P.; Doreleijers, T. Gross motor performance and self-perceived motor competence in children with emotional, behavioural, and pervasive developmental disorders: A review. *Dev. Med. Child Neurol.* **2009**, *51*, 501–517. [CrossRef]
101. Neporent, L. *Fitness Walking for Dummies*; John Wiley & Sons: New York, NY, USA, 2011.
102. Siri, K.; Lyons, T. *Cutting-Edge Therapies for Autism*; Skyhorse Publishing Inc.: New York, NY, USA, 2014.
103. Mayall, L.A.; D'Souza, H.; Hill, E.L.; Karmiloff-Smith, A.; Tolmie, A.; Farran, E.K. Motor Abilities and the Motor Profile in Individuals with Williams Syndrome. *Adv. Neurodev. Disord.* **2020**, *8*, 1–15. [CrossRef]
104. Wilson, R.B.; Enticott, P.G.; Rinehart, N.J. Motor development and delay: Advances in assessment of motor skills in autism spectrum disorders. *Curr. Opin. Neurol.* **2018**, *31*, 134–139. [CrossRef] [PubMed]
105. Jasmin, E.; Couture, M.; McKinley, P.; Reid, G.; Fombonne, E.; Gisel, E. Sensori-motor and daily living skills of preschool children with autism spectrum disorders. *J. Autism Dev. Disord.* **2009**, *39*, 231–241. [CrossRef]
106. MacDonald, M.; Lord, C.; Ulrich, D.A. The relationship of motor skills and social communicative skills in school-aged children with autism spectrum disorder. *Adapt. Phys. Act. Q.* **2013**, *30*, 271–282. [CrossRef]
107. Purpura, G.; Fulceri, F.; Puglisi, V.; Masoni, P.; Contaldo, A. Motor coordination impairment in children with autism spectrum disorder: A pilot study using Movement Assessment Battery for Children-2 Checklist. *Minerva Pediatrica* **2016**, *72*. [CrossRef] [PubMed]

13

The 15q11.2 BP1–BP2 Microdeletion Syndrome

Devin M. Cox †,* **and Merlin G. Butler** †

Departments of Psychiatry & Behavioral Sciences, University of Kansas Medical Center, 3901 Rainbow Boulevard, MS 4015, Kansas City, KS 66160, USA; mbutler4@kumc.edu

* Author to whom correspondence should be addressed; dcox2@kumc.edu

† These authors contributed equally to this work.

Academic Editor: Cesar Borlongan

Abstract: Patients with the 15q11.2 BP1–BP2 microdeletion can present with developmental and language delay, neurobehavioral disturbances and psychiatric problems. Autism, seizures, schizophrenia and mild dysmorphic features are less commonly seen. The 15q11.2 BP1–BP2 microdeletion involving four genes (*i.e.*, *TUBGCP5*, *CYFIP1*, *NIPA1*, *NIPA2*) is emerging as a recognized syndrome with a prevalence ranging from 0.57%–1.27% of patients presenting for microarray analysis which is a two to four fold increase compared with controls. Review of clinical features from about 200 individuals were grouped into five categories and included developmental (73%) and speech (67%) delays; dysmorphic ears (46%) and palatal anomalies (46%); writing (60%) and reading (57%) difficulties, memory problems (60%) and verbal IQ scores ≤75 (50%); general behavioral problems, unspecified (55%) and abnormal brain imaging (43%). Other clinical features noted but not considered as common were seizures/epilepsy (26%), autism spectrum disorder (27%), attention deficit disorder (ADD)/attention deficit hyperactivity disorder (ADHD) (35%), schizophrenia/paranoid psychosis (20%) and motor delay (42%). Not all individuals with the deletion are clinically affected, yet the collection of findings appear to share biological pathways and presumed genetic mechanisms. Neuropsychiatric and behavior disturbances and mild dysmorphic features are associated with genomic imbalances of the 15q11.2 BP1–BP2 region, including microdeletions, but with an apparent incomplete penetrance and variable expressivity.

Keywords: 15q11.2 BP1–BP2 microdeletion; Burnside-Butler syndrome; clinical and behavioral phenotype; chromosome breakpoints BP1 and BP2; Prader-Willi and Angelman syndromes; language and motor delays; autism; review

1. Introduction

Chromosome 15 contains five common breakpoint sites along the proximal long arm; they are commonly referred to as BP1–BP5. There is a cluster of low copy DNA repeats located within this chromosome region which can facilitate mis-alignment during meiosis leading to non-allelic homologous recombination [1,2]. These low copy repeat sequences are called duplicons and contain pseudogenes [3]. Duplicons found within breakpoints BP1, BP2 and BP3 have been characterized by the presence of the *HERC2* gene (at BP3) and *HERC2* pseudogenes (at BP1 and BP2) [2].

Prader-Willi syndrome (PWS) and Angelman syndrome are typically caused by a deletion of different parental origin involving the distal breakpoint BP3 and proximally placed breakpoints BP1 or BP2. These cytogenetic deletions of chromosome 15q11–q13 region are classified as typical type I (involving BP1 and BP3) or typical type II (involving BP2 and BP3) (see Figure 1). Type I deletions have an average genomic length of 6.58 Mb while type II deletions have a mean length of 5.33 Mb [4]. Several studies have shown that individuals with the larger typical 15q11–q13 type I deletion which is found in both Prader-Willi and Angelman syndromes are reported to have more severe neurodevelopmental symptoms as compared to those individuals with the smaller typical type II deletion [5–10]. Initially, Butler *et al.* [5] found that several behavioral and intelligence measures were statistically different between the two PWS deletion types (type I and type II). PWS individuals with type I deletions showed more compulsive and self-injurious behaviors and visual perception impairment along with lower intelligence, reading and math scores than in those with type II deletions. Furthermore, Bittel *et al.* [6] reported that the amount of mRNA isolated from lymphoblastoid cell lines established from individuals with PWS for the four genes (*i.e.*, *NIPA1*, *NIPA2*, *CYFIP1*, *TUBGCP5*) found in the genomic area between BP1 and BP2 in the 15q11.2 chromosome band explained between 24% to 99% of the phenotypic variability in behavioral and academic measures. The *NIPA2* gene accounted for the largest number of significant correlations between the mRNA levels and phenotypic features.

In other studies, Varela *et al.* [10] found that individuals with PWS having 15q11–q13 type I deletions acquired speech later than those with type II deletions. Hartley *et al.* [7] also found that individuals with PWS having type I deletions had significantly higher Reiss maladaptive behavior scores for depression (physical signs) than individuals with type II deletions. Similarly, Sahoo *et al.* [9] reported that in individuals with Angelman syndrome and the 15q11–q13 type I deletion had significantly more behavioral and cognitive impairments with lower expressive and total language abilities and a higher likelihood of features for autism spectrum disorder.

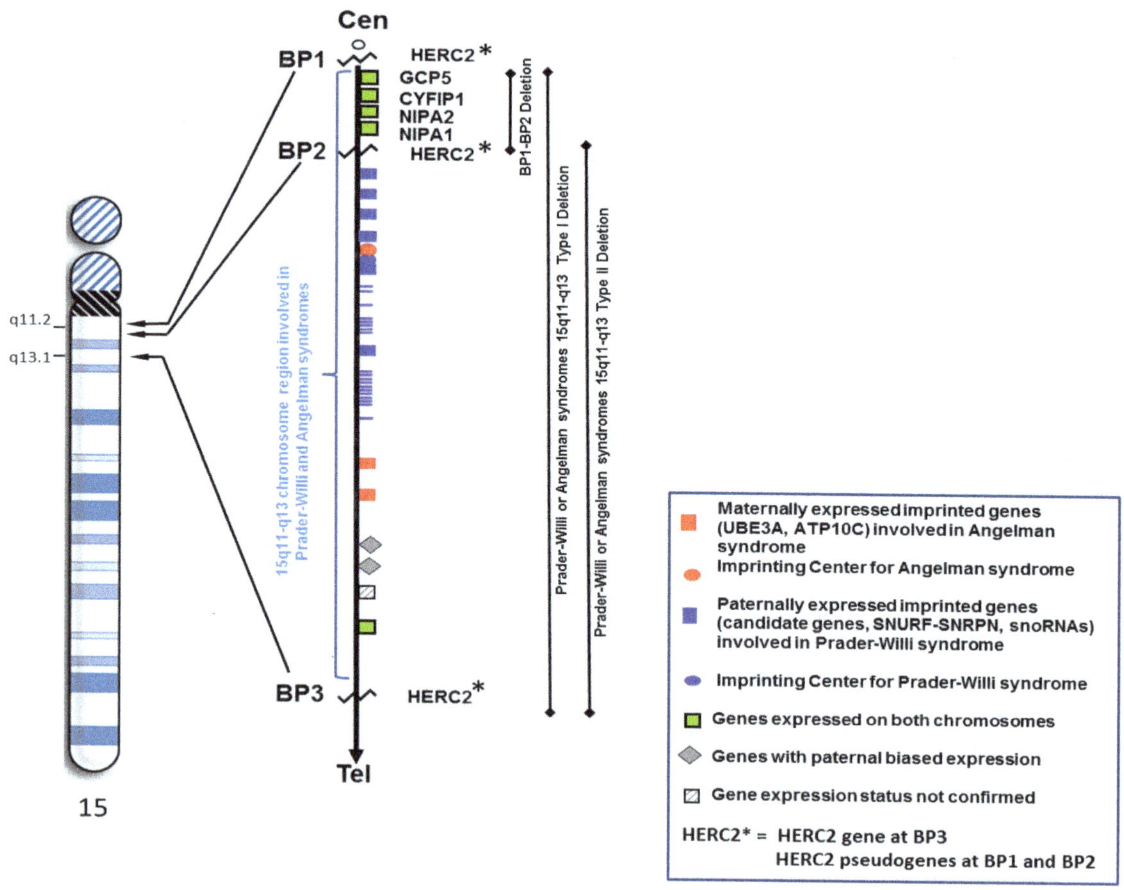

Figure 1. High resolution ideogram representing chromosome 15 showing location of breakpoints BP1 and BP2 (at 15q11.2 band) and BP3 (at 15q13.1 band) involving HERC2 and position of the non-imprinted genes between BP1 and BP2. The three deletion types involving the 15q11–q13 region (*i.e.*, BP1–BP2, typical type I, typical type II) are represented.

Valente *et al.* [11] also reported in Angelman syndrome that those with the 15q11–q13 type I deletion had more severe seizures and were refractory to treatment compared with those having the type II deletion. In a separate study Milner *et al.* [8] found significantly higher verbal IQ scores in individuals with PWS and type II deletions *versus* those with type I deletions. They further reported that those with type I deletions performed more poorly on all measures of ability even though they were not significantly different from the patients with type II deletions.

A report by Dykens and Roof [12] examined behaviors in PWS using a mixed cohort of young and old subjects (n = 88) and showed a relationship between genetic subtypes and ages. They found negative associations between age and behavior in the 15q11–q13 type I deletion subtype only which implicated non-imprinted genes between breakpoints BP1 and BP2, specifically the *CYFIP1* gene. Disturbed expression of *CYFIP1* is seen in other developmental disabilities including those with 15q disorders without PWS. Although they reported no significant behavioral findings when combining data from subjects at all ages, significant differences were found in those with type I *versus* type II deletions with age. The individuals with the 15q11–q13 type I deletion consistently had lower targeted problem behaviors and adaptive skills and externalizing symptoms with advancing age.

As several studies have shown evidence of disturbed gene expression patterns and behavioral findings in subjects with either PWS or Angelman syndrome with different genetic deletion subtypes implicating genes within the BP1 and BP2 genomic region, Burnside *et al.* [13] summarized the literature and surveyed the first large cohort of patients presenting for genetic testing using high resolution microarrays. They found that 0.86% of the approximate 17,000 individuals had an abnormality (deletion or duplication) of the 15q11.2 BP1–BP2 region. Specifically, 69 subjects were found with the 15q11.2 microdeletion and 77 subjects were found with a microduplication of the same region. They proposed that this genomic area was a susceptibility region for neurological dysfunction, impaired development and characteristic phenotypic features which was initially raised by Butler *et al.* [5] in a study of PWS individuals with the larger 15q11–q13 type I deletion including the four genes in the BP1 and BP2 area and having a more severe behavior phenotype compared with those with the smaller type II deletion. Collectively, they summarized that a deletion involving this genomic region correlated with language or motor delays, behavioral problems, autism, seizures and occasionally mild dysmorphic features. The collection of clinical findings in the microdeletion in a large cohort of patients with the 15q11.2 BP1–BP2 presenting for genetic services supported the original observations by Butler *et al.* [14] of behavioral disturbances seen in PWS patients with the larger 15q11–q13 type I deletion compared with the smaller type II deletion which stimulated interest in additional studies of this chromosome region and, hence, coined the Burnside-Butler syndrome.

Preliminary clinical information about the 15q11.2 microdeletion alone without PWS was first reported by Murthy *et al.* [15] in 2007 in two individuals in a consanguineous family and later by Doornbos *et al.* [16] in 2009 in nine individuals. The vast majority of their combined subjects presented with behavioral or neurological problems. Later, Abdelmoity *et al.* [17] reported a cohort of 1654 consecutive pediatric patients presenting with a range of neurological disorders and found that 21% or 1.27% of the patients carried a 15q11.2 BP1–BP2 deletion. They found that 87.5% of the patients with the deletion had developmental delay or intellectual disability. More recently, Cafferkey *et al.* [18] presented data from 14,605 patients (primarily pediatric) referred for genetic testing using microarray analysis and found 83 (0.57%) with the 15q11.2 BP1–BP2 microdeletion. The majority of their patients presented with some form of behavioral disturbance or developmental/motor delays as summarized by Burnside *et al.* [13]. The area between BP1 and BP2 is approximately 500 kb in size and includes the *NIPA1, NIPA2, TUBGCP5,* and *CYFIP1* genes and prone to both microdeletions and microduplications. In this review, we summarize information regarding the 15q11.2 BP1–BP2 microdeletion. A review of information regarding the microduplication is beyond the scope of this report.

Chai *et al.* [19] showed that these four genes are highly conserved and biallelically expressed. *NIPA1* or non-imprinted in Prader-Willi/Angelman syndrome 1 gene is the best studied gene within this region and associated with autosomal dominant hereditary spastic paraplegia [20,21]. There has been no case to date where haploinsufficiency of *NIPA1* due to a deletion has led to hereditary spastic paraplegia. *NIPA1* also mediates Mg^{2+} transport and is highly expressed in neuronal tissue [22]. The *NIPA2* or non-imprinted in Prader-Willi/Angelman syndrome 2 gene is used in renal Mg^{2+} transport [22]. Jiang *et al.* [23] examined patients with childhood absence epilepsy and found mutations in *NIPA2* with unknown functional effects. The *TUBGCP5* gene or tubulin gamma complex associated protein 5 gene is involved in neurobehavioral disorders including ADHD and OCD [24]. The final gene within this region is *CYFIP1* or cytoplasmic fragile X mental retardation 1 (FMR1) interacting protein 1 gene. This gene product interacts with FMRP in a ribonucleoprotein complex. FMRP is the product of the *FMR1* gene which is associated with fragile X syndrome, the most common cause of familial intellectual disability that primarily affects males [25]. Both of these gene products play important roles in the regulation of brain mRNAs [24]. Bozdagi *et al.* [26] showed that haploinsufficiency of *CYFIP1* resembles important aspects found in knockout FMR1 mice.

Not all individuals with defects within the 15q11.2 band (*i.e.*, microdeletions or microduplications) share a clinical phenotype or are clinically affected. Therefore, this region contains genetic material showing incomplete penetrance or low penetrance of pathogenicity along with variable expressivity. For example, a review of reported data from control cohorts (n = 66,462 subjects) summarized to date show that about 0.25% of controls are found with the 15q11.2 BP1–BP2 microdeletion [18,27–31]. The penetrance of the 15q11.2 BP1–BP2 microdeletion has also been estimated at 10.4% [28] or an approximate two fold increase over the general population risk but may be due to paucity of inheritance data. Other estimates have been lower but results consistently show this region to play a role in autism [32]. The penetrance for the 15q11.2 microdeletion is low compared to other microdeletion syndromes such as the 16p11.2 deletion with a penetrance estimated at 62.4% [28]. A higher penetrance is often seen in copy number variants (CNVs) that have higher *de novo* frequencies while low penetrance estimates may reflect a subclinical presentation or manifestation of features that are recognized as components of disorders such as neuropsychiatric disturbances in parents of affected individuals (e.g., autism in 15q11.2 BP1–BP2 deletion) or in control cohorts. Not only are microarray studies needed on other family members (and parents) of those with the 15q11.2 BP1–BP2 deletion but also neuropsychiatric and behavioral testing as well to appreciate the variability of expression and level of penetrance. The review of literature from six published reports summarized by Cafferkey *et al.* [18] regarding information on the inheritance of the 15q11.2 BP1–BP2 microdeletion indicates that 22/43 (51%) of individuals with the microdeletion, where parental data were available, inherited their deletion from an apparently healthy parent while 10/29 (35%) of individuals inherited their deletion from an abnormal parent [13,15–17,33,34]. The phenotypic information was unavailable or incomplete for all parents found to carry the deletion. The reported *de novo* deletion frequency ranged from 1/21 (5%) [13] to 2/9 (22%) [16] in subjects reviewed by Cafferkey *et al.* [18]. It would be of importance to undertake DNA sequencing analyses of the 15q11.2 BP1–BP2 genomic region to identify subtle deletions or mutations of the non-deleted allele and determine the genetic status of this "normal allele". Other modifying genes outside of the chromosome region may also play a role and will require further investigations.

Recently, individuals have been reported with the 15q11.2 BP1–BP2 microdeletion and additional non-neurological clinical findings. These findings included congenital cataracts [14,35], proximal esophageal atresia and distal tracheoesophageal fistula (type C) [35] and congenital arthrogryposis [36]. These clinical reports lend support for further phenotypic expansion of this susceptibility region impacted by the 15q11.2 BP1–BP2 microdeletion. Our report will focus on the review of the clinical features now recognized in this microdeletion syndrome.

2. Results and Discussion

2.1. *Growth and Development*

A review of the literature on growth and development in individuals with 15q11.2 BP1–BP2 microdeletions involving a susceptibility region for neurological dysfunction with general developmental and motor delay with speech problems as primary components of this disorder. General developmental delay occurred in 73% of individuals and speech delay occurred in 67% as reported in the literature suggesting characteristic features for this microdeletion syndrome (see Table 1). These features may correlate with the neuronal components of the genes within this deleted region. *NIPA1*, *NIPA2*, and *CYFIP1* are highly expressed in neuronal tissue of the central nervous system and *TUBGCP5* is highly expressed in the subthalamic nuclei [22,24].

Motor delay and microcephaly were considered important features of this microdeletion syndrome after a review of the literature. Motor delay was seen in 42% of individuals and microcephaly was seen in 24%. Occasional features found were intrauterine growth retardation (18%), short stature (10%), and macrocephaly (8%) (see Table 1).

2.2. *Dysmorphic Features*

A review of the literature on the dysmorphic features for those individuals with the 15q11.2 BP1–BP2 microdeletion or Burnside-Butler syndrome showed that this disorder does not appear to have a clear dysmorphic phenotype (see Table 2). This is supported by studies by Butler *et al.* [5] in examining individuals with Prader-Willi syndrome with 15q11–q13 type I deletion or type II deletion and observing behavioral and cognitive differences but not in growth parameters or other clinical findings indicating that the four genes present within the BP1–BP2 genomic area and when disturbed can lead to neurological or behavioral outcomes.

2.3. *Intelligence and Academic Achievement*

General, non-specified, dysmorphic features were seen in 55 out of 141 individuals or 39% of those reported within the literature. The only common dysmorphic feature found from a review of the literature was palatal abnormalities with 46% of individuals being reported with these findings. Occasional dysmorphic features included broad forehead (21%), hypertelorism (18%), slender fingers (15%), pectus excavatum (13%), plagiocephaly (10%), dysmorphic nose (8%), dysmorphic teeth (8%), and contractures/arthrogryposis (8%). Reported dysmorphic features that, at present, are uncommon or not associated with this syndrome based on a literature review and include short fingers (5%), long narrow face (3%), small face (3%), and hypotelorism (3%) (see Table 2).

Intelligence and academic achievement for individuals with 15q11.2 BP1–BP2 microdeletions were reviewed (see Table 3). Common reported features included writing difficulties (60%), memory problems (60%), reading difficulties (57%), and a verbal IQ score equal to or below 75 (50%). However, very few individuals were reported within the literature regarding these findings so further studies are needed to determine if they are associated findings. Occasional findings within the literature included intellectual disability (37%) and performance IQ which was equal to or below 75 (33%). There were 43 out of 116 individuals reported within the literature who had intellectual disability; however, there were only 1 out of 3 individuals reportedly with a low performance IQ. Stefansson *et al.* [38] found a modest effect on verbal IQ (effect = 0.38, $p = 0.033$) and performance IQ (effect = 0.43, $p = 0.018$) from the 15q11.2 deletion.

Table 1. Literature Review of Growth and Development for Individuals with Chromosome 15q11.2 BP1–BP2 Microdeletion Syndrome.

Feature	Murthy *et al.* [15]	Doornbos *et al.* [16]	Von der Lippe *et al.* [34]	Burnside *et al.* [13]	Abdelmoity *et al.* [17]	Madrigal *et al.* [33]	Wong *et al.* [35]	Cafferkey *et al.* [18]	Usrey *et al.* [36]	Rudd *et al.* [37]	Jerkovich & Butler [14]	Total (%)
IUGR [1]	0/1	3/9	0/5	N/A	N/A	N/A	1/2	N/A	0/2	0/2	0/1	4/22 (18)
Short stature	0/1	1/9	1/5	N/A	N/A	N/A	0/2	N/A	0/2	N/A	0/1	2/20 (10)
Microcephaly	0/1	1/9	0/5	N/A	4/16	2/2	0/2	N/A	1/2	N/A	1/1	9/38 (24)
Macrocephaly	0/1	0/9	1/5	N/A	2/16	0/2	0/2	N/A	0/2	N/A	0/1	3/38 (8)
Developmental delay (general)	2/2	7/8	4/7	33/56	13/15 *	2/2	0/2	65/77	N/A	0/2	0/1	**126/172 (73)**
Motor delay	1/2	8/9	5/7	20/56	N/A	2/2	1/2	29/77	N/A	0/2	0/1	66/158 (42)
Speech delay	2/2	8/8	5/5	44/49	N/A	2/2	0/2	37/77	N/A	0/2	1/1	**99/148 (67)**

[1] Intrauterine growth retardation; * indicated both Intellectual disability or Global developmental delay; Bold indicate categories that represent 50% or greater incidence within the literature.

Table 2. Literature Review of Dysmorphic Features for Individuals with Chromosome 15q11.2 BP1–BP2 Microdeletion Syndrome.

Feature	Doornbos *et al.* [16]	Von der Lippe *et al.* [34]	Burnside *et al.* [13]	Abdelmoity *et al.* [17]	Madrigal *et al.* [33]	Wong *et al.* [35]	Cafferkey *et al.* [18]	Usrey *et al.* [36]	Rudd *et al.* [37]	Jerkovich & Butler [14]	Total (%)
Dysmorphism, unspecified	N/A	N/A	27/56	N/A	N/A	N/A	28/83	N/A	0/2	N/A	55/141 (39)
Plagiocephaly	4/9	0/7	N/A	0/16	0/2	0/2	N/A	0/2	N/A	0/1	4/39 (10)
Broad forehead	5/9	0/7	N/A	1/16	2/2	0/2	N/A	0/2	N/A	0/1	8/39 (21)
Long narrow face	0/9	1/7	N/A	0/16	0/2	0/2	N/A	0/2	N/A	0/1	1/39 (3)
Small face	0/9	1/7	N/A	0/16	0/2	0/2	N/A	0/2	N/A	0/1	1/39 (3)
Hypertelorism	5/9	1/7	N/A	1/16	0/2	0/2	N/A	0/2	N/A	0/1	7/39 (18)
Hypotelorism	0/9	1/7	N/A	0/16	0/2	0/2	N/A	0/2	N/A	0/1	1/39 (3)
Abnormal nose	0/9	2/7	N/A	1/16	0/2	0/2	N/A	0/2	N/A	0/1	3/39 (8)
Dysmorphic ears	6/9	0/7	N/A	1/16	2/2	0/2	N/A	0/2	N/A	1/1	9/39 (46)
Palatal abnormalities	4/9	0/7	N/A	2/16	2/2	1/2	N/A	0/2	N/A	0/1	9/39 (46)
Abnormal teeth	0/9	2/7	N/A	1/16	0/2	0/2	N/A	0/2	N/A	0/1	3/39 (8)
Pectus excavatum	2/9	0/7	N/A	1/16	0/2	1/2	N/A	0/2	N/A	1/1	5/39 (13)
Contractures/arthrogryposis	0/9	1/7	N/A	0/16	0/2	0/2	N/A	2/2	N/A	0/1	3/39 (8)
Short fingers	0/9	1/7	N/A	1/16	0/2	0/2	N/A	0/2	N/A	0/1	2/39 (5)
Slender fingers	5/9	1/7	N/A	0/16	0/2	0/2	N/A	0/2	N/A	0/1	6/39 (15)

2.4. *Behavioral and Psychiatric Problems*

Behavioral features including autism spectrum disorder and schizophrenia have been studied as features of the 15q11.2 BP1–BP2 microdeletion [32,33,37–40]. A review of the behavioral and psychiatric features reported within the literature found that 55% of those reported had general behavior problems that were not otherwise specified (see Table 4). Common behavioral features included Attention Deficit Disorder or Attention Deficit Hyperactivity Disorder (35%), Autism Spectrum Disorder (27%), obsessive compulsive disorder (26%), self-injurious behaviors (26%), oppositional defiant disorder (24%), and schizophrenia or paranoid psychosis (20%). Studies have been performed to determine if the 15q11.2 BP1–BP2 microdeletion is a susceptibility locus for schizophrenia [37–40]. Rees *et al.* [40] found a significant association between the microdeletion and schizophrenia with the frequency of individuals having schizophrenia and the microdeletion from their study was 0.64 (44/6882). The 15q11.2 BP1–BP2 microdeletion has also been studied regarding potential susceptibility for autism [32]. Chaste *et al.* [32] found a small risk regarding this microdeletion and autism but a greater effect on the autism phenotype in males and when maternally inherited. They reported an overall modest effect for this copy number variant for autism in studying a sample of 2525 families with autism [32]. They suggested that carriers may need additional copy number variants along with the 15q11.2 microdeletion in order to be diagnosed with autism [32]. Occasionally, reported behavioral features within the literature included an unusually happy expression (12%) and anxiety (6%) [16,34].

2.5. *Other Related Medical Concerns*

The 15q11.2 BP1–BP2 microdeletion or Burnside-Butler syndrome has been reported with various medical concerns or conditions (see Table 5). A review of the literature indicated that 43% of these individuals had abnormal brain imaging (MRI, EEG, *etc.*) with common clinical features of seizures or epilepsy (26%) and ataxia or balance (coordination) problems (28%). The medical literature surrounding this microdeletion syndrome and seizures indicate that this chromosomal anomaly may be a risk factor for epilepsy [29,41–43]. Occasional features seen within the literature regarding medical conditions included congenital heart defect (9%), genital abnormalities (7%), recurrent infections (7%), cataracts (4%), hearing loss or impairment (4%), tracheoesophageal fistula (2%), and omphalocele (2%). Whether these additional findings represent further phenotypic expansion of the syndrome as raised by others is unknown [14,35,36].

Table 3. Literature Review of Intelligence and Academic Achievement for Individuals with Chromosome 15q11.2 BP1–BP2 Microdeletion Syndrome.

Feature	Murthy *et al.* [15]	Doornbos *et al.* [16]	De Kovel *et al.* [29]	Von der Lippe *et al.* [34]	Burnside *et al.* [13]	Abdelmoity *et al.* [17]	Madrigal *et al.* [33]	Mullen *et al.* [43]	Jahn *et al.* [42]	Usrey *et al.* [36]	Rudd *et al.* [37]	Jerkovich & Butler [14]	Total (%)
ID */FSIQ [1] ≤ 75/special education	2/2	6/12	0/11	5/11	11/49	13/15	2/2	1/6	2/3	1/1	0/3	0/1	43/116 (37)
Verbal IQ ≤ 75	N/A	1/1	N/A	N/A	N/A	N/A	N/A	N/A	N/A	N/A	1/3	N/A	**2/4 (50)**
Performance IQ ≤ 75	N/A	N/A	N/A	N/A	N/A	N/A	N/A	N/A	N/A	N/A	1/3	N/A	1/3 (33)
Reading difficulties	N/A	N/A	N/A	4/7	N/A	N/A	N/A	N/A	N/A	N/A	N/A	N/A	**4/7 (57)**
Writing difficulties	N/A	N/A	N/A	3/5	N/A	N/A	N/A	N/A	N/A	N/A	N/A	N/A	**3/5 (60)**
Memory problems	N/A	N/A	N/A	2/4	N/A	N/A	N/A	N/A	N/A	N/A	N/A	1/1	**3/5 (60)**

* Intellectual disability; [1] Full scale intelligence quotient; Bold indicate categories that represent 50% or greater incidence within the literature.

Table 4. Literature Review of Behavioral and Psychiatric Problems for Individuals with Chromosome 15q11.2 BP1–BP2 Microdeletion Syndrome.

Feature	Murthy *et al.* [15]	Doornbos *et al.* [16]	Von der Lippe *et al.* [34]	Burnside *et al.* [13]	Abdelmoity *et al.* [17]	Madrigal *et al.* [33]	Cafferkey *et al.* [18]	Rudd *et al.* [37]	Jerkovich & Butler [14]	Total (%)
General behavior problems, unspecified	2/2	N/A	N/A	35/56	N/A	2/4	35/73	N/A	1/1	**75/136 (55)**
Autism Spectrum Disorder	1/2	4/9	1/7	14/49	2/16	2/4	19/73	N/A	0/1	43/161 (27)
Schizophrenia/paranoid psychosis	N/A	0/9	1/7	N/A	N/A	N/A	N/A	3/3	0/1	4/20 (20)
OCD [1]	0/2	2/9	0/7	16/49 *	N/A	N/A	N/A	N/A	0/1	18/68 (26)
ODD [2]	0/2	0/9	0/7	16/49 *	N/A	N/A	N/A	N/A	0/1	16/68 (24)
ADD [3]/ADHD [4]	2/2	2/9	0/7	16/49	7/12	N/A	N/A	N/A	1/1	28/80 (35)
Self-injurious behaviors	0/2	2/9	0/7	16/49 *	N/A	N/A	N/A	N/A	0/1	18/68 (26)
Anxiety	N/A	0/9	1/7	N/A	N/A	N/A	N/A	N/A	0/1	1/17 (6)
Happy expression	N/A	2/9	0/7	N/A	N/A	N/A	N/A	N/A	0/1	2/17 (12)

[1] Obsessive compulsive disorder; [2] Oppositional defiant disorder; [3] Attention deficit disorder; [4] Attention deficit hyperactivity disorder; * indicates obsessive compulsive disorder, oppositional defiant disorder, self-injury, tantrums, *etc*; Bold indicate categories that represent 50% or greater incidence within the literature.

Table 5. Literature Review of Other Related Medical Concerns for Individuals with Chromosome 15q11.2 BP1–BP2 Microdeletion Syndrome.

Feature	Murthy *et al.* [15]	Doornbos *et al.* [16]	De Kovel *et al.* [29]	Von der Lippe *et al.* [34]	Burnside *et al.* [13]	Abdelmoity *et al.* [17]	Madrigal *et al.* [33]	Wong *et al.* [35]	Mullen *et al.* [43]	Cafferkey *et al.* [18]	Jahn *et al.* [42]	Usrey *et al.* [36]	Rudd *et al.* [37]	Jerkovich & Butler [14]	Total (%)
Seizures/epilepsy	0/2	2/8	8/23	0/7	14/56	2/16	0/2	0/2	6/6	13/83	4/5	1/2	0/3	0/1	57/216 (26)
Cataracts	0/1	0/9	N/A	0/7	N/A	0/16	0/2	1/2	N/A	N/A	0/3	0/2	0/3	1/1	2/46 (4)
Congenital heart defect	0/1	2/9	N/A	0/7	N/A	0/16	0/2	2/2	N/A	N/A	0/3	0/2	0/3	0/1	4/46 (9)
Genital abnormalities	0/1	2/9	N/A	1/7	N/A	0/16	0/2	0/2	N/A	N/A	0/3	0/2	N/A	0/1	3/46 (7)
Recurrent infections	0/1	2/9	N/A	0/7	N/A	N/A	0/2	0/2	N/A	N/A	0/3	0/2	N/A	0/1	2/30 (7)
Ataxia/balance issues	1/2	4/8	N/A	0/7	15/49	N/A	2/2	0/2	N/A	N/A	0/3	0/1	0/3	0/1	22/78 (28)
TE fistula	0/1	0/9	N/A	0/7	N/A	0/16	0/2	1/2	N/A	N/A	0/3	0/2	0/3	0/1	1/49 (2)
Hearing loss/impairment	0/1	1/9	N/A	0/7	N/A	1/16	0/2	0/2	N/A	N/A	0/3	0/2	0/3	0/1	2/49 (4)
Omphalocele	0/1	1/9	N/A	0/7	N/A	0/16	0/2	0/2	N/A	N/A	0/3	0/2	0/3	0/1	1/49 (2)
Abnormal brain imaging	N/A	0/4	N/A	1/2	20/56 *	2/3	N/A	N/A	N/A	N/A	5/5	1/2	3/3	N/A	32/75 (43)

* indicates cases with insomnia, abnormal brain MRI or EEG, *etc*.

3. Conclusions

The 15q11.2 BP1–BP2 microdeletion (Burnside-Butler) syndrome is now a recognized condition with over 200 individuals identified from the literature using chromosomal microarray analysis. Clinically, neurological dysfunction, developmental and language delay are the most commonly associated findings followed by motor delay, ADD/ADHD and autism spectrum disorder showing incomplete penetrance and variable expressivity. The four non-imprinted biallelically expressed genes (*TUBGCP5, CFYIP1, NIPA1, NIPA2*) in this microdeletion were initially noted to impact severity of clinical presentation and neurological impairment in two classical genomic imprinting disorders (*i.e.*, Prader-Willi and Angelman syndromes) with typical 15q11–q13 deletions depending on the absence or presence of the genomic area between breakpoints BP1 and BP2 containing the four genes leading to studies recognizing this syndrome. The 15q11.2 BP1–BP2 microdeletion syndrome has a reported *de novo* frequency between 5%–22%, with 51% having inherited the microdeletion from an apparently unaffected parent and 35% having inherited the microdeletion from an affected parent. Low penetrance estimates may relate to subclinical manifestations of neuropsychiatric/behavioral problems or incomplete information about the parents of individuals with 15q11.2 BP1–BP2 microdeletion or members of control cohorts [44]. From reported patient cohorts presenting for genetic services and microarray analysis, this microdeletion syndrome can now be recognized as the most common cytogenetic abnormality found in autism spectrum disorder.

Acknowledgments: We thank Carla Meister for preparation of this manuscript and support from NICHD (National Institute of Child Health and Human Development) HD02528 grant.

Author Contributions: Merlin G. Butler conceived the study and wrote and contributed to the manuscript. Devin M. Cox reviewed the literature and wrote and contributed to the content of the manuscript.

References

1. Locke, D.P.; Segraves, R.; Nicholls, R.D.; Schwartz, S.; Pinkel, D.; Alberston, D.G.; Eichler, E.E. BAC microarray analysis of 15q–q13 rearrangements and the impact of segmental duplications. *J. Med. Genet.* **2004**, *41*, 175–182. [CrossRef] [PubMed]
2. Pujana, M.A.; Nadal, M.; Guitart, M.; Armengol, L.; Gratacos, M.; Estivill, X. Human Chromosome 15q11–q14 regions of rearrangements contain clusters of LCR15 duplicons. *Eur. J. Hum. Genet.* **2002**, *10*, 26–35. [CrossRef] [PubMed]
3. Eichler, E.E. Masquerading repeats: Paralogous pitfalls of the human genome. *Genome Res.* **1998**, *8*, 758–762. [PubMed]
4. Butler, M.G.; Fischer, W.; Kibiryeva, N.; Bittel, D.C. Array comparative genomic hybridization (aCGH) analysis in Prader-Willi syndrome. *Am. J. Med. Genet. A* **2008**, *146A*, 854–860. [CrossRef]
5. Butler, M.G.; Bittel, D.C.; Kibiryeva, N.; Talebizadeh, Z.; Thompson, T. Behavioral differences among subjects with Prader-Willi syndrome and type I or type II deletion and maternal disomy. *Pediatrics* **2004**, *113*, 565–573. [CrossRef] [PubMed]
6. Bittel, D.C.; Kibiryeva, N.; Butler, M.G. Expression of 4 genes between chromosome 15 breakpoints 1 and 2 and behavioral outcomes in Prader-Willi syndrome. *Pediatrics* **2006**, *118*, e1276–e1283. [CrossRef] [PubMed]
7. Hartley, S.L.; Maclean, W.E., Jr.; Butler, M.G.; Zarcone, J.; Thompson, T. Maladaptive behaviors and risk factors among the genetic subtypes of Prader-Willi syndrome. *Am. J. Med. Genet. A* **2005**, *136*, 140–145. [CrossRef] [PubMed]
8. Milner, K.M.; Craig, E.E.; Thompson, R.J.; Veltman, M.W.; Thomas, N.S.; Roberts, S.; Bellamy, M.; Curran, S.R.; Sporikou, C.M.; Bolton, P.F. Prader-Willi syndrome: Intellectual abilities and behavioural features by genetic subtype. *J. Child Psychol. Psychiatry* **2005**, *46*, 1089–1096. [CrossRef] [PubMed]
9. Sahoo, T.; Bacino, C.A.; German, J.R.; Shaw, C.A.; Bird, L.M.; Kimonis, V.; Anselm, I.; Waisbren, S.; Beaudet, A.L.; Peters, S.U. Identification of novel deletions of 15q11q13 in Angelman syndrome by array-CGH: Molecular characterization and genotype-phenotype correlations. *Eur. J. Hum. Genet.* **2007**, *15*, 943–949. [CrossRef] [PubMed]

10. Varela, M.C.; Kok, F.; Setian, N.; Kim, C.A.; Koiffmann, C.P. Impact of molecular mechanisms, including deletion size, on Prader-Willi syndrome phenotype: Study of 75 patients. *Clin. Genet.* **2005**, *67*, 47–52. [CrossRef] [PubMed]
11. Valente, K.D.; Varela, M.C.; Koiffmann, C.P.; Andrade, J.Q.; Grossmann, R.; Kok, F.; Marques-Dias, M.J. Angelman syndrome caused by deletion: A genotype-phenotype correlation determined by breakpoint. *Epilepsy Res.* **2013**, *105*, 234–239. [CrossRef] [PubMed]
12. Dykens, E.M.; Roof, E. Behavior in Prader-Willi syndrome: Relationship to genetic subtypes and age. *J. Child. Psychol. Psychiatry* **2008**, *49*, 1001–1008. [CrossRef] [PubMed]
13. Burnside, R.D.; Pasion, R.; Mikhail, F.M.; Carroll, A.J.; Robin, N.H.; Youngs, E.L.; Gadi, I.K.; Keitges, E.; Jaswaney, V.L.; Papenhausen, P.R.; *et al.* Microdeletion/microduplication of proximal 15q11.2 between BP1 and BP2: A susceptibility region for neurological dysfunction including developmental and language delay. *Hum. Genet.* **2011**, *130*, 517–528. [CrossRef] [PubMed]
14. Jerkovich, A.M.; Butler, M.G. Further phenotypic expansion of 15q11.2 BP1–BP2 microdeletion (Burnside-Butler) syndrome. *J. Pediatr. Genet.* **2014**, *3*, 41–44. [PubMed]
15. Murthy, S.K.; Nygren, A.O.H.; El Shakankiry, H.M.; Schouten, J.P.; Al Khayat, A.I.; Righa, A.; Al Ali, M.T. Detection of a novel familial deletion of four genes between BP1 and BP2 of the Prader-Willi/Angelman syndrome critical region by oligo-array CGH in a child with neurological disorder and speech impairment. *Cytogenet. Genome Res.* **2007**, *116*, 135–140. [CrossRef] [PubMed]
16. Doornbos, M.; Sikkema-Raddatz, B.; Ruijvenkamp, C.A.L.; Dijkhuizen, T.; Bijlsma, E.K.; Gijsbers, A.C.J.; Hihorst-Hofstee, Y.; Hordijk, R.; Verbruggen, K.T.; Kerstjens-Frederikse, W.S.M.; *et al.* Nine patients with a microdeletion 15q11.2 between breakpoints 1 and 2 of the Prader-Willi critical region, possibly associated with behavioral disturbances. *Eur. J. Med. Genet.* **2009**, *52*, 108–115. [CrossRef] [PubMed]
17. Abdelmoity, A.T.; LePichon, J.B.; Nyp, S.S.; Soden, S.E.; Daniel, C.A.; Yu, S. 15q11.2 proximal imbalances associated with a diverse array of neuropsychiatric disorders and mild dysmorphic features. *J. Dev. Behav. Pediatr.* **2012**, *33*, 570–576. [CrossRef] [PubMed]
18. Cafferkey, M.; Ahn, J.W.; Flinter, F.; Ogilvie, C. Phenotypic features in patients with 15q11.2 (BP1–BP2) deletion: Further delineation of an emerging syndrome. *Am. J. Med. Genet. Part A* **2013**, *164A*, 1916–1922. [CrossRef]
19. Chai, J.H.; Locke, D.P.; Greally, J.M.; Knoll, J.H.; Ohta, T.; Dunai, J.; Yavor, A.; Eichler, E.E.; Nicholls, R.D. Identification of four highly conserved genes between breakpoint hotspots BP1 and BP2 of the Prader-Willi/Angelman syndromes deletion region that have undergone evolutionary transposition mediated by flanking duplicons. *Am. J. Hum. Genet.* **2003**, *73*, 898–925. [CrossRef] [PubMed]
20. Chen, S.; Song, C.; Guo, H.; Xu, P.; Huang, W.; Zhou, Y.; Sun, J.; Li, C.X.; Du, Y.; Li, X.; *et al.* Distinct novel mutations affecting the same base in the *NIPA1* gene cause autosomal dominant hereditary spastic paraplegia in two Chinese families. *Hum. Mutat.* **2005**, *25*, 135–141. [CrossRef] [PubMed]
21. Rainier, S.; Chai, J.H.; Tokarz, D.; Nicholls, R.D.; Fink, J.K. *NIPA1* gene mutations cause autosomal dominant hereditary spastic paraplegia (SPG6). *Am. J. Hum. Genet.* **2003**, *73*, 967–971. [CrossRef] [PubMed]
22. Goytain, A.; Hines, R.M.; El-Husseini, A.; Quamme, G.A. NIPA1 (SPG6), the basis for autosomal dominant form of hereditary spastic paraplegia, encodes a functional $Mg2^{+}$ transporter. *J. Biol. Chem.* **2007**, *282*, 8060–8068. [CrossRef] [PubMed]
23. Jiang, Y.; Zhang, Y.; Zhang, P.; Sang, T.; Zhang, F.; Ji, T.; Huang, Q.; Xie, H.; Du, R.; Cai, B.; *et al.* NIPA2 located in 15q11.2 is mutated in patients with childhood absence epilepsy. *Hum. Genet.* **2012**, *131*, 1217–1224. [CrossRef] [PubMed]
24. De Wolf, V.; Brison, N.; Devriendt, K.; Peeters, H. Genetic counseling for susceptibility loci and neurodevelopmental disorders: The del15q11.2 as an example. *Am. J. Med. Genet. Part A* **2013**, *161A*, 2846–2854. [CrossRef]
25. Hagerman, R.J.; Hagerman, P.J. *Fragile X Syndrome: Diagnosis, Treatment and Research*, 3rd ed.; The John Hopkins University Press: Baltimore, MD, USA, 2002.
26. Bozdagi, O.; Sakurai, T.; Dorr, N.; Pilorge, M.; Takahashi, N.; Buxbaum, J.D. Haploinsufficiency of Cyfip1 produces fragile X-like phenotypes in mice. *PLoS One* **2012**, *7*, e42422. [CrossRef] [PubMed]
27. Cooper, G.M.; Coe, B.P.; Girirajan, S.; Rosenfeld, J.A.; Vu, T.; Baker, C.; Williams, C.; Stalker, H.; Hamid, R.; Hannig, V.; *et al.* A copy number variation mobidity map of developmental delay. *Nat. Genet.* **2011**, *43*, 838–846. [CrossRef] [PubMed]

28. Rosenfeld, J.A.; Coe, B.P.; Eichler, E.E.; Cuckle, H.; Shaffer, L.G. Estimates of penetrance for recurrent pathogenic copy-number variants. *Genet Med.* **2013**, *15*, 478–481. [CrossRef] [PubMed]
29. De Kovel, C.G.; Trucks, H.; Helbig, I.; Mefford, H.C.; Baker, C.; Leu, C.; Kluck, C.; Muhle, H.; von Spiczak, S.; Ostertag, P.; *et al.* Recurrent microdeletions at 15q11.2 and 16p13.11 predispose to idiopathic generalized epilepsies. *Brain* **2010**, *133*, 23–32. [CrossRef] [PubMed]
30. Itsara, A.; Cooper, G.M.; Baker, C.; Girirajan, S.; Li, J.; Absher, D.; Krauss, R.M.; Myers, R.M.; Ridker, P.M.; Chasman, D.I.; Mefford, H.; Ying, P.; Nickerson, D.A.; Eichler, E.E. Population analysis of large copy number variants and hotspots of human genetic disease. *Am. J. Hum. Genet.* **2009**, *84*, 148–161. [CrossRef] [PubMed]
31. Stefansson, H.; Rujescu, D.; Cichon, S.; Pietilainen, O.P.; Ingason, A.; Steinberg, S.; Fossdal, R.; Sigurdsson, E.; Sigmundsson, T.; Buizer-Voskamp, J.E.; *et al.* Large recurrent microdeletions associated with schizophrenia. *Nature* **2008**, *455*, 232–236. [CrossRef] [PubMed]
32. Chaste, P.; Sanders, S.J.; Mohan, K.N.; Klei, L.; Song, Y.; Murtha, M.T.; Hus, V.; Lowe, J.K.; Willsey, A.J.; Moreno-De-Luca, D.; *et al.* Modest impact on risk for Autism Spectrum Disorder of rare copy number variants at 15q11.2, specifically breakpoints 1 to 2. *Autism Res.* **2014**, *7*, 355–362. [CrossRef] [PubMed]
33. Madrigal, I.; Rodriguez-Revenga, L.; Xuncla, M.; Mila, M. 15q11.2 microdeletion and FMR1 premutation in a family with intellectual disabilities and autism. *Gene* **2012**, *508*, 92–95. [CrossRef] [PubMed]
34. Von der Lippe, C.; Rustad, C.; Heimdal, K.; Rodningen, O.K. 15q11.2 microdeletion—Seven new patients with delayed development and/or behavioral problems. *Eur. J. Med. Genet.* **2011**, *54*, 357–360. [CrossRef] [PubMed]
35. Wong, D.; Johnson, S.M.; Young, D.; Iwamoto, L.; Sood, S.; Slavin, T.P. Expanding the BP1–BP2 15q11.2 microdeletion phenotype: Tracheoesophageal fistula and congenital cataracts. *Case Rep. Genet.* **2013**, *2003*. [CrossRef]
36. Usrey, K.M.; Williams, C.A.; Dasouki, M.; Fairbrother, L.C.; Butler, M.G. Congenital arthrogryposis: An extension of the 15q11.2 BP1–BP2 microdeletion syndrome? *Case Rep. Genet.* **2014**, *2004*. [CrossRef]
37. Rudd, D.S.; Azelsen, M.; Epping, E.A.; Andreasen, N.C.; Wassink, T.H. A genome-wide CNV analysis of schizophrenia reveals a potential role for a multiple-hit model. *Am. J. Med. Genet. Part. B* **2014**, *165B*, 619–626. [CrossRef]
38. Stefansson, H.; Meyer-Lindenberg, A.; Steinberg, S.; Magnusdottir, B.; Morgen, K.; Arnarsdottir, S.; Bjornsdottir, G.; Walters, G.B.; Jonsdottir, G.A.; Doyle, O.M.; *et al.* CNVs conferring risk of autism or schizophrenia affect cognition in controls. *Nature* **2014**, *505*, 361–366. [CrossRef] [PubMed]
39. Kirov, G.; Grozeva, D.; Norton, N.; Ivanov, D.; Mantripragada, K.K.; Holmans, P.; International Schizophrenia Consortium; Wellcome Trust Case Control Consortium; Craddock, N.; Owen, M.J.; *et al.* Support for the involvement of large copy number variants in the pathogenesis of schizophrenia. *Hum. Mol. Genet.* **2009**, *18*, 1497–1503.
40. Rees, E.; Walters, J.T.R.; Georgieva, L.; Isles, A.R.; Chambert, K.D.; Richards, A.L.; Mahoney-Davies, G.; Legge, S.E.; Moran, J.L.; McCarroll, S.A.; *et al.* Analysis of copy number variations at 15 schizophrenia-associated loci. *Br. J. Psychiatry* **2014**, *204*, 108–114. [CrossRef] [PubMed]
41. Helbig, I.; Hartmann, C.; Mefford, H.C. The unexpected role of copy number variations in juvenile myocolonic epilepsy. *Epilepsy Behav.* **2012**, *28*, S66–S68. [CrossRef]
42. Jahn, J.A.; von Spiczak, S.; Muhle, H.; Obermeier, T.; Franke, A.; Mefford, H.C.; Stephani, U.; Helbig, I. Iterative phenotyping of 15q11.2, 15q13.3 and 16p13.11 microdeletion carriers in pediatric epilepsies. *Epilepsy Res.* **2014**, *108*, 109–116. [CrossRef] [PubMed]
43. Mullen, S.A.; Carvill, G.L.; Bellows, S.; Bayly, M.A.; Berkovic, S.F.; Dibbens, L.M.; Scheffer, I.E.; Mefford, H.C. Copy number variants are frequent in genetic generalized epilepsy with intellectual disability. *Neurology* **2013**, *81*, 1507–1514. [CrossRef] [PubMed]
44. Girirajan, S.; Rosenfeld, J.A.; Cooper, G.M.; Antonacci, F.; Siswara, P.; Itsara, A.; Vives, L.; Walsh, T.; McCarthy, S.E.; Baker, C.; *et al.* A recurrent 16p12.1 microdeletion supports a two-hit model for severe developmental delay. *Nat. Genet.* **2010**, *42*, 203–209. [CrossRef] [PubMed]

14

Phenotypic and Molecular Convergence of 2q23.1 Deletion Syndrome with Other Neurodevelopmental Syndromes Associated with Autism Spectrum Disorder

Sureni V. Mullegama [1], Joseph T. Alaimo [1], Li Chen [1,2] and Sarah H. Elsea [1,*]

[1] Department of Molecular and Human Genetics, Baylor College of Medicine, Houston, TX 77030, USA; mullegam@bcm.edu (S.V.M.); alaimo@bcm.edu (J.T.A.); li.chen@bcm.edu (L.C.)

[2] Department of Cellular and Genetic Medicine, School of Basic Medical Sciences, Fudan University, Shanghai 200032, China

[*] Author to whom correspondence should be addressed; elsea@bcm.edu

Academic Editor: Merlin G. Butler

Abstract: Roughly 20% of autism spectrum disorders (ASD) are syndromic with a well-established genetic cause. Studying the genes involved can provide insight into the molecular and cellular mechanisms of ASD. 2q23.1 deletion syndrome (causative gene, *MBD5*) is a recently identified genetic neurodevelopmental disorder associated with ASD. Mutations in *MBD5* have been found in ASD cohorts. In this study, we provide a phenotypic update on the prevalent features of 2q23.1 deletion syndrome, which include severe intellectual disability, seizures, significant speech impairment, sleep disturbance, and autistic-like behavioral problems. Next, we examined the phenotypic, molecular, and network/pathway relationships between nine neurodevelopmental disorders associated with ASD: 2q23.1 deletion Rett, Angelman, Pitt-Hopkins, 2q23.1 duplication, 5q14.3 deletion, Kleefstra, Kabuki make-up, and Smith-Magenis syndromes. We show phenotypic overlaps consisting of intellectual disability, speech delay, seizures, sleep disturbance, hypotonia, and autistic-like behaviors. Molecularly, MBD5 possibly regulates the expression of *UBE3A*, *TCF4*, *MEF2C*, *EHMT1* and *RAI1*. Network analysis reveals that there could be indirect protein interactions, further implicating function for these genes in common pathways. Further, we show that when *MBD5* and *RAI1* are haploinsufficient, they perturb several common pathways that are linked to neuronal and behavioral development. These findings support further investigations into the molecular and pathway relationships among genes linked to neurodevelopmental disorders and ASD, which will hopefully lead to common points of regulation that may be targeted toward therapeutic intervention.

Keywords: *MBD5*; ASD; networks; overlapping phenotypes; *UBE3A*; *TCF4*; *MEF2C*; *EHMT1*; *RAI1*; transcriptional regulation; pathways; network analysis

---

1. Introduction

Autism spectrum disorder (ASD) is a growing public health concern that affects millions of individuals worldwide [1]. ASD is a broad term encompassing a heterogeneous group of complex, highly heritable neurodevelopmental disorders in which individuals have impairments in social interaction and communication coupled with repetitive and restricted behaviors [2]. Other morbidities such as intellectual disability, epilepsy, neurological disabilities (ataxia and hypotonia), and other behavioral disorders have been associated with ASD [3]. The molecular etiology of ASD involves the interplay of many genes [4]. A contributor to the risk of ASD resides in high-impact rare variants, such as chromosomal abnormalities, copy number variation (CNV), and mutations in genes previously linked to classic monogenenic genetic disorders such as fragile X syndrome (FXS) (MIM 300624), Rett syndrome (RTT) (MIM 312750), Angelman syndrome (AS) (MIM 105830), and Smith-Magenis syndrome (SMS) (MIM 182290) [2,5,6].

With the advancement of genetic diagnostic technologies such as chromosomal microarray analysis, the identification of novel genetic subtypes of ASD and their associated genes have come to light, such as 16p11.2 deletion (MIM 611913, gene unknown), 2q23.1 deletion syndrome (MIM 156200, *MBD5*), Pitt-Hopkins syndrome (PTHS MIM 610954, *TCF4*), 5q14.3 deletion syndrome (MIM 613443, *MEF2C*), and Kleefstra syndrome (MIM 610253, *EHMT1*). Many of these genes are involved in neuronal functions (synaptic transmission and cell-cell interaction), chromatin modification, methylation, and transcriptional regulation [7]. The identification of these disease genes associated with ASD has led to many theories regarding the pathogenesis of ASD. One theory that has garnered support from some in the ASD community proposes that the pathogenesis is due to the disruption of neurodevelopment, which is triggered by genes with global effects on expression (chromatin modification, methylation, and transcriptional regulation) of other genes that are specifically involved in neuronal functions [7]. Further, these genes are thought to be most likely involved in common ASD-associated pathways such as cell adhesion, cadherin signaling, WNT signaling, PTEN signaling, mTOR signaling, PI3K-Akt signaling, and circadian rhythm [4,8].

Corroborating studies have suggested that a disease phenotype is rarely a consequence of an abnormality in a single gene product but a reflection of dysfunction in a variety of genes and pathobiological processes that interact in complex networks and pathways [9–11]. Many neurodevelopmental genetic disorders associated with ASD share common phenotypic features despite their genetic heterogeneity, which further suggests that these genes may act together in complex interconnected pathways that, when perturbed, manifest similar phenotypes.

2q23.1 deletion syndrome (MIM 156200), previously known as "pseudo-Angelman syndrome," was initially identified in one of the first comparative genomic hybridization (CGH) surveys of developmental disorders [12]. Patients are characterized by severe intellectual disability, seizures, significant speech impairment, and autistic-like behavioral problems [13]. 2q23.1 deletion syndrome is caused by deletion in the chromosomal region 2q23.1 or gene specific deletions in methy-CpG-binding domain 5 (MBD5, MIM 611472). Deletions of 2q23.1 range from small deletions of 38 kb to >19 Mb [13]. While some large deletions extend in the chromosomal region 2q22.3, these deletions do not include the zinc finger E box-binding homeobox 2 gene (*ZEB2*, MIM 605802), the causative gene for Mowat-Wilson syndrome (MIM 235730). *MBD5* is part of the methyl-CpG-binding domain (MBD) family, which consists of a well-known ASD-associated gene, *MECP2*, which is the causative gene in Rett syndrome. MBD5 has two known isoforms [14] and is thought to have a role in epigenetic modification [7,14–18]. Further, MBD5/Mbd5 has been shown to regulate expression of genes, suggesting it acts as a transcription factor [15,17,19].

In this study, we conducted a comprehensive phenotypic overview of 2q23.1 deletion syndrome and then briefly examined the phenotypic and molecular relationships between 2q23.1 deletion syndrome and neurodevelopmental disorders associated with ASDs. Finally, we examined the pathways in common between 2q23.1 deletion syndrome and Smith-Magenis syndrome.

2. Results and Discussion

2.1. 2q23.1 Deletion Syndrome Clinical Review

To further update our phenotypic knowledge of 2q23.1 deletion syndrome, we surveyed the most prevalent phenotypic features of all 2q23.1 deletion cases (*MBD5*-specific deletions and 2q23.1 deletions) using the two largest phenotypic studies on 2q23.1 deletion syndrome [13,20] and case reports that were published subsequently after these studies [15,16,19,21–24]. Overall, phenotypic findings are comparable across the 74 cases reported [13,15,16,20–23,25–30], and the frequently reported neurological, neurobehavioral, and craniofacial features associated within syndrome are seen and listed in Figure 1 and Table 1 [13,20]. Neurological and behavioral features are the most prevalent findings in 2q23.1 deletion syndrome patients, while the other abnormalities, such as craniofacial abnormalities and skeletal abnormalities, are not consistently the same among individuals with this deletion (Figure 1).

Developmental delay and motor delay were present in 100% of the 2q23.1 deletion cases studied. Previous reports have identified seizures and severe language impairment as two primary features of 2q23.1 deletion syndrome, and we further show that 94.4% and 84.9% of the 2q23.1 deletion cases exhibit these features, respectively [13,15,16,20–23,25–30]. Infantile hypotonia and feeding difficulties were also present in greater than 85% of reported 2q23.1 deletion cases (Table 1). Autistic-like behaviors and behavioral problems were reported in 98.4%. The most prevalent behaviors were distractibility/short attention span (100%) and sleep disturbances (78.8%). These studies also showed that there is a clear lack of precise documentation by clinicians regarding the exact autistic-like behaviors of individuals with 2q23.1 deletion syndrome. Nonetheless, impairments in communication, social interaction and repetitive behaviors are key behavioral criteria for ASD, which are also present in the majority of 2q23.1 deletion syndrome patients. Overall, these patients should be assessed by ADI-R and ADOS to identify specific ASD phenotypes present in individuals with 2q23.1 deletion syndrome. It is apparent that while craniofacial abnormalities are present in children with 2q23.1 deletion, the features are variable across the population. While mild dysmorphic craniofacial features were present at >70% in reported cases, including broad forehead, arched/thick eyebrows, eye abnormalities, nasal abnormalities, downturned corners of the mouth, open mouth, thin upper lip, tented upper lip, and thick or everted lower lip, a consistent and thorough evaluation, measurement, and documentation of craniofacial and skeletal abnormalities is necessary for an accurate and full understanding of the commonly observed associations with 2q23.1 deletion syndrome (Figure 1).

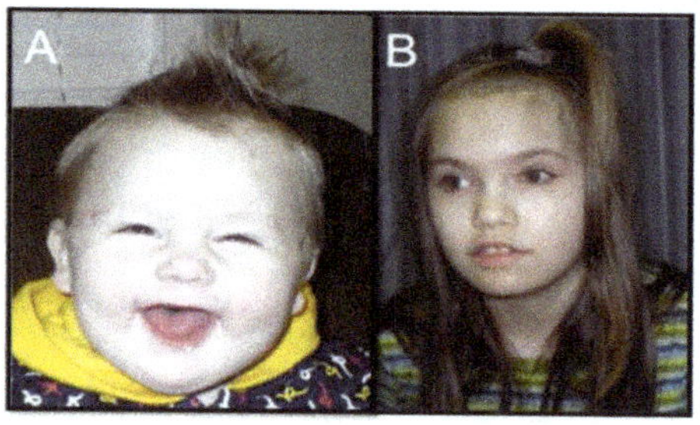

Figure 1. Craniofacial features of 2q23.1 deletion syndrome. Children with 2q23.1 deletion syndrome exhibit broad forehead, open mouth, and tented, thin upper lip. (**A**) 1 year old male. (**B**) 13 year old female. Approvals from parents were obtained to publish these photos.

Table 1. Prevalent features of 2q23.1 deletion syndrome.

2q23.1 Deletion [1]		
Common Features	**Frequency**	**Percentage (%)**
Neurological		
Developmental delay	74/74	100
Motor delay	45/45	100
Language impairment	51/54	94.4
Ataxia	22/32	68.7
Infantile hypotonia	28/30	93.3
Infantile feeding difficulties	17/20	85.0
Seizures	45/53	84.9
Behavioral		
Autistic-like behaviors	60/61	98.4
Behavioral problems	60/61	98.4
Aggression/temper tantrums	13/21	62.9
Distractibility/short attention span	21/21	100
Hyperphagia	8/16	50.0
Self-injurious behaviors	21/33	63.6
Sleep disturbances	41/52	78.8

Table 1. *Cont.*

2q23.1 Deletion [1]		
Common Features	**Frequency**	**Percentage (%)**
Neurological		
Growth/Endocrine Abnormalities		
Postnatal growth retardation	25/51	49.0
Obesity	6/17	35.3
Short stature (<5th percentile)	30/43	69.8
Craniofacial Abnormalities		
Cranium		
Brachycephaly	12/36	33.3
Broad forehead	21/30	70.0
Microcephaly	28/46	60.9
Eyes		
Arched/thick eyebrows	19/24	79.2
Myopia/hypermetropia/corrective lenses	8/11	72.7
Synophrys	13/28	46.4
Nose/Ear		
Nasal abnormalities	42/43	97.7
Outer ear abnormalities	22/29	75.9
Mouth/Chin		
Dental abnormalities	18/35	51.4
Downturned corners of the mouth	20/28	71.4
Macroglossia or protruding tongue	8/33	24.2
Micrognathia/retrognathia	16/30	53.3
Open mouth	26/34	76.5
Tented upper lip	19/30	63.3
Thin upper lip	21/28	75.0
Thick or everted lower lip	19/26	73.1
Wide mouth	15/25	60.0
Skeletal Extremity Abnormalities		
Brachydactyly	14/33	42.4
Clinodactyly, 5th finger	24/38	63.2
Sandal gap	12/32	37.5
Short fifth digit	16/37	43.2
Small hands and feet	25/37	67.6

[1] Cases came from [13,15,20–24].

2.2. Overlapping Phenotypes across 2q23.1 Deletion Syndrome and Other Autism Spectrum Disorders

2q23.1 deletion has been aptly termed a "potent masquerader", wherein the clinical features of the disorder were initially thought to be due to other well-known genetic syndromes [20]. Since the neurodevelopmental and behavioral characteristics common to 2q23.1 deletion syndrome are nonspecific and commonly found in multiple other neurodevelopmental disorders associated with ASD [20], many 2q23.1 deletion syndrome patients were initially tested for a variety of disorders, including Rett, Angelman, and Smith-Magenis syndromes [26]. As previously mentioned, Mowat-Wilson syndrome and 2q23.1 deletion syndrome are on neighboring chromosome bands, patients with 2q23.1 deletion do not share key anomalies associated with Mowat-Wilson syndrome, such as Hirschsprung disease, congenital heart defects, genitourinary anomalies, and eye defects; thus, Mowat-Wilson syndrome is not in the differential diagnosis for 2q23.1 deletion syndrome patients [31,32]. Here, we reviewed the neurological and behavioral features of 2q23.1 deletion syndrome and eight other disorders that have been phenotypically linked to or considered in the differential diagnosis for 2q23.1 deletion syndrome [31,32]. The reported phenotypic features of 2q23.1 deletion syndrome, RTT, AS, PTHS, 2q23.1 duplication syndrome, 5q14.3 deletion syndrome, Kleefstra syndrome (KFS), Kabuki syndrome (MIM 147920), and SMS show they share neurological and behavioral co-morbidities coupled with ID, including motor impairments and gaiting abnormalities, hypotonia, language impairments, seizures, sleep disturbance, autistic-like behaviors, and other distinctive behaviors (Table 2). The similar features among many highly penetrant neurodevelopmental disorders associated with ASD allow us to hypothesize several models for

ASD etiology and pathogenesis. First, the ASD-associated genes linked to known neurodevelopmental disorders govern similar cellular functions. Second, the genes play a role in specific cellular functions that converge into common molecular pathways that are associated with specific phenotypes. Third, these genes are involved in entirely different molecular pathways that converge to a common phenotype.

2.3. MBD5 Regulates Disorder-Specific Genes

Due to the high degree of phenotypic similarity between RTT (*MECP2*), AS (*UBE3A*), PTHS (*TCF4*), 2q23.1 duplication syndrome (*MBD5*), 5q14.3 deletion syndrome (*MEF2C*), KFS (*EHMT1*), Kabuki syndrome (*KMT2D* and *KDM6A*), and SMS (*RAI1*) relative to 2q23.1 deletion syndrome (Table 2), we examined the co-expression relationships of these genes to MBD5 toward assessing their involvement in the phenotype of 2q23.1 deletion syndrome. We hypothesized that these genes may be dysregulated in 2q23.1 deletion syndrome and therefore assessed expression of *MECP2, UBE3A, TCF4, MEF2C, EHMT1, KMT2D, KDM6A*, and *RAI1* in 2q23.1 deletion syndrome patient lymphoblastoid cell lines (LCLs) that had various deletions of *MBD5*. As expected, mRNA levels of *MBD5* were significantly down regulated in 2q23.1 deletion syndrome LCLs ($p < 0.0001$), confirming previously reported results [13] (Figure 2). Overall, we observed 5/8 (62.5%) of the tested genes had significantly altered mRNA levels when *MBD5* was haploinsufficient. *TCF4* and *UBE3A* expression levels were elevated to ~1.5-fold (*TCF4*, $p = 0.012$; *UBE3A*, $p < 0.0001$). However, *MEF2C, EHMT1*, and *RAI1* expression levels were significantly reduced to ~0.5-fold (*MEF2C*, $p = 0.016$; *EHMT1*, $p = 0.0004$; *RAI1*, $p < 0.0001$). *MECP2, KMT2D*, and *KDM6A* had no significant change of expression.

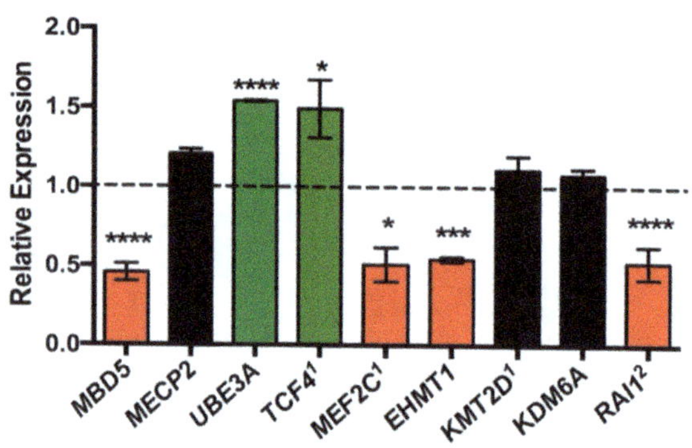

Figure 2. Dysregulation of associated genes in 2q23.1 deletion syndrome. *MBD5, MEF2C, EHTM1*, and *RAI1* were significantly down regulated (red bars) while *UBE3A* and *TCF4* were significantly up regulated (green bars). *MECP2, KMT2D*, and *KDM6A* did not have altered mRNA levels (black bars). Gene expression is shown relative to control set to 1.0 (black line). Graphs represent mean ± SEM (* $p < 0.05$, *** $p < 0.01$, **** $p < 0.0001$). 1 = Manuscript in review, 2 = [20].

Our co-expression data indicate that *MBD5* functions, either directly or indirectly, in the regulation of the expression of other ASD-associated genes (*TCF4, MEF2C, EHTM1, RAI1*, and *UBE3A*), which supports the common pathway ASD pathogenesis hypothesis. *MBD5* and the genes with altered expression possibly converge on common pathways that contribute to the phenotype of 2q23.1 deletion syndrome and genetic neurodevelopmental syndromes associated with ASD. While *MECP2, KMT2D*, and *KDM6A*, did not have altered mRNA levels, these genes may share a molecular connection to *MBD5* beyond co-expression, such as physical interactions. Thus, MBD5 and *MECP2, KMT2D*, and *KDM6A* could be involved in different genetic pathways that result in a similar phenotypic output, which may indicate the presence of redundant pathways. Alternatively, *MECP2, KMT2D*, and *KDM6A* may be in the same or overlapping pathways but may function upstream of MBD5. Our phenotypic and gene expression data (Table 2 and Figure 2) implicate some form of pathway overlap or interaction when *MBD5* is haploinsufficient.

Table 2. Common phenotypes between 2q23.1 deletion syndrome and Rett, Angelman, Pitt-Hopkins, 2q23.1 duplication, 5q14.3 deletion, Kleefstra, Kabuki, and Smith-Magenis syndromes.

DISORDER	2q23.1 del	RTT	AS	PTHS	2q23.1 dup	5q14.3 del	KFS	KMS	SMS
Key References	[13,20]	[33,34]	[31,35]	[36,37]	[38,39]	[40]	[41]	[42,43]	[44]
Causative Gene	*MBD5*	*MECP2*	*UBE3A*	*TCF4*	*MBD5*	*MEF2C*	*EHMT1*	*KMT2D, KDM6A*	*RAI1*
Neurological/Behavioral Characteristics									
Intellectual disability [a]	+++	+++	+++	+++	++	+++	+++	++	++
Speech delay [b]	+++	+++	+++	+++	++	+++	++	++	+
Seizures [c]	+++	+++	+++	++	++	++	++	+	+
Sleep disturbance [d]	+++	+	+++	++	++	+	+	+	+++
Delayed walking [e]	++	+++	++	++	+	+++	+	+	+
Hypotonia	+	+	+	+	+	+	+	+	+
Autism-like behaviors	+	+	+	+	+	+	+[f]	+	+
Feeding difficulties	+	+	+	-	+	+	+	+	+
Stereotypic behaviors	+	+	+	+	+	+	-	+	+
Ataxia	+	+	+	+	+	+	-	+	-
Happy disposition (frequent or inappropriate laughing)	+	+	+	+	+	NR	-	+	-
Hyperactivity/short attention span	+	-	+	+	+	-	-	+	+
Self-injurious behavior	+	-	-	-	-	-	+	-	+
Aggressive behavior	-	-	-	+	-	-	+	-	+

2q23.1 del = 2q23.1 deletion syndrome, RTT = Rett syndrome, AS = Angelman syndrome, PTHS = Pitt-Hopkins syndrome, 2q23.1 dup = 2q23.1 duplication syndrome, 5q14.3 del = 5q14.3 deletion syndrome, KFS = Kleefstra syndrome, KMS = Kabuki make-up syndrome, and Smith-Magenis syndrome, [a] + = mild; ++ = moderate; +++ = severe, [b] + = moderate; ++ = severe; +++ = absent, [c] + = 0%–40%; ++ = 41%–70%; +++ 71%–100%, [d] + = 0%–40%; ++ 40%–70%; +++ 71%–100%, [e] + = 1–3 y; ++ = 4–6 y; +++ = >6 y or limited mobility, [f] only in childhood, NR = not reported.

2.4. MBD5 Network

Recent studies suggest that genes involved in common endpoints (e.g., phenotypes) show an increased tendency to have protein-protein interactions, similar expression patterns in specific tissues, and exhibit synchronized expression as a group [45,46]. In this study, we observed co-expression relationships between *MBD5* and ASD-associated genes (Figure 2). To comprehensively understand MBD5-dependent genetic pathways relative to these genes, we utilized bioinformatics resources and the network tool, Cognoscente (http://vanburenlab.tamhsc.edu/), to uncover related protein interactions (Figure 3). While data do not exist in the literature to support the key genes (in red boxes) directly interacting with each other, we did observe that some hubs (central network connections) all intervened with one another (Figure 3). This finding could suggest there are intermediary genes that molecularly connect the genes directly involved in known disorders. Interestingly, from this network, several other genes linked to ASD were identified, including *CDKL5*, *HDAC4*, *EP300*, *FMR1*, *SMARCA4*, and *ATRX*, each previously linked to a neurodevelopmental disorder with overlapping or similar phenotypes, as listed in Table 2 (Figure 2). In Mullegama *et al.* (2014), we observed overexpression of *FMR1* in 2q23.1 deletion syndrome cell lines [19]. Additional expression studies of these ASD-associated genes in 2q23.1 deletion syndrome would prove interesting. A limitation using such tools to explore molecular networks, as we demonstrated in Figure 2, is that all programs that generate networks, like Cognoscente, rely on the published literature [47]. This fact revealed that there is clearly a lack of research and understanding of the interactions among the genome and proteome in ASD. Thus, undoubtedly, concerted efforts need to be made to study molecular interactions between these genes collectively to further elucidate the genetic etiology of these and other monogenic neurodevelopmental disorders associated with ASDs. Futures studies such as RNA-seq, methylation sequencing, whole-genome miRNA analysis, and chromatin immunoprecipitation sequencing (ChIP-seq) studies of these disorder-causing genes will allow us to further elucidate the levels of molecular convergence between these disorders.

2.5. Molecular Relationships between MBD5 and RAI1

We propose that functional relationships between genes serve as a strong indicator for involvement in key pathways responsible for phenotypic outcomes. An example of this concept is the relationship between MBD5 and RAI1. We have shown that 2q23.1 deletion syndrome and Smith-Magenis syndrome have overlapping phenotypes (see Table 2). From the data we presented here, it appears that *RAI1* could be regulated directly or indirectly by MBD5. Our previously published work also suggested that *RAI1* is dysregulated when *MBD5* is knocked down through siRNA technology in neuroblastoma SH-SY5Y cell lines [19]. Therefore, we wanted to further examine the functional pathways common to *MBD5* and *RAI1*.

From previously published microarray data [19] where *MBD5* and *RAI1* were knocked down through siRNA technology individually in neuroblastoma cell lines, we conducted Ingenuity Pathway Analysis (IPA) on these microarray data to identify the common pathways that are perturbed when *MBD5* and *RAI1* are haploinsufficient. We propose that these pathways could be key contributors to the overlapping phenotypes we see in both syndromes. IPA was used to determine which biological pathways and function involving genes were differentially expressed in *MBD5* and *RAI1* knockdown SH-SY5Y cell lines. A p-value of less than 0.05 for each pathway was determined using Fisher's exact tests to determine the likelihood of those genes assigned by chance. IPA shows that *MBD5* and *RAI1* are implicated in many neurological, cell growth and developmental pathways ($p < 0.05$) (Tables 3 and 4). The top common pathways reveal many interesting and important pathways altered due to *MBD5* and *RAI1* haploinsufficiency. Previously mentioned pathways that are associated with autism and sleep, circadian rhythm signaling, and mTOR signaling pathways are present (Tables 3 and 4) [19]. The CDK5 signaling pathway is crucial to neuronal activity, neuronal migration during development and neurite growth [48]. In previous mouse studies of Mbd5, reduced neurite outgrowth was observed [49]. Further, the *Xenopus laevis* rai1 morphants exhibit aberrant neural crest migration [50]. Thus, the CDK5 signaling pathway could be contributing to the features seen in the above studies. The apoptosis signaling pathway (see Table 4) is involved in the determination of the size and shape of the brain and it regulates the wiring of developing neuronal networks [51]. It is thought that dysregulation of this pathway can lead to neuroanatomic abnormalities and developmental disabilities [51]. There are growing associations between neural cell death and autism [51]. Thus, the involvement of the apoptosis signaling pathway in 2q23.1 deletion syndrome and Smith-Magenis syndrome should be further investigated. Overall, extensive molecular studies on how these shared pathways contribute to the phenotypes present in 2q23.1 deletion syndrome and Smith-Magenis syndrome is necessary. In addition, these results provide further evidence that monogenic neurodevelopmental disorders associated with ASD share common pathways and are crucial to study in regards to phenotypic development.

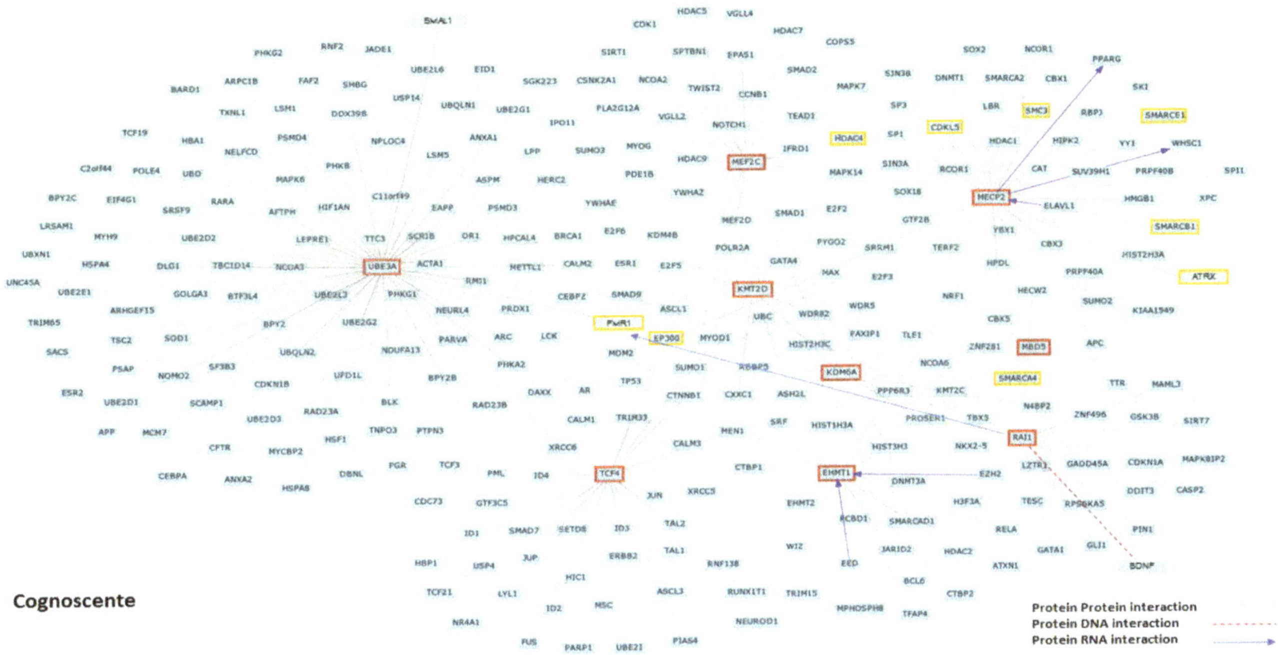

Figure 3. 2q23.1 deletion syndrome gene interaction network. Cognoscente was used to generate direct protein-protein (grey line), protein-DNA (red dash line), and protein-RNA (blue arrow line) interactions of genes previously implicated in ASD: *MBD5*, *MECP2*, *UBE3A*, *TCF4*, *MEF2C*, *EHMT1*, *KMT2D*, *KDM6A* and *RAI1* (red box). The human orthologs of genes of many of the protein products that came up in this network are involved in neuronal functions, chromatin modification, methylation and transcriptional regulation. In addition, other genes associated with ASD also were identified (yellow box).

Table 3. Common neurological pathways in both *MBD5* and *RAI1* knockdown SH-SY5Y cells.

Ingenuity Canonical Pathways *
Acetate conversion to acetyl-CoA
Agrin interactions at neuromuscular junction
Aldosterone signaling in epithelial cells
Amyotrophic lateral sclerosis signaling
Axonal guidance signaling
Cyclin-dependent kinsase 5 signaling
Choline degradation I
Circadian rhythm signaling
Ciliary neurotrophic factor signaling
Docosahexaenoic acid signaling

Table 3. *Cont.*

Ingenuity Canonical Pathways *
Dolichol and dolichyl phosphate biosynthesis
Eukaryotic initiation factor 2 signaling
Ephrin A signaling
Ephrin B signaling
Ephrin receptor signaling
Epidermal growth factor receptor signaling
G protein signaling mediated by Tubby
Gap junction signaling
Glial cell line-derived neurotrophic factors family ligand-receptor interactions
Glioma signaling
Melanoma signaling
Mechanistic target of rapamycin signaling
Netrin signaling
Neuregulin signaling

* All pathways had a *p*-value <0.05 as determined by Fisher Exact Test within Ingenuity Pathway Analysis.

Table 4. Common cell growth and developmental pathways in both *MBD5* and *RAI1* knockdown SH-SY5Y cells.

Ingenuity Canonical Pathways *
14-3-3-mediated signaling
1D-myo-inositol hexakisphosphate biosynthesis II (mammalian)
Acetate conversion to acetyl-CoA
Agrin interactions at neuromuscular junction
Aldosterone signaling in epithelial cells
Angiopoietin signaling
Apoptosis signaling
Aryl hydrocarbon receptor signaling
Assembly of RNA polymerase II complex
Assembly of RNA polymerase III complex
Ataxia telangiectasia mutated signaling
Bone morphogenetic protein signaling
CD40 signaling
Cell division control protein 42 homolog signaling
Cytidine diphosphate diacylglycerol-diacylglycerol biosynthesis I
Cell cycle control of chromosomal replication
Cell Cycle: G1/S checkpoint regulation
Cell Cycle: G2/M DNA damage checkpoint regulation
Ceramide signaling
Cholecystokinin/gastrin-mediated signaling
Choline degradation I
Circadian rhythm signaling
Citrulline-nitric oxide cycle
Clathrin-mediated endocytosis signaling

* All pathways had a *p*-value <0.05 as determined by Fisher Exact Test within Ingenuity Pathway Analysis.

3. Experimental Section

3.1. Patients and Cell Culture Studies

All samples and information were collected after informed consent was obtained and in accordance with Institutional Review Board (IRB) approved protocols from Baylor College of Medicine. Lymphoblastoid cell lines (LCLs) (Epstein–Barr virus-transformed human lymphocytes) were cultured as previously described [25]. LCLs utilized in this study included: 2q23.1 deletion syndrome

(SMS367 [25], SMS185 [25], SMS361 [13], SMS373 [13], SMS375 [13], and SMS368 [13] and five normal control lines).

3.2. Expression Analyses

RNA was isolated from cultured patient and control lymphoblastoid cell lines via TRIzol (Invitrogen, Carlsbad, CA, USA) according to standard protocols. All cell lines were cultured for the same period of time to the same cell density. RNA was quantified using the NanoDrop® ND-100 Spectrophotometer (NanoDrop Technologies, Inc., Wilmington, DE, USA). First-strand cDNA synthesis was carried out using qSCRIPT cDNA SuperMix (Quanta Biosciences, Inc., Gaithersburg, MD, USA) (with 1 μg of RNA) according to the manufacturer's protocol. For quantitative real-time PCR, predesigned Taqman MGB probes from Assays-on-Demand Gene Expression Products (ABI) (Life Technologies Inc., Carlsbad, CA, USA) were used for all genes. A minimum of three unrelated patient samples were run in triplicate in 10 μL reaction volumes. PCR conditions were the default settings of the ABI Prism 7900 HT Sequence Detection System (Life Technologies Inc., Carlsbad, CA, USA). The cycle threshold (C_t) was determined during the geometric phase of the PCR amplification plots as recommended by the manufacturer. Relative differences in transcript levels were quantified with the ΔΔCt method with *GAPDH* (MIM138400) (Hs99999905_m1) mRNA as an endogenous control. All expression values were calculated relative to control levels set at 1.0.

3.3. Network Analysis

Cognoscente (http://vanburenlab.tamhsc.edu/) was used to identify the biomolecular interactions that have been documented in the literature of the genes listed in Table 2. Cognoscente is a highly curated freely available database that identifies interacting components of protein networks and the primary literature to support such interactions [47].

3.4. Ingenuity Pathway Analysis (IPA)

IPA was used to identify biological functions, gene networks and pathways, and likely upstream regulators that were significantly more altered in knockdown cells than in controls. Significant interactions were determined using the Ingenuity Pathway Knowledge Base and a Fisher's exact test to calculate a p-value determining the probability that each function network or pathway assigned to that data set is due to chance alone. Statistical significance was determined at a cutoff of $p \leq 0.05$.

3.5. Statistical Analyses

Statistical analysis for gene expression data was performed with Prism 4 version 4.0b (GraphPad Software, Inc., San Diego, CA, USA). Statistical significance was determined at a cutoff of $p \leq 0.05$.

4. Conclusions

In conclusion, we show that 2q23.1 deletion syndrome shares common neurological and behavioral phenotypes with other monogenic neurodevelopmental disorders associated with autism spectrum disorders. Furthermore, haploinsufficiency of *MBD5* impacts expression of several ASD-implicated genes, including *UBE3A*, *TCF4 MEF2C*, *EHMT1*, and *RAI1*; supporting MBD5 as a transcriptional regulator. Further, data suggest that these genes associated with ASD, *MBD5*, *MECP2*, *UBE3A*, *TCF4 MEF2C*, *EHMT1*, *KMT2D* and *KDM6A*, and *RAI1* may be part of a gene network that converges into common or overlapping pathways that results in similar phenotypes when perturbed. As an example, we show that when *MBD5* and *RAI1* are both haploinsufficient they share common perturbed pathways that likely contribute to the overlapping phenotypes exhibited by 2q23.1 deletion syndrome and Smith-Magenis syndrome patients. Overall, future studies identifying and dissecting the genetic and downstream molecular pathways in monogenic neurodevelopmental disorders associated with

ASD may reveal common points of regulation and promote gene candidates for targeted therapeutic and pharmacological intervention.

Acknowledgments: We are deeply indebted to the study participants and their families, as well as support from the Fondation Jérôme Lejeune. This work was supported in part by the resources from Baylor College of Medicine, the Jan and Dan Duncan Neurological Research Institute, and the Texas Children's Hospital. Li Chen was funded by the National Science Foundation-China (NSFC) grant 31200937 and Shanghai Health and Family Planning Commission grant 20144Y0106.

Author Contributions: Sureni V. Mullegama conceived the study, conducted the experiments, analyzed the data and wrote the manuscript. Joseph T. Alaimo and Li Chen helped create figures and critically edited the manuscript. Sarah H. Elsea is the principal investigator and critically edited the manuscript.

References

1. Spooren, W.; Lindemann, L.; Ghosh, A.; Santarelli, L. Synapse dysfunction in autism: A molecular medicine approach to drug discovery in neurodevelopmental disorders. *Trends Pharmacol. Sci.* **2012**, *33*, 669–684. [CrossRef] [PubMed]
2. Ceroni, F.; Sagar, A.; Simpson, N.H.; Gawthrope, A.J.; Newbury, D.F.; Pinto, D.; Francis, S.M.; Tessman, D.C.; Cook, E.H.; Monaco, A.P.; *et al.* A deletion involving CD38 and BST1 results in a fusion transcript in a patient with autism and asthma. *Autism Res.* **2014**, *7*, 254–263. [CrossRef] [PubMed]
3. Pendergrass, S.; Girirajan, S.; Selleck, S. Uncovering the etiology of autism spectrum disorders: Genomics, bioinformatics, environment, data collection and exploration, and future possibilities. *Pac. Symp. Biocomput.* **2014**, 422–426.
4. De Rubeis, S.; He, X.; Goldberg, A.P.; Poultney, C.S.; Samocha, K.; Cicek, A.E.; Kou, Y.; Liu, L.; Fromer, M.; Walker, S.; *et al.* Synaptic, transcriptional and chromatin genes disrupted in autism. *Nature* **2014**, *515*, 209–215. [CrossRef] [PubMed]
5. Marshall, C.R.; Noor, A.; Vincent, J.B.; Lionel, A.C.; Feuk, L.; Skaug, J.; Shago, M.; Moessner, R.; Pinto, D.; Ren, Y.; *et al.* Structural variation of chromosomes in autism spectrum disorder. *Am. J. Hum. Genet.* **2008**, *82*, 477–488. [CrossRef] [PubMed]
6. Betancur, C. Etiological heterogeneity in autism spectrum disorders: More than 100 genetic and genomic disorders and still counting. *Brain Res.* **2011**, *1380*, 42–77. [CrossRef] [PubMed]
7. Blumenthal, I.; Ragavendran, A.; Erdin, S.; Klei, L.; Sugathan, A.; Guide, J.R.; Manavalan, P.; Zhou, J.Q.; Wheeler, V.C.; Levin, J.Z.; *et al.* Transcriptional consequences of 16p11.2 deletion and duplication in mouse cortex and multiplex autism families. *Am. J. Hum. Genet.* **2014**, *94*, 870–883. [CrossRef] [PubMed]
8. Pasciuto, E.; Bagni, C. Snapshot: Fmrp interacting proteins. *Cell* **2014**, *159*, 218–218.e1. [CrossRef] [PubMed]
9. Van Bokhoven, H. Genetic and epigenetic networks in intellectual disabilities. *Annu. Rev. Genet.* **2011**, *45*, 81–104. [CrossRef] [PubMed]
10. Urdinguio, R.G.; Sanchez-Mut, J.V.; Esteller, M. Epigenetic mechanisms in neurological diseases: Genes, syndromes, and therapies. *Lancet Neurol.* **2009**, *8*, 1056–1072. [CrossRef] [PubMed]
11. Oti, M.; Huynen, M.A.; Brunner, H.G. Phenome connections. *Trends Genet.* **2008**, *24*, 103–106. [CrossRef] [PubMed]
12. Vissers, L.E.; de Vries, B.B.; Osoegawa, K.; Janssen, I.M.; Feuth, T.; Choy, C.O.; Straatman, H.; van der Vliet, W.; Huys, E.H.; van Rijk, A.; *et al.* Array-based comparative genomic hybridization for the genomewide detection of submicroscopic chromosomal abnormalities. *Am. J. Hum. Genet.* **2003**, *73*, 1261–1270. [CrossRef] [PubMed]
13. Talkowski, M.E.; Mullegama, S.V.; Rosenfeld, J.A.; van Bon, B.W.; Shen, Y.; Repnikova, E.A.; Gastier-Foster, J.; Thrush, D.L.; Kathiresan, S.; Ruderfer, D.M.; *et al.* Assessment of 2q23.1 microdeletion syndrome implicates MBD5 as a single causal locus of intellectual disability, epilepsy, and autism spectrum disorder. *Am. J. Hum. Genet.* **2011**, *89*, 551–563. [CrossRef] [PubMed]
14. Laget, S.; Joulie, M.; le Masson, F.; Sasai, N.; Christians, E.; Pradhan, S.; Roberts, R.J.; Defossez, P.A. The human proteins MBD5 and MBD6 associate with heterochromatin but they do not bind methylated DNA. *PLoS ONE* **2010**, *5*, e11982. [CrossRef] [PubMed]
15. Bonnet, C.; Ali Khan, A.; Bresso, E.; Vigouroux, C.; Beri, M.; Lejczak, S.; Deemer, B.; Andrieux, J.; Philippe, C.; Moncla, A.; *et al.* Extended spectrum of mbd5 mutations in neurodevelopmental disorders. *Eur. J. Hum. Genet.* **2013**, *21*, 1457–1461. [CrossRef] [PubMed]

16. Cukier, H.N.; Lee, J.M.; Ma, D.; Young, J.I.; Mayo, V.; Butler, B.L.; Ramsook, S.S.; Rantus, J.A.; Abrams, A.J.; Whitehead, P.L.; *et al.* The expanding role of mbd genes in autism: Identification of a mecp2 duplication and novel alterations in mbd5, mbd6, and setdb1. *Autism Res.* **2012**, *5*, 385–397. [CrossRef] [PubMed]
17. Du, Y.; Liu, B.; Guo, F.; Xu, G.; Ding, Y.; Liu, Y.; Sun, X.; Xu, G. The essential role of MBD5 in the regulation of somatic growth and glucose homeostasis in mice. *PLoS ONE* **2012**, *7*, e47358. [CrossRef] [PubMed]
18. Ladha, S. Getting to the bottom of autism spectrum and related disorders: MBD5 as a key contributor. *Clin. Genet.* **2012**, *81*, 363–364. [CrossRef] [PubMed]
19. Mullegama, S.V.; Pugliesi, L.; Burns, B.; Shah, Z.; Tahir, R.; Gu, Y.; Nelson, D.L.; Elsea, S.H. MBD5 haploinsufficiency is associated with slee disturbance and disrupts circadian pathways common to smith-magenis and fragile X syndromes. *Eur J. Hum. Genet.* **2014**. [CrossRef]
20. Hodge, J.C.; Mitchell, E.; Pillalamarri, V.; Toler, T.L.; Bartel, F.; Kearney, H.M.; Zou, Y.S.; Tan, W.H.; Hanscom, C.; Kirmani, S.; *et al.* Disruption of mbd5 contributes to a spectrum of psychopathology and neurodevelopmental abnormalities. *Mol. Psychiatry* **2014**, *19*, 368–379. [CrossRef] [PubMed]
21. Du, X.; An, Y.; Yu, L.; Liu, R.; Qin, Y.; Guo, X.; Sun, D.; Zhou, S.; Wu, B.; Jiang, Y.H.; *et al.* A genomic copy number variant analysis implicates the mbd5 and hnrnpu genes in chinese children with infantile spasms and expands the clinical spectrum of 2q23.1 deletion. *BMC Med. Genet.* **2014**, *15*, 62. [CrossRef] [PubMed]
22. Lund, C.; Brodtkorb, E.; Rosby, O.; Rodningen, O.K.; Selmer, K.K. Copy number variants in adult patients with lennox-gastaut syndrome features. *Epilepsy Res.* **2013**, *105*, 110–117. [CrossRef] [PubMed]
23. Shichiji, M.; Ito, Y.; Shimojima, K.; Nakamu, H.; Oguni, H.; Osawa, M.; Yamamoto, T. A cryptic microdeletion including MBD5 occurring within the breakpoint of a reciprocal translocation between chromosomes 2 and 5 in a patient with developmental delay and obesity. *Am. J. Med. Genet. A* **2013**, *161*, 850–855. [CrossRef]
24. Girirajan, S.; Dennis, M.Y.; Baker, C.; Malig, M.; Coe, B.P.; Campbell, C.D.; Mark, K.; Vu, T.H.; Alkan, C.; Cheng, Z.; *et al.* Refinement and discovery of new hotspots of copy-number variation associated with autism spectrum disorder. *Am. J. Hum. Genet.* **2013**, *92*, 221–237. [CrossRef] [PubMed]
25. Williams, S.R.; Mullegama, S.V.; Rosenfeld, J.A.; Dagli, A.I.; Hatchwell, E.; Allen, W.P.; Williams, C.A.; Elsea, S.H. Haploinsufficiency of mbd5 associated with a syndrome involving microcephaly, intellectual disabilities, severe speech impairment, and seizures. *Eur. J. Hum. Genet.* **2010**, *18*, 436–441. [CrossRef]
26. Van Bon, B.W.; Koolen, D.A.; Brueton, L.; McMullan, D.; Lichtenbelt, K.D.; Ades, L.C.; Peters, G.; Gibson, K.; Moloney, S.; Novara, F.; *et al.* The 2q23.1 microdeletion syndrome: Clinical and behavioural phenotype. *Eur J. Hum. Genet.* **2010**, *18*, 163–170.
27. Noh, G.J.; Graham, J.M., Jr. 2q23.1 microdeletion of the MBD5 gene in a female with seizures, developmental delay and distinct dysmorphic features. *Eur. J. Med. Genet.* **2012**, *55*, 59–62. [CrossRef] [PubMed]
28. Motobayashi, M.; Nishimura-Tadaki, A.; Inaba, Y.; Kosho, T.; Miyatake, S.; Niimi, T.; Nishimura, T.; Wakui, K.; Fukushima, Y.; Matsumoto, N.; *et al.* Neurodevelopmental features in 2q23.1 microdeletion syndrome: Report of a new patient with intractable seizures and review of literature. *Am. J. Med. Genet. A* **2012**, *158*, 861–868. [CrossRef]
29. Chung, B.H.; Stavropoulos, J.; Marshall, C.R.; Weksberg, R.; Scherer, S.W.; Yoon, G. 2q23 de novo microdeletion involving the mbd5 gene in a patient with developmental delay, postnatal microcephaly and distinct facial features. *Am. J. Med. Genet. A* **2011**, *155*, 424–429. [CrossRef]
30. Wagenstaller, J.; Spranger, S.; Lorenz-Depiereux, B.; Kazmierczak, B.; Nathrath, M.; Wahl, D.; Heye, B.; Glaser, D.; Liebscher, V.; Meitinger, T.; *et al.* Copy-number variations measured by single-nucleotide-polymorphism oligonucleotide arrays in patients with mental retardation. *Am. J. Hum. Genet.* **2007**, *81*, 768–779. [CrossRef] [PubMed]
31. Tan, W.H.; Bird, L.M.; Thibert, R.L.; Williams, C.A. If not angelman, what is it? A review of angelman-like syndromes. *Am. J. Med. Genet. A* **2014**, *164*, 975–992. [CrossRef]
32. Kleefstra, T.; Kramer, J.M.; Neveling, K.; Willemsen, M.H.; Koemans, T.S.; Vissers, L.E.; Wissink-Lindhout, W.; Fenckova, M.; van den Akker, W.M.; Kasri, N.N.; *et al.* Disruption of an ehmt1-associated chromatin-modification module causes intellectual disability. *Am. J. Hum. Genet.* **2012**, *91*, 73–82. [CrossRef] [PubMed]
33. Smeets, E.E.; Pelc, K.; Dan, B. Rett syndrome. *Mol. Syndromol.* **2012**, *2*, 113–127. [CrossRef] [PubMed]
34. Neul, J.L. The relationship of Rett syndrome and MECP2 disorders to autism. *Dialogues Clin. Neurosci.* **2012**, *14*, 253–262. [PubMed]
35. Kyllerman, M. Angelman syndrome. *Handb. Clin. Neurol.* **2013**, *111*, 287–290. [PubMed]

36. Whalen, S.; Heron, D.; Gaillon, T.; Moldovan, O.; Rossi, M.; Devillard, F.; Giuliano, F.; Soares, G.; Mathieu-Dramard, M.; Afenjar, A.; *et al.* Novel comprehensive diagnostic strategy in Pitt-hopkins syndrome: Clinical score and further delineation of the TCF4 mutational spectrum. *Hum. Mutat.* **2012**, *33*, 64–72. [CrossRef] [PubMed]
37. Marangi, G.; Ricciardi, S.; Orteschi, D.; Tenconi, R.; Monica, M.D.; Scarano, G.; Battaglia, D.; Lettori, D.; Vasco, G.; Zollino, M. Proposal of a clinical score for the molecular test for Pitt-hopkins syndrome. *Am. J. Med. Genet. A* **2012**, *158*, 1604–1611. [CrossRef]
38. Chung, B.H.; Mullegama, S.; Marshall, C.R.; Lionel, A.C.; Weksberg, R.; Dupuis, L.; Brick, L.; Li, C.; Scherer, S.W.; Aradhya, S.; *et al.* Severe intellectual disability and autistic features associated with microduplication 2q23.1. *Eur. J. Hum. Genet.* **2012**, *20*, 398–403. [CrossRef] [PubMed]
39. Mullegama, S.V.; Rosenfeld, J.A.; Orellana, C.; van Bon, B.W.; Halbach, S.; Repnikova, E.A.; Brick, L.; Li, C.; Dupuis, L.; Rosello, M.; *et al.* Reciprocal deletion and duplication at 2q23.1 indicates a role for MBD5 in autism spectrum disorder. *Eur. J. Hum. Genet.* **2014**, *22*, 57–63. [CrossRef] [PubMed]
40. Novara, F.; Rizzo, A.; Bedini, G.; Girgenti, V.; Esposito, S.; Pantaleoni, C.; Ciccone, R.; Sciacca, F.L.; Achille, V.; Della Mina, E.; *et al.* Mef2c deletions and mutations versus duplications: A clinical comparison. *Eur. J. Med. Genet.* **2013**, *56*, 260–265. [CrossRef] [PubMed]
41. Willemsen, M.H.; Vulto-van Silfhout, A.T.; Nillesen, W.M.; Wissink-Lindhout, W.M.; van Bokhoven, H.; Philip, N.; Berry-Kravis, E.M.; Kini, U.; van Ravenswaaij-Arts, C.M.; Delle Chiaie, B.; *et al.* Update on Kleefstra syndrome. *Mol. Syndromol.* **2012**, *2*, 202–212. [PubMed]
42. Banka, S.; Lederer, D.; Benoit, V.; Jenkins, E.; Howard, E.; Bunstone, S.; Kerr, B.; McKee, S.; Lloyd, I.C.; Shears, D.; *et al.* Novel KDM6A (UTX) mutations and a clinical and molecular review of the X-linked Kabuki syndrome (KS2). *Clin. Genet.* **2015**, *87*, 252–258. [CrossRef] [PubMed]
43. Bogershausen, N.; Wollnik, B. Unmasking Kabuki syndrome. *Clin. Genet.* **2013**, *83*, 201–211. [CrossRef] [PubMed]
44. Elsea, S.H.; Girirajan, S. Smith-magenis syndrome. *Eur. J. Hum. Genet.* **2008**, *16*, 412–421. [CrossRef] [PubMed]
45. Goh, K.I.; Cusick, M.E.; Valle, D.; Childs, B.; Vidal, M.; Barabasi, A.L. The human disease network. *Proc. Natl. Acad. Sci. USA* **2007**, *104*, 8685–8690. [CrossRef] [PubMed]
46. Goh, K.I.; Choi, I.G. Exploring the human diseasome: The human disease network. *Brief. Funct. Genomics* **2012**, *11*, 533–542. [CrossRef] [PubMed]
47. Jupiter, D.C.; VanBuren, V. A visual data mining tool that facilitates reconstruction of transcription regulatory networks. *PLoS ONE* **2008**, *3*, e1717. [CrossRef] [PubMed]
48. Duhr, F.; Deleris, P.; Raynaud, F.; Seveno, M.; Morisset-Lopez, S.; Mannoury la Cour, C.; Millan, M.J.; Bockaert, J.; Marin, P.; Chaumont-Dubel, S. Cdk5 induces constitutive activation of 5-HT_6 receptors to promote neurite growth. *Nat. Chem. Biol.* **2014**, *10*, 590–597. [CrossRef] [PubMed]
49. Camarena, V.; Cao, L.; Abad, C.; Abrams, A.; Toledo, Y.; Araki, K.; Araki, M.; Walz, K.; Young, J.I. Disruption of mbd5 in mice causes neuronal functional deficits and neurobehavioral abnormalities consistent with 2q23.1 microdeletion syndrome. *EMBO Mol. Med.* **2014**, *6*, 1003–1015. [CrossRef] [PubMed]
50. Tahir, R.; Kennedy, A.; Elsea, S.H.; Dickinson, A.J. Retinoic acid induced-1 (Rai1) regulates craniofacial and brain development in *Xenopus*. *Mech. Dev.* **2014**, *133*, 91–104. [CrossRef] [PubMed]
51. Wei, H.; Alberts, I.; Li, X. The apoptotic perspective of autism. *Int. J. Dev. Neurosci.* **2014**, *36*, 13–18. [CrossRef] [PubMed]

15

Unbalance between Excitation and Inhibition in Phenylketonuria: A Genetic Metabolic Disease Associated with Autism

Antonella De Jaco [1,*], Dalila Mango [2], Federica De Angelis [1], Flores Lietta Favaloro [1], Diego Andolina [3,4], Robert Nisticò [5], Elena Fiori [2,3,6], Marco Colamartino [3,4] and Tiziana Pascucci [3,4]

1 Department of Biology and Biotechnologies "Charles Darwin", Sapienza University of Rome, 00185 Rome, Italy; federica.deangelis@uniroma1.it (F.D.A.); floresl@libero.it (F.L.F.)
2 EBRI-European Brain Research Institute, 00143 Rome, Italy; dalilamango@gmail.com (D.M.); elena.fiori@uniroma1.it (E.F.)
3 Department of Psychology, "Daniel Bovet", Neurobiology Research Center, Sapienza University of Rome, 00185 Rome, Italy; diego.andolina@uniroma1.it (D.A.); marco.colamartino@uniroma1.it (M.C.); tiziana.pascucci@uniroma1.it (T.P.)
4 Foundation Santa Lucia, IRCCS, 00143 Rome, Italy
5 Department of Biology, University of Tor Vergata, 00133 Rome, Italy; robert.nistico@uniroma1.it
6 Cell Biology and Neurobiology Institute, National Research Council, 00143 Rome, Italy
* Correspondence: antonella.dejaco@uniroma1.it

Academic Editor: Merlin G. Butler

Abstract: Phenylketonuria (PKU) is the most common genetic metabolic disease with a well-documented association with autism spectrum disorders. It is characterized by the deficiency of the phenylalanine hydroxylase activity, causing plasmatic hyperphenylalaninemia and variable neurological and cognitive impairments. Among the potential pathophysiological mechanisms implicated in autism spectrum disorders is the excitation/inhibition (E/I) imbalance which might result from alterations in excitatory/inhibitory synapse development, synaptic transmission and plasticity, downstream signalling pathways, and intrinsic neuronal excitability. Here, we investigated functional and molecular alterations in the prefrontal cortex (pFC) of BTBR-Pah^{enu2} (ENU2) mice, the animal model of PKU. Our data show higher frequency of inhibitory transmissions and significant reduced frequency of excitatory transmissions in the PKU-affected mice in comparison to wild type. Moreover, in the pFC of ENU2 mice, we reported higher levels of the post-synaptic cell-adhesion proteins neuroligin1 and 2. Altogether, our data point toward an imbalance in the E/I neurotransmission favouring inhibition in the pFC of ENU2 mice, along with alterations of the molecular components involved in the organization of cortical synapse. In addition to being the first evidence of E/I imbalance within cortical areas of a mouse model of PKU, our study provides further evidence of E/I imbalance in animal models of pathology associated with autism spectrum disorders.

Keywords: neurotransmission; excitation and inhibition balance; cognitive delay; prefrontal cortex; neuroligins

1. Introduction

Several reports suggest an association between autism and inherited metabolic diseases among which phenylketonuria (PKU), suggesting that autism spectrum disorders might represent the end result of a dysfunction caused by a metabolic block in the brain [1]. PKU is the prototypical human Mendelian disease (OMIM 261600; overall incidence of 1 in 10,000) resulting from impaired activity of phenylalanine hydroxylase (PAH), the enzyme necessary to convert phenylalanine (PHE) to tyrosine. This deficiency causes hyperphenylalaninemia (HPA), which is especially harmful for the brain during the first years of life, resulting in variable neurological and mental impairments [2–4]. Previous evidence from our group demonstrated that the accumulation of PHE in the brain of BTBR-Pah^{enu2} (ENU2) mice impairs protein levels and enzymatic activity of the tryptophan hydroxylase, the rate-limiting enzyme responsible for serotonin biosynthesis [5], and that the serotonin reduction in the brain causes cortical morphological alterations such as a reduction in the dendritic spine density and maturation [6]. Restoring normal levels of brain serotonin in the ENU2 mice, during the third post-natal week, allowed the recovery of some cognitive functions as well as the morphological maturation of pyramidal neuron dendritic spines in the prefrontal cortex (pFC) [6].

We have investigated functional alterations and molecular rearrangements typically associated with neurodevelopmental disorders in an animal model of PKU in order to explore possible common molecular mechanisms in comorbidity with autism. Alterations in excitatory/inhibitory (E/I) ratio in cortical circuitry have been reported in several animal models for neurodevelopmental disorders in association with cognitive delay [7], providing experimental models to define abnormal molecular mechanisms and to identify new therapeutic targets. Since synaptic transmission is regulated by a plethora of molecules where cell-adhesion molecules are emerging as crucial players [8], we have studied the neuroligin/neurexin (NLGN/NRXN) pathway involved in the maturation of the inhibitory and excitatory synapses [9]. Moreover, genes directly involved in the regulation of the ratio between excitation and inhibition represent risk candidate genes [10]. Copy number variations and/or several single point mutations in the NLGN/NRXN synaptic pathway have been detected in association to neurodevelopmental disorders [11] including autism spectrum disorders [12–17].

Here we investigate, for the first time, the functional and molecular features underlying the morphological and biochemical phenotype reported in the pFC of ENU2 mice, the genetic murine model of the most common metabolic inborn error. Our data support the hypothesis that in PKU, unknown mechanisms linked to PHE accumulation lead to a E/I imbalance shifting toward inhibition, accompanied by altered expression levels of specific members of the synaptic family of the Neuroligin proteins, classically linked to autism.

2. Results

2.1. *Analysis of Inhibitory and Excitatory Transmission in Layer II/III of ENU2 pFC*

ENU2-mutant mice exhibit abnormal behaviors that mimic the intellectual disability symptoms observed in human PKU untreated patients. In order to assess whether immature spine morphology and cognitive impairments described for PKU in the ENU2 mice [6] reflect functionally a different cortical activity in comparison to parental controls, we have measured the spontaneous inhibitory postsynaptic currents (sIPSC) and spontaneous excitatory postsynaptic currents (sEPSC) from layer II/III of brain pFC by using whole-cell patch clamp recordings. We have analyzed synaptic transmission by assessing amplitude and frequency of action potential dependent inhibitory and excitatory spontaneous events from slices obtained by ENU2 and relative control mice at postnatal day 60 (PND 60). We have measured cumulative probability of amplitude and inter-event interval of frequency for sIPSC and sEPSC. As shown in Figure 1a, we have found higher frequency of sIPSC in ENU2 mice compared to wild-type (WT) (K–S test $p < 0.001$, t-test $p = 0.0412$ ENU2 $n = 8$ vs. WT $n = 7$, Figure 1A) and significant reduced frequency of sEPSC in ENU2 mice compared to WT (K–S test $p = 0.0091$, t-test $p = 0.0433$ ENU2 $n = 7$ vs. WT $n = 6$, Figure 1B). Consistently, the E/I ratio was also significantly reduced in ENU2 mice compared to WT (t-test $p = 0.0306$, ENU2 $n = 6$ vs. WT $n = 6$ Figure 1C).

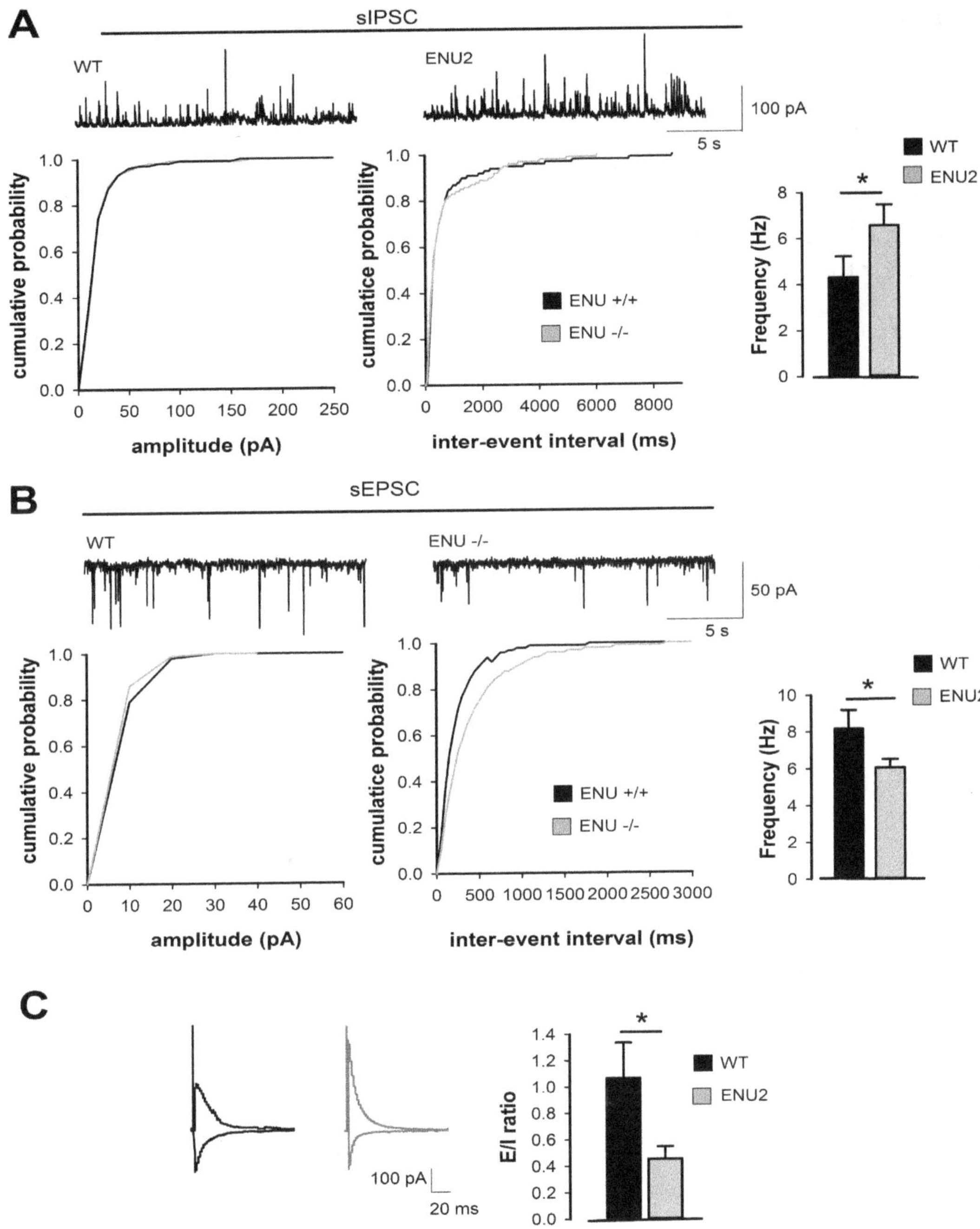

Figure 1. BTBR-Pah^{enu2} (ENU2) mice show altered excitatory/inhibitory (E/I) balance. (**A**) Pooled cumulative distributions of spontaneous inhibitory post synaptic currents (sIPSCs) amplitude (**left**; bin size 10 pA) and inter-event interval (**right**; bin size 50 ms) recorded from neurons of wild type (WT, $n = 8$) and ENU2 ($n = 7$) mice. Representative traces are shown on top. (**B**) Pooled cumulative distributions of spontaneous excitatory post synaptic currents (sEPSCs) amplitude (**left**) and inter-event interval (**right**) recorded from neurons of WT ($n = 7$) and ENU2 ($n = 6$) mice. Histograms are averages (mean ± S.E.M) of the corresponding median values of sEPSCs frequency for the same neurons. Representative traces are shown on top. (**C**) Histograms are averages (mean ± S.E.M) of E/I ratio recorded from WT ($n = 6$) and ENU2 ($n = 6$). Representative traces are shown on the left. (* $p < 0.05$).

The reported electrophysiological alterations resemble those typically associated with other neurodevelopmental disorders [7], such as autism, where the excitatory and inhibitory balance is functionally impaired and might account for the cognitive phenotype.

2.2. *Protein Levels of Synaptic Cell Adhesion Molecules in the pFC of ENU2 Mice*

Synaptic cell adhesion molecules operate in concert with neurotransmitter receptors to ensure proper function of synaptic circuits [18]. The NLGN/NRXN pathway is currently one of the most studied trans-synaptic codes acting in the organization of the excitatory and inhibitory synapses. The NLGN family is made of four members (1, 2, 3, 4), encoded by different genes, with NLGN1 being specifically localized to excitatory postsynaptic densities while NLGN2 is found in inhibitory postsynaptic specializations and NLGN3 is present at both [19]. NLGNs play a crucial role in the recruitment of neurotransmitter receptors at the synapse and in the control of the E/I balance in the brain [20].

We have initially quantified the levels of all the NLGNs by western blot using a PAN-antibody. Analysis of NLGNs levels revealed an increasing trend in the ENU2 mice that however did not present significant results in comparison to WT mice (t-test $p = 0.2162$, ENU2 $n = 8$ vs. WT $n = 7$ Figure 2A). We have then investigated the levels of each family member by using antibodies specific for each of the NLGNs forms. We found that NLGN1 (t-test $p = 0.0142$, ENU2 $n = 14$ vs. WT $n = 18$ Figure 2B) and NLGN2 (t-test $p = 0.0266$, ENU2 $n = 14$ vs. WT $n = 13$, Figure 2C) resulted in increased ENU2 in comparison to WT mice. Non-significant differences were observed for NLGN3 between ENU2 and WT mice (t-test $p = 0.543$, ENU2 $n = 14$ vs. WT $n = 17$ Figure 2D). These observations suggest that the functional differences in the ENU2 pFC reflect a different regulation of molecular synaptic components.

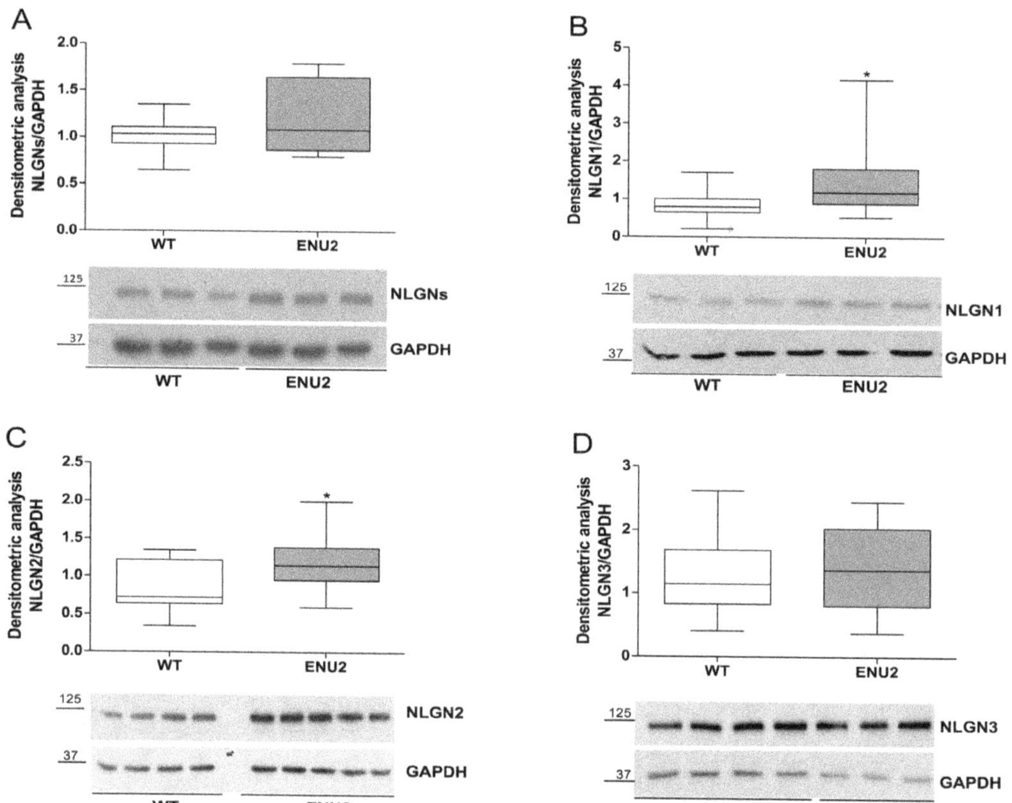

Figure 2. Neuroligins (NLGNs) levels in the pFC of ENU2 mice. Protein levels were quantified by densitometry after western blot analysis for total NLGNs and for NLGN1, 2, and 3 family members. Values were normalized to GAPDH loading control and are represented as a box plot of their distribution (min/max *e* median). (**A**) NLGNs (WT $n = 7$, ENU2 $n = 8$, $p = 0.2162$); (**B**) NLGN1 (WT $n = 18$, ENU2 $n = 13$, $p = 0.0142$); (**C**) NLGN2 (WT $n = 13$, ENU2 $n = 14$, $p = 0.0266$); and (**D**) NLGN3 (WT $n = 17$, ENU2 $n = 14$, $p = 0.5430$). Statistical analysis compared ENU2 values versus WT (* $p < 0.05$). Representative images of western blot analysis are shown. Molecular masses are indicated on the blots in kDa.

3. Discussion

Dysregulation of the excitation/inhibition equilibrium has been postulated to represent a hallmark of neuropsychiatric disorders, including autism and some forms of mental retardation. Several mouse models reproducing behavioral phenotypes common to neurodevelopmental syndromes show alterations of the E/I balance. In particular, a mouse model of Rett syndrome showed a shift favoring inhibition in the pFC [21]. Increased inhibition was observed in the somatosensory cortex of mice expressing the R451C autism-related mutation in NLGN3, and this was associated with impairments in social interaction [22]. In general, while a decrease in inhibition is currently associated with autism spectrum disorders, an excess of inhibition has been described to occur in mental retardation syndromes such as Down [23–25] and Rett syndromes [21]. Interestingly, by using an optogenetic approach to study real-time effects of elevation of cellular E/I balance in vivo, it was shown that elevated E/I balance resulted in impairments on social behavior that are specific for pFC [26].

Although compelling evidence points toward a link between dysregulation of E/I ratio and behavioral phenotypes resembling those observed in neuropsychiatric disorders, the molecular machinery involved in the regulation of this balance remains unclear.

PKU mice, created by chemically induced genetic mutation, display a phenotype that closely resembles untreated human PKU, characterized by reduced PAH activity, PHE plasma levels 10–20 times greater than those of healthy littermates, impaired cerebral protein synthesis, neurochemical reductions in different brain regions, particularly in serotonergic metabolism in prefrontal cortical areas, reduced functional and morphological synaptic plasticity, and cognitive and other behavioral abnormalities [27].

We have postulated that cognitive impairments might be linked to E/I imbalance and found that there was a resultantly higher inhibition and reduced excitation in the layer II/III of ENU2 pFC, suggesting an overall reduced activity in cortical circuits as observed in other animal models of neurodevelopmental disorders where a shift in the balance between excitation and inhibition—favoring inhibition—has been reported [7].

In recent years, several lines of evidence suggest a possible link between the levels of neuroligins and neurotransmission dysfunctions in association to autism spectrum disorders [28]. Gain and loss of function studies in vitro and in vivo have provided experimental support to the hypothesis that the regulation of the levels of the neuroligin proteins might correlate with alteration of the E/I balance. Transgenic mice where NLGN2 expression has been enhanced showed higher frequency of mIPSC in the pFC and an overall reduction in the E/I ratio [29]. NLGN2 function in modulating inhibitory synaptic currents was further highlighted by the selective deletion of NLGN2 in the medial pFC in a conditional knock-out mouse strain. This resulted in chronic changes in E/I balance characterized by a reduction in frequency and amplitude of inhibitory sIPSCs and by cognitive behavioral changes [30]. This has led us to investigate whether the E/I unbalance in the pFC of ENU2 mice might correlate with altered levels of the NLGNs family members. Indeed, in ENU2 mice we have found different levels of neuroligin proteins in comparison to the parental healthy mice. In particular, our data show unchanged levels for NLGN3 along with higher protein levels for NLGN2 and NLGN1. Enhanced NLGN2 protein levels in the pFC of ENU2 mice correlate with the increased inhibitory transmission observed in the layer II/III and strengthen the hypothesis of a shift in the E/I balance favoring inhibition in the ENU2 mice. In fact, NLGN2 is found in inhibitory postsynaptic specializations [31] where it plays a specific role in the regulation of inhibitory synaptic terminals and in the maintenance of E/I balance in the brain [32]. NLGN2 interacts with collybistin and gephyrin in order to recruit and anchoring GABAA receptors to the post-synaptic membrane [33], favoring the maturation of the inhibitory synapses [34]. At this stage, we have not investigated whether the enhancement of sIPSC is due to an increase of the number of inhibitory synapses. However, the increased levels of NLGN2 cannot explain the decrease in the excitatory neurotransmission in ENU2 mice. Recently, it has been shown that selectively deleting NLGN2 from the II/III layer of pFC leads to a decrease in spontaneous mIPSC without affecting mEPSC [30].

The prominent deficit of serotonin in pFC of PKU mice is well documented [5,35] and also a crucial role is played by serotonin in regulating maturational events such as spine morphology through the activation of the serotonin 2A receptor (5HT2A) receptor, expressed in excitatory synapses [36]. Our previous work showed that cortical spine maturation, and consequently cognitive deficits, are affected in ENU2 mice through a serotonin-dependent pathway [6]. Thus, the reduced serotonin release in ENU2 [5] might result in a lower excitatory activity 5HT2A-dependent. This would agree with the data we show in regard to the lower rates of spontaneous EPSCs in the II/III layers of pFC. Our data show a statistically significant increase for NLGN1 in ENU2 mice, classically localized to excitatory synapses [34]. This increase does not agree with the reduced excitatory transmissions found in the layer II/III of the pFC in ENU2 mice. This might be due to the western blot analysis being performed from punchings of the pFC, comprising all of the cortical layers, in contrast to the electrophysiological recordings restricted to layer II/III.

The shift in the ratio from excitation to inhibition is however differentially regulated by the association of the NLGNs with elements critical for synapse formation such as postsynaptic scaffolding proteins, PSD-95 (at the excitatory synapses), and gephryn (at the inhibitory synapses) and to the presynaptic proteins NRXNs [37–39]. Therefore, a further analysis of these components will help clarify the mechanism.

The data presented shows the first evidence of E/I cortical imbalance in a genetic murine model of inherited metabolic disease, PKU. The unbalance toward inhibitory transmission in the pFC of ENU2 mice might impact on the proper development of brain circuits involved in cognitive function. The cascade of events that lead from high blood PHE levels to the E/I cortical imbalance in PKU however is still not understood.

Finally, investigating the molecular and physiological mechanisms underlying cognitive disability in PKU mice can provide insights for autism spectrum disorders, as well as for all syndromes characterized by similar pathogenic mechanisms.

4. Materials and Methods

4.1. Animal Protocols and Housing

All experiments were approved by the ethics committee of the Italian Ministry of Health and conducted under license/approval ID #: 10/2011-B, according with Italian regulations on the use of animals for research (legislation DL 116/92) and the Council Directive 2010/63EU of the European Parliament and the Council of 22 September 2010 on the protection of animals used for scientific purposes. Homozygote (−/−) Pah^{Enu2} (ENU2) and Homozygote (+/+) Pah^{Enu2} (WT) BTBR mice were issued from heterozygous mating. Genetic characterization was performed on DNA prepared from tail tissue using the Easy DNA Kit (Invitrogen, Carlsbad, CA, USA). The ethylnitrosourea (ENU2) mutation was detected after PCR amplification of exon 7 of the Pah gene and digestion with BsmAI restriction enzyme (NEB, USA) as previously described [40]. At PND28, animals (sex matched) were housed 2–4 per standard breeding cage with food and water ad libitum on a 12:12 h dark: light cycle (light on 07.00 a.m.–07.00 p.m. h).

Brain tissue was collected at PND80 from male ENU2 and WT mice. All animals were killed and the brain was removed and stored depending on the experimental procedures. Every effort was made to alleviate animal discomfort and cervical dislocation was applied as the appropriate method of sacrifice.

4.2. Slice Preparation for Electrophysiological Recordings

The brain was rapidly removed from the skull and coronal slices (250 μm thick) were cut with a vibratome (VT 1200S, Leica) in cold (0 °C) artificial cerebrospinal fluid (aCSF) containing (in mM): NaCl 124; KCl 3; $MgSO_4$ 1; $CaCl_2$ 2; NaH_2PO_4 1.25; $NaHCO_3$ 26; glucose 10; saturated with 95% O_2, 5% CO_2 (pH 7.4), and left to recover for 1 h in aCSF at room temperature.

4.3. Whole-Cell Patch Clamp Recordings

Individual slices were placed in a recording chamber, on the stage of an upright microscope (Zeiss, Munich, Germany) and submerged in a continuously flowing (3 mL/min) solution at 30°C (±2 °C). Individual neurons were visualized through a 40× water-immersion objective (Olympus, Tokyo, Japan) connected to infrared video microscopy (Hamamatsu, Hamamatsu City, Japan). Borosilicate glass electrodes (5–7 MΩ), pulled with a PP 83 Narishige puller, were filled with a solution containing the following (in mM): $CsCH_3SO_3$ 115; CsCl 10; KCl 10; $CaCl_2$ 0.45; EGTA 1; Hepes 10; QX-314 5; Na_3-GTP 0.3; Mg-ATP 4.0; pH adjusted to 7.3 with CsOH.

Whole cell patch-clamp recordings have been performed from layer II/III pyramidal neurons of pFC brain slice of WT and ENU2 mice. To isolate sEPSCs and sIPSCs from the same neurons we recorded in voltage clamp mode while maintaining the membrane potential either at the reversal potential for GABA receptor for EPSCs (−70 mV) or at the reversal potential for ionotropic glutamate receptors for IPSCs (+10 mV). To record evoked responses elicited by monopolar stimulating electrodes placed in layer I of pFC, EPSCs and IPSCs were monitored sequentially in the presence of 50 μm APV at postsynaptic holding voltages of −60 and 0 mV, respectively. The E/I ratio is computed as the ratio of excitatory to inhibitory charges, obtained by the integration of the measured currents from the network response triggered by extracellular stimulations [41]. Kolmogorov–Smirnov test (K–S test) and unpaired Student's *t*-test (*t*-test) have been applied as statistical test with α value set at 0.05, *n* reflected the number of neurons recorded.

4.4. SDS PAGE and Western Blot

For protein analysis, frozen brains were removed and dissected to obtain punches of the pFC from brain slices (coronal sections) not thicker than 300 μm. Stainless steel tubes of 1.0 mm inside diameter were used and the coordinates were measured as previously reported [42].

Samples derived from pFC punching were homogenized by sonication using RIPA buffer (Life Technologies, Monza, Italy) to extract total proteins and total protein concentration was determined by Bradford assay (Biorad, Rome, Italy). Around 70 micrograms of total proteins were loaded for each sample. Immunoblotting used previously optimized standard techniques [43] including 10% *w*/*v* SDS-PAGE (Biorad, Rome, Italy) and immobilon transfer membranes (Millipore, Bedford, MA, USA).

Detection of NLGN proteins employed commercial primary antibodies from Synaptic Systems, used at the 1:1000 dilution: anti-NLGN pan mouse monoclonal antibody (clone 4F9, Cat. No. 129-011); anti-NLGN1 mouse monoclonal (Cat. No. 129-111); anti-NLGN2 polyclonal rabbit (Cat. No. 129-203); anti-NLGN3 polyclonal rabbit (Cat. No. 129-113). The anti-GAPDH polyclonal rabbit antibody (abcam ab37168) was used as a loading control. The anti-mouse-HRP and anti-rabbit-HRP (Sigma-Aldrich, Milan, Italy) secondary antibodies were diluted 1:10,000. The HRP signal was developed using the LiteAblot PLUS and TURBO extra sensitive chemiluminescent substrates (Euroclone, Milan, Italy) and exposed to autoradiographic films (Santa Cruz Biotechnology, through Aurogene, Rome, Italy) or revealed by using the ChemiDoc™ MP System (Biorad, Rome, Italy). Densitometry was performed using the Image-J software (version 1.43, NIH, Bethesda, MD, USA). Punching samples were derived from 7 to 18 animals per group and unpaired Student's *t*-test (*t*-test) statistical analysis was used to compare values from ENU2 and WT mice.

Acknowledgments: This work was supported by the Comitato Telethon Fondazione ONLUS grant (Grant GGP09254) and Scientific Research grants 2010, 2011 and 2015 by Sapienza University of Rome to Tiziana Pascucci and by the Compagnia San Paolo and Pasteur Institute and Cenci Bolognetti Foundation grants and Scientific Research grants 2010, 2011, 2012, 2013 and 2014 to Antonella De Jaco.

Author Contributions: Antonella De Jaco designed the research strategy and wrote the manuscript. Dalila Mango performed the electrophysiological recordings. Federica De Angelis and Flores Lietta Favaloro analyzed protein levels by western blot. Diego Andolina and Elena Fiori conducted mouse colony handling, dissection, and punching for protein analysis. Robert Nisticò contributed to the experimental design and the interpretation of the results. Marco Colamartino performed genetic characterization of ENU2 mice. Tiziana Pascucci conceived the study and contributed to writing the manuscript.

Abbreviations

sEPSC	spontaneous excitatory postsynaptic potential
sIPSC	spontaneous inhibitory postsynaptic potential
NLGNs	neuroligins
HRP	horseradish peroxidase
SDS	sodium dodecyl sulfate
PAGE	polyacrylamide gel electrophoresis
pFC	prefrontal cortex
LTP	long term potentiation
LTD	long term depression

References

1. Ghaziuddin, M.; Al-Owain, M. Autism spectrum disorders and inborn errors of metabolism: An update. *Pediatr. Neurol.* **2013**, *49*, 232–236. [CrossRef] [PubMed]
2. DeRoche, K.; Welsh, M. Twenty-five years of research on neurocognitive outcomes in early-treated phenylketonuria: Intelligence and executive function. *Dev. Neuropsychol.* **2008**, *33*, 474–504. [CrossRef] [PubMed]
3. Stemerdink, B.A.; Kalverboer, A.F.; van der Meere, J.J.; van der Molen, M.W.; Huisman, J.; de Jong, L.W.; Slijper, F.M.; Verkerk, P.H.; van Spronsen, F.J. Behaviour and school achievement in patients with early and continuously treated phenylketonuria. *J. Inherit. Metab. Dis.* **2000**, *23*, 548–562. [CrossRef] [PubMed]
4. Diamond, A.; Prevor, M.B.; Callender, G.; Druin, D.P. Prefrontal cortex cognitive deficits in children treated early and continuously for PKU. *Monogr. Soc. Res. Child Dev.* **1997**, *62*. [CrossRef]
5. Pascucci, T.; Andolina, D.; Mela, I.L.; Conversi, D.; Latagliata, C.; Ventura, R.; Puglisi-Allegra, S.; Cabib, S. 5-Hydroxytryptophan rescues serotonin response to stress in prefrontal cortex of hyperphenylalaninaemic mice. *Int. J. Neuropsychopharmacol.* **2009**, *12*, 1067–1079. [CrossRef] [PubMed]
6. Andolina, D.; Conversi, D.; Cabib, S.; Trabalza, A.; Ventura, R.; Puglisi-Allegra, S.; Pascucci, T. 5-Hydroxytryptophan during critical postnatal period improves cognitive performances and promotes dendritic spine maturation in genetic mouse model of phenylketonuria. *Int. J. Neuropsychopharmacol.* **2011**, *14*, 479–489. [CrossRef] [PubMed]
7. Nelson, S.B.; Valakh, V. Excitatory/Inhibitory Balance and Circuit Homeostasis in Autism Spectrum Disorders. *Neuron* **2015**, *87*, 684–698. [CrossRef] [PubMed]
8. Bemben, M.A.; Shipman, S.L.; Nicoll, R.A.; Roche, K.W. The cellular and molecular landscape of neuroligins. *Trends Neurosci.* **2015**, *38*, 496–505. [CrossRef] [PubMed]
9. Krueger, D.D.; Tuffy, L.P.; Papadopoulos, T.; Brose, N. The role of neurexins and neuroligins in the formation, maturation, and function of vertebrate synapses. *Curr. Opin. Neurobiol.* **2012**, *22*, 412–422. [CrossRef] [PubMed]
10. Lee, E.; Lee, J.; Kim, E. Excitation/Inhibition Imbalance in Animal Models of Autism Spectrum Disorders. *Biol. Psychiatry* **2017**, *81*, 838–847. [CrossRef] [PubMed]
11. De la Torre-Ubieta, L.; Won, H.; Stein, J.L.; Geschwind, D.H. Advancing the understanding of autism disease mechanisms through genetics. *Nat. Med.* **2016**, *22*, 345–361. [CrossRef] [PubMed]
12. Jamain, S.; Quach, H.; Betancur, C.; Råstam, M.; Colineaux, C.; Gillberg, I.C.; Soderstrom, H.; Giros, B.; Leboyer, M.; Gillberg, C.; et al. Paris Autism Research International Sibpair Study Mutations of the X-linked genes encoding neuroligins NLGN3 and NLGN4 are associated with autism. *Nat. Genet.* **2003**, *34*, 27–29. [CrossRef] [PubMed]
13. Laumonnier, F.; Bonnet-Brilhault, F.; Gomot, M.; Blanc, R.; David, A.; Moizard, M.-P.; Raynaud, M.; Ronce, N.; Lemonnier, E.; Calvas, P.; et al. X-linked mental retardation and autism are associated with a mutation in the NLGN4 gene, a member of the neuroligin family. *Am. J. Hum. Genet.* **2004**, *74*, 552–557. [CrossRef] [PubMed]
14. Chih, B.; Afridi, S.K.; Clark, L.; Scheiffele, P. Disorder-associated mutations lead to functional inactivation of neuroligins. *Hum. Mol. Genet.* **2004**, *13*, 1471–1477. [CrossRef] [PubMed]

15. Comoletti, D.; de Jaco, A.; Jennings, L.L.; Flynn, R.E.; Gaietta, G.; Tsigelny, I.; Ellisman, M.H.; Taylor, P. The Arg451Cys-neuroligin-3 mutation associated with autism reveals a defect in protein processing. *J. Neurosci. Off. J. Soc. Neurosci.* **2004**, *24*, 4889–4893. [CrossRef] [PubMed]
16. De Jaco, A.; Lin, M.Z.; Dubi, N.; Comoletti, D.; Miller, M.T.; Camp, S.; Ellisman, M.; Butko, M.T.; Tsien, R.Y.; Taylor, P. Neuroligin trafficking deficiencies arising from mutations in the α/β-hydrolase fold protein family. *J. Biol. Chem.* **2010**, *285*, 28674–28682. [CrossRef] [PubMed]
17. Cao, X.; Tabuchi, K. Functions of synapse adhesion molecules neurexin/neuroligins and neurodevelopmental disorders. *Neurosci. Res.* **2017**, *116*, 3–9. [CrossRef] [PubMed]
18. Siddiqui, T.J.; Craig, A.M. Synaptic organizing complexes. *Curr. Opin. Neurobiol.* **2011**, *21*, 132–143. [CrossRef] [PubMed]
19. Südhof, T.C. Neuroligins and neurexins link synaptic function to cognitive disease. *Nature* **2008**, *455*, 903–911. [CrossRef] [PubMed]
20. Maćkowiak, M.; Mordalska, P.; Wędzony, K. Neuroligins, synapse balance and neuropsychiatric disorders. *Pharmacol. Rep.* **2014**, *66*, 830–835. [CrossRef] [PubMed]
21. Dani, V.S.; Chang, Q.; Maffei, A.; Turrigiano, G.G.; Jaenisch, R.; Nelson, S.B. Reduced cortical activity due to a shift in the balance between excitation and inhibition in a mouse model of Rett syndrome. *Proc. Natl. Acad. Sci. USA* **2005**, *102*, 12560–12565. [CrossRef] [PubMed]
22. Tabuchi, K.; Blundell, J.; Etherton, M.R.; Hammer, R.E.; Liu, X.; Powell, C.M.; Südhof, T.C. A neuroligin-3 mutation implicated in autism increases inhibitory synaptic transmission in mice. *Science* **2007**, *318*, 71–76. [CrossRef] [PubMed]
23. Belichenko, P.V.; Kleschevnikov, A.M.; Masliah, E.; Wu, C.; Takimoto-Kimura, R.; Salehi, A.; Mobley, W.C. Excitatory-inhibitory relationship in the fascia dentata in the Ts65Dn mouse model of Down syndrome. *J. Comp. Neurol.* **2009**, *512*, 453–466. [CrossRef] [PubMed]
24. Fernandez, F.; Garner, C.C. Over-inhibition: A model for developmental intellectual disability. *Trends Neurosci.* **2007**, *30*, 497–503. [CrossRef] [PubMed]
25. Kleschevnikov, A.M.; Belichenko, P.V.; Villar, A.J.; Epstein, C.J.; Malenka, R.C.; Mobley, W.C. Hippocampal long-term potentiation suppressed by increased inhibition in the Ts65Dn mouse, a genetic model of Down syndrome. *J. Neurosci. Off. J. Soc. Neurosci.* **2004**, *24*, 8153–8160. [CrossRef] [PubMed]
26. Yizhar, O.; Fenno, L.E.; Prigge, M.; Schneider, F.; Davidson, T.J.; O'Shea, D.J.; Sohal, V.S.; Goshen, I.; Finkelstein, J.; Paz, J.T.; et al. Neocortical excitation/inhibition balance in information processing and social dysfunction. *Nature* **2011**, *477*, 171–178. [CrossRef] [PubMed]
27. De Groot, M.J.; Hoeksma, M.; Blau, N.; Reijngoud, D.J.; van Spronsen, F.J. Pathogenesis of cognitive dysfunction in phenylketonuria: Review of hypotheses. *Mol. Genet. Metab.* **2010**, *99*, S86–S89. [CrossRef] [PubMed]
28. Levinson, J.N.; El-Husseini, A. Building excitatory and inhibitory synapses: Balancing neuroligin partnerships. *Neuron* **2005**, *48*, 171–174. [CrossRef] [PubMed]
29. Hines, R.M.; Wu, L.; Hines, D.J.; Steenland, H.; Mansour, S.; Dahlhaus, R.; Singaraja, R.R.; Cao, X.; Sammler, E.; Hormuzdi, S.G.; et al. Synaptic imbalance, stereotypies, and impaired social interactions in mice with altered neuroligin 2 expression. *J. Neurosci.* **2008**, *28*, 6055–6067. [CrossRef] [PubMed]
30. Liang, J.; Xu, W.; Hsu, Y.-T.; Yee, A.X.; Chen, L.; Südhof, T.C. Conditional neuroligin-2 knockout in adult medial prefrontal cortex links chronic changes in synaptic inhibition to cognitive impairments. *Mol. Psychiatry* **2015**, *20*, 850–859. [CrossRef] [PubMed]
31. Varoqueaux, F.; Jamain, S.; Brose, N. Neuroligin 2 is exclusively localized to inhibitory synapses. *Eur. J. Cell Biol.* **2004**, *83*, 449–456. [CrossRef] [PubMed]
32. Poulopoulos, A.; Aramuni, G.; Meyer, G.; Soykan, T.; Hoon, M.; Papadopoulos, T.; Zhang, M.; Paarmann, I.; Fuchs, C.; Harvey, K.; et al. Neuroligin 2 drives postsynaptic assembly at perisomatic inhibitory synapses through gephyrin and collybistin. *Neuron* **2009**, *63*, 628–642. [CrossRef] [PubMed]
33. Soykan, T.; Schneeberger, D.; Tria, G.; Buechner, C.; Bader, N.; Svergun, D.; Tessmer, I.; Poulopoulos, A.; Papadopoulos, T.; Varoqueaux, F.; et al. A conformational switch in collybistin determines the differentiation of inhibitory postsynapses. *EMBO J.* **2014**, *33*, 2113–2133. [CrossRef] [PubMed]
34. Chubykin, A.A.; Atasoy, D.; Etherton, M.R.; Brose, N.; Kavalali, E.T.; Gibson, J.R.; Südhof, T.C. Activity-dependent validation of excitatory versus inhibitory synapses by neuroligin-1 versus neuroligin-2. *Neuron* **2007**, *54*, 919–931. [CrossRef] [PubMed]

35. Pascucci, T.; Ventura, R.; Puglisi-Allegra, S.; Cabib, S. Deficits in brain serotonin synthesis in a genetic mouse model of phenylketonuria. *Neuroreport* **2002**, *13*, 2561–2564. [CrossRef] [PubMed]
36. Jones, K.A.; Srivastava, D.P.; Allen, J.A.; Strachan, R.T.; Roth, B.L.; Penzes, P. Rapid modulation of spine morphology by the 5-HT2A serotonin receptor through kalirin-7 signaling. *Proc. Natl. Acad. Sci. USA* **2009**, *106*, 19575–19580. [CrossRef] [PubMed]
37. Prange, O.; Wong, T.P.; Gerrow, K.; Wang, Y.T.; El-Husseini, A. A balance between excitatory and inhibitory synapses is controlled by PSD-95 and neuroligin. *Proc. Natl. Acad. Sci. USA* **2004**, *101*, 13915–13920. [CrossRef] [PubMed]
38. Ko, J.; Choii, G.; Um, J.W. The balancing act of GABAergic synapse organizers. *Trends Mol. Med.* **2015**, *21*, 256–268. [CrossRef] [PubMed]
39. Graf, E.R.; Zhang, X.; Jin, S.-X.; Linhoff, M.W.; Craig, A.M. Neurexins induce differentiation of GABA and glutamate postsynaptic specializations via neuroligins. *Cell* **2004**, *119*, 1013–1026. [CrossRef] [PubMed]
40. Pascucci, T.; Andolina, D.; Ventura, R.; Puglisi-Allegra, S.; Cabib, S. Reduced availability of brain amines during critical phases of postnatal development in a genetic mouse model of cognitive delay. *Brain Res.* **2008**, *1217*, 232–238. [CrossRef] [PubMed]
41. Delattre, V.; La Mendola, D.; Meystre, J.; Markram, H.; Markram, K. NLGN4 knockout induces network hypo-excitability in juvenile mouse somatosensory cortex in vitro. *Sci. Rep.* **2013**, *3*, 2897. [CrossRef] [PubMed]
42. Puglisi-Allegra, S.; Cabib, S.; Pascucci, T.; Ventura, R.; Cali, F.; Romano, V. Dramatic brain aminergic deficit in a genetic mouse model of phenylketonuria. *Neuroreport* **2000**, *11*, 1361–1364. [CrossRef] [PubMed]
43. Ulbrich, L.; Favaloro, F.L.; Trobiani, L.; Marchetti, V.; Patel, V.; Pascucci, T.; Comoletti, D.; Marciniak, S.J.; De Jaco, A. Autism-associated R451C mutation in neuroligin3 leads to activation of the unfolded protein response in a PC12 Tet-On inducible system. *Biochem. J.* **2016**, *473*, 423–434. [CrossRef] [PubMed]

16

High-Resolution Chromosome Ideogram Representation of Currently Recognized Genes for Autism Spectrum Disorders

Merlin G. Butler *, Syed K. Rafi † and Ann M. Manzardo †

Departments of Psychiatry & Behavioral Sciences and Pediatrics, University of Kansas Medical Center, Kansas City, KS 66160, USA; rafigene@yahoo.com (S.K.R.); amanzardo@kumc.edu (A.M.M.)

* Author to whom correspondence should be addressed; mbutler4@kumc.edu

† These authors contributed to this work equally.

Academic Editor: William Chi-shing Cho

Abstract: Recently, autism-related research has focused on the identification of various genes and disturbed pathways causing the genetically heterogeneous group of autism spectrum disorders (ASD). The list of autism-related genes has significantly increased due to better awareness with advances in genetic technology and expanding searchable genomic databases. We compiled a master list of known and clinically relevant autism spectrum disorder genes identified with supporting evidence from peer-reviewed medical literature sources by searching key words related to autism and genetics and from authoritative autism-related public access websites, such as the Simons Foundation Autism Research Institute autism genomic database dedicated to gene discovery and characterization. Our list consists of 792 genes arranged in alphabetical order in tabular form with gene symbols placed on high-resolution human chromosome ideograms, thereby enabling clinical and laboratory geneticists and genetic counsellors to access convenient visual images of the location and distribution of ASD genes. Meaningful correlations of the observed phenotype in patients with suspected/confirmed ASD gene(s) at the chromosome region or breakpoint band site can be made to inform diagnosis and gene-based personalized care and provide genetic counselling for families.

Keywords: high-resolution chromosome ideograms; autism; genetic evidence; autism spectrum disorders (ASD); ASD genes

1. Introduction

Classical autism or autistic disorder is common, with developmental difficulties noted by three years of age. It belongs to a group of heterogeneous conditions known as autism spectrum disorders (ASDs) with significant impairments in verbal and non-verbal communication and social interactions with restricted repetitive behaviors, specifically in movements and interests [1–3]. Other symptoms include lack of eye contact or focus, sleep disturbances and tactile defensiveness beginning at an early age. Several validated rating scales are used at a young age to help establish the diagnosis, including the autism diagnostic observation schedule (ADOS) and the autism diagnostic interview-revised (ADI-R) supported by pertinent medical history and clinical findings [4–6]. ASD affects about 1% of children in the general U.S. population with a 4:1 male to female ratio, usually without congenital anomalies or growth retardation [7,8].

Autism was first used as a term by Kanner in 1943 when describing a group of children lacking the ability to establish interpersonal contact and communication [9]. About one-fourth of children with autism are diagnosed by 2–3 years of age and show regression of skills in about 30% of cases. About 60% of ASD subjects show intellectual disabilities at a young age [10,11]. When comparing the prevalence of health disorders involving the central nervous system, autism ranks higher than epilepsy (6.5 cases per 1000), brain paralysis or dementia (2.5 cases/1000 for each) and Parkinson disease (two cases per 1000); genetic factors are related to many of these disorders [12,13]. Autism also occurs more commonly than congenital malformations in the general population, but dysmorphic findings are present in about 25% of children with autism. Microcephaly is seen in about 10% of cases, but macrocephaly is documented with larger frontal and smaller occipital lobes in about 20% of children with autism. Those with autism and extreme macrocephaly are at a greater risk to have *PTEN* tumor suppressor gene mutations [14], while another autism-related gene (*CHD8*) can also lead to macrocephaly and autism [15].

Autism is due to a wide range of genetic abnormalities, as well as non-genetic causes, including the environment, environmental and gene interaction (epigenetics) and metabolic disturbances (e.g., mitochondrial dysfunction), with the recurrence risk dependent on the family history and presence or absence of dysmorphic features. Candidate genes for ASD are identified by different means, including cytogenetic abnormalities (*i.e.*, translocations at chromosome breakpoints or deletions (e.g., the 22q11.2 deletion) indicating the location or loss of specific genes) in individuals with ASD along with overlapping linkage and functional data related to the clinical presentation, with certain chromosome regions identified by genetic linkage using DNA markers that co-inherit with the specific phenotype [16,17]. A representative example for such an occurrence is the proto-oncogene (MET) involved in pathways related to neuronal development [18] and found to be linked to the chromosome 7q31 band, where this gene is located. Decreased activity of the gene promoter was recognized when specific single nucleotide polymorphisms (SNPs) were present in this region by linkage studies. However, genetic linkage studies have received only limited success in the study of the genetics of autism. On the other hand, chromosomal microarray analysis using DNA probes disturbed across the genome can be used to detect chromosomal abnormalities at >100-times smaller than seen in high-resolution chromosome studies. Microarray studies have also become the first tier of genetic testing for this patient population and are recommended for all ASD patients [19]. Greater than 20% of studied patients with microarray analysis are found to have submicroscopic deletions or duplications in the genome containing genes that play a role in causing autism [20,21]. Identification of causative mutations is important to guide treatment selection and to manage medical co-morbidities, such as risks for seizures, developmental regression or for cancer (e.g., the *PTEN* gene).

Routine cytogenetic studies have shown abnormalities of chromosomes 2, 3, 4, 5, 7, 8, 11, 13, 15, 16, 17, 19, 22 and X, including deletions, duplications, translocations and inversions involving specific chromosome regions where known or candidate genes for ASD are located [22]. These studies further support the role of genetic factors in the causation of this common neurodevelopment disorder. Specifically, cytogenetic abnormalities involving the 15q11–q13 region are found in at least 1% of individuals with ASD and include *CYFIP1*, *GABRB3* and *UBE3A* genes in this chromosome region [23] and most recently the 15q11.2 BP1-BP2 microdeletion (Burnside-Butler) syndrome [24]. DNA copy number changes have also shown recurrent small deletions or duplications of the chromosome 16p11.2 band using microarray analysis [25,26] and the chromosome 15q13.2–q13.3 region [27], whereas copy number changes are noted throughout the genome in individuals with ASD, indicating the presence of multiple candidate genes on every human chromosome. These copy number changes are more often of the deletion type.

For idiopathic or non-syndromic autism, the empirical risk for siblings to be similarly affected is between 2% and 8% with an average of 4% [28]. In multiplex families having two or more affected children with autism, the recurrence risk may be as high as 25%, but generally ranges from 13% [29] to 19% [30] if due to single-gene disturbances as the cause, a major focus of this illustrative review. Advances in genetic technology beyond linkage or cytogenetic analysis of affected families with ASD or other complex disorders have led to genome-wide association studies (GWAS) involving hundreds of affected and control individuals by analyzing the distribution and clustering of hundreds and thousands of SNPs that have successfully been searched for candidate genes. The first GWAS for ASD was undertaken by Lauritsen *et al.* in 2006 [31] using 600 DNA markers in an isolated population of affected individuals from the Faroe Islands. They found an association of the chromosome 3p25.3 band, and later, other investigators studied more subjects with larger collections of genotyped markers and found several chromosome bands and regions ascertained when specific SNPs were over-represented in the ASD subjects, including 5p14.1, 5p15 and 16p13–p21 [32–37]. The studies implicated several gene families, including the cadherin family, encoding proteins for neuronal cell adhesion, while other genes (e.g., *SEMA5A*) were implicated in axonal guidance with lower gene expression levels in brain specimens from individuals with ASD [33], reviewed by Holt and Monaco [17]. Since that time, several additional studies searching for clinically relevant and known genes for ASD have identified a new collection of ASD genes [38–53].

The ability to identify an increased number of SNPs with advanced genetic platforms and extensive approaches using bioinformatics have led to improved access and a more thorough analysis. This has led to comparing genotyping data from GWAS and DNA copy number variants (CNVs) with the identification of structural genetic defects, such as submicroscopic deletions or duplications of the genome, which was not possible a few years ago. Separate studies using array comparative genomic hybridization or microarray analysis to investigate those individuals with ASD continue to yield useful data in identifying candidate genes for ASD in affected individuals [20,21,54]. The yield for microarray analysis is reported to be approximately 20% for identifying deletions or duplications at sites where known or candidate ASD genes are present. The use of more advanced technology, such as next-generation sequencing (whole genome or exome) will yield additional valuable information on the location and description of lesions of genes contributing to ASD with increasing evidence for specific and recurring mutations of single genes involved with neurodevelopment and function, leading to potential therapeutic discoveries and interventions.

Autism is frequent in single-gene conditions, such as fragile X syndrome, tuberous sclerosis, Rett syndrome or neurofibromatosis, but single-gene disorders as a whole account for less than 20% of all cases; therefore, most individuals with ASD are non-syndromic. The heritability of ASD, which takes into consideration the extent of genetic factors contributing to autism, is estimated to be as high as 90% [55]; hence the relevance and continued importance of investigating the role of genetics in the causation of ASD and expanded diagnostic testing to inform and guide treatment for individuals with identifiable genetic disturbances.

A current list of clinically relevant and known candidate genes for ASD is needed for diagnostic testing and genetic counselling purposes in the clinical setting. Historically, a previous list of known or candidate genes showing an association with ASD was reported in 2011 by Holt and Monaco [17] with the placement of 175 genes on chromosome ideograms. A much greater number of validated genes are now recognized as playing a pivotal role in ASD, warranting an updated, revised summary. We will utilize high-resolution chromosome ideograms (850 band level) to plot the location of genes now recognized by searching the literature and website information as playing a documented role in ASD. In tabular form, we will list the individual gene symbol, expanded name or description and chromosome location.

2. Results and Discussion

The diagnostic approach for an individual with ASD should include a clinical genetics evaluation with interviews of parents and health caregivers for the collection and overview of historical problems, a three-generation family pedigree, recording of developmental milestones and description of atypical behaviors along with medical and surgical procedures and a current list of medications and ongoing treatments. Laboratory tests should include lead, thyroid function, lactate and pyruvate levels in order to assess metabolic and mitochondrial functions that may be impacted by an underlying genetic disturbance along with cholesterol and urine collection for organic acid levels. Brain imaging and electroencephalogram patterns should be reviewed, if available. In addition, the ADI-R and ADOS instruments are used to test the diagnosis of ASD.

To further increase the diagnostic yield in individuals with ASD presenting for genetic service, Schaefer *et al.* [19] proposed and utilized a three-tier approach to include a genetic work-up by a clinical geneticist with expertise in dysmorphology to identify known syndromes with or without dysmorphic features (e.g., birth marks), growth anomalies (e.g., microcephaly, macrocephaly and short stature), viral titers (e.g., rubella) and metabolic screening (urine for organic acids and mucopolysaccharides, plasma lactate and amino acid levels). DNA testing for fragile X syndrome and Rett syndrome in females and males is also available, along with chromosomal and DNA microarrays to examine structural DNA lesions in those with a sporadic form of autism and the use of SNP arrays to examine for regions of homozygosity or uniparental disomy, whereby both members of a chromosome pair come from one parent [56]. Exome sequencing is now available particularly to those affected subjects with a positive family history of autism (multiplex families), if other diagnostic tests are uninformative. *PTEN* gene mutation screening would be indicated in those patients with extreme macrocephaly (head size > 2 SD) [14], if not previously done, and a review of brain MRI results. Serum and urine uric acid levels and assays for adenylate succinase deficiency should be done to include biochemical genetic studies and mitochondrial genome screening and function [57] if the above testing protocols are not diagnostic. Up to one in five children with ASD show findings of mitochondrial dysfunction [57], and a detailed genetic work-up will significantly increase the yield for the diagnosis of ASD, leading to a better understanding of causation, treatment and more accurate genetic counselling for those presenting for genetic services [20,21,54].

Advances made in genetic technology and bioinformatics have led to vastly improved genetic testing options for application in the clinical setting in patients presenting for genetic services [54]. Significant discoveries have been made with the recognition of genetic defects in the causation of ASD using microarray technology and, now, next generation sequencing. This technology has flourished with a combination of DNA probes used for both copy number variation and SNPs being required to identify segmental deletions and duplications in the genome and regions of homozygosity for the determination of identical by descent for the calculation of inbreeding coefficients or consanguinity status along with uniparental disomy of individual chromosomes [56].

Next generation exome DNA sequencing and RNA sequencing allows for discoveries of disease-causing genes and regulatory sequences required for normal function. Identifying and characterizing molecular signatures for novel or disturbed gene or exon expression and disease-specific profiles and patterns with expression heat maps have led to the recognition of interconnected disturbed gene pathways in many diseases, including a growing body of genetic evidence for autism and other psychiatric or aberrant behavioral disorders [54].

The position for each known or candidate gene for ASD susceptibility is plotted on high-resolution chromosome ideograms (850 band level), as shown in Figure 1 below. We have included gene symbols and expanded names along with the chromosome band location in Table 1 for the 792 genes recognized as playing a role in ASD.

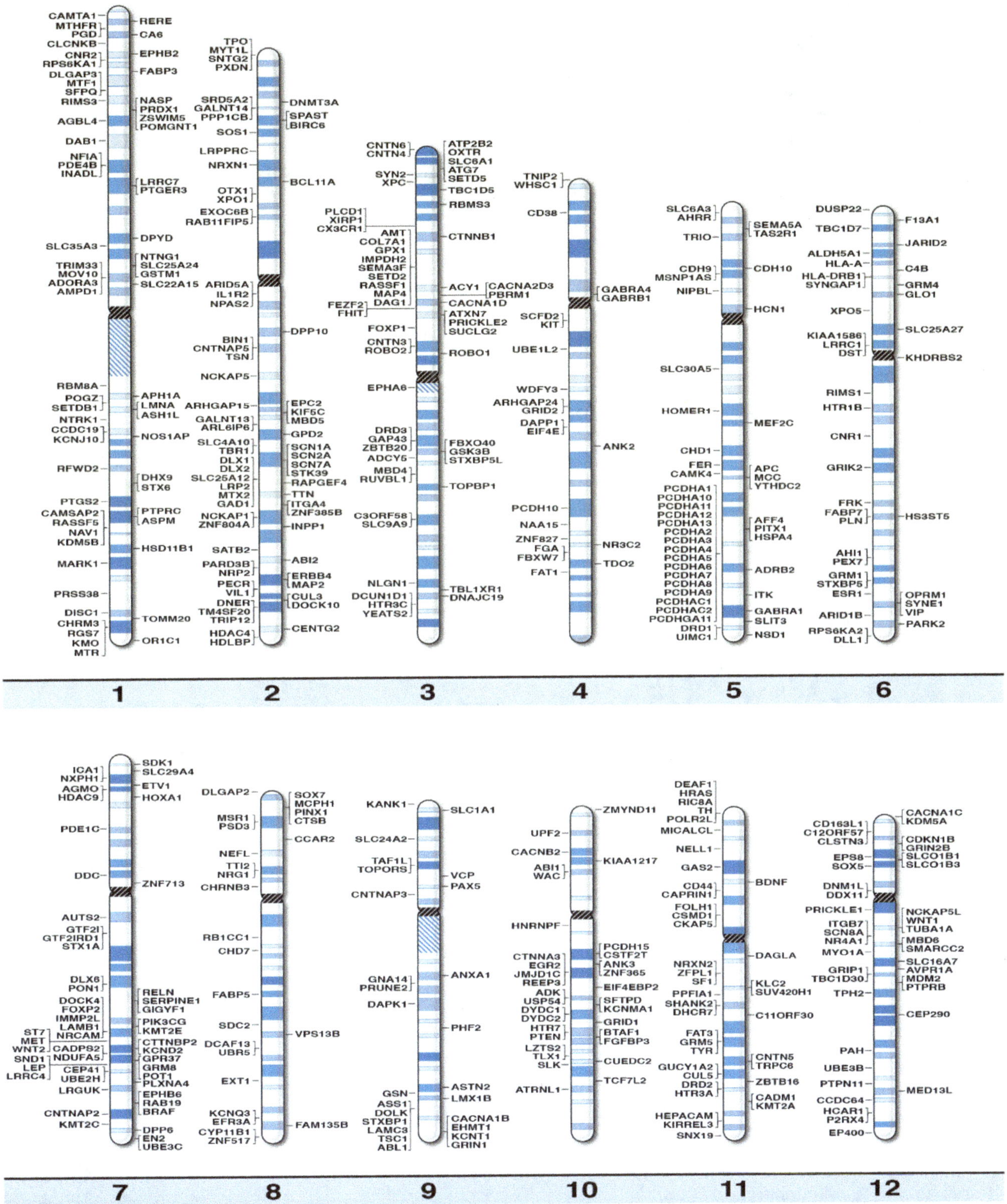

Figure 1. *Cont.*

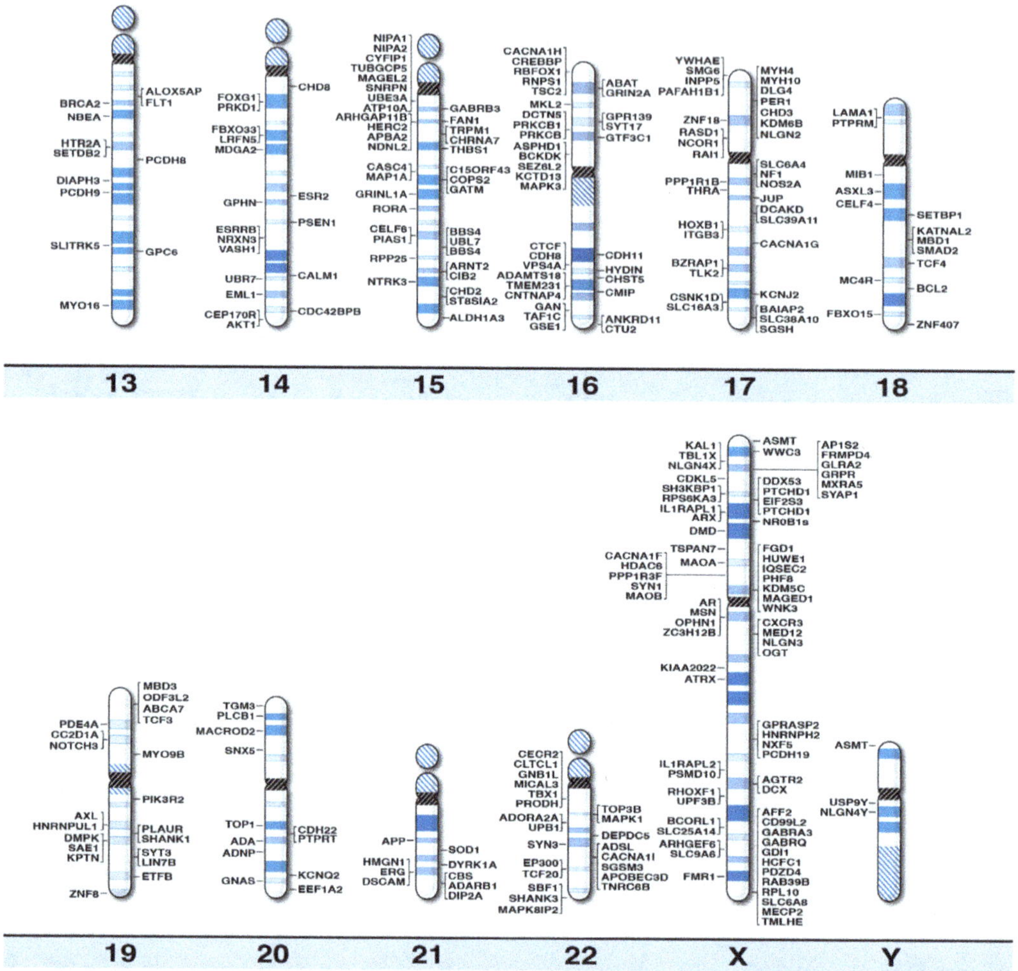

Figure 1. High-resolution human chromosome ideograms (850 band level) with the ASD gene symbol placed at the chromosomal band location. The centromere area, highlighted in black, separates the upper short "p" arm and lower long "q" arm for each chromosome. The gene symbols are arranged in alphabetical order with the expanded name and chromosome band position listed in Table 1.

Table 1. Recognized genes for autism spectrum disorders (ASD) and their chromosome locations.

Gene Symbol	Gene Name	Location
ABAT	4-aminobutyrate aminotransferase	16p13.2
ABCA7	ATP-binding cassette, sub-family A (ABC1), member 7	19p13.3
ABI1	Abl-interactor 1	10p12.1
ABI2	Abl-interactor 2	2q33.2
ABL1	C-Abl oncogene 1, non-receptor tyrosine kinase	9q34.12
ACY1	Aminoacylase 1	3p21.2
ADA	Adenosine deaminase	20q13.12
ADAMTS18	A disintegrin-like and metalloproteinase with thrombospondin type 1 motif, 18	16q23.1
ADARB1	Adenosine deaminase, RNA-specific, B1	21q22.3
ADCY5	Adenylate cyclase 5	3q21.1
ADK	Adenosine kinase	10q22.2
ADNP	Activity-dependent neuroprotector homeobox	20q13.13

Table 1. *Cont.*

Gene Symbol	Gene Name	Location
ADORA2A	Adenosine A2A receptor	22q11.23
ADORA3	Adenosine A3 receptor	1p13.2
ADRB2	Adrenergic, β 2 receptor	5q32
ADSL	Adenylosuccinate lyase	22q13.1
AFF2	AF4/fragile X mental retardation 2 (FMR2) family, member 2	Xq28
AFF4	AF4/fragile X mental retardation 2 (FMR2) family, member 4	5q31.1
AGBL4	ATP/GTP binding protein-like 4	1p33
AGMO	Alkylglycerol monooxygenase	7p21.1
AGTR2	Angiotensin II receptor, type 2	Xq23
AHI1	Abelson helper integration site 1	6q23.3
AHRR	Aryl hydrocarbon receptor repressor	5p15.33
AKT1	v-Akt murine thymoma viral oncogene homolog 1	14q32.33
ALDH1A3	Aldehyde dehydrogenase 1 family, member A3	15q26.3
ALDH5A1	Aldehyde dehydrogenase 5 family, member A1	6p22.3
ALOX5AP	Arachidonate 5-lipoxygenase-activating protein	13q12.3
AMPD1	Adenosine monophosphate deaminase 1	1p13.2
AMT	Aminomethyltransferase	3p21.31
ANK2	Ankyrin 2	4q25
ANK3	Ankyrin 3	10q21.2
ANKRD11	Ankyrin repeat domain 11	16q24.3
ANXA1	Annexin A1	9q21.13
AP1S2	Adaptor-related protein complex 1, sigma 2 subunit	Xp22.2
APBA2	Amyloid β precursor protein-binding, family A, member 2	15q13.1
APC	Adenomatosis polyposis coli	5q22.2
APH1A	APH1A γ secretase subunit	1q21.2
APOBEC3D	Apolipoprotein B mRNA editing enzyme, catalytic polypeptide-like 3D	22q13.1
APP	Amyloid β precursor protein	21q21.3
AR	Androgen receptor	Xq12
ARHGAP11B	Rho GTPase activating protein 11B	15q13.2
ARHGAP15	Rho GTPase activating protein 15	2q22.2
ARHGAP24	Rho GTPase activating protein 24	4q22.1
ARHGEF6	RAC/CDC42 guanine nucleotide exchange factor (GEF) 6	Xq26.3
ARID1B	AT rich interactive domain 1B (SWI1-like)	6q25.3
ARID5A	AT rich interactive domain 5A (MRF1-like)	2q11.2
ARL6IP6	ADP-ribosylation-like factor 6 interacting protein 6	2q23.3
ARNT2	Aryl-hydrocarbon receptor nuclear translocator 2	15q25.1
ARX	Aristaless related homeobox	Xp21.3
ASH1L	Ash1 (absent, small, or homeotic)-like (Drosophila)	1q22
ASMT	Acetylserotonin *O*-methyltransferase, X-chromosomal	Xp22.33
ASMT	Acetylserotonin *O*-methyltransferase, Y-chromosomal	Yp11.32
ASPHD1	Aspartate β-hydroxylase domain containing 1	16p11.2
ASPM	Asp (abnormal spindle) homolog, microcephaly associated	1q31.3
ASS1	Argininosuccinate synthetase	9q34.1
ASTN2	Astrotactin 2	9q33.1
ASXL3	Additional sex combs-like 3	18q12.1
ATG7	Autophagy related 7	3p25.3
ATP10A	ATPase, Class V, type 10A	15q11.2
ATP2B2	ATPase, Ca++ transporting, plasma membrane 2	3p25.3
ATRNL1	Attractin-like 1	10q25.3
ATRX	α thalassemia/mental retardation syndrome X-linked	Xq21.1
ATXN7	Ataxin 7	3p14.1
AUTS2	Autism susceptibility candidate 2	7q11.22
AVPR1A	Arginine vasopressin receptor 1A	12q14.2
AXL	AXL receptor tyrosine kinase	19q13.2
BAIAP2	BAI1-associated protein 2	17q25.3
BBS4	Bardet-Biedl syndrome 4	15q24.1
BCKDK	Branched chain ketoacid dehydrogenase kinase	16p11.2
BCL11A	B-Cell CLL/lymphoma 11A (zinc finger protein)	2p16.1
BCL2	B-cell CLL/lymphoma 2	18q21.33

Table 1. *Cont.*

Gene Symbol	Gene Name	Location
BCORL1	Bc16 co-repressor-like 1	Xq26.1
BDNF	Brain-derived neurotrophic factor	11p14.1
BIN1	Bridging integrator 1	2q14.3
BIRC6	Baculoviral IAP repeat containing 6	2p22.3
BRAF	v-Raf murine sarcoma viral oncogene homolog B	7q34
BRCA2	Breast cancer 2, early onset	13q13.1
BTAF1	RNA polymerase II, B-TFIID transcription factor-associated, 170 kDa (Mot1 homolog, *S. cerevisiae*)	10q23.32
BZRAP1	Benzodiazepine receptor (peripheral) associated protein 1	17q23.2
C11ORF30	Chromosome 11 open reading frame 30	11q13.5
C12ORF57	Chromosome 12 open reading frame 57	12p13.31
C15ORF43	Chromosome 15 open reading frame 43	15q21.1
C3ORF58	Chromosome 3 open reading frame 58	3q24
C4B	Complement component 4B	6p21.33
CA6	Carbonic anhydrase VI	1p36.2
CACNA1B	Calcium channel, voltage-dependent, N type, α 1B subunit	9q34.3
CACNA1C	Calcium channel, voltage-dependent, L type, α 1C subunit	12p13.33
CACNA1D	Calcium channel, voltage-dependent, L type, α 1D subunit	3p14.3
CACNA1F	Calcium channel, voltage-dependent, α 1F subunit	Xp11.23
CACNA1G	Calcium channel, voltage-dependent, T type, α 1G subunit	17q21.33
CACNA1H	Calcium channel, voltage-dependent, α 1H subunit	16p13.3
CACNA1I	Calcium channel, voltage-dependent, T type, α 1I subunit	22q13.1
CACNA2D3	Calcium channel, voltage-dependent, α 2/δ subunit 3	3p21.1
CACNB2	Calcium channel, voltage-dependent, β 2 subunit	10p12.33
CADM1	Cell adhesion molecule 1	11q23.3
CADPS2	Ca++-dependent activator protein for secretion 2	7q31.32
CALM1	Calmodulin 1 (phosphorylase kinase, δ)	14q32.11
CAMK4	Calcium/calmodulin-dependent protein kinase	5q22.1
CAMSAP2	Calmodulin regulated spectrin-associated protein family, member 2	1q32.1
CAMTA1	Calmodulin binding transcription activator 1	1p36.31
CAPRIN1	Cell cycle associated protein 1	11p13
CASC4	Cancer susceptibility candidate 4	15q15.3
CBS	Cystathionine β-synthase	21q22.3
CCAR2	Cell cycle and apoptosis regulator 2	8p21.3
CC2D1A	Coiled-coil and C2 domain-containing 1A	19p13.12
CCDC19	Coiled-coil domain-containing protein 19	1q23.2
CCDC64	Coiled-coil domain-containing 64	12q24.23
CD38	CD38 molecule	4p15.32
CD44	CD44 molecule	11p13
CD163L1	CD163 molecule-like 1	12p13.31
CD99L2	CD99 molecule-like 2	Xq28
CDC42BPB	CDC42 binding protein kinase β (DMPK-like)	14q32.32
CDH10	Cadherin 10, type 2	5p14.2
CDH22	Cadherin-like 22	20q13.1
CDH8	Cadherin 8, type 2	16q22.1
CDH9	Cadherin 9, type 2	5p14.1
CDH11	Cadherin 11, type 2	16q21
CDKL5	Cyclin-dependent kinase-like 5	Xp22.13
CDKN1B	Cyclin-dependent kinase inhibitor 1B	12p13.1
CECR2	Cat eye syndrome chromosome region, candidate 2	22q11.21
CELF4	CUGBP, Elav-like family, member 4	18q12.2
CELF6	CUGBP, Elav-like family, member 6	15q23
CENTG2	Centaurin γ-2	2q37.2
CEP170R	Centrosomal protein 170B	14q32.33
CEP290	Centrosomal protein 290 kDa	12q21.32
CEP41	Centrosomal protein 41 kDa	7q32.2
CHD1	Chromodomain helicase DNA binding protein 1	5q21.1
CHD2	Chromodomain helicase DNA binding protein 2	15q26.1

Table 1. *Cont.*

Gene Symbol	Gene Name	Location
CHD3	Chromodomain helicase DNA binding protein 3	17p13.1
CHD7	Chromodomain helicase DNA binding protein 7	8q12.2
CHD8	Chromodomain helicase DNA binding protein 8	14q11.2
CHRM3	Cholinergic receptor, muscarinic 3	1q43
CHRNA7	Cholinergic receptor, neuronal nicotinic, α 7	15q13.3
CHRNB3	Cholinergic receptor, neuronal nicotinic, β 3	8p11.21
CHST5	Carbohydrate sulfotransferase 5	16q22.3
CIB2	Calcium and integrin binding family member 2	15q25.1
CKAP5	Cytoskeleton associated protein 5	11p11.2
CLCNKB	Chloride channel voltage-sensitive kidney, B	1p36.13
CLSTN3	Calsyntenin 3	12p13.31
CLTCL1	Clathrin, heavy chain-like 1	22q11.21
CMIP	c-MAF inducing protein	16q23.2
CNR1	Cannabinoid receptor 1	6q15
CNR2	Cannabinoid receptor 2	1p36.11
CNTN3	Contactin 3	3p12.3
CNTN4	Contactin 4	3p26.3
CNTN5	Contactin 5	11q22.1
CNTN6	Contactin 6	3p26.3
CNTNAP2	Contactin associated protein-like 2	7q35
CNTNAP3	Contactin associated protein-like 3	9p13.1
CNTNAP4	Contactin associated protein-like 4	16q23.1
CNTNAP5	Contactin associated protein-like 5	2q14.3
COL7A1	Collagen, type VII, α 1	3p21.31
COPS2	Thyroid hormone receptor interactor 15	15q21.1
CREBBP	CREB binding protein	16p13.3
CSMD1	Cytoskeleton associated protein 5	11p11.2
CSNK1D	Casein kinase 1, δ	17q25
CSTF2T	Cleavage stimulation factor, 3' pre-RNA, subunit 2, 64 kDa, tau	10q21.1
CTCF	CCCTC-binding factor	16q22.1
CTNNA3	Catenin (cadherin-associated protein), α 3	10q21.3
CTNNB1	Catenin (cadherin-associated protein), β 1, 88 kDa	3p22.1
CTSB	Cathepsin B	8p23.1
CTTNBP2	Cortactin binding protein 2	7q31.31
CTU2	Cytosolic thiouridylase subunit 2 homolog (S. pombe)	16q24.3
CUEDC2	CUE domain containing 2	10q24.32
CUL5	Cullin 5	11q22.3
CUL3	Cullin 3	2q36.2
CX3CR1	Chemokine (C-X3-C motif) receptor 1	3p22.2
CXCR3	Chemokine, CXC motif, receptor 3	Xq13.1
CYFIP1	Cytoplasmic FMRP interacting protein 1	15q11.2
CYP11B1	Cytochrome P450, subfamily XIB, polypeptide 1	8q24.3
DAB1	Disabled homolog 1	1p32.2
DAG1	Dystroglycan 1 (dystrophin-associated glycoprotein 1)	3p21.31
DAGLA	Diacylglycerol lipase, α	11q12.2
DAPK1	Death-associated protein kinase 1	9q21.33
DAPP1	Dual adaptor of phosphotyrosine and 3-phosphoinositides 1	4q23
DCAF13	DDB1 and CUL4 associated factor 13	8q22.3
DCAKD	Dephospho-CoA kinase domain-containing protein	17q21.31
DCTN5	Dynactin 5	16p12.2
DCUN1D1	DCN1, domain containing protein 1	3q27.1
DCX	Doublecortin	Xq23
DDC	DOPA decarboxylase	7p12.1
DDX11	DEAD (Asp-Glu-Ala-Asp)/H box 11	12p11.21
DDX53	DEAD (Asp-Glu-Ala-Asp) box polypeptide 53	Xp22.11
DEAF1	DEAF1 transcription factor	11p15.5
DEPDC5	DEP domain containing 3 protein 5	22q12.2
DHCR7	7-dehydrocholesterol reductase	11q13.4

Table 1. *Cont.*

Gene Symbol	Gene Name	Location
DHX9	DEAH (Asp-Glu-Ala-His) box helicase 9	1q25.3
DIAPH3	Diaphanous, Drosophila, homolog 3	13q21.2
DIP2A	DIP2 disco-interacting protein 2 homolog A (Drosophila)	21q22.3
DISC1	Disrupted in schizophrenia 1	1q42.2
DLG4	Discs, large, Drosophila, homolog 4	17p13.1
DLGAP2	Discs, large- associated protein 2	8p23.3
DLGAP3	Discs, large- associated protein 3	1p34.3
DLL1	δ-like 1 (Drosophila)	6q27
DLX1	Distal-less homeobox 1	2q31.1
DLX2	Distal-less homeobox 2	2q31.1
DLX6	Distal-less homeobox 6	7q21.3
DMD	Dystrophin	Xp21.1
DMPK	Dystrophia myotonica-protein kinase	19q13.32
DNAJC19	DNAJ Hsp40 homolog, subfamily C, member 19	3q26.33
DNER	δ- and notch-like epidermal growth factor-related receptor	2q36.3
DNM1L	Dynamin 1-like	12p11.21
DNMT3A	DNA (cytosine-5)-methyltransferase 3 α	2p23.3
DOCK4	Dedicator of cytokinesis 4	7q31.1
DOCK10	Dedicator of cytokinesis 10	2q36.2
DOLK	Dolichol kinase	9q34.1
DPP10	Dipeptidyl peptidase 10	2q14.1
DPP6	Dipeptidyl peptidase 6	7q36.2
DPYD	Dihydropyrimidine dehydrogenase	1p21.3
DRD1	Dopamine receptor D1	5q35.2
DRD2	Dopamine receptor D2	11q23.2
DRD3	Dopamine receptor D3	3q13.31
DSCAM	Down syndrome cell adhesion molecule	21q22.2
DST	Dystonin	6p12.1
DUSP22	Dual specificity phosphatase 22	6p25.3
DYDC1	DPY30 domain containing 1	10q23.1
DYDC2	DPY30 domain containing 2	10q23.1
DYRK1A	Dual-specificity tyrosine-phosphorylation-regulated kinase 1A	21q22.13
EEF1A2	Eukaryotic translation elongation factor 1 α 2	20q13.33
EFR3A	EFR3 homolog A (*S. cerevisiae*)	8q24.22
EGR2	Early growth response 2	10q21.3
EHMT1	Euchromatic histone methyltransferase 1	9q34.3
EIF2S3	Eukaryotic translation initiation factor 2, subunit 3 γ	Xp22.11
EIF4E	Eukaryotic translation initiation factor 4E	4q23
EIF4EBP2	Eukaryotic translation initiation factor 4E binding protein 2	10q22.1
EML1	Echinoderm microtubule associated protein like 1	14q32.2
EN2	Engrailed 2	7q36.3
EP300	E1A binding protein p300	22q13.2
EP400	E1A binding protein p400	12q24.33
EPC2	Enhancer of polycomb, Drosophila homolog of 2	2q23.1
EPHA6	Ephrin receptor A6	3q11.2
EPHB2	Ephrin receptor B2	1p36.12
EPHB6	Ephrin receptor B6	7q34
EPS8	Epidermal growth factor receptor pathway substrate 8	12p12.3
ERBB4	v-ERB-A avian erythroblastic leukemia viral oncogene homolog 4	2q34
ERG	v-ETS avian erythroblastosis virus E26 oncogene homolog	21q22.2
ESR1	Estrogen receptor 1	6q25.1
ESR2	Estrogen receptor 2	14q23.2
ESRRB	Estrogen-related receptor β	14q24.3
ETFB	Electron-transfer-flavoprotein, β polypeptide	19q13.41
ETV1	Ets variant 1	7p21.2
EXOC6B	Exocyst complex component 6B	2p13.2
EXT1	Exostosin 1	8q24.11
F13A1	Factor XIII, A1 subunit	6p25.1

Table 1. *Cont.*

Gene Symbol	Gene Name	Location
FABP3	Fatty acid binding protein 3, muscle and heart (mammary-derived growth inhibitor)	1p35.2
FABP5	Fatty acid binding protein 5	8q21.13
FABP7	Fatty acid binding protein 7	6q22.31
FAM135B	Family with sequence similarity 135, member B	8q24.23
FAN1	FANCD2/FANCI-associated nuclease 1	15q13.2
FAT1	FAT tumor suppressor, Drosophila homolog of, 1	4q35.2
FAT3	FAT tumor suppressor, Drosophila homolog of , 3	11q14.3
FBXO15	F-box protein 15	18q22.3
FBXO33	F-box protein 33	14q21.1
FBXO40	F-box protein 40	3q13.33
FBXW7	F-box and WD repeat domain containing 7, E3 ubiquitin protein	4q31.3
FER	FPS/FES related tyrosine kinase	5q21.3
FEZF2	FEZ family zinc finger 2	3p14.2
FGA	Fibrinogen, A α polypeptide	4q31.3
FGD1	FYVE, Rho GEF and PH domain containing 1	Xp11.22
FGFBP3	Fibroblast growth factor binding protein 3	10q23.32
FHIT	Fragile histidine triad	3p14.2
FLT1	c-FMS-related tyrosine kinase 1	13q12.3
FMR1	Fragile X mental retardation 1 (FMR1)	Xq27.3
FOLH1	Folate hydrolase 1	11p11.2
FOXG1	Forkhead box G1	14q12
FOXP1	Forkhead box P1	3p13
FOXP2	Forkhead box P2	7q31.1
FRK	FYN-related kinase	6q22.1
FRMPD4	FERM and PDZ domain containing protein 4	Xp22.2
GABRA1	γ-aminobutyric acid A receptor, α 1	5q34
GABRA3	γ-aminobutyric acid receptor, α 3	Xq28
GABRA4	γ-aminobutyric acid receptor, α 4	4p12
GABRB1	γ-aminobutyric acid receptor, β 1	4p12
GABRB3	γ-aminobutyric acid receptor, β 3	15q12
GABRQ	γ-aminobutyric acid receptor, θ	Xq28
GAD1	Glutamate decarboxylase 1 (brain, 67 kDa)	2q31.1
GALNT13	UDP-*N*-acetyl-α-D-galactosamine:polypeptide *N*-acetylgalactosaminyl-transferase 13	2q23.3
GALNT14	UDP-*N*-acetyl-α-D-galactosamine:polypeptide *N*-acetylgalactosaminyl-transferase 14	2p23.1
GAN	Gigaxonin	16q24.1
GAP43	Growth associated protein 43	3q13.31
GAS2	Growth arrest-specific 2	11p14.3
GATM	Glycine amidinotransferase (L-arginine:glycine amidinotransferase)	15q21.1
GDI1	GDP dissociation inhibitor 1	Xq28
GIGYF1	GRB10 interacting GYF protein 1	7q22.1
GLO1	Glyoxalase I	6p21.2
GLRA2	Glycine receptor, α 2 subunit	Xp22.2
GNA14	Guanine nucleotide-binding protein, α 14	9q21.2
GNAS	Guanine nucleotide-binding protein, α-stimulating activity polypeptide I complex locus	20q13.32
GNB1L	Guanine nucleotide-binding protein, β 1-like	22q11.21
GPC6	Glypican 6	13q31.3
GPD2	Glycerol-3-phosphate dehydrogenase 2	2q24.1
GPHN	Gephyrin	14q23.3
GPR139	G protein-coupled receptor 139	16p12.3
GPR37	G protein-coupled receptor 37	7q31.33
GPRASP2	G protein-coupled receptor associated sorting protein 2	Xq22.1
GPX1	Glutathione peroxidase 1	3p21.31
GRID1	Glutamate receptor, ionotropic, δ 1	10q23.2
GRID2	Glutamate receptor, ionotropic, δ 2	4q22.1

Table 1. *Cont.*

Gene Symbol	Gene Name	Location
GRIK2	Glutamate receptor, ionotropic, kainate 2	6q16.3
GRIN1	Glutamate receptor, ionotropic, *N*-methyl D-aspartate 1	9q34.3
GRIN2A	Glutamate receptor, ionotropic, *N*-methyl D-aspartate 2A	16p13.2
GRIN2B	Glutamate receptor, ionotropic, *N*-methyl D-aspartate 2B	12p13.1
GRINL1A	GRINL1A complex locus 1	15q21.3
GRIP1	Glutamate receptor interacting protein 1	12q14.3
GRM1	Glutamate receptor, metabotropic 1	6q24.3
GRM4	Glutamate receptor, metabotropic 4	6p21.31
GRM5	Glutamate receptor, metabotropic 5	11q14.3
GRM8	Glutamate receptor, metabotropic 8	7q31.33
GRPR	Gastrin-releasing peptide receptor	Xp22.2
GSE1	Gse1 coiled-coil protein	16q24.1
GSK3B	Glycogen synthase kinase 3 β	3q13.33
GSN	Gelsolin	9q33.2
GSTM1	Glutathione *S*-transferase M1	1p13.3
GTF2I	General transcription factor III	7q11.23
GTF2IRD1	GTF2I repeat domain containing 1	7q11.23
GTF3C1	General transcription factor IIIC, polypeptide 1, α	16p12.1
GUCY1A2	Guanylate cyclase 1, soluble, α 2	11q22.3
HCAR1	Hydroxycarboxylic acid receptor 1/G protein-coupled receptor 81	12q24.31
HCFC1	Host cell factor C1	Xq28
HCN1	Hyperpolarization activated cyclic nucleotide-gated potassium channel 1	5p12
HDAC4	Histone deacetylase 4	2q37.3
HDAC6	Histone deacetylase 6	Xp11.23
HDAC9	Histone deacetylase 9	7p21.1
HDLBP	High density lipoprotein binding protein	2q37.3
HEPACAM	Hepatic and glial cell adhesion molecule	11q24.2
HERC2	HECT domain and RCC1-like domain 2	15q13.1
HLA-A	Major histocompatibility complex, class I, A	6p22.1
HLA-DRB1	Major histocompatibility complex, class II, DR β 1	6p21.32
HMGN1	High mobility group nucleosome binding domain 1	21q22.2
HNRNPF	Heterogeneous nuclear ribonucleoprotein F	10q11.21
HNRNPH2	Heterogeneous nuclear ribonucleoprotein H2	Xq22.1
HNRNPUL1	Heterogeneous nuclear ribonucleoprotein U-like 1	19q13.2
HOMER1	Homer, Drosophila, homolog 1 of 1	5q14.1
HOXA1	Homeobox A1	7p15.3
HOXB1	Homeobox B1	17q21.32
HRAS	v-HA-RAS Harvey rat sarcoma viral oncogene homolog	11p15.5
HS3ST5	Heparan sulfate 3-*O*-sulfotransferase 5	6q22.31
HSD11B1	11-β-hydroxysteroid dehydrogenase type 1	1q32.2
HSPA4	Heat shock 70 kDa protein 4	5q31.1
HTR1B	5-hydroxytryptamine receptor 1B	6q14.1
HTR2A	5-hydroxytryptamine receptor 2A	13q14.2
HTR3A	5-hydroxytryptamine receptor 3A	11q23.2
HTR3C	5-hydroxytryptamine receptor 3, family member C	3q27.1
HTR7	5-hydroxytryptamine receptor 7	10q23.31
HUWE1	HECT, UBA and WWE domain containing 1, E3 ubiquitin protein ligase	Xp11.22
HYDIN	Hydrocephalus-inducing, mouse, homolog of	16q22.2
ICA1	Islet cell autoantigen 1	7p21.3
IL1R2	Interleukin 1 receptor, type II	2q11.2
IL1RAPL1	Interleukin 1 receptor accessory protein-like 1	Xp21.3
IL1RAPL2	Interleukin 1 receptor accessory protein-like 2	Xq22.3
IMMP2L	Inner mitochondrial membrane peptidase, subunit 2, *S. cerevisiae*, homolog of	7q31.1
IMPDH2	Inosine-5-prime monophosphate dehydrogenase 2	3p21.31
INADL	Inactivation no after-potential D-like	1p31.3
INPP1	Inositol polyphosphate-1-phosphatase	2q32.2
INPP5	Inositol polyphosphate-5-phosphatase	17p13.3
IQSEC2	IQ motif and Sec7 domain 2	Xp11.22
ITGA4	Integrin, α 4	2q31.3

Table 1. *Cont.*

Gene Symbol	Gene Name	Location
ITGB3	Integrin, β 3	17q21.32
ITGB7	Integrin, β 7	12q13.13
ITK	IL20 inducible t-cell kinase	5q33.3
JARID2	Jumonji, AT rich interactive domain 2	6p22.3
JMJD1C	Jumonji domain containing 1C	10q21.3
JUP	Junction plakoglobin	17q21.2
KAL1	Kallmann syndrome interval 1	Xp22.31
KANK1	KN motif and ankyrin repeat domains 1	9p24.3
KATNAL2	Katanin p60 subunit A-like 2	18q21.1
KCND2	Potassium voltage-gated channel, Shal-related subfamily, member 2	7q31.31
KCNJ2	Potassium inwardly-rectifying channel, subfamily J, member 2	17q24.3
KCNJ10	Potassium inwardly-rectifying channel, subfamily J, member 10	1q23.2
KCNMA1	Potassium large conductance calcium-activated channel, subfamily M, α member 1	10q22.3
KCNQ2	Potassium voltage-gated channel, KQT-like subfamily, member 2	20q13.3
KCNQ3	Potassium voltage-gated channel, KQT-like subfamily, member 3	8q24.22
KCNT1	Potassium channel, subfamily T, member 1	9q34.3
KCTD13	Potassium channel tetramerization domain containing protein 13	16p11.2
KDM5A	Lysine (K)-specific demethylase 5A	12p13.33
KDM5B	Lysine (K)-specific demethylase 5B	1q32.1
KDM5C	Lysine (K)-specific demethylase 5C	Xp11.22
KDM6B	Lysine (K)-specific demethylase 6B	17p13.1
KHDRBS2	KH domain containing, RNA binding, signal transduction associated protein 2	6q11.1
KIAA1217	Sickle tail protein homolog	10p12.31
KIAA1586	KIAA1586	6p12.1
KIAA2022	KIAA2022	Xq13.3
KIF5C	Kinesin family member 5C	2q23.1
KIRREL3	Kin of IRRE like 3	11q24.2
KIT	v-KIT Hardy-Zuckerman 4 feline sarcoma viral oncogene homolog	4q12
KLC2	Kinesin light chain 2	11q13.2
KMO	Kynurenine 3-monooxygenase	1q43
KMT2A	Lysine (K)-specific methyltransferase 2A	11q23.3
KMT2C	Lysine (K)-specific methyltransferase 2C	7q36.1
KMT2E	Lysine (K)-specific methyltransferase 2E	7q22.3
KPTN	Kaptin (actin binding protein)	19q13.32
LAMA1	Laminin, α 1	18p11.23
LAMB1	Laminin, β 1	7q31.1
LAMC3	Laminin, γ 3	9q34.1
LEP	Leptin	7q32.1
LIN7B	Lin-7 homolog B (*C. elegans*)	19q13.33
LMNA	Lamin A/C	1q22
LMX1B	LIM homeobox transcription factor 1, β	9q33.3
LRFN5	Leucine-rich repeats and fibronectin type III domain containing 5	14q21.1
LRGUK	Leucine-rich repeats and guanylate kinase domain containing	7q33
LRP2	Low density lipoprotein receptor-related protein 2	2q31.1
LRPPRC	Leucine-rich PPR motif containing protein	2p21
LRRC1	Leucine-rich repeat-containing protein 1	6p12.1
LRRC4	Leucine-rich repeat-containing protein 4	7q32.1
LRRC7	Leucine-rich repeat-containing protein 7	1p31.1
LZTS2	Leucine zipper, putative tumor suppressor 2	10q24.31
MACROD2	Macro domain containing 2	20p12.1
MAGED1	Melanoma antigen family D, 1	Xp11.22
MAGEL2	MAGE-like 2	15q11.2
MAOA	Monoamine oxidase A	Xp11.3
MAOB	Monoamine oxidase B	Xp11.23
MAP1A	Microtubule-associated protein 1A	15q15.3
MAP2	Microtubule-associated protein (MAP) 2	2q34
MAP4	Microtubule-associated protein (MAP) 4	3p21.31

Table 1. *Cont.*

Gene Symbol	Gene Name	Location
MAPK1	Mitogen-activated protein kinase 1	22q11.22
MAPK3	Mitogen-activated protein kinase 3	16p11.2
MAPK8IP2	Mitogen-activated protein kinase 8 interacting protein 2	22q13.33
MARK1	MAP/microtubule affinity-regulating kinase 1	1q41
MBD1	Methyl-CpG binding domain protein 1	18q21.1
MBD3	Methyl-CpG binding domain protein 3	19p13.3
MBD4	Methyl-CpG binding domain protein 4	3q21.3
MBD5	Methyl-CpG binding domain protein 5	2q23.1
MBD6	Methyl-CpG binding domain protein 6	12q13.2
MC4R	Melanocortin 4 receptor	18q21.32
MCC	Mutated in colorectal cancers	5q22.2
MCPH1	Microcephalin 1	8p23.1
MDGA2	Mephrin, A5 antigen, protein tyrosine phosphatase mu (MAM) domain containing glycosylphosphatidylinositol anchor 2	14q21.3
MDM2	MDM2 oncogene, E3 ubiquitin protein ligase	12q15
MECP2	Methyl CpG binding protein 2	Xq28
MED12	Mediator complex subunit 12	Xq13.1
MED13L	Mediator complex subunit 13-like	12q24.21
MEF2C	MADS box transcription myocyte enhancer factor 2, polypeptide C	5q14.3
MET	Met proto-oncogene	7q31.2
MIB1	Mind bomb E3 ubiquitin protein ligase 1	18q11.2
MICAL3	Microtubule-associated monooxygenase, calponin and lim domains-containing, 3	22q11.21
MICALCL	MICAL C-terminus-like protein	11p15.3
MKL2	Myocardin-like 2	16p13.12
MOV10	Moloney leukemia virus 10, mouse, homolog of	1p13.2
MSN	Moesin	Xq12
MSNP1AS	Moesin pseudogene 1 antisense	5p14.1
MSR1	Macrophage scavenger receptor	8p22
MTF1	Metal-regulatory transcription factor 1	1p34.3
MTHFR	5-10-methylene-tetrahydrofolate reductase	1p36.22
MTR	5-methyltetrahydrofolate-homocysteine *S*-methyltransferase	1q43
MTX2	Metaxin 2	2q31.1
MXRA5	Matrix-remodelling associated 5	Xp22.2
MYH4	Myosin, heavy chain 4, skeletal muscle	17p13.1
MYH10	Myosin, heavy chain 10, non-muscle	17p13.1
MYO16	Myosin XVI	13q33.3
MYO1A	Myosin IA	12q13.3
MYO9B	Myosin IXB	19p13.11
MYT1L	Myelin transcription factor 1-like	2p25.3
NAA15	*N*(α)-acetyltransferase 15, NatA auxiliary subunit	4q31.1
NASP	Nuclear autoantigenic sperm protein (histone-binding)	1p34.1
NAV1	Neuron navigator 1	1q32.1
NBEA	Neurobeachin	13q13.3
NCKAP1	NCK-associated protein 1	2q32.1
NCKAP5	NCK-associated protein 5	2q21.2
NCKAP5L	NCK-associated protein 5-like	12q13.12
NCOR1	Nuclear receptor corepressor 1	17p11.2
NDNL2	Necdin-like gene 2	15q13.1
NDUFA5	NADH-ubiquinone oxidoreductase 1 α subcomplex, 5	7q31.32
NEFL	Neurofilament protein, light polypeptide	8p21.2
NELL1	NEL-like 1	11p15.1
NF1	Neurofibromin 1	17q11.2
NFIA	Nuclear factor I/A	1p31.3
NIPA1	Non imprinted gene in Prader-Willi/Angelman syndrome chromosomal region 1	15q11.2
NIPA2	Non imprinted gene in Prader-Willi/Angelman syndrome chromosomal region 2	15q11.2
NIPBL	Nipped-B-like	5p13.2
NLGN1	Neuroligin 1	3q26.31
NLGN2	Neuroligin 2	17p13.1

Table 1. *Cont.*

Gene Symbol	Gene Name	Location
NLGN3	Neuroligin 3	Xq13.1
NLGN4X	Neuroligin 4, X-linked	Xp22.31
NLGN4Y	Neuroligin 4, Y-linked	Yq11.221
NOS1AP	Nitric oxide synthase 1 (neuronal) adaptor protein	1q23.3
NOS2A	Nitric oxide synthase 2A	17q11.2
NOTCH3	Notch 3	19p13.12
NPAS2	Neuronal PAS domain protein 2	2q11.2
NR0B1	Nuclear receptor subfamily 0, group B, member 1	Xp21.2
NR3C2	Nuclear receptor subfamily 3, group C, member 2	4q31.23
NR4A1	Nuclear receptor subfamily 4, group A, member 1	12q13.13
NRCAM	Neuronal cell adhesion molecule	7q31.1
NRG1	Neuregulin 1	8p12
NRP2	Neuropilin 2	2q33.3
NRXN1	Neurexin I	2p16.3
NRXN2	Neurexin II	11q13.1
NRXN3	Neurexin III	14q24.3
NSD1	Nuclear receptor-binding Sa-var, enhancer of zeste, and trithorax domain protein 1	5q35.3
NTNG1	Netrin G1	1p13.3
NTRK1	Neurotrophic tyrosine kinase, receptor, type 1	1q23.1
NTRK3	Neurotrophic tyrosine kinase, receptor, type 3	15q25.3
NXF5	Nuclear RNA export factor 5	Xq22.1
NXPH1	Neurexophilin 1	7p21.3
ODF3L2	Outer dense fiber of sperm tails 3-like 2	19p13.3
OGT	O-linked *N*-acetylglucosamine transferase	Xq13.1
OPHN1	Oligophrenin 1	Xq12
OPRM1	Opioid receptor, mu 1	6q25.2
OR1C1	Olfactory receptor, family 1, subfamily C, member 1	1q44
OTX1	Orthodenticle Drosophila, homolog of	2p15
OXTR	Oxytocin receptor	3p25.3
P2RX4	Purinergic receptor P2X, ligand-gated ion channel, 4	12q24.31
PAFAH1B1	Platelet-activating factor acetylhydrolase 1B, regulatory subunit 1	17p13.3
PAH	Phenylalanine hydroxylase	12q23.2
PARD3B	PAR-3 family cell polarity regulator β	2q33.3
PARK2	Parkin	6q26
PAX5	Paired box 5	9p13.2
PBRM1	Polybromo 1	3p21.1
PCDH10	Protocadherin 10	4q28.3
PCDH15	Protocadherin 15	10q21.1
PCDH19	Protocadherin 19	Xq22.1
PCDH8	Protocadherin 8	13q14.3
PCDH9	Protocadherin 9	13q21.32
PCDHA1	Protocadherin α 1	5q31.3
PCDHA10	Protocadherin α 10	5q31.3
PCDHA11	Protocadherin α 11	5q31.3
PCDHA12	Protocadherin α 12	5q31.3
PCDHA13	Protocadherin α 13	5q31.3
PCDHA2	Protocadherin α 2	5q31.3
PCDHA3	Protocadherin α 3	5q31.3
PCDHA4	Protocadherin α 4	5q31.3
PCDHA5	Protocadherin α 5	5q31.3
PCDHA6	Protocadherin α 6	5q31.3
PCDHA7	Protocadherin α 7	5q31.3
PCDHA8	Protocadherin α 8	5q31.3
PCDHA9	Protocadherin α 9	5q31.3
PCDHAC1	Protocadherin α subfamily C, member 1	5q31.3
PCDHAC2	Protocadherin α subfamily C, member 2	5q31.3
PCDHGA11	Protocadherin γ subfamily A, member 11	5q31.3
PDE1C	Phosphodiesterase 1C	7p14.3

Table 1. *Cont.*

Gene Symbol	Gene Name	Location
PDE4A	Phosphodiesterase 4A, cAMP-specific	19p13.2
PDE4B	Phosphodiesterase 4B, cAMP-specific	1p31.3
PDZD4	PDZ domain containing 4	Xq28
PECR	Peroxisomal trans-2-enoyl-CoA reductase	2q35
PER1	Period, Drosophila, homolog of	17p13.1
PEX7	Peroxisomal biogenesis factor 7	6q23.3
PGD	Phosphogluconate dehydrogenase	1p36.22
PHF2	PHD finger protein 2	9q22.31
PHF8	PHD finger protein 8	Xp11.22
PIAS1	Protein inhibitor of activated STAT, 1	15q23
PIK3CG	Phosphatidylinositol-3-kinase, catalytic, γ	7q22.3
PIK3R2	Phosphatidylinositol-3-kinase, regulatory subunit 2	19q13.11
PINX1	PIN2 interacting protein 1	8p23.1
PITX1	Paired-like homeodomain transcription factor 1	5q31.1
PLAUR	Plasminogen activator receptor, urokinase-type	19q13.31
PLCB1	Phospholipase C, β 1	20p12.3
PLCD1	Phospholipase C, δ 1	3p22.2
PLN	Phospholamban	6q22.31
PLXNA4	Plexin A4	7q32.3
POGZ	POGO transposable element with ZNF domain	1q21.3
POLR2L	Polymerase (RNA) II (DNA directed) polypeptide L, 7.6 kDa	11p15.5
POMGNT1	Protein *O*-mannose β-1, 2-*N*-acetylglucosaminyl-transferase	1p34.1
PON1	Paraoxonase 1	7q21.3
POT1	Protection of telomeres 1	7q31.33
PPFIA1	Protein tyrosine phosphatase, receptor type, F polypeptide, interacting protein, α 1	11q13.3
PPP1CB	Protein phosphatase 1, catalytic subunit, β isozyme	2p23.2
PPP1R1B	Protein phosphatase 1, regulatory (inhibitor) subunit 1B	17q12
PPP1R3F	Protein phosphatase 1, regulatory (inhibitor) subunit 3F	Xp11.23
PRODH	Proline dehydrogenase (oxidase) 1	22q11.21
PRICKLE1	Prickle, Drosophila, homolog of, 1	12q12
PRICKLE2	Prickle, Drosophila, homolog of, 2	3p14.1
PRKCB	Protein kinase C, β	16p12.2
PRKCB1	Protein kinase C, β-1	16p12.2
PRKD1	Protein kinase D1	14q12
PRDX1	Peroxiredoxin 1	1p34.1
PRSS38	Protease, serine, 38	1q42.13
PRUNE2	Prune, Drosophila, homolog of, 2	9q21.2
PSD3	Pleckstrin and Sec7 domains-containing protein 3	8p22
PSEN1	Presenilin 1	14q24.2
PSMD10	Proteasome 26S subunit, non-ATPase, 10	Xq22.3
PTCHD1	Patched domain containing protein 1	Xp22.11
PTEN	Phosphatase and tensin homolog	10q23.31
PTGER3	Prostaglandin E receptor 3, EP3 subtype	1p31.1
PTGS2	Prostaglandin-endoperoxide synthase 2	1q31.1
PTPN11	Protein tyrosine phosphatase, non-receptor type 11	12q24.13
PTPRB	Protein tyrosine phosphatase, receptor type, B	12q15
PTPRC	Protein tyrosine phosphatase, receptor type, C	1q31.3
PTPRM	Protein tyrosine phosphatase, receptor type, M	18p11.23
PTPRT	Protein tyrosine phosphatase, receptor type, T	20q13.11
PXDN	Peroxidasin, Drosophila homolog of	2p25.3
RAB11FIP5	RAB11 family-interacting protein 5	2p13.2
RAB19	RAB19, member RAS oncogene family	7q34
RAB39B	RAS-associated protein RAB39B	Xq28
RAI1	Retinoic acid induced gene 1	17p11.2
RAPGEF4	Rap guanine nucleotide exchange factor	2q31.1
RASD1	RAS protein, dexamethasone-induced, 1	17p11.2
RASSF1	RAS association (ralGDS/AF-6) domain family member 1	3p21.31
RASSF5	RAS association domain family protein 5	1q32.1

Table 1. *Cont.*

Gene Symbol	Gene Name	Location
RB1CC1	RB1-inducible coiled-coil 1	8q11.23
RBFOX1	RNA binding protein FOX-1, *C. elegans*, homolog of, 1	16p13.3
RBM8A	RNA binding motif protein 8A	1q21.1
RBMS3	RNA binding motif protein, single stranded interacting, 3	3p24.1
REEP3	Receptor expression-enhancing protein 3	10q21.3
RELN	Reelin	7q22.1
RERE	RE-repeats encoding gene	1p36.23
RFWD2	Ring finger and WD repeat domains-containing protein 2	1q25.2
RGS7	Regulator of G protein signaling 7	1q43
RHOXF1	RHOX homeobox family, member 1	Xq24
RIC8A	RIC8 guanine nucleotide exchange factor A	11p15.5
RIMS1	Regulating synaptic membrane exocytosis 1	6q13
RIMS3	Protein regulating synaptic membrane exocytosis 3	1p34.2
RNPS1	RNA binding protein S1	16p13.3
ROBO1	Roundabout, Drosophila, homolog of, 1	3p12.2
ROBO2	Roundabout, Drosophila, homolog of, 2	3p12.3
RORA	RAR-related orphan receptor A	15q22.2
RPL10	Ribosomal protein L10	Xq28
RPP25	Ribonuclease P/MRP 25 kDa subunit	15q24.2
RPS6KA1	Ribosomal protein S6 kinase, 90 kDa, polypeptide 1	1p36.11
RPS6KA2	Ribosomal protein S6 kinase, 90 kDa, polypeptide 2	6q27
RPS6KA3	Ribosomal protein S6 kinase, 90 kDa, polypeptide 3	Xp22.12
RUVBL1	RuvB-E. coli, homolog-like 1	3q21.3
SAE1	SUMO1 activating enzyme, subunit 1	19q13.32
SATB2	Special AT-rich sequence-binding protein 2	2q33.1
SBF1	SET binding factor 1	22q13.33
SCFD2	Sec1 family domain containing 2	4q12
SCN1A	Sodium channel, neuronal, type I, α subunit	2q24.3
SCN2A	Sodium channel, voltage-gated, type II, α subunit	2q24.3
SCN7A	Sodium channel, voltage-gated, type VII, α subunit	2q24.3
SCN8A	Sodium channel, voltage-gated, type VIII, α subunit	12q13.13
SDC2	Syndecan 2	8q22.1
SDK1	Sidekick cell adhesion molecule 1	7p22.2
SEMA3F	Sema domain, immunoglobulin domain (Ig), short basic domain, secreted, (semaphorin) 3F	3p21.31
SEMA5A	Semaphorin 5A	5p15.31
SERPINE1	Serpin peptidase inhibitor, clade E (nexin, plasminogen activator inhibitor type 1), member 1	7q22.1
SETBP1	SET binding protein 1	18q12.3
SETD2	SET domain containing protein 2	3p21.31
SETD5	SET domain containing protein 5	3p25.3
SETDB1	SET domain, bifurcated, 1	1q21.3
SETDB2	SET domain, bifurcated, 2	13q14.2
SEZ6L2	Seizure related 6 homolog (mouse)-like 2	16p11.2
SF1	Splicing factor 1	11q13.1
SFPQ	Splicing factor proline/glutamine-rich	1p34.3
SFTPD	Surfactant, pulmonary-associated protein D	10q22.3
SGSH	*N*-sulfoglucosamine sulfohydrolase	17q25.3
SGSM3	Small G protein signaling modulator 3	22q13.1
SH3KBP1	SH3-domain kinase binding protein 1	Xp22.12
SHANK1	SH3 and multiple ankyrin repeat domains 1	19q13.3
SHANK2	SH3 and multiple ankyrin repeat domains 2	11q13.4
SHANK3	SH3 and multiple ankyrin repeat domains 3	22q13.33
SLC16A3	Solute carrier family 16 (monocarboxylic acid transporter), member 3	17q25
SLC16A7	Solute carrier family 16 (monocarboxylic acid transporter), member 7	12q14.1
SLC1A1	Solute carrier family 1 (neuronal/epithelial high affinity glutamate transporter), member 1	9p24.2
SLC22A15	Solute carrier family 22, (organic cation transporter), member 15	1p13.1

Table 1. *Cont.*

Gene Symbol	Gene Name	Location
SLC24A2	Solute carrier family 24 (sodium/potassium/calcium exchanger), member 2	9p22.1
SLC25A12	Solute carrier family 25 (mitochondrial carrier, Aralar), member 12	2q31.1
SLC25A14	Solute carrier family 25 (mitochondrial carrier, brain), member 14	Xq26.1
SLC25A24	Solute carrier family 25 (mitochondrial carrier, phosphate carrier), member 24	1p13.3
SLC25A27	Solute carrier family 25, member 27	6p12.3
SLC29A4	Solute carrier family 29 (equilibrative nucleoside transporter), member 4	7p22.1
SLC30A5	Solute carrier family 30 (zinc transporter), member 5	5q13.1
SLC35A3	Solute carrier family 35 (UDP-*N*-acetylglucosamine transporter), member 3	1p21.2
SLC38A10	Solute carrier family 38, member 10	17q25.3
SLC39A11	Solute carrier family 39 (metal ion transporter), member 11	17q21.31
SLC4A10	Solute carrier family 4 (sodium bicarbonate transporter-like), member 10	2q24.2
SLC6A1	Solute carrier family 6 (neurotransmitter transporter), member 1	3p25.3
SLC6A3	Solute carrier family 6 (neurotransmitter transporter, dopamine), member 3	5p15.33
SLC6A4	Solute carrier family 6 (neurotransmitter transporter, serotonin), member 4	17q11.2
SLC6A8	Solute carrier family 6 (neurotransmitter transporter, creatine), member 8	Xq28
SLC9A6	Solute carrier family 9 (sodium/hydrogen exchanger), member 6	Xq26.3
SLC9A9	Solute carrier family 9 (sodium/hydrogen exchanger), member 9	3q24
SLCO1B1	Solute carrier organic anion transporter family, member 1B1	12p12.2
SLCO1B3	Solute carrier organic anion transporter family, member 1B3	12p12.2
SLIT3	Slit, Drosophila, homolog of, 3	5q35.1
SLITRK5	SLIT and NTRK-like family, member 5	13q31.2
SLK	STE20-like kinase	10q24.33
SMAD2	SMAD family member 2	18q21.1
SMARCC2	SWI/SNF related, matrix associated, actin dependent regulator of chromatin, subfamily C, member 2	12q13.2
SMG6	SMG 6, *C. elegans*, homolog of	17p13.3
SND1	EBNA2 coactivator p100	7q32.1
SNRPN	Small nuclear ribonucleoprotein polypeptide N	15q11.2
SNTG2	Syntrophin, γ 2	2p25.3
SNX19	Sorting nexin 19	11q25
SNX5	Sorting nexin 5	20p11.23
SOD1	Superoxide dismutase 1, soluble	21q22.11
SOS1	Son of sevenless (SOS), Drosophila, homolog 1	2p22.1
SOX5	SRY (sex determining region Y)-box 5	12p12.1
SOX7	SRY (sex determining region Y)-box 7	8p23.1
SPAST	Spastin	2p22.3
SRD5A2	Steroid-5-α-reductase, 2	2p23.1
ST7	Suppressor of tumorigenicity 7	7q31.2
ST8SIA2	ST8 α-*N*-acetyl-neuraminide α-2,8-sialyltransferase 2	15q26.1
STK39	Serine/threonine protein kinase 39	2q24.3
STX6	Syntaxin 6	1q25.3
STX1A	Syntaxin 1A	7q11.23
STXBP1	Syntaxin-binding protein 1	9q34.1
STXBP5	Syntaxin-binding protein 5	6q24.3
STXBP5L	Syntaxin-binding protein 5-like	3q13.33
SUCLG2	Succinate-CoA ligase, GDP-forming, β subunit	3p14.1
SUV420H1	Suppressor of variegation 4–20, Drosophila, homolog of, 1	11q13.2
SYAP1	Synapse associated protein 1	Xp22.2
SYN1	Synapsin 1	Xp11.23
SYN2	Synapsin II	3p25.2
SYN3	Synapsin III	22q12.3
SYNE1	Spectrin repeat containing nuclear envelope 1	6q25.2
SYNGAP1	Synaptic RAS-GTPase-activating protein 1	6p21.32
SYT17	Synaptotagmin XVII	16p12.3
SYT3	Synaptotagmin III	19q13.33
TAF1C	TATA box-binding protein-associated factor 1C	16q24.1
TAF1L	TATA box-binding protein-associated factor 1-like	9p21.1
TAS2R1	Taste receptor, type 2, member 1	5p15.31

Table 1. *Cont.*

Gene Symbol	Gene Name	Location
TBC1D30	TBC1 domain family, member 30	12q14.3
TBC1D5	TBC1 domain family, member 5	3p24.3
TBC1D7	TBC1 domain family, member 7	6p24
TBL1X	Transducin-β-like 1, X-linked	Xp22.31
TBL1XR1	Transducin-β-like 1 receptor 1	3q26.32
TBR1	T-box, brain, 1	2q24.2
TBX1	T-box 1	22q11.21
TCF3	Transcription factor 3	19p13.3
TCF4	Transcription factor 4	18q21.2
TCF20	Transcription factor 20 (AR1)	22q13.2
TCF7L2	Transcription factor 7-like 2 (t-cell specific, HMG-box)	10q25.2
TDO2	Tryptophan 2,3-dioxygenase	4q32.1
TGM3	Transglutaminase 3	20p13
TH	Tyrosine hydroxylase	11p15.5
THBS1	Thrombospondin 1	15q14
THRA	Thyroid hormone receptor, α-1	17q21.1
TLK2	Tousled-like kinase 2	17q23.2
TLX1	T-cell leukemia homeobox 1	10q24.31
TM4SF20	Transmembrane 4 L6 family, member 20	2q36.3
TMEM231	Transmembrane protein 231	16q23.1
TMLHE	Epsilon-trimethyllysine hydroxylase	Xq28
TNIP2	TNFAIP3 interacting protein 2	4p16.3
TNRC6B	Trinucleotide repeat containing 6B	22q13.1
TOMM20	MAS20P, *S. cerevisiae*, homolog of	1q42.3
TOP1	Topoisomerase, DNA, I	20q12
TOP3B	Topoisomerase, DNA, III, β	22q11.22
TOPBP1	Topoisomerase (DNA) II-binding protein 1	3q22.1
TOPORS	Topoisomerase I-binding, arginine/serine-rich, E3 ubiquitin protein ligase	9p21.1
TPH2	Tryptophan hydroxylase 2	12q21.1
TPO	Thyroid peroxidase	2p25.3
TRIM33	Tripartite motif containing protein 33	1p13.2
TRIO	Trio Rho guanine nucleotide exchange factor	5p15.2
TRIP12	Thyroid hormone receptor interactor 12	2q36.3
TRPC6	Transient receptor potential cation channel, subfamily C, member 6	11q22.1
TRPM1	Transient receptor potential cation channel, subfamily M, member 1	15q13.3
TSC1	Tuberous sclerosis 1	9q34.1
TSC2	Tuberous sclerosis 2	16p13.3
TSN	Translin	2q14.3
TSPAN7	Tetraspanin 7	Xp11.4
TTI2	TELO2-interacting protein 2	8p12
TTN	Titin	2q31.2
TUBA1A	Tubulin, α-1A	12q13.12
TUBGCP5	Tubulin-γ complex-associated protein 5	15q11.2
TYR	Tyrosinase	11q14.3
UBE1L2	Ubiquitin-activating enzyme, E1-like 2	4q13.2
UBE2H	Ubiquitin-conjugating enzyme E2H	7q32.2
UBE3A	Ubiquitin protein ligase E3A	15q11.2
UBE3B	Ubiquitin protein ligase E3B	12q24.11
UBE3C	Ubiquitin protein ligase E3C	7q36.3
UBL7	Ubiquitin-like 7	15q24.1
UBR5	Ubiquitin protein ligase E3 component *N*-recognin 5	8q22.3
UBR7	Ubiquitin protein ligase E3 component *N*-recognin 7	14q32.12
UIMC1	Ubiquitin interaction motif containing 1	5q35.2
UPB1	Ureidopropionase, β 1	22q11.23
UPF2	UPF2, yeast, homolog of	10p14
UPF3B	UPF3, yeast, homolog of, B	Xq24
USP54	Ubiquitin specific peptidase 54	10q22.2
USP9Y	Ubiquitin specific protease 9, Y-chromosome	Yq11.21

Table 1. *Cont.*

Gene Symbol	Gene Name	Location
VASH1	Vasohibin 1	14q24.3
VCP	Valosin containing protein	9p13.3
VIL1	Villin 1	2q35
VIP	Vasoactive intestinal peptide (VIP)	6q25.2
VPS13B	Vacuolar protein sorting 13, yeast, homolog of, B	8q22.2
VPS4A	Vacuolar protein sorting 4 homolog A (*S. cerevisiae*)	16q22.1
WAC	WW domain containing adaptor with coiled-coil	10p12.1
WDFY3	WD repeat and FYVE domain containing 3	4q21.23
WHSC1	Wolf-Hirschhorn syndrome candidate 1	4p16.3
WNK3	Protein kinase lysine deficient 3	Xp11.22
WNT1	Wingless-type MMTV integration site family, member 1	12q13.12
WNT2	Wingless-type MMTV integration site family, member 2	7q31.2
WWC3	WWC family member 3	Xp22.32
XIRP1	Cardiomyopathy-associated protein 1	3p22.2
XPC	Xeroderma pigmentosum complementation group C	3p25.1
XPO1	Exportin 1	2p15
XPO5	Exportin 5	6p21.1
YEATS2	YEATS domain containing 2	3q27.1
YTHDC2	YTH domain containing 2	5q22.2
YWHAE	Tyrosine 3-monooxygenase, tryptophan 5-monooxygenase activation protein, epsilon isoform	17p13.3
ZBTB16	Zinc finger- and BTB domain-containing protein 16	11q23.1
ZBTB20	Zinc finger- and BTB domain-containing protein 20	3q13.31
ZC3H12B	Zinc finger CCCH domain-containing protein 12B	Xq12
ZFPL1	Zinc finger protein-like 1	11q13.1
ZMYND11	Zinc finger, MYND-type containing 11	10p15.3
ZNF18	Zinc finger protein 18	17p12
ZNF365	Zinc finger protein 365	10q21.2
ZNF385B	Zinc finger protein 385B	2q31.3
ZNF407	Zinc finger protein 407	18q23
ZNF517	Zinc finger protein 517	8q24.3
ZNF8	Zinc finger protein 8	19q13.43
ZNF713	Zinc finger protein 713	7p11.2
ZNF804A	Zinc finger protein 804A	2q32.1
ZNF827	Zinc finger protein 827	4q31.22
ZSWIM5	Zinc finger, SWIM-type containing 5	1p34.1

3. Experimental Section

We used computer-based internet websites and PubMed (https://www.ncbi.nlm.nih.gov/pubmed) to search key words for genetics and autism. This included the integrated catalogue of human genetic studies related to autism found at the Simons Foundation Autism Research Initiative (SFARI) website (https://gene.sfari.org), which currently lists 667 genes reported as of 25 February 2015. This public access initiative is an ongoing curated collection of clinically proven ASD genes supported by clinical and autism experts, medical geneticists and laboratory specialists in the study of autism. This site includes gene description and evidence of support for causation with cited literature reports. We examined peer-reviewed articles found in the medical literature following our search for genetic evidence (*i.e.*, gene variants, mutations or disturbed gene function) and the involvement of genetics playing a role in autism. Sources included whole-genome sequencing of ASD families randomly selected with at least one unaffected sibling [40] or gene expression profiles in ASD [39] along with other informative websites (e.g., Online Mendelian Inheritance in Man, www.OMIM.org). We then compiled the list of genes from these major sources for a total of 792 genes, whereby at least one mechanism was involved for each gene that could lead to ASD, a heterogeneous condition involving many genes; as our report is focused on the compilation of ASD genes from peer-reviewed research articles and authoritative computer website genomic databases for autism and not necessarily related to causal relationships between the individual gene and ASD. Those genes recognized, to date, as playing a role in ASD susceptibility and causation generally appear to impact chromatin remodeling, metabolism, mRNA translation, cell adhesion and synaptic function [39].

SFARI is a publicly available manually curated web-based searchable site of human genes with links to ASD and includes genes in catalogue form based on five categories—genetic association, syndromic, rare single-gene variant and functional and multi-genetic copy number variation—supported by cited research publications for each. Additional literature sources in our study consisted of both primary research articles and reviews summarizing genetic evidence. Many of the listed genes were identified in multiple research studies and widely reported in literature reviews, data repositories and/or computer genomic-based websites for autism (e.g., SFARI). A large number of genes showed a varied relationship to autism and neurodevelopment, but the mass of the literature surveyed limits the reliability of our relative strength estimates for the ASD and gene associations. The gene would be included if cited and recognized in peer-reviewed publications (e.g., PubMed) with supportive genetic evidence (e.g., genetic linkage, GWAS, functional gene expression patterns, informative SNPs, CNVs or identified gene mutations). Other supporting genetic evidence can be found at Simons Foundation Autism Research Initiative (SFARI) at https://sfari.org/sfari-initiatives/simons-simplex-collection, the National Institutes of Health (NIH) at https://www.ncbi.nlm.nih.gov/gap, the Online Inheritance in Man (OMIM) at www.omim.org or Genecards at https://www.genecards.org.

4. Conclusions

Readily available tissue sources, such as peripheral blood, established lymphoblastoid cell lines and saliva, hold promise for more advances in ASD by enabling the identification of new genes and a better understanding of the causation and disease mechanisms to further stimulate research with the hope to discover new treatment modalities impacted by the recognition of known disease-causing or candidate genes for ASD. We illustrated the master list of clinically relevant and known ASD genes in our summary by plotting individual genes on high-resolution chromosome ideograms and generated a tabular form to increase the awareness required for genetic testing and counselling purposes for family members presenting for genetic services. Creating a master list of genes related to ASD is a complicated process; new genes are continually identified, but not all genes are equally important or certain to be causative. Additional research is needed to further investigate the causal relationships between the specific gene and ASD. The authors encourage the use of this collection of known and clinically relevant candidate genes for ASD in their evaluation of patients and families presenting for genetic testing options and for accurate genetic counselling.

Acknowledgments: We thank Carla Meister for expert preparation of the manuscript and Lorie Gavulic for excellent artistic design and preparation of chromosome ideograms. We acknowledge support from National Institute of Child Health and Human Development (NICHD) HD02528.

Author Contributions: Merlin G. Butler conceived of the study, reviewed data from ASD gene literature reports and wrote the manuscript; Syed K. Rafi obtained and reviewed articles pertaining to ASD genes and summarized the master gene list; and Ann M. Manzardo contributed to gene data review and interpretation, contributed to the content of the manuscript and reviewed the literature.

References

1. American Psychiatric Association. *Diagnostic and Statistical Manual of Mental Disorders*, 4th ed.; American Psychiatric Association: Washington, DC, USA, 2000.
2. Johnson, C.P.; Myers, S.M.; American Academy of Pediatrics Counsel on Children with Disablities. Identifiction and evaluation of children with autism spectrum disorders. *Pediatrics* **2007**, *120*, 1183–1215. [CrossRef]
3. Hughes, J.R. Update on autism: A review of 1300 reports published in 2008. *Epilepsy Behav.* **2009**, *16*, 569–589. [CrossRef] [PubMed]

4. Lord, C.; Risi, S.; Lambrecht, L.; Cook, E.H., Jr.; Leventhal, B.L.; DiLavore, P.C.; Pickles, A.; Rutter, M. The autism diagnostic observation schedule-generic: A standard measure of social and communication deficits associated with the spectrum of autism. *J. Autism Dev. Disord.* **2000**, *30*, 205–223. [CrossRef] [PubMed]
5. Le Couteur, A.; Lord, C.; Rutter, M. *Autism Diagnostic Interview-Reviewed (ADI-R)*; Western Psychological Services: Los Angeles, CA, USA, 2003.
6. Constantino, J.N.; Davis, S.A.; Todd, R.D.; Schindler, M.K.; Gross, M.M.; Brophy, S.L.; Metzger, L.M.; Shoushtari, C.S.; Splinter, R.; Reich, W. Validation of a brief quantitative measure of autistic traits: Comparison of the social responsiveness scale with the autism diagnostic interview-revised. *J. Autism Dev. Disord.* **2003**, *33*, 427–433. [CrossRef] [PubMed]
7. Rice, C. Prevalence of autism spectrum disorders-autism and developmental disabilities monitoring network, United States, 2006. *MMWR Surveill. Summ.* **2009**, *58*, 3–8.
8. Fombonne, E. Epidemiology of autistic disorder and other pervasive developmental disorders. *J. Clin. Psychiatry* **2005**, *66* (Suppl. 10), 3–8. [PubMed]
9. Kanner, L. Autistic psychopathy in childhood. *Nerv. Child.* **1943**, *2*, 217–250.
10. Rapin, I. Autistic regression and disintegrative disorder: How important the role of epilepsy? *Semin. Pediatr. Neurol.* **1995**, *2*, 278–285. [CrossRef] [PubMed]
11. Geschwind, D.H.; Levitt, P. Autism spectrum disorders: Developmental disconnection syndromes. *Curr. Opin. Neurobiol.* **2007**, *17*, 103–111. [CrossRef] [PubMed]
12. Kurtzke, J. Neuroepidemiology. In *Neurology in Clinical Practice*; Bradley, W., Daroff, R., Fenichel, G., Marsden, C., Eds.; Butterworth-Heinemann: Stoneham, MA, USA, 1991; pp. 545–560.
13. Gadia, C.A.; Tuchman, R.; Rotta, N.T. Autism and pervasive developmental disorders. *J. Pediatr.* **2004**, *80*, S83–S94.
14. Butler, M.G.; Dasouki, M.J.; Zhou, X.P.; Talebizadeh, Z.; Brown, M.; Takahashi, T.N.; Miles, J.H.; Wang, C.H.; Stratton, R.; Pilarski, R.; *et al.* Subset of individuals with autism spectrum disorders and extreme macrocephaly associated with germline PTEN tumour suppressor gene mutations. *J. Med. Genet.* **2005**, *42*, 318–321. [CrossRef]
15. Prontera, P.; Ottaviani, V.; Toccaceli, D.; Rogaia, D.; Ardisia, C.; Romani, R.; Stangoni, G.; Pierini, A.; Donti, E. Recurrent approximately 100 kb microdeletion in the chromosomal region 14q11.2, involving *CHD8* gene, is associated with autism and macrocephaly. *Am. J. Med. Genet. A* **2014**, *164*, 3137–3141. [CrossRef]
16. Benvenuto, A.; Moavero, R.; Alessandrelli, R.; Manzi, B.; Curatolo, P. Syndromic autism: Causes and pathogenetic pathways. *World J. Pediatr.* **2009**, *5*, 169–176. [CrossRef] [PubMed]
17. Holt, R.; Monaco, A.P. Links between genetics and pathophysiology in the autism spectrum disorders. *EMBO Mol. Med.* **2011**, *3*, 438–450. [CrossRef] [PubMed]
18. Campbell, D.B.; Sutcliffe, J.S.; Ebert, P.J.; Militerni, R.; Bravaccio, C.; Trillo, S.; Elia, M.; Schneider, C.; Melmed, R.; Sacco, R.; *et al.* A genetic variant that disrupts MET transcription is associated with autism. *Proc. Natl. Acad. Sci. USA* **2006**, *103*, 16834–16839. [CrossRef]
19. Schaefer, G.B.; Starr, L.; Pickering, D.; Skar, G.; Dehaai, K.; Sanger, W.G. Array comparative genomic hybridization findings in a cohort referred for an autism evaluation. *J. Child Neurol.* **2010**, *25*, 1498–1503. [CrossRef] [PubMed]
20. Roberts, J.L.; Hovanes, K.; Dasouki, M.; Manzardo, A.M.; Butler, M.G. Chromosomal microarray analysis of consecutive individuals with autism spectrum disorders or learning disability presenting for genetic services. *Gene* **2014**, *535*, 70–78. [CrossRef] [PubMed]
21. Butler, M.G.; Usrey, K.; Roberts, J.L.; Schroeder, S.R.; Manzardo, A.M. Clinical presentation and microarray analysis of Peruvian children with atypical development and/or aberrant behavior. *Genet. Res. Int.* **2014**, *2014*, 408516. [PubMed]
22. Miles, J.H. Autism spectrum disorders—A genetics review. *Genet. Med.* **2011**, *13*, 278–294. [CrossRef] [PubMed]
23. Liu, X.; Takumi, T. Genomic and genetic aspects of autism spectrum disorder. *Biochem. Biophys. Res. Commun.* **2014**, *452*, 244–253. [CrossRef] [PubMed]
24. Cox, D.M.; Butler, M.G. The 15q11.2 BP1-BP2 microdeletion syndrome: A review. *Int. J. Mol. Sci.* **2015**, *16*, 4068–4082. [CrossRef] [PubMed]

25. Hempel, M.; Rivera Brugues, N.; Wagenstaller, J.; Lederer, G.; Weitensteiner, A.; Seidel, H.; Meitinger, T.; Strom, T.M. Microdeletion syndrome 16p11.2-p12.2: Clinical and molecular characterization. *Am. J. Med. Genet. A* **2009**, *149*, 2106–2112. [CrossRef]
26. Fernandez, B.A.; Roberts, W.; Chung, B.; Weksberg, R.; Meyn, S.; Szatmari, P.; Joseph-George, A.M.; Mackay, S.; Whitten, K.; Noble, B.; *et al.* Phenotypic spectrum associated with de novo and inherited deletions and duplications at 16p11.2 in individuals ascertained for diagnosis of autism spectrum disorder. *J. Med. Genet.* **2010**, *47*, 195–203. [CrossRef]
27. Miller, D.T.; Shen, Y.; Weiss, L.A.; Korn, J.; Anselm, I.; Bridgemohan, C.; Cox, G.F.; Dickinson, H.; Gentile, J.; Harris, D.J.; *et al.* Microdeletion/duplication at 15q13.2q13.3 among individuals with features of autism and other neuropsychiatric disorders. *J. Med. Genet.* **2009**, *46*, 242–248. [CrossRef]
28. Ritvo, E.R.; Jorde, L.B.; Mason-Brothers, A.; Freeman, B.J.; Pingree, C.; Jones, M.B.; McMahon, W.M.; Petersen, P.B.; Jenson, W.R.; Mo, A. The UCLA-university of Utah epidemiologic survey of autism: Recurrence risk estimates and genetic counseling. *Am. J. Psychiatry* **1989**, *146*, 1032–1036. [CrossRef] [PubMed]
29. Sandin, S.; Lichtenstein, P.; Kuja-Halkola, R.; Larsson, H.; Hultman, C.M.; Reichenberg, A. The familial risk of autism. *JAMA* **2014**, *311*, 1770–1777. [CrossRef] [PubMed]
30. Sebat, J.; Lakshmi, B.; Malhotra, D.; Troge, J.; Lese-Martin, C.; Walsh, T.; Yamrom, B.; Yoon, S.; Krasnitz, A.; Kendall, J.; *et al.* Strong association of de novo copy number mutations with autism. *Science* **2007**, *316*, 445–449. [CrossRef] [PubMed]
31. Lauritsen, M.B.; Als, T.D.; Dahl, H.A.; Flint, T.J.; Wang, A.G.; Vang, M.; Kruse, T.A.; Ewald, H.; Mors, O. A genome-wide search for alleles and haplotypes associated with autism and related pervasive developmental disorders on the Faroe islands. *Mol. Psychiatry* **2006**, *11*, 37–46. [CrossRef] [PubMed]
32. Ma, D.; Salyakina, D.; Jaworski, J.M.; Konidari, I.; Whitehead, P.L.; Andersen, A.N.; Hoffman, J.D.; Slifer, S.H.; Hedges, D.J.; Cukier, H.N.; *et al.* A genome-wide association study of autism reveals a common novel risk locus at 5p14.1. *Ann. Hum. Genet.* **2009**, *73*, 263–273. [CrossRef]
33. Weiss, L.A.; Arking, D.E.; Gene Discovery Project of Johns Hopkins & the Autism Consortium; Daly, M.J.; Chakravarti, A. A genome-wide linkage and association scan reveals novel loci for autism. *Nature* **2009**, *461*, 802–808. [CrossRef] [PubMed]
34. Anney, R.; Klei, L.; Pinto, D.; Regan, R.; Conroy, J.; Magalhaes, T.R.; Correia, C.; Abrahams, B.S.; Sykes, N.; Pagnamenta, A.T.; *et al.* A genome-wide scan for common alleles affecting risk for autism. *Hum. Mol. Genet.* **2010**, *19*, 4072–4082. [CrossRef]
35. Wang, K.; Zhang, H.; Ma, D.; Bucan, M.; Glessner, J.T.; Abrahams, B.S.; Salyakina, D.; Imielinski, M.; Bradfield, J.P.; Sleiman, P.M.; *et al.* Common genetic variants on 5p14.1 associate with autism spectrum disorders. *Nature* **2009**, *459*, 528–533. [CrossRef]
36. Pinto, D.; Pagnamenta, A.T.; Klei, L.; Anney, R.; Merico, D.; Regan, R.; Conroy, J.; Magalhaes, T.R.; Correia, C.; Abrahams, B.S.; *et al.* Functional impact of global rare copy number variation in autism spectrum disorders. *Nature* **2010**, *466*, 368–372. [CrossRef]
37. Pagnamenta, A.T.; Khan, H.; Walker, S.; Gerrelli, D.; Wing, K.; Bonaglia, M.C.; Giorda, R.; Berney, T.; Mani, E.; Molteni, M.; *et al.* Rare familial 16q21 microdeletions under a linkage peak implicate cadherin 8 (CDH8) in susceptibility to autism and learning disability. *J. Med. Genet.* **2011**, *48*, 48–54. [CrossRef]
38. Klei, L.; Sanders, S.J.; Murtha, M.T.; Hus, V.; Lowe, J.K.; Willsey, A.J.; Moreno-De-Luca, D.; Yu, T.W.; Fombonne, E.; Geschwind, D.; *et al.* Common genetic variants, acting additively, are a major source of risk for autism. *Mol. Autism* **2012**, *3*, 9. [CrossRef]
39. Campbell, M.G.; Kohane, I.S.; Kong, S.W. Pathway-based outlier method reveals heterogeneous genomic structure of autism in blood transcriptome. *BMC Med. Genomics* **2013**, *6*, 34. [CrossRef] [PubMed]
40. Jiang, Y.H.; Yuen, R.K.; Jin, X.; Wang, M.; Chen, N.; Wu, X.; Ju, J.; Mei, J.; Shi, Y.; He, M.; *et al.* Detection of clinically relevant genetic variants in autism spectrum disorder by whole-genome sequencing. *Am. J. Hum. Genet.* **2013**, *93*, 249–263. [CrossRef] [PubMed]
41. Huguet, G.; Ey, E.; Bourgeron, T. The genetic landscapes of autism spectrum disorders. *Ann. Rev. Genomics Hum. Genet.* **2013**, *14*, 191–213. [CrossRef]
42. Correia, C.; Oliveira, G.; Vicente, A.M. Protein interaction networks reveal novel autism risk genes within gwas statistical noise. *PLoS One* **2014**, *9*, e112399. [CrossRef] [PubMed]

43. Merikangas, A.K.; Segurado, R.; Heron, E.A.; Anney, R.J.; Paterson, A.D.; Cook, E.H.; Pinto, D.; Scherer, S.W.; Szatmari, P.; Gill, M.; *et al.* The phenotypic manifestations of rare genic CNVs in autism spectrum disorder. *Mol. Psychiatry* **2014**. [CrossRef]
44. Lossifov, I.; O'Roak, B.J.; Sanders, S.J.; Ronemus, M.; Krumm, N.; Levy, D.; Stessman, H.A.; Witherspoon, K.T.; Vives, L.; Patterson, K.E.; *et al.* The contribution of de novo coding mutations to autism spectrum disorder. *Nature* **2014**, *515*, 216–221. [CrossRef] [PubMed]
45. Goldani, A.A.S.; Downs, S.R.; Widjaja, F.; Lawton, B.; Hendren, R.L. Biomarkers in autism. *Front. Psychiatry* **2014**, *5*, 100. [CrossRef] [PubMed]
46. Ch'ng, C.; Kwok, W.; Rogic, S.; Pavlidis, P. Meta-analysis of gene expression in autism spectrum disorder. **2015**. [CrossRef]
47. Uddin, M.; Tammimies, K.; Pellecchia, G.; Alipanahi, B.; Hu, P.; Wang, Z.; Pinto, D.; Lau, L.; Nalpathamkalam, T.; Marshall, C.R.; *et al.* Brain-expressed exons under purifying selection are enriched for de novo mutations in autism spectrum disorder. *Nat. Genet.* **2014**, *46*, 742–747. [CrossRef] [PubMed]
48. De Rubeis, S.; He, X.; Goldberg, A.P.; Poultney, C.S.; Samocha, K.; Cicek, A.E.; Kou, Y.; Liu, L.; Fromer, M.; Walker, S.; *et al.* Synaptic, transcriptional and chromatin genes disrupted in autism. *Nature* **2014**, *515*, 209–215. [CrossRef] [PubMed]
49. Hadley, D.; Wu, Z.L.; Kao, C.; Kini, A.; Mohamed-Hadley, A.; Thomas, K.; Vazquez, L.; Qiu, H.; Mentch, F.; Pellegrino, R.; *et al.* The impact of the metabotropic glutamate receptor and other gene family interaction networks on autism. *Nat. Commun.* **2014**. [CrossRef]
50. Butler, M.G.; Rafi, S.K.; Hossain, W.; Stephan, D.A.; Manzardo, A.M. Whole exome sequencing in females with autism implicates novel and candidate genes. *Int. J. Mol. Sci.* **2015**, *16*, 1312–1335. [CrossRef] [PubMed]
51. Yuen, R.K.; Thiruvahindrapuram, B.; Merico, D.; Walker, S.; Tammimies, K.; Hoang, N.; Chrysler, C.; Nalpathamkalam, T.; Pellecchia, G.; Liu, Y.; *et al.* Whole-genome sequencing of quartet families with autism spectrum disorder. *Nat. Med.* **2015**, *21*, 185–191. [CrossRef] [PubMed]
52. Willsey, J.A.; State, M.W. Autism spectrum disorders: From genes to neurobiology. *Curr. Opin. Neurobiol.* **2015**, *30*, 92–99. [CrossRef] [PubMed]
53. Hormozdiari, F.; Penn, O.; Borenstein, E.; Eichler, E.E. The discovery of integrated gene networks for autism and related disorders. *Genome Res.* **2015**, *25*, 142–154. [CrossRef] [PubMed]
54. Butler, M.G.; Youngs, E.L.; Roberts, J.L.; Hellings, J.A. Assessment and treatment in autism spectrum disorders: A focus on genetics and psychiatry. *Autism Res. Treat.* **2012**. [CrossRef]
55. Herman, G.E.; Henninger, N.; Ratliff-Schaub, K.; Pastore, M.; Fitzgerald, S.; McBride, K.L. Genetic testing in autism: How much is enough? *Genet. Med.* **2007**, *9*, 268–274. [CrossRef] [PubMed]
56. Butler, M.G. Prader-willi syndrome: Obesity due to genomic imprinting. *Curr. Genomics* **2011**, *12*, 204–215. [CrossRef] [PubMed]
57. Dhillon, S.; Hellings, J.A.; Butler, M.G. Genetics and mitochondrial abnormalities in autism spectrum disorders: A review. *Curr. Genomics* **2011**, *12*, 322–332. [CrossRef] [PubMed]

Permissions

All chapters in this book were first published by MDPI; hereby published with permission under the Creative Commons Attribution License or equivalent. Every chapter published in this book has been scrutinized by our experts. Their significance has been extensively debated. The topics covered herein carry significant findings which will fuel the growth of the discipline. They may even be implemented as practical applications or may be referred to as a beginning point for another development.

The contributors of this book come from diverse backgrounds, making this book a truly international effort. This book will bring forth new frontiers with its revolutionizing research information and detailed analysis of the nascent developments around the world.

We would like to thank all the contributing authors for lending their expertise to make the book truly unique. They have played a crucial role in the development of this book. Without their invaluable contributions this book wouldn't have been possible. They have made vital efforts to compile up to date information on the varied aspects of this subject to make this book a valuable addition to the collection of many professionals and students.

This book was conceptualized with the vision of imparting up-to-date information and advanced data in this field. To ensure the same, a matchless editorial board was set up. Every individual on the board went through rigorous rounds of assessment to prove their worth. After which they invested a large part of their time researching and compiling the most relevant data for our readers.

The editorial board has been involved in producing this book since its inception. They have spent rigorous hours researching and exploring the diverse topics which have resulted in the successful publishing of this book. They have passed on their knowledge of decades through this book. To expedite this challenging task, the publisher supported the team at every step. A small team of assistant editors was also appointed to further simplify the editing procedure and attain best results for the readers.

Apart from the editorial board, the designing team has also invested a significant amount of their time in understanding the subject and creating the most relevant covers. They scrutinized every image to scout for the most suitable representation of the subject and create an appropriate cover for the book.

The publishing team has been an ardent support to the editorial, designing and production team. Their endless efforts to recruit the best for this project, has resulted in the accomplishment of this book. They are a veteran in the field of academics and their pool of knowledge is as vast as their experience in printing. Their expertise and guidance has proved useful at every step. Their uncompromising quality standards have made this book an exceptional effort. Their encouragement from time to time has been an inspiration for everyone.

The publisher and the editorial board hope that this book will prove to be a valuable piece of knowledge for researchers, students, practitioners and scholars across the globe.

List of Contributors

Sabina Barrios-Fernández
Medical-Surgical Therapeutics Department, University of Extremadura, 10003 Cáceres, Spain

Margarita Gozalo
Psychology and Anthropology Department, University of Extremadura, 10003 Cáceres, Spain

Beatriz Díaz-González
Nursing and Occupational Therapy College, University of Extremadura, 10003 Cáceres, Spain

Andrés García-Gómez
Education Sciences Department, University of Extremadura, 10003 Cáceres, Spain

Alma Y. Galvez-Contreras
Department of Neuroscience, Centro Universitario de Ciencias de la Salud, University of Guadalajara, Guadalajara 44340, Mexico

Oscar Gonzalez-Perez
Laboratory of Neuroscience, School of Psychology, University of Colima, Colima 28040, Mexico

David Zarate-Lopez and Ana L. Torres-Chavez
Laboratory of Neuroscience, School of Psychology, University of Colima, Colima 28040, Mexico
Physiological Sciences PhD Program, School of Medicine, University of Colima, Colima 28040, Mexico

Michelle L. Mackenzie and Andrea M. Haqq
Department of Pediatrics, Faculty of Medicine and Dentistry, University of Alberta, 11405 87 Avenue, Edmonton, AB T6G1C9, Canada

Jeffrey A. Bennett and Lonnie Zwaigenbaum
Department of Pediatrics, Faculty of Medicine and Dentistry, University of Alberta, 11405 87 Avenue, Edmonton, AB T6G1C9, Canada
Autism Research Centre-E209, Glenrose Rehabilitation Hospital, 10230 111 Avenue, Edmonton, AB T5G 0B7, Canada

Sandra Hodgetts
Faculty of Rehabilitation Medicine, University of Alberta, 8205 114 Street, Edmonton, AB T6G 2G4, Canada

Amy Jane Griffiths and Sneha Kohli Mathur
Attallah College of Educational Studies, Chapman University, One University Drive, Orange, CA 92866, USA

Elisa Leonardi, Francesca Isabella Famà, Cristina Carrozza, Letteria Spadaro, Flavia Marino, Gennaro Tartarisco, David Vagni, Giovanni Pioggia and Liliana Ruta
Institute for Biomedical Research and Innovation (IRIB), National Research Council of Italy, 98164 Messina, Italy

Antonio Cerasa
Institute for Biomedical Research and Innovation (IRIB), National Research Council of Italy, 98164 Messina, Italy
S. Anna Institute and Research in Advanced Neurorehabilitation (RAN), 88900 Crotone, Italy

Renato Scifo and Sabrina Baieli
Centre for Autism Spectrum Disorders, Child Psychiatry Unit, Provincial Health Service of Catania (ASP CT), 95100 Catania, Italy

Amy Hurley Hanson and Cristina M. Giannantonio
Argyros School of Business and Economics, Chapman University, One University Drive, Orange, CA 92866, USA

Kayleigh Hyde
Schmid College of Science and Technology, Chapman University, One University Drive, Orange, CA 92866, USA

Erik Linstead
Fowler School of Engineering, Chapman University, One University Drive, Orange, CA 92866, USA

Jessica Barsotti, Gloria Mangani, Roberta Nencioli, Lucia Pfanner, Raffaella Tancredi, Angela Cosenza, Paola Cipriani and Anna Maria Chilosi
IRCCS Stella Maris Foundation, Calambrone, 56018 Pisa, Italy

Filippo Muratori
IRCCS Stella Maris Foundation, Calambrone, 56018 Pisa, Italy
Department of Clinical and Experimental Medicine, University of Pisa, Via Savi, 10, 56126 Pisa, Italy

Christoph Weber
Research Institute of Developmental Medicine, Johannes Kepler University, 4020 Linz, Austria
Department for Inclusive Education, University of Education Upper Austria, 4020 Linz, Austria

Patricia Garcia Primo
Research Institute of Developmental Medicine, Johannes Kepler University, 4020 Linz, Austria

Manuel Posada de la Paz
Institute of Rare Diseases Research (IIER) & CIBERER, Instituto de Salud Carlos III, 28029 Madrid, Spain

Anna Dirmhirn
Institut für Sinnes- und Sprachneurologie, Konventhospital Barmherzige Brüder, 4020 Linz, Austria

Johannes Fellinger
Research Institute of Developmental Medicine, Johannes Kepler University, 4020 Linz, Austria
Institut für Sinnes- und Sprachneurologie, Konventhospital Barmherzige Brüder, 4020 Linz, Austria
Division of Social Psychiatry, Medical University of Vienna, 1010 Vienna, Austria

Daniel Holzinger
Research Institute of Developmental Medicine, Johannes Kepler University, 4020 Linz, Austria
Institut für Sinnes- und Sprachneurologie, Konventhospital Barmherzige Brüder, 4020 Linz, Austria
Institute of Linguistics, Karl-Franzens University of Graz, 8010 Graz, Austria

Opal Ousley and Michael J. Morrier
Emory Autism Center, Department of Psychiatry and Behavioral Sciences, Emory University School of Medicine, 1551 Shoup Court, Atlanta, GA 30322, USA

A. Nichole Evans and Karlene Coleman
Marcus Autism Center, Children's Healthcare of Atlanta, 1920 Briarcliff Road, Atlanta, GA 30329, USA

Samuel Fernandez-Carriba
Marcus Autism Center, Children's Healthcare of Atlanta, 1920 Briarcliff Road, Atlanta, GA 30329, USA
Marcus Autism Center, Department of Pediatrics, Emory University School of Medicine, 1920 Briarcliff Road, Atlanta, GA 30329, USA

Erica L. Smearman
Department of Psychology, Emory University, Psychology and Interdisciplinary Studies (PAIS) Building, 36 Eagle Row, Atlanta, GA 30322, USA

Joseph Cubells and Kimberly Rockers
Emory Autism Center, Department of Psychiatry and Behavioral Sciences, Emory University School of Medicine, 1551 Shoup Court, Atlanta, GA 30322, USA
Department of Human Genetics, Emory University School of Medicine, 615 Michael Street, Whitehead Biomedical Research Building, Suite 301, Atlanta, GA 30322, USA

David W. Evans
Department of Psychology, Bucknell University, 1 Dent Drive, Lewisburg, PA 17837, USA

Chiara Cristofani, Paola Cristofani, Pamela Fantozzi, Emanuela Inguaggiato, Pietro Muratori, Chiara Pfanner, Lisa Polidori, Laura Ruglioni, Elena Valente, Gabriele Masi and Annarita Milone
IRCCS Stella Maris Foundation, 56128 Pisa (Calambrone), Italy

Antonio Narzisi
IRCCS Stella Maris Foundation, 56128 Pisa (Calambrone), Italy
IRCCS Stella Maris Foundation, Calambrone, 56018 Pisa, Italy

Gianluca Sesso
IRCCS Stella Maris Foundation, 56128 Pisa (Calambrone), Italy
Department of Clinical and Experimental Medicine, University of Pisa, 56126 Pisa, Italy
IRCCS Stella Maris Foundation, Calambrone, 56018 Pisa, Italy

Simone Pisano
Department of Neuroscience, AORN Santobono-Pausilipon, 80122 Naples, Italy
Department of Translational Medical Sciences, Federico II University, 80138 Naples, Italy

Stefano Damiani, Natascia Brondino and Pierluigi Politi
Department of Brain and Behavioral Sciences, University of Pavia, 27100 Pavia, Italy

Pietro Leali
Faculty of Medicine, University of Pavia, 27100 Pavia, Italy

Guido Nosari
Department of Neurosciences and Mental Health, IRCCS Ca' Granda Ospedale Maggiore Policlinico, 20122 Milan, Italy

Monica Caviglia
RSD Cascina Rossago, 27050 Ponte Nizza, Italy

Mariangela V. Puci and Maria Cristina Monti
Department of Public Health, Experimental and Forensic Medicine, University of Pavia, 27100 Pavia, Italy

José Guevara-Campos
"Felipe Guevara Rojas" Hospital, Pediatrics Service, University of Oriente, El Tigre-Anzoátegui, 6034 Venezuela, Spain

Lucía González-Guevara
"Felipe Guevara Rojas" Hospital, Epilepsy and Encephalography Unit, El Tigre-Anzoátegui, 6034 Venezuela, Spain

Omar Cauli
Department of Nursing, University of Valencia, 46010 Valencia, Spain

Rehab H. Alsaedi
Faculty of Education, Queensland University of Technology (QUT), Brisbane 4059, Australia
Department of Special Education, Taibah University, Madinah 41477, Saudi Arabia

Devin M. Cox
Departments of Psychiatry & Behavioral Sciences, University of Kansas Medical Center, 3901 Rainbow Boulevard, MS 4015, Kansas City, KS 66160, USA

Merlin G. Butler
Departments of Psychiatry & Behavioral Sciences, University of Kansas Medical Center, 3901 Rainbow Boulevard, MS 4015, Kansas City, KS 66160, USA
Departments of Psychiatry & Behavioral Sciences and Pediatrics, University of Kansas Medical Center, Kansas City, KS 66160, USA

Sureni V. Mullegama, Joseph T. Alaimo and Sarah H. Elsea
Department of Molecular and Human Genetics, Baylor College of Medicine, Houston, TX 77030, USA

Li Chen
Department of Molecular and Human Genetics, Baylor College of Medicine, Houston, TX 77030, USA
Department of Cellular and Genetic Medicine, School of Basic Medical Sciences, Fudan University, Shanghai 200032, China

Antonella De Jaco, Federica De Angelis and Flores Lietta Favaloro
Department of Biology and Biotechnologies "Charles Darwin", Sapienza University of Rome, 00185 Rome, Italy

Dalila Mango
EBRI-European Brain Research Institute, 00143 Rome, Italy

Diego Andolina, Marco Colamartino and Tiziana Pascucci
Department of Psychology, "Daniel Bovet", Neurobiology Research Center, Sapienza University of Rome, 00185 Rome, Italy
Foundation Santa Lucia, IRCCS, 00143 Rome, Italy

Robert Nisticò
Department of Biology, University of Tor Vergata, 00133 Rome, Italy

Elena Fiori
EBRI-European Brain Research Institute, 00143 Rome, Italy
Department of Psychology, "Daniel Bovet", Neurobiology Research Center, Sapienza University of Rome, 00185 Rome, Italy
Cell Biology and Neurobiology Institute, National Research Council, 00143 Rome, Italy

Syed K. Rafi and Ann M. Manzardo
Departments of Psychiatry & Behavioral Sciences and Pediatrics, University of Kansas Medical Center, Kansas City, KS 66160, USA

Index

www.ingramcontent.com/pod-product-compliance
Lightning Source LLC
LaVergne TN
LVHW081024210926
848485LV00004B/940
* 9 7 8 1 6 3 9 2 7 9 0 0 5 *